Misappropriation of Human Rights

International Studies in Human Rights

VOLUME 152

The titles published in this series are listed at *brill.com/ishr*

Misappropriation of Human Rights

Elements, Fora, Actors and Critiques

Edited by

Cathérine Van de Graaf, Júlia Miklasová
and Paula Rhein-Fischer

BRILL | NIJHOFF

Funded by the Volkswagen Foundation – 0071374-00.

ISSN 0924-4751
ISBN 978-90-04-73706-8
ISBN 978-90-04-76300-5 (PDF)
DOI https://doi.org/10.1163/9789004763005

Library of Congress Control Number: 2026947899

Brill Nijhoff and Koninklijke Brill BV are part of De Gruyter Brill.
www.degruyterbrill.com

Questions about General Product Safety Regulation: productsafety@degruyterbrill.com

Contents

Notes on Contributors

Mariana Amaral
is a PhD student in the Department of Anthropology of Princeton University. She holds a Master's degree in Sociology and a Law degree, both from the University of São Paulo (USP). She worked as a researcher at LAUT, an independent think tank focusing on rights and rising authoritarianism in Brazil, where she integrated the project 'Reactionary movements and the new grammars of rights'. Her research explores the relationship between state, care, and control, with a focus on drug policy, mental health, and the criminal justice system – as well as contemporary forms of authoritarianism and neoliberal governance. Co-author of the books *The Law of the Bullet, the Beef and the Bible: Democratic Culture in Crisis Amid Disputes over Rights* (Tinta da China, 2024) and *The Path of Autocracy: Current Strategies for Democratic Erosion* (Tinta da China, 2022), both in Portuguese.

Işıl Aral
is Assistant Professor of International Law at Koç University, Istanbul and the Director of KÜREMER (the Center for Global Public Law). She is the co-editor of *International Law and Universality* (Oxford University Press) and the co-author of *Expansionism in International Human Rights Law* (Brill). Her articles have been published in the *Leiden Journal of International Law*, the *Journal of the History of International Law*, and the *Journal on the Use of Force and International Law*. Her forthcoming monograph, *International Law as a Set of Narratives*, will be published by Cambridge University Press.

Dorjana Bojanovska Popovska
is a postdoctoral researcher at the CEU Democracy Institute working at the intersection of law, religion, and illiberalism. She holds an SJD in Comparative Constitutional Law (CEU, 2022, summa cum laude), an LLM in Comparative Constitutional Law (CEU, 2017), and an LLM in Constitutional Law (Iustinianus Primus, Skopje, 2014). She is an alumna of the ICLRS Young Scholars Fellowship on Religion and the Rule of Law and has been a visiting scholar at the Department of Law, University of Milan (2019), and the Europa Institute, Leiden Law School (2017). She has taught and lectured at universities across Europe, including CEU (Budapest and Vienna), Bard College Berlin, the University of Milan, the University of Bologna, and Eötvös Loránd University in Budapest.

Elif Çelik
is Associate Professor of Human Rights at Eskişehir Osmangazi University. She received her PhD in Human Rights from Hacettepe University, Ankara, with a dissertation titled 'From Human Dignity to Human Vulnerability: Rethinking the Foundational Concepts of Human Rights'. Drawing from both legal and political theory, her work engages with the shifting conceptual foundations of human rights and the tensions they produce across different legal and social contexts, particularly in relation to vulnerable groups. More recently, her research has turned toward examining how human rights discourse functions in contested domains involving social norms, legal recognition, and embodied rights. Her recent work also reflects a growing interest in the institutional and procedural dimensions of human rights law, including how legal frameworks accommodate emerging forms of engagement and advocacy. Her academic work appears in both Turkish and international publications.

Gráinne de Búrca
is Professor of Constitutional Law at the EUI, on leave from New York University. Her fields of interest are European Union law, Human Rights law and Transnational Governance. She is co-editor of the OUP series *Oxford Studies in European Law*, co-author of the OUP textbook *EU Law*, and author of *Reframing Human Rights in a Turbulent Era*. She is coeditor-in-chief of the *International Journal of Constitutional Law* (I·CON) and a member of the board of editors of the American Journal of International Law.

Rosa Freedman
is the inaugural Professor of Law, Conflict and Global Development at the University of Reading and a visiting professor at Reichman University (Israel). She is a barrister and an academic panel member of 4–5 Gray's Inn Square. She has published extensively on the United Nations and human rights, including three monographs, five co-edited collections, and articles in the leading international law journals. She regularly is instructed to provide expert advice and reports for national governments and multilateral institutions, and appears frequently in the international media. She has served as a member of the UN Secretary-General's Civil Society Advisory Board on prevention of sexual exploitation and abuse, a Specialist Adviser on safeguarding to the UK government International Development Committee, and currently sits on a UK FCDO Steering Committee.

Egbert Fortuin
is Professor of Russian Linguistics at Leiden University. His research focuses on semantics, pragmatics, and argumentation, with particular attention to the use of language in Russian propaganda, including the rhetorical manipulation of terms such as 'genocide' in the context of Russia's discourse on Ukraine.

Robert Horvath
lectures in Russian politics at La Trobe University, Melbourne. His scholarship is focused on Russian nationalism, civil society, and the evolution of the Putin regime. He is the author of *The Legacy of Soviet Dissent* (2005), *Putin's Preventive Counter-Revolution* (2013) and *Putin's Fascists* (2020). His research on human rights includes a study of the nationalist ideologue Nataliya Narochnitskaya's influence on the Putin regime's 'traditional values' agenda, and articles for *Human Rights Quarterly* about the 'Solzhenitsyn Effect' and the Initiative Group for the Defence of Human Rights in the USSR.

Henrike Jansen
is Associate Professor of Argumentation Theory at Leiden University. She has published extensively on legal argumentation, as well as on the relationship between argumentation and populism.

Elena Lipatova
is a lawyer and researcher specialising in the right to freedom of assembly. She conducted the research for this article while affiliated with OVD-Info, where she worked on protecting protesters in Russian courts and coordinated the submission of over 3,000 complaints on freedom of assembly to the European Court of Human Rights as part of a joint campaign with Memorial Human Rights Centre. She holds a master's degree in International Relations and Political Science from the University of Manchester. Currently, she works as a lawyer at OVD-Info, focusing on human rights strategic litigation.

Eve Lister
is a PhD candidate and Graduate Lecturer in Public Law at University College London. Eve's research explores entitlement to adequate housing in England, and involves analysis of overlapping statute, case law, policy and commentary. She also works as a Research Assistant to Tom Hickman KC of Blackstone Chambers, and is assisting on the long-awaited book 'Constitutional Fracture'. She is broadly interested in public law and socioeconomic rights and their role within case law and policy across Europe. She is also a Paralegal at a Welfare

Benefits Legal Advice clinic, where she enjoys working with clients in the local community. She welcomes discussion and outreach in light of her paper.

Melaniya Maslova
is a human rights defender and researcher from Russia holding a master's degree in European and International Human Rights Law from Leiden University. Her topics of interest include freedom of assembly, LGBTQI+ rights, and various issues related to the war in Ukraine. The present article was written while in affiliation with OVD-Info, a Russian human rights organisation working on the issues of freedom of assembly and political persecution in Russia.

Júlia Miklasová
is a postdoctoral researcher at the Academy for European Human Rights Protection, University of Cologne. She earned her PhD in International Law (summa cum laude avec les félicitations du jury) from the Graduate Institute of International and Development Studies (IHEID) in Geneva. Her monograph *Secession in International Law with a Special Reference to the Post-Soviet Space* was published open access by Brill in 2024. Her research focuses on public international law, particularly the law of statehood and secession, territorial disputes, the use of force, peremptory norms, and international responsibility. She also works on international and European human rights law and their intersection with general international law. She has been a visiting researcher at the Lauterpacht Centre for International Law (Cambridge), a junior visiting fellow at the Institute for Human Sciences (Vienna), a research assistant at the Global Migration Centre, and a legal assistant to a UN ILC member.

Ignatius Yordan Nugraha
is a postdoctoral researcher at Friedrich-Alexander-Universität Erlangen-Nürnberg, part of the Cluster of Excellence "Transforming Human Rights", in Nuremberg, Germany. Previously, he was a postdoctoral researcher at the Centre for Fundamental Rights at the Hertie School in Berlin, as part of the project Deep Impact through Soft Jurisprudence? The Contribution of United Nations Treaty Body Case Law to the Development of International Human Rights Law. He earned his doctoral degree from Hasselt University on 30 January 2024. This chapter was first drafted at Hasselt University and finalised at the Hertie School in Berlin. He has broad expertise in comparative constitutional law, ECHR law, and UN human rights law. He is particularly interested in how law articulates different ways of imagining and making sense of reality. His current work explores the vernacularisation of constitutionalism and

human rights, as well as the effects of modernisation and secularisation on how we understand law.

Levina de Wolf
holds a bachelor's and master's degree in Russian Studies, and is now a PhD candidate at Leiden University, where she works within a research group that focuses on the language and argumentation of Russian propaganda. Her PhD research concentrates on the Russian-language propaganda that the Kremlin and state-controlled media use to rally domestic audiences behind the 'special military operation' against Ukraine. She is particularly interested in the argumentative-rhetorical strategies that characterise the war legitimisations given in this conflict, and employs the theoretical framework of pragma-dialectics to gain more insight in Russia's war argumentation and the nature of propaganda more generally.

Wiktor Pawłowski
holds a master's degree in Russian and Eurasian Studies. His research concentrates on the linguistic aspects of Russian propaganda abroad in the context of the ongoing war in Ukraine. He is particularly interested in how language is used to frame political and ideological narratives for international audiences. His work primarily employs mixed-methods research designs, in which computational large-scale text analysis is used to support and inform qualitative linguistic analysis.

Paula Rhein-Fischer
is Postdoctoral Researcher at the Academy for European Human Rights Protection of University of Cologne (Germany). She is Principal Investigator of the German, Lithuanian and Portuguese research consortium 'Mnemonic Reality' and was a Postdoctoral researcher of the Danish, Dutch, German and Polish research consortium 'Memocracy, both funded by the Volkswagen Foundation. She holds both German state exams in law as well as a Maîtrise en Droit from Université Paris I Panthéon Sorbonne. She completed her PhD at the Institute for International Peace and Security Law at the University of Cologne with a dissertation on the prohibition to use force and factual mistakes (Nomos, 2020). Her current research focusses on law and time, memory laws, human rights and constitutional law.

Adriane Sanctis de Brito
is an associate at Harvard University's Department of History. She co-founded LAUT, an independent think tank focusing on rights and rising authoritarian-

ism in Brazil, where she served at the board of directors and co-led the project 'Reactionary movements and the new grammars of rights'. She was a Kathleen Fitzpatrick Fellow at the University of Melbourne and a visiting researcher at the Max Planck Institute of Luxembourg and at the University of Helsinki. She holds a PhD from the University of São Paulo (USP) and held an adjunct teaching position at its International Relations Institute. Her research focuses on international legal histories. Co-author of the book *The Law of the Bullet, the Beef and the Bible: Democratic Culture in Crisis Amid Disputes over Rights* (Tinta da China, 2024) (in Portuguese).

Luciana Silva Reis
is Professor of Law at the University of São Paulo (USP) and Associate Researcher at the Law and Democracy Unit of the Brazilian Center for Analysis and Planning (CEBRAP). She is a co-founder of LAUT, an independent think tank focusing on rights and rising authoritarianism in Brazil, where she serves as Vice-President and co-leads the research project 'Reactionary Movements and the New Grammars of Rights'. She holds a bachelor's, master's, and PhD in Law from the University of São Paulo. Her teaching and research focus on legal theory, political philosophy, history of legal thought, and critical theories of rights and democracy, with current emphasis on contemporary authoritarianism, post-positivism and interpretive jurisprudence, and the analytic turn in Left Hegelianism. She is co-author of the book *The Law of the Bullet, the Beef and the Bible: Democratic Culture in Crisis Amid Disputes over Rights* (Tinta-da-China, 2024) (in Portuguese).

Ana Silva Rosa
has a PhD and Master's in Political Science from the Institute of Social and Political Studies of the State University of Rio de Janeiro. She is a coordinator at LAUT, an independent think tank focusing on rights and rising authoritarianism in Brazil, where she also takes part in the project 'Reactionary Movements and the New Grammars of Rights' as a researcher. Her research focuses on political theory and Brazilian political thought, especially the history of Brazilian 19th-century political ideas, political languages, and ideologies in contemporary Brazil. Co-author of the book *The Law of the Bullet, the Beef and the Bible: Democratic Culture in Crisis Amid Disputes over Rights* (Tinta da China, 2024) (in Portuguese).

Cathérine Van de Graaf
is a postdoctoral researcher at the Human Rights Centre (Ghent University) and the Academy for European Human Rights Protection (University of Cologne).

She is a principal investigator on the joint project 'Who Is the Court For? Bringing the Human Back into Human Rights Research' funded by the Volkswagen Foundation in which she focuses on the examination of discrimination complaints before the European Court of Human Rights. She is an editor at the Strasbourg Observers blog and regularly contributes to the submission of third-party interventions to the Court. She obtained her PhD from Ghent University with a thesis focusing on procedural justice theory, perceived discrimination and Islamophobia under the supervision of Prof. Dr. Eva Brems and an LLM in International Human Rights Law from Lund University and the Raoul Wallenberg Institute.

Cai Wilkinson (she/they)
is Associate Professor in International Relations at Deakin University, Australia. Her research focuses on societal security in the post-Soviet space, with a particular focus on LGBTQ human rights and 'traditional values' in Kyrgyzstan and Russia, as well as on interrogating the role of genders and sexualities in international politics and the discipline of International Relations. Her work has been published in journals including *Security Dialogue*, the *Journal of Human Rights*, *Nationalities Papers*, and *Critical Studies on Security*. Together with Jasmine Dall'Agnola, she is the co-editor of *LGBTQ+ Visibilities in the Caucasus and Central Asia* (Routledge, 2025), and they are one of the editors of *Thinking World Politics Otherwise: A Diverse Introduction to International Relations* (Oxford University Press, 2025). She has also contributed chapters to volumes on securitisation theory, LGBT activism in Central Asia, fieldwork-based research methods, and feminist and queer IR.

Katharine G. Young
is Professor and Robert A. Trevisani Dean's Faculty Fellow at Boston College Law School. Her fields of research include Comparative Constitutional Law and Human Rights Law. In addition to authoring *Constituting Economic and Social Rights* (2012), she has edited *The Future of Economic and Social Rights* (2019), co-edited *The Public Law of Gender* (2016) and *The Oxford Handbook of Economic and Social Rights*. She has a law degree from University of Melbourne, and a doctoral SJD degree from Harvard University. Her recent publications include 'The Misappropriation of Human Rights' (*International Journal of Constitutional Law*) (with Gráinne de Búrca) and 'Human Rights Originalism' (*Georgetown Law Journal*).

Introduction

Júlia Miklasová, Paula Rhein-Fischer and Cathérine Van de Graaf

US Vice President Vance expressed concerns about "the retreat of Europe from some of its most fundamental values" at the Munich Security Conference in February 2025, pointing to "digital censorship" in the EU and a "backslide away from conscience rights" and basic liberties of religion, given the criminal conviction of an army veteran for having prayed 50 meters from an abortion clinic in the UK.[1] What Vance portrayed as a critique of human rights violations in Europe may also be seen from a different angle: a use of human rights language for ulterior purposes, hierarchising certain "fundamental" human rights – like the freedom of religion – in the interest of a conservative state policy.

Across diverse contexts – from authoritarian regimes to ostensibly democratic societies – individuals, communities, and also nation states continue to face systemic injustices and violations – and this, paradoxically, under the guise of human rights rhetoric. Globally, various actors employ the language of human rights to advance agendas that are exclusionary, repressive, or antithetical to pluralism, often regressing or overturning prior commitments while also trying to evade external scrutiny and preventing accountability. Yet, it is also inherent in the nature of human rights as a legal framework, value system, and platform for mobilisation to be used to fit the divergent aims of various actors, sometimes pushing the law or the concept to its limits. As such, human rights have consistently been a battleground of contention and discord. In order to deal with this impression of the malicious (over)flexing of human rights and its symptomatic manifestations, de Búrca and Young introduced the term "(mis)appropriation" to conceptualise the above-mentioned phenomenon of distortion and abuse. In their scholarship, they defined misappropriation as the "deployment by a particular set of actors of a range of strategies and arguments [...] advanced in the language of protecting 'human rights,' but generally seeking to reverse or undo previous human rights developments and commitments."[2]

1 B Franke (ed), *Selected Speeches Held at the Munich Security Conference 2025*, vol 2 (Mittler 2025) 16 ff.

2 G de Búrca and K Young, 'The (Mis)appropriation of Human Rights by the New Global Right: An Introduction to the Symposium' (2023) 21 International Journal of Constitutional Law 205, 207.

This edited volume aims to build on the writings of de Búrca and Young and put them to the test by further exploring the complex dynamics underpinning this phenomenon, offering an examination of its elements, the actors employing it, the fora in which its manifestations occur, and the scholarly critique of the concept's relevance and limitations. This inquiry unpacks the mechanisms through which such misappropriations occur, drawing on interdisciplinary perspectives to illuminate the intersecting forces of power, ideology, and historical legacies at play.

The central questions to which this edited volume wants to provide an answer to are as follows: What are the constitutive elements of misappropriation? What distinguishes misappropriation from 'ordinary' abuse and distortion? What are the motives for human rights to be misappropriated? Where and through what forms does misappropriation take place? What agents are the driving forces behind it? And to what extent can the concept be criticised as drawing on subjective value judgments made along the lines of power, ignoring diversified and non-Western approaches to human rights?

To answer these questions convincingly, we need to rely on both "research in law" and "research about law."[3] Thus, we include in this edited volume both doctrinal contributions that use the legal system as the primary source of concepts and critically reflect on how these fit within a variety of parallel legal (national, regional and international) systems (research in law) as well as research that approaches law from an independent theoretical framework, which consists of concepts that are primarily borrowed not from the legal system itself, but from other disciplines.[4] From this latter group (research about law), we include contributions from sociology of law, critical legal studies, linguistics, law and politics and studies of law in context among others. Taking these questions as a departure point, answers are provided by zooming in on various actors across national and supranational systems. In this edited volume, scholars from law and social sciences are brought together to reflect on this newly coined notion, its contours, contributions, and implications for (international) human rights law. With this collection of chapters, we therefore aim to bring together a myriad of research strands to engage with misappropriation in all its facets. Indeed, the example of the US Vice President's

---

3 See the categorisation of H W Arthurs, *Law and Learning: Report to the Social Sciences and Humanities Research Council of Canada by the Consultative Group on Research and Education in Law* (Social Sciences and Humanities Research Council of Canada 1983) 63.

4 See for this distinction P Westerman, 'Open or Autonomous? The Debate on Legal Methodology as a Reflection of the Debate on Law', in M van Hoecke (ed), *Methodology of Legal Research* (Hart Publishing 2011), 87, 94 et seq., terming both approaches "legal doctrine" and "legal science."

speech in Munich, discussed earlier, leaves no doubt that the processes outlined in this volume have taken centre stage, raising further questions about their implications for the human rights project as such.

1 How this Volume Relates to the 2023 Symposium by de Búrca and Young

This edited volume builds on and challenges the findings and analyses presented in a 2023 symposium published by the *International Journal of Constitutional Law* titled "The (Mis)appropriation of Human Rights by the New Global Right."[5] As mentioned earlier, this symposium had a seminal significance as it introduced this notion in human rights law for the first time and offered several supporting case study analyses. In particular, in the symposium's introduction, de Búrca and Young instigated the debate about the phenomenon that certain actors invoke the language, tools, and framework of human rights to reverse or undo previous human rights developments and commitments.[6] Drawing on the symposium's case studies of Putin's Russia, Erdogan's Turkey, Modi's India, Bolsonaro's Brazil, the United States under the first Trump administration, and Uganda, Nigeria, and Ghana, de Búrca and Young identified eight indicators of "ultraconservative or illiberal human rights (mis) appropriation": (1) an exclusionary, repressive, or anti-pluralist aim or effect of the human rights interpretation, (2) a departure from the existing international human rights law, and particularly from developments post-dating the Universal Declaration of Human Rights (UDHR) (3) the creation of a hierarchy of human rights (4) attempts to scapegoat certain groups or to identify groups who are said not to be entitled to claim rights, (5) attempts to impose restrictions on civil society or resorts to strategic lawsuits against public participation, (6) evidence of clear falsehood, subterfuge, camouflage, intentional distortion, (7) the fact that the human rights invocation is a reversal of previous rhetorical or legal strategies of the actor, suggestive of bad faith or disingenuous purposes, and (8) moves to evade or reject external monitoring or independent mechanisms of accountability.[7]

The symposium concentrates on actors of the "global right," namely national and transnational coalitions of populist and conservative political and reli-

5 The conveners of this symposium – De Búrca and Young – offer an epilogue to this edited volume.

6 De Búrca and Young (n 2) 205, 207.

7 Ibid., 213.

gious actors.[8] Accordingly, when distorting human rights language, these actors are driven by religious, power, and economic interests.[9] As Stoeckl elaborates in the symposium for the Russian Orthodox Church, one of the strategies used is to rely on an ostensibly literal reading of human rights norms and to "freeze" human rights in a past semantic and historical context.[10] This applies in particular to provisions of the UDHR on religious freedom, on the right to property, on the family and on duties, as Huckerby and Knuckey confirm most clearly in relation to the Pompeo Commission on Unalienable Rights in the United States.[11] Other mechanisms include familiar populist strategies, such as authoritarian forms of legalism as well as lawfare for repressive and anti-pluralist purposes.[12] Huckerby and Knuckey emphasise the strategic relevance of the supposed legitimacy of the messenger of the distortive human rights interpretation, of its deliberation process, of its motives for interpreting and defining rights, and of the substance of the defined rights as well as a tactical norm diffusion.[13] Non-legal strategies of misappropriation can be seen in "political correctness" speech and attempts to distinguish between "legitimate" right holders and those who should not possess any rights.[14] Progressive NGOs have tried to refute the claims that lead to misappropriation of human rights, interestingly using similar strategies as the actors involved.[15] Huckerby and Knuckey identify various strategies, including court filings, the use of human rights mechanisms, monitoring, shaming, and media strategies as well as the creation of reports refuting the assertions.[16]

As innovative and rich as these first analyses conceptualising the notion of misappropriation are, many gaps remain to be filled. Here is where the edited volume steps in. First, the volume, in particular, in its parts 1 and 2, aims at deepening some of the findings of de Búrca's and Young's symposium. Hence, drawing on other case studies, it tracks strategies of misappropriation in other contexts and delves deeper into the reasons why misappropriation is preferred over outright rejection of human rights. Related to that, to further the

8 Ibid., 207.

9 See Ibid., 214 ff.

10 K Stoeckl, 'Traditional Values, Family, Homeschooling: The Role of Russia and the Russian Orthodox Church in Transnational Moral Conservative Networks and the Efforts at Reshaping Human Rights' (2023) 21 International Journal of Constitutional Law 224, 238.

11 J Huckerby and S Knuckey, 'Appropriation and the Rewriting of Rights' (2023) 21 International Journal of Constitutional Law 243, 257.

12 De Búrca and Young (n 2) 217.

13 Huckerby and Knuckey (n 11) 247–264.

14 De Búrca and Young (n 2) 217 f.

15 Huckerby and Knuckey (n 11) 262.

16 Ibid., 249, 253, 260 f.

understanding of the notion, the volume sheds light on the actors misappropriating human rights and the fora in which this occurs. Second, the volume takes up and tests the suggested concept. It asks whether the proposed indicators adequately describe the phenomenon and are workable in practice to distinguish regular uses of human rights law from misappropriation. This exercise results in a significant clarification of the relevant indicators identifying misappropriation. Very much linked to this, Part 3 of the volume cedes considerable space to critiques of the concept. In this respect, it critically asks to what extent there is a difference between "misappropriations" and regular "appropriations" or simply novel argumentation based on human rights, as well as between misappropriation and regular contestation of human rights law. The still very unclear relationship with "abuse" of human rights law is also illuminated. Third, the volume problematises the concept's complex relationship with the old debate between universalism and relativism of human rights.[17] In this respect, it tries to answer to what extent the concept of misappropriation requires acknowledging a core of universal human rights and how this can be reconciled with specific regional human rights practices.

2 Delineating the Notion

"Misappropriation of human rights" is not a legal concept with any defined legal effects under international law, but an analytical category. Still, to serve any analytical purpose[18] it is necessary to delineate the notion that forms the object of this volume. However, to do so is a complex exercise, not only due to the notion's novelty but arguably also due to a certain element of fluctuation or instability at its core. This is already detectable when zooming in on the two definitional components outlined by de Búrca and Young. As mentioned earlier, these scholars define "(mis)appropriation" as the "deployment by a particular set of actors of a range of strategies and arguments [...] advanced in the language of protecting 'human rights,' but generally seeking to reverse or undo previous human rights developments and commitments."[19] Two components

17 See only J Donnelly, 'Cultural Relativism and Universal Human Rights' (1984) 6 Human Rights Quarterly 400; and 'The Relative Universality of Human Rights', (2007) 29(2) Human Rights Quarterly 281; E Brems, *Human Rights: Universality and Diversity* (Martinus Nijhoff 2001).

18 For the purposes we think this concept serves, see the concluding chapter.

19 De Búrca and Young (n 2) 207.

entail: first, the use of (distorted) conception of human rights, and second, the use of such language to undermine human rights developments.[20]

First, the very possibility of assessing distortion concerning the invocation of human rights presupposes some shared substantive understanding of human rights against which this can be evaluated. In human rights law, for some scholars, the task of defining this common baseline raises difficulties, given the long-standing contestation of any consensus view and the open-ended character of human rights provisions. States and other actors are not prohibited from, and indeed sometimes do, advance novel, outlandish, unorthodox or even untenable[21] legal claims concerning human rights, for instance when defending their actions before international and domestic legal fora. Importantly, in international law, the arguments and communications of States not only have policy ramifications or legal effects in specific cases, but may also generate broader legal implications. If certain conditions are met, they may ultimately lead to the "silent modification" of the treaty rights or contribute to a change in the State practice and *opinio juris* with respect to particular rights under customary international law.[22]

In this context, the line between the appropriation and misappropriation of human rights may appear rather tenuous. In general English, the verb "appropriate" can be defined as "to take something for your own use, usually without permission."[23] As such, the term can be either neutral or negative, depending on the context. Conversely, the verb "misappropriate" means "to take (something, such as money) dishonestly for your own use: to appropri-

20 The object of de Búrca and Young's study entails "a deliberate strategy to refute the existing commitments and parameters of the human rights system as they have developed, consolidated, and gained fairly widespread recognition over the decades, while *at the same time* consciously promoting a distinctive – and, we argue, distorted – overall conception of human rights, whether by emphasizing different sources, values, or particular rights, or by seeking to exclude certain groups or rights from protection." De Búrca and Young (n 2) 207 (*emphasis added*).

21 J Miklasová, 'Russian Approaches to Post-Soviet Secessions: Bad Faith Argumentation and Its Limits' (2023) 22 Baltic Yearbook of International Law 64, 75.

22 Vienna Convention on the Law of Treaties (adopted 23 May 1969, entered into force 27 January 1980) 1155 UNTS 331, Art 31(3)(a)(b) ("VCLT"). G Futhazar and A Peters, 'Good Faith' in JE Vinuales (ed), *The UN Friendly Relations Declaration at 50* (CUP 2020) 204–205.

23 'Appropriate' (*Cambridge Dictionary*) <https://dictionary.cambridge.org/dictionary/english/appropriating> accessed 6 November 2025.

ate (something) wrongly."[24] Generally, the prefix "mis-" indicates that "the action referred to by the verb has been done wrongly or badly."[25]

Notably, the 2023 symposium to which this volume refers employs a more ambivalent notion of "(mis)appropriation." The authors use parentheses to convey that "appropriative moves" under the umbrella of (mis)appropriation may seek to undo or erode previous human rights commitments, "while acknowledging the space for contestation around that designation."[26]

At the same time, the authors associate the term with legal claims "transgressing the plausible boundaries of the field."[27] De Búrca and Young admit that "it is not obvious that any particular interpretative move – whether conservative or progressive –" can be defined as such.[28] Nevertheless, the two scholars posit that "certain core features of human rights" can offer "guidance as to the plausibility of proposed interpretations, and their fit with the broad parameters, premises and basic commitments to human rights."[29] These concern "the basic commitments to recognition and protection for the equal human dignity, human freedom, and human welfare of all persons."[30]

As suggested, other authors are more sceptical regarding this aspect.[31] However, de Búrca and Young emphasise that rather than isolated interpretations, what matters are the interpretative patterns inimical to these commitments occurring over time and consistently.[32] Moreover, they argue that the set of eight criteria that they propose "help distinguish between genuine, even if contested, invocations of human rights, on the one hand, and uses which may be pretextual or which breach core commitments of the field, on the other."[33] Ultimately, while this volume employs the term 'misappropriation' without the parentheses to simplify the text, several of its contributions as

24 'Misappropriate' (*The Britannica Dictionary*) <https://www.britannica.com/dictionary/misappropriate> accessed 6 November 2025.

25 'Mis-' (*Cambridge Dictionary*) <https://dictionary.cambridge.org/dictionary/english/mis#google_vignette> accessed 6 November 2025.

26 De Búrca and Young (n 2) 207.

27 Ibid., 208.

28 Ibid., 208.

29 Ibid., 208–209.

30 Ibid., 208–209.

31 According to Mégret, the populist challenge ultimately reveals how its "discourse is in fact not that different from the common vernacular of rights and how, conversely, the human rights movement's hold on the meaning of rights is tenuous." F Mégret, 'Human Rights Populism' (2022) 13 Humanity: An International Journal of Human Rights, Humanitarianism, and Development 240, 247. See the concluding chapter for the synthesis of the views expressed across this volume and the editors' reflections.

32 De Búrca and Young (n 2) 210. See the concluding chapter.

33 Ibid., 212.

well as its conclusion focus on the (seemingly) blurred line between appropriation and misappropriation.[34]

The second difficulty stems from the fact that de Búrca and Young refer to the deployment of human rights language "*generally seeking* to reverse or undo previous human rights developments and commitments" (emphasis added).[35] This seems to suggest that the *intended effects* of the given use of human rights language are the decisive element. The question thus arises whether misappropriation requires an element of abusive or malicious intent in employing the human rights language to such ends. In fact, some of de Búrca and Young's indicators inherently point to the element of bad faith, including the criterion concerning "evidence of clear falsehood, subterfuge, 'camouflage', intentional distortion, or deliberate polarization" (6); the volte-face on the actor's previous human rights positions suggestive of bad faith (7); and actions aimed at limiting or refusing external monitoring or accountability mechanisms (8).[36]

The notion of abuse in international law is linked to the doctrine of abuse of rights, which, among others things, refers to the use of a legal right for an end different from that for which it was conferred.[37] In general English, bad-faith behaviour is defined as "done in a dishonest way with the *intention* of tricking someone."[38] In international law, the principle of good faith is central to the inquiry regarding *mala fide* behaviour. Beyond governing the formation, implementation, and interpretation of legal obligations, its role in international law is broad and structural.[39] According to Virally, "[g]ood faith excludes any separation between reality and appearances."[40]

---

34 See chapters by Aral, Nugraha, and Lister.

35 De Búrca and Young (n 2) 207.

36 Ibid., 213.

37 A Kiss, 'Abuse of Rights' MPEPIL (online edn OUP 2006) par 1.

38 'Bad Faith' (*Cambridge Dictionary*) <https://dictionary.cambridge.org/dictionary/english/bad-faith> accessed 6 November 2025 (*emphasis added*).

39 Charter of the United Nations (adopted 26 June 1945, entered into force 24 October 1945) 1 UNTS xvi, Art 2(2); Declaration on Principles of International Law concerning Friendly Relations and Co-operation among States in accordance with the Charter of the United Nations, UNGA Res 2625 (xxv) (24 October 1970) UN Doc A/RES/2625(xxv); *Nuclear Tests (Australia v France)* (Judgment) [1974] ICJ Rep 253, para 46; VCLT, Arts 26, 31; Miklasová (n 21) 80–81; B Çalı, 'Proving Bad Faith in International Law: Lesson from the Article 18 Case Law of the European Court of Human Rights' in G Kajtár et al (eds), *Secondary Rules of Primary Importance – Attribution, Causality, Standard of Review and Evidentiary Rules in International Law* (OUP 2022) 184; M Virally, 'Review Essay: Good Faith in Public International Law' 77 Am J Int'l L (1983) 130, 132. See *infra* (n 49 and 58).

40 Virally (n 39) 131.

By definition, states do not articulate the illegitimate purposes underpinning human rights misappropriation directly. The process of demonstrating that the state – an abstract legal entity – has acted *mala fide* faces "serious evidentiary challenges."[41] The problems are known from other subjective elements in international law.[42] Apart from the uncertainties relating to the exact circumstances from which a malicious mindset can be inferred, the question is whose mindset should be attributed to the state at all: all state agents, only the state leaders, or only the person who makes the statement that misappropriates human rights? It is thus notoriously difficult to differentiate between state arguments made in good faith and those advanced in bad faith.[43]

A focus on a subjective intent is a standard, albeit not exclusive scholarly way of understanding bad faith. For example, Çali notes that in public international law it is unclear whether to demonstrate bad faith requires "subjective intention to act maliciously" or "whether a more objective evidentiary standard can be set."[44] In the context of abusive constitutional borrowing, Dixon and Landau distinguish between thinner and thicker understanding of abuse. While the former centres on the effects of the relevant activity "on the minimum core of democracy," the latter requires that "would-be authoritarians knowingly or *intentionally* take aim at the democratic minimum core."[45] In their work, Dixon and Landau mostly espouse the abuse in the latter, intent-based sense of abuse. Similarly, Pozen conceptually distinguishes between objective and subjective constitutional bad faith – the former being derived from the standard of unreasonableness in the contract law, "tested against the norms of legally relevant community."[46] Petrov, in turn, moves away both from

---

41 Çalı (n 39) 185.

42 On similar debates in the context of genocidal intent, see R Mazzeschi and E Carli, 'Proof of Specific Intent in the Crime of genocide' (2024) 22 Journal of International Criminal Justice 429, 433; see also H van der Wilt, 'Genocide and International v. Domestic Jurisdiction – Reflections on the van Anraat Case' (2006) 4 Journal on International Criminal Justice 239, 241 et seq.; similar problems emerge with regard to the *animus aggressionis*, a disputed intentional element of the aggression as gravest form of inter-state use of force, see P Fischer, *Irrtumsrisiko bei den Ausnahmen des völkerrechtlichen Gewaltverbotes* (Nomos 2020) 312–316; specifically on the problem to prove *animus aggressionis*, see UNGA 'Report of the Special Committee on the Question of Defining Aggression' (13 July – 14 August 1970) UN Doc A/8019 (1970) para 39.

43 Miklasová (n 21) 81; Çalı (n 39) 185; J Petrov, 'How to Detect Abusive Constitutional Practices' (2024) 2 European Constitutional Law Review 1, 9–12.

44 Çalı (n 39) 185.

45 D Landau and R Dixon, *Abusive Constitutional Borrowing. Legal Globalization and the Subversion of Liberal Democracy* (Oxford University Press 2021) 27 (*emphasis in original*).

46 DE Pozen, 'Constitutional Bad Faith' (2016) 129 Harvard Law Review 885. According to Pozen, subjective bad faith "may involve the use of deception to conceal or obscure a

the intent-oriented analysis and objective bad-faith standard and developing instead "the foreseeable effects test" to detect abusive constitutional practices.[47] In international law, Futhazar and Peters outline two ways of understanding good faith – namely subjectively and objectively.[48] Regarding the latter sense, the authors view it as "a rough synonym for 'reasonable'" and note that, being a standard, it "does not in itself impose any obligation but is only a modality, a way of applying (making, interpreting, enforcing etc.) *other* legal norms."[49]

The debate in international criminal law is akin to the much older controversy of how the different stages of *mens rea* can be distinguished from each other in criminal law along objective and subjective elements. In that context, courts and scholars have had to determine the exact content of borderline categories situated between intention and mere negligence, such as recklessness (in common law systems) or *dolus eventualis* (in continental systems like Germany, Italy, or the Netherlands).[50] A debated question in this respect is whether these categories let an (extreme) objective unreasonableness suffice or whether they presuppose some volitional element beyond the mere knowledge of the circumstances.[51]

However, upon closer examination, a sharp distinction between the subjective and objective standards of bad faith appears somewhat illusory, "since as a practical matter, ordinarily the only way to prove bad motive is by inferences drawn from objective conduct."[52] To ascertain the abusive intent, Dixon and Landau, thus point to several factors. Beyond substantive analysis of con-

---

material fact, a malicious purpose, or an improper motive or belief, including the belief that one's own conduct is unlawful." Ibid., 892. One of the definitions of the objective constitutional bad faith concern "interpretative arguments that are so unreasonable as to betray a furtive design or malicious state of mind." Ibid., 933.

47 Petrov (n 43). See below (n 52).

48 Futhazar and Peters (n 22) 190–191.

49 Ibid., 191 (*emphasis in original*).

50 See generally on these concepts in their comparison A Duff and T Hörnle, Crimes of Endangerment, in K Ambos, A Duff, A Heinze, J Roberts and T Weigend (eds), *Core Concepts in Criminal Law and Criminal Justice*, vol 2 (CUP 2022), 132, 138 et seq.

51 For English-language criticism against a volitional element of *dolus eventualis*, see T Weigend, 'Subjective Elements of Criminal Liability', in M Dubber and T Hörnle (eds), *The Oxford Handbook of Criminal Law* (OUP 2015) 501–502; for a defence, see B Krebs, *Joint Criminal Enterprise in English and German Law* (PhD Thesis, Oxford University 2015) 61–73; in a similar vein, emphasising negligence's element of "awareness of risk in terms of the defendant's belief"; F Stark, *Culpable Carelessness* (CUP 2017), especially Chapters 4–6.

52 L Ponoroff, 'The Limits of Good Faith Analyses: Unraveling and Redefining Bad Faith in Involuntary Bankruptcy Proceedings' (1992) 71 Nebraska Law Review 209, 222 n 44 cited

stitutional changes, and their impact on democratic minimum core, these include what the actors say and do before and after a particular constitutional change, procedural irregularities, and the broader context in which the change occurs.[53] Identifying abuse therefore requires taking into account a combination of these elements.[54]

In light of these reflections, it is argued here that bad faith intent is normally an element of misappropriation of human rights and that it should be understood as the *deliberate employment of human rights discourse for purposes other than those normally associated with human rights argumentation.* Several chapters in this volume outline such ulterior motivations. Beyond the general motivation of eroding achievements of human rights project, these include, for example, the objective of evading accountability, deflecting attention from a State's own human rights violations, or undermining the mobilisatory potential of human rights.[55] Although this standard is mainly subjective – drawing on the purpose pursued by the speaker – it can be deduced from the context in which human rights discourse is employed.[56]

This is not to deny that there will be some borderline cases where it is difficult to prove bad faith intent as understood here. Arguably, the presence of some or several indicators combined, can help assessing whether there is a misappropriation in the sense outlined here.[57]

Ultimately, international law requires that treaties be interpreted and reinterpreted in good faith, as it does for the formation of customary international

---

in Pozen (n 46) ftn 37. Petrov views its effects test "as a complementary or alternative method to intent analysis." Petrov (n 43) 4.

53 R Dixon and D Landau, 'Abusive Constitutional Borrowing: A Reply to Commentators' (2021) 7 The Canadian Journal of Comparative and Contemporary Law 49, 64–73. See Contra Petrov who views the idea of focusing on context as "rather vague and potentially all-encompassing." Petrov (n 43) 10.

54 Dixon and Landau, 'Reply' (n 53) 68.

55 See chapters by Horvath, Fortuin et al., and Freedman.

56 See the concluding chapter for the specifications of context relevant here. In the related area of the *mala fide* restrictions of rights under Article 18 ECHR, Çalı shows that there has been a clear shift in the jurisprudence of the ECtHR concerning, among others, the move away from requiring direct to circumstantial evidence of ulterior purpose of the State authorities. The Court showed openness to a more expanded outlook of circumstantial evidence of bad faith restrictions, in particular to evidence that shows that restriction is not an isolated incident, "but flows from motives that can be deduced from the health of human rights protections, rule of law and democracy in particular country." Çalı (n 39) 198.

57 De Búrca and Young (n 2) 214. For further discussion on this issue, see the concluding chapter.

law,[58] arguably providing additional legal ground for rejecting this type of human rights discourse.

In sum, against the backdrop of the reflections and efforts to delineate the notion of misappropriation of human rights, this edited volume situates its inquiry. In particular, it scrutinises the indicators of (mis)appropriation of human rights formulated by de Búrca and Young and zooms in on the elements of misappropriation, in particular, the strategies and tactics used, as well as on the actors and fora in which they occur.

3 Strategies, Fora, Actors, and Related Concepts: Antecedents of Misappropriation in Scholarship

This edited volume builds on rich scholarship which has centred on the ***strategies*** employed by the States within their domestic jurisdictions or in litigations before domestic or international courts that can be viewed through the lenses of misappropriation of human rights. An important theme analysed in existing literature focuses on the ways in which the States used this approach to undermine LGBT rights. For example, Wilkinson has shown how the Russian government's promotion of "traditional values" in relation to human rights was used, among others, to introduce anti-homopropaganda laws in Russia.[59] Similarly, Kos has identified, among Hungary's post-2010 strategies of non-compliance before the European Court of Human Rights, the strategy of "disguised non-compliance" whereby states offer 'merely rhetorical lip service to formal obligations'.[60] Another example can be found in Kocemba's

58 "In the same way that good faith undergirds the legal possibility of developing a treaty, it also undergirds the emergence and modification of customary rules. In both cases, State expectations, trust and confidence are upheld by a uniform practice and beliefs in a community of States." Futhazar and Peters (n 22) 205.

59 C Wilkinson, 'Putting "Traditional Values" Into Practice: The Rise and Contestation of Anti-Homopropaganda Laws in Russia' (2014) 13 Journal of Human Rights 363; similar trends can be found in other countries, see, eg, A Adebanjo, 'Culture, Morality and the Law: Nigeria's Anti-Gay Law in Perspective' (2015) 15 International Journal of Discrimination and the Law 256; B Bompani, 'Sexualizing Politics: The Anti-Homosexuality Bill, Party-Politics and the New Political Dispensation in Uganda' (2017) 9 Critical African Studies 52.

60 U Kos, 'Controlling the Narrative: Hungary's Post-2010 Strategies of Non-Compliance before the European Court of Human Rights' (2023) 19 European Constitutional Law Review 195, 208–209.

analysis of Poland's use of constitutional law in the course of legal mobilisation against abortion.[61]

Next, the edited volume, by examining (mis)uses of human rights law language within international human rights ***fora***, creates links to legal scholars that have observed and criticised the "politicisation" of the United Nations Human Rights Council's (UNHRC) functioning, particularly through the activities of the regional groups and bloc politics.[62] Recently, in her 2023 Report for the European Parliament, Freedman identified the activities of certain States (ie China, Cuba, Egypt, India, Pakistan, Russia) undertaken at the multilateral fora, especially the UN human rights bodies, or bilaterally, as "advancing competing human rights narratives."[63] The defining feature of this approach is that the relevant States, rather than rejecting the human rights project outright, promote competing human rights discourses and interact with the human rights institutions, yet they do so to weaken and erode the rights from within.[64] Similarly, focusing on Russia's promotion of the "traditionalist agenda"[65] at the UNHRC between 2009 and 2016, Stoeckl and Medvedeva argued that this agenda is not a continuation of cultural relativism, but rather "represents a form of illiberal norm protagonism in the human rights sphere," one that incorporates novel aspects.[66] One of the employed strategies involves constructing alternative narratives about what human rights were historically and what they ought to represent today with the aim of challenging liberal understanding of human rights, delegitimising the West and undermining the UN.[67] Importantly, unlike the previous universal-contextualist debate, this argumentative strategy has garnered signifi-

---

61 K Kocemba, 'Right-Wing Legal Mobilization against Abortion: the Case of Poland' (EUI Working Paper 2023/02).

62 See, eg R Freedman, 'The Human Rights Council' in F Mégret and P Alston (eds), *The United Nations: A Critical Appraisal* (2nd edn, OUP 2020) 203; A-L Chané and A Sharma, 'Universal Human Rights? Exploring Contestation and Consensus in the UN Human Rights Council' (2016) 10 Human Rights & Intl Legal Discourse 219, 223–224.

63 R Freedman, *The Opposition of Models and Narratives in the Field of Human Rights: In-Depth Analysis* (European Union 2023) EP/EXPO/DROI/FW/2019-01/Lot6/1/23. Freedman's contribution to this volume is based on her research conducted for this report.

64 Ibid., 26.

65 See, eg, UNHRC Resolution 12/21 (2009) 'Promoting Human Rights and Fundamental Freedom through a Better Understanding of Traditional Values of Humankind' UN Doc A/HRC/RES/12/21; UNHRC Resolution 26/11 (2014) 'Protection of the Family' UN Doc A/HRC/RES/26/11.

66 K Stoeckl and K Medvedeva, 'Double Bind at the UN: Western Actors, Russia, and the Traditionalist Agenda' (2018) 7 Global Constitutionalism 383, 386.

67 Ibid., 387.

cant support from Western NGOs and "has turned a formerly contextualist topic into a transversal cause."[68]

Similarly, the literature has moved beyond a purely State-centric paradigm, highlighting the roles and strategies of various non-State ***actors***, in particular, religions and related NGOs as well as right-wing groups operating at local, international, or even transnational levels. Regarding the activities of religious actors in the human rights sphere, Stoeckl's scholarship on the Russian Orthodox Church (ROC) is particularly relevant.[69] Similarly, Horsfjord sheds light on the ROC's activities in promoting "traditional values" at the UNHRC, highlighting that "cooperation between different conservative religious forces," especially between Russia and the ROC and Muslim leaders, was particularly significant in this context.[70] In the same vein, Öztürk investigates how the Turkish Directorate of Religious Affairs (the *Diyanet*) has been "transformed into a pliable state apparatus geared towards implementing the political ideology of the ruling cadre," recurring to values such as religion.[71] Moreover, the literature has also analysed the increasingly important role of religious NGOs and right-wing or governmental associations, in particular when they operate transnationally.[72] These organisations invoke rights not only when influencing legislation through lobbying, but also when instigating legal mobilisation and litigation.[73] In this respect, literature has pointed to the significance of government-organised NGOs (GONGOs).[74]

---

68 Ibid., 395.

69 See K Stoeckl, *The Russian Orthodox Church and Human Rights* (Routledge, 2014); K Stoeckl, 'The Russian Orthodox Church as Moral Norm Entrepreneur' (2016) 44(2) Religion, State and Society 131. See above Stoeckl's contribution to de Búrca's and Young's symposium (n 10) and the corresponding text.

70 VL Horsfjord, 'The Russian Orthodox Church at the United Nations Human Rights Council (UNHRC) in A Stensvold (ed), *Religion, State and the United Nations: Value Politics* (Routledge 2017) 75.

71 A Öztürk, Turkey's Diyanet under AKP Rule: From Protector to Imposer of State Ideology', in K Öktem and K Akkoyunlu (eds), *Exit from Democracy* (Routledge 2018); see also B Çalı and E Demir-Gürsel, 'Continuity and Change in Human Rights Appropriation: The Case of Turkey' (2023) 21(1) International Journal of Constitutional law, 266, 274, 275, this article is part of de Búrca's and Young's mentioned symposium.

72 See, generally, C McCrudden, 'Transnational Culture Wars' (2015) 13 International Journal of Constitutional Law 434.

73 On litigation, see, eg, G Baranowska, 'Protecting the Good Name of the Nation as Memory Law' (2024) 19(4) European Constitutional Law Review, 623, 637.

74 R Hasmath, T Hildebrandt and J Hsu, 'Conceptualizing Government-organized Nongovernmental Organizations' (2019) 15 Journal of Civil Society 267.

While the notion of misappropriation itself is relatively new in the context of human rights law, comparable dynamics have been observed by scholars using ***related concepts***. Mégret, in his examination of the populist challenge to human rights,[75] coined the notion of 'human rights populism' defining it as "the use of human rights discourse by those whose politics are grounded in an appeal to ordinary 'people' against an elite, even as their politics have been understood traditionally as anti-human rights."[76] According to Mégret the origins of this type of populism can be traced to "intermediary" political systems, namely in the West, where it is impossible to simply discard the human rights project as such, given its strong legacy there.[77] Mégret argues that human rights populism exploits the long-existing tensions within the conceptual framework of the human right's project.[78]

Similarly, this volume links in with the considerable body of scholarship on the phenomenon of "abusive constitutional borrowing" defined as "appropriation of liberal democratic constitutional designs, concepts, and doctrines in order to advance authoritarian projects."[79] Misappropriation of human rights follows similar techniques and goals in that it invokes widely accepted concepts – human rights – to ultimately reduce the level of human rights protection.

This phenomenon can also be situated alongside literature on the concept of "distortion." This notion has appeared in "legal transplant" literature to denote the transposition of a legal rule or concept from one legal order into another where the legal rule "loses all material similarity with the original and retains only a surface, textual similarity."[80] This notion can again be put in context with the notion of "vernacularisation" that Merry has defined as "the extraction of ideas and practices from the universal sphere of international

75 See the literature on this subject broadly P Alston, 'The Populist Challenge to Human Rights' (2017) 9 Journal of Human Rights Practice 1; J Petrov, 'The Populist Challenge to the European Court of Human Rights' (2020) 18 Int J Const L 476; J Ford, *Human Rights and Populism* (Routledge 2024).

76 Mégret (n 31) 241.

77 Ibid., 242.

78 Ibid., 246.

79 Landau and Dixon (n 45) 3. D Landau, 'Abusive Constitutionalism' (2013) 47 University of California, Davis 189; Dixon and Landau, 'Reply' (n 53); See also J Scholtes, 'Abusing Constitutional Identity' (2021) 22 German Law Journal 534; Pozen (n 46); Petrov (n 43).

80 M Cohn, 'Legal Transplant Chronicles: The Evolution of Unreasonableness and Proportionality Review of the Administration in the United Kingdom' (2010) 58 The American Journal of Comparative Law 583.

organizations and their translation into ideas and practices that resonate with the values and ways of doing things in local contexts."[81]

The neighbouring scientific fields have also explored related phenomena. For example, in the field of international relations and political science, Bettiza and Lewis defined four modes of normative contestation employed over the past two decades by the authoritative powers, such as Russia and China.[82] Among them, "liberal mimicry" is defined as "a type of contestation, which consists in adopting the *form* of liberal discourses and practices, while simultaneously giving these a non-liberal *content*."[83] The authors claim that the implication of such approach is that when a non-liberal actor imitates liberalism by adapting liberal norms to align with its own interests, it raises "the possibility that apparently universalistic norms do not represent universalist claims after all, but are merely the projection of particularist European or American worldviews and interests."[84] Similarly, Bob has distinguished several ways in which rights can be "weaponised," among them their uses as rallying cries to mobilise support,[85] as camouflage to mask motives,[86] or as barriers to suppress subordinates.[87] In public international law, Mälksoo described Russia's use of certain notions in this field as "a simulacrum or concave mirror to Western uses," pointing that "[t]he words are the same but the meanings are different and, from the Western point of view, even distorted."[88] Mälksoo also highlighted how deep-rooted Russia's positioning is, given "its own claim to truth and universality."[89] In addition, especially, in the wake of Russia's (pseudo)legal justifications for its all-out invasion of Ukraine, several authors

---

81 S Engle Merry, 'The Global Travel of Women's Human Rights' (New York University 2017) https://as.nyu.edu/content/dam/nyu-as/asSilverDialogues/documents/S%20Merry%20Resonance%20Dilemma%20silver%20prof%20article1.pdf accessed 5 November 2025. S Engle Merry, *The Seductions of Quantification: Measuring Human Rights, Gender Violence, and Sex Trafficking* (The University of Chicago Press 2016) 110–111.

82 G Bettiza and D Lewis, 'Authoritarian Powers and Norm Contestation in the Liberal International Order: Theorizing the Power Politics of Ideas and Identity' (2020) 5 Journal of Global Security Studies 1, 2.

83 Ibid., 9.

84 Ibid., see also E Burai, 'Parody as Norm Contestation: Russian Normative Justifications in Georgia and Ukraine and Their Implications for Global Norms' (2016) 30 Global Society 67.

85 C Bob, *Rights as Weapons: Instruments of Conflict, Tools of Power* (Princeton University Press 2019) 27 ff.

86 Ibid., 65 ff.

87 Ibid., 151 ff.

88 L Mälksoo, *Russian Approaches to International Law* (OUP 2015) 185.

89 Ibid.

offered their perspectives on the conditions and parameters of abusive argumentation in international law argumentation.[90]

This volume attempts to tie up the loose ends of these neighbouring concepts. Thus, it aims to clarify the relationship between the notion of misappropriation and pre-existing ideas and shed light on the blind spots in the existing literature.

4 Structure of This Volume

Part 1 of this volume focuses on delineating the *elements* included in the misappropriation of human rights. For the misappropriation framework to be a useful addition to human rights scholarship, increased clarity is necessary as to what is considered to be covered by it. The running definition allows for a vast selection of tactics and interpretative methods to be included. This also stems from the fact that de Búrca and Young's approach remains explicitly modest when they describe their criteria as mere "indicators" that "particularly when considered together, may help to identify some of the contemporary forms of ultraconservative or illiberal human rights (mis)appropriation."[91] Yet, this diversity appears to contribute to conceptual unclarity. As such, in this section, several elements that have earlier been identified as part of the 'misappropriation tactical toolbox' are investigated in a particular national context, such as the novel nature of the appropriation, or the selectivity in appropriating, resulting in a lowering of individual human rights protection.

First, we include selective judicial dialogue and inaccurate cherry-picking of jurisprudence by national courts to support a reading of human rights provisions (such as freedom of assembly) that offer less individual protection.

90 F Zarbiyev, 'Of Bullshit, Lies and "Demonstrably Rubbish" Justifications in International Law' (*Völkerrechtsblog*, 18 March 2022) <https://voelkerrechtsblog.org/of-bullshit-lies-and-demonstrably-rubbish-justifications-in-international-law/> accessed 23 April 2024. J-E Perrin, 'La Russie en Ukraine: un cas d'école de l'instrumentalisation du droit international' (*le rubicon*, 28 March 2022) <https://lerubicon.org/la-russie-en-ukraine-un-cas-decole-de-linstrumentalisation-du-droit-international/#:~:text=Comment%20les%20autorités%20russes%20instrumentalisent,de%20Donetsk%20et%20de%20Lougansk%20».> accessed 23 April 2024; M Jorgensen, 'The Weaponisation of International Law in Ukraine' (*Völkerrechtsblog*, 15 March 2022 <https://voelkerrechtsblog.org/the-weaponisation-of-international-law-in-ukraine/> accessed 23 April 2024; E Domínguez-Redondo, 'Russian Misuse of International Law is Final Nail in Coffin of Post WW2 Order' (Middlesex University London, 9 March 2022) <https://mdxminds.com/2022/03/09/ukraine-russia-war-security-council/> 23 April 2024. Miklasová (n 21).

91 De Búrca and Young (n 2) 213.

Then, the section examines how national equality bodies (with questionable independence) engage in selective initiation of hate speech claims against members of disadvantaged groups in the interest of a conservative religious elite. Here, it is discussed how legitimate aims based on majoritarian concepts such as "traditional (family) values" are mobilised to interfere with human rights of minorities (sexual minorities or women). Finally, Part 1 includes an investigation of "bad faith" interests when non-state actors engage in mobilisation through human rights norms which they had previously rejected as an illegitimate colonialist imposition on the Global South or where state actors utilise human rights language to legitimise of a military invasion in another country.

In Chapter 1, *Ignatius Yordan Nugraha* examines the limits of the concept of human rights misappropriation through the case of the Family Love Alliance (Aliansi Cinta Keluarga, AILA) in Indonesia. While de Búrca and Young developed the misappropriation framework to identify regressive uses of human rights by ultraconservative actors, Nugraha argues that the category cannot be applied universally, as it overlooks the cultural and political specificity of local contexts. Focusing on AILA, a group of modernist Islamic women academics opposing feminism and LGBT rights, the chapter shows how human rights language can be appropriated and reshaped – vernacularised – without necessarily aligning with the "New Global Right" or Western notions of misappropriation. AILA combines human rights discourse with anti-colonial rhetoric and modernist Islamic ideas, illustrating that vernacularisation can transform global norms in ways that are meaningful locally but may appear regressive from an external perspective. Nugraha thus calls for greater attention to the interplay between misappropriation and vernacularisation in comparative legal research.

In Chapter 2, *Melaniya Maslova* and *Elena Lipatova* explore how the Russian authorities misappropriate human rights discourse to justify systematic restrictions on the freedom of assembly, all while maintaining the appearance of adherence to international norms. Drawing on qualitative content analysis of judicial decisions under Article 20.2 of the Russian Code of Administrative Offences (2019–2023) (relating to protests), as well as legislative and policy reviews, they uncover how courts, police, and administrative authorities collectively reproduce legal and institutional practices that legitimise repression through the language of rights. By tracing the selective invocation of European Court of Human Rights jurisprudence, the chapter exposes how references to international standards are strategically employed to mask violations and sustain an illusion of legality within an authoritarian framework.

In Chapter 3, *Cai Wilkinson* examines how the promotion of "traditional values" and the rejection of LGBT rights have become central to Russia's domestic and foreign policy since the early 2010s. The chapter situates Russian political homophobia within a broader strategy of statecraft aimed at reasserting national and moral sovereignty as part of the project to "make Russia great again." Central to this analysis is the misappropriation of human rights, where rights discourse is selectively deployed to justify restrictions and reinforce state authority. Wilkinson argues that Russia's approach goes beyond challenging international human rights standards, representing a deliberate rejection of the liberal democratic order, and transforming human rights language into a tool for consolidating authoritarian power and moral control over society. The chapter also highlights how this strategy is embedded in both domestic legislation and Russia's international rhetoric, linking internal governance with geopolitical objectives.

In Chapter 4, *Elif Çelik* examines how human rights discourse in Turkey has been strategically misappropriated to serve the objectives of an authoritarian state. Over the past two decades, the government has not rejected human rights language but has selectively redefined and deployed it to restrict dissent, discipline political expression, and legitimise conservative, exclusionary policies. Focusing on the instrumentalisation of hate speech, the chapter highlights how legal interpretations, court practices, and institutions such as the Human Rights and Equality Institution of Turkey (TİHEK) and the Radio and Television Supreme Council (RTÜK) reinforce the state's ideological priorities. Çelik situates this process within the broader evolution of human rights in Turkey, showing how globally resonant concepts of rights are vernacularised and transformed to align with domestic political agendas. The chapter demonstrates that this misappropriation enables the state to maintain the appearance of compliance with international norms while consolidating power, shaping the boundaries of citizenship, and entrenching authoritarian governance under the guise of rights protection.

Lastly, in Chapter 5, *Egbert Fortuin, Henrike Jansen, Levina de Wolf*, and *Wiktor Pawłowski* examine the elements of human rights misappropriation through the lenses of argumentation theory (Pragma-Dialectics) and communication theory (Grice's theory of communication and framing theory). Their chapter analyses Russia's rationale for its full-scale invasion of Ukraine in February 2022, focusing on claims grounded in human rights and international law, particularly the so-called "Liberation from Genocide" argument. By applying argumentative theory, the authors reveal several strategies underpinning Russia's narrative, including creation of all-encompassing but factually unfounded storyline of past, present and future, the use of vague, irrelevant or misleadingly detailed human rights arguments, and the incorrect application of commonly accepted argumentative schemes. These features collectively distort and misappropriate human rights discourse, exposing the ulterior motives behind its use. The chapter ultimately demonstrates how argumentative analysis can serve as a valuable tool for identifying and assessing instances of human rights misappropriation.

In *Part 2*, the focus lies on the *actors* that engage in misappropriation and the *fora* they use for this engagement. Chapter 6 by *Rosa Freedman* explores how some states, through diplomatic and practical tactics, misappropriate human rights language with the aim to undermine their universal character within the UN Human Rights Council, other multilateral arenas and through bilateral frameworks. By zooming in on the current battlegrounds and sites of contestation, the research contributes to scholarship on different forms of politicisation of human rights. It identifies several tactics employed in this context, including through the invocation of the rights of non-human entities to restrict existing human rights or those of specific minorities, and the promotion of development at the expense of human rights. Particular attention is devoted to the activities spearheaded by China.

In Chapter 7, *Robert Horvath*, examines how Vladimir Putin's regime in Russia has "misappropriated the norms, language and procedures of international criminal justice, a field closely related to international human rights law and often concerned with the most egregious violations of human rights." The chapter traces the evolution of this practice by Russian authorities and identifies several key instances. It explores how the Russian government sought to undermine the credibility and objectivity of the International Criminal Tribunal for the former Yugoslavia through public pronouncements by politicians and diplomats in international arenas, the activities of Kremlin-aligned groups operating in Europe, and annual interventions at the UN Security Council. It further analyses how Russia has sought to present itself as the custodian of the Nuremberg legacy, including by sponsoring anti-racism resolutions at the UN Human Rights Council, and how it misappropriated the language of genocide prevention through performative domestic prosecutions against forces of neighbouring States, and high-profile statements by Russian officials. The chapter reveals how this cynical rhetoric undermines the credibility of international institutions, debases the language of international justice, and shields the perpetrators from accountability.

Next, Chapter 8 by *Adriane Sanctis de Brito*, *Luciana Silva Reis*, *Ana Silva Rosa Mariana*, and *Celano de Souza Amaral* examines how conservative and reactionary actors in Brazil have sought to advance their values and interests in the socio-environmental, moral-religious, and public security spheres ("Beef,

Bible, Bullets") by employing the language of victimhood. The authors analyse the legal arguments of the so-called BBB coalition beyond its parliamentary representatives, encompassing a range of civil society actors. Drawing on publicly available documents submitted to the legislative, executive, and judicial branches of government, the chapter traces how the mobilisation of "victim identity" serves to promote a limited understanding of citizenship. In the narrative advanced by these actors, "the State no longer guarantees universal rights but becomes a tool to directly fulfil the rights of a specific group – the victims."

Finally, *Part 3* sheds light on the ***critiques*** of misappropriation of human rights as a novel framework. Specifically, this part questions the separate need for the concept of misappropriation within the vast scholarship on abusive methods for human rights regression. It critically investigates whether the framework of misappropriation is able to withstand a test of conceptual objectivity or whether – in fact – it relies on incorrect self-referential assumptions and thus constitutes, as Aral puts it, an "empty frame."

In her Chapter 9, *Işıl Aral* goes as far as turning the concept against the very scholars defending it. She argues that scholarly writings that support the concept of misappropriation of human rights themselves misappropriate human rights discourses. She reaches this conclusion by a discourse analysis where she dismantles the concept of misappropriation as a narrative, identifying three elements of narrativisation. The first element ("formal element") anchors the narrative in international law, thus explaining why the investigated phenomenon concerns international law. It is here where Aral situates her critique that the "narrative of misappropriation" avoids any clear definition of what precise human rights are being misappropriated and what is the exact content of these rights. This "obscurity [...] enables the narrative to sound in the register of international law while avoiding the need to specify what this law requires." In her second element ("temporal element"), Aral challenges the presentation of misappropriation of human rights as a narrative of regress in opposition to the history of human rights presented as a linear and progressive trajectory. Thirdly, she unpacks the "spatial element" of the misappropriation narrative, namely that concept's focus on non-Western states. She opposes that focus with the lack of universalisation of a Western understanding of human rights, reproaching the concept of misappropriation "neo-colonial undertones."

In Chapter 10, *Eve Lister* joins Aral in her criticism putting an emphasis on the argument that the concept of misappropriation is unduly broad, and the suggested indicators fail delineating the notion. Rather, she finds, they open the door for injecting dominant cultural values. She demonstrates this claim applying the indicators to euthanasia and the right to life. She argues that there is no "settled body of law" in the law on euthanasia making the misappropriation indicator "departure from a settled body of law" inherently unsettled. Similarly, she argues that the socio-legal concepts included in the indicators "dignity-reducing rather than dignity-enhancing," "repressive or exclusionary aims" as well as "deliberate polarisation" vary greatly among people as the difficult case of euthanasia shows – an "innately polarising" subject where rules and procedures that are dignity-enhancing for some may be dignity-reducing for others.

Following this critique, *Dorjana Bojanovska Poposvka*, in Chapter 11, examines how the misappropriation of rights operates as a central strategy in contemporary efforts to undermine liberal democracy. Drawing on the post-1989 European context, she shows how illiberal actors exploit the unfinished project of liberal constitutionalism, using its institutions and principles to concentrate power while appearing to remain within the rules of democracy. Bojanovska Popovska situates misappropriation not merely as a micro-strategy but as a structural mechanism that works in tandem with other tools to recalibrate legal hierarchies, reinterpret values, and reshape the public sphere, ultimately eroding egalitarian foundations and promoting exclusionary definitions of citizenship. The chapter highlights complementary strategies employed at both national and supranational levels, emphasising the multidirectional and multilevel nature of these efforts. She argues that misappropriation of rights transforms human rights and democratic norms from within, allowing illiberal actors to legitimise power consolidation without presenting a coherent alternative ideology.

In the volume's concluding chapter, we assess the volume's contribution to the concept of misappropriation of human rights and add our own reflection on the elements, fora, actors, and strategies, and – most importantly – the critiques of that notion. The volume is closed by an epilogue in which we give the floor to the two leading voices behind the introduction of misappropriation as a conceptual tool to tackle the misuse of human rights language. *De Búrca and Young* reflect on the contribution of misappropriation as a concept when aiming to uncover an exclusionary, repressive, or anti-pluralist agenda in human rights research.

Bibliography

Monographs

Arthurs HW, *Law and Learning: Report to the Social Sciences and Humanities Research Council of Canada by the Consultative Group on Research and Education in Law* (Social Sciences and Humanities Research Council of Canada 1983).

Bob C, *Rights as Weapons: Instruments of Conflict, Tools of Power* (Princeton University Press 2019).

Brems E, *Human Rights: Universality and Diversity* (Martinus Nijhoff 2001).

Engle Merry S, *The Seductions of Quantification: Measuring Human Rights, Gender Violence, and Sex Trafficking* (The University of Chicago Press 2016).

Fischer P, *Irrtumsrisiko bei den Ausnahmen des völkerrechtlichen Gewaltverbotes* (Nomos 2020).

Ford J, *Human Rights and Populism* (Routledge 2024).

Landau D and Dixon R, *Abusive Constitutional Borrowing. Legal Globalization and the Subversion of Liberal Democracy* (Oxford University Press 2021).

Mälksoo L, *Russian Approaches to International Law* (OUP 2015).

Stark F, *Culpable Carelessness* (CUP 2017).

Stoeckl K, *The Russian Orthodox Church and Human Rights* (Routledge, 2014).

Journal Articles

Adebanjo A, 'Culture, Morality and the Law: Nigeria's Anti-Gay Law in Perspective' (2015) 15 International Journal of Discrimination and the Law 256.

Alston P, 'The Populist Challenge to Human Rights' (2017) 9 Journal of Human Rights Practice 1.

Baranowska G, 'Protecting the Good Name of the Nation as Memory Law' (2024) 19(4) European Constitutional Law Review, 623.

Bettiza G and Lewis D, 'Authoritarian Powers and Norm Contestation in the Liberal International Order: Theorizing the Power Politics of Ideas and Identity' (2020) 5 Journal of Global Security Studies 1.

Bompani B, 'Sexualizing Politics: The Anti-Homosexuality Bill, Party-Politics and the New Political Dispensation in Uganda' (2017) 9 Critical African Studies 52.

Burai E, 'Parody as Norm Contestation: Russian Normative Justifications in Georgia and Ukraine and Their Implications for Global Norms' (2016) 30 Global Society 67.

Chané A-L and Sharma A, 'Universal Human Rights? Exploring Contestation and Consensus in the UN Human Rights Council' (2016) 10 Human Rights & Intl Legal Discourse 219.

Cohn M, 'Legal Transplant Chronicles: The Evolution of Unreasonableness and Proportionality Review of the Administration in the United Kingdom' (2010) 58 The American Journal of Comparative Law 583.
Çalı Band Demir-Gürsel E, 'Continuity and Change in Human Rights Appropriation: The Case of Turkey' (2023) 21(1) International Journal of Constitutional law, 266.
De Búrca G and Young K, 'The (Mis)appropriation of Human Rights by the New Global Right: An Introduction to the Symposium' (2023) 21 International Journal of Constitutional Law 205.
Dixon R and Landau D, 'Abusive Constitutional Borrowing: A Reply to Commentators' (2021) 7 The Canadian Journal of Comparative and Contemporary Law 49.
Donnelly J, 'Cultural Relativism and Universal Human Rights' (1984) 6 Human Rights Quarterly 400.
Donnelly J, 'The Relative Universality of Human Rights', (2007) 29(2) Human Rights Quarterly 281.
Hasmath R, Hildebrandt T and Hsu J, 'Conceptualizing Government-organized Non-governmental Organizations' (2019) 15 Journal of Civil Society 267.
Huckerby J and Knuckey S, 'Appropriation and the Rewriting of Rights' (2023) 21 International Journal of Constitutional Law 243.
Kos U, 'Controlling the Narrative: Hungary's Post-2010 Strategies of Non-Compliance before the European Court of Human Rights' (2023) 19 European Constitutional Law Review 195.
Landau D, 'Abusive Constitutionalism' (2013) 47 University of California, Davis 189.
Mazzeschi R and Carli E, 'Proof of Specific Intent in the Crime of genocide' (2024) 22 Journal of International Criminal Justice 429.
McCrudden C, 'Transnational Culture Wars' (2015) 13 International Journal of Constitutional Law 434.
Mégret F, 'Human Rights Populism' (2022) 13 Humanity: An International Journal of Human Rights, Humanitarianism, and Development 240.
Miklasová J, 'Russian Approaches to Post-Soviet Secessions: Bad Faith Argumentation and Its Limits' (2023) 22 Baltic Yearbook of International Law 64.
Petrov J, 'The Populist Challenge to the European Court of Human Rights' (2020) 18 Int J Const L 476.
Petrov J, 'How to Detect Abusive Constitutional Practices' (2024) 2 European Constitutional Law Review 1.
Ponoroff L, 'The Limits of Good Faith Analyses: Unraveling and Redefining Bad Faith in Involuntary Bankruptcy Proceedings' (1992) 71 Nebraska Law Review 209.
Pozen DE, 'Constitutional Bad Faith' (2016) 129 Harvard Law Review 885.
Scholtes J, 'Abusing Constitutional Identity' (2021) 22 German Law Journal 534.
Stoeckl K, 'The Russian Orthodox Church as Moral Norm Entrepreneur' (2016) 44(2) Religion, State and Society 131.

Stoeckl K, 'Traditional Values, Family, Homeschooling: The Role of Russia and the Russian Orthodox Church in Transnational Moral Conservative Networks and the Efforts at Reshaping Human Rights' (2023) 21 International Journal of Constitutional Law 224.

Stoeckl K and Medvedeva K, 'Double Bind at the UN: Western Actors, Russia, and the Traditionalist Agenda' (2018) 7 Global Constitutionalism 383.

Van der Wilt H, 'Genocide and International v. Domestic Jurisdiction – Reflections on the van Anraat Case' (2006) 4 Journal on International Criminal Justice 239.

Virally M, 'Review Essay: Good Faith in Public International Law' 77 Am J Int'l L (1983) 130.

Wilkinson C, 'Putting "Traditional Values" Into Practice: The Rise and Contestation of Anti-Homopropaganda Laws in Russia' (2014) 13 Journal of Human Rights 363.

Contributions in Edited Volumes

Çalı B, 'Proving Bad Faith in International Law: Lesson from the Article 18 Case Law of the European Court of Human Rights' in Kajtár G et al (eds), *Secondary Rules of Primary Importance – Attribution, Causality, Standard of Review and Evidentiary Rules in International Law* (OUP 2022).

Duff A and Hörnle T, 'Crimes of Endangerment' in Ambos K, Duff A, Heinze A, Roberts J and Weigend T (eds), *Core Concepts in Criminal Law and Criminal Justice*, vol 2 (CUP 2022).

Franke B (ed), *Selected Speeches Held at the Munich Security Conference 2025*, vol 2 (Mittler 2025).

Freedman R, 'The Human Rights Council' in Mégret F and Alston P (eds), *The United Nations: A Critical Appraisal* (2nd edn, OUP 2020).

Futhazar G and Peters A, 'Good Faith' in Vinuales JE (ed), *The UN Friendly Relations Declaration at 50* (CUP 2020).

Kiss A, 'Abuse of Rights' MPEPIL (online edn, OUP 2006).

Horsfjord VL, 'The Russian Orthodox Church at the United Nations Human Rights Council (UNHRC) in Stensvold A (ed), *Religion, State and the United Nations: Value Politics* (Routledge 2017) 75.

Öztürk A, Turkey's Diyanet under AKP Rule: From Protector to Imposer of State Ideology', in Öktem K and Akkoyunlu K (eds), *Exit from Democracy* (Routledge 2018).

Westerman P, 'Open or Autonomous? The Debate on Legal Methodology as a Reflection of the Debate on Law', in Van Hoecke M (ed), *Methodology of Legal Research* (Hart Publishing 2011).

Weigend T, 'Subjective Elements of Criminal Liability', in Dubber M and Hörnle T (eds), *The Oxford Handbook of Criminal Law* (OUP 2015)

Working Papers and Online Publications

Engle Merry S, 'The Global Travel of Women's Human Rights' (New York University 2017) https://as.nyu.edu/content/dam/nyu-as/asSilverDialogues/documents/S%20Merry%20Resonance%20Dilemma%20silver%20prof%20article1.pdf accessed 5 November 2025.

Kocemba K, 'Right-Wing Legal Mobilization against Abortion: the Case of Poland' (EUI Working Paper 2023/02).

Reports

Freedman R, *The Opposition of Models and Narratives in the Field of Human Rights: In-Depth Analysis* (European Union 2023) EP/EXPO/DROI/FW/2019-01/Lot6/1/23.

Theses

B Krebs, *Joint Criminal Enterprise in English and German Law* (PhD Thesis, Oxford University 2015)-

Blogs

Domínguez-Redondo E, 'Russian Misuse of International Law is Final Nail in Coffin of Post WW2 Order' (Middlesex University London, 9 March 2022) <https://mdxminds.com/2022/03/09/ukraine-russia-war-security-council/> 23 April 2024.

Jorgensen M, 'The Weaponisation of International Law in Ukraine' (*Völkerrechtsblog*, 15 March 2022 <https://voelkerrechtsblog.org/the-weaponisation-of-international-law-in-ukraine/> accessed 23 April 2024.

Perrin J-E, 'La Russie en Ukraine: un cas d'école de l'instrumentalisation du droit international' (*le rubicon*, 28 March 2022) <https://lerubicon.org/la-russie-en-ukraine-un-cas-decole-de-linstrumentalisation-du-droit-international/#:~:text=Comment%20les%20autorités%20russes%20instrumentalisent,de%20Donetsk%20et%20de%20Lougansk%20».> accessed 23 April 2024.

Zarbiyev F, 'Of Bullshit, Lies and "Demonstrably Rubbish" Justifications in International Law' (*Völkerrechtsblog*, 18 March 2022) <https://voelkerrechtsblog.org/of-bullshit-lies-and-demonstrably-rubbish-justifications-in-international-law/> accessed 23 April 2024.

PART 1

Elements of Human Rights Misappropriation

CHAPTER 1

Misappropriation or Vernacularisation in the Global South? The 'Family Love Alliance' and the Modernist Islamic Appropriation of Human Rights in Indonesia

Ignatius Yordan Nugraha

> We have the right to adopt good laws from England, or Japan, from Uruguay or Finland if they are not in conflict with our religion. (Mohammad Natsir)[1]

1 Introduction

The debate on whether human rights are universal or particular is nothing new.[2] After decades of never-ending discussions, most human rights scholars today concur that universality does not imply uniformity and that there is room for legitimate variations of human rights.[3] They also advocate for an approach that combines the universality of human rights with the accommodation of cultural pluralism.[4] However, there is no consensus as to the extent to which legitimate variations should be accepted; in the words of Marie-

1 Audrey R Kahin, *Islam, Nationalism and Democracy: A Political Biography of Mohammad Natsir* (NUS Press 2012) 21.

2 Jack Donnelly, *Universal Human Rights in Theory and Practice* (3rd edn, Cornell University Press 2013) 103.

3 See Sébastien Touzé, 'Les pays arabo-musulmans et les traités universels de protection des droits de l'homme' in Mustapha Afroukh (ed), *L'islam en droit international des droits de l'homme* (Institut Universitaire Varenne 2019) 104; Carlos Iván Fuentes, René Provost, and Samuel G Walker, 'E Pluribus Unum – Bhinneka Tunggal Ika? Universal Human Rights and the Fragmentation of International Law' in René Provost and Colleen Sheppard (eds), *Dialogues on Human Rights and Legal Pluralism* (Springer 2013) 41 & 52.

4 Donnelly (n 2) 103–104; Eva Brems, 'Reconciling Universality and Diversity in International Human Rights Law' in András Sajó (ed), *Human Rights with Modesty: The Problem of Universalism* (Springer 2004) 223–228; Abdullahi Ahmed An-Na'im, 'Toward a Cross-Cultural Approach to Defining International Standards of Human Rights: The Meaning of Cruel, Inhuman, or Degrading Treatment or Punishment' in Abdullahi Ahmed An-Na'im (ed), *Human Rights in Cross-Cultural Perspectives. A Quest for Consensus* (University of Pennsylvania Press 1992) 20–21.

Bénédicte Dembour, a potential solution to the debate between universality and relativism is to 'err uncomfortably between the two poles'.[5]

As the world is witnessing a resurgence of primordial identities and traditionalism since the 2010s,[6] reactionary groups have appropriated the language of 'human rights' and filled it with their own religious conceptions.[7] While non-liberal engagement with human rights itself is nothing new,[8] this phenomenon has raised a concern that illiberal and reactionary groups do not actually find 'human rights' meaningful, but are instead abusing it for their own nefarious purposes.[9] This is where Gráinne de Búrca and Katharine Young stepped in out of their concern for the rise of the 'New Global Right': they posited that human rights have been 'misappropriated' by 'ultraconservative' and 'illiberal' actors to undermine the dignity of vulnerable groups, deny their equality, assert a sovereigntist conception of human rights, reduce the welfare of society, and reject mechanisms of accountability.[10] In their view, interpretations of human rights must not 'reverse or undo previous human rights developments and commitments'.[11]

The purpose of this contribution is to critically assess the analytical value of de Búrca and Young's framework in comparing and understanding the process of human rights appropriation across the world. My main observation is that 'misappropriation' has its limits as an analytical category because it does not set a clear line between malicious abuse of human rights and what legal anthropologists call 'vernacularisation', where global concepts of human

---

5 See Marie-Benedicte Dembour, 'Following the Movement of a Pendulum: Between Universalism and Relativism' in Jane K Cowan, Marie-Bénédicte Dembour, and Richard A Wilson (eds), *Culture and Rights: Anthropological Perspectives* (CUP 2001) 59.

6 Francis Fukuyama, *Identity: The Demand for Dignity and the Politics of Resentment* (Farrar, Straus and Giroux 2018).

7 Kristina Stoeckl, 'Traditional Values, Family, Homeschooling: The Role of Russia and the Russian Orthodox Church in Transnational Moral Conservative Networks and Their Efforts at Reshaping Human Rights' (2023) 21 International Journal of Constitutional Law 224, https://doi.org/10.1093/icon/moad026; Kapya Kaoma, 'The Interaction of Human Rights and Religion in Africa's Sexuality Politics' (2023) 21 International Journal of Constitutional Law 339, https://doi.org/10.1093/icon/moad031.

8 Alexandra Huneeus, 'When Illiberals Embrace Human Rights' (2019) 113 AJIL Unbound 380, https://doi.org/10.1017/aju.2019.67.

9 Gráinne de Búrca and Katharine G Young, 'The (Mis)appropriation of Human Rights by the New Global Right: An Introduction to the Symposium' (2023) 21 International Journal of Constitutional Law 205, https://doi.org/10.1093/icon/moad019.

10 Ibid., 210.

11 Ibid., 206–207.

Online Resources

'Appropriate' (*Cambridge Dictionary*) <https://dictionary.cambridge.org/dictionary/english/appropriating> accessed 6 November 2025.

'Bad Faith' (*Cambridge Dictionary*) <https://dictionary.cambridge.org/dictionary/english/bad-faith> accessed 6 November 2025.

'Misappropriate' (*The Britannica Dictionary*) <https://www.britannica.com/dictionary/misappropriate> accessed 6 November 2025.

'Mis-' (*Cambridge Dictionary*) <https://dictionary.cambridge.org/dictionary/english/mis#google_vignette> accessed 6 November 2025.

Treaties

Charter of the United Nations (adopted 26 June 1945, entered into force 24 October 1945) 1 unts xvi.

Vienna Convention on the Law of Treaties (adopted 23 May 1969, entered into force 27 January 1980) 1155 UNTS 331.

UN Documents

UNGA 'Report of the Special Committee on the Question of Defining Aggression' (13 July – 14 August 1970) UN Doc. A/8019 (1970).

Declaration on Principles of International Law concerning Friendly Relations and Co-operation among States in accordance with the Charter of the United Nations, UNGA Res 2625 (xxv) (24 October 1970) UN Doc A/RES/2625(xxv).

UNHRC Resolution 12/21 (2009) 'Promoting Human Rights and Fundamental Freedom through a Better Understanding of Traditional Values of Humankind' UN Doc A/HRC/RES/12/21.

UNHRC Resolution 26/11 (2014) 'Protection of the Family' UN Doc A/HRC/RES/26/11.

Case Laws

Nuclear Tests (Australia v France) (Judgment) [1974] ICJ Rep 253.

rights are 'reinterpreted, redefined, and relocated in a different context'.[12] I argue that 'misappropriation' fails to take into account that human rights are inevitably vernacularised by local actors as they diffuse in society.[13]

I further argue that 'misappropriation' cannot be applied universally as a scientific framework because it is embedded within the specific cultural and political context of the authors. As a consequence, if we were to apply 'misappropriation' to a society with an utterly distinct context, it would lead to a distorted picture of reality. Local understandings of human rights, which have existed for a long time, risk being labelled as a 'misappropriation' simply because the content seems to converge with the conceptions of the so-called 'New Global Right'.

To unpack these arguments, this article focuses on the example of the Family Love Alliance (*Aliansi Cinta Keluarga*, AILA) in Indonesia. AILA is a 'family advocacy' association established by a group of Islamic women academics in February 2014.[14] This association, whose worldview can be categorised as 'modernist Islamic', sought to defend the family from so-called 'sexual immorality', which includes 'pornography, prostitution, fornication (*zina*), free sex (*seks bebas*), and homosexuality'.[15] The women activists of AILA are well-educated and operate in the Jakarta metropolitan area. For instance, a member of AILA's advisory board, Euis Sunarti, is a professor of family security at the Bogor Agricultural Institute, a leading academic institution in Indonesia,[16] whereas the Chairwoman of AILA, Rita Soebagio, is a researcher at an Islamic think tank in Jakarta.[17]

AILA received national spotlight on 19 April 2016, when it filed a petition to the Indonesian Constitutional Court in a case which I shall call *Euis Sunarti and Others*.[18] Spearheaded by Professor Sunarti, AILA lamented that the Indonesian Criminal Code at that time, which was directly inherited from the

12 Sally Engle Merry, *The Seductions of Quantification: Measuring Human Rights, Gender Violence, and Sex Trafficking* (The University of Chicago Press 2016) 110–111.

13 Peggy Levitt and Sally Merry, 'Vernacularization on the Ground: Local Uses of Global Women's Rights in Peru, China, India and the United States' (2009) 9 Global Networks 441, https://doi.org/10.1111/j.1471-0374.2009.00263.x.

14 Afifur Rochman Sya'rani, 'Muslim Women Against Feminism: The Family Love Alliance (Aliansi Cinta Keluarga) and Its Impact on Women's and Sexual Rights in Contemporary Indonesia' (2024) 12 TRaNS: Trans-Regional and -National Studies of Southeast Asia 156, 161, https://doi.org/10.1017/trn.2023.6.

15 Ibid.

16 Ibid., 165.

17 Ibid., 161 fn 6.

18 Constitutional Court of the Republic of Indonesia, Judgment for Case Number 46/PUU-XIV/2016, 14 December 2017 (hereinafter *Euis Sunarti and Others*).

Dutch colonial era, did not criminalise *zina* and homosexual sex. Thus, AILA implored the Court to expand the scope of the existing criminal law provisions.[19] Eventually, the Constitutional Court rejected this petition in a narrow 5–4 ruling.[20] Notably, in building its case, AILA has appropriated 'human rights' to such an extent that the substance has become utterly unrecognisable in comparison to international human rights standards.[21] In its publication, AILA has also assumed the language of 'anti-colonialism'. A collaborator of AILA even appropriated the Third World approaches to international law (TWAIL) and filled it with modernist Islamic substance to reject mainstream human rights standards as a 'Western imposition'.[22]

This article focuses on AILA as an apt illustration of why 'misappropriation' has its limits as an analytical framework. This women academics organisation does not fit the cliché of the unholy alliance between 'ultraconservative' religious actors and the 'illiberal' state.[23] Most importantly, AILA is not known to foster any ties with 'a growing array of national and transnational coalitions of populist and conservative political and religious actors – what [de Búrca and Young] refer[red] to as the New Global Right'.[24] Yet, AILA's hostility to feminism and LGBT rights is more in line with this so-called 'New Global Right', which makes it particularly tempting for international human rights jurists to apply the label of 'misappropriation'. Regardless, as I shall argue in this article, doing so would lead to an inaccurate picture of the cultural and political contexts where AILA operates, which throws into question the analytical value of 'misappropriation' for comparative legal research. 'Misappropriation' also does not account for the fact that 'appropriation' of global concepts (such as 'democracy' and 'human rights') has a long history among modernist Muslims who have strong commitments to democracy,[25] and the resulting vernacularised conceptions may not necessarily align with our own sensibilities.

This chapter is structured as follows. Section 2 argues why 'misappropriation' is not a universally applicable analytical category, but rather a norma-

19 Ibid.

20 Ibid.

21 See Section 3.1.

22 See Section 3.2.

23 See Lucy Ash, *The Baton and the Cross: Russia's Church Under Putin* (Icon Books 2024); Marta R de Assis Machado, 'Antiabortion Legal Mobilization in Brazil: Human Rights as a Field of Contention' (2023) 21 International Journal of Constitutional Law 308, https://doi.org/10.1093/icon/moad030.

24 De Búrca and Young (n 9) 207.

25 Gwenaël Feillard, 'Adapting to Reformasi: Democracy, Human Rights, and Civil Society in the Indonesian Islamist Discourse' (2004) 7 Moussons 17, https://doi.org/10.4000/moussons.2461.

tive term specific to the cultural and political contexts of the authors. Subsequently, Section 3 unpacks how AILA and its collaborators have appropriated the language of 'human rights' as well as anti-colonialism, including TWAIL. Section 4 then argues why 'misappropriation' is inappropriate to be applied in the context of AILA. Finally, Section 5 reflects on the implication of the AILA case study to the 'misappropriation' framework as a whole.

2 Distinguishing Misappropriation from Vernacularisation?

The possibility that human rights may be misappropriated by an illiberal populist leader has been tackled in the comparative constitutional law scholarship under the banner of 'abusive constitutionalism' or 'abusive constitutional borrowings'.[26] In their landmark publication, Rosalind Dixon and David Landau observed that constitutional doctrines that were originally meant to prevent the concentration and abuse of power can be misappropriated for anti-democratic purposes.[27] Under this framework, a populist executive abuses human rights when they advance an interpretation of rights that erodes the democratic order.[28] The examples include the use of gender quota in the parliament to entrench the authoritarian rule of Paul Kagame in Rwanda,[29] or the invocation of the right to political participation in Bolivia to remove presidential term limits and thus pave the way for Evo Morales to remain in power.[30] In this regard, abusive constitutionalism is assessed based on whether there is an attempt to subvert democracy and usher in an illiberal, if not outright authoritarian, regime.

Gráinne de Búrca and Katharine G Young then stepped in to provide a more detailed framework on the 'misappropriation' of human rights in a 2023 symposium for the International Journal of Constitutional Law.[31] They posited that while the content of human rights is subject to reasonable disagreement, certain interpretations may be considered a form of 'misappropriation', which they defined as 'the deployment by a particular set of actors of a range of strategies and arguments [...] advanced in the language of protecting "human rights," but generally seeking to reverse or undo previous human rights devel-

26 Rosalind Dixon and David Landau, *Abusive Constitutional Borrowing: Legal Globalization and the Subversion of Liberal Democracy* (OUP 2021).

27 Ibid., 3.

28 See Ibid., 56 et seq.

29 Ibid., 73–74.

30 Huneeus (n 8) 381–382.

31 De Búrca and Young (n 9).

opments and commitments'.[32] Focusing on what they called the 'New Global Right', namely 'a growing array of national and transnational coalitions of populist and conservative political and religious actors', de Búrca and Young observed that these actors do not reject human rights outright, but rather take advantage of the language of human rights to advance their agenda.[33]

To further unpack the meaning of 'misappropriation', de Búrca and Young argued that human rights have 'certain core features', which include 'the basic commitments to recognition and protection for the equal human dignity, human freedom and human welfare of all persons'.[34] In relation to these basic commitments, they spelt out the following normative criteria:

> legal protection for human rights should be dignity-enhancing rather than dignity-undermining, recognizing rather than denying the equality of humans, universalist in orientation rather than strictly sovereigntist, welfare-promoting rather than welfare-reducing, and accepting rather than rejecting of mechanisms of accountability.[35]

De Búrca and Young acknowledged that these 'general indicators' may not offer full guidance as to whether a differing interpretation of rights is a right or wrong, 'particularly if proposed as part of an exception or derogation'.[36] Nonetheless, they posited that 'if a set of interpretations over time is consistently at odds with these core commitments, there is reason to consider that what is being promoted is fundamentally inconsistent with the essential premises of human rights'.[37]

On top of that, based on their observation of the modus operandi of what they called the 'New Global Right', de Búrca and Young formulated eight specific indicators to identify a 'misappropriation'.[38] These include: (1) whether particular human rights interpretation is exclusionary, repressive, or anti-pluralist, (2) whether a particular interpretation departs from the existing international human rights standards, (3) whether there is an attempt to assert that certain rights are more fundamental than others, (4) whether there is an attempt to scapegoat certain groups or consider them as not deserving to claim rights, (5) whether there is an attempt to repress civil soci-

32 Ibid., 206–207.
33 Ibid., 207.
34 Ibid., 209.
35 Ibid., 210.
36 Ibid.
37 Ibid.
38 Ibid., 213–214.

ety, (6) whether there is evidence of 'clear falsehood, subterfuge, "camouflage," intentional distortion, or deliberate polarization', (7) whether the human rights claim constitutes a reversal of previous strategies, which suggest bad faith or disingenuous purpose, and (8) whether there is an effort to repudiate or evade external monitoring or independent mechanisms of accountability.[39]

With regard to the general indicators, de Búrca and Young seem to view 'dignity', 'freedom', and 'welfare' as universal categories which hold true irrespective of time, space, and culture. However, in this diverse world, different societies understand these terms differently.[40] With regard to 'dignity', for instance, Oscar Schachter observed that international human rights instruments do not define this term, and '[i]ts intrinsic meaning has been left to intuitive understanding, conditioned in large measure by cultural factors'.[41] Christopher McCrudden has also argued that 'dignity carried an enormous amount of content, but different content for different people'.[42] Thus, in his view, human dignity 'is exposed as culturally relative, deeply contingent on local politics and values, resulting in significantly diverging, even conflicting, conceptions'.[43]

More importantly, de Búrca and Young have not factored the ineluctable reality that human rights assume different substances as they diffuse into a particular society.[44] Here, I am not alluding to the widely discredited cultural relativism,[45] but rather what the eminent anthropologist Sally Engle Merry called 'vernacularisation'.[46] In her words, '[v]ernacularization refers to a pro-

39 Ibid., 213.

40 See, for instance, Josiah AM Cobbah. 'African Values and the Human Rights Debate: An African Perspective' (1987) 9 Human Rights Quarterly 309.

41 Oscar Schachter, 'Human Dignity as a Normative Concept' (1983) 77 American Journal of International Law 848, 849.

42 Christopher McCrudden, 'Human Dignity and Judicial Interpretation of Human Rights' (2008) 19 EJIL 655, 678, https://doi.org/10.1093/ejil/chn043.

43 Ibid., 698.

44 Daniel M Goldstein, 'Whose Vernacular? Translating Human Rights in Local Contexts' in Mark Goodale (ed), *Human Rights at the Crossroads* (OUP 2014), https://doi.org/10.1093/acprof:osobl/9780199376414.003.0008.

45 See Bonny Ibhawoh, 'Between Culture and Constitution: Evaluating the Cultural Legitimacy of Human Rights in the African State' (2000) 22 Human Rights Quarterly 838, 841; Sally Engle Merry, 'Human Rights Law and the Demonization of Culture (And Anthropology Along the Way)' (2003) 26 Political and Legal Anthropology Review 55, 72, https://doi.org/10.1525/pol.2003.26.1.55.

46 Merry (n 12) 110.

cess by which global ideas, such as those of human rights [...], enter into local situations and are refashioned in local contexts'.[47] In short, vernacularisation involves 'the process of appropriation and local adoption of globally generated ideas'.[48] It is to be distinguished from, in the words of Mark Goodale, 'the mere translation of international norms into "local" linguistic or cultural categories'.[49]

Through vernacularisation, human rights concepts would 'take on some of the ideological and social attributes of the place, but also retain some of their original formulation'.[50] This vernacularisation of global concepts is performed by those whom Merry called 'vernacularisers', namely 'people in between, conversant with both sides of the exchange but able to move across borders of ideas and approaches', such as social movement activists and members of non-governmental organisations (NGOs).[51] Thus, Merry observed that each community has its own vernacularisers who would 'convey ideas from one context to another, adapting and reframing them from the way they attach to a source context to one that resonates with the new location'.[52]

As it turns out, Merry eventually discovered that vernacularisation has 'its limits' due to the pre-existing values, tradition, and ideology.[53] For instance, during their fieldwork among impoverished women in Lima, whose lives are shaped by 'the Andean traditions', Levitt and Merry discovered that '[b]ecause their strong sense of community clashed with the individualized discourse of rights, they reinterpreted rights as more communally based'.[54] As a consequence, when these women were encouraged by a feminist non-governmental organisation to 'embrace their sexuality and become more comfortable with their bodies', these women were resistant to what they perceived as 'an anti-male stance'.[55] Similarly, Beth Lyon and Pranoto Iskandar's fieldwork in West

47 Ibid., See also Tom Boellstorff, 'Dubbing Culture: Indonesian 'Gay' and 'Lesbi' Subjectivities and Ethnography in an Already Globalized World' (2008) 30 American Ethnologist 225, 232 & 237, https://doi.org/10.1525/ae.2003.30.2.225 (exploring how the sense of being 'gay' and 'lesbi', while realised through globalised mass media, 'is usually experienced locally' in Indonesia).

48 Levitt and Merry (n 13) 446.

49 See Mark Goodale, 'Justice in the Vernacular: An Anthropological Critique of Commensuration' (2024) 49 Law & Social Inquiry 7, 21, https://doi.org/10.1017/lsi.2022.107.

50 Levitt and Merry (n 13) 446.

51 Ibid., 449.

52 Ibid.

53 Ibid., 451. See also David M Engel, 'Rights as Wrongs: Legality and Sacrality in Thailand' (2014) 39 Asian Studies Review 38, https://doi.org/10.1080/10357823.2014.990356.

54 Levitt and Merry (n 13) 451.

55 Ibid.

Java, Indonesia, found that the local farmworkers have a sense of 'relational self' where personhood is inseparable from communal relationships.[56] As a result, 'rights-based claims are perceived [by local farmworkers] as self-interested and materialistic, given that they fail to embody the collective interests of the community'.[57]

Thus, it is to be expected that, as observed by Levitt and Merry, vernacularisation 'produces a set of ideas and practices that are remote from the original documents and intentions and that may differ from ideas that international organizations and agreements produce'.[58] Daniel Goldstein has also observed that vernacularisation involves 'a dialectic in which transnational conceptions are made meaningful within [...] local realities, themselves already conditioned by their broader inclusion within transnational frameworks of economics, politics, and culture'.[59] In this light, while Merry seems to conceive 'vernacularisation' as a top-down process initiated by local human rights activists to 'bring human rights home',[60] local knowledge and context are an essential condition in shaping and forming the resulting 'vernacularised' rights. As further observed by Sumi Madhok:

> vernacular rights cultures are not wholly derivative from or entirely oppositional to Western notions and conventions of human rights or, indeed, entirely discrete in form, in that one would be hard pressed to find hermetically sealed or "pure" indigenous rights traditions. They are instead interlocked into relations that are historically, productively, intimately, and coercively produced and experienced.[61]

Given that vernacularisation is a 'widespread practice' and continuously occurs across the globe,[62] it is essential to be able to distinguish between 'misappropriation' and genuine appropriation of universalistic concepts that

---

56 Beth Lyon and Pranoto Iskandar, 'Relational Self and Farmworker Law Reform: The Case of Indonesia' (2024) 56 Legal Pluralism and Critical Social Analysis 616, 620, https://doi.org/10.1080/27706869.2024.2374631.

57 Ibid., 629.

58 Levitt and Merry (n 13) 458. See also Mark Goodale, 'Human Rights After the Post-Cold War' in Mark Goodale (ed), *Human Rights at the Crossroads* (OUP 2014) 9, https://doi.org/10.1093/acprof:osobl/9780199376414.003.0001.

59 Goldstein (n 44) 112.

60 Merry (n 45) 72.

61 Sumi Madhok, 'On Vernacular Rights Cultures and the Political Imaginaries of Haq' (2017) 8 Humanity: An International Journal of Human Rights, Humanitarianism, and Development 485, 486, https://dx.doi.org/10.1353/hum.2017.0029.

62 Levitt and Merry (n 13) 458.

are made meaningful to a particular society; otherwise, we risk disparaging vernacular perspectives from the Global South. However, when international human rights law is vernacularised in different societies, the resulting hybrid may not necessarily align with how we conceive dignity, freedom, and welfare.[63] On the very contrary, vernacular human rights, as conditioned by local knowledge and values, may strike international human rights lawyers as 'revers[ing] or undo[ing] previous human rights developments and commitments' at the global level,[64] even though from a local perspective, it is neither a 'progress' nor 'regress'.[65]

In comparison, the framework of 'abusive constitutionalism', while also founded on a profound commitment to 'constitutional democracy', contains a clear element of intent: we can speak of an abuse of human rights when it is deployed by an authoritarian populist leader to concentrate and entrench their own power.[66] In de Búrca and Young's 'misappropriation', the focus is more on whether an interpretation is by nature *regressive* compared to what has been achieved at the international level thus far, irrespective of whether a vernaculariser genuinely believes in this particular interpretation and finds it truly meaningful. 'Misappropriation' is hence an inherently normative framework, where a 'regressive' belief is denigrated as nefarious, malicious, or abusive, as opposed to an analytical concept that seeks 'to focus [...] on the social processes of human rights implementation and resistance'.[67]

In fact, de Búrca and Young's 'misappropriation' is rooted in a specific cultural context.[68] 'Progress' and 'regress' are not objective realities to be discovered in nature; underlying these terms lies a deep cultural assumption concerning 'the eternal progress and infinite task of humanity perfecting itself', which is characteristic of Western societies following the Age of

63 See Goodale (n 58) 16.

64 De Búrca and Young (n 9) 206–207.

65 See, for instance, Alexander Hinton, *The Justice Facade: Trials of Transition in Cambodia* (OUP 2018) 138: according to 'a Buddhist vernacular conception of time mediating lived experience in Cambodia [...], our being is constituted and reconstituted in a cyclical fashion. On a cosmic level, the universe is created and then degrades before being renewed'. He further added, '[t]his Buddhist vernacular of time is at odds with the linearity and progressive teleology of juridical time'. In other words, other cultures do not necessarily have the same worldview of mankind's continuous progress towards utopia.

66 See David Landau, 'Abusive Constitutionalism' (2013) 47 UC Davis Law Review 189.

67 Sally Engle Merry, 'Transnational Human Rights and Local Activism: Mapping the Middle' (2006) 108 American Anthropologist 38, 39, https://doi.org/10.1525/aa.2006.108.1.38.

68 Gershom Scholem, *The Messianic Idea in Judaism: And Other Essays on Jewish Spirituality* (Schocken Books 1995) 26.

Enlightenment.[69] As declared by the renowned Enlightenment thinker Marquis de Condorcet, 'the perfectibility of man is absolutely indefinite; that the progress of this perfectibility [...] has no other limit than the duration of the globe upon which nature has placed us'.[70]

De Búrca and Young's framework denotes such a linear progressive imagination of history,[71] since they believe that human rights must always be 'dignity-enhancing rather than dignity-undermining' or 'welfare-promoting rather than welfare-reducing'.[72] For them, the correct human rights interpretation must not 'reverse or undo previous human rights developments and commitments'.[73] This is to be contrasted with traditional societies in Java and Bali; under their Dharmic-influenced worldview, history is not a linear 'progression' of continuous 'dignity-enhancement' and 'welfare-promotion', but rather 'repeat[ing] in cycles and one keeps going back to the time before'.[74]

Furthermore, 'misappropriation' is also embedded within the specific political context of the authors. De Búrca and Young specifically formulated this framework as a response to the 'New Global Right'. This political underpinning is made explicit by de Búrca and Young's own statement that the eight specific indicators were formulated 'to identify some of the contemporary forms of *ultraconservative or illiberal* human rights (mis)appropriation'.[75] Therefore, as well acknowledged by de Búrca and Young themselves, 'misappropriation' denotes a direct academic response to the 'threat' of 'conserva-

69 Ibid., 37. See also Hinton (n 65) 8.

70 Marquis de Condorcet, *Outlines of An Historical View of the Progress of the Human Mind* (G Fryer 1802) <www.archive.org/details/outlinesofhistoroocon/page/214/mode/2up> accessed 23 May 2025, 215–216. See also W Warren Wagar, 'Modern Views of the Origins of the Idea of Progress' (1967) 28 Journal of the History of Ideas 55, 60.

71 See Pranoto Iskandar, 'Pancasila Nation: Indonesia's Folk Constitutionalism' (DPhil thesis, McGill University 2024) 40–41.

72 De Búrca and Young (n 9) 210.

73 Ibid., 206–207.

74 Clifford Geertz, *The Religion of Java* (The University of Chicago Press 1976) 231. See also Iskandar (n 71) 40–41; Benedict R O'G Anderson, 'The Idea of Power in Javanese Culture' in Claire Holt (ed), *Culture and Politics in Indonesia* (1972) 20. It is worth noting that pre-Enlightenment Europe itself had a different understanding of history. As lucidly explained by Anderson, 'the mediaeval Christian mind had no conception of history as an endless chain of cause and effect or of radical separations between past and present. [...] [P]eople thought they must be near the end of time, in the sense that Christ's second coming could occur at any moment [...]. See Benedict Anderson, *Imagined Communities: Reflections on the Origin and Spread of Nationalism* (Verso 1991) 23.

75 De Búrca and Young (n 9) 213–214, emphasis added.

tive global alliances'.[76] It is a product of our time,[77] a globalised era when nationalism, identity, and traditionalism are resurging around the globe to challenge the post–Cold War consensus on democracy, constitutionalism, and the rule of law.[78] 'Misappropriation' denotes an academic reaction and opposition to this resurgence.

Hence, the term as used by de Búrca and Young should be seen in this light; 'misappropriation' is only meaningful within the specific political and cultural context of the authors, instead of a universal analytic category applicable in all cultures.[79] After all, the spotlight on the 'New Global Right' itself already denotes a Western-centric assumption that all societies are divided based on the left-right political spectrum or that there is a dichotomy between 'conservatives' and 'progressives'.[80] As I shall show in the following sections, the 'misappropriation' framework shows its limits when applied to the example of the 'ultraconservative religious' AILA: their understanding of human rights is clearly incompatible with the values that both I and de Búrca and Young subscribe to, yet forcing the framework of 'misappropriation' would lead to a distorted picture of reality.

3 Family Love Alliance and Modernist Islamic Appropriation of Human Rights

'Misappropriation' denotes an opposition to the 'New Global Right', which is part of the political and cultural dynamics in much of the Western hemisphere. Before examining why 'misappropriation' is incongruous when applied to

76 Ibid., 211.

77 As a note, I understand 'culture' here as webs of meaning pervading a particular community. See Clifford Geertz, *The Interpretation of Cultures: Selected Essays* (Basic Books 1973) 5.

78 See Fukuyama (n 6).

79 See Mark Goodale, *Anthropology and Law: A Critical Introduction* (NYU Press 2017) 15–16; Merry (n 67) 41.

80 As an example of a society where the left-right political spectrum is of limited applicability and does not make sense when applied to a different society, see Ignatius Yordan Nugraha and Abdurrachman Satrio, 'Is This a Constitutional Democracy: Familial Harmony, Pancasila, and Javanese Values in Indonesia's New Government' (*Verfassungsblog*, 7 November 2024) <www.verfassungsblog.de/is-this-a-constitutional-democracy/> accessed 10 February 2025, https://dx.doi.org/10.59704/055af6dc9b63dbfc. See also Edward Aspinall, Diego Fossati, Burhanuddin Muhtadi, and Eve Warburton, 'Mapping the Indonesian Political Spectrum' (*New Mandala*, 24 April 2018) <www.newmandala.org/mapping-indonesian-political-spectrum/> accessed 10 February 2025.

AILA, it is essential to understand how this non-governmental organisation has appropriated *hak asasi manusia* (human rights). This section therefore unpacks how members of AILA and their collaborators understand 'human rights' and fill this term with modernist Islamic norms, with repercussions for gender equality and sexual minority rights. It also explores how AILA and its collaborators appropriate the language of anti-colonialism and even 'TWAIL' to reject international human rights standards.

3.1 'Human Rights' with Modernist Islamic Substance

In *Euis Sunarti and Others*, AILA filed a petition to the Indonesian Constitutional Court to expand the scope of the Criminal Code to cover *zina* and homosexual sex, which was eventually rejected in a narrow 5–4 ruling.[81] In building their case, AILA appropriated the language of 'human rights'. Members of AILA claimed that the State had violated their fundamental rights because of the failure to criminalise sex outside marriage and homosexual sex. The rights that they invoked were multifarious, such as 'the right to found a family and to continue the progeny through a lawful marriage', the right of the child to protection, the right to protection of oneself and family,[82] and even women's right to health.[83] Strikingly, to argue for the criminalisation of homosexual acts, they also invoked the right to legal guarantee, protection, and certainty and to equal treatment before the law.[84]

If we seek to understand AILA's submission from a purely legal-doctrinal perspective,[85] we will be utterly perplexed beyond belief. To put it mildly, members of AILA, as well as their own legal counsel, do not follow the mainstream canon of rights interpretation as can be found in Global North jurisdictions. Instead, their arguments are often circular and not systematic, which is typical of legal writings in Indonesia.[86] Their submission would also strike a reasonable person in the international legal academia as reek of slippery-slope

81 *Euis Sunarti and Others* (n 18).
82 Ibid., 7.
83 Ibid., 36.
84 Ibid., 54.
85 For what I meant with 'legal-doctrinal', see Suzanne Egan, 'The Doctrinal Approach in International Human Rights Law Scholarship' in Lee McConnell and Rhona Smith (eds), *Research Methods in Human Rights* (Routledge 2018).
86 See Pranoto Iskandar, 'Why Are Indonesian Law (Schools) No Good' (2019) 6 The Indonesian Journal of International & Comparative Law 607, 608: 'No surprise that reading an inordinately hefty tome of a doctoral thesis that is not uncommon to reach more than 500 pages has left one with nothing but a sense of bewilderment. [...] The extreme case, but not by any means should be considered as uncommon, is the unceasing production

and lacking robust scientific evidence. For instance, AILA claimed that the failure of the Criminal Code to criminalise sex outside of marriage and homosexual sex threatens 'family security' in Indonesia, which could lead to the 'destruction' of the nation itself.[87] It is easy to dismiss and ridicule AILA's arguments as 'not human rights', since, to borrow Merry's words, 'the name and transnational referent are retained but the content of the ideas [...] is dramatically changed'.[88]

Nonetheless, AILA's understanding of rights can be understood if we take a step back and engage in an interpretive method, where we try to uncover the webs of meaning, values, and norms underlying the use of certain terms.[89] In this regard, when AILA invokes the language of *hak asasi manusia* in its constitutional petition, the term acquires a radically different meaning in their imaginary compared to *human rights* as understood at the international level. *Hak* (rights), to borrow the terms of Madhok, 'is not only always sovereign, individualist, discrete, or indeed privately articulated one. It is predominantly expressed collectively and in religious [...] terms'.[90]

First, the term *hak*, which is a loanword from Arabic *haqq* meaning 'truth', 'reality', or 'validity',[91] immediately assumes a religious meaning in the imaginary universe of AILA members. *Hak* in the Indonesian context does not denote a set of enforceable claims against the state to prevent the abuse of power.[92] Instead, 'rights' are believed to be 'inherent in the essence and existence of humans as the creations of All-One God' and 'gifted by Him', as enshrined under Article 1(1) of Law No 39 of 1999 on Human Rights.[93] In this respect, AILA is not alone in imagining rights as being ordained by God.[94] Belief in

of unintelligible and, certainly, nonsense scholarly writing genre that speaks volumes about nothing'.

87 *Euis Sunarti and Others* (n 18) 20.

88 Merry (n 67) 44.

89 See Geertz (n 77) 312 & 314.

90 See Madhok (n 61) 487.

91 Clifford Geertz, *Local Knowledge: Further Essays in Interpretive Anthropology* (Basic Books 1983) 185.

92 See Daniel J Elazar, *Covenant and Commonwealth: From Christian Separation Through the Protestant Reformation the Covenant Tradition in Politics* (Routledge 2018) 138; Michael Ignatieff, *Human Rights as Politics and Idolatry* (Princeton University Press 2003) 83–84.

93 Law No 39 of 1999 on Human Rights.

94 See Pranoto Iskandar, 'Religious Constitutionalism: An Indonesian-esque Interpretive Venture' (2019) Oxford University Comparative Law Forum <https://ouclf.law.ox.ac.uk/religious-constitutionalism-an-indonesian-esque-interpretive-venture/> accessed 10 February 2025. See also *Euis Sunarti and Others* (n 18) 124–127.

God is fervent among the population and even forms part of the state's constitutional identity.[95]

However, AILA and its collaborators are 'modernist' or 'reformist' Muslims in the sense that they rely on their pure reason to understand and internalise the original sources of the Sharia: the Quran and the Hadith.[96] In the Indonesian context, modernist Muslims are to be contrasted with 'traditionalist' Muslims influenced by Indonesia's Shivaist-Buddhist past who are 'best known for integrating Sufi, folk Javanese, and Javanese court traditions within a broadly Islamic frame'.[97] Modernist Muslims seek to purify Islam from un-Islamic practices, yet at the same time they 'readily adopted the organizational and educational methods and ideas of the West, including those of Christian missionaries, as long as these were not in violation of the principles of Islam'.[98]

As part of the modernist movement, members of AILA are deeply influenced by what Clifford Geertz called Islamic 'scripturalism',[99] which is 'scholastic, legalistic, and doctrinal' and represents 'the turn toward the Koran, the Hadith, and the Sharia, together with various standard commentaries upon them, as the only acceptable bases of religious authority'.[100] This is to be contrasted with the traditionalist Muslims of Indonesia; as aptly observed by Pranoto Iskandar, their religious tradition is 'rooted in immanentism [...], indicated by *Kawulo Manunggaling Gusti* or unio mystica as its main tenet'.[101] After all, the folk religious traditions of Indonesia 'emphasise adherence to the correct conduct, form, or ritual ("orthopraxy")', whereas 'the "modern" or "universal" religions [...] value the importance of following the correct conceptual understanding or dogma ("orthodoxy")'.[102]

95 See Ignatius Yordan Nugraha, 'Godly Constitution and Divine Enlightenment: The Indonesian Constitutional Court's Recent Theocratic Judgment' (*Verfassungsblog*, 13 January 2025) <www.verfassungsblog.de/godly-constitution-and-divine-enlightenment/> accessed 10 February 2025, https://dx.doi.org/10.59704/1bf50643de038c99.

96 See Muhamad Ali, 'Categorizing Muslims in Postcolonial Indonesia' (2007) 11 Moussons 33, https://doi.org/10.4000/moussons.1746.

97 Nancy J Smith-Hefner, *Islamizing Intimacies: Youth, Sexuality, and Gender in Contemporary Indonesia* (University of Hawaii Press 2019) 20.

98 Ibid., 20.

99 See Clifford Geertz, *Islam Observed: Religious Development in Morocco and Indonesia* (The University of Chicago Press 1971) 60.

100 Ibid., 62 & 65.

101 Iskandar (n 71) 211.

102 Ibid., 75.

As a consequence, the imaginary of members of AILA is also shaped by this scripturalism and orthodoxy. *Hak asasi manusia*, in this regard, is inseparable from 'obligations'.[103] Geertz further elaborated that *haqq*:

> anchors a theory of duty as a set of sheer assertions, so many statements of brute fact, in a vision of reality as being in its essence imperative, a structure not of objects but of wills. The moral and ontological change places, at least from our point of view. It is the moral, where we see the "ought," which is a thing of descriptions, the ontological, for us the home of the "is," which is one of demands.[104]

Consequently, *haqq* as reality 'is a deeply moralized, active, demanding real, not a neutral, metaphysical "being," merely sitting there awaiting observation and reflection; a real of prophets not philosophers'.[105] In other words, the descriptive is inherently prescriptive: *haqq* implies a reality to which every human being must submit.[106]

The fusion between the descriptive and the prescriptive, or 'is' and 'ought',[107] in *haqq* explains why AILA's submissions are mostly based on assertions of 'facts', instead of a carefully constructed legal argument based on prescriptive norms. For instance, AILA claimed in its constitutional petition that the word 'family' in human rights provisions implies a biological relationship between mother, father, and children.[108] This is not a mere assertion of a sociological or biological 'fact' but incorporates a prescriptive outlook that family *must* consist of the traditional nuclear family. From the perspective of the women of AILA, going against this would be tantamount to defying 'reality' itself, including Allah, one of whose 99 names include *al-Haqq*.[109]

Hence, it is not surprising that AILA's submissions to the Constitutional Court are riddled with slippery slopes, because according to their imaginary, one would be facing the direct repercussions of defying the 'reality', or *haqq*, of Allah. For instance, AILA confidently asserted, without scientific evidence,

---

103 Feillard (n 25) para 43; Madhok (n 61) 488.

104 Geertz (n 91) 187.

105 Ibid., 188.

106 Ibid.

107 This is to be contrasted with David Hume's 'guillotine', where he argued that *is* and *ought* occupy separate domains and cannot be conflated with each other. See David Hume, *A Treatise of Human Nature* (John Noon 1739) 469–470, <https://en.wikisource.org/wiki/Treatise_of_Human_Nature/Book_3:_Of_morals/Part_1/Section_1> accessed 10 February 2025.

108 *Euis Sunarti and Others* (n 18) 20.

109 Geertz (n 91) 188.

that 'if families in the Republic of Indonesia are not strong, the nation and state of the Republic of Indonesia will be threatened by destruction that can lead to the disintegration of the nation and the state or the easiness for the state to be controlled by foreign parties'.[110] This observation denotes the belief that the nation itself would be devastated if it were to violate the *haqq* of Allah. AILA also submitted that *zina* or 'unlawful sexual intercourse', which is considered a 'shameful deed' (*fahisha*) under the Sharia,[111] will destroy population growth in Indonesia and reduce the quality of Indonesian families because relationship outside marriage is considered 'prone to violence, infidelity, and will end up in uncertainty over the goal of marriage relationship itself [...]'.[112] As 'evidence', AILA pointed out that a number of Western countries 'believe in free sex and thus their population growth becomes 0 (zero)'.[113] This apocalyptic vision is consistent with the saying of Prophet Muhammad himself, as narrated in a *shahih* (valid) Hadith narrated by 'Abdullah bin 'Umar:

> [*Fahisha*] never appears among a people to such an extent that they commit it openly, but plagues and diseases that were never known among the predecessors will spread among them. They do not cheat in weights and measures but they will be stricken with famine, severe calamity and the oppression of their rulers.[114]

Furthermore, with regard to homosexual sex, AILA contended that the failure to criminalise this act 'destroys the institution of the family and desacralises the institution of marriage'.[115] AILA even claimed that if 'lewd' (*cabul*) same-sex activities between adults were let to 'increasingly become a plague', the future generation will no longer feel the need to establish a family, and thus the family will be destroyed.[116] In this context, AILA launched a petition to the Constitutional Court not to 'restrain [the states'] power and tame their authority' or 'to protect individuals against the lure of arbitrariness',[117] but rather to

110 *Euis Sunarti and Others* (n 18) 20.
111 Ibid., 35. AILA is specifically referring to Surah al-Isra 17:32.
112 Ibid., 22.
113 Ibid., 37–38.
114 Sunan Ibn Majah 4019 <www.sunnah.com/ibnmajah:4019> accessed 10 February 2025.
115 *Euis Sunarti and Others* (n 18) 57.
116 Ibid., 61.
117 Laurence Burgorgue-Larsen, *The 3 Regional Human Rights Courts in Context.* (OUP 2024) 1, https://doi.org/10.1093/oso/9780192871459.003.0001.

uphold the *haqq* of Allah.[118] Indeed, AILA insisted that acceptance of its constitutional petition 'eventually will create a healthy environment for the development of the institution of marriage, the institution of the family, that will lead to national security in Indonesia'.[119]

Integral to AILA's imagination of *hak asasi manusia* is the concepts of *fitrah* ('original disposition') and *kodrat* ('God's natural law'). As lucidly described by Afifur Rochman Sya'rani, based on his interview with AILA members:

> In the eyes of AILA women activists, women's status and roles are not socially constructed but have been determined by divine revelation as explained in the Qur'an and the Prophetic tradition. Their understanding of women's status and roles are articulated through the idea of *fitrah* or *kodrat*, meaning women's social roles are based on their biological nature. Based on this belief, the roles of women as mothers and housewives and men as breadwinners are considered inherently natural [...]. The concept of motherhood is also articulated in terms of its function as "the very first school for their children (*al-umm madrasat al-ula*)." Accordingly, women are primarily supposed to nurture and educate their children and build the moral fabric of future generations. In their view, since this gender difference has been determined by Islamic provision, it is fixed, absolute, and unchangeable regardless of socio-cultural context. [...].[120]

Thus, it is not surprising that AILA members categorically rejected the distinction between 'biological' sex and 'socially constructed' gender. For them, individuals do not have the autonomy to discover and pursue their own gender roles beyond the gender binary. Instead, the women of AILA believe that gender roles that are/must be assumed by women, as well as men, are inseparable from their *fitrah* and *kodrat*.[121] To have 'women's rights' indispensably means to have 'women's duties' before society and Allah; as summarised by Sya'rani, 'AILA women activists acknowledge the equality of men and women before God and their equal rights and responsibilities in Islamic obligations and

---

118 cf the following Islamist publication in Indonesia, which speaks of 'the right (*hak*) of Allah' over humans: Anshory Huzaimi, 'Menjaga Hak Allah dan Hak Sesama' [Safeguarding the Rights of Allah and the Rights of Fellow Human Being] (*Hidayatullah*, 16 November 2022) <www.hidayatullah.com/kajian/oase-iman/2022/11/16/240196/menjaga-hak-allah-dan-hak-sesama.html> accessed 23 May 2025. Islamists in Indonesia often invoke 'the right of Allah' to argue for the imposition of Sharia criminal law nationwide. *Hak* here does not imply that God has a legal entitlement from the State; instead, it means the totalising reality to which all humans must submit.

119 *Euis Sunarti and Others* (n 18) 65.

120 Sya'rani (n 14) 162.

121 Ibid., 164.

teachings'.[122] Thus, there is 'a set of religious duties that both men and women must uphold',[123] which would include not engaging in sex outside marriage and homosexual sex. Indeed, they framed 'homosexual sex' as a deed that goes against the *fitrah*, as implied by the title of their 2019 publication, *Transformation into Fitrah: LGBT in Indonesian Perspective*.[124]

Additionally, it is worth highlighting that even the notion of 'dignity' has assumed a radically different, modernist Islamic meaning in the minds of AILA members. AILA invoked Article 28G(1) of the Constitution, which enshrines the right to protection of oneself, family, honour, and 'dignity'. Here, 'dignity' is linked with one's *fitrah* and *kodrat*. As a consequence, AILA claimed that Article 28G(1) of the Constitution was violated by the failure to criminalise homosexual acts because, as a consequence of this legal vacuum, 'families cannot defend their honour' if one of their adult family members 'became a victim', which would lead to the person's dignity being 'debased'.[125] Strikingly, in its third-party submission to *Euis Sunarti and Others*, the hard-lined Indonesian Ulema Council even invoked Article 28G (2) of the Constitution on the right to be free from torture or inhuman or degrading treatment.[126] According to the Council, the criminal law provision that fails to penalise same-sex activities between adults 'degrades human dignity'.[127] This interpretation of the prohibition of torture and cruel, inhuman, or degrading treatment is highly unconventional to say the least, but within the imaginary of modernist Muslims, it flows directly from the concepts of *fitrah* and *kodrat*.

3.2 AILA's Anti-colonialism and the Appropriation of TWAIL

International human rights law forms what Peggy Levitt and Sally Merry called 'global values package', which is 'inherently powerful because they are imbued with the appeal, power, and legitimacy of the international'.[128] AILA is deeply suspicious of such 'global values package' and branded it as a form of

122 Ibid., 162.
123 Ibid.
124 See Dinar Dewi Kania, Meyrinda Rahmawaty Hilipito, Qurrata Ayuni, Rita H Soebagio, Fajri Matahati Muhammadin, Tiar Anwar Bachtiar, Hasbi Aswar, Evi Risna Yanti, and Ariesa Ulfa, *Transformasi Menuju Fitrah: LGBT dalam Perspektif Keindonesiaan* (Yayasan Dompet Dhuafa Republika 2019).
125 *Euis Sunarti and Others* (n 18) 57.
126 Ibid., 391.
127 Ibid.
128 Levitt and Merry (n 13) 447.

'value colonialism'.[129] As firmly asserted by the chairwoman of AILA, Rita Soebagio, in a 2016 interview:

> The makers of women's programs which result from CEDAW [Convention on the Elimination of All Forms of Discrimination against Women], are our enemy. Why do they impose it on the Muslim world while America has never ratified it? Moreover, Ulamas have been reminded about this due to its danger. People who undertake this departs from an ideology. Including LGBT, it is part of an ideology [...].[130]

In its 2019 publication, AILA also repudiated international human rights standards on sexual minority rights. They considered them 'particular human rights values of Western countries that cannot be applied universally to the whole world. [...] Human rights concepts definitely have to be released from the shackle of interpretations based on Western modernity'.[131] Additionally, AILA called for the United Nations to 'realise that all forms of campaign and propagation of beliefs that declare the normalcy of LGBT behaviour is a form of value colonialism [...]'.[132] It even claimed that campaigns to foster acceptance of homosexuality 'is a form of intolerance [towards anti-LGBT beliefs] that is contrary to true human rights'.[133]

Interestingly, the Third World approaches to international law (TWAIL) have also been appropriated and filled with modernist Islamic substance. A notable figure in this regard is Fajri Matahati Muhammadin, an international law scholar at the prestigious University of Gadjah Mada who is also a co-author of the above-mentioned 2019 AILA publication. Fajri fits into the category of 'vernaculariser' par excellence, because as a legal scholar trained in public international law at the University of Edinburgh, he is 'conversant with both sides of the exchange but able to move across borders of ideas and approaches'.[134] In 2019, he published his research on whether lashing as a Sharia punishment in the Province of Aceh, which may be imposed on those convicted of *zina*, *liwat* (male sodomy), and *musahaqah* (lesbian sex), is consistent with the United Nations Convention Against Torture (UNCAT).[135] To

129 Kania et al (n 124) xii–xiii.
130 Sya'rani (n 14) 168.
131 Kania et al (n 124) 129.
132 Ibid., 132.
133 Ibid.
134 Levitt and Merry (n 13) 449.
135 Fajri Matahati Muhammadin, Dian Agung Wicaksono, Almonika Cindy Fatika Sari, and Ola Anisa Ayutama, 'Lashing in Qanun Aceh and the Convention against Torture: A

justify a modernist Islamic reading of the UNCAT (and, in the process, ignore the interpretations of the official treaty body of the convention), Fajri drew upon TWAIL,[136] including the works of Antony Anghie.[137] He wrote:

> are we witnessing more evidence the 'West regime of international law' trying to reinforce its colonialism-based intellectual hegemony in a postcolonial world? The truth is that there are compelling arguments explaining the colonial origins of this 'Eurocentric international law' (Anghie, 2004). [...] In context of international human rights law, has developed into today's regime of a falsely-claimed 'universal human rights' regime. Human rights [have] never been truly universal, but it is always claimed to be universal as a means for the Western powers to push their intellectual hegemony to the rest of the world [...].[138]

He even condemned the United Nations, which, in his view, 'claims universality, but they seem to only include those within their "magic circle" (i.e. the Westerners, as an exclusive group) from which to consider what is universal [...]'.[139] Thus, he called for more critical approaches to international law, particularly from the perspective of the Muslim world.[140]

In the spirit of these 'critical approaches', Fajri made a radical suggestion: replacing 'Western' universalism with 'Islamic universalism', since 'Islam is universal and its teachings are beneficial to all [humans]'.[141] Together with Mohd Hisham Mohd Kamal, a scholar from Malaysia, they suggested, in a modernist Islamic manner, that the only valid source of 'human rights' is the Quran and the Hadith:

> [T]he Qur'ān is the literal and verbatim of Allah's Words to Prophet Muḥammad PBUH, and not written or made by the latter who definitely was not merely 'inspired'. Therefore, as the Qur'ān is not a human product according to the Islamic belief, it cannot be assumed to share the human limitations of its socio-

---

Critical Appraisal' (2019) 7 Malaysian Journal of Syariah and Law 11, https://doi.org/10.33102/mjsl.v7i1.173.

136 Ibid., 20.

137 Antony Anghie, *Imperialism, Sovereignty, and the Making of International Law* (CUP 2004).

138 Muhammadin et al (n 135) 20.

139 Ibid., 21.

140 Ibid.

141 Fajri Matahati Muhammadin and Mohd Hisham Mohd Kamal, 'The Western Universalism v. Cultural Relativism Debate on Human Rights' (2019) 21 Afkar 175, 201–202, https://doi.org/10.22452/afkar.vol21no2.6.

> historical background. Rather, it transcends the boundaries of time, space, and cultures, because it is the Words of Allah.[142]

Consequently, Fajri and Hisham rejected the suggestion that the Islamic *ḥudūd* (penalties provided in the Quran and Hadith) need reforms to be compatible with international human rights law, since 'the Qur'ān and the Sunnah are to be by default taken literally'.[143] In their view, '[a Muslim] person implementing non-Islamic laws due to the belief that such a law is better than the Qur'ān and the Sunnah is considered as a *murtad* [apostate] for committing such an act of *kufr* (disbelief)'.[144] Hence, Fajri and Hisham insisted that 'the path for a Muslim scholar of international law which is consistent with the Islamic *'aqīdah* [creed] is to advocate the Islamic concept of human rights as a universally applicable norm'.[145] This demonstrates how AILA and Fajri have also appropriated decolonial approaches to human rights to be more fitting with their own modernist Islamic sensibility.

4 AILA's 'Human Rights': A Misappropriation?

In the previous section, we have seen how AILA has appropriated the language of 'human rights' and refitted the content in line with their own modernist Islamic sensibility. It goes without saying that the substance is not compatible with mainstream human rights standards: under the jurisprudence of the United Nations human rights treaty bodies, the criminalisation of sex outside marriage and homosexual sex violates the right to privacy and non-discrimination.[146] AILA's repudiation of gender equality and LGBT rights may also draw parallels with the so-called 'New Global Right', since their interpretations would strike a Western(ised) observer as being anti-pluralist, sexist, homophobic, and sovereigntist.[147] In this light, it is easy to suspect that their 'unconventional' interpretation constitutes a form of 'misappropriation'. As observed by Alexandra Huneeus, '[i]t can be tempting to minimize non-liberal engagement with human rights as politicized and therefore somehow disingenuous [...]'.[148]

142 Ibid., 187.
143 Ibid., 188.
144 Ibid., 191–192.
145 Ibid., 203.
146 See Flamer-Caldera v. Sri Lanka (2022) UN Doc CEDAW/C/81/D/134/2018.
147 cf de Búrca and Young (n 9) 219.
148 Huneeus (n 8) 380.

However, as I have argued in Section 2, 'misappropriation' is a term that is only meaningful within a particular societal and cultural context. The general indicators provided by de Búrca and Young denote a particular normative commitment, which I share, to the 'global values package' of international human rights law. Meanwhile, the specific indicators reflect the societal and political contexts of opposition to the 'New Global Right', and thus 'misappropriation' denotes the belief that these right-wing conservative actors are not only 'wrong' in their interpretation, but also 'malicious' in their intention.

In fact, 'misappropriation' is inappropriate to be used by comparative scholars as a universal analytical category, as it simplifies the specific context of various societies into the narrative of 'the nefarious weaponisation of human rights by the New Global Right'. Hence, the drawback of their framework is not the typical cultural relativist argument that there are different understandings of 'dignity', 'freedom', and 'equality' that deserve 'tolerance' or even 'respect'. Instead, as an analytical category to be used in comparative legal research, 'misappropriation' is utterly incongruous when applied to societies with different contexts. What I meant with 'incongruous' is that 'misappropriation' has an embedded meaning within a particular societal and political context, which cannot simply be transposed to other societies. If the facts on the ground in an entirely different society were forced to fit this category, it would lead to a distorted description of reality.

Applying the category of 'misappropriation' on AILA's interpretation means denigrating and condemning it as a 'wrong' and 'malicious' interpretation, and at the same time also extending the categories of 'right-wing' and 'ultraconservative' to this organisation. Doing so implies transposing the left-right divide in the Western world to Indonesia, even though such a division is largely meaningless in the Indonesian context.[149] Instead, as observed by Edward Aspinall and others, '[Indonesian political] parties differentiate primarily – if not solely – in terms of how they view the role of Islam in public and political life'.[150] Additionally, the widely recognised division in Indonesian Islam is between 'traditionalists' who are influenced by Shivaist-Buddhist traditions and 'modernists' who rely on pure reason to interpret the Quran and the Hadith.[151] This is what I meant by 'distorted reality': it creates a simplified narrative of a 'right-wing ultraconservative' actor with transnational links

149 See Diego Fossati, 'The Resurgence of Ideology in Indonesia: Political Islam, Aliran and Political Behaviour' (2019) 38 Journal of Current Southeast Asian Affairs 119, https://doi.org/10.1177/1868103419868400.

150 Aspinall et al (n 80).

151 Ali (n 96).

seeking to 'subvert' human rights and suppress vulnerable minorities.[152] AILA cannot be classified as 'right-wing' because the left-right political and economic spectrum is inapplicable in Indonesia. AILA is also not 'ultraconservative', but rather 'reformist', since its members directly use their own pure reason to study the Quran and the Hadith and do not conform (*taqlid*) to the sacred authority of the *kyai* (spiritual teachers) as the traditionalists do.[153]

Furthermore, AILA does not fit the cliché of the 'unholy' alliance between the illiberal state and 'ultraconservative' religious actors working together to accumulate power and destroy constitutional democracy. While it is a reactionary group hostile to the 'global values package' of international human rights law, AILA remains a small organisation with no governmental endorsement. The party with whom AILA sustains a link, the Prosperous Justice Party, never received more than 8.5% of the votes in Indonesian legislative elections.[154] In fact, AILA filed a constitutional petition precisely because of insufficient political backing in the parliament.[155] Additionally, during the second

152 In fact, this narrative seems to be pervasive among public law scholars that when I presented this work (and other related articles), I kept receiving questions on whether AILA is influenced by or sustains links with 'American Evangelicals'. One audience even told me to look for a possible Hungarian influence, since the Orbán government has been awarding scholarships to Indonesian students. However, many AILA members received their education at national universities, while one member who was among the petitioners to the Constitutional Court, Qurrata Ayuni, earned her master's degree at James Cook University in Australia. Interestingly, Fajri Muhammadin, a modernist Islamic legal scholar who has written that lashing as a corporal punishment is not a form of torture, received his Master's degree at the University of Edinburgh. It is more likely that his modernist Islamic outlook was strengthened by his doctorate education at the International Islamic University of Malaysia. Furthermore, Atip Latipulhayat, an expert witness who supported AILA in *Euis Sunarti and Others*, earned both his Master's and doctorate degrees at Monash University, Australia. Indeed, many modernist Muslim scholars in Indonesia are educated in Western universities. Furthermore, as I discuss below, modernist Islamic appropriation of 'democracy' and 'human rights' is nothing new in Indonesia and can be traced long before Viktor Orbán was even born.

153 Smith-Hefner (n 97) 27.

154 Alexander R Arifianto, 'PKS Electoral Setbacks in the Indonesian Regional Elections: Pragmatism at the Cost of Losing Core Constituencies' (*IDSS Paper*, 12 December 2024) <www.rsis.edu.sg/wp-content/uploads/2024/12/IP24104.pdf> accessed 10 February 2025.

155 While Indonesia did enact a new Criminal Code in 2022, the criminalisation of sex outside marriage remains largely symbolic, with enforcement being made exceedingly difficult, whereas same-sex activities are only criminalised if committed in public, with force or violence, or published as a pornography. See Ignatius Yordan Nugraha, 'Inherently Repugnant'? Indonesia and the Criminalisation of Sex Outside Marriage' (*Verfassungsblog*, 7 December 2022) <www.verfassungsblog.de/inherently-repugnant/> accessed 10 February 2025, https://dx.doi.org/10.17176/20221207-121611-0. The Islamists were angered by the fact that the Criminal Code did not fully penalise zina and homosexual acts and also

term of President Joko Widodo in 2019–2024, he launched a crackdown on Islamist groups, which culminated in the banning of not only the pan-Islamist Hizb ut-Tahrir, but also the 'Islamic Defender Front', a vigilante group who advocated for the imposition of Sharia criminal law nation-wide.[156] While Indonesia is known for its 'Godly' constitutional identity, this arrangement reflects 'a nationalist vision influenced by the nation's Shivaist-Buddhist past, where different [religions] are viewed as the manifestations of the same one "reality"',[157] instead of the Islamists' long-held desire to constitutionalise the Sharia as the only possible religious truth.[158]

Even if we were to ignore the possibly distorted image that 'misappropriation' implies, this framework still does not distinguish between dishonest and nefarious appropriation from the inevitable 'vernacularisation' of human rights as it diffuses within a society. After all, as observed by Kristina Stoeckl:

> rights appropriation is not something that is specific to certain groups of actors and ideological worldviews. All actors that engage in actions and politics around human rights in one way or the other make rights "their own" and fill human-rights provisions with meanings and ends that are relevant in their concrete historical, social, and political context.[159]

Indeed, in the Indonesian context, modernist Muslims have a long history of 'appropriating' Western concepts and fitting them with their own sensibility.[160] A leading figure of modernist Islam, Mohammad Natsir (1908–1993), was known for his advocacy of 'democracy' and 'human rights' filled with an Islamic understanding.[161] As observed by Audrey Kahin, a biographer of Nat-

---

criminalised 'marital rape', which fulfilled the aspiration of mainstream women's rights activists. There was even an attempt of suicide bombing in protest of the new Criminal Code, which the perpetrator claimed to be a form of *shirk* (idolatry). See Bima Bagaskara, 'Motor "KUHP Syirik" Pelaku Bom Bunuh Diri di Astana Anyar Berpelat Solo' [Motorbike with "The Criminal Code is Shirk" Owned by Perpetrator of Suicide Bombing in Astana Anyar Has the Number Plate of Surakarta] (*Detik*, 7 December 2022) <https://news.detik.com/berita/d-6447995/motor-kuhp-syirik-pelaku-bom-bunuh-diri-di-astana-anyar-berpelat-solo> accessed 10 February 2025.

156 John McBeth, 'Widodo Bites Back at Islamic Militants in Indonesia' (*Asia Times*, 31 December 2020) <www.asiatimes.com/2020/12/widodo-bites-back-at-islamic-militants-in-indonesia/> accessed 10 February 2025.

157 Nugraha (n 95).

158 See RE Elson, 'Two Failed Attempts to Islamize the Indonesian Constitution' (2013) 28 Sojourn: Journal of Social Issues in Southeast Asia 379, http://doi.org/10.1355/sj28-3a.

159 Stoeckl (n 7) 227.

160 Feillard (n 25); Smith-Hefner (n 97) 20.

161 Kahin (n 1) 188–189.

sir, '[h]e believed that Islamic values would necessarily exert major influence in a democratic state with a majority Muslim population'.[162] Consequently, while he 'continued to admire the basic concepts underlying Western political thought and to embrace the core democratic values of egalitarianism and social justice, together with belief in a multi-party system and separation of powers', he was also firmly opposed to 'behavior forbidden under Islam', which included drugs and alcohol consumption, gambling, and adultery, as well as Christian proselytisation activities.[163]

Similarly, the only modernist Muslim President in Indonesian history, BJ Habibie, outlined his vision of *masyarakat madani* as a direct equivalent of 'civil society', consisting of six principles: independence, freedom, pluralism, human rights balanced with obligations, moral and ethical values, and justice and welfare.[164] Among modernist Muslims, however, the term connotes their desire to emulate the first Islamic state founded by Prophet Muhammad in Medina. It thus follows that global concepts forming part of *masyarakat madani*, such as freedom, pluralism, and human rights, are to be interpreted and internalised in line with the Sharia.[165] As explained by Anwar Ibrahim in 1995, the then Deputy Prime Minister of Malaysia who first coined the term, '[i]t was Islam, for the first time, which gave us, on these shores, the ideals of social justice and the formation of a *masyarakat madani*, that is, a civil society with a democratic spirit'.[166]

Anis Matta, the former President of the Prosperous Justice Party, also wrote in 2002 that 'democracy' is overall positive for not only bringing equality, freedom of expression, freedom of possession, and freedom to engage in a commercial activity, but also allowing Islamic missionary activities (*dakwah*) without restrictions.[167] At the same time, he regretted that democracy 'does give freedom of expression to [...] those Matta calls "evil doers" (*pelaku kemungkaran*), such as homosexuals or any other individuals who disrespect the precepts of Islam'.[168] Thus, he called for Muslims to convince the public 'so that

162 Ibid., 188.
163 Ibid., 189.
164 Muhamad Wahyuni, 'Habibie Sebut Enam Prinsip Terwujudnya Masyarakat Madani' (*Antara News*, 18 July 2012) <https://jogja.antaranews.com/berita/302062/habibie-sebut-enam-prinsip-terwujudnya-masyarakat-madani> accessed 23 May 2025.
165 See Iskandar (n 71) 128. See also Feillard (n 25).
166 Feillard (n 25).
167 Ibid.
168 See Ibid.

Islamic principles can be accepted through the legal process and through state institutions'.[169]

Such process of appropriation continues to the present day, as can be seen in the 'expert testimony' of Atip Latipulhayat in *Euis Sunarti and Others*.[170] Atip is a professor of international law at the University of Padjadjaran, whose public law researchers are renowned for their defence of 'democracy', 'the rule of law', and 'human rights'.[171] He is also actively involved in a modernist Muslim organisation called the Islamic Union (PERSIS),[172] of which Natsir was once a notable member.[173] Atip supported AILA's petition and appropriated concepts such as the 'margin of appreciation' of the European Court of Human Rights to argue that the criminalisation of sex outside marriage and homosexual sex is not contrary to human rights.[174]

Given this common tendency of modernist Muslims to appropriate Western concepts and fill the substance with their own Islamic understanding,[175] 'misappropriation' would fail to take into account the possibility that they did so not out of malicious intention, but rather of a genuine and profound conviction in Islam, which does not necessarily exclude a commitment to what they understand as 'democracy' and 'human rights'. Modernist Muslims such as Habibie and Ibrahim profoundly believe in both the democratic ideals and Islam, and they envisioned a *masyarakat madani* or civil society with 'a prosperous social system that has as its principle the balancing between the rights of the individual and the stability of society'.[176] Yet applying the label of 'misappropriation' to modernist Muslim groups such as AILA, simply because

169 Ibid.

170 *Euis Sunarti and Others* (n 18) 124–127.

171 See Abdurrachman Satrio, 'Scholars and the (Un)Virtuous Roots of Abusive Constitutional Borrowing in Indonesia: A Tale from the Land of Gods' (2023) 10 Indonesian Journal of International & Comparative Law 239. Of course, 'democracy', 'the rule of law', and 'human rights' here are vernacularised with a modernist Islamic understanding. Satrio, in his criticism, discussed a PhD dissertation defended at the University of Padjadjaran, where the candidate appropriated 'democracy' and 'constitutional convention' to argue that non-Muslims are constitutionally banned from running for president. This thesis received praises from his examiners, including from Professor Susi Dwi Harijanti, who was lauded as 'the most progressive constitutional law professor' in Indonesia.

172 He was appointed as the Vice Chairman of the Central Leadership of PERSIS for the 'jihad' period of 2022–2027. He then became Deputy Minister of Primary and Secondary Education on 21 October 2024 as part of President Prabowo Subianto's attempt to embrace all political currents in Indonesia, including modernist Muslims.

173 Kahin (n 1) 19.

174 See *Euis Sunarti and Others* (n 18) 124–127.

175 Smith-Hefner (n 97) 20.

176 Feillard (n 25).

their interpretations may be similar to the 'New Global Right' with regards to gender and sexuality, would imply that their belief is not only 'wrong', but also 'malicious', an assumption that would fail to factor in the inevitable vernacularisation of global concepts.

Therefore, 'misappropriation' shows its limits when applied universally in comparative legal research: its value is purely normative within the societal and political contexts of the authors. In this regard, AILA's attempt to engage with human rights fits more with the analytical category of 'vernacularisation', as its members seek to understand 'rights' based on their own sensibility and modernist Islamic zeal, even though the resulting interpretations are so far removed from the mainstream global approach. Most importantly, 'vernacularisation' does not distort the context where AILA operates. On the very contrary, the concept of vernacularisation allows us to gain an understanding of how modernist Muslim women in Indonesia appropriate and interpret human rights in light of their own sensibility, instead of merely condemning their interpretation as normatively undesirable.

5 Conclusion

Islamic groups in Indonesia have traditionally been suspicious of human rights as an instrument of 'Western imperialism',[177] but at the same time modernist Muslims have a long history of appropriating both 'democracy' and 'human rights'.[178] In this regard, AILA has unconventionally appropriated 'human rights' and refitted the content with modernist Islamic conceptions. They have also appropriated decolonial approaches. In the process, universal 'human rights' have been transmogrified in such a manner that makes it not only 'unrecognisable' for a Western(ised) observer, but also unintelligible unless we deploy an interpretive method. This Islamic vernacularisation is perhaps inevitable; Geertz even argued, based on his study of Islam in Indonesia and Morocco, that '[i]n a curiously ironical way, intense involvement with the West moved religious faith closer to the center of our peoples' self-definition than it had been before'.[179]

---

177 Knut Asplund, 'Resistance to Human Rights in Indonesia: Asian Values and Beyond' (2009) 10 Asia-Pacific Journal on Human Rights and the Law 27, 40–41, https://doi.org/10.1163/138819009X12589762582538.

178 See Feillard (n 25).

179 Geertz (n 99) 65.

In comparative terms, AILA's understanding of human rights may seem to resemble the 'New Global Right' when it comes to gender equality and LGBT rights. Moreover, they both share the same scepticism about, if not outright contempt for mainstream human rights standards. However, the category of 'misappropriation' turns out to be only meaningful within the societal and political contexts where de Búrca and Young operate. When it is applied to the context of AILA, it leads to a distorted picture of reality. Furthermore, it also does not factor the inevitable fact of vernacularisation. After all, the webs of meanings underlying *haqq* are very distinct compared to those permeating in the Western world, including within the imaginary of 'New Global Right' actors themselves.

Therefore, the AILA case study provides a cautionary tale of the perils of applying concepts rooted in a particular context onto distinct realities. This does not mean that de Búrca and Young's framework is without merits; their framework should be understood as being purely normative and denoting their admirable and profound commitment to the 'global values package' of international human rights law. Regardless, when studying non-liberal engagements with human rights, the framework of 'vernacularisation' is more fitting, since it focuses on the process itself, and at the same time it also keeps an open mind that there may be multifarious understanding of rights from the Global South that may not necessarily fit with our own sensibilities.

Bibliography

Articles

Ali M, 'Categorizing Muslims in Postcolonial Indonesia' (2007) 11 Moussons 33, https://doi.org/10.4000/moussons.1746.

Asplund K, 'Resistance to Human Rights in Indonesia: Asian Values and Beyond' (2009) 10 Asia-Pacific Journal on Human Rights and the Law 27, https://doi.org/10.1163/138819009X12589762582538.

Boellstorff T, 'Dubbing Culture: Indonesian 'Gay' and 'Lesbi' Subjectivities and Ethnography in an Already Globalized World' (2008) 30 American Ethnologist 225, https://doi.org/10.1525/ae.2003.30.2.225.

Cobbah JAM. 'African Values and the Human Rights Debate: An African Perspective' (1987) 9 Human Rights Quarterly 309.

De Assis Machado MR, 'Antiabortion Legal Mobilization in Brazil: Human Rights as a Field of Contention' (2023) 21 International Journal of Constitutional Law 308, https://doi.org/10.1093/icon/moad030.

De Búrca G and Young KG, 'The (Mis)appropriation of Human Rights by the New Global Right: An Introduction to the Symposium' (2023) 21 International Journal of Constitutional Law 205, https://doi.org/10.1093/icon/moad019.

Elson RE, 'Two Failed Attempts to Islamize the Indonesian Constitution' (2013) 28 Sojourn: Journal of Social Issues in Southeast Asia 379, http://doi.org/10.1355/sj28-3a.

Engel DM, 'Rights as Wrongs: Legality and Sacrality in Thailand' (2014) 39 Asian Studies Review 38, https://doi.org/10.1080/10357823.2014.990356.

Feillard G, 'Adapting to Reformasi: Democracy, Human Rights, and Civil Society in the Indonesian Islamist Discourse' (2004) 7 Moussons 17, https://doi.org/10.4000/moussons.2461.

Goodale M, 'Justice in the Vernacular: An Anthropological Critique of Commensuration' (2024) 49 Law & Social Inquiry 7, https://doi.org/10.1017/lsi.2022.107.

Huneeus A, 'When Illiberals Embrace Human Rights' (2019) 113 AJIL Unbound 380, https://doi.org/10.1017/aju.2019.67.

Ibhawoh B, 'Between Culture and Constitution: Evaluating the Cultural Legitimacy of Human Rights in the African State' (2000) 22 Human Rights Quarterly 838.

Iskandar P, 'Religious Constitutionalism: An Indonesian-esque Interpretive Venture' (2019) Oxford University Comparative Law Forum <https://ouclf.law.ox.ac.uk/religious-constitutionalism-an-indonesian-esque-interpretive-venture/> accessed 10 February 2025.

Iskandar P, 'Why Are Indonesian Law (Schools) No Good' (2019) 6 The Indonesian Journal of International & Comparative Law 607.

Kaoma K, 'The Interaction of Human Rights and Religion in Africa's Sexuality Politics' (2023) 21 International Journal of Constitutional Law 339, https://doi.org/10.1093/icon/moad031.

Landau D, 'Abusive Constitutionalism' (2013) 47 UC Davis Law Review 189.

Levitt P and Merry S, 'Vernacularization on the Ground: Local Uses of Global Women's Rights in Peru, China, India and the United States' (2009) 9 Global Networks 441, https://doi.org/10.1111/j.1471-0374.2009.00263.x.

Lyon B and Iskandar P, 'Relational Self and Farmworker Law Reform: The Case of Indonesia' (2024) 56 Legal Pluralism and Critical Social Analysis 616, https://doi.org/10.1080/27706869.2024.2374631.

Madhok S, 'On Vernacular Rights Cultures and the Political Imaginaries of Haq' (2017) 8 Humanity: An International Journal of Human Rights, Humanitarianism, and Development 485, https://dx.doi.org/10.1353/hum.2017.0029.

McCrudden C, 'Human Dignity and Judicial Interpretation of Human Rights' (2008) 19 EJIL 655, 678, https://doi.org/10.1093/ejil/chn043.

Merry SE, 'Human Rights Law and the Demonization of Culture (And Anthropology Along the Way)' (2003) 26 Political and Legal Anthropology Review 55, https://doi.org/10.1525/pol.2003.26.1.55.

Merry SE, 'Transnational Human Rights and Local Activism: Mapping the Middle' (2006) 108 American Anthropologist 38, https://doi.org/10.1525/aa.2006.108.1.38.

Muhammadin FM et al, 'Lashing in Qanun Aceh and the Convention against Torture: A Critical Appraisal' (2019) 7 Malaysian Journal of Syariah and Law 11, https://doi.org/10.33102/mjsl.v7i1.173.

Muhammadin FM and Kamal MHM, 'The Western Universalism v. Cultural Relativism Debate on Human Rights' (2019) 21 Afkar 175, 201–202, https://doi.org/10.22452/afkar.vol21no2.6.

Satrio A, 'Scholars and the (Un)Virtuous Roots of Abusive Constitutional Borrowing in Indonesia: A Tale from the Land of Gods' (2023) 10 Indonesian Journal of International & Comparative Law 239.

Schachter O, 'Human Dignity as a Normative Concept' (1983) 77 American Journal of International Law 848.

Stoeckl K, 'Traditional Values, Family, Homeschooling: The Role of Russia and the Russian Orthodox Church in Transnational Moral Conservative Networks and Their Efforts at Reshaping Human Rights' (2023) 21 International Journal of Constitutional Law 224, https://doi.org/10.1093/icon/moad026.

Sya'rani AR, 'Muslim Women Against Feminism: The Family Love Alliance (Aliansi Cinṭa Keluarga) and Its Impact on Women's and Sexual Rights in Contemporary Indonesia' (2024) 12 TRaNS: Trans-Regional and -National Studies of Southeast Asia 156, https://doi.org/10.1017/trn.2023.6.

Books

Anghie A, *Imperialism, Sovereignty, and the Making of International Law* (CUP 2004).

Ash L, *The Baton and the Cross: Russia's Church Under Putin* (Icon Books 2024).

Burgorgue-Larsen L, *The 3 Regional Human Rights Courts in Context.* (OUP 2024), https://doi.org/10.1093/oso/9780192871459.003.0001.

De Condorcet M, *Outlines of An Historical View of the Progress of the Human Mind* (G Fryer 1802) <www.archive.org/details/outlinesofhistor00con/page/214/mode/2up> accessed 23 May 2025.

Dixon R and Landau D, *Abusive Constitutional Borrowing: Legal Globalization and the Subversion of Liberal Democracy* (OUP 2021).

Donnelly J, *Universal Human Rights in Theory and Practice* (3rd edn, Cornell University Press 2013).

Elazar DJ, *Covenant and Commonwealth: From Christian Separation Through the Protestant Reformation the Covenant Tradition in Politics* (Routledge 2018).

Fukuyama F, Identity: *The Demand for Dignity and the Politics of Resentment* (Farrar, Straus and Giroux 2018).

Geertz C, *Islam Observed: Religious Development in Morocco and Indonesia* (The University of Chicago Press 1971).

Geertz C, *The Interpretation of Cultures: Selected Essays* (Basic Books 1973).

Geertz C, *Local Knowledge: Further Essays in Interpretive Anthropology* (Basic Books 1983).

Goodale M, *Anthropology and Law: A Critical Introduction* (NYU Press 2017).

Hinton A, *The Justice Facade: Trials of Transition in Cambodia* (OUP 2018).

Hume D, *A Treatise of Human Nature* (John Noon 1739) <https://en.wikisource.org/wiki/Treatise_of_Human_Nature/Book_3:_Of_morals/Part_1/Section_1> accessed 10 February 2025.

Ignatieff M, *Human Rights as Politics and Idolatry* (Princeton University Press 2003).

Kahin AR, *Islam, Nationalism and Democracy: A Political Biography of Mohammad Natsir* (NUS Press 2012).

Kania DD et al, *Transformasi Menuju Fitrah: LGBT dalam Perspektif Keindonesiaan* (Yayasan Dompet Dhuafa Republika 2019).

Machmudi Y, *Islamising Indonesia: The Rise of Jemaah Tarbiyah and the Prosperous Justice Party (PKS)* (ANU Press 2008)

Merry SE, *The Seductions of Quantification: Measuring Human Rights, Gender Violence, and Sex Trafficking* (The University of Chicago Press 2016).

Rosen L, *The Justice of Islam: Comparative Perspectives on Islamic Law and Society* (OUP 2000).

Scholem G, *The Messianic Idea in Judaism: And Other Essays on Jewish Spirituality* (Schocken Books 1995).

Smith-Hefner NJ *Islamizing Intimacies: Youth, Sexuality, and Gender in Contemporary Indonesia* (University of Hawaii Press 2019).

Vleugel V, *Culture in the State Reporting Procedure of the UN Human Rights Treaty Bodies: How the HRC, the CESCR and the CEDAWCee Use Human Rights as a Sword to Protect and Promote Culture, and as a Shield to Protect against Harmful Culture* (Intersentia 2020).

Book Chapters

An-Na'im AA, 'Toward a Cross-Cultural Approach to Defining International Standards of Human Rights: The Meaning of Cruel, Inhuman, or Degrading Treatment or Punishment' in An-Na'im AA (ed), *Human Rights in Cross-Cultural Perspectives. A Quest for Consensus* (University of Pennsylvania Press 1992).

Anderson BRO'G, 'The Idea of Power in Javanese Culture' in Holt C (ed), *Culture and Politics in Indonesia* (1972).

Brems E, 'Reconciling Universality and Diversity in International Human Rights Law' in Sajó A (ed), *Human Rights with Modesty: The Problem of Universalism* (Springer 2004).

Dembour M, 'Following the Movement of a Pendulum: between Universalism and Relativism' in Cowan JK, Dembour M, and Wilson RA (eds), *Culture and Rights: Anthropological Perspectives* (CUP 2001).

Egan S, 'The Doctrinal Approach in International Human Rights Law Scholarship' in McConnell L and Smith R (eds), *Research Methods in Human Rights* (Routledge 2018).

Fuentes CI, Provost R, and Walker SG, 'E Pluribus Unum – Bhinneka Tunggal Ika? Universal Human Rights and the Fragmentation of International Law' in Provost R and Sheppard C (eds), *Dialogues on Human Rights and Legal Pluralism* (Springer 2013).

Goldstein DM, 'Whose Vernacular? Translating Human Rights in Local Contexts' in Goodale M (ed), *Human Rights at the Crossroads* (OUP 2014), https://doi.org/10.1093/acprof:osobl/9780199376414.003.0008.

Goodale M, 'Human Rights after the Post-Cold War' in Goodale M (ed), *Human Rights at the Crossroads* (OUP 2014), https://doi.org/10.1093/acprof:osobl/9780199376414.003.0001.

Touzé S, 'Les Pays Arabo-Musulmans Et Les Traités Universels de Protection Des Droits de L'Homme' in Afroukh M (ed), *L'islam en droit international des droits de l'homme* (Institut Universitaire Varenne 2019).

Decisions and Judgment

Constitutional Court of the Republic of Indonesia, Judgment for Case Number 46/PUU-XIV/2016, 14 December 2017 (*Euis Sunarti and Others*).

Flamer-Caldera v. Sri Lanka (2022) UN Doc CEDAW/C/81/D/134/2018.

Online Sources

Arifianto AR, 'PKS Electoral Setbacks in the Indonesian Regional Elections: Pragmatism at the Cost of Losing Core Constituencies' (*IDSS Paper*, 12 December 2024) <www.rsis.edu.sg/wp-content/uploads/2024/12/IP24104.pdf> accessed 10 February 2025.

Aspinall E, Fossati D, Muhtadi B, and Warburton E, 'Mapping the Indonesian Political Spectrum' (*New Mandala*, 24 April 2018) <www.newmandala.org/mapping-indonesian-political-spectrum/> accessed 10 February 2025.

Bagaskara B, 'Motor "KUHP Syirik" Pelaku Bom Bunuh Diri di Astana Anyar Berpelat Solo' [Motorbike with "The Criminal Code is Shirk" Owned by Perpetrator of Suicide Bombing in Astana Anyar Has the Number Plate of Surakarta] (*Detik*, 7 December 2022) <https://news.detik.com/berita/d-6447995/motor-kuhp-syirik-pelaku-bom-bunuh-diri-di-astana-anyar-berpelat-solo> accessed 10 February 2025.

McBeth J, 'Widodo Bites Back at Islamic Militants in Indonesia' (*Asia Times*, 31 December 2020) <www.asiatimes.com/2020/12/widodo-bites-back-at-islamic-militants-in-indonesia/> accessed 10 February 2025.

Nugraha IY, 'Inherently Repugnant'? Indonesia and the Criminalisation of Sex Outside Marriage' (*Verfassungsblog*, 7 December 2022) <www.verfassungsblog.de/inherently-repugnant/> accessed 10 February 2025, https://dx.doi.org/10.17176/20221207-121611-0.

Nugraha IY, 'Godly Constitution and Divine Enlightenment: Thc Indonesian Constitutional Court's Recent Theocratic Judgment' (*Verfassungsblog*, 13 January 2025) <www.verfassungsblog.de/godly-constitution-and-divine-enlightenment/> accessed 10 February 2025, https://dx.doi.org/10.59704/1bf50643de038c99.

Nugraha IY and Satrio A, 'Is This a Constitutional Democracy: Familial Harmony, Pancasila, and Javanese Values in Indonesia's New Government' (*Verfassungsblog*, 7 November 2024) <www.verfassungsblog.de/is-this-a-constitutional-democracy/> accessed 10 February 2025, https://dx.doi.org/10.59704/055af6dc9b63dbfc.

CHAPTER 2

Formalising the Right to Freedom of Assembly in Russia

Elena Lipatova and Melaniya Maslova

1 Introduction

Putin's regime in Russia has developed a sophisticated approach to human rights in general and freedom of assembly in particular. This attitude is characterised by an outward acceptance of the arguments, language, and logic of freedom of assembly as defined in core international treaties, while, in fact, perpetrating multiple and systematic human rights violations. Russian authorities appear to be employing an approach called 'misappropriation', using human rights norms for the sake of protection of human rights but in fact seeking to reverse or undo previous human rights developments and commitments.[1]

The relationship between Russia and the European Court of Human Rights (Court, ECtHR) perfectly illustrates this misappropriation dynamic. Russia ratified the European Convention on Human Rights (Convention, ECHR) on 30 March 1998. It had been under the jurisdiction of the ECtHR for more than 24 years, until 16 September 2022, when Russia ceased to be a High Contracting Party to the Convention. Although tensions between Russia and the Council of Europe (CoE) had been escalating for several years, the start of the full-scale invasion of Ukraine seriously aggravated them. Before, Russian authorities were engaged in a dialogue with the CoE. The Constitutional Court cited the ECtHR judgements in its case law and even built some of its key practices around them.[2] Then, the Constitutional Court rendered a decision concluding that the Constitution takes precedence over ECtHR jurisprudence.[3] Finally, as a consequence of the invasion, Russia's membership in the CoE was suspended

1 Gráinne De Búrca and Katharine G Young, 'The (mis)appropriation of human rights by the new global right: An introduction to the Symposium' (2023) 21(1) *International Journal of Constitutional Law* 205.

2 1344-O-P [2009] Constitutional Court of Russia.

3 For example, in its judgement N 21-P [2015], the Constitutional Court came to the conclusion that in case an ECtHR judgement is contradictory to the Constitution it cannot be enforced.

and then terminated. The ECtHR published a statement, according to which it kept its jurisdiction over the violations that took place before 16 September 2022.[4] Russian authorities, in turn, denounced the Convention.[5] Nevertheless, as described in Section 3.4 of this article, Russian courts continue to reference ECtHR case law in their decisions.

Although the implementation of the ECtHR judgements benefited the Russian legal system by humanising many aspects of it, practice reveals that in dealing with politicised issues such as the right to freedom of assembly, Russian authorities have made little effort to genuinely comply with the Convention, systematically violating this right. According to the research of Crew Against Torture, an independent human rights organisation, the ECtHR found a violation of Article 11 in relation to 527 assemblies held between 2010 and 2022. And the number of individuals whose right to freedom of assembly has been violated exceeds 6,000.[6] As of February 2024, OVD-Info[7] has sent 3,109 communications to the ECtHR regarding public protests since 2019. The number of freedom of assembly violations is so serious that the Court has categorised the problem as systematic. For instance, in *Lashmankin and others v Russia*,[8] the ECtHR found that the Russian authorities violated the applicants' right to freedom of assembly by arbitrarily restricting the time, place, and manner of peaceful protests, applying overly strict regulations, and failing to provide effective legal remedies, resulting in the dispersal and arrest of participants without sufficient justification. In other assembly cases, the Court similarly emphasised that when participants in unauthorised demonstrations do not engage in violence, public authorities are expected to demonstrate a

---

4 Andrew Drzemczewski and Rick Lawson, 'Exclusion of the Russian Federation from the Council of Europe and the ECHR: An Overview' (2022) 21 *Baltic Yearbook of International Law*.

5 Interfax, The State Duma terminated international treaties of the Council of Europe [2023] <https://www.interfax.ru/russia/886500> accessed 15 April 2025.

6 Crew Against Torture, 'Schyotchik kompensatsii. Rossiya ne vyplatila milliony evro po postanovleniyam ESPCh' (2025) <https://pytkam.net/schetchikECHR/> accessed 27 October 2025.

7 OVD-Info is an independent human rights media project dedicated to political persecution in Russia. OVD-Info provides legal help to those who are persecuted for realising the right to freedom of assembly and other basic political rights. See <https://en.ovdinfo.org> accessed 14 April 2025.

8 *Lashmankin and others v Russia* App no 57818/09 (ECtHR, 7 September 2017).

certain level of tolerance toward peaceful gatherings and refrain from prosecuting individuals solely for their participation.[9]

While systematically suppressing the freedom of assembly, the authorities simultaneously and explicitly affirmed their commitment to respecting human rights.[10] The state's submissions to the ECtHR in assembly cases show that it views its approach, examined in detail in this article, as fully compatible with international law.[11]

We aim to reveal how these contradictory attitudes coexist, providing a unified picture. Our research question is: How does the strategy of human rights misappropriation operate in the regulation of the right to freedom of assembly in Russia? To address this question, we consider the following sub-questions: What legal framework do the authorities construct to justify violations of the freedom of assembly? What tools do they use, and which actors are involved? Addressing these questions might aid in planning international efforts for peace and democratisation, as well as advocating for the rights of individuals whose rights have been violated.

2 Conceptual Framework

States often display contradictory attitudes towards international human rights obligations, raising important questions. Do the authorities intend to adhere to the Convention but lack the capacity to do so, or does the outward acceptance of the international norms serve other purposes? Previous research has shown that this approach may be a deliberate strategy. Scholars demonstrated that non-democratic governments may ratify human rights treaties or otherwise uphold human rights to gain reputational benefits,[12] as well as to use these tools for undemocratic purposes, such as advancing illiberal agendas and values or shielding themselves from criticism.[13]

9 *Navalnyy and Yashin v. Russia* App no. 76204/11 (ECtHR, 4 December 2014), para. 63; *Lashmankin and others v Russia* App no 57818/09 (ECtHR, 7 September 2017), para. 423; *Oya Ataman v. Turkey*, App no 74552/01 (ECtHR, 5 December 2006), paras. 41–42; *Bukta and Others v. Hungary* App. no. 25691/04 (ECtHR, 17 July 2007), para. 34.

10 For example, Russian Federation, Eighth Report submitted by the Russian Federation under Article 40 of the Covenant (2019), para 302.

11 See *Bodalev v Russia* App no 67200/12 (ECtHR, 6 September 2022), paras. 69 and 74.

12 Mathis Lohaus and Sören Stapel, 'Who commits to regional human rights treaties? Reputational benefits, sovereignty costs, and regional dynamics' (2022) 22 *Journal of Human Rights* 386.

13 Tom Ginsburg, 'Authoritarian International Law?' (2020) 114(2) *American Journal of International Law* 221.

Within this broader discussion, the concept of human rights *misappropriation* has been developed to capture how states strategically reinterpret or selectively invoke human rights norms for purposes contrary to their original spirit. Scholars have contributed significantly to understanding these misappropriation strategies.[14] Much of this literature focuses on right-wing populist or conservative actors. For instance, Kristina Stoeckl demonstrates how Russian authorities and the Russian Orthodox Church utilise selected provisions of the Universal Declaration of Human Rights, particularly those related to religion and family, while rejecting or marginalising more recent international human rights instruments.[15] Such selective use of human rights discourse serves an illiberal conservative agenda, centred on morality, family, and sovereignty. Similarly, the notion of sovereignty stands as a fundamental pillar upon which Russia's vision of human rights is built.[16]

We contribute to the literature on human rights misappropriation in two important ways. First, while existing research has mainly focused on strategies that ideologically reinterpret human rights, comparatively little attention has been paid to approaches that operate without invoking such ideological narratives. In the context of the right to freedom of assembly, this approach is distinctive because it follows a formal and depoliticised logic. Its legitimacy stems not from moral or ideological connotations attached to human rights, but from the apparent coherence of legislation and jurisprudence. Second, our article presents the first in-depth examination of the right to freedom of assembly within the conceptual framework of human rights misappropriation.

3 Data and Methods

This study employs a multi-method approach, combining both primary and secondary data to examine how the right to freedom of assembly is implemented in practice. Given the complexity of this right, which involves the interaction of multiple actors, the analysis integrates several complementary methods.

---

14 De Búrca and Young (n 4).

15 Kristina Stoeckl, 'Traditional values, family, homeschooling: The role of Russia and the Russian Orthodox Church in transnational moral conservative networks and their efforts at reshaping human rights' (2023) 21(1) *International Journal of Constitutional Law* 224.

16 Lauri Mälksoo, *Russian Approaches to International Law* (Oxford, 2015; online edn, Oxford Academic, 21 May 2015).

Firstly, to establish the legal framework, we employed a qualitative and normative legal analysis. This includes an examination of the relevant provisions of Russian legislation that guarantee the right to freedom of assembly and establish the grounds for its restriction, which were then contrasted with the ECtHR standing.

Secondly, to capture the administrative and police practices that shape the exercise of this right, we relied on secondary sources, primarily reports of independent human rights organisations. These materials provide crucial factual context on how the law is applied.

Finally, the core method of this study is a qualitative content analysis of judicial decisions,[17] which is divided into two parts. The first part includes the dataset of Russian cassation courts' and the Supreme Court's decisions regarding the implementation of article 20.2 of the Code of Administrative Offences (CAO), which establishes responsibility for organising and participating in protests.[18,19] It encompasses all decisions between 1 October 2019 (the start of the cassation court system) and 22 April 2022 that were published at the time of the analysis.[20] There were 785 decisions in this area. Data from the Cassation Court were not available for the requested cases at the time of data collection. The texts of court decisions were obtained using a custom script from the courts' websites.[21] The dataset was organised using Airtable,

17 Ali Fuad Selvi, 'Qualitative Content Analysis' (Routledge, 2019).

18 Code of Administrative Offences of the Russian Federation (Federal Law No 195-FZ of 30 December 2001) art 20.2.

19 In Russia, there are several cassation courts organised regionally to review judicial decisions for legal compliance. The cassation system is divided into cassation courts situated within each federal district, currently numbering nine courts. These courts ensure the uniform application of the law by reviewing lower court rulings and possess the authority to overturn or amend decisions. Case law is streamlined through this system by applying consistent legal interpretations across the regions, guided by rulings and clarifications issued by the Supreme Court of Russia, which aim to unify jurisprudence.

20 The dataset of judicial decisions was initially compiled by the authors within a separate research project conducted by OVD-Info, which aimed to document courts' standing related to public assemblies. At that stage, volunteers assisted with data collection and partial annotation. However, for this article, the authors independently conducted a full manual analysis of the decisions relevant to the scope of this research, following the methodological criteria described above.

21 1st Cassation Court of Russia <https://1kas.sudrf.ru/> accessed 30 May 2025; 2nd Cassation Court of Russia <https://2kas.sudrf.ru/> accessed 30 May 2025; 3rd Cassation Court of Russia <https://3kas.sudrf.ru/> accessed 30 May 2025; 4th Cassation Court of Russia <https://4kas.sudrf.ru/> accessed 30 May 2025; 5th Cassation Court of Russia <https://5kas.sudrf.ru/> accessed 30 May 2025; 6th Cassation Court of Russia <https://6kas.sudrf.ru/> accessed 30 May 2025; 7th Cassation Court of Russia <https://7kas.sudrf.ru/> accessed 30 May 2025; 8th Cassation Court of Russia <https://8kas.sudrf.ru/> accessed

a cloud-based spreadsheet and database platform. In the present study, we do not provide the whole dataset due to its large volume; instead, we cite some cases as examples. The full list of referenced cases for this part we give in Table 1. Since article 20.2 of the CAO penalises both unlawful participation in assemblies and their organisation, we selected and analysed only those decisions explicitly related to participation, namely parts 5, 6.1, and 8 of the article. Here, we manually analysed what legal norms judges cited and what reasoning they used to uphold or dismiss the case. This approach enabled us to identify recurring patterns in judicial reasoning systematically.

We based the second part of qualitative content analysis on a sample of 20 court decisions under article 20.2 of the CAO that reference the ECtHR judgments. These decisions we summarised in Table 2. To collect the decisions, we used OVD-Info's judicial data-gathering bot Sudmonster that compiles court decisions from the websites of regional and district courts in Russia, as well as from the governmental website Pravosudie,[22] a publicly accessible database of court proceedings. In this part, we manually analysed which international standards the judges cited, how they interpreted them, and how they incorporated them into their reasoning.

4 Results

We reveal how the misappropriation strategy operates across various levels of the legal and institutional framework governing the right to freedom of assembly. This strategy is evident in the design of laws regulating assemblies, the bureaucratic obstacles, and discretionary practices involved in the authorisation process, the enforcement practices of the police, and the interpretive approaches adopted by the judiciary. A significant aspect of this misappropriation is the selective and, at times, distorted referencing of the ECtHR case law by national courts, particularly after Russia's expulsion from the Council of Europe.

We argue that the right to freedom of assembly in Russia is shaped by a set of procedural limitations and *assumptions* embedded in the practices of administrative authorities, the police, and the judiciary (see Figure 1). By assumptions, we refer to the underlying normative and procedural premises

---

30 May 2025; 9th Cassation Court of Russia <https://9kas.sudrf.ru/> accessed 30 May 2025.

22 State Automated System of the Russian Federation 'Pravosudie' <https://sudrf.ru> accessed 30 May 2025.

that severely constrain the practical realisation of this right. First, participants are prosecuted not for participating in the assembly itself, but for failing to comply with the 'lawful' orders of police officers, typically orders to disperse from unauthorised events. Second, administrative bodies authorising public events employ layers of procedural requirements that make the authorisation impossible in practice. Third, the judiciary routinely upholds assembly cases without scrutinising the legality of the police orders, thereby reinforcing administrative and police discretion.

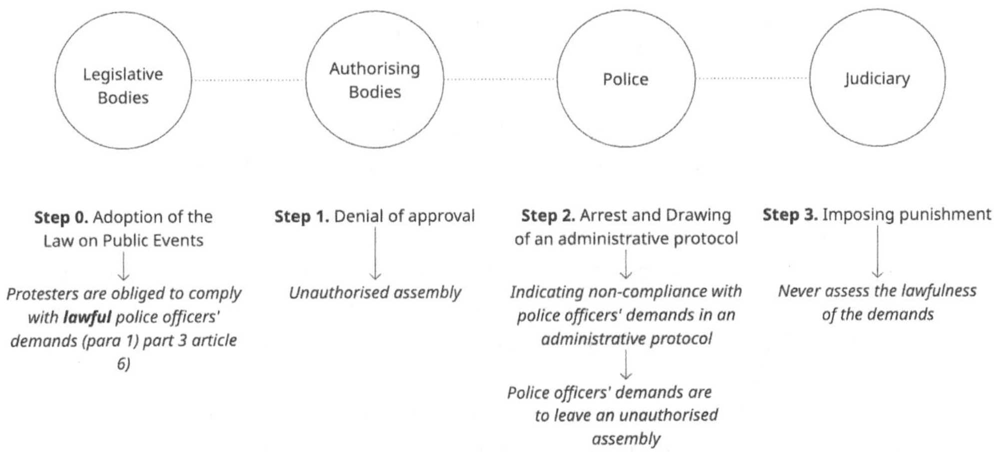

FIGURE 1 Strategies of Misappropriation at a Systemic Level.

These assumptions enable state actors to maintain the appearance of compliance with international human rights standards while in practice systematically restricting the right to assemble. They also facilitate portraying protesters as lawbreakers, shift the focus from the right itself to alleged violations of public order, and ultimately undermine the meaningful exercise of the right to protest.

To reconstruct this narrative in more detail, we structure our overview of results as follows: (4.1) Legal Framework for Restricting the Right to Freedom of Assembly; (4.2) Role of the Executive Powers, addressing authorisation processes and policing practices; (4.3) Role of the Judiciary; and (4.4) Referencing ECtHR Case Law Before and After the Expulsion from the Council of Europe, further divided into four distinct characteristics of judicial referencing practices.

4.1 Legal Framework for Restricting the Right to Freedom of Assembly

The right to freedom of assembly in Russia is enshrined at the highest level of domestic law. Article 31 of the Russian Constitution states that citizens of the Russian Federation shall have the right to assemble peacefully, without arms, to hold meetings, rallies, demonstrations, marches, and picketings. The existence of this right in the Constitution was never questioned, as was done with provisions on international law and others in 2020.[23]

At the same time, Russian domestic law has developed certain limitations on the right, granting authorities the power to prosecute some assembly participants selectively.[24] To understand how these restrictions are applied, it is essential first to acknowledge that in Russia, participants in peaceful assemblies can be held accountable if they violate the procedures governing the event. The two main laws that regulate this are the Public Event Act and the Code of Administrative Offences (CAO). The former enshrines the obligations and prohibitions for participants of assemblies, while the latter establishes penalties for violating these provisions.

During participation in an assembly, its participants shall: (1) comply with all lawful orders of the organiser of the public event, or police officers; (2) comply with public order and the regulations for holding a public event; (3) comply with the requirements to ensure transport and road safety, if the public event is held with the use of vehicles. Participants must not: (1) conceal their face; (2) carry weapons, ammunition, or stabbing and cutting objects; (3) be at the venue of an assembly in a state of intoxication; (4) use distinctive signs of media representatives.[25]

The main judicial act interpreting these provisions, the Resolution of the Plenum of the Supreme Court No. 28 adopted on 26 June 2018 (the Resolution), stipulates that administrative liability under article 20.2(5) of the

23 Venice Commission Opinion CDL-AD(2020)009 on draft amendments to the Constitution (as signed by the President of the Russian Federation on 14 March 2020) related to the execution in the Russian Federation of decisions by the European Court of Human Rights [2020] <https://www.coe.int/en/web/venice-commission/-/CDL-AD(2020)009-e> accessed 14 April 2025; William E Pomeranz, 'Putin's 2020 Constitutional Amendments: What Changed? What Remained the Same?' (2021) 6(1) *Russian Politics* 6.

24 Katerina Tertytchnaya and Madeleine Tiratsoo, 'Legal Repression in Russia' (2024) *Oxford Research Encyclopedia of Politics* <https://oxfordre.com/politics/view/10.1093/acrefore/9780190228637.001.0001/acrefore-9780190228637-e-2247> accessed 14 April 2025.

25 Public Events Act 2004 art 6 (3) and (4) (as amended).

CAO may take place only in case of non-fulfillment of mentioned above obligations and prohibitions outlined in Public Events Act 2004, article 6(3) and (4).[26]

Do these limitations comply with international human rights standards? These provisions are permissible as long as they are not applied arbitrarily. In their current form, they do not establish direct punishment for mere participation in an unauthorised assembly, which is not in line with ECtHR case law.[27] Although the Resolution did not lead to a significant change in judicial practice, its introduction was regarded positively. In particular, the Committee of Ministers commended the Plenum's Resolution as being in line with the Convention.[28] As stated in the Communication from the Russian Federation concerning the case of *Lashmankin and others v Russia*, the Resolution was delivered 'in order to improve judicial practice and increase the effectiveness of domestic judicial remedies'.[29]

Nevertheless, enforcing these provisions has resulted in numerous penalties for peaceful protests. The Resolution did not change the practice, as it did not address the issue comprehensively enough. In particular, it did not indicate that orders by police officers to leave an unauthorised event should not be presumed legal.

4.2 Role of the Executive Powers

Participation in unauthorised protests is not penalised directly – another formal cause is used instead. What constitutes the formal cause for liability is not a participation in an unauthorised assembly *per se*, but the failure to comply with police officers' orders. In practice, the provision concerning the failure to comply with police officers' 'lawful' orders (article 6(3) (1) of Public Event Act)

26 Resolution 'On certain issues arising before the courts when considering administrative cases and cases on administrative offences related to the application of legislation on public events' No. 28 (Plenum of the Supreme Court) 2018, para 33.

27 The ECtHR has consistently held that participation in a peaceful, non-prohibited demonstration cannot, in itself, constitute grounds for punishment (see *Kudrevičius and others v. Lithuania* App no. 37553/05 (ECtHR, 15 October 2015), para. 149; *Kasparov and others v Russia* App no 21913/07 (ECtHR, 3 October 2013), para. 92).

28 Committee of Ministers Interim Resolution CM/ResDH(2022)54 on the Execution of the Judgments of the European Court of Human Rights in Lashmankin group v Russian Federation (2022).

29 Communication of Russian Federation concerning the case of Lashmankin and Others v Russian Federation (Application No 57818/09), para. 10.1 <https://hudoc.exec.coe.int/eng?i=004-47097 accessed 14 April 2025.

is the one most frequently applied in such cases, as also shown by the qualitative text analysis of our study.[30] These orders are often framed as orders to disperse an unauthorised assembly. This is how the misappropriation strategy we described above manifests itself: prosecution of people for mere participation in an assembly would be a clear violation of the right to freedom of assembly. In contrast, prosecution on such a pretext creates the illusion of compliance with international standards.

For this reasoning to hold, certain assumptions must be met. The first assumption is that the assembly must be unauthorised, a condition for which the executive authorities bear responsibility. Consequently, the systematic violation of the right to freedom of assembly is perpetuated through widespread refusals to grant authorisation for assemblies.[31] The procedure itself makes it difficult to obtain approval for an assembly in Russia.[32] There are only 5 to 12 days to submit a notice of a planned assembly, depending on the type.[33] Legislation in this area lacks consistency and integrity. There is an extensive list of locations where holding an assembly is prohibited.[34] After all, authorities often use various formal and illegitimate pretexts to deny approval, such as fictitious repair works of the assembly venue.[35] This makes the approval procedure practically unfeasible.

Compounding these difficulties, in 2020, authorities enacted a near-total ban on public events under the pretext of COVID-19 spreading.[36] With the onset of the full-scale invasion of Ukraine on 24 February 2022 and the intro-

30 See, for example, 16-8352/2021 [2021] 8th Cassation Court of Russia; 16-211/2022 [2021] 8th Cassation Court of Russia; 16-2098/2022 [2022] 8th Cassation Court of Russia.

31 Information about refusals to authorise public assemblies in Russia is fragmented but illustrative. For example, in 2020, over 60% of all public events in Moscow were unauthorised, with 526 refusals being challenged in court for the first half of the year ('Ombudsman: Bolee 60% ot vsekh publichnykh aktsiy v Moskve v 2020g byli nesanktsionirovannymi' (Interfax Russia, 20 February 2020) <https://www.interfax-russia.ru/moscow/main/ombudsmen-bolee-60-ot-vseh-publichnyh-akciy-v-moskve-v-2020g-byli-nesankcionirovannymi> accessed 11 June 2025; OVD-Info, 'Unresolved Freedom of Assembly Issues in Russia in 2020' (2021) <https://ovd.info/en/lashmankin-et-al-v-russia> accessed 11 June 2025); Similarly, in 2023, 117 refusals were recorded nationwide (OVD-Info, 'Repression in Russia 2023: OVD-Info Overview' (2023) <https://ovd.info/en/repression-russia-2023-ovd-info-overview> accessed 11 June 2025).

32 OVD-Info, 'The Art of Ban' (2019) <https://ovd.info/en/art-ban> accessed 14 April 2025.

33 Public Events Act 2004 art 7 (as amended).

34 OVD-Info, 'Territoriia "nel'zia"' (2018) <https://tn.ovdinfo.org/> accessed 14 April 2025.

35 OVD-Info, 'The Art of Ban' (n 33).

36 OVD-Info, 'Svoboda Sobranii na Fone Pandemii' (2020) <https://reports.ovd.info/svoboda-sobraniy-na-fone-pandemii> accessed 3 September 2025.

duction of new repressive legislation targeting anti-war dissent,[37] assemblies related to criticism of the government and its actions in Ukraine were effectively banned in the public space.

The second assumption is that administrative liability for participating in an unauthorised assembly is typically triggered by claims that the individual failed to comply with a police officer's order to leave the event. In practice, the authority responsible for making the arrest and preparing the administrative offence protocol – in Russia, the police – records this claim in the case file. Police officers may not be physically present at the assembly to issue such orders. Instead, a simple note in the administrative offence report stating that the person failed to comply with a police order is treated as sufficient for prosecution. Courts routinely accept these reports as valid evidence without verifying whether police actually gave such orders.

4.3 Role of the Judiciary

The third assumption turns us to the approach of the judiciary in assembly cases. Russian courts do not evaluate the legality of police officers' orders. Instead, they only determine whether there was a case of non-compliance with those orders. Courts repeatedly emphasise that in the proceedings, they cannot assess the legality of the arrest and that for this purpose, detainees should file a separate administrative claim.[38] Regarding the lawfulness of the police officers' claims, the courts rely on the assumption that there is no reason to question the police officers' testimony and that they, likewise, act in accordance with the law. This wording is prevalent in the analysed judicial acts.[39]

In our analysis, we examined the reasons why courts overturned or modified decisions of first- or lower-instance courts, as well as the frequency of such reversals. In doing so, we sought to determine whether any jurisprudence fully aligns with international standards, specifically, whether there were cases in which the court found that a mere indication of non-compliance with police officers' orders was insufficient, or that it was necessary to assess the legality of such orders. Our findings were, however, disappointing.

---

37 Criminal Code of the Russian Federation (1996) art 280.3 and 207.3; Code of Administrative Offences of the Russian Federation (Federal Law No 195-FZ of 30 December 2001) art 20.3.3.

38 Natalia Smirnova and Denis Shedov, 'Russia on the Path to Freedom of Assembly: Problems and Tools for Change' (2021) <https://reforum.io/contents/uploads/2021/06/ovd-web.pdf> accessed 14 April 2025.

39 See for example, 16-1988/2021 [2021] 9th Cassation Court of Russia; 16-3516/2021 [2021] 9th Cassation Court of Russia.

Decisions in assembly cases are rarely overturned, and when they are, it is almost always on procedural rather than substantive grounds. By procedural grounds, we mean errors or violations in the legal process, such as a missed limitation period or procedural irregularities. This contrasts with substantive grounds, which concern the absence of an actual violation or wrongdoing, for instance, when the act in question does not constitute an offence. In our dataset, one case was dismissed due to double jeopardy,[40] three cases were dismissed due to the lack of proper notification of the hearing,[41] and two cases were dismissed because the prosecutor did not consent since the person was a member of an election committee.[42] Several cases were dismissed due to judicial errors[43] or police mistakes.[44]

Courts sometimes overturn decisions on substantive grounds. We found that the second-instance courts overturned several decisions due to a lack of any indications in the case files regarding non-compliance with police officers' orders. Consequently, courts chose to dismiss cases because protocols on administrative offences did not specify which actions committed by a protestor fell under the restrictions listed in article 6(3) and (4) of the Public Event Act.[45] However, sometimes, when an essential detail of non-compliance with police officers' orders is not indicated in the protocol, which can happen by mistake, the courts still hold victims responsible. This, in our opinion, reflects more on the unscrupulousness of the courts, which become trapped in the formalisation of the entire process. In both scenarios, the courts do not go beyond the logic of misappropriation.

All the conclusions we have reached can be illustrated by the following scheme (see Figure 1). We have observed how the strategy of misappropriation operates at the systemic level, involving various authorities, including legislative, executive, and judicial. In judicial practice, the acknowledgement of freedom of assembly is emphasised as aligning with international human rights standards, particularly those of the ECtHR. Many court decisions directly ref-

40 16-2798/2020 [2021] 7th Cassation Court of Russia.

41 16-6272/2020 [2020] 2nd Cassation Court of Russia; 16-1545/2021 [2021] 3rd Cassation Court of Russia; 16-817/2022 [2022] 9th Cassation Court of Russia.

42 16-5388/2021 [2021] 8th Cassation Court of Russia; 16-5499/2021 [2021] 2nd Cassation Court of Russia.

43 16-8040/2021 [2021] 8th Cassation Court of Russia).

44 16-2175/2021 [2021] 8th Cassation Court of Russia.

45 16-5611/2020 [2020] 7th Cassation Court of Russia; 16-588/2021-16-5842/2020 [2021] 7th Cassation Court of Russia; 16-1196/2021-16-6753/2020 [2021] 7th Cassation Court of Russia; 16-1197/2021-16-6754/2020 [2021] 7th Cassation Court of Russia; 16-1206/2021-16-6763/2020 [2021] 7th Cassation Court of Russia.

erence ECtHR case law – this complex dialogue will be explored in the following paragraphs.

4.4 Referencing ECtHR Case Law before and after the Expulsion from the Council of Europe

Interestingly enough, despite being expelled from the Council of Europe, Russian courts continue to reference the ECtHR's judgements in their own decisions.

In the cases on the freedom of assembly, Russian courts utilised judgements of the ECtHR quite frequently. Having analysed judgements of different Russian courts (see Table 2), we can highlight the main characteristics of these references:

(1) The references only concern the most basic aspects of the Court's jurisprudence on the freedom of assembly and freedom of expression;
(2) The references were incomplete, as they did not represent the Court's practice in an accurate or reliable way;
(3) The references were incomplete because they merely cited judgments and did not explain their relevance to the case or the subsequent legal argument;
(4) The references were always used in order to justify a restriction.

4.4.1 Characteristic 1: Referencing the Basics

We found that the courts referenced the same provisions of the Convention, as well as the same cases of the ECtHR. In every single judgement listed in Table 2, courts included the same paragraph, using the same or almost the same wording. This paragraph highlights that the right to freedom of assembly, enshrined in Article 11 of the Convention, is a 'fundamental right in a democratic society', and that, according to Article 11(2) of the Convention, it can be subject to limitations. The paragraph then lists the cases of *Makhmudov v Russia*,[46] *Djavit An v Turkey*,[47] and *Christian Democratic People's Party v Moldova*[48] and states that in these cases the Court confirmed that freedom of assembly is not absolute and can be subject to restrictions. The courts do not actually describe the cases or give any additional information about their con-

46 *Makhmudov v. Russia* App. no. 35082/04 (ECtHR, 26 July 2007).

47 *Djavit An v Turkey* App. no. 20652/92 (ECtHR, 20 February 2003).

48 *Christian Democratic People's Party v Moldova* App. no. 28793/02 (ECtHR, 14 February 2006)

tents. Finally, the paragraph includes a list of grounds for such restrictions from Article 11(2) of the Convention (national security or public safety, prevention of disorder or crime, etc.). The inclusion of this information is not problematic on its own; however, in all judgements we have analysed, the courts limit themselves to this paragraph and do not explore relevant international law provisions any further (see Characteristic 3).

4.4.2 Characteristic 2: Warping the Case Law

In their judgments, Russian courts did not strive to use the case law of the ECtHR in a manner that would adequately present its key cases or findings. The courts only cited the part of the ECtHR judgements that would fit their point of view and did not delve into their essence. In all three ECtHR cases cited by Russian courts, the ECtHR found a violation of Article 11. This part, however, was left out by the Russian courts. National courts also did not explain the facts of the case, the legal issues raised in them, or the arguments of the Court regarding these issues. This was done strategically: the jurisprudence of the ECtHR clearly prohibits prosecuting people for peaceful participation in protests and other types of peaceful expression, even if such assemblies have not been authorised beforehand.[49] Therefore, Russian courts needed to leave out these parts of the ECtHR judgements, as otherwise, they would have to agree with the protesters and acquit them.

4.4.3 Characteristic 3: Referencing for the Sake of Referencing

The judgments did not provide any explanation as to what purpose the reference to the ECtHR case law was meant to serve. After the paragraph on the applicable international standards described above (that ended with a list of permissible grounds for restrictions under the Convention), the courts went on to state that the Public Events Act also provides limitations to the freedom of assembly. However, they did not specify which of the grounds was applicable in the case they were dealing with; they also did not explain why and how the reference to the human rights law was relevant in the first place. Therefore, it appears that the national courts cited ECtHR cases just for the sake of referencing, to highlight the fact that the judges are aware of the provisions of the

49 Navalnyy and Yashin v. Russia App no. 76204/11 (ECtHR, 4 December 2014), para. 63; Lashmankin and others v Russia App no 57818/09 (ECtHR, 7 September 2017), para. 423; Oya Ataman v. Turkey, App no 74552/01 (ECtHR, 5 December 2006), paras. 41–42; Bukta and Others v. Hungary App. no. 25691/04 (ECtHR, 17 July 2007), para. 34.

human rights instruments and to give more credibility and legitimacy to their findings.

4.4.4 Characteristic 4: ECtHR Case Law as a Justification for Restrictions

As highlighted in the previous section of this chapter, Russian courts have established a set of jurisprudence, which only allows participants in assemblies to be acquitted on procedural grounds or due to errors in a case file. We have found no less than 84,066 court decisions on administrative proceedings held from January 2008 to March 2024 under article 20.2 of the CAO in the courts of the first and second instances. Of these decisions, 9,400 contain references to the ECtHR case law. Out of this vast number of court decisions, there were only 43 dismissals that cited the ECtHR case law. Interestingly, these decisions cite the same provisions of the ECHR and the same cases of the Court as the ones where a person gets convicted for participating in an assembly. Therefore, references to the ECtHR served a merely formalistic function in a practice where an overwhelming majority of protestors were sentenced for participation in an assembly.

To summarise the findings of this section, we argue that Russian courts do mention ECtHR cases on the freedom of assembly. However, what is referenced are the short passages of the legal reasoning concerning grounds for restrictions under international human rights law, which do not paint a full picture of the Court's jurisprudence. Referencing the ECtHR jurisprudence is done merely to justify the restrictions imposed on the freedom of assembly in Russia. This way, Russian courts contribute to the broader strategy of misappropriation of human rights narratives by selectively invoking international human rights standards to legitimise state-imposed limitations, rather than to protect the right to peaceful assembly.

5 Conclusion

This study demonstrates the sophisticated use of laws governing assemblies by the Russian authorities, both before and after the 2022 invasion of Ukraine. By exploiting seemingly legitimate regulations and invoking international human rights instruments such as the ECHR, authorities impose technically feasible limitations on this right. These limitations include a challenging and unpredictable approval process, embedded assumptions in police and judicial practices, and a carefully constructed legal narrative.

Several key observations emerge. First, the system operates in a coordinated manner: various branches – including legislative, executive, and judicial – act in synergy, with their practices mutually reinforcing rather than being random. Courts adopt a consistent approach, refraining from assessing the legality of police orders and uniformly referencing ECtHR case law. Police officers systematically report alleged non-compliance of their orders in administrative protocols. While minor divergences exist, such as how courts treat omissions in the protocols, overall, the evidence points to a harmonised system, maintained through implicit rules and shared assumptions. There are, however, no publicly observable rules governing these uniform practices, which could potentially serve as important areas for future research.

Second, the findings reveal a creation of the appearance of compliance with human rights standards. The formal acknowledgement of the right to freedom of assembly and references to international law function primarily to legitimise restrictions rather than protect rights. Assumptions not evident to the broader public, allow authorities to prosecute individuals for mere participation in peaceful assemblies. These practices constitute a strategy of human rights misappropriation: the authorities exploit a seemingly liberal legal framework, invoking universally recognised international laws, to infringe upon the right to freedom of assembly.

Looking ahead, as repression has intensified, public protests have shifted mainly from physical spaces to virtual realms, where they fall under the protection of freedom of expression.[50] Regarding freedom of expression, the evolution of the Russian legal system has been characterised by significant regression rather than progress. Comparatively, provisions targeting war critics (article 20.3.3 of the CAO) do not exhibit a strategy of misappropriation. On the contrary, the implementation of these provisions is clearly arbitrary, and the law itself evidently fails to pursue a legitimate aim. We can not see any effort by the authorities to imitate a legitimate legal order. While some scholars argue that the situation concerning anti-war legislation is not substantially different from laws regulating assemblies, we assert that our perspective highlights the key distinctions between these two areas.[51] Moreover, the arbitrary nature of recent rulings by the Supreme Court is equally evident. Particularly, the declaration of the 'International Public LGBT Movement' as

---

50 OVD-Info, 'Persecution of the Anti-war Movement report: Three Years into Russia's Full-Scale Invasion of Ukraine. February 2025' (2025) <https://ovd.info/en/antiwar_3_years> accessed 14 April 2025.

51 Lauren A McCarthy, Douglas Rice and Aleks Lokhmutov, 'Four Months of "Discrediting the Military": Repressive Law in Wartime Russia' (2023) 31 Demokratizatsiya: The Journal of Post-Soviet Democratization 125.

an extremist organisation, without any evidence of its existence, serves as one example.[52] Similarly, the designation of the fictitious 'Anti-Russian Separatist Movement' as an extremist organisation has turned into reality the persecution of numerous unrelated decolonial organisations and groups.[53] These examples raise a critical question: Is there currently any effort in Russia to create a facade of legal order, or are we witnessing a situation better described as 'rule without law'?

Bibliography

European Court of Human Rights Cases

Bodalev v Russia App no 67200/12 (ECtHR, 6 September 2022)
Bukta and Others v Hungary App no 25691/04 (ECtHR, 17 July 2007)
Christian Democratic People's Party v Moldova App no 28793/02 (ECtHR, 14 February 2006)
Djavit An v Turkey App no 20652/92 (ECtHR, 20 February 2003)
Kasparov and Others v Russia App no 21913/07 (ECtHR, 3 October 2013)
Kudrevičius and Others v Lithuania App no 37553/05 (ECtHR, 15 October 2015)
Lashmankin and Others v Russia App no 57818/09 (ECtHR, 7 September 2017)
Navalnyy and Yashin v Russia App no 76204/11 (ECtHR, 4 December 2014)
Oya Ataman v Turkey, App no 74552/01 (ECtHR, 5 December 2006)

National Courts 1

1344-O-P № 3-P [1999] Constitutional Court of Russia
16-6272/2020 [2020] 2nd Cassation Court of Russia
16-5611/2020 [2020] 7th Cassation Court of Russia
16-1196/2021–16-6753/2020 [2021] 7th Cassation Court of Russia
16-1197/2021–16-6754/2020 [2021] 7th Cassation Court of Russia
16-1206/2021–16-6763/2020 [2021] 7th Cassation Court of Russia

---

52 'The Destruction of Traditional Values and Feminatives: "Svobodnye Novosti" Publishes the Full Text of the Supreme Court of Russia's Decision Recognising the "LGBT Movement" as Extremist' (Svobodnye Novosti, 3 October 2024) <https://fn-volga.ru/news/view/id/219533> accessed 14 April 2025.

53 'The Supreme Court declared the "Anti-Russian Separatist Movement", likely non-existent organisation, "extremist"' (OVD-Info, 7 June 2024) <https://ovd.info/express-news/2024/06/07/vs-priznal-ekstremistskim-veroyatno-nesuschestvuyuschee-antirossiyskoe> accessed 14 April 2025.

16-588/2021–16-5842/2020 [2021] 7th Cassation Court of Russia
16-1545/2021 [2021] 3rd Cassation Court of Russia
16-5499/2021 [2021] 2nd Cassation Court of Russia
16-1988/2021 [2021] 9th Cassation Court of Russia
16-3516/2021 [2021] 9th Cassation Court of Russia
16-2175/2021 [2021] 8th Cassation Court of Russia
16-5388/2021 [2021] 8th Cassation Court of Russia
16-8040/2021 [2021] 8th Cassation Court of Russia
16-8352/2021 [2021] 8th Cassation Court of Russia
16-2798/2020 [2021] 7th Cassation Court of Russia
16-211/2022 [2021] 8th Cassation Court of Russia
16-817/2022 [2022] 9th Cassation Court of Russia
16-2098/2022 [2022] 8th Cassation Court of Russia

National Courts 2

5-53/2024 [2024] Sterlitamaksky city court of Bashkortostan region
5-52/2024 [2024] Sterlitamaksky city court of Bashkortostan region
5-47/2024 [2024] Sterlitamaksky city court of Bashkortostan region
5-46/2024 [2024] Sterlitamaksky city court of Bashkortostan region
5-2081/2023 [2023] Lyublinsky district court of Moscow
5-2069/2023 [2023] Lyublinsky district court of Moscow
5-236/2022 [2023] Moscow city court
7-6225/2023 [2023] Moscow city court
5-174/23 [2023] Preobrazhenskiy district court of Moscow
7-5047/2023 [2023] Moscow city court
7-4698/2023 [2023] Moscow city court
7-4729/2023 [2023] Moscow city court
5-173/23 [2023] Preobrazhenskiy district court of Moscow
5-175/23 [2023] Preobrazhenskiy district court of Moscow
5-82/2023 [2023] Oktyabrskiy district court of Saint-Petersburg
7-5102/2023 [2023] Moscow city court
7-5110/2023 [2023] Moscow city court
7-5111/2023 [2023] Moscow city court
7-4745/2023 [2023] Moscow city court
7-2755/2023 [2023] Moscow city court

Legislation and Official Documents

Code of Administrative Offences of the Russian Federation (2001)

Committee of Ministers, Interim Resolution CM/ResDH(2022)54 on the Execution of the Judgments of the European Court of Human Rights in Lashmankin group v Russian Federation (2022)

Communication of the Russian Federation concerning the case of Lashmankin and Others v Russian Federation (App no 57818/09)

Criminal Code of the Russian Federation (1996)

Russian Federation, Eighth Report Submitted by the Russian Federation under Article 40 of the Covenant (UN Doc CCPR/C/RUS/8, 2019)

Venice Commission, Opinion CDL-AD(2020)009 on draft amendments to the Constitution (as signed by the President of the Russian Federation on 14 March 2020) related to the execution in the Russian Federation of decisions by the European Court of Human Rights (2020)

Secondary Sources

Selvi AF, 'Qualitative Content Analysis' (Routledge 2019)

De Búrca G and Young KG, 'The (mis)appropriation of human rights by the new global right: An introduction to the Symposium' (2023) 21 *International Journal of Constitutional Law* 205

Drzemczewski A and Lawson R, 'Exclusion of the Russian Federation from the Council of Europe and the ECHR: An Overview' (2022) 21 *Baltic YB Intl L*

Ginsburg T, 'Authoritarian International Law?' (2020) *114 AJIL* 221

Lohaus M and Stapel S, 'Who commits to regional human rights treaties? Reputational benefits, sovereignty costs, and regional dynamics' (2022) 22 *Journal of Human Rights* 386

Mälksoo L, *Russian Approaches to International Law* (Oxford University Press 2015)

McCarthy LA, Rice D and Lokhmutov A, 'Four Months of "Discrediting the Military": Repressive Law in Wartime Russia' (2023) 31 *Demokratizatsiya* 125

Pomeranz WE, 'Putin's 2020 Constitutional Amendments: What Changed? What Remained the Same?' (2021) 6 *Russian Politics* 6

Smirnova N and Shedov D, 'Russia on the Path to Freedom of Assembly: Problems and Tools for Change' (*OVD-Info*, 2021) <https://reforum.io/contents/uploads/2021/06/ovd-web.pdf> accessed 14 April 2025

Stoeckl K, 'Traditional values, family, homeschooling: The role of Russia and the Russian Orthodox Church in transnational moral conservative networks and their efforts at reshaping human rights' (2023) 21 *International Journal of Constitutional Law* 224

Tertytchnaya K and Tiratsoo M, 'Legal Repression in Russia' (2024) *Oxford Research Encyclopedia of Politics* <https://oxfordre.com/politics/view/10.1093/acrefore/9780190228637.001.0001/acrefore-9780190228637-e-2247> accessed 14 April 2025

Web and News Sources

——, 'Schyotchik kompensatsii. Rossiya ne vyplatila milliony evro po postanovleniyam ESPCh' (*Crew Against Torture*, 2025) <https://pytkam.net/schetchikECHR/> accessed 27 October 2025

——, 'Ombudsman: Bolee 60% ot vsekh publichnykh aktsiy v Moskve v 2020g byli nesanktsionirovannymi' (*Interfax*, 20 February 2020) <https://www.interfax-russia.ru/moscow/main/ombudsmen-bolee-60-ot-vseh-publichnyh-akciy-v-moskve-v-2020g-byli-nesankcionirovannymi> accessed 11 June 2025

——, 'Persecution of the Anti-war Movement report: Three Years into Russia's Full-Scale Invasion of Ukraine. February 2025' (*OVD-Info*, 2025) <https://ovd.info/en/antiwar_3_years> accessed 14 April 2025

——, 'Repression in Russia 2023' (*OVD-Info*, 2023) <https://ovd.info/en/repression-russia-2023-ovd-info-overview> accessed 11 June 2025

State Automated System of the Russian Federation 'Pravosudie' <https://sudrf.ru> accessed 30 May 2025

——, 'Svoboda Sobranii na Fone Pandemii' (*OVD-Info*, 2020) <https://reports.ovd.info/svoboda-sobraniy-na-fone-pandemii> accessed 3 September 2025

——, 'Territoriia "nel'zia"' (*OVD-Info*, 2018) <https://tn.ovdinfo.org> accessed 14 April 2025

——, 'The Art of Ban' (*OVD-Info*, 2019) <https://ovd.info/en/art-ban> accessed 14 April 2025

——, 'The Destruction of Traditional Values and Feminatives: "Svobodnye Novosti" Publishes the Full Text of the Supreme Court of Russia's Decision Recognising the "LGBT Movement" as Extremist' (*Svobodnye Novosti*, 3 October 2024) <https://fn-volga.ru/news/view/id/219533> accessed 14 April 2025

——, 'The State Duma terminated international treaties of the Council of Europe' (*Interfax*, 16 February 2023) <https://www.interfax.ru/russia/886500> accessed 15 April 2025

——, 'The Supreme Court declared the "Anti-Russian Separatist Movement", likely non-existent organisation, "extremist"' (*OVD-Info*, 7 June 2024) <https://ovd.info/express-news/2024/06/07/vs-priznal-ekstremistskim-veroyatno-nesuschestvuyuschee-antirossiyskoe> accessed 14 April 2025

——, 'Unresolved Freedom of Assembly Issues in Russia in 2020' (*OVD-Info*, 2021) <https://ovd.info/en/lashmankin-et-al-v-russia> accessed 11 June 2025

CHAPTER 3

Beyond LGBT Rights: Russia's "Traditional Values" Statecraft

Cai Wilkinson

1 Introduction

Since the early 2010s, Russia has not only actively opposed the development of LGBT rights as a new human rights norm but has also made its opposition a central feature of both its foreign and domestic policies. At the UN, Russia's representatives have invested significant effort in "actively neutering rights agreements across the globe"[1] including fostering alliances with other states to support its anti-LGBT position,[2] as well as on gender rights more widely.[3] More widely, Russia's involvement in transnational right-wing and anti-gender networks is well documented.[4] It has played a self-proclaimed leading role in "The Moralist International" – a transnational network of conservative political and religious actors–that constitutes one faction of the "global culture

1 Paul Chaney, "Civil Society, 'Traditional Values' and LGBT Resistance to Heteronormative Rights Hegemony: Analysis of the UN Universal Periodic Review in the Russian Federation" (2018) 70 Europe-Asia Studies 638.

2 Emil Edenborg, "Anti-Gender Politics as Discourse Coalitions: Russia's Domestic and International Promotion of 'Traditional Values'" [2021] Problems of Post-Communism 1.

3 Jelena Cupać and Irem Ebetürk, "The Personal Is Global Political: The Antifeminist Backlash in the United Nations" (2020) 22 The British Journal of Politics and International Relations 702.

4 Edenborg, "Anti-Gender Politics as Discourse Coalitions: Russia's Domestic and International Promotion of 'Traditional Values'"; Kevin Moss, "Russia as the Saviour of European Civilization: Gender and the Geopolitics of Traditional Values" in Roman Kuhar and David Paternotte (eds), *Anti-Gender Campaigns in Europe* (Rowman & Littlefield 2017); KRISTINA STOECKL and KSENIYA MEDVEDEVA, "Double Bind at the UN: Western Actors, Russia, and the Traditionalist Agenda" (2018) 7 Global Constitutionalism 383; Julia Mourão Permoser and Kristina Stoeckl, "Reframing Human Rights: The Global Network of Moral Conservative Homeschooling Activists" (2021) 21 Global Networks 681; Kristina Stoeckl, "Traditional Values, Family, Homeschooling: The Role of Russia and the Russian Orthodox Church in Transnational Moral Conservative Networks and Their Efforts at Reshaping Human Rights" (2023) 21 International Journal of Constitutional Law 224; Kristina Stoeckl, "The Rise of the Russian Christian Right: The Case of the World Congress of Families" (2020) 48 Religion, State & Society 223.

wars" – a media-friendly shorthand term to describe "a division between progressive and conservative values and between the individuals, groups and countries that identify with one or the other".[5]

Within these culture wars, questions of sexual and gender diversity have emerged as particularly contentious issues. The framing of LGBT rights as human rights has been strongly supported by progressive actors, who view it as in keeping with the concept of universal human rights and a way to strengthen human rights as a core liberal and democratic value,[6] and equally strongly condemned by conservative ones who view it as creating a category of special rights that undermines the international human rights regime and the principle of universality.[7]

Positions on both sides have not been confined to debate and declarations but rather have been reflected in policy and legislation as well as public opinion. The result has been the development of a situation of international polarisation over LGBT rights,[8] which is reflected in contradictory trends. On the one hand, the global trend is towards greater support for LGBT rights: the number of countries criminalising consensual same-sex sexual acts has fallen from 113 to 64 since 1990;[9] same-sex marriage has been legalised in 38 countries with a further 54 providing more limited rights such as civil unions or domestic partnerships;[10] more than 135 countries provide at least some protection against discrimination based on sexual orientation and/or gender identity.[11] These developments have been accompanied by an overall trend towards greater public support for LGBT rights in many countries.[12] On the other hand, however, the pace at which anti-discrimination and other protect-

5 Dmitry Uzlaner and Kristina Stoeckl, *The Moralist International* (Fordham University Press 2022).

6 Ronald Holzhacker and Zehra F Kabasakal Arat, "'Gay Rights Are Human Rights': The Framing of New Interpretations of International Human Rights Norms" in George Andrepoulos (ed), *The Uses and Misuses of Human Rights, A Critical Approach to Advocacy* (Palgrave MacMillan 2014); Anthony J Langlois, "Making LGBT Rights into Human Rights" in Michael J Bosia, Sandra M McEvoy and Momin Rahman (eds), *The Oxford Handbook of Global LGBT and Sexual Diversity Politics* (Oxford University Press 2020).

7 M Joel Voss, "Contesting Sexual Orientation and Gender Identity at the UN Human Rights Council" (2018) 19 Human Rights Review 1.

8 Jonathan Symons and Dennis Altman, "International Norm Polarization: Sexuality as a Subject of Human Rights Protection" (2015) 7 International Theory 61.

9 https://database.ilga.org/criminalisation-consensual-same-sex-sexual-acts.

10 https://www.equaldex.com/issue/marriage.

11 https://www.equaldex.com/issue/discrimination.

12 Byung-Deuk Woo and others, "Public Support for Gay Rights Across Countries and Over Time" (2025) 106 Social Science Quarterly.

ive legislation is enacted has slowed significantly, and at regional and national levels there are notable trends towards greater restrictions on LGBT people's rights in the form of anti-LGBT legislation targeting freedoms of expression and association.[13]

Against the wider backdrop of growing disenchantment with globalisation and democracy and spread of populism and authoritarianism, "queer wars"[14] have thus taken on far greater significance than just about whether the human rights of sexual and gender minorities should be recognised and protected. Rather, as Russian sexologist Igor Kon argued, the issue of LGBT rights has become "a litmus test for democracy".[15] Research has shown correlation between state-sanctioned targeting of LGBT people and their rights and the likelihood of "democratic backsliding" occurring.[16] The use of political homophobia, often in combination with wider anti-gender rhetoric and policies, by populist and authoritarian actors seeking to advance illiberal agendas has been evidenced extensively and repeatedly in a wide range of countries.[17] In many cases, as Ayoub and Stoeckl have comprehensively demonstrated, the same arguments used to advance LGBT rights has been redeployed by an array of conservative groups and actors to refute them.[18]

Such anti-LGBT tactics clearly meet de Búrca and Young's definition of human rights misappropriation insofar as they draw on "the language of pro-

---

13 Lucas Ramon Mendos and Dhia Rezki Rohaizad, "Laws On Us: A Global Overview of Legal Progress and Backtracking on Sexual Orientation, Gender Identity, Gender Expression, and Sex Characteristics" (ILGA World 2024) <https://ilga.org/news/laws-on-us-2024-lgbti-human-rights/>.

14 Dennis Altman and Jonathan Symons, *Queer Wars* (Polity Press 2016).

15 I Kon, "Homophobia as a Litmus Test of Russian Democracy" (2010) 51 Russian Social Science Review 16.

16 Andrew R Flores, Miguel Fuentes Carreño and Ari Shaw, "Democratic Backsliding and LGBTI Acceptance" (Williams Institute 2023) <https://williamsinstitute.law.ucla.edu/publications/dem-backsliding-gai/>.

17 Meredith L Weiss and Michael J Bosia (eds), *Global Homophobia: States, Movements, and the Politics of Oppression* (University of Illinois Press 2013); Roman Kuhar and David Paternotte (eds), *Anti-Gender Campaigns in Europe* (Rowman & Littlefield International 2017); Gisela Zaremberg, Constanza Tabbush and Elisabeth Jay Friedman, "Feminism(s) and Anti-Gender Backlash: Lessons from Latin America" (2021) 23 International Feminist Journal of Politics 527; Agnieszka Graff and Elżbieta Korolczuk, *Anti – Gender Politics in the Populist Moment* (Routledge 2022); Ov Cristian Norocel and David Paternotte, "The Dis/Articulation of Anti-Gender Politics in Eastern Europe: Introduction" (2023) 70 Problems of Post-Communism 123; Jerker Edström and others, "Introduction: Understanding Gender Backlash Across Regions" (2024) 55 IDS Bulletin 1.

18 Phillip M Ayoub and Kristina Stoeckl, *The Global Fight Against LGBTI Rights* (New York University Press 2024) <https://nyupress.org/9781479824793/the-global-fight-against-lgbti-rights/>.

tecting 'human rights', but generally [seek] to reverse or undo previous human rights developments and commitments".[19] Similarly, the negative consequences of anti-LGBT politics are not in doubt, with increases in violence against LGBT people recorded in almost all parts of the world in recent years, including those often regarded as "LGBT friendly" such as Europe and the US.[20] Yet to date there has been less attention paid to the wider motivations and aims of those engaging in human rights misappropriation – and it is this aspect that is the focus of this chapter.

Using the case of Russia's implementation of anti-LGBT legislation since 2013, I trace how this initial human rights misappropriation has increasingly served as a vehicle for Russia to challenge the international liberal order itself and advance an alternative view of how states and societies should be structured. In the following section, I provide an overview of the trajectory of LGBT rights in Russia, with particular focus on developments since 2013 and how political homophobia has been a central vector for the creation of an intimate regulatory regime of sexuality and gender that extends far beyond the rejection of LGBTQ rights, with gender becoming a powerful lever for the Putin regime's consolidation of authoritarian rule. I then situate the evolution of this intimate regime in relation to Russia's pursuit of absolute sovereignty and how threat narratives of an "unholy queer peril" have been utilised to assert the necessity of not only territorial and cultural sovereignty but moral sovereignty as a condition for Russia's security and survival. This extensive securitisation of sexual and gender diversity has played a central role in the implementation of a *de facto* state ideology of "traditional Russian spiritual-moral values" that reflects Russia's claimed identity as a "state-civilisation" with a unique role to play in world affairs.[21] Accordingly, from a Russian perspective, far from misappropriating human rights, their actions are necessary responses to counter liberalism and the threat it poses to Russia's existence.

---

19 Gráinne de Búrca and Katharine G Young, "The (Mis)Appropriation of Human Rights by the New Global Right: An Introduction to the Symposium" (2023) 21 International Journal of Constitutional Law 205.

20 Ilan H Meyer and Andrew R Flores, "Anti-LGBT Victimization in the United States" (Williams Institute, School of Law, UCLA 2022) <https://williamsinstitute.law.ucla.edu/publications/anti-lgbt-victimization-us/>; European Union Agency for Fundamental Rights, "LGBTIQ Equality at a Crossroads: Progress and Challenges" (Publications Office of the European Union 2024) <https://fra.europa.eu/en/news/2024/harassment-and-violence-against-lgbtiq-people-rise>.

21 Igor Torbakov, "The 'Special Path' of Russian State-Civilization: The Genealogy of Vladimir Putin's Geopolitical Metaphor" [2023] The Russia Program at GW Online Papers < https://therussiaprogram.org/onlinepaper_9>.

2 Anti-queer Politics in Russia

In this section, I provide an overview of the development of "anti-queer" politics in Russia since 2012, when Vladimir Putin commenced his third presidential term. My use of "anti-queer", rather than simply anti-LGBT, points to how the initial misappropriation of human rights that was used to justify the introduction of restrictions on so-called "homopropaganda" has evolved into a wider narrative about the incompatibility of sexual and gender diversity – understood as any deviance from the "natural" cisheteropatriarchal gender order and gendered norms – with "traditional values". This discursive move has then been extended to present any manifestation of gender non-conformity as an intolerable threat to Russia's existence via the construction of an "Unholy Queer Peril"[22] that, as I discuss in the following section, has been used to elevate "traditional values" from a justification for human rights misappropriation to the status of *de facto* state ideology.

2.1 Anti-LGBT Legislation

Putin's third term was not the starting point of political homophobia in Russia. Setting aside the Soviet period,[23] after a brief decade in which consensual sexual relations between men were decriminalised, homosexuality was officially depathologised and LGBT people became visible in popular culture,[24] from the early 2000s a "conservative turn" in relation to matters of gender and sexuality was increasingly evident.[25] One of the most tangible manifestations of the authorities' growing resistance to liberal sexual norms was the repeated refusal to issue permits for Moscow Pride from 2006 onwards, with activists exercising their rights to freedom of assembly and association often being

22 Cai Wilkinson, "Mother Russia in Queer Peril: The Gender Logic of the Hypermasculine State" in Swati Parashar, J Ann Tickner and Jacqui True (eds), *Revisiting Gendered States: Feminist Imaginings of the State in International Relations* (2018).

23 For a concise history of homophobia in the Soviet Union and consideration of how it has influenced post-Soviet LGBT politics, see Dan Healey and Francesca Stella, "Sexual and Gender Dissent in the USSR and Post-Soviet Space. Introduction" (2021) 62 Cahiers du monde russe. Russie – Empire russe – Union soviétique et États indépendants 225; Dan Healey, *Russian Homophobia from Stalin to Sochi* (Bloomsbury Academic 2018).

24 Cai Wilkinson, "LGBT Rights in the Former Soviet Union: The Evolution of Hypervisibility" in Michael J Bosia, Sandra M McEvoy and Momin Rahman (eds) (2020).

25 Maria Davidenko and Valeriya Utkina, "The Conservative Turn in Post-Soviet Russia" (2024) 76 Europe-Asia Studies 135.

subjected to homophobic violence and arrest.[26] The discriminatory nature of such bans on public LGBT parades, rallies and protests has been upheld in European Court of Human Rights judgements, but has not led to a change in position.[27] Indeed, following the ECtHR issuing of its first judgement in favour of LGBT activist Nikolai Alekseyev in October 2011,[28] in 2012 the Moscow city government imposed a 100-year ban on gay pride marches.[29]

The mid-2000s also marked the beginning of trend to outlaw "propaganda of homosexuality" among minors at the sub-national level. Ryazan Oblast was the first region to enact legislation in 2006, with Arkhangelsk Oblast following suit in 2011 and a further seven regional or municipal governments passing similar bills in 2012.[30] Of this latter group, the legislation adopted in St Petersburg attracted particular international attention due to the sweeping scope of the ban, which prohibited "public actions aimed at propagandising sodomy, lesbianism, bisexualism and transgenderism among minors", as well as the bill's inclusion of a second article prohibiting "propaganda of paedophilia" that was widely seen as "more or less inserting an equal sign between the two".[31]

By the end of 2012, a draft federal bill prohibiting homopropaganda was under consideration in the State Duma.[32] The proposal sought to introduce amendments to three pieces of legislation: the federal law "On Protecting Chil-

26 Francesca Stella, "Queer Space, Pride, and Shame in Moscow" (2013) 72 Slavic Review 458; Alice EM Underwood, "The Politics of Pride: The LGBT Movement and Post-Soviet Democracy" (2011) 33 Harvard International Review 42.

27 Lisa McIntosh Sundstrom and Valerie Sperling, "Seeking Better Judgment: LGBT Discrimination Cases in Russia and at the European Court of Human Rights" (2020) 24 The International Journal of Human Rights 750.

28 Kristen L Thomas, "We're Here, We're Queer, Get Used to It: Freedom of Assembly and Gay Pride in Alekseyev v. Russia" (2012) 14 Oregon Review of International Law 473.

29 BBC News, "Gay Parades Banned in Moscow for 100 Years" *BBC News* (2012) <https://www.bbc.com/news/world-europe-19293465>.

30 Francesca Ugolino, "In Russia Was Passed the Law Prohibiting Propaganda of 'Non-Traditional Relationships' in the Presence of Minors, at the Federal Level. Protection of Minors or Discrimination Based on Sexual Orientation?" (2013) N° 31 Civitas Europa 331.

31 Julia Ioffe, "What's Russian for 'Homosexual Propaganda'?" *The New Yorker* (2011) <https://www.newyorker.com/news/news-desk/whats-russian-for-homosexual-propaganda>.

32 Miriam Elder, "Russian Parliament to Consider Federal Anti-Gay Law" *The Guardian* (2012) <https://www.theguardian.com/world/2012/nov/30/russian-parliament-federal-anti-gay-law>. Законопроект № 44554–6 «о внесении изменений в статью 5 Федерального закона «о защите детей от информации, причиняющей вред их здоровьюи развитию» и отдельные законодательные акты

dren from Information Harmful to Their Health and Development",[33] the federal law "On Basic Guarantees for the Rights of the Child in the Russian Federation",[34] and the Code of the Russian Federation on Administrative Offences.[35] The bill passed its first reading in January 2013, and then its second and third readings on the same day in early June 2013 and was signed into law by President Vladimir Putin before the end of the month.[36] Notably, between January and June the proposed wording changed from specifying the "propaganda of homosexualism among minors" to the "propaganda of non-traditional sexual relations among minors" – the first time such phrasing had been used in a federal law, according to the NGO Civil Rights Defenders.[37]

Despite the change of wording, the federal law was understood by international human rights experts as targeting the LGBT community.[38] It was criticised extensively both prior to and after adoption for breaching international human rights standards and obligations by imposing "illegitimate restrictions on freedom of expression, [discriminating] against Lesbian, Gay, Bisexual, and Transgender (LGBT) persons, [impeding] pluralistic and open discussion on matters of sexual identity, equality and tolerance, and [harming] the rights of children it ostensibly seeks to promote".[39] This was unsurprising, especially in light of the aforementioned ECtHR judgement as well as the UN Human Rights Committee's November 2012 decision in favour of LGBT

Российской Федерации в целях защиты детей отинформации, пропагандирующей отрицание традиционных семейных ценностей».

33 Федеральный закон "О защите детей от информации, причиняющей вред их здоровью и развитию" от 29.12.2010 N 436-ФЗ (последняя редакция). https://www.consultant.ru/document/cons_doc_LAW_108808/.

34 Федеральный закон "Об основных гарантиях прав ребенка в Российской Федерации" от 24.07.1998 N 124-ФЗ (последняя редакция) https://www.consultant.ru/document/cons_doc_LAW_19558/.

35 Проект федерального закона «о внесении изменений в Кодекс Российской Федерации обадминистративных правонарушениях».

36 Civil Rights Defenders, "Duma Prohibits 'Propaganda' of Non-Traditional Relations" (2013) <https://crd.org/2013/06/12/duma-prohibits-propaganda-of-non-traditional-relations/>; ABC News, "Russia's Vladimir Putin Signs 'anti-Gay Propaganda' Bill into Law" *ABC News* (2013) <https://www.abc.net.au/news/2013-06-30/russia27s-putin-signs-27anti-gay-propaganda27-bill-into-law/4790498>.

37 Defenders.

38 Maria Issaeva and Maria Kiskachi, "Immoral Truth vs. Untruthful Morals? Attempts to Render Rights and Freedoms Conditional upon Sexual Orientation in Light of Russia's International Obligations" (2015) 2 Russian Law Journal 81.

39 Article 19, "Russia: Federal Laws Introducing Ban of Propaganda of Non-Traditional Sexual Relationships" (2013) Legal analysis <https://www.refworld.org/reference/research/art19/2013/en/95025>.

activist Irina Fedotova regarding her 2009 conviction under the Ryazan Oblast law.[40]

Russia's response to international criticism of the new legislation demonstrated clearly how human rights language and logics had been misappropriated. Two angles were emphasised: first, that, far from being discriminatory against LGBT people, the law simply balanced their rights with the rights of children, and second, that the Russian government was being accountable by implementing the legislation and protecting not only children's rights, but also cultural rights. These rebuttals were clearly evident in Putin's remarks at a press conference in January 2014 ahead of the Sochi Winter Olympicsforexample:

> "We do not have a ban on non-traditional sexual relationships," said Putin in comments reported by Russian agencies. "We have a ban on the propaganda of homosexuality and paedophilia. I want to underline this. Propaganda among children. These are absolutely different things – a ban on something or a ban on the propaganda of that thing."
> [...].
>
> "We are not forbidding anything and nobody is being grabbed off the street, and there is no punishment for such kinds of relations," said Putin. "You can feel relaxed and calm [in Russia], but leave children alone please," said Putin.
> [...].
>
> Earlier this week, Putin said the Games would be held "without discrimination on any grounds". But he added on Friday that Russia was a traditional country, and refused to accept European values on sexual orientation, claiming that some countries were even discussing the legalisation of paedophilia. He declined to specify which countries, saying it was easy to find out about such things on the internet.
>
> Putin said: "What, are we supposed to follow along like obedient lapdogs, towards whatever consequences await? We have our own traditions, our own

40 Thomas; International Commission of Jurists, "Russia: Human Rights Groups Hail Historic Decision on Homosexual Propaganda Ban" (*International Commission of Jurists*, 2012) <https://www.icj.org/russia-human-rights-groups-hail-historic-decision-on-homosexual-propaganda-ban/>.

> culture. We have respect for all of our international partners and ask that they also respect our own traditions and culture."[41]

Despite Putin's explanation for the reasonableness and necessity of the legislation – which is built on the spurious conflation of homosexuality and paedophilia and the presumed incompatibility of homosexuality with Russian culture – all elements of rights misappropriation are evident: universality is replaced by a hierarchy of rights with children's rights prioritised over those of LGBT people; the intent is exclusionary and anti-pluralist insofar as the legislation deliberately restricts LGBT people's access to public spaces and presents them as danger to children; and while accountability is invoked, it is in relation to the Russian state's duty to protect traditional values, not to uphold international human rights norms. Indeed, Putin's concluding remark calling for "respect" from international partners can be read as an active rejection of such accountability.

In June 2017, the ECtHR ruled in *Bayev and Others v. Russia* that the legislative amendments introduced by the 2013 federal bill violated Article 10 (freedom of expression) and Article 14 (prohibition of discrimination) of the European Convention on Human Rights.[42] The Kremlin's argument about the necessity of the law to protect children and morals was roundly rejected, with the decision further noting that the ban "reinforced stigma and prejudice and encouraged homophobia, which was incompatible with the values – of equality, pluralism and tolerance – of a democratic society".[43]

The judgement was ignored by the Kremlin. This was unsurprising given Russian perceptions about the Council of Europe's "politicisation of human rights" (not only in relation to LGBT rights),[44] but also because of Russia's development between 2015 and 2020 of an interpretation of constitutional law that has given the Constitutional Court of the Russian Federation increasing jurisdiction to determine compliance with ECtHR judgements.[45] In com-

41 Shaun Walker, "Vladimir Putin: Gay People at Winter Olympics Must 'Leave Children Alone'" *The Guardian* (2014) <https://www.theguardian.com/world/2014/jan/17/vladimir-putin-gay-winter-olympics-children>.

42 Registrar of the European Court of Human Rights, "Judgment Bayev and Others v. Russia – Legislation Banning the Promotion of Homosexuality" (European Court of Human Rights, 2017) <https://hudoc.echr.coe.int/eng-press?i=003-5755355-7315126>.

43 Ibid.

44 Tom Casier, "A Classic Dilemma: Russia's Threat to Withdraw from the Council of Europe" *Heinrich Böll Stiftung Brussels* (2018) <https://eu.boell.org/en/2018/02/21/classic-dilemma-russias-threat-withdraw-council-europe>.

45 Bill Bowring, "Russia and the European Convention (or Court) of Human Rights: The End?" [2021] Revue québécoise de droit international 201.

bination with amendments to the Constitution of the Russian Federation in 2020 that included defining marriage as "a union between a man and a woman",[46] this meant that the ECtHR's judgement in July 2021 regarding the case *Fedotova and Others v. Russia*,[47] which had been brought to challenge "the lack of legal recognition in same-sex relationships in the Russian legal system", was deemed "contrary to the Constitution".[48]

Against the backdrop of the 2020 changes to the Constitution, which, in addition to defining marriage as a heterosexual union, affirmed children as the priority of state and laid significant groundwork for "traditional values" to move from principles to policy,[49] in 2022–2024 there has been a dramatic intensification of Russia's anti-LGBT legislation. In late 2022, amendments to federal laws "On Information, Information Technologies and Protection of Information",[50] "On Mass Media",[51] "On the Protection of Children from Information Harmful to Their Health and Development",[52] "On Advertising",[53] and "On State Support of Cinematography of the Russian Federation",[54] as well as corresponding amendments to the Code on Administrative Violations, were adopted. Collectively, these amendments extended the scope of the 2013 law to people of any age, expanded the types of prohibited information to include

46 Elizabeth Teague, "Russia's Constitutional Reforms of 2020" (2020) 5 Russian Politics 301. Закон РФ о поправке к Конституции РФ от 14.03.2020 N 1-ФКЗ "О совершенствовании регулирования отдельных вопросов организации и функционирования публичной власти", https://www.consultant.ru/document/cons_doc_LAW_346019/.

47 ECtHR, Fedotova and others v. Russia, Judgment of 13 July 2021, Applications Nos. 40792/10, 30538/14, 43439/14 <https://hudoc.echr.coe.int/fre?i=001-211016>.

48 Dmitri Bartenev, "Will Russia Yield to the ECtHR?: Fedotova and Others v. Russia: Yet Another Test Case of Russia's Resistance to the European Human Rights Standards" (*VerfBlog*, 2021) <https://verfassungsblog.de/will-russia-yield-to-the-ecthr/>.

49 Teague.

50 Федеральный закон от 27.07.2006 N 149-ФЗ (ред. от 24.06.2025) "Об информации, информационных технологиях и о защите информации" (с изм. и доп., вступ. в силу с 01.09.2025) <https://www.consultant.ru/document/cons_doc_LAW_61798/c5051782233acca771e9adb35b47d3fb82c9ff1c/>.

51 Закон РФ от 27.12.1991 N 2124-1 (ред. от 23.07.2025) "О средствах массовой информации" <https://www.consultant.ru/document/cons_doc_LAW_1511/>.

52 Федеральный закон "О защите детей от информации, причиняющей вред их здоровью и развитию" от 29.12.2010 N 436-ФЗ (последняя редакция) <https://www.consultant.ru/document/cons_doc_LAW_108808/>.

53 Федеральный закон "О рекламе" от 13.03.2006 N 38-ФЗ (последняя редакция) <https://www.consultant.ru/document/cons_doc_LAW_58968/>.

54 Федеральный закон "О государственной поддержке кинематографии Российской Федерации" от 22.08.1996 N 126-ФЗ (последняя редакция) <https://www.consultant.ru/document/cons_doc_LAW_11454/>.

materials "capable of causing children to wish to change sex", and outlawed "demonstration of non-traditional sexual relations or preferences" in advertising and films.[55] Then, in July 2023, a bill adding an article to the federal law "On the Foundations of Public Health in the Russian Federation" that outlawed the provision of gender affirming care to transgender people and altering gender in public records was adopted.[56] Finally, in November 2023, Russia's Supreme Court ruled that the "international LGBT movement" is an "extremist organisation" in response to a lawsuit brought by the Ministry of Justice alleging that it incites social and religious discord.[57] As a result, Katsuba observes, there has been a "hybrid recriminalisation" of homosexuality insofar as while being homosexual and engaging in consensual same-sex intimacy in private is not illegal, any manifestation of "LGBT-ness" in public is a violation of at least one of the laws described above. "Essentially", he concludes, "we are back to the situation before 1993".[58] Moreover, while the 'we' to which Katsuba refers may be construed as LGBT people and their allies, his observation also points to Russia's wider retreat from universal human rights norms and democratic principles.

2.2 Regulating Sex and Gender: An Intimate Regime

The trajectory of anti-LGBT legislation described in the previous section has not occurred in isolation. Rather, as USAID's Samantha Power observes, "LGBTQI+ crackdowns are the 'canary in the coal mine' for declining freedoms".[59] In this sense, anti-LGBT legislation points not only to the Russian

---

55 Государственная Дума, "Приняты Законопроекты о Защите Традиционных Ценностей" *Государственная Дума* (2022) <http://duma.gov.ru/news/55609/>.

56 Yana Kirey-Sitnikova, "'You Should Care by Prohibiting All This Obscenity': A Public Policy Analysis of the Russian Law Banning Medical and Legal Transition for Transgender People" (2024) 40 Post-Soviet Affairs 452. Федеральный закон от 21.11.2011 N 323-ФЗ (ред. от 23.07.2025) "Об основах охраны здоровья граждан в Российской Федерации" (с изм. и доп., вступ. в силу с 01.09.2025) < https://www.consultant.ru/document/cons_doc_LAW_121895/902a58ee0b9a7017e3e5a77464c63deadaf6c5fc/>.

57 Human Rights Watch, "Russia: Supreme Court Bans 'LGBT Movement' as 'Extremist'" *Human Rights Watch* (2023) <https://www.hrw.org/news/2023/11/30/russia-supreme-court-bans-lgbt-movement-extremist>.

58 Sergey Katsuba, "30 Years of LGBTQ+ History in Russia: From Decriminalisation in 1993 to 'Extremist' Status in 2023" (*The Conversation*, 2024) <https://theconversation.com/30-years-of-lgbtq-history-in-russia-from-decriminalisation-in-1993-to-extremist-status-in-2023-220569>.

59 Atlantic Council, "USAID's Samantha Power: LGBTQI+ Crackdowns Are 'the Canary in the Coal Mine' for Declining Freedoms (Transcript)" (2023) <https://www.atlanticcoun

state's political homophobia, but its ongoing efforts to regulate the sexuality and gender of all citizens in accordance with the state's interests and priorities. As such, the resultant "intimate regime" reflects the hypermasculinst logics of Putin's regime,[60] which relies on "a set of interlocking gender systems" to consolidate power and delegitimise opposition as well as democratic principles.[61] Controlling how gender – which includes sexuality, insofar as it is conventionally defined in gendered terms – is defined and performed therefore central to all manifestations of state power.

The functioning of this intimate regime begins to become clear when the societal consequences of the 2013 anti-homopropaganda bill are considered. At least until 2022, the greatest impact of anti-LGBT legislation was achieved not via actual enforcement of the ban – there were only 52 convictions between 2013 and 2022[62] – but via the insecurity it created for LGBT people. This was not primarily due to the uncertainty regarding how the legislation would be interpreted by police and prosecutors given the lack of a clear definition of "propaganda of non-traditional sexual relations". Rather, the ban heightened awareness of the possibility of being subjected to homophobic violence and the extremely low chance that the state would provide any protection – an assessment borne out by analyses of hate crime data against LGBTQ people in Russia.[63] Reports of vigilante gangs "hunting" queers with impunity,[64] gay

cil.org/news/transcripts/usaids-samantha-power-lgbtqi-crackdowns-are-the-canary-in-the-coal-mine-for-declining-freedoms/> accessed May 5, 2025.

60 Wilkinson, "Mother Russia in Queer Peril: The Gender Logic of the Hypermasculine State."

61 Elizabeth A Wood, "Gender Systems in the Putin Autocracy" (2024) 9 Frontiers in Sociology 1327946; Valerie Sperling, *Sex, Politics, and Putin: Political Legitimacy in Russia* (Oxford University Press 2014).

62 Sergey Katsuba, "The Decade of Violence: A Comprehensive Analysis of Hate Crimes Against LGBTQ in Russia in the Era of the 'Gay Propaganda Law' (2010–2020)" (2023) ahead-of-print Victims & Offenders 1.

63 Ibid; Alexander Kondakov, "The Influence of the 'Gay-Propaganda' Law on Violence against LGBTIQ People in Russia: Evidence from Criminal Court Rulings" (2021) 18 European Journal of Criminology 940.

64 Paul Gallagher and Vanessa Thorpe, "Russian Anti-Gay Gang Violence Seen for the First Time on Camera" *The Guardian* (2014) <https://www.theguardian.com/world/2014/feb/01/russia-anti-gay-gang-violence-homophobic-olympics>; Radzhana Buyantueva, "LGBT Rights Activism and Homophobia in Russia" (2018) 65 Journal of Homosexuality 456; Sergei Katsuba, "Premeditated, Organized and Impactful: Dating Violence as a Method of Committing Hate Crimes Against LGBTQ People in Russia" [2023] Journal of Family Violence 1.

purges in Chechnya,[65] as well as increasingly overt homophobia in the media,[66] further reinforced LGBT people's awareness of being rendered systematically insecure and the risks of being visible.[67] Essentially, the ban on the promotion of non-traditional sexual relations functioned as an implicit threat about the consequences for queers of non-compliance with the Kremlin's intimate regime. As Kondakov observes, staying on the right side of the law is not enough to be safe in circumstances when law itself is the trigger for anti-queer violence.[68]

Importantly, however, the Kremlin's regulation of gender and sexuality is not just anti-LGBT, but anti-queer in terms of imposing highly normative gendered expectations on all Russians. In other words, the principal aim of the intimate regime is not to prevent manifestations of sexual and gender diversity in the public sphere, but to encourage compliance with state's preferred norms of gender and sexuality. Russia's approach to achieving this family-centred societal order has shifted considerably over time. Prior to the early 2010s, while the language of "family values" and tradition was evident,[69] the government's primary approach was through the implementation of pronatalist policies that would improving the material conditions for families and especially children. This, it was hoped, would lead to increased birthrates and help reverse Russia's demographic crisis, which was explicitly recognised as a matter of national security as early as 1998.[70] The limited success of these policies,[71] however, coupled with increasing concerns about Western-led efforts to promote women's rights and LGBT rights as human rights,[72]

65 Maria Brock and Emil Edenborg, "'You Cannot Oppress Those Who Do Not Exist'Gay Persecution in Chechnya and the Politics of In/Visibility" (2020) 26 GLQ: A Journal of Lesbian and Gay Studies 673.

66 Anna Khlusova, "Legitimising Political Homophobia: Sexual Minorities and Russian Television News" in R Sanz Sabido (ed), *Representing Communities, Discourse and Contexts* (Palgrave Macmillan 2017).

67 Wilkinson, "LGBT Rights in the Former Soviet Union: The Evolution of Hypervisibility."

68 Alexander Sasha Kondakov, *Violent Affections: Queer Sexuality, Techniques of Power, and Law in Russia* (UCL Press 2022).

69 See for example Putin's speech at the Opening Ceremony for the Year of the Family in Russia in December 2007 <http://en.kremlin.ru/events/president/transcripts/24746>.

70 Ekaterina Vasilieva, Tamara Rostovskaya and Ebulfez Süleymanlý, "Demographic Threats to National Security in the Political Discourse of the Russian Federation (1992–2019)" (2021) 26 Vestnik Volgogradskogo gosudarstvennogo universiteta. Serija 4. Istorija. Regionovedenie. Mezhdunarodnye otnoshenija 255.

71 Tomas Frejka and Sergei Zakharov, "The Apparent Failure of Russia's Pronatalist Family Policies" (2013) 39 Population and Development Review 635.

72 Cai Wilkinson, "Putting 'Traditional Values' Into Practice: The Rise and Contestation of Anti-Homopropaganda Laws in Russia" (2014) 13 Journal of Human Rights 363; Vikki

resulted in the adoption of an approach increasingly centred on the need to promote and protect "traditional values".

The invocation of "traditional values" has become increasingly evident in Russia's justification for implementing anti-LGBT legislation,[73] as well as a range of other policies and laws, especially pertaining to matters such as abortion,[74] divorce,[75] domestic violence[76] and children's rights.[77] The effect of these state initiatives, which have been actively supported by the Russian Orthodox Church,[78] has been the continuing intensification of "retraditionalisation" of the family since 2013.[79] This discourse is deeply gendered, presenting motherhood as women's primary role and the patriarchal family as natural and essential for the well-being of Russian society and culture. The extent of this reframing can be seen in the speech by Vladimir Putin at the All-Russian Family Forum to launch the Year of the Family in Russia in January 2024.

Turbine, "Women's Human Rights in Russia: Outmoded Battlegrounds, or New Sites of Contentious Politics?" (2015) 31 East European Politics 326.

73 Edenborg, "Anti-Gender Politics as Discourse Coalitions: Russia's Domestic and International Promotion of 'Traditional Values'"; Emil Edenborg, "'Traditional Values' and the Narrative of Gay Rights as Modernity: Sexual Politics beyond Polarization" (2023) 26 Sexualities 37; Chaney; Stehn A Mortensen, "Discursive Propagation in Putin's Russia: Prohibiting 'Propaganda of Non-Traditional Sexual Relations'" [2016] Zeitschrift für Slavische Philologie 1 <https://www.jstor.org/stable/26583038>; Emil Edenborg, "Russia's Spectacle of 'Traditional Values': Rethinking the Politics of Visibility" (2019) 22 International Feminist Journal of Politics 1; Cai Wilkinson, "Intersection of 'Traditional Values' and LGB Rights" in Paula Gerber (ed), *Worldwide Perspectives on Lesbians, Gays and Bisexuals: Culture, History and Law* (Praeger Press 2021); Wilkinson, "LGBT Rights in the Former Soviet Union: The Evolution of Hypervisibility."

74 Michele Rivkin-Fish, *Unmaking Russia's Abortion Culture: Family Planning and the Struggle for a Liberal Biopolitics* (Vanderbilt University Press 2024).

75 Current Time and Chris Rickleton, "Russia's 'Year Of The Family' Has Meant A War On Abortion And Divorce" *Radio Free Europe Radio Liberty* (2025) <https://www.rferl.org/a/33273068.html>.

76 Olimpiada Usanova, "Russia's 'Traditional Values' and Domestic Violence" (2020) 54 Kennan Cable 55; Janet Elise Johnson, "Russia's Authoritarian Policymaking: The Politics of Domestic Violence after Partial Decriminalization" (2024) 71 Problems of Post-Communism 557.

77 Государственная Дума, "Как Законы Защищают Безопасность Детей" (2022) <http://duma.gov.ru/news/54460/>; ЕМ Павленко, "Обеспечение Наилучших Интересов и Безопасности Детей: Международные Стандарты и Практика в России" (2021) 44 Вестник МГПУ «Юридические науки» 75.

78 Pål Kolstø, *Family, Sex, and Faith: The Biopolitics of the Russian Orthodox Church* (Cornell University Press 2024).

79 Marianna Muravyeva, "Traditional Values and Modern Families: Legal Understanding of Tradition and Modernity in Contemporary Russia" (2014) 12 The Journal of Social Policy Studies 625.

Having observed that "The main purpose of the family is about having children, about procreation, and thus, the perpetuation of our people and our centuries-old history", Putin stated that "The family should be at the centre of all state policy", and highlighted the release of a new Executive Order to provide state support for families with three or more children. He then moved to the broader significance of the family:

> It is important that the family is again acquiring a high moral value in Russian society. Today I would like to thank the spiritual shepherds of Russia's traditional religions, schoolteachers, representatives of public organisations – everyone who contributes to preserving and strengthening our traditional family values, such as strong and reliable ties between generations, respect for parents, care for elders, and our grandparents' love, which remains with us forever. [...].
>
> As I said, we will continue to give priority attention to strengthening the institution of the family, improving the prestige of motherhood and fatherhood, to comprehensive protection of childhood and demographic programmes. And I want to stress that for us this is not just a key area of the country's development, of the work at all levels of authority, but the most important part of our sovereign worldview, our vision of the future of our people.[80]

The framing of the family is part of a wider discourse of "traditional values" as, to use Stepanova's phrase, "everything good against everything bad".[81] Consequently, what is meant by traditional values has evolved from being defined only as that which is not non-traditional – as in the case of anti-LGBT legislation – into a concept that intertwines religion, culture and national identity. The most explicit articulation of this to date has been in the "Foundations of State Policy for the Preservation and Strengthening of Traditional Russian Spiritual-Moral Values", which was confirmed by presidential decree in November 2022.[82] In the first part of the document, traditional values are defined as

80 President of Russia, "Launching the Year of the Family in Russia" (2024) <http://en.kremlin.ru/events/president/news/73297>.

81 Elena A Stepanova, "'Everything Good against Everything Bad': Traditional Values in the Search for New Russian National Idea" (2023) 7 Zeitschrift für Religion, Gesellschaft und Politik 97.

82 Указ Президента РФ от 09.11.2022 N 809 "Об утверждении Основ государственной политики по сохранению и укреплению традиционных российских

> [...] the moral reference points that form Russian citizen's worldview, which are transferred from generation to generation and which lie at the foundation of all-Russian civic identity and the country's unified cultural realm, strengthening civic unity that takes its unique and original manifestation from the spiritual, historical and cultural development of Russia's multi-ethnic peoples.
>
> Traditional values include: life, dignity, human rights and freedoms, patriotism, civic duty, serving the Fatherland and responsibility for its fate, high moral ideals, strong family, creative work, prioritising the spiritual over the material, humanism, compassion, justice, collectivism, mutual assistance and mutual respect, historical memory and the continuity of generations, the unity of Russia's peoples.[83]

With such a broad list, it is perhaps unsurprising that references to "everything bad" are used extensively to help articulate what traditional values mean in practice. It is also unsurprising that references to gender and sexuality play a central role in these discourses, pointing to the final element of the intime regime that has been constructed to support implementation of the Russian state's "traditional values" agenda: the framing of all non-compliance with "traditional" norms of gender and sexuality as a threat.

In the case of anti-LGBT laws, as discussed earlier, the main justification was the need to protect minors from harmful information. Beyond the legislation itself, this argument has been evident in public narratives of homosexuality as incompatible with children's wellbeing.[84] Over time, this framing has broadened to position all deviation from the traditional gender order envisaged by the Kremlin as a threat not only to children, but Russian society as a whole. Putin's 2021 speech at the Valdai Discussion Club made explicit the logic underlying this narrative:

> In a number of Western countries, the debate over men's and women's rights has turned into a perfect phantasmagoria. Look, beware of going where the Bolsheviks once planned to go – not only communalising chickens, but also communalising women. One more step and you will be there.

духовно-нравственных ценностей" <https://www.consultant.ru/document/cons_doc_LAW_430906/> (translation by author).

83 Part 1, Articles 4 and 5.

84 Yulia Ioffe and Hedi Viterbo, "Homophobia Disguised as Children's Rights in Russia's Constitutional Referendum" (*VerfBlog*, June 29, 2020) <https://verfassungsblog.de/homophobia-disguised-as-childrens-rights-in-russias – constitutional-referendum/>.

> Zealots of these new approaches even go so far as to want to abolish these concepts altogether. Anyone who dares mention that men and women actually exist, which is a biological fact, risk being ostracised. "Parent number one" and "parent number two," "'birthing parent" instead of "mother," and "human milk" replacing "breastmilk" because it might upset the people who are unsure about their own gender. I repeat, this is nothing new; in the 1920s, the so-called Soviet Kulturtraegers also invented some newspeak believing they were creating a new consciousness and changing values that way. And, as I have already said, they made such a mess it still makes one shudder at times.
>
> Not to mention some truly monstrous things when children are taught from an early age that a boy can easily become a girl and vice versa. That is, the teachers actually impose on them a choice we all supposedly have. They do so while shutting the parents out of the process and forcing the child to make decisions that can upend their entire life. They do not even bother to consult with child psychologists – is a child at this age even capable of making a decision of this kind? Calling a spade a spade, this verges on a crime against humanity, and it is being done in the name and under the banner of progress.[85]

In Putin's account, the threat to children is about their immediate safety and wellbeing, but it is also about the threat that the erosion of the institutions of the family – marriage, motherhood and fatherhood – poses to children as emblematic of Russia's future. Put bluntly, the nation must reproduce if it is to survive. This reality has driven continued initiatives aimed at encouraging women to have more children intense enough to be described as "maternity by mandate" in their use of material incentives with legislative regulation that in November 2024 extended to banning "childfree propaganda".[86]

However, in the face of the reality that the impact of pronatalist policies are more symbolic than substantive,[87] the final component of the Kremlin's intimate regime has been the wholesale securitisation of gender and sexuality along highly normative lines: LGBTQ people, feminists, childfree people, atheists and any other heterosexual and/or cisgender people who reject or simply fail to conform with the gendered requirements of "traditional values" as

---

85 President of Russia, "Valdai Discussion Club Meeting" (*President of Russia Events*, 2021) <http://en.kremlin.ru/events/president/news/66975>.

86 Daria Boll-Palievskaya, "Maternity by Mandate" (*IPS Journal*, 2024) <https://www.ips-journal.eu/topics/democracy-and-society/maternity-by-mandate-7909/>.

87 Vladimir N Arkhangelskiy, Svetlana Yu Sivoplyasova and Evgeniya M Moiseeva, "Exploring Fertility Dynamics and Factors Shaping Russia's Demographic Prospects" (2024) 8 Changing Societies & Personalities 291.

defined by the Kremlin have been cast as an "unholy queer peril" that is an existential threat to Russia.[88] The only way to repel this threat is by embracing "traditional values" as fully as possible not only at the societal level, but also at the level of the state. Correspondingly, as is demonstrated in the next section, "traditional values" have become a central component of the Russian Federation's statecraft.

3 "Traditional Values" as Statecraft

From the starting premise of protecting minors, non-traditional manifestations of gender and sexuality have increasingly come to be regarded by Russia as a threat to national security, a threat to Western civilisation, and a threat to the future of humankind. To be clear, this logic has been evident from early on in Russia's traditional turn, as exemplified in Putin's speech at the Valdai International Discussion Club in September 2013, in which he argued

> We can see how many of the Euro-Atlantic countries are actually rejecting their roots, including the Christian values that constitute the basis of Western civilisation. They are denying moral principles and all traditional identities: national, cultural, religious and even sexual. They are implementing policies that equate large families with same-sex partnerships, belief in God with the belief in Satan.[89]

Such progressive models of society, he continued, constitute "a direct path to degradation and primitivism, resulting in a profound demographic and moral crisis" that can only stopped by a return to living in accordance with "traditional values":

> Without the values embedded in Christianity and other world religions, without the standards of morality that have taken shape over millennia, people will inevitably lose their human dignity. We consider it natural and right to defend these values. One must respect every minority's right to be different, but the rights of the majority must not be put into question.[90]

88 Wilkinson, "Mother Russia in Queer Peril: The Gender Logic of the Hypermasculine State."

89 President of Russia, "Meeting of the Valdai International Discussion Club" (2013) <http://en.kremlin.ru/events/president/news/19243>.

90 Ibid.

Putin was also clear in his 2013 speech that the need for "traditional values" to be upheld was geopolitical as well as societal, addressing this directly after his affirmation of Russia's intention to defend them:

> At the same time, we see attempts to somehow revive a standardised model of a unipolar world and to blur the institutions of international law and national sovereignty. Such a unipolar, standardised world does not require sovereign states; it requires vassals. In a historical sense this amounts to a rejection of one's own identity, of the God-given diversity of the world.
>
> Russia agrees with those who believe that key decisions should be worked out on a collective basis, rather than at the discretion of and in the interests of certain countries or groups of countries. Russia believes that international law, not the right of the strong, must apply. And we believe that every country, every nation is not exceptional, but unique, original and benefits from equal rights, including the right to independently choose their own development path.[91]

Yet Putin's criticisms of other countries were still expressed in the language of democracy and the liberal order in 2013, allowing for the assumption that the traditional values agenda would be primarily a domestic and societally orientated project. What has subsequently become starkly evident is that the intimate regime that has been developed is has a considerably more ambitious aim than simply retraditionalising the Russian nation. Rather, as I outline in following section, it has served as vehicle for the redefinition of sovereignty through the prism of "traditional Russian spiritual-moral values". I argue that the resultant claim of Russia's "moral sovereignty" as a state-civilisation constitutes a refutation of the liberal order, with Russia actively working to impose its alternative conceptualisation of how both states and societies should be ordered.

3.1 Russian Sovereignty and Traditional Values

Sovereignty is viewed as the defining feature of statehood and the modern international system. It is widely understood as the institutionalisation of political legitimacy and territoriality and has often been regarded as a "static, fixed concept: a set of ideas that underlies international relations but is not

---

91 Ibid.

changed along with them".[92] Within International Relations, the Peace of Westphalia has been particularly influential on conceptualisations of sovereignty, serving as an origin story for the formation of a system of sovereign states organised around the inviolable principles of mutual recognition, territoriality and non-interference in the affairs of other states.[93] Despite this, Krasner explains,

> The term sovereignty has been commonly used in at least four different ways: domestic sovereignty, referring to the organization of public authority within a state and to the level of effective control exercised by those holding authority; interdependence sovereignty, referring to the ability of public authorities to control transborder movements; international legal sovereignty, referring to the mutual recognition of states or other entities; and Westphalian sovereignty, referring to the exclusion of external actors from domestic authority configurations.[94]

Importantly, he notes, "These four meanings of sovereignty are not logically coupled, nor have they covaried in practice."[95] In other words, the concept of sovereignty is not internally coherent, and this is reflected in how states organise themselves and interact with each other. Traditional sovereignty, Krasner concludes, is "best conceptualized as [...] organized hypocrisy" insofar as while it is "defined by widely understood rules", violations of these rules are the norm, rather than the exception.[96]

In many ways, Russia's uses of sovereignty accord with Krasner's assessment. This has been demonstrated by Deyermond, who identifies contrasting approaches to state sovereignty in international fora versus within the post-Soviet space that speaks to "the principal significance of the idea of sovereignty in Russian foreign policy in the twenty-first century [being] instrumen-

---

92 J Samuel Barkin and Bruce Cronin, "The State and the Nation: Changing Norms and the Rules of Sovereignty in International Relations" (1994) 48 International Organization 107.

93 Andreas Osiander, "Sovereignty, International Relations, and the Westphalian Myth" (2001) 55 International Organization 251; Luke Glanville, "The Myth of 'Traditional' Sovereignty" (2013) 57 International Studies Quarterly 79.

94 Stephen D Krasner, *Sovereignty : Organized Hypocrisy* (Princeton University Press 1999).

95 Ibid.

96 Ibid. Note that I am using "traditional sovereignty" as a combined term for international legal sovereignty and Westphalian sovereignty as the two forms that tend to be contested in international relations.

tal, not ideational".[97] Yet, the increasing prominence of traditional values in Russian political discourse since 2013 suggests that sovereignty has become increasingly significant ideationally. First, references to state sovereignty convey Russia's aim of regaining its status as a great power, despite repeated attempts by Western countries to undermine its national interests and "right to freely and independently determine its fate, or political, social and economic models of its development".[98] Second, sovereignty is used to signal Russia's view that the current liberal international order has departed from the principles of traditional sovereignty,[99] which, alongside the West's embrace of non-traditional values, is the cause of its decline. And third, it positions Russia as a leader of a new and legitimate international order in which, to quote Putin, "traditional values, as well as peoples' desire for true freedom, justice, and sovereignty, will serve as the foundation for a multipolar world".[100]

These three ideational functions in combination mean that "while all states have an interest in safeguarding their own sovereignty, the present Russian regime is *obsessed* with it".[101] The achievement of absolute state sovereignty is an existential imperative for Russia as a "state-civilisation" with a historical global mission. The idea of Russia as a civilisation with a distinctive identity emerged in the 1990s as part of debates over Russian national identity and search for a new "national idea" in the wake of the Soviet Union's collapse.[102] However, it took until 2012 for a political "civilisational discourse" to emerge, when Putin began emphasising Russia as a "state-civilisation" frequently in his

97 Ruth Deyermond, "The Uses of Sovereignty in Twenty-First Century Russian Foreign Policy" (2016) 68 Europe-Asia Studies 957.

98 Embassy of the Russian Federation in South Africa, "National Sovereignty – the Pillar of Russia's Statehood" (2024) <https://russianembassyza.mid.ru/en/press-centre/news/national_sovereignty_the_pillar_of_russia_s_statehood/>.

99 Roy Allison, "Russian Revisionism, Legal Discourse and the 'Rules-Based' International Order" (2020) 72 Europe-Asia Studies 976.

100 Russia, "Launching the Year of the Family in Russia."

101 Jardar Østbø, "The Sources of Russia's Transgressive Conservatism:Cultural Sovereignty and the Monopolization of Bespredel," *The Cultural is Political: Intersections of Russian Art and State Politics* (2020). Page 14 emphasis in original.

102 Victor Shnirelman, "Russia between a Civilization and a Civic Nation" in Kåre Johan Mjør and Sanna Turoma (eds), *Russia as Civilization: Ideological Discourses in Politics, Media and Academia* (Routledge 2020); Kåre Johan Mjør, "A Morphology of Russia? The Russian Civilisational Turn and Its Cyclical Idea of History" in Katja Lehtisaari and Arto Mustajoki (eds), *Philosophical and Cultural Interpretations of Russian Modernisation* (Routledge 2016).

speeches and writings.[103] In doing so, Putin sought to advance a conceptualisation of Russian state sovereignty in which the state, its people and culture are indivisible and mutually reinforcing. On the one hand, Linde explains, "The crucial importance of the state, it is claimed, has been an essential and inalienable feature of Russian history." On the other, she continues, "Russia's identity as a distinct civilisation is seen as the enduring foundation on which the state as a political entity rests".[104]

By 2023, this statist and sovereignist narrative of Russia's identity and place in the world had gained sufficient traction to form the basis for the country's new foreign policy concept. While previously implicit, the concept is the first time that "Russia's special position as a unique country civilization and a vast Eurasian and Euro-Pacific power" is asserted directly and without qualification in an official document.[105] Russia, it is claimed, is "one of the sovereign centres of global development performing a historically unique mission aimed at maintaining global balance of power and building a multipolar international system".[106]

The articulation of Russia's role in the world is presented in the context of the decline of the liberal order and opposition to the West. The "formation of a more equitable multipolar world order", the Concept states, "are not welcomed by a number of states being used to the logic of global dominance and neocolonialism":

> These countries refuse to recognize the realities of a multipolar world and to agree on the parameters and principles of the world order accordingly. Attempts are made to restrain the natural course of history, to eliminate competitors in the politico-military and economic spheres, and to suppress dissent. A wide range of illegal instruments and methods is being used, including the introduction of coercive measures (sanctions) in circumvention of the UN Security Council, provocation of coups d'état and military conflicts, threats, blackmailing, manipulation of the consciousness of certain social groups and entire nations, offensive and subversive actions in the information space. A widespread form of interference in the internal affairs of sovereign states has become

103 Fabian Linde, "State Civilisation: The Statist Core of Vladimir Putin's Civilisational Discourse and Its Implications for Russian Foreign Policy" (2016) 12 Politics in Central Europe 21.

104 Ibid.

105 Torbakov.

106 Ministry of Foreign Affairs of the Russian Federation, "The Concept of the Foreign Policy of the Russian Federation (Unofficial Translation)" (2023) <https://mid.ru/en/foreign_policy/fundamental_documents/1860586/>.

> the imposition of destructive neoliberal ideological attitudes that run counter to traditional spiritual and moral values. As a result, the destructive effect extends to all spheres of international relations.[107]

For Russia to protect its national interests and achieve its foreign policy goals, therefore, it must ensure "sovereignty in all domains",[108] including that of morality.

3.2 Moral Sovereignty

"Moral sovereignty" describes "the idea that states have the right to decide and actively enforce society's moral norms, or traditional values, and that this right takes precedence over international norms and obligations".[109] It is interlinked to cultural sovereignty, with a common narrative of the existential threat posed to Russia by Western promotion of liberalism and understanding "spiritual-moral values" as the only effective defence.[110] In contrast to the broader term of cultural sovereignty, however, the term draws attention to the crucial role that moral issues, such as opposition to LGBT rights, have played in defining Russia's understanding of sovereignty and the strategies used to pursue it both within its borders and internationally. In this respect, moral sovereignty highlights not only the statism in Russia's sovereignty, but its absolutism. Sovereignty unaligned with traditional Russian spiritual-moral values is insufficient and intolerable.

Domestically, this logic is reflected in the institutionalisation of traditional Russian spiritual-moral values into the state. While the 2022 Foundations of State Policy for the Preservation and Strengthening of Traditional Russian Spiritual-Moral Values is the most explicit articulation of traditional values to date, the scope of the policy is significantly wider, encompassing "a whole range of coordinated measures that are implemented by the President of the Russian Federation and other organs of public authority with the participation of civil society institutions in order to counter sociocultural threats to the Russian Federation's national security that, in part, include the defence of

107 Ibid.

108 Ibid.

109 Wilkinson, "Putting 'Traditional Values' Into Practice: The Rise and Contestation of Anti-Homopropaganda Laws in Russia."

110 Østbø; Federica Prina, "Fantasies of Cultural Sovereignty and National Unity: Russia?S Ontological (in)Security and Its Assertion of ?Spiritual-Moral Values??" [2024] International Politics 1.

transitional values".[111] Thus, as of 2023, traditional Russian spiritual-moral values already featured explicitly in at least ten state strategy documents including the 2021 Strategy for the National Security of the Russian Federation, 2020 Strategy to Combat Extremism in the Russian Federation until 2025,[112] and the 2023 Strategy for the Comprehensive Security of Children in the Russian Federation for the period until 2030.[113]

Echoing the role of scholarship in establishing the justification for anti-LGBT legislation,[114] legal academics are now exploring the potential for further institutionalisation. Recent examples of this trend include articles arguing that traditional Russian spiritual-moral values are "fundamental for the entire Russian legal system",[115] and that their "constitutionalisation" would help to "strengthen mechanisms for the implementation and protection of human rights and freedoms".[116] There have also been publications discussing the possibility of legal recognition of traditional Russian spiritual-moral values as an official state ideology[117] – something banned under the current Constitution of the Russian Federation.[118]

The ongoing institutionalisation of traditional Russian spiritual-moral values and reinforces the intimate regime that has been constructed for the regulation of sexuality and gender. With the link to sovereignty as well as security

111 Elmira Faritovna Abubikerova, "Конституционализация Традиционных Российских Духовно-Нравственных Ценностей" (2025) 25 Вестник Поволжского института управления 82. P. 87.

112 Replaced in late 2024 by an updated version (N. 1124).

113 Ekaterina Kashkina, "Legal Regulation of Conservation and Strengthening Traditional Russian Spiritual and Moral Values Within Strategic Planning" [2023] Vestnik Advanced Training Institute of The MIA of Russia 78.

114 Kevin Moss, "Russia's Queer Science, or How Anti-LGBT Scholarship Is Made" (2021) 80 The Russian Review 17.

115 КА Чуйченко, НМ Кропачев and ВЕ Кондуров, "Традиционные Россиийскуе Духовно-Нравственние Ценности в Контексте Современной Правовой По литики" (2024) 68 Правоведение 156; Oksana Huzhina, "Traditional Spiritual and Moral Values in Russian Law: Formulation of a Scientific Problem" (2023) 2023 Legal Science and Practice: Journal of Nizhny Novgorod Academy of the Ministry of Internal Affairs of Russia 39.

116 Abubikerova.

117 ND Shikher, "Ideological Tendencies of Modern Russian Legislation" (2023) 23 Vestnik Povolzhskogo instituta upravleniya 36; ВБ Рожковский and ОМ Михайловна, "Традиционные Духовно-Нравственные Ценности в Государственной Идеологии Современной России" (2024) 111 Философия права 222.

118 Anna Zotééva and Martin Kragh, "From Constitutional Identity to the Identity of the ConstitutionSolving the Balance of Law and Politics in Russia" (2021) 54 Communist and Post-Communist Studies 176.

established, the debate is no longer about whether the rules of the game are being observed, but who makes the rules. For Russia, there is only one answer.

4 Conclusion: Misappropriation and World Orders

This chapter has charted how "traditional values" have been used increasingly extensively and intensively as a central strategy of Russian statecraft since the beginning of Putin's third presidential term in 2013. Starting from the implementation of legislation restricting the rights of LGBT people in ways that are at odds with prevailing international human rights interpretations, it has been demonstrated how anti-gay laws have been used to implement an "intimate" regime focused on regulating gender and sexuality for all Russians, regardless of their sexual orientation and/or gender identity. Within this regime, "traditional values" have been uses both to articulate the Russian state's gendered ideals, which have often been expressed through references to 'the family' and children.

Connecting this intimate regime to Russia's more recent move to establish traditional Russian spiritual-moral values as state policy and de facto ideology then sheds light on the full significance of instances of human rights misappropriation. Given Russia's long-standing opposition to LGBT rights and international advocacy for traditional values prior to 2013,[119] the initial adoption of federal anti-homopropaganda legislation undoubtedly constituted a misappropriation aimed at reshaping the field of international human rights norms. However, the subsequent expansions of the legislation alongside Russia's development of a wider intimate regulatory regime and increasingly explicit policy position aimed at promoting and protecting its moral sovereignty highlights that misappropriations should be viewed as part of broader anti-democratic trends domestically and internationally. While the progression to broader illiberal policies is not inevitable, the correlation between misappropriations targeting LGBT human rights and increasingly authoritarian policies is by now well established – as evidenced not only by Russia, but elsewhere including Hungary, Colombia, Brazil and the US.[120] In all these cases, misappropriations have been justified by the purported threat that internationally sponsored LGBT rights pose to "traditional values", with the

119 Wilkinson 2014.

120 Mauricio Albarracín-Caballero, "How Targeting LGBTQ+ Rights Are Part of the Authoritarian Playbook" (*Human Rights Watch*, 2022) <https://www.hrw.org/news/2022/09/06/how-targeting-lgbtq-rights-are-part-authoritarian-playbook>.

language of human rights redeployed to present discrimination and exclusion as necessary to protect the rights of the state's cisheterosexual majority and their way of life. In doing so, governments are also contesting the meaning of sovereignty and, by extension, challenging the international order and its foundation in liberal democratic principles. While the scale and scope of Russia's increasingly robust assertion of moral sovereignty as a precondition for its statehood and existence may be viewed as exceptional, it also highlights that human rights misappropriations are far from only about human rights. Rather, as the case of Russia makes clear, misappropriations are a key strategy in opposing the international liberal order itself.

Bibliography

ABC News, "Russia's Vladimir Putin Signs 'anti-Gay Propaganda' Bill into Law" *ABC News* (2013) <https://www.abc.net.au/news/2013-06-30/russia27s-putin-signs-27anti-gay-propaganda27-bill-into-law/4790498>.

Abubikerova EF, "Конституционализация Традиционных Российских Духовно-Нравственных Ценностей" (2025) 25 Вестник Поволжского института управления 82.

Allison R, "Russian Revisionism, Legal Discourse and the 'Rules-Based' International Order" (2020) 72 Europe-Asia Studies 976.

Albarracín-Caballero M, "How Targeting LGBTQ+ Rights Are Part of the Authoritarian Playbook" *Human Rights Watch* (2022) <https://www.hrw.org/news/2022/09/06/how-targeting-lgbtq-rights-are-part-authoritarian-playbook>.

Altman D and Symons J, *Queer Wars* (Polity Press 2016).

Arkhangelskiy VN, Sivoplyasova SY and Moiseeva EM, "Exploring Fertility Dynamics and Factors Shaping Russia's Demographic Prospects" (2024) 8 Changing Societies & Personalities 291.

Article 19, "Russia: Federal Laws Introducing Ban of Propaganda of Non-Traditional Sexual Relationships" (2013) Legal analysis <https://www.refworld.org/reference/research/art19/2013/en/95025>.

Atlantic Council, "USAID's Samantha Power: LGBTQI+ Crackdowns Are 'the Canary in the Coal Mine' for Declining Freedoms (Transcript)" (2023) <https://www.atlanticcouncil.org/news/transcripts/usaids-samantha-power-lgbtqi-crackdowns-are-the-canary-in-the-coal-mine-for-declining-freedoms/>.

Ayoub PM and Stoeckl K, *The Global Fight Against LGBTI Rights* (New York University Press 2024) <https://nyupress.org/9781479824793/the-global-fight-against-lgbti-rights/>.

Barkin JS and Cronin B, "The State and the Nation: Changing Norms and the Rules of Sovereignty in International Relations" (1994) 48 International Organization 107.

Bartenev D, "Will Russia Yield to the ECtHR?: Fedotova and Others v. Russia: Yet Another Test Case of Russia's Resistance to the European Human Rights Standards" (*VerfBlog*, 2021) <https://verfassungsblog.de/will-russia-yield-to-the-ecthr/>.

BBC News, "Gay Parades Banned in Moscow for 100 Years" *BBC News* (2012) <https://www.bbc.com/news/world-europe-19293465>.

Boll-Palievskaya D, "Maternity by Mandate" (*IPS Journal*, 2024) <https://www.ips-journal.eu/topics/democracy-and-society/maternity-by-mandate-7909/>.

Bowring B, "Russia and the European Convention (or Court) of Human Rights: The End?" [2021] Revue québécoise de droit international 201.

Brock M and Edenborg E, "'You Cannot Oppress Those Who Do Not Exist' Gay Persecution in Chechnya and the Politics of In/Visibility" (2020) 26 GLQ: A Journal of Lesbian and Gay Studies 673.

Búrca G de and Young KG, "The (Mis)Appropriation of Human Rights by the New Global Right: An Introduction to the Symposium" (2023) 21 International Journal of Constitutional Law 205.

Buyantueva R, "LGBT Rights Activism and Homophobia in Russia" (2018) 65 Journal of Homosexuality 456.

Casier T, "A Classic Dilemma: Russia's Threat to Withdraw from the Council of Europe" *Heinrich Böll Stiftung Brussels* (2018) <https://eu.boell.org/en/2018/02/21/classic-dilemma-russias-threat-withdraw-council-europe>.

Chaney P, "Civil Society, 'Traditional Values' and LGBT Resistance to Heteronormative Rights Hegemony: Analysis of the UN Universal Periodic Review in the Russian Federation" (2018) 70 Europe-Asia Studies 638.

Civil Rights Defenders, "Duma Prohibits 'Propaganda' of Non-Traditional Relations" (2013) <https://crd.org/2013/06/12/duma-prohibits-propaganda-of-non-traditional-relations/>.

Cupać J and Ebetürk I, "The Personal Is Global Political: The Antifeminist Backlash in the United Nations" (2020) 22 The British Journal of Politics and International Relations 702.

Davidenko M and Utkina V, "The Conservative Turn in Post-Soviet Russia" (2024) 76 Europe-Asia Studies 135.

Deyermond R, "The Uses of Sovereignty in Twenty-First Century Russian Foreign Policy" (2016) 68 Europe-Asia Studies 957.

Edenborg E, "Russia's Spectacle of 'Traditional Values': Rethinking the Politics of Visibility" (2019) 22 International Feminist Journal of Politics 1.

Edenborg E, "Anti-Gender Politics as Discourse Coalitions: Russia's Domestic and International Promotion of 'Traditional Values'" (2021) Problems of Post-Communism 1.

Edenborg E, "'Traditional Values' and the Narrative of Gay Rights as Modernity: Sexual Politics beyond Polarization" (2023) 26 Sexualities 37.

Edström J and others, "Introduction: Understanding Gender Backlash Across Regions" (2024) 55 IDS Bulletin 1.

Elder M, "Russian Parliament to Consider Federal Anti-Gay Law" *The Guardian* (2012) <https://www.theguardian.com/world/2012/nov/30/russian-parliament-federal-anti-gay-law>.

Embassy of the Russian Federation in South Africa, "National Sovereignty – the Pillar of Russia's Statehood" (2024) <https://russianembassyza.mid.ru/en/press-centre/news/national_sovereignty_the_pillar_of_russia_s_statehood/>.

European Court of Human Rights, "Judgment Bayev and Others v. Russia – Legislation Banning the Promotion of Homosexuality" (European Court of Human Rights, 2017) <https://hudoc.echr.coe.int/eng-press?i=003-5755355-7315126>.

European Union Agency for Fundamental Rights, "LGBTIQ Equality at a Crossroads: Progress and Challenges" (Publications Office of the European Union 2024) <https://fra.europa.eu/en/news/2024/harassment-and-violence-against-lgbtiq-people-rise>.

Flores AR, Carreño MF and Shaw A, "Democratic Backsliding and LGBTI Acceptance" (Williams Institute 2023) <https://williamsinstitute.law.ucla.edu/publications/dem-backsliding-gai/>.

Frejka T and Zakharov S, "The Apparent Failure of Russia's Pronatalist Family Policies" (2013) 39 Population and Development Review 635.

Gallagher P and Thorpe V, "Russian Anti-Gay Gang Violence Seen for the First Time on Camera" *The Guardian* (2014) <https://www.theguardian.com/world/2014/feb/01/russia-anti-gay-gang-violence-homophobic-olympics>.

Glanville L, "The Myth of 'Traditional' Sovereignty" (2013) 57 International Studies Quarterly 79.

Graff A and Korolczuk E, *Anti – Gender Politics in the Populist Moment* (Routledge 2022).

Healey D, *Russian Homophobia from Stalin to Sochi* (Bloomsbury Academic 2018).

Healey D and Stella F, "Sexual and Gender Dissent in the USSR and Post-Soviet Space. Introduction" (2021) 62 Cahiers du monde russe. Russie – Empire russe – Union soviétique et États indépendants 225.

Holzhacker R and Arat ZFK, "'Gay Rights are Human Rights': The Framing of New Interpretations of International Human Rights Norms" in George Andrepoulos (ed), *The Uses and Misuses of Human Rights, A Critical Approach to Advocacy* (Palgrave MacMillan 2014).

Human Rights Watch, "Russia: Supreme Court Bans 'LGBT Movement' as 'Extremist'" *Human Rights Watch* (2023) <https://www.hrw.org/news/2023/11/30/russia-supreme-court-bans-lgbt-movement-extremist>.

Huzhina O, "Traditional Spiritual and Moral Values in Russian Law: Formulation of a Scientific Problem" (2023) 2023 Legal Science and Practice: Journal of Nizhny Novgorod Academy of the Ministry of Internal Affairs of Russia 39.

International Commission of Jurists, "Russia: Human Rights Groups Hail Historic Decision on Homosexual Propaganda Ban" (*International Commission of Jurists*, 2012) <https://www.icj.org/russia-human-rights-groups-hail-historic-decision-on-homosexual-propaganda-ban/>.

Ioffe J, "What's Russian for 'Homosexual Propaganda'?" *The New Yorker* (2011) <https://www.newyorker.com/news/news-desk/whats-russian-for-homosexual-propaganda>.

Ioffe Y and Viterbo H, "Homophobia Disguised as Children's Rights in Russia's Constitutional Referendum" (*VerfBlog*, June 29, 2020) <https://verfassungsblog.de/homophobia-disguised-as-childrens-rights-in-russias–constitutional-referendum/>.

Issaeva M and Kiskachi M, "Immoral Truth vs. Untruthful Morals? Attempts to Render Rights and Freedoms Conditional upon Sexual Orientation in Light of Russia's International Obligations" (2015) 2 Russian Law Journal 81.

Johnson JE, "Russia's Authoritarian Policymaking: The Politics of Domestic Violence after Partial Decriminalization" (2024) 71 Problems of Post-Communism 557.

Kashkina E, "Legal Regulation of Conservation and Strengthening Traditional Russian Spiritual and Moral Values Within Strategic Planning" [2023] Vestnik Advanced Training Institute of The MIA of Russia 78.

Katsuba S, "Premeditated, Organized and Impactful: Dating Violence as a Method of Committing Hate Crimes Against LGBTQ People in Russia" [2023] Journal of Family Violence 1.

Katsuba S, "The Decade of Violence: A Comprehensive Analysis of Hate Crimes Against LGBTQ in Russia in the Era of the 'Gay Propaganda Law' (2010–2020)" (2023) ahead-of-print Victims & Offenders 1.

Katsuba S, "30 Years of LGBTQ+ History in Russia: From Decriminalisation in 1993 to 'Extremist' Status in 2023" (*The Conversation*, 2024) <https://theconversation.com/30-years-of-lgbtq-history-in-russia-from-decriminalisation-in-1993-to-extremist-status-in-2023-220569>.

Khlusova A, "Legitimising Political Homophobia: Sexual Minorities and Russian Television News" in R Sanz Sabido (ed), *Representing Communities, Discourse and Contexts* (Palgrave Macmillan 2017).

Kirey-Sitnikova Y, "'You Should Care by Prohibiting All This Obscenity': A Public Policy Analysis of the Russian Law Banning Medical and Legal Transition for Transgender People" (2024) 40 Post-Soviet Affairs 452.

Kolstø P, *Family, Sex, and Faith: The Biopolitics of the Russian Orthodox Church* (Cornell University Press 2024).

Kon I, “Homophobia as a Litmus Test of Russian Democracy” (2010) 51 Russian Social Science Review 16.

Kondakov A, “The Influence of the ‘Gay-Propaganda’ Law on Violence against LGBTIQ People in Russia: Evidence from Criminal Court Rulings” (2021) 18 European Journal of Criminology 940.

Kondakov AS, *Violent Affections: Queer Sexuality, Techniques of Power, and Law in Russia* (UCL Press 2022).

Krasner SD, *Sovereignty : Organized Hypocrisy* (Princeton University Press 1999).

Kuhar R and Paternotte D (eds), *Anti-Gender Campaigns in Europe* (Rowman & Littlefield International 2017).

Langlois AJ, “Making LGBT Rights into Human Rights” in Michael J Bosia, Sandra M McEvoy and Momin Rahman (eds), *The Oxford Handbook of Global LGBT and Sexual Diversity Politics* (Oxford University Press 2020).

Linde F, “State Civilisation: The Statist Core of Vladimir Putin’s Civilisational Discourse and Its Implications for Russian Foreign Policy” (2016) 12 Politics in Central Europe 21.

Mendos LR and Rohaizad DR, “Laws On Us: A Global Overview of Legal Progress and Backtracking on Sexual Orientation, Gender Identity, Gender Expression, and Sex Characteristics” (ILGA World 2024) <https://ilga.org/news/laws-on-us-2024-lgbti-human-rights/>.

Meyer IH and Flores AR, “Anti-LGBT Victimization in the United States” (Williams Institute, School of Law, UCLA 2022) <https://williamsinstitute.law.ucla.edu/publications/anti-lgbt-victimization-us/>.

Ministry of Foreign Affairs of the Russian Federation, “The Concept of the Foreign Policy of the Russian Federation (Unofficial Translation)” (2023) <https://mid.ru/en/foreign_policy/fundamental_documents/1860586/>.

Mjør KJ, “A Morphology of Russia? the Russian Civilisational Turn and Its Cyclical Idea of History” in Katja Lehtisaari and Arto Mustajoki (eds), *Philosophical and Cultural Interpretations of Russian Modernisation* (Routledge 2016).

Mortensen SA, “Discursive Propagation in Putin’s Russia: Prohibiting ‘Propaganda of Non-Traditional Sexual Relations’” [2016] Zeitschrift für Slavische Philologie 1 <https://www.jstor.org/stable/26583038>.

Moss K, “Russia as the Saviour of European Civilization: Gender and the Geopolitics of Traditional Values” in Roman Kuhar and David Paternotte (eds), *Anti-Gender Campaigns in Europe* (Rowman & Littlefield 2017)

Moss K, “Russia’s Queer Science, or How Anti-LGBT Scholarship Is Made” (2021) 80 The Russian Review 17.

Muravyeva M, “Traditional Values and Modern Families: Legal Understanding of Tradition and Modernity in Contemporary Russia” (2014) 12 The Journal of Social Policy Studies 625.

Norocel OC and Paternotte D, "The Dis/Articulation of Anti-Gender Politics in Eastern Europe: Introduction" (2023) 70 Problems of Post-Communism 123.

Osiander A, "Sovereignty, International Relations, and the Westphalian Myth" (2001) 55 International Organization 251.

Østbø J, "The Sources of Russia's Transgressive Conservatism: Cultural Sovereignty and the Monopolization of Bespredel," *The Cultural is Political: Intersections of Russian Art and State Politics* (2020).

Permoser JM and Stoeckl K, "Reframing Human Rights: The Global Network of Moral Conservative Homeschooling Activists" (2021) 21 Global Networks 681.

President of Russia, "Meeting of the Valdai International Discussion Club" (2013) <http://en.kremlin.ru/events/president/news/19243>.

President of Russia, "Valdai Discussion Club Meeting" (*President of Russia Events*, 2021) <http://en.kremlin.ru/events/president/news/66975>.

President of Russia, "Launching the Year of the Family in Russia" (2024) <http://en.kremlin.ru/events/president/news/73297>.

Prina F, "Fantasies of Cultural Sovereignty and National Unity: Russia's Ontological (in)Security and Its Assertion of 'Spiritual-Moral Values'" [2024] International Politics 1.

Rivkin-Fish M, *Unmaking Russia's Abortion Culture : Family Planning and the Struggle for a Liberal Biopolitics* (Vanderbilt University Press 2024).

Shikher ND, "Ideological Tendencies of Modern Russian Legislation" (2023) 23 Vestnik Povolzhskogo instituta upravleniya 36.

Shnirelman V, "Russia between a Civilization and a Civic Nation" in Kåre Johan Mjør and Sanna Turoma (eds), *Russia as Civilization: Ideological Discourses in Politics, Media and Academia* (Routledge 2020).

Sperling V, *Sex, Politics, and Putin: Political Legitimacy in Russia* (Oxford University Press 2014).

Stella F, "Queer Space, Pride, and Shame in Moscow" (2013) 72 Slavic Review 458.

Stepanova EA, "'Everything Good against Everything Bad': Traditional Values in the Search for New Russian National Idea" (2023) 7 Zeitschrift für Religion, Gesellschaft und Politik 97.

Stoeckl K, "The Rise of the Russian Christian Right: The Case of the World Congress of Families" (2020) 48 Religion, State & Society 223.

Stoeckl K, "Traditional Values, Family, Homeschooling: The Role of Russia and the Russian Orthodox Church in Transnational Moral Conservative Networks and Their Efforts at Reshaping Human Rights" (2023) 21 International Journal of Constitutional Law 224.

Stoeckl K and Medvedeva K, "Double Bind at the UN: Western Actors, Russia, and the Traditionalist Agenda" (2018) 7 Global Constitutionalism 383.

Sundstrom LM and Sperling V, “Seeking Better Judgment: LGBT Discrimination Cases in Russia and at the European Court of Human Rights” (2020) 24 The International Journal of Human Rights 750.

Symons J and Altman D, “International Norm Polarization: Sexuality as a Subject of Human Rights Protection” (2015) 7 International Theory 61.

Teague E, “Russia’s Constitutional Reforms of 2020” (2020) 5 Russian Politics 301.

Thomas KL, “We’re Here, We’re Queer, Get Used to It: Freedom of Assembly and Gay Pride in Alekseyev v. Russia” (2012) 14 Oregon Review of International Law 473.

Time C and Rickleton C, “Russia’s ‘Year Of The Family’ Has Meant A War On Abortion And Divorce” *Radio Free Europe Radio Liberty* (2025) <https://www.rferl.org/a/33273068.html>.

Torbakov I, “The ‘Special Path’ of Russian State-Civilization: The Genealogy of Vladimir Putin’s Geopolitical Metaphor” [2023] The Russia Program at GW Online Papers <https://therussiaprogram.org/onlinepaper_9>.

Turbine V, “Women’s Human Rights in Russia: Outmoded Battlegrounds, or New Sites of Contentious Politics?” (2015) 31 East European Politics 326.

Ugolino F, “In Russia Was Passed the Law Prohibiting Propaganda of ‘Non-Traditional Relationships’ in the Presence of Minors, at the Federal Level. Protection of Minors or Discrimination Based on Sexual Orientation?” (2013) N° 31 Civitas Europa 331.

Underwood AEM, “The Politics of Pride: The LGBT Movement and Post-Soviet Democracy” (2011) 33 Harvard International Review 42.

Usanova O, “Russia’s ‘Traditional Values’ and Domestic Violence” (2020) 54 Kennan Cable 55.

Uzlaner D and Stoeckl K, *The Moralist International* (Fordham University Press 2022).

Vasilieva E, Rostovskaya T and Süleymanlý E, “Demographic Threats to National Security in the Political Discourse of the Russian Federation (1992–2019)” (2021) 26 Vestnik Volgogradskogo gosudarstvennogo universiteta. Serija 4. Istorija. Regionovedenie. Mezhdunarodnye otnoshenija 255.

Voss MJ, “Contesting Sexual Orientation and Gender Identity at the UN Human Rights Council” (2018) 19 Human Rights Review 1.

Walker S, “Vladimir Putin: Gay People at Winter Olympics Must ‘Leave Children Alone’” *The Guardian* (2014) <https://www.theguardian.com/world/2014/jan/17/vladimir-putin-gay-winter-olympics-children>.

Weiss ML and Bosia MJ (eds), *Global Homophobia: States, Movements, and the Politics of Oppression* (University of Illinois Press 2013).

Wilkinson C, “Putting ‘Traditional Values’ Into Practice: The Rise and Contestation of Anti-Homopropaganda Laws in Russia” (2014) 13 Journal of Human Rights 363.

Wilkinson C, “Mother Russia in Queer Peril: The Gender Logic of the Hypermasculine State” in Swati Parashar, J Ann Tickner and Jacqui True (eds), *Revisiting Gendered States: Feminist Imaginings of the State in International Relations* (2018).

Wilkinson C, "LGBT Rights in the Former Soviet Union: The Evolution of Hypervisibility" in Michael J Bosia, Sandra M McEvoy and Momin Rahman (eds) *The Oxford Handbook of Global LGBT and Sexual Diversity Politics* (Oxford University Press 2020).

Wilkinson C, "Intersection of 'Traditional Values' and LGB Rights" in Paula Gerber (ed), *Worldwide Perspectives on Lesbians, Gays and Bisexuals: Culture, History and Law* (Praeger Press 2021).

Woo B, Ko H, Tai YC, Hu Y and Solt F, "Public Support for Gay Rights Across Countries and Over Time" (2025) 106 Social Science Quarterly e13478.

Wood EA, "Gender Systems in the Putin Autocracy" (2024) 9 Frontiers in Sociology 1327946.

Zaremberg G, Tabbush C and Friedman EJ, "Feminism(s) and Anti-Gender Backlash: Lessons from Latin America" (2021) 23 International Feminist Journal of Politics 527.

Zotééva A and Kragh M, "From Constitutional Identity to the Identity of the Constitution Solving the Balance of Law and Politics in Russia" (2021) 54 Communist and Post-Communist Studies 176.

Государственная Дума, "Как Законы Защищают Безопасность Детей" (2022) <http://duma.gov.ru/news/54460/>.

Государственная Дума, "Приняты Законопроекты о Защите Традиционных Ценностей" *Государственная Дума* (2022) <http://duma.gov.ru/news/55609/>.

Павленко ЕМ, "Обеспечение Наилучших Интересов и Безопасности Детей: Международные Стандарты и Практика в России" (2021) 44 Вестник МГПУ «Юридические науки» 75.

Рожковский ВБ and Михайловна ОМ, "Традиционные Духовно-Нравственные Ценности в Государственной Идеологии Современной России" (2024) 111 Философия права 222.

Чуйченко КА, Кропачев НМ and Кондуров ВЕ, "Традиционные Российискуе Духовно-Нравственние Ценности в Контексте Современной Правовой Политики" (2024) 68 Правоведение 156.

CHAPTER 4

The Strategic Deployment of 'Hate Speech' in Turkey: Misappropriation of Human Rights?

Elif Çelik

1 Introduction

States around the world systematically appropriate human rights, and Turkey, which has developed an increasingly troubling record over the past decade, is no exception.[1] The term 'human rights misappropriation' is characterised by de Búrca and Young as the exploitation of the human rights language to promote agendas that are "exclusionary, repressive or anti-pluralist in character, highly retrogressive or reversing of previous commitments, and evasive of external monitoring or accountability".[2] This phenomenon can be explained by the long-standing centrality of human rights within international law and global governance; a position that has enabled its transformation into a common political language, yet one often appropriated by states to legitimise authority over their citizens or external intervention.[3] Accordingly, states wish to project an image consistent with the discourse of human rights, irrespective of their particular characteristics and underlying motivations.[4] Though overt conservative resistance to human rights has long been documented, this latest form is cloaked in the very language of human rights[5] and weaponised through advocacy strategies. The evolution of this trend, for example, has

1 Freedom House, *Turkey: Freedom in the World 2025* (Freedom House, 2025) <https://freedomhouse.org/country/turkey/freedom-world/2025> accessed 1 August 2025.

2 Gráinne de Búrca and Katharine G Young, 'The (Mis)appropriation of Human Rights by the New Global Right: An Introduction to the Symposium' (2023) 21 *International Journal of Constitutional Law* 205.

3 Costas Douzinas, *Human Rights and Empire: The Political Philosophy of Cosmopolitanism* (Routledge-Cavendish 2007) 33.

4 Makau Mutua, *Human Rights: A Political and Cultural Critique* (University of Pennsylvania Press 2002) 43, 57.

5 Kim Lane Scheppele, while relying on the term 'autocratic legalism', notes that: since the new autocrats know the scenarios that will attract immediate and overwhelming reaction, they govern in the name of their democratic mandates, and rather than destroying state institutions, they repurpose them. Kim Lane Scheppele, 'Autocratic Legalism' (2018) 85(2) *University of Chicago Law Review* 545, 573–575.

HTTPS://DOI.ORG/10.1163/9789004763005-006

been captured by Stoeckl in the Russian context, particularly through the instrumentalisation of the Russian Orthodox Church, with such efforts extending beyond the domestic sphere and circulating transnationally through deliberate advocacy and organised networks of actors.[6] Such strategic use of human rights discourse allows governments and states to justify exclusionary policies while preserving the appearance of commitment to law and democratic principles.[7]

The term 'human rights misappropriation' also seems to intersect with the concept of 'human rights populism', which describes the strategic invocation of rights language to advance illiberal or majoritarian ends. Although Mégret, who uses the term, suggests that such populism is more typical of states with strong liberal traditions,[8] one could go further and argue that in contexts such as Turkey, where the interpretation of rights has historically been shaped by shifting political priorities, such discourse may be even more viable since this flexibility enables the selective and strategic redefinition of human rights claims. Given the widely acknowledged decline in the rule of law and judicial independence in Turkey, as documented in international reports,[9] the state is nevertheless required to present an image of adherence to human rights commitments. Within this framework, concepts derived from human rights discourse may at times be selectively instrumentalised to serve political objectives. Building on prior scholarly work on the 'old and new forms of human rights appropriation in Turkey',[10] this chapter investigates how 'hate speech' is strategically mobilised as a tool within consolidated right-wing authoritarian governance, in order to critically examine the extent to which this may represent a misappropriation of human rights discourse. The study, despite

6 Kristina Stoeckl, 'Traditional Values, Family, Homeschooling: The Role of Russia and the Russian Orthodox Church in Transnational Moral Conservative Networks and Their Efforts at Reshaping Human Rights' (2023) 21 *International Journal of Constitutional Law* 225; Frédéric Mégret, 'Human Rights Populism' (2022) 13 *Humanity: An International Journal of Human Rights, Humanitarianism, and Development* 240, 242.

7 Susanna Mancini and Michel Rosenfeld, 'Nationalism, Populism, Religion, and the Quest to Reframe Fundamental Rights' (2020) 42 *Cardozo Law Review* 464, 469.

8 Mégret contends that the integration of human rights principles into populist discourse is most evident in states with a strong historical commitment to human rights norms – and that leaders of governments such as Turkey and Hungary exhibit what he describes as 'more vulgar' forms of populism, which are generally less inclined to adopt such strategies. Mégret, 'Human Rights Populism' (n 6) 242.

9 World Justice Project, *Rule of Law Index 2023: Turkey Country Data* (World Justice Project, 2023) <https://worldjusticeproject.org/rule-of-law.index/country/2023/Turkey> accessed 1 August 2025.

10 Başak Çalı and Esra Demir-Gürsel, 'Continuity and Change in Human Rights Appropriation: The Case of Turkey' (2023) 21 *International Journal of Constitutional Law* 266.

some evidentiary limitations,[11] seeks to trace how the hate speech argument selectively applied to suppress dissent, delegitimise minority expression, and reinforce the ruling power's right-wing conservative populist agenda thereby shaping the boundaries of citizenship.

To provide context, the chapter first offers a concise overview of how human rights discourse, particularly around expression, has evolved in Turkey since the early 2000s. It then turns to the role of contemporary institutional actors whose legal independence is shaped by political forces and whose roles have become increasingly pivotal to the instrumentalisation of hate speech as a tool of ideological control and censorship. The chapter unfolds under four sections. It begins with an analysis of how human rights discourse has been strategically reframed by also emphasising the structural constrains on freedom of expression. Then, it examines the legal and judicial treatment of hate speech and court practices and finally considers how institutions such as the Human Rights and Equality Institution of Turkey (TİHEK) and the Radio and Television Supreme Council (RTÜK) have come to play key roles in the instrumentalisation of hate speech regulation.

2 Strategic Reframing of Human Rights in Contemporary Turkey

While the scope of this study does not allow for an extensive discussion of Turkey's human rights history throughout the twentieth century, it is important to acknowledge the broader context in which more recent developments have unfolded. Throughout the late twentieth century, while Turkey adopted the language of human rights to project alignment with the West,[12] it consistently subordinated individual freedoms in the national context to state prior-

11 These limitations stem from several interrelated factors such as: the lack of consistent application of a clear and universally accepted legal definition or regulatory framework for hate speech; the tendency to invoke hate speech argument in a discretionary rather than legally grounded manner; the fact that many investigations initiated by citizens who are subjected to this type of speech are dismissed or result in non-prosecution thus legal tracking being difficult; and the inaccessibility of some decisions by quasi-independent administrative bodies that issue sanctions or rulings based on hate speech allegations.

12 Zehra F Kabasakal Arat, 'Collisions and Crossroads: Introducing Human Rights in Turkey' in Zehra F Kabasakal Arat (ed), *Human Rights in Turkey* (University of Pennsylvania Press 2007) 3.

ities such as secularism, national unity and security.[13] From the early 2000s onwards, Turkey entered an era of intensified engagement with international political processes, particularly those related to European Union accession.[14] The legal and institutional reforms pursued during this period, made it increasingly difficult for the State to completely disregard the language of human rights.[15] Consequently, human rights discourse began to occupy a visible space within the dominant political narrative. Although this incorporation did not always reflect a genuine commitment to the normative foundations of human rights, it nevertheless signalled a transformation in official rhetoric.

The growing emphasis on international human rights standards in the early 2000s coincided with the rise of the Justice and Development Party (AKP), which initially framed its political agenda around promises of democratisation. Over time, however, President Erdoğan, once a 'critic' of repression,[16] increasingly used the language of rights strategically – invoking it when politically useful and dismissing it when it posed limits. Since coming to power in the early 2000s, Erdoğan's AKP has maintained uninterrupted control over government, gradually reshaping the country's political system.[17] Over the ruling party's two-decade rule, human rights in Turkey have experienced a steady deterioration.[18] In this new phase of human rights reinterpretation, it became clear that while the early years of the Erdoğan regime invoked the idea of co-

13 Ceren Belge, 'Friends of the Court: The Republican Alliance and Selective Activism of the Constitutional Court of Turkey' (2006) 40(3) *Law & Society Review* 653, 656; Başak Çalı, 'Human Rights Discourse and Domestic Human Rights NGOs' in Zehra F Kabasakal Arat (ed), *Human Rights in Turkey* (University of Pennsylvania Press 2007) 220.

14 Ergun Özbudun, 'Democratization Reforms in Turkey, 1993–2004' (2007) 8(2) *Turkish Studies* 179.

15 Elif M Babül, *Bureaucratic Intimacies: Translating Human Rights in Turkey* (Stanford University Press 2017).

16 In 1997, Erdoğan was jailed for reading a poem that challenged the secular state's restrictions on religious expression, an event that shaped his image as 'once a victim'. Petra de Bruijn, 'Of Minarets and Bayonets: The Poem that Landed Erdoğan in Jail' in Alp Yenen and Erik-Jan Zürcher (eds), *A Hundred Years of Republican Turkey: A History in a Hundred Fragments* (Leiden University Press 2023) 198–201.

17 The regime has increasingly been characterised as authoritarian, whether in its competitive or consolidated form. Berk Esen, 'Competitive Authoritarianism in Turkey under the AKP Rule' in Emel Akçalı (ed), *The Routledge Handbook on Contemporary Turkey* (Routledge 2021); Koray Çalışkan, 'Toward a New Political Regime in Turkey: From Competitive toward Full Authoritarianism' (2018) 58 *New Perspectives on Turkey* 5.

18 Human Rights Watch, *World Report 2022: Turkey* (HRW, 2022) <www.hrw.org/world-report/2022/country-chapters/turkey> accessed 1 August 2025.

existence to promote selective human rights, its shift toward an authoritarian stance transformed this approach into a form of bestowed tolerance.[19]

Although Turkey's historical approach to human rights has largely been characterised by a state-centric interpretation informed by national security concerns, and although concepts such as national security, public order, and secularism have traditionally been invoked to justify restrictions on rights, the current political discourse increasingly relies on more ambiguous and subjective value judgments.[20] Notably, phrases like 'our sensitivities' (*hassasiyetlerimiz*), frequently invoked by President Erdoğan, have supplanted earlier justifications while remaining undefined and ideologically flexible.[21] The 'sensitivities' are rarely defined and are instead understood through the framework of the regime-endorsed notion of being 'local and national' (*yerli ve milli*) which appeals to a constructed sense of national authenticity. These very 'sensitivities' have been cited, for example, in Erdoğan's justification for Turkey's withdrawal from the Istanbul Convention,[22] and more recently in the declaration of 2025 as the 'Year of the Family', despite the ongoing prevalence of violence and femicides against women and children.[23] They have also underpinned the growing influence and budget of the Diyanet (Turkish Directorate of Religious Affairs), whose mission to raise a pious generation is increasingly aligned with Erdoğan's political agenda.[24]

---

19 One illustrative example of the asymmetrical power dynamics between the 'tolerant' and the 'tolerated' is President Erdoğan's ironic statement at a United Nations event on hate speech – an event ostensibly aimed at promoting religious diversity. His words: 'even though there are pork eaters in the country we don't interfere' illustrate this notion of 'tolerance' as a conditional and discretionary privilege rather than a fundamental right. Bianet, 'Erdoğan at UN Hate Speech Event: "There Are Pork-Eaters in Our Country, We Don't Interfere"' (25 September 2019) <https://bianet.org/haber/erdogan-at-un-hate-speech-event-there-are-pork-eaters-in-our-country-we-don-t-interfere-213553> accessed 1 August 2025.

20 Çalı and Demir-Gürsel (n 10) 268.

21 Tanıl Bora, *Zamanın Kelimeleri: Türkiye'nin Siyasi Dili* (İletişim Yayınları 2018) 192, 274.

22 Republic of Turkey Directorate of Communications, *Statement Regarding Turkey's Withdrawal from the Istanbul Convention* (20 March 2021) <www.iletisim.gov.tr/english/haberler/detay/statement-regarding-turkeys-withdrawal-from-the-istanbul-convention > accessed 1 August 2025.

23 We Will Stop Femicides Platform, *2025 Report for First 6 Months* (Kadın Cinayetlerini Durduracağız Platformu, 1 July 2025) <https://kadincinayetlerinidurduracagiz.net/veriler/3146/we-will-stop-femicides-platform-2025-report-for-first-6-months> accessed 1 August 2025.

24 Nil Mutluer, 'Diyanet's Role in Building the "Yeni (New) Milli" in the AKP Era' (2018) 27 *European Journal of Turkish Studies* 1, 4.

While analyses of Turkey often foreground the prevalence of human rights violations, it is essential to also recognise the parallel and underexamined dynamic wherein the discourse of human rights is strategically appropriated by the ruling power and its allies to legitimise a conservative agenda. A commitment to selected human rights topics is now observed in the party statutes and programmes of the current regime's allies, despite their Islamist and nationalist agendas.[25] Within this context, it appears that the ruling ideology embraces a culturally relativist approach to human rights, marking a departure from the previous regime's emphasis on statism and secularism.

Given that the constitutional framework does not always lend itself to the political objectives of the conservative ruling bloc, alternative institutional actors have at times been tasked with roles that align more closely with prevailing ideological agendas, even when these diverge from their original legal mandates. While other scholars have noted such actors as the Directory of Religious Affairs and National Human Rights Institution and ministries such as the Ministry of Education,[26] one could also include the Presidency's Directorate of Communications and the Radio and Television Supreme Council among these. This broader institutional dynamic plays a role in reshaping contemporary interpretation of human rights.

3 The Structural Limits of Expression: A Fragile Culture of Free Speech

Turkey has earned a reputation for being one of the most limiting environments for civil liberties within the Council of Europe, in particular regarding freedom of expression. Notably, judgments against Turkey constitute nearly half of the European Court of Human Rights' total decisions on free speech issues, significantly influencing the Court's jurisprudence and standards in this area, including its case law on hate speech.[27] Even though freedom of expression has consistently been a contested political domain worldwide, and recent trends in countries traditionally advertised as exemplars of demo-

25 Yeniden Refah Partisi, *Party Statute* <https://yenidenrefahpartisi.org.tr/page/parti-tuzugu/12>; HÜDA PAR, *Party Statute* (*English*) <https://files.hudapar.org/media/StatikIcerikGorselleri/Yayinlar/PdfDosyalari/ingilizce.pdf>; MHP, *2024 Party Program* <www.mhp.org.tr/usr_img/_mhp2007/kitaplar/mhp_partiprogrami_2024.pdf> accessed 1 August 2025.

26 Çalı and Demir-Gürsel (n 10) 274.

27 *Sürek v Turkey* (No 1) App no 26682/95 (ECHR, 8 July 1999); *Gündüz v Turkey* App no 35071/97 (ECHR, 4 December 2003).

cratic freedoms[28] indicate a worrying regression, the situation in Turkey follows somewhat a different trajectory. Rather than a straightforward regression, it is better understood as the continuation of a long-standing pattern of political appropriation of freedom of expression, one that is now reinforced by emerging discursive tools. In this context, its distinctly contemporary form in some respects represents not just a mere appropriation but a deliberate and strategic distortion of the concept itself.

Throughout the history of the modern republic, incidents involving critical speech on certain sensitive subjects, which are perceived as fundamental to the identity of the 'ideal' Turkish citizen, have repeatedly affected journalists, artists,[29] academics,[30] and ordinary people. As a result, a distinct judicial-political culture has developed,[31] shaped by this historical tradition and an internalised perception of taboos and the boundaries of acceptable discourse within the socio-political context.[32] The persistence of these has contributed to widespread mechanisms of self-censorship in everyday civic practices, performances, and political discourse.[33] Although specific constitutional provisions and articles in the penal code have historically restricted freedom of expression, particularly on issues such as terrorism, incitement to violence, the degradation of particular groups, or insults to Turkish identity, the concept of 'hate' in relation to speech, or more precisely the deployment of the term *hate speech*, has only recently emerged within this restrictive legal and

28 UN Human Rights Office of the High Commissioner, 'USA: Free Speech on Campus Needs to Be Protected, Not Attacked, Say Experts' (OHCHR, 25 July 2024) <www.ohchr.org/en/press-releases/2024/07/usa-free-speech-campus-needs-be-protected-not-attacked-say-experts> accessed 1 August 2025.

29 A particularly absurd anecdote concerns the famous modernist painter Fikret Mualla. In 1936, at a well-known café of the era, Mualla criticised the artistic quality of a portrait of Atatürk that hung on the wall, which led to his arrest on charges of insulting Atatürk. He was taken into custody, reportedly tortured, and ultimately forced to choose between imprisonment and confinement in a mental institution to serve his sentence. Hıfzı Topuz, *Paris'te Bir Türk Ressam: Fikret Mualla'nın Yaşamı* (6th edn, Remzi Kitabevi 2014) 30–31.

30 One such example from an academic aspect is *Altuğ Taner Akçam v Turkey* App no 27520/07 (ECtHR, 25 October 2011).

31 It was not until the 1961 Constitution that the right to freedom of expression was formally included in Turkey's constitutional framework. In this light, the legal recognition of freedom of thought and expression in Turkey remains relatively recent and institutionally fragile.

32 For certain contexts in which a performance of Turkishness, including discursive expressions, takes shape see Barış Ünlü, *Türklük Sözleşmesi* (Dipnot Yayınları 2019) 208–219.

33 Susma Platformu, *Ocak-Aralık 2024 İzleme Raporu* (Susma Platformu 2025) 16 <https://susma24.com/raporlar> accessed 1 August 2025.

political landscape. Incorrect references to *hate speech* and *hate crime*, often conflating the two, are now common in the political discourse of all parties.

In line with the psychosocial context outlined above, Turkey has associated specific articles of its penal code with the criminalisation of speech.[34] While certain of these laws have been abolished, others have undergone amendments, and some have merely been presented in a new guise such as the article 301 of the Penal Code.[35] Until the late-2000s, a significant proportion of freedom of speech judgments related to Turkish national identity, national security, or criticism of Atatürk.[36] While this trend persists, during the last decade of the AKP rule, the focus has also shifted toward cases involving alleged offences against religion and the government.[37] Scholars have observed this shift as an evolution from previously rigid methods to a more intricate, carefully structured, and analytically nuanced approach in which restrictions are framed as being in accordance with the law.[38] Furthermore the crime of insulting the president, a specific article of the penal code that had been largely forgotten before Erdoğan's leadership, has come to the forefront over the past decade[39] despite repeated criticism and warnings from international legal bodies regarding its existence.[40] As of today, even children and the eld-

34 Studies, including this comparative analysis of Italian and Turkish penal systems, display that although Turkey formally adopted the Italian Criminal Code and retains certain structural similarities, the Turkish context has evolved in a markedly different direction. In particular, the entanglement of opinion crimes with hate speech provisions in Turkey has produced a legal framework that enables broad and politically motivated restrictions on expression, posing serious risks to democratic discourse and the protection of fundamental rights. Sofia Verza, *Opinion Crimes in Italy and in Turkey: Balancing the Right to Freedom of Expression with the Defence of National Security and Public Order* (Master's thesis, Università di Trento 2016) 207–211.

35 Bülent Algan, 'The Brand New Version of Article 301 of the Turkish Penal Code and Its Loss of Legitimacy' (2008) 9(12) *German Law Journal* 2237, 2239.

36 Human Rights Watch, *Turkey: Ongoing Restrictions on Freedom of Expression* (12 April 2007) <https://www.hrw.org/news/2007/04/12/turkey-ongoing-restrictions-freedom-expression> accessed 1 August 2025.

37 Yaman Akdeniz and Kerem Altıparmak, *Turkey: Freedom of Expression in Jeopardy* (ARTICLE 19, July 2016) 5 <www.article19.org/resources/turkey-freedom-of-expression-in-jeopardy/ > accessed 1 August 2025.

38 Ibid.

39 Reuters, 'Nearly 2,000 Legal Cases Opened for Insulting Turkey's Erdogan' (2 March 2016) <www.reuters.com/article/world/nearly-2000-legal-cases-opened-for-insulting-turkeys-erdogan-idUSKCN0W42HM> accessed 1 August 2025.

40 *Vedat Şorli v Turkey* App no 42048/19 (ECtHR, 19 October 2021) para 17,18,19.

erly can be deemed perpetrators of this 'crime'.[41] Although the offences of insulting religion and the president differ legally, their parallel rise under Erdoğan has blurred public perception, leading many to view criticism of the president or certain values as attacks on the sacred. This has made it increasingly unclear when criticism of emerging 'sensitivities' may be treated as hate speech and criminalised.

4 Hate Speech in Context: Legal Ambiguity and Ideological Flexibility

Hate speech analysis in Turkey, with respect to potential misappropriation, presents an intricate challenge, particularly because this form of speech frequently serves as a component of populist and authoritarian discourse[42] where certain communities and groups have consistently been subjected to targeted hate speech.[43] The problem intensifies notably during election periods, a time when protective legal and institutional mechanisms intended to prevent such abuses tend to operate ineffectively or fail altogether.[44] Compounding the issue, the penal code provision most relevant to combating hate speech is frequently used not against perpetrators, but rather against individuals who are expressing critical or dissenting views that challenge dominant political narratives[45] as elaborated further below.

41 Bianet, 'Insulting Erdoğan: Nearly 10,000 People Stood Trial in a Year, including 290 Children' (6 September 2021) <https://bianet.org/haber/insulting-erdogan-nearly-10-000-people-stood-trial-in-a-year-including-290-children-247507> accessed 1 August 2025.

42 As also observed in other regimes such as Modi's India. Human Rights Watch, *India: Hate Speech Fueled Modi's Election Campaign* (14 August 2024) <https://www.hrw.org/news/2024/08/14/india-hate-speech-fueled-modis-election-campaign> accessed 1 August 2025.

43 Hrant Dink Foundation, *Hate Speech and Discriminatory Discourse in Media: 2019 Report* (November 2020) <https://hrantdink.org/attachments/article/2727/Hate-Speech-and-Discriminatory-Discourse-in-Media-2019.pdf> accessed 1 August 2025.

44 Hrant Dink Foundation, *Between Two Elections – Z Report on Hate Speech on Twitter* (2023) <https://hrantdink.org/en/asulis/activities/projects/media-watch-on-hate-speech/3986-between-two-elections-z-report-on-hate-speech-on-twitter> accessed 1 August 2025.

45 Kasım Akbaş and İlker Gökhan Şen, 'How Did a Safeguard for Disadvantaged Groups Turn into the Weapon of Oppression?: Normative Distortion of the Article 216 of the Turkish Penal Code' (2020) 7 *Ankara Bar Rev* 1.

4.1 Article 216 as a Tool of Control: From Legal Provision to Political Weapon

While hate speech as a distinct concept is not defined in the national legal framework, it is often linked to Article 216 of the current Penal Code[46] which reads as follows:

> (1) A person who publicly provokes hatred or hostility in one section of the public against another section which has a different characteristic based on social class, race, religion, sect or regional difference, which creates an explicit and imminent danger to public security, shall be sentenced to a penalty of imprisonment for a term of one to three years. (2) A person who publicly degrades a section of the public on grounds of social class, race, religion, sect, gender or regional differences shall be sentenced to a penalty of imprisonment for a term of six months to one year (3) A person who publicly degrades the religious values of a section of the public shall be sentenced to a penalty of imprisonment for a term of six months to one year, where the act is capable of disturbing public peace.

Although it was noted that Article 216 was invoked less frequently to restrict freedom of expression following the Penal Code reforms of the early 2000s,[47] it has nonetheless assumed increasing significance over the past decade, particularly in the context of a progressively narrowing space for dissent and critical expression.[48] Given its frequent and controversial application, Article 216, along with other commonly invoked provisions of the Turkish Penal Code, has also been subject to critical scrutiny by the Venice Commission.[49] The Commission raised concerns regarding the vague and overly broad formulation of the provision, noting the absence of essential safeguards such as necessity and proportionality. It further observed that these deficiencies render the article incompatible with the standards established under Article 10 of the

46 This article has been presented as part of Turkey's legal compliance under the International Convention on the Elimination of All Forms of Racial Discrimination (CERD) but the CERD Committee has identified several shortcomings of it in addressing racial discrimination. CERD/C/TUR/CO/4–6 (11 January 2016) para. 21, 22.

47 Zühtü Arslan, 'Türkiye'de İstisna Hâli, Terör ve İfade Özgürlüğü' (2007) 71 *Türkiye Barolar Birliği Dergisi* 201, 204.

48 Venice Commission, *Opinion on Articles 216, 299, 301 and 314 of the Penal Code of Turkey* CDL-AD (2016)002 (11–12 March 2016) <www.venice.coe.int/webforms/documents/default.aspx?pdffile=CDL-AD(2016)002-e > accessed 1 August 2025.

49 Ibid.

European Convention on Human Rights, particularly the requirement that any restriction on expression be justified by a pressing social need and that it ensures adequate protection for dissenting or minority views.[50] Since these criticisms were raised, its use has, on the contrary, steadily increased, and in this context, the series of cases initiated under the article can be aptly characterised as a form of 'judicial harassment', as noted by other scholars.[51]

Moreover, in its application of Article 216(3) of the Penal Code, Turkey frequently criminalises blasphemy, a form of expression that is conceptually distinct from religious hate speech and, according to international human rights bodies, should not be subject to criminal sanctions.[52] This distinction has been highlighted by the Council of Europe's Parliamentary Assembly in Resolution 1805 (2011), the Venice Commission's 2013 report, and the United Nations Human Rights Committee in General Comment No. 34, all of which support the decriminalisation of blasphemy while maintaining legal protections against incitement to discrimination, hostility or violence.[53] The prevailing tendency in Turkey to conflate criticism of religion with Article 216(3) of the Penal Code – originally intended as a hate speech provision but often interpreted as a blasphemy clause – not only deepens existing conceptual ambiguities but also risks undermining the normative coherence and legal precision of hate speech law. As it was observed by another scholar in the *Fazıl Say* case,[54] Turkish courts often treat criticism of religious values not as

50 Ibid.

51 This term with respect to article 216 was used by Tolga Şirin, in Mine Yıldırım, Rümeysa Çamdereli, Tolga Şirin, *A Human Rights Perspective on the Multi-faceted Right (Not) to Believe in Türkiye* (Norwegian Helsinki Committee, Freedom of Belief Initiative Report, 2025) 83.

52 On the other hand, the distinction between blasphemy and religious hate speech remains also unsettled in the jurisprudence of the European Court of Human Rights, a point that has drawn scholarly criticism. While in *E.S. v. Austria*, the Court upheld the applicant's conviction for making disparaging remarks about the Prophet Muhammad, prioritising religious sensitivity over freedom of expression; more recently in *Rabczewska v. Poland*, the Court found a violation of Article 10 in response to critical statements directed at Christianity. The Court stressed the need for contextual analysis and reaffirmed that freedom of expression includes the right to challenge dominant religious beliefs. This approach, however, did not go unchallenged, as one of the dissenting judges in *Rabczewska* expressed concern over the inconsistency of affording protection to certain faiths while permitting criticism of others.

53 Parliamentary Assembly of the Council of Europe (PACE), *Resolution 1805 (2007) para 4.* UN Human Rights Committee, *General Comment No 34: Article 19: Freedoms of Opinion and Expression* (12 September 2011) UN Doc CCPR/C/GC/34, para 48.

54 Kerem Altıparmak, *Fazıl Say'ın Tweet'leri ve Doğru Sandığınız Yedi Yanlış* (2013) <https://www.keremaltiparmak.com/fazil-sayin-tweetleri-ve-dogru-sandiginiz-yedi-yanlis/> accessed 1 August 2025.

protected speech but as an offence under Article 216 (3), effectively transforming a hate speech provision into a functional blasphemy law. Approximately a decade ago, pianist *Say* was charged under Article 216 for retweeting a poem attributed to Omar Khayyam, which can be translated as close to original as: "you say that rivers of wine will flow; is Heaven a tavern? You say each believer will receive two houris; is Heaven a brothel" and was alleged to constitute defamation of religion.[55] Right-wing politicians, including then Foreign Minister Ahmet Davutoğlu, as well as pro-government media, characterised the pianist's actions as 'hate speech'.[56] Despite the prevailing climate of fear and censorship of this case, insufficient attention has been paid to the fact that the Court of Cassation ultimately ruled that the content of Say's tweets did not constitute a criminal offense and were protected under the right to freedom of expression, resulting in the reversal of his conviction.[57] Nevertheless such responses have contributed significantly to the misconception that criticism or satirical commentary on religious matters constitutes universally recognised hate speech. In reality, this reflects a broader pattern in which lower courts, often acting under political pressure, issue rulings that foster a climate of fear and shape public perception regarding the boundaries of permissible speech. Although these decisions can be overturned by higher courts, as in the case of *Say*, the underlying approach and its chilling effect on free expression tend to persist. A recent and illustrative example of this ongoing pattern is the case of the Turkish satirical magazine *Leman*[58] which was subjected to an ex officio investigation, a police raid, and the use of force following the publication of a cartoon depicting two winged figures, Mohammed and Moses, greeting each other over a bombed city. The authorities immediately claimed the

55 It appears from the details of the case that Say was not charged solely for this tweet, but also for several others, some including: "Is God something you live for, die for, or descend into savagery to kill for? Reflect on that as well," and "Have you noticed? Wherever there is a creep, a lowlife, a gossipmonger, a thief or a clown, they are all God-fearing. Is this a paradox?" Turkish Court of Cassation, 8th Criminal Chamber, E 2014/35434, K 2015/22535, 12 October 2015.

56 Ahmet Davutoğlu'ndan Fazıl Say yorumu, *CNN Türk* <www.youtube.com/watch?v=1MCDtWjdI6k> accessed 1 August 2025.

57 Turkish Court of Cassation, 8th Criminal Chamber, E 2014/35434, K 2015/22535, 12 October 2015.

58 Bethan McKernan, 'Protests in Turkey over satirical magazine's alleged Prophet Muhammad cartoon' *The Guardian* (London, 1 July 2025) <https://www.theguardian.com/world/2025/jul/01/istanbul-turkey-leman-magazine-alleged-prophet-muhammad-cartoon-protests-arrests> accessed 1 August 2025.

cartoon insulted religious values and initiated legal action,[59] including the confiscation of the magazine and the detention of several staff members.

Misappropriation of Article 216 of the Turkish Penal Code is not limited to subsection (3). In some instances, cases initially brought under Article 216 (3) have also resulted in the application of Article 216 (1), the provision most closely aligned with hate speech, even in the absence of any incitement to hostility or imminent threat.[60] A notable example is the prosecution of journalists who shared Charlie Hebdo caricatures in 2015 as an act of solidarity. The case was marked by significant political interference: it was publicly provoked by the Prime Minister at the time, and the President Erdoğan's daughter, son, and son-in-law participated as complainants. Istanbul criminal court sentenced the journalist with two years of imprisonment.[61] One particularly striking, though not formally acknowledged, aspect of the case is that individuals who had not directly suffered harm from the alleged offence were nevertheless allowed to intervene as parties to the proceedings. This procedural decision was subsequently deemed legally flawed by the Court of Cassation yet this aspect of the case did not receive much attention.[62]

Despite persistent criticism regarding its arbitrary application, the use of Article 216 of the Turkish Penal Code has markedly increased over the past decade,[63] encompassing prosecutions of social media users,[64] lawyers,[65] and

---

59 In a tweet adressing the manner the Minister of Interior remarked: "I once again condemn those who try to sow seeds of discord by caricaturing our Prophet (PBUH). The individual named as D.P., who created this offensive drawing, has been captured and detained. I reiterate: These scoundrels will be held accountable by the law." Euronews, 'Turkish police detain cartoonist over Prophet Muhammad caricature' (1 July 2025) <https://www.euronews.com/culture/2025/07/01/turkish-police-detain-cartoonist-over-prophet-muhammad-caricature> accessed 1 August 2025.

60 For some examples of this usage see Yıldırım, Çamdereli and Şirin (n 51) 84.

61 Human Rights Watch, *Silencing Turkey's Media: The Government's Deepening Assault on Critical Journalism* (15 December 2016) 28 <https://www.hrw.org/sites/default/files/report_pdf/turkey1216_web.pdf> accessed 1 August 2025.

62 Yargıtay 8. Ceza Dairesi, E 2020/8472, K 2022/3517, 1 March 2022. However, while the media widely covered the two-year prison sentence back in 2016, none reported that the ruling was overturned due to its legal defects; a silence that may be read as evidence that the intended chilling effect on the public has already been achieved.

63 Adalet Bakanlığı, *Adalet İstatistikleri 2024-Turkish and English Judicial Statistics* (2024). <https://adlisicil.adalet.gov.tr/Resimler/SayfaDokuman/7042025092455Adalet_İstatistikleri_2024%20Türkçe_Ingilizce.pdf> accessed 1 August 2025.

64 <www.duvarenglish.com/turkish-court-arrests-two-minors-over-degrading-religious-values-news-63149> accessed 1 August 2025.

65 <www.duvarenglish.com/famous-turkish-lawyer-feyza-altun-detained-over-sharia-remark-news-63861> accessed 1 August 2025.

even street interview participants[66] for remarks ranging from criticism of government policy and religious discourse to satirical or personal expressions made in public or digital spaces. This growing trend reflects a broader pattern in which ideologically driven narratives dominate public discourse, creating a climate where those advocating for equality, human rights, and the protection of marginalised communities are increasingly silenced.

4.2 Judicial Reluctance to Engage with Hate Speech Complaints

There is no doubt that hate speech has an intrinsic relationship with the notion of discrimination, as it both reflects and reinforces existing social hierarchies and exclusionary structures.[67] The legal framework governing discrimination in Turkey is, however, markedly limited in scope, particularly from the perspective of criminal law, which significantly hinders the effective protection of groups potentially targeted by such acts.[68] Turkish first-degree courts frequently exhibit reluctance to prosecute hate speech cases, particularly those initiated by groups directly targeted or adversely affected by such speech.[69] Furthermore, prosecutors often refrain from initiating proceedings in response to hate speech complaints, or decide that the expression is within freedom of speech.[70] Reports produced on hate speech in Turkey reveal that,

66 <www.duvarenglish.com/turkish-court-arrests-woman-for-insulting-president-in-street-interview-news-64798> accessed 1 August 2025.

67 The United Nations Rabat Plan of Action explicitly recognises this link, emphasising that certain forms of hate speech that incite discrimination, hostility, or violence, can create an enabling environment for broader patterns of exclusion and inequality. United Nations Office of the High Commissioner for Human Rights, *Rabat Plan of Action on the Prohibition of Advocacy of National, Racial or Religious Hatred that Constitutes Incitement to Discrimination, Hostility or Violence* (OHCHR 2012) para 21.

68 According to Article 122, it is a criminal offence to obstruct a person's access to goods, services, employment, or economic activity on the basis of language, race, nationality, colour, gender, disability, political opinion, philosophical belief, religion, or sect. However, the 2014 amendment introduced a requirement that these acts must be committed 'with hatred' in order to constitute a crime. Venice Commission, *Opinion on Article 122 of the Turkish Penal Code* CDL-REF(2016)011 <www.venice.coe.int/webforms/documents/default.aspx?pdffile=CDL-REF(2016)011-e> accessed 1 August 2025.

69 In this regard, judicial search database (LEXPERA) show no cases at the first-instance court level that directly address complaints involving hate speech or include the phrase 'hate speech' in their reasoning. For the regional administrative and appellate courts – authorised to uphold or overturn lower court decisions – 88 such cases are recorded. In nearly all of these, the concept of hate speech only appears in a generic and formulaic expression, consistently framed in connection with terrorism-related offences.

70 Bianet, 'Pro-Government Daily Yeni Akit Not Prosecuted for Calling LGBTI+s "Dishonourable Faggots"' (11 March 2020) <https://bianet.org/haber/pro-government-daily-yeni-

when the term is applied in line with its conventional meaning, the principal targets of such speech in Turkey are Kurds, Armenians, Jews, Greek Cypriots, Syrians, refugees, and individuals of LGBT+.[71] Yet given their existing social vulnerability and reluctance to initiate legal action, there is limited data on the extent to which such individuals are able to access judicial remedies, as well as on the effectiveness of the legal avenues available to them.

Effective from 2012, Turkey implemented the individual application procedure before the Constitutional Court, providing a domestic remedy for claims related to violations of rights guaranteed both by the Constitution and the European Convention of Human Rights (ECHR)[72] As of 2025, the Constitutional Court's database contains 82 rulings in which the term 'hate speech' appears. However, it would be inaccurate to assert that the concept is central to the substance of all these cases. Conversely, applications in which individuals claim to have been direct targets of hate speech remain limited.[73] Nonetheless, the majority of these applications have been deemed inadmissible, either on the grounds of non-exhaustion of domestic remedies or due to deficiencies concerning the applicants' legal standing. Although the Court has referred to international standards in the cases explicitly alleging hate speech,[74] it has not yet found a violation on that basis. A recent case which was ultimately dismissed as inadmissible concerned an application by an LGBT+ organisation claiming a violation of the right to protection of honour and reputation in relation to a prosecutor's decision not to pursue charges against a news article allegedly inciting hatred or degrading the public. The

akit-not-prosecuted-for-calling-lgbti-s-dishonorable-faggots-218651> accessed 1 August 2025.

71 *Hate Speech and Discriminatory Discourse in Media 2018 Report*, 20 <https://hrantdink.org/en/asulis/publications/75-media-watch-on-hate-speech-reports/2304-hate-speech-and-discriminatory-discourse-in-media-2018-report> accessed 1 August 2025.

72 Venice Commission, *Opinion on the Legal Framework for the Individual Application to the Constitutional Court of Turkey* (CDL-AD(2011)040, 12–13 December 2011) <https://venice.coe.int/webforms/documents/default.aspx?pdffile=CDL-AD(2011)040-e> accessed 1 August 2025.

73 The instances where alleged hate speech has been invoked by applicants have largely been framed under claims relating to the right to equality before the law (art 10), the right to personal inviolability and the corporeal and spiritual integrity of the individual (art 17), and the right to legal remedies (art 36) AYM *Fetullah Gülen* App nos: 2014/12225; 2014/11499; 2014/8951; 2014/12225; AYM *Mehmet Aytaç* App no 2017/26514); AYM *Sinem Hun* App no 2013/5356; AYM *Aytuğ Atıcı* App no 2018/21055; AYM *Cemal Halis* App no 2014/118; AYM *Eksen Bilimsel A.Ş ve Özel Yaprak A.Ş* App no 2015/1341; AYM *Kaos GL Derneği* App nos 2014/18891; 2018/20035; AYM *Osman Hilmi Özdil* App no 2014/14934; AYM *Nur Neşe Karahan ve Yeşil Artvin Derneği* App no 2016/79283.

74 *Fetullah Gülen* App no 2014/12225 para. 14,19,20,24.

article appeared in a pro-government newspaper and labelled the LGBT+ organisation as "deviant". In its decision, while the Court referred to the definition of the concept hate speech with respect to its earlier case law,[75] it avoided engaging with the vulnerability or historical marginalisation of the targeted group,[76] despite its earlier decisions having acknowledged that hate speech need not incite violence or crime[77] and that it was sufficient for such speech to be directed at specific individuals or groups based on identifiable characteristics.[78] In this case, the Court concluded that the newspaper was merely expressing conservative views and reasoned that public debate on such topics inherently involves hostility. Crucially, the Court failed to recognise that the targeted group constituted a distinct social category.[79] Although individual applications to the Constitutional Court could be seen as a remedy for the lower courts' failure to apply Article 216 effectively in combating hate speech, the Court's stance in the case involving sexual minorities, while seemingly in favour of freedom of expression, appears worthy of scrutiny as a possible case of misappropriation of that very principle.

5 Beyond the Courts: Instrumentalising Hate Speech through Institutional Practice

When existing legal frameworks and conventional legal paths remain insufficient in realising authoritarian aims, other institutional mechanisms are repurposed to pursue those objectives under the guise of performative legalism.[80] In the context of Turkey, public bodies vested with administrative regulatory powers have increasingly taken on such responsibilities. This section focuses on two key institutions in this regard: the Human Rights and Equality Institution of Turkey (TİHEK) and the Radio and Television Supreme Council (RTÜK). It explores whether these bodies have contributed to a redef-

75 *KAOS GL Association* App no 2018/20035 paras 28,29,30,31.

76 This issue with respect to LGBT+ people have been addressed in the concurring opinion of Justice Engin Yıldırım, with reference to recent ECtHR judgments. *KAOS GL Association* App no 2018/20035 paras 22, 27, 31–32 (concurring opinion of Judge Engin Yıldırım); also see Engin Yıldırım, 'Missing a Landmark Moment or Treading on Thin Ice: Sexual Orientation and Gender Identity and the Turkish Constitutional Court' (2021) *Turkish Studies* 1, 10.

77 *Mehmet Aytaç* App no 2017/26514 para 52; *Kaos GL Derneği* App no 2014/18891 para 46.

78 *Fetullah Gülen* App no 2014/12225 para 41.

79 *Kaos GL Derneği* App no 2018/20035 para 33.

80 Scheppele (n 5) 547–549.

inition of hate speech in a manner that aligns with conservative policy preferences, potentially legitimising restrictions on freedom of expression and limiting space for critical discourse.

5.1 National Human Rights Institution's Selective Engagement with Human Rights and Hate Speech

Since its inception,[81] TİHEK has been subject to critique,[82] particularly regarding the legal framework underpinning the institution and the procedures followed during its establishment. Within the framework of the Paris Principles, institutional independence is regarded as a fundamental requirement for national human rights bodies yet TİHEK has been subject to substantial critique at the national level,[83] concerning its institutional independence and the criteria employed in the appointment of its board members.[84] The current structure, whereby board members are appointed directly by the President[85] and where safeguards against potential ideological influence are limited, raises concerns about the institution's impartiality and capacity to operate effectively, particularly in relation to politically sensitive matters.[86] Observers have also noted that the institution's priorities appear to align closely with governmental policy preferences often selectively engaging with human rights issues that reflect dominant conservative and relativist narratives.[87] In con-

---

81 The Human Rights Institute of Turkey was established in 2012 and was later restructured and transformed into the Human Rights and Equality Institution of Turkey (TİHEK) in 2016.

82 Kerem Altıparmak, *Köprüden Önce Son Çıkış: Türkiye İnsan Hakları Kurumu Kanun Tasarısı'nın Eleştirel Değerlendirilmesi* (AÜ SBF İnsan Hakları Merkezi Yayını, İnsan Hakları Çalışma Metinleri XIII, 2010) <www.academia.edu/10119470/K%C3%B6pr%C3%BCden_%C3%96nce_Son_%C3%87%C4%B1k%C4%B1%C5%9F_T%C3%BCrkiye_%C4%B0nsan_Haklar%C4%B1_Kurumu_Kanun_Tasar%C4%B1s%C4%B1n%C4%B1n_Ele%C5%9Ftirel_De%C4%9Ferlendirilmesi> accessed 1 August 2025.

83 Ulaş Karan, 'Bir İnsan Hakları Koruma Mekanizması Olarak Ulusal Eşitlik Kurumları: Kamu Denetçiliği Kurumu ve Türkiye İnsan Hakları ve Eşitlik Kurumu Örneği' in Ulaş Karan and D Çidem Sever, *Bir İnsan Hakları Koruma Mekanizması Olarak Ulusal Eşitlik Kurumları* (Eşit Haklar İçin İzleme Derneği 2020)

84 Law No 6701 on the Human Rights and Equality Institution of Turkey, art 8 (1) <www.tihek.gov.tr/en/pages/Law-on-the-Human-Rights-and-Equality-Institution-of-Turkiye> accessed 1 August 2025.

85 Law No 6701 art 10 (2).

86 Turan Kayaoğlu and Devran Gülel, 'National Human Rights Institutions and the Appropriation of Human Rights: The Case of the Human Rights and Equality Institution of Turkey' (2023) 29(2) *Australian Journal of Human Rights* 354, 365.

87 Karan (n 83) 20; Çalı and Demir-Gürsel (n 10) 275.

texts where a genuinely independent national human rights institution would be expected to address the broader human rights implications, the Institute's selective focus reinforces concerns about its autonomy and role within an increasingly constrained civic space.[88]

According to the TİHEK Law, the Institution may act upon individual applications, initiate investigations on its own initiative in cases of human rights and anti-discrimination violations, and carry out monitoring activities including thematic reports and unannounced visits to places where individuals are deprived of their liberty.[89] Despite the broad mandate granted under Article 9 of its founding law, TİHEK's authority to initiate investigations has exhibited a pattern of inconsistency and procedural ambiguity, as highlighted in a dedicated report on the issue.[90] It is also worth noting that more than half of the official statements concerning targeted national contexts and most of its decisions are absent from the Institute's English-language website.[91] It appears that the selective visibility of content on the Institute's multilingual platforms reflects more than a matter of translation or prioritisation.[92] The current English-language version of the Institute's website predominantly features state-

88 A recent example occurred during the March 2025 demonstrations, which followed the detention and subsequent arrest of Istanbul's elected mayor. While international human rights bodies and global media drew attention to concerns over disproportionate use of force and arbitrary detentions, TİHEK's only public intervention was a statement cautioning against insults allegedly made towards the President, his family, and his late mother. Türkiye İnsan Hakları ve Eşitlik Kurumu (TİHEK), 'İstanbul Saraçhane'de Gerçekleştirilen Gösteriler Hakkında Basın Açıklaması' (28 March 2025) <www.tihek.gov.tr/istanbul-sarachanede-gerceklestirilen-gosteriler-hakkinda-basin-aciklamasi> accessed 1 August 2025.

89 Law No 6701 on the Human Rights and Equality Institution of Turkey (n 80) art 9.

90 D Çiğdem Sever, *Türkiye İnsan Hakları ve Eşitlik Kurumu'nun Kabul Edilmezlik Kararları ve Resen İnceleme Yetkisine İlişkin Tutumu* (2024) <www.academia.edu/121558599/T%C3%BCrkiye_%C4%B0nsan_Haklar%C4%B1_ve_E%C5%9Fitlik_Kurumunun_Kabul_Edilmezlik_Kararlar%C4%B1_ve_Resen_%C4%B0nceleme_Yetkisine_%C4%B0li%C5%9Fkin_Tutumu> accessed 1 August 2025.

91 While it is not possible to fully substantiate this claim in the absence of comprehensive institutional transparency, a preliminary comparison of the press releases available on the English and Turkish versions of the Institute's website is indicative. As of August 2025, the earliest press releases available in the English-language section dates back to 2019, with a total of 91 press releases listed. In contrast, the Turkish-language section displays 199 press releases. This discrepancy suggests a selective international projection of the Institute's work, which may influence external perceptions of its activity and scope. <www.tihek.gov.tr/en/> accessed 1 August 2025.

92 As Derrida reminds us: 'there is no political power without control of the archive.' Jacques Derrida, *Archive Fever: A Freudian Impression* (Eric Prenowitz tr, University of Chicago Press 1996) 11.

ments on issues such as commemoration of international days and select discrimination concerns primarily relating to women, the elderly or migrants but places particular emphasis on topics that align with Turkey's contemporary foreign policy objectives such as combatting Islamophobia elsewhere[93] or only more recently on the humanitarian situation in Gaza.[94] This approach of the Institute projects a universalist image in matters of international responsibility, while withholding from global audiences more relativist statements and decisions in the national context.

The organisation's mandate does not explicitly encompass combating hate speech yet one might reasonably infer that a body dedicated primarily to countering discrimination could effectively undertake this role, even in the absence of an explicit mention. However, the Institute has demonstrated a notably inconsistent approach in accepting applications related to addressing hate speech.[95] As of 2025, only six publicly available decisions by the Institution explicitly address the term 'hate speech', five of which were found inadmissible.[96] Three of these applications concerned discriminatory statements targeting the Roma community, but all were rejected on the grounds that the applicant, an association advocating for Roma rights, had not been directly affected as a victim.[97] Of the two remaining cases, one was brought by an NGO requesting the Institution to take action against hate speech during election campaigns, which was also dismissed for lack of victim status.[98] The other involved allegations of hate speech based on disability and was deemed inadmissible on the basis that the expression had not resulted in a discriminatory act affecting the applicant.[99] Finally, a complaint brough by a pro-government union concerning a social media post by an academic criticising veiled women in the psychology profession was likewise found inadmissible due to the applicant's lack of victim status. However, in this instance, the Institution

---

93 Alexander Brown and Adriana Sinclair, *The Politics of Hate Speech Laws* (Routledge 2019) 80.

94 It is significant that Turkey's declaration of intervention in the *South Africa v. Israel* proceedings was submitted comparatively late, on 7 August 2024. <https://www.icj-cij.org/case/192/intervention> accessed 1 August 2025.

95 Sever (n 90) 12.

96 One must note that inconsistencies exist regarding the public availability of the of the Institute's decisions.

97 TİHEK, K. No: 2023/221, B. No: 2023/1293; TİHEK, *K. No: 2022/210, B. No: 2022/1196;* TİHEK, *K. No: 2023/44, B. No: 2023/121* <https://www.tihek.gov.tr/public/images/kararlar/cugzxr.03> accessed 1 August 2025.

98 TİHEK, *K. No: 2023/205, B. No: 2023/1322.*

99 TİHEK, K. No: 2024/311, B. No: 2024/15 <https://www.tihek.gov.tr/public/images/kararlar/4m8qeo.pdf> accessed 1 August 2025.

announced that it would nevertheless initiate an ex-officio investigation.[100] The fact that the Institution considered it necessary to act ex-officio in a case involving conservative and government-aligned concerns, while choosing not to do so in cases involving the Roma, a clearly identifiable and historically marginalised social group, raises concerns about the consistency, objectivity, and neutrality of its approach to hate speech. Although according to TİHEK technically neither applicant held victim status, the Institution's decision to act only in one of the two comparable contexts suggests a selective interpretation of its authority.

Institute's available public announcements indicate that its counter-hate speech interventions may be applied in a selective manner. For example, in one case involving hate speech based on religion published in a media organ, the Institute issued a broadly worded and symbolic statement without identifying the responsible media organ which was a pro-government newspaper.[101] In another incident, where a public figure was associated with similarly characterised hate speech, the Institute acted on its own initiative to condemn and explicitly disclosed the individual's identity.[102] In other words, while one condemnation focused on the nature of the discourse, the other centred on the identity of the offender concerned. The contrast between these responses raises questions regarding the consistency and neutrality of the standards applied in such determinations

In 2023 the Institution addressed hate speech along with discrimination based on religious ground in a politically sensitive case concerning statements made by a prominent pop singer, widely recognised for her liberal public image, and imposed an administrative fine in response.[103] During a performance with a limited audience, a humorous exchange between the singer and a

---

100 TİHEK, *K. No: 2023/245, B. No: 2023/1570*, para 3 <https://www.tihek.gov.tr/public/images/kararlar/cugzxr.03> accessed 1 August 2025.

101 Türkiye İnsan Hakları ve Eşitlik Kurumu (TİHEK), 'Alevilik İnancına Sahip Bireylere Yönelik Nefret Söylemi Barındıran İfadeler Hakkında Basın Açıklaması' (2022) <www.tihek.gov.tr/alevilik-inancina-sahip-bireylere-yonelik-nefret-soylemi-barindiran-ifadeler-hakkinda-basin-aciklamasi/> accessed 1 August 2025.

102 Türkiye İnsan Hakları ve Eşitlik Kurumu (TİHEK), 'Ses Sanatçısı Leman Sam'ın Farklı Milliyetten Kişilere Yönelik Ayrımcı İfadeleri Hakkında Basın Açıklaması' (5 August 2022) <www.tihek.gov.tr/ses-sanatcisi-leman-samin-farkli-milliyetten-kisilere-yonelik-ayrimci-ifadeleri-hakkinda-basin-aciklamasi> accessed 1 August 2025.

103 Although this case is cited in the Institute's annual report as an example of its actions against discrimination and hate speech, it is worth noting that the full decision is no longer accessible/available through the Institute's online database which reaffirms the criticisms concerning transparency of the Institute's decisions and actions further. <www.tihek.gov.tr/kategori/pages/kararlar> accessed 1 August 2025.

stage member about religious schools (*Imam Hatip*)[104] became the subject of a criminal investigation. During the performance, the singer remarked about her band member: "I think he studied at an Imam Hatip School; his perversion stems from there". However, the statement had actually been made nearly a year before the complaints were filed. The singer was charged under thecontroversial Article 216 of the Turkish Penal Code and was subsequently imprisoned for several days before being placed under house arrest.[105] Although, according to Article 45(1)(c) of the Regulation on the Implementation of the Law on the Human Rights and Equality Institution of Turkey (TİHEK), the Institution is not authorised to process applications that are already the subject of judicial proceedings, it nonetheless made assessments in this case while it was actively pending before the court, despite lacking jurisdiction.[106] In this case, which has been dominated by the public statements of the ruling party's head and ministers targeting the singer,[107] this pro-

104 While prior to the 2000s, graduates of Imam Hatip schools faced certain forms of discrimination, particularly in accessing higher education due to policies enforced by the Council of Higher Education (YÖK), this situation has changed markedly over the past two decades. Erdoğan has consistently expressed strong support for these schools, to the extent that referencing one's Imam Hatip background has become a common and even favourable element in résumés. The certain case, thus, became highly political due to the significance and mission Erdoğan attributes to Imam Hatip Schools. Bianet, 'PM Erdoğan Believes Religious Education Will Breed Obedience' (30 October 2012) <https://bianet.org/haber/pm-erdogan-believes-religious-education-will-breed-obedience-140924> accessed 1 August 2025.

105 It must be noted that although the singer was charged under Article 216/1 of the Turkish Criminal Code, she was ultimately sentenced to 10 months of imprisonment under Article 216/2 for publicly denigrating a section of the public, with the announcement of the verdict deferred. The criminal proceedings against the singer resulted in a ruling for the postponement of the pronouncement of the judgment (HAGB), a mechanism that was still in force at the time. As such rulings do not constitute final convictions, they are typically not made publicly accessible in full through open judicial databases. In a landmark decision delivered in August 2023, the Constitutional Court of Turkey annulled the legal provision regulating HAGB on the grounds that it violated the right to a fair trial by undermining the accused's ability to participate effectively in the proceedings and seek judicial remedies. The annulment took effect as of August 2024.

106 The Regulation further clarifies that if a case is brought before a court after an application is filed, the Institution must issue a decision of non-examination (art. 73). *Türkiye İnsan Hakları ve Eşitlik Kurumu Kanununun Uygulanmasına İlişkin Usul ve Esaslar Hakkında Yönetmelik*, RG no 29940 (24 November 2016) <https://kms.kaysis.gov.tr/Home/Goster/137654?AspxAutoDetectCookieSupport=1> accessed 1 August 2025.

107 İfade Özgürlüğü Derneği, *Gülşen Çolakoğlu Case Monitoring Report* (2023) <https://ifade.org.tr/reports/IFOD_GulsenColakoglu_MonitoringReport.pdf> para. 4, 5, 12. Accessed 1 August 2025.

cedural limitation was disregarded,[108] and the Institute proceeded to act upon three different yet simultaneous individual applications.[109] In their complaints, all three applicants grounded their claims of victimhood on the fact that they were graduates of these schools, alleging that the statement in question discriminated against them by inciting hostility and hatred, thereby stigmatising individuals associated with such educational backgrounds.[110]

TİHEK reviewed the application and the allegations concerning freedom of religion and discrimination, and, in this context, made reference to the ECtHR *Kokkinakis v. Greece* judgment, particularly the paragraph emphasising the importance of pluralism.[111] The decision also cited General Comment No. 22 of the ICCPR, interpreting it to affirm that freedom of religion includes the right to establish and attend religious schools in line with one's beliefs. TİHEK went further by linking attendance at *Imam Hatip* schools for religious vocational purposes to the protection of freedom of religion, in the context of the use of the term 'pervert'. According to TİHEK, the statements were deemed to promote hate based on religious intolerance, particularly given their delivery during a public concert and subsequent media amplification, and concluded that the expressions lacked an objective basis, heightened social tension, and crossed the threshold from legitimate criticism into discriminatory speech.[112]

Several factors, as also noted by other scholars, render the outcome of this decision controversial.[113] First and foremost, as it was addressed also in the dissenting opinions to the decision,[114] the complainants were neither part of the limited audience present at the event nor had they attempted to partici-

108 Zülfiye Yılmaz, '2023/345, 2023/346 ve 2023/347 Sayılı Kararlarına Dair Tespitler' (Eşitlik İzleme Merkezi, 5 January 2024) <www.esithaklar.org/2024/01/05/karar-analiz-dizisi-1-tihek-gulsen-karari/> accessed 1 August 2025.

109 TİHEK, B. No: 2022/1365, K. No: 2023/347, 2/5/2023; TİHEK, B. No: 2022/1307, K. No: 2023/346, 2/5/2023; TİHEK, B. No: 2022/1306, K. No: 2023/345, 2/5/2023 para 2. It must be emphasised that the official documents related to these decisions were either inaccessible or removed from the Institute's official decision database, and were instead obtained through the Association for Monitoring Equal Rights (AMER), an NGO actively working in this field.

110 Ibid para 2(ç).

111 Ibid paras 19, 21 Kokkinakis decision was somehow linked with the "forum externum" dimension of religion with respect to attending religious schools.

112 Ibid para 30.

113 Yılmaz (n 108).

114 Dissenting vote by Muharrem Kılıç and Dilek Ertürk on K. No: 347/2023; 345/2023; 346/2023.

pate in it.[115] Thus they lacked the victim status.[116] However, by disregarding both procedural and substantive legal standards as explained above, TİHEK proceeded to assess an alleged rights violation without meeting the fundamental criteria. Furthermore, although not elaborated or justified anywhere in the decision, it was based on the premise that graduates of religious schools constitute a distinct group allegedly subjected to discrimination on the grounds of religious belief. Yet the ruling contains no reference to any structural disadvantage or minority status, both of which are typically required in hate speech assessments. Ultimately, the decision lacks any reasoning on structural disadvantage or marginalisation, making it untenable to conclude that the singer intended to discriminate the group through hate speech. Yet the political character of the issue ultimately overrode both procedural safeguards and substantive merits, as centred squarely on the 'sensitivities' heavily emphasised by the ruling power. The entire project of disciplining society and shaping the borders of acceptable speech was indeed conducted under the banner of human rights; specifically, through the institutional framework of a national human rights body.

5.2 From Oversight to Overreach: RTÜK's Political Function in Turkey's Hate Speech Discourse

Institutional mechanisms in Turkey have increasingly been used to consolidate executive influence and suppress dissent. One such body in this regard is the Radio and Television Supreme Council (RTÜK), which was formally established in 1994 to regulate and liberalise the broadcasting sector.[117] RTÜK oversees radio, television, and on-demand broadcasts through a combination of

115 According to the Article 30 of the *Regulation on the Procedures and Principles Regarding the Implementation of the Law on TIHEK*, any natural or legal person who *benefits* from, has *applied to benefit from*, or *seeks information about services* such as education, judiciary, law enforcement, health care, transportation, communication, social security, social services, social assistance, sports, accommodation, culture, tourism, and similar public services, shall have *the right to apply* to the Institution on the grounds of *having suffered from a violation of the prohibition of discrimination*. (emphasis added).

116 It is particularly worth emphasising, as raised in dissenting views, that interpreting the concept of 'harm' too broadly or flexibly may lead to an unforeseeable expansion of the notion of 'victim', thereby allowing individuals who are not personally and directly affected by a discriminatory act to claim victimhood based on abstract or indirect grievances.

117 Mahir Akser and Burak Baybars, 'Repressed Media and Illiberal Politics in Turkey: The Persistence of Fear' (2022) 23 *Southeast European and Black Sea Studies* 159, 160.

regulatory approaches: direct inspections carried out by its experts, assessment of viewer complaints submitted via hotlines and digital platforms, and self-monitoring by broadcasters guided by ethical broadcasting principles and audience representatives.[118] RTÜK's institutional independence has been a persistent concern, given that its members are appointed by parliament based on nominations from political parties in proportion to their representation. Although this appointment method appears rational at first glance, the parliamentary majority is directly reflected in the Council's composition, raising concerns over institutional impartiality.[119] RTÜK has frequently been the subject of criticism for alleged partiality in its regulatory decisions, particularly for imposing disproportionate sanctions on media organs critical of government policies.[120] Attempts to initiate parliamentary inquiries into RTÜK's sanctioning practices have also been blocked by the ruling coalition,[121] further reinforcing concerns regarding political interference and the lack of regulatory independence. Even though the decisions made by the Council are open to judicial review by administrative courts, its power to impose administrative fines, suspend programs, or halt broadcasts poses serious concerns, as the immediate enforcement of such measures not only blocks the public's right to receive information but also exerts a chilling effect on journalistic freedom and critical expression.[122] Moreover, the fact that its decisions are enforceable without delay results in broadcast interruptions during periods when the public's right to receive information and access truthful reporting is critically needed.[123]

---

118 Dilek Kurban, Ceren Sözeri, *İktidarın Çarkında Medya: Türkiye'de Medya Bağımsızlığı ve Özgürlüğü Önündeki Siyasi, Yasal ve Ekonomik Engeller* (TESEV Yayınları 2012) 21 <https://www.tesev.org.tr/wp-content/uploads/rapor_Iktidarin_Carkinda_Medya.pdf> accessed 1 August 2025.

119 Law No 6112 on the Establishment of Radio and Television Enterprises and Their Media Services (15 February 2011, RG No 27863) art 35.

120 Council of Europe Commissioner for Human Rights, *Memorandum on Freedom of Expression and Media Freedom in Turkey* (15 February 2017) CommDH(2017)5, para 29 <https://rm.coe.int/ref/CommDH(2017)5> accessed 1 August 2025.

121 <www.tbmm.gov.tr/Denetim/Meclis-Arastirma-Onergesi-Detay/f72877c2-412a-037b-e050-007f01005610> accessed 1 August 2025.

122 Council of Europe Commissioner for Human Rights, *Memorandum on Freedom of Expression and of the Media, Human Rights Defenders and Civil Society in Türkiye* (15 February 2023) CommDH(2023)10, para 13 <www.coe.int/en/web/commissioner/-/turkiye-authorities-should-restore-full-enjoyment-of-fundamental-freedoms> accessed 1 August 2025.

123 <https://bianet.org/haber/pro-opposition-tv-channel-handed-10-day-blackout-over-imamoglu-protest-coverage-305913> accessed 1 August 2025.

Research has pointed to a pattern in which the Council's interpretations of terms such as 'neutrality' and 'public morality' have been selectively applied, often in a manner that affects coverage of politically sensitive issues, including opposition viewpoints, minority rights, and LGBT+ representation.[124] Article 8 of the RTÜK Law, titled 'Principles of Broadcasting Services', is intended to safeguard freedom of expression by prohibiting certain forms of harmful content. Two specific provisions are most relevant for potentially addressing hate speech:

> (b) broadcasts may not incite hatred and hostility in society or provoke feelings of hatred by making distinctions based on race, language, religion, gender, class, region, or sect; and (e) they shall not include or promote content that discriminates against or denigrates individuals on the basis of race, colour, language, religion, nationality, gender, disability, political or philosophical belief, sect, or similar grounds.[125]

RTÜK's implementation of such provisions over the years has given rise to concerns over selective and inconsistent enforcement. In decisions where RTÜK has imposed sanctions on the grounds of hate speech, the protected individual group or value has often been identified as the AKP voters,[126] the 'political position where AKP defines itself'[127] the Presidency, or the Directorate of Religious Affairs.[128] This politically selective and unsubstantiated use of the hate speech framework has, in effect, positioned the institution as an actor in re-defining and interpreting what constitutes hate speech, and risks transforming the concept into a catch-all justification for restricting content that is merely unfavourable.[129] One way to observe the inconsistency of RTÜK's 'sen-

---

124 Kurban and Sözeri, n (118), 41.

125 Law No 6112 (n 106) art 8(b), (e).

126 RTÜK, Karar No. 39, T. No. 2023/51; RTÜK, Karar No. 14, T. No. 2023/44; RTÜK, Karar No. 25, T. No. 2024/11. In all of these examples, commentators appearing on television programs made remarks about the electoral process, during which they criticised voters who supported the AKP and its allied parties by portraying them as "ignorant", "unconscious" or possessing a "disturbed mental state". Consequently, such discourse has been classified under the category of hate speech in RTÜK decisions.

127 RTÜK, Karar No. 30, T. No. 2016/15.

128 RTÜK, Karar No. 10, T. No. 2020/27; RTÜK, Karar No. 7, T. No. 2022/32.

129 One of the earliest references of this kind can be found in a 2014 decision, issued prior to the coup attempt, in which a programme referring to a group of individuals as "plot martyrs" (*kumpas şehidi*) was classified as hate speech – specifically in relation to individuals and groups later understood to be linked to the coup attempt. RTÜK, Karar No. 15, T. No. 2014/30.

sitivity' toward hate speech is through the record-high penalty it imposed in 2023 on Halk TV, after Esmeray, a trans woman and political figure, spoke about hate crimes against LGBT+ people and affirmed her existence by stating that living in Turkey as a trans woman meant the country belonged to her too, which RTÜK deemed contrary to public morality, national values, and the protection of the family.[130] As this example also illustrates, the Council's regulatory practices towards combating hate appear to align more closely with prevailing political agendas than with the promotion of pluralistic discourse.[131] Furthermore, while RTÜK legislation does not explicitly prohibit 'insulting religion' and only prohibits discrimination on religious and other grounds; religious criticism is frequently treated as sanctionable.[132] In this context, RTÜK fined Halk TV, one of the most frequently sanctioned channels due to its critical stance toward the government, for allegedly violating the principle prohibiting discriminatory or degrading content. The sanction was triggered by the remarks of a commentator, who referred to the problems and underdevelopment in Islamic geographies with a comparison to the "Middle Ages". This observation alone was sufficient to activate RTÜK's institutional 'sensitivities' and led the authority to reframe the matter under the guise of hate speech and discrimination.[133]

The examination of the Institute's available decisions[134] reveals how the concept of hate speech and provoking to hatred is inconsistently cited and applied in different contexts. A recent and particularly ironic example in this sense is the case of Açık Radyo.[135] Although according to media watch re-

130 RTÜK, Karar No 42, T. No 2023/51.

131 In this respect, monitoring reports have highlighted that cases in which the Council issued sanctions in response to hate speech directed at minority groups remain exceptionally limited. Kurban and Sözeri, (n 113) 41.

132 Yıldırım, Çamdereli and Şirin (n 51 *Hate Speech and Discriminatory Discourse in Media: 2019 Report*) 72; Media and Law Studies Association, *30 Years of Censorship: 30th Anniversary of the Radio and Television Supreme Council* (MLSA 2024) 6, 21. <www.mlsaturkey.com/images/RAPORLAR/RTUK%20REPORT%20ENGLISH%20Version.pdf> accessed 1 August 2025.

133 RTÜK, K. No: 20419 <https://www.rtuk.gov.tr/UstKurulKarar/Detay/20419> accessed 1 August 2025.

134 A search conducted on a case law database LEXPERA, which also includes the institution's decisions, revealed 216 rulings containing only the word 'hate' as of May 2025. When the search is expanded to 'hate crime', the number of relevant decisions drops to 73. If the search is limited strictly to the phrase "hate speech", the number further decreases to 17 decisions, the earliest of which dates back to 2012. All of these 17 decisions have been reviewed by the author.

135 Freedom House, 'Turkey: Freedom of Press and Expression Groups Condemn Broadcast Regulator's Silencing of Açık Radyo' (Freedom House, 3 July 2024) <https://free

ports[136] Armenian citizens are among the minority groups most frequently targeted by hate speech, RTÜK claimed that the use of the term 'Armenian genocide' during a radio program on Açık Radyo incited hatred and hostility. On this basis, it imposed a monetary fine and suspended the broadcast, and eventually revoked the station's license altogether.[137] In doing so, RTÜK, by relying on the concept of hate, decided to punish a historical expression, which has, in fact, been explicitly found not to constitute a criminal offence and to be protected under freedom of expression by both the Constitutional Court and the ECtHR.[138]

In cases involving television programmes broadcast on channels closely linked to the ruling party, statements against minorities appear to be interpreted in the most lenient way[139] whereas similar or milder statements on government critical channels are often subjected to much stricter scrutiny.[140] In instances where critical artistic content is perceived to bear even a slight resemblance to the ruling party, RTÜK tends to scrutinise and overinterpret metaphors or symbolic expressions in detail, sometimes invoking the concept of hate speech and resulting in punitive measures.[141] The largest fine ever imposed in RTÜK's history in this sense was issued to Fox TV during the presidential elections in response to a journalist's remarks made during a live broadcast, particularly focusing on the statement "democracy is not limited to the ballot box".[142] Although the decision cited this statement as incitement to hatred and hostility among the public, the legal reasoning fails to establish how the journalist's words constituted hate speech. While the decision references sources ranging from Baudrillard's theory of hyperreality to the ECtHR judgment in *Times Newspapers Ltd v United Kingdom*, no concrete legal explanation is offered as to how the journalist's expression provoked feelings of

---

domhouse.org/article/turkey-freedom-press-and-expression-groups-condemn-broad cast-regulators-silencing-acik> accessed 1 August 2025.

136 *Hate Speech and Discriminatory Discourse in Media: 2019 Report* n (43).

137 RTÜK, Karar No. 21, T. No. 2024/20 T. 22.5.2024.

138 Constitutional Court of Turkey, *İlker Deniz Yücel*, App No 2017/16589, 28 May 2019, § 85; *Altuğ Taner Akçam v Turkey* App no 27520/07.

139 RTÜK, Karar No 38, T. No 2012/62; RTÜK, Karar No 13, T. No 2023/23; RTÜK, Karar No 6, T. No 2020/21;

140 In this sense the clauses of the RTÜK Law that are applicable to hate speech and incitement to hate is mostly used against certain media organs. Only some these decisions are: RTÜK, Karar No. 39, T. No. 2023/51; RTÜK, Karar No. 14, T. No. 2023/44; RTÜK, Karar No. 25, T. No. 2024/11; RTÜK, Karar No: 7, T No: 2026/25; RTÜK, Karar No: 16, T No: 2025/10.

141 Kurban and Sözeri n (118).

142 RTÜK, Karar No 13, T. No 2023/23.

hatred by making distinctions based on race, language, religion, gender, class, region, or sect.[143]

It appears that the Institute at times invokes international human rights norms and decisions in an effort to enhance its legitimacy. However, in displaying this kind of 'performative legalism' through selectively quoting ECtHR case law, it occasionally relies on irrelevant or decontextualised sources.[144] This suggests an instrumental use of legal references aimed more at supporting predetermined claims than at engaging with legal standards in a coherent or consistent manner. Despite RTÜK's stated commitment to addressing hate speech, including through panel discussions,[145] in a context of political alignment and institutional control, the regulatory body not only fails to safeguard minority groups or prevent discriminatory speech,[146] but also appears to instrumentalise the concept of hate speech in a selectively manner.

6 Conclusion

In the context of Turkey, the concept hate speech has been selectively redeployed in line with the ideological and moral 'sensibilities' of the current political regime. Although derived from international human rights frameworks, its practical application increasingly reflects political imperatives rather than a consistent legal commitment to pluralism or freedom of expression. Rather than constraining the abuse of power, hate speech related regulation now functions predominantly as a mechanism for disciplining dissent and reinforcing dominant narratives. This transformation is particularly evident in the operations of quasi-independent institutions such as RTÜK and TİHEK, whose interventions often mirror executive-defined sensitivities rather than universal rights-based standards.

Importantly, this pattern does not emerge in isolation. While the current political logic is shaped by authoritarian-populist tendencies, it is facilitated by historical constraints on freedom of expression and a legal tradition that prioritises state-defined moral unity over open contestation. Moreover, these developments unfold within a broader context of democratic erosion and the weakening of institutional guarantees for human rights in Turkey. Although

143 Ibid.

144 Such as the ILO's definition of workplace discrimination. RTÜK, Karar No. 29, T. No. 2024/43.

145 <www.rtuk.gov.tr/medyada-nefret-soylemi-paneli/4730> accessed 1 August 2025.

146 <www.mlsaturkey.com/en/rtuek-fines-for-lgbt-representation-supports-anti-lgbt-hate-rally > accessed 1 August 2025.

today's context differs in form and intensity from the past, past and present converge in sustaining a restrictive framework that limits the boundaries of permissible speech and institutionalises ideological selectivity.

In this light, Turkey's case presents strong indicators of what may be understood as a form of rights misappropriation. While not an exact fit with any singular definition, the observed patterns closely resemble a process in which the language of human rights is retained but repurposed to legitimise ideological control. Hate speech, in this context, is no longer invoked to combat exclusion or harm, but to protect political orthodoxy. The implications of this shift go beyond legal interpretation, pointing to a broader transformation in the function of rights discourse, from a constraint on authority to a strategic extension of it.

Bibliography

Adalet Bakanlığı, Adalet İstatistikleri 2024-Turkish and English Judicial Statistics(2024) <https://adlisicil.adalet.gov.tr/Resimler/SayfaDokuman/7042025092455Adalet_İstatistikleri_2024%20Türkçe_Ingilizce.pdf> accessed 1 August 2025.

'Ahmet Davutoğlu'ndan Fazıl Say yorumu' (*YouTube*, 5 March 2014) <www.youtube.com/watch?v=1MCDtWjdI6k> accessed 1 August 2025.

Akbaş K and Şen İG, 'How Did a Safeguard for Disadvantaged Groups Turn into the Weapon of Oppression?: Normative Distortion of the Article 216 of the Turkish Penal Code' (2020) 7 *Ankara Bar Review* 1.

Akdeniz Y and Altıparmak K, *Turkey: Freedom of Expression in Jeopardy* (ARTICLE 19, July 2016) <www.article19.org/resources/turkey-freedom-of-expression-in-jeopardy> accessed 1 August 2025.

Akser M and Baybars B, 'Repressed Media and Illiberal Politics in Turkey: The Persistence of Fear' (2022) 23 *Southeast European and Black Sea Studies* 159.

Algan B, 'The Brand New Version of Article 301 of the Turkish Penal Code and Its Loss of Legitimacy' (2008) 9(12) *German Law Journal* 2237.

Altıparmak K, *Köprüden Önce Son Çıkış: Türkiye İnsan Hakları Kurumu Kanun Tasarısı'nın Eleştirel Değerlendirilmesi* (AÜ SBF İnsan Hakları Merkezi Yayını, İnsan Hakları Çalışma, Metinleri XIII, 2010) <www.academia.edu/10119470> accessed 1 August 2025.

Arat Kabasakal ZF, 'Collisions and Crossroads: Introducing Human Rights in Turkey' in Kabasakal Arat ZF (ed), *Human Rights in Turkey* (University of Pennsylvania Press 2007) 1.

Arslan Z, 'Türkiye'de İstisna Hâli, Terör ve İfade Özgürlüğü' (2007) 71 *Türkiye Barolar Birliği Dergisi* 201.

Babül E M, *Bureaucratic Intimacies: Translating Human Rights in Turkey* (Stanford University Press 2017).

Belge C, 'Friends of the Court: The Republican Alliance and Selective Activism of the Constitutional Court of Turkey' (2006) 40(3) *Law & Society Review* 653.

Between Two Elections – Z Report on Hate Speech on Twitter (2023) <https://hrantdink.org/en/asulis/activities/projects/media-watch-on-hate-speech/3986-between-two-elections-z-report-on-hate-speech-on-twitter> accessed 1 August 2025.

Bianet, 'Erdoğan at UN Hate Speech Event: "There Are Pork-Eaters in Our Country, We Don't Interfere"' (25 September 2019) <https://bianet.org/haber/erdogan-at-un-hate-speech-event-there-are-pork-eaters-in-our-country-we-don-t-interfere-213553> accessed 1 August 2025.

Bianet, 'Pro-Government Daily Yeni Akit Not Prosecuted for Calling LGBTI+s "Dishonorable Faggots"' (11 March 2020) <https://bianet.org/haber/pro-government-daily-yeni-akit-not-prosecuted-for-calling-lgbti-s-dishonorable-faggots-218651> accessed 1 August 2025.

Bianet, 'Insulting Erdoğan: Nearly 10,000 People Stood Trial in a Year, Including 290 Children' (6 September 2021) <https://bianet.org/haber/insulting-erdogan-nearly-10-000-people-stood-trial-in-a-year-including-290-children-247507> accessed 1 August 2025.

Bianet, 'PM Erdoğan Believes Religious Education Will Breed Obedience' (30 October 2012) <https://bianet.org/haber/pm-erdogan-believes-religious-education-will-breed-obedience-140924> accessed 1 August 2025.

Bora T, *Zamanın Kelimeleri: Türkiye'nin Siyasi Dili* (İletişim Yayınları 2018).

Brown A and Sinclair A, *The Politics of Hate Speech Laws* (Routledge 2019).

Çalı B, 'Human Rights Discourse and Domestic Human Rights NGOs' in Kabasakal Arat ZF (ed), *Human Rights in Turkey* (University of Pennsylvania Press 2007).

Çalı B and Demir-Gürsel E, 'Continuity and Change in Human Rights Appropriation: The Case of Turkey' (2023) 21 *International Journal of Constitutional Law* 266.

Çalışkan K, 'Toward a New Political Regime in Turkey: From Competitive toward Full Authoritarianism' (2018) 58 *New Perspectives on Turkey* 5.

Council of Europe Commissioner for Human Rights, *Memorandum on Freedom of Expression and Media Freedom in Turkey* (15 February 2017) CommDH (2017) 5 <https://rm.coe.int/ref/CommDH(2017)5> accessed 1 August 2025.

Council of Europe Commissioner for Human Rights, *Memorandum on Freedom of Expression and of the Media, Human Rights Defenders and Civil Society in Türkiye* (15 February 2023) CommDH(2023)10 <www.coe.int/en/web/commissioner/-/turkiye-authorities-should-restore-full-enjoyment-of-fundamental-freedoms> accessed 1 August 2025.

de Bruijn P, 'of Minarets and Bayonets: the Poem that Landed Erdoğan in Jail' in Yenen A and Zürcher E-J (eds), *A Hundred Years of Republican Turkey: A History in a Hundred Fragments* (Leiden University Press 2023) 412.

de Búrca G and Young KG, 'The (Mis)appropriation of Human Rights by the New Global Right: An Introduction to the Symposium' (2023) 21 *International Journal of Constitutional Law* 205.

Derrida J, *Archive Fever: A Freudian Impression* (Eric Prenowitz tr, University of Chicago Press 1996).

Douzinas C, *Human Rights and Empire: The Political Philosophy of Cosmopolitanism* (Routledge-Cavendish 2007).

Famous Turkish lawyer Feyza Altun detained over sharia remark <www.duvarenglish.com/famous-turkish-lawyer-feyza-altun-detained-over-sharia-remark-news-63861> accessed 1 August 2025.

Esen B, 'Competitive Authoritarianism in Turkey under the AKP Rule' in Akçali E (ed), *The Routledge Handbook on Contemporary Turkey* (Routledge 2021) 153.

Freedom House, *Turkey: Freedom in the World 2025* (Freedom House, 2025) <https://freedomhouse.org/country/turkey/freedom-world/2025> accessed 1 August 2025.

Hate Speech and Discriminatory Discourse in Media: 2019 Report (November 2020) <https://hrantdink.org/attachments/article/2727/Hate-Speech-and-Discriminatory-Discourse-in-Media-2019.pdf> accessed 1 August 2025.

Hate Speech and Discriminatory Discourse in Media 2018 Report, 20 <https://hrantdink.org/en/asulis/publications/75-media-watch-on-hate-speech-reports/2304-hate-speech-and-discriminatory-discourse-in-media-2018-report> accessed 1 August 2025.

Human Rights Watch, World Report 2022: Turkey (HRW, 2022) <https://www.hrw.org/world-report/2022/country-chapters/turkey> accessed 1 August 2025.

HÜDA PAR, *Party Statute (English)* <https://files.hudapar.org/media/StatikIcerikGorselleri/Yayinlar/PdfDosyalari/ingilizce.pdf> accessed 1 August 2025.

İfade Özgürlüğü Derneği, *Gülşen Çolakoğlu Case Monitoring Report* (2023) <https://ifade.org.tr/reports/IFOD_GulsenColakoglu_MonitoringReport.pdf> accessed 1 August 2025.

Karan U, 'Bir İnsan Hakları Koruma Mekanizması Olarak Ulusal Eşitlik Kurumları: Kamu Denetçiliği Kurumu Ve Türkiye İnsan Hakları Ve Eşitlik Kurumu Örneği' in Karan U and Sever DÇ, *Bir İnsan Hakları Koruma Mekanizması Olarak Ulusal Eşitlik Kurumları* (Eşit Haklar İçin İzleme Derneği 2020).

Kayaoğlu T and Gülel D, 'National Human Rights Institutions and the Appropriation of Human Rights: The Case of the Human Rights and Equality Institution of Turkey' (2023) 29(2) *Australian Journal of Human Rights* 354.

Kurban D and Sözeri C, *İktidarın Çarkında Medya: Türkiye'de Medya Bağımsızlığı ve Özgürlüğü Önündeki Siyasi, Yasal ve Ekonomik Engeller* (TESEV Yayınları 2012) <https://tesev.org.tr/yayin/iktidarin-carkinda-medya-turkiyede-medya-bagimsizl

igi-ve-ozgurlugu-onundeki-siyasi-yasal-ve-ekonomik-engeller/> accessed 1 August 2025.

Mancini S and Rosenfeld M, 'Nationalism, Populism, Religion, and the Quest to Reframe Fundamental Rights' (2020) 42 *Cardozo Law Review* 464.

Meclis Araştırma Önergesi <https://www.tbmm.gov.tr/Denetim/Meclis-Arastirma-Onergesi-Detay/f72877c2-412a-037b-e050-007f01005610> accessed 1 August 2025.

Medyada Nefret Söylemi Paneli <https://www.rtuk.gov.tr/medyada-nefret-soylemi-paneli/4730> accessed 1 August 2025.

McKernan B, 'Protests in Turkey over satirical magazine's alleged Prophet Muhammad cartoon' *The Guardian* (London, 1 July 2025) <https://www.theguardian.com/world/2025/jul/01/istanbul-turkey-leman-magazine-alleged-prophet-muhammad-cartoon-protests-arrests> accessed 1 August 2025.

Mégret F, 'Human Rights Populism' (2022) 13 *Humanity: An International Journal of Human Rights, Humanitarianism, and Development* 240.

MHP, *2024 Party Program* <https://www.mhp.org.tr/usr_img/_mhp2007/kitaplar/mhp_partiprogrami_2024.pdf> accessed 1 August 2025.

Mutluer N, 'Diyanet's Role in Building the "Yeni (New) Milli" in the AKP Era' (2018) 27 *European Journal of Turkish Studies* 1.

Mutua M, *Human Rights: A Political and Cultural Critique* (University of Pennsylvania Press 2002).

Özbudun E, 'Democratization Reforms in Turkey, 1993–2004' (2007) 8(2) *Turkish Studies* 179.

Parliamentary Assembly of the Council of Europe (PACE), Resolution 1805 (2007).

Presidency of the Republic of Türkiye, 'We Will Continue to Spearhead All Efforts to Actively Fight against Rising Islamophobia, Racism and Hate Speech' (5 March 2024)<https://www.tccb.gov.tr/en/news/542/109827/-we-will-continue-to-spear-head-all-efforts-to-actively-fight-against-rising-islamophobia-racism-and-hate-sp-eech-> accessed 1 August 2025.

Pro-opposition TV channel handed 10-day blackout over İmamoğlu protest coverage <https://bianet.org/haber/pro-opposition-tv-channel-handed-10-day-blackout-ov-er-imamoglu-protest-coverage-305913> accessed 1 August 2025.

Republic of Turkey Directorate of Communications, *Statement Regarding Turkey's Withdrawal from the Istanbul Convention* (20 March 2021) <https://www.iletisim.gov.tr/english/haberler/detay/statement-regarding-turkeys-withdrawal-from-the-istanbul-convention> accessed 1 August 2025.

Reuters, 'Nearly 2,000 Legal Cases Opened for Insulting Turkey's Erdogan' (2 March 2016) <https://www.reuters.com/article/world/nearly-2000-legal-cases-opened-for-insulting-turkeys-erdogan-idUSKCN0W42HM> accessed 1 August 2025.

RTÜK Fines for LGBT Representation, Supports Anti-LGBT Hate Rally' <https://www.mlsaturkey.com/en/rtuek-fines-for-lgbt-representation-supports-anti-lgbt-hate-rally> accessed 1 August 2025.

Sever DÇ, *Türkiye İnsan Hakları ve Eşitlik Kurumu'nun Kabul Edilmezlik Kararları ve Resen İnceleme Yetkisine İlişkin Tutumu* (2024) <https://www.academia.edu/121558599> accessed 1 August 2025

Scheppele KL, 'Autocratic Legalism' (2018) 85(2) *University of Chicago Law Review* 545.

Stoeckl K, 'Traditional Values, Family, Homeschooling: The Role of Russia and the Russian Orthodox Church in Transnational Moral Conservative Networks and Their Efforts at Reshaping Human Rights' (2023) 21 *International Journal of Constitutional Law* 224.

Susma Platformu, *Ocak-Aralık 2024 İzleme Raporu* (Susma Platformu 2025) 16 <https://susma24.com/raporlar> accessed 1 August 2025.

Topuz H, *Paris'te Bir Türk Ressam: Fikret Mualla'nın Yaşamı* (6th edn, Remzi Kitabevi 2014).

Türkiye İnsan Hakları ve Eşitlik Kurumu (TİHEK), 'İstanbul Saraçhane'de Gerçekleştirilen Gösteriler Hakkında Basın Açıklaması' (28 March 2025) <https://www.tihek.gov.tr/istanbul-sarachanede-gerceklestirilen-gosteriler-hakkinda-basin-aciklamasi> accessed 1 August 2025.

UN Human Rights Committee, General Comment No 34: Article 19: Freedoms of Opinion and Expression (12 September 2011) UN Doc CCPR/C/GC/34.

UN News, 'UN Human Rights Office "Deeply Concerned" by Turkey's New Disinformation Law' (2022) <https://news.un.org/en/story/2022/10/1129567> accessed 1 August 2025.

Turkish court arrests two minors over degrading religious values <www.duvarenglish.com/turkish-court-arrests-two-minors-over-degrading-religious-values-news-63149> accessed 1 August 2025.

Turkish court arrests woman for insulting president in street interview <www.duvarenglish.com/turkish-court-arrests-woman-for-insulting-president-in-street-interview-news-64798> accessed 1 August 2025.

Türkiye İnsan Hakları ve Eşitlik Kurumu (TİHEK), 'Alevilik İnancına Sahip Bireylere Yönelik Nefret Söylemi Barındıran İfadeler Hakkında Basın Açıklaması' (2022) <www.tihek.gov.tr/alevilik-inancina-sahip-bireylere-yonelik-nefret-soylemi-barindiran-ifadeler-hakkinda-basin-aciklamasi/> accessed 1 August 2025.

Türkiye İnsan Hakları ve Eşitlik Kurumu (TİHEK), 'Ses Sanatçısı Leman Sam'ın Farklı Milliyetten Kişilere Yönelik Ayrımcı İfadeleri Hakkında Basın Açıklaması' (2022) <www.tihek.gov.tr/ses-sanatcisi-leman-samin-farkli-milliyetten-kisilere-yonelik-ayrimci-ifadeleri-hakkinda-basin-aciklamasi> accessed 1 August 2025.

UN Human Rights Office of the High Commissioner, 'USA: Free Speech on Campus Needs to Be Protected, Not Attacked, Say Experts' (OHCHR, 25 July 2024)

<www.ohchr.org/en/press-releases/2024/07/usa-free-speech-campus-needs-be-protected-not-attacked-say-experts> accessed 1 August 2025.

UN Human Rights Committee, *General Comment No 34: Article 19: Freedoms of Opinion and Expression* (12 September 2011) UN Doc CCPR/C/GC/34.

United Nations Office of the High Commissioner for Human Rights, *Rabat Plan of Action on the Prohibition of Advocacy of National, Racial or Religious Hatred that Constitutes Incitement to Discrimination, Hostility or Violence* (OHCHR 2012).

Ünlü B, *Türklük Sözleşmesi* (Dipnot Yayınları 2019).

Venice Commission, *Turkey – Opinion on the Amendments to the Criminal Code by Law No 7418 of 13 October 2022 and Their Application*, CDL-PI(2022)032 (19 December 2022).

Venice Commission, *Opinion on Articles 216, 299, 301 and 314 of the Penal Code of Turkey* CDL-AD(2016)002 (11–12 March 2016).

Venice Commission, *Report on the Relationship between Freedom of Expression and Freedom of Religion: The Issue of Regulation and Prosecution of Blasphemy, Religious Insult and Incitement to Religious Hatred* CDL-AD(2008)026.

Venice Commission, *Opinion on Article 122 of the Turkish Penal Code* CDL-REF (2016)011.

Verza S, *Opinion Crimes in Italy and in Turkey: Balancing the Right to Freedom of Expression with the Defence of National Security and Public Order* (Master's thesis, Università di Trento 2016).

World Justice Project, *Rule of Law Index 2023: Turkey Country Data* (World Justice Project, 2023) <https://worldjusticeproject.org/rule-of-law-index/country/2023/Turkey> accessed 1 August 2025.

Yaman S and Hürtaş S, *Liberal Perspektif Rapor: Yapısal Reformlar Projesi RTÜK*, no 38 (Freedom Research Association 2024).

Yeniden Refah Partisi, *Party Statute* <https://yenidenrefahpartisi.org.tr/page/parti-tuzugu/12> accessed 1 August 2025.

Yıldırım M, Çamdereli R and Şirin T, *A Human Rights Perspective on the Multi-faceted Right (Not) to Believe in Türkiye* (Norwegian Helsinki Committee, Freedom of Belief Initiative Report 2025) <https://inancozgurlugugirisimi.org/en/new-report-a-human-rights-perspective-on-the-multi-faceted-right-not-to-believe-in-turkiye/> accessed 1 August 2025.

Yıldırım E, 'Missing a Landmark Moment or Treading on Thin Ice: Sexual Orientation and Gender Identity and the Turkish Constitutional Court' (2021) *Turkish Studies* 119.

Yılmaz Z, '2023/345, 2023/346 ve 2023/347 Sayılı Kararlarına Dair Tespitler' (Eşitlik İzleme Merkezi, 5 January 2024) <www.esithaklar.org/2024/01/05/karar-analiz-dizisi-1-tihek-gulsen-karari/> accessed 1 August 2025.

Zürcher E J, *Turkey: A Modern History, Revised Edition* (I.B. Tauris 2004).

CHAPTER 5

Russia's Arguments to Justify the War in Ukraine and Their Abuse of Human Rights Appeals

Egbert Fortuin, Henrike Jansen, Wiktor Pawłowski and Levina de Wolf

1 Introduction

This contribution examines the arguments put forth by the Russian Federation to justify its full-scale invasion of Ukraine on 24 February 2022, which followed the invasion of 2014. To this end, we will make use of the Pragma-Dialectical theory of argumentation and insights about language use based on Grice (1975). As will be demonstrated, Russia frequently invokes the discourse of human rights – particularly the rights of Russian-speaking populations of Ukraine – as well as international agreements and rules to legitimise its actions. The objective of this contribution is to provide a systematic analysis and evaluation of the arguments employed by Russia to invade Ukraine, which can be characterised in terms of misappropriation of human rights or, more broadly, misappropriation of legal principles. In this context, the term 'misappropriation of human rights' is understood as the misuse, distortion, or exploitation of the concept of human rights for purposes that contradict their original intent and undermine their core values. This misappropriation of human rights and the mimicry of the language characteristic of them is part of a contemporary global trend of nationalist, populist, and authoritarian groups and actors that instrumentalise legal principles and rights as part of rhetorical and legal strategies to silence opponents and gain support for what typically are repressive and illiberal agendas.[1] In the process of doing so, these

1 Clifford Bob, *Rights as Weapons: Instruments of Conflict, Tools of Power* (Princeton University Press 2019) 4, 13–15; Frédéric Mégret, 'Human Rights Populism' (2022) 13 Humanity: An International Journal of Human Rights, Humanitarianism, and Development 240, 241, 255–256 <DOI: 10.1353/hum.2022.0010>; Gráinne De Búrca and Katharine G Young, 'The (Mis)Appropriation of Human Rights by the New Global Right: An Introduction to the Symposium' (2023) 21 International Journal of Constitutional Law 205, 207, 210, 213, 222 <DOI: 10.1093/icon/moad019>.

groups and actors often present themselves as important defenders of human rights.[2]

The central research questions guiding this study can be formulated as follows:

I. What arguments appealing to human rights does Russia use to justify the war against Ukraine?
II. How can these arguments be evaluated based on standards of sound communication and argumentation?
III. What can we learn from this when it comes to the misappropriation of human rights?

Our contribution has the following structure. In Section 2, we provide the theoretical framework for our analysis. In Section 3, we provide a general overview of Russia's justification (argumentation) of the war as put forward in three important speeches by Russian president Vladimir Putin. In Section 4, we provide an analysis of the arguments used by Russia to start the war, focusing on the argument of the violation of human rights of Russians by Ukraine. In Section 5, we present a more general discussion of the argumentation that is used by Russia with respect to human rights, applying insights from argumentation theory and communication theory. This section provides a more general approach of how to determine misappropriation of human rights, and how one can use insights from argumentation theories and theories of communication. In Section 6, we provide our conclusion.

2 Theoretical Embedding

The utterances of Russian government officials can be studied as instances of political discourse, but they can also be seen as part of the Russian propaganda. The term 'propaganda' is defined differently by different people.[3] Using insights from these various studies, we use the term as follows:

---

2 Mégret, 'Human Rights Populism' (n 1) 241.

3 For various definitions see for example J Michael Sproule, 'Channels of Propaganda' (ERIC/EDINFO Press, Indiana University 1994) 2; Stanley B Cunningham, *The Idea of Propaganda: A Reconstruction* (Praeger 2002); Garth Samuel Jowett and Victoria O'Donnell, *Propaganda and Persuasion* (5th edn, Sage 2008) 6; Jason Stanley, *How Propaganda Works* (Princeton University Press 2015) 39 <DOI: 10.1515/9781400865802>; Bruce L Smith, 'Propaganda', *Encyclopedia Britannica* (2016) <www.britannica.com/topic/propaganda> accessed 23 April 2022.

Propaganda:
A form of communication intended to influence public opinion and thus gain support for certain political views or positions. Propaganda is characterised by the systematic provision of one-sided information, which may or may not be (partly) false, with certain facts being selectively emphasised and others deliberately left out. Propaganda is a form of (manipulative) persuasion, which means that rhetorical means such as language, image, or a combination, and argumentation are used to influence people's opinions. In the case of propaganda, governments or politicians intend to influence public opinion. For this, they use various types of media and various ways to express their message in an effective and attractive way.

In the case of Russia, misappropriation of human rights is part of propaganda, and in order to analyse this misappropriation, theories of argumentation (Pragma-Dialectics) and communication (Grice's theory of communication and framing theory) provide important theoretical tools to gain more understanding of what misappropriation exactly is.

The Pragma-Dialectical theory of argumentation can provide insight into the way arguments are used and abused in propaganda. This theory provides a systematic method for analysing and evaluating argumentation.[4] In both tasks, the ideal model of a 'critical discussion' is crucial. This model stipulates how a discussion should look when discussants seriously aim at a reasonable resolution of a difference of opinion, i.e., by critically testing the standpoint that is at stake. On the one hand, the model defines the four discussion stages that constitute a critical discussion, and the moves that are relevant within each of those stages. As such, the model provides a lens, which enables an analyst of real discourse to find the relevant elements in that discourse; this is the model's *heuristic* function.[5] On the other hand, the model of a critical discussion states the rules that regulate the discussion, such as the prohib-

4 Frans H van Eemeren and Rob Grootendorst, 'A Pragma-Dialectical Procedure for a Critical Discussion' (2003) 17 Argumentation 365 <DOI: 10.1023/A:1026334218681>; Frans H van Eemeren and Rob Grootendorst, *A Systematic Theory of Argumentation: The Pragma-Dialectical Approach* (Cambridge University Press 2004); Frans H van Eemeren, *Strategic Maneuvering in Argumentative Discourse: Extending the Pragma-Dialectical Theory of Argumentation* (John Benjamins Publishing 2010); Frans H van Eemeren, *Argumentation Theory: A Pragma-Dialectical Perspective* (Springer 2018).

5 In addition to the tools that the model offers, a Pragma-dialectical analysis is also based on (pragma-)linguistic insights about communication and genres, by which the interpretation of utterances in real discourse can be accounted for. Moreover, it is also steered by theoretical concepts such as 'type of difference of opinion', 'implicit premise', and 'argument scheme'.

itions to make use of vague language or irrelevant arguments, and the commandment that a standpoint that was not sufficiently defended must be retracted. The rules, of which a complete overview is given in the Appendix,[6] give the model a *critical* function, since they can be used to ascertain what goes wrong in an actual discussion.[7]

A first thing to note with respect to the subject of this contribution is that the rules regulating the critical discussion are not incompatible with the rules of a relevant particular (institutional) context, such as, in the case at hand, rules of international law. In fact, the model provides the norms, while the criteria to establish whether a norm has been violated should be derived from the institutional preconditions of the particular context at hand, i.e., the formal and informal rules and conventions playing a role in that context.[8] With regard to the acceptability of an argument, it is important to note that it ultimately depends on its agreement with generally shared starting points. In the case at hand, those starting points consist of, for instance, factual statements of internationally recognised institutions like the UN and the legal rules of international treaties.

A second thing to note is that applying the model to argumentative discourse does not have to be limited to an explicit dialogical situation in which two or more discussants are sitting together and exchanging arguments. It may also be used, for example, with respect to a speech by Putin addressing why Russia invaded Ukraine. Since such a speech uses argumentation, it presupposes that the audience of the speech aims to convince the audience to accept a certain standpoint. In fact, it is highly likely that Putin, in his speeches, takes into account what imaginary opponents or discussion partners think, and how they would respond, when developing his argumentation.[9] Therefore, monological discourse, provided that it contains argumentation, can also presuppose a discussion, even though the audience itself is not able to communicate with the speaker or writer.

6 Section 5 contains a discussion of some rules.

7 It is important to stress that a critical discussion is not an empirical category: it does not describe reality. After all, in reality, people rather aim at winning a discussion than to critically test a standpoint and frequently commit fallacies by violating discussion rules. However, it is also not true that the model has nothing to do with reality, since even people who just want to win an argument make use of argumentation, and generally want to project an image of reasonableness. This is also the case with Putin, who, as we will show, does in fact go through great lengths to explain when and why he thinks it is justified to invade Ukraine, and how human rights play a part in this.

8 Van Eemeren, *Strategic Maneuvering in Argumentative Discourse* (n 4) 197.

9 Van Eemeren, *Argumentation Theory: A Pragma-Dialectical Perspective* (n 4) 59.

We will also draw insights from the theory of communication developed by Grice, who defines rules for successful communication,[10] and we will use insights from the theory of framing.[11] As we will show, Russian political discourse about human rights contains rhetorical frames, which consists of key words which shape how the world is conceived and communicated. Terminology from human rights or the term human rights itself is part of a rhetorical frame developed by Russia.

In sum, in order to understand why one can speak of misappropriation of human rights, it is important to see this misappropriation as part of propaganda, for which analysis insights from argumentation theory and theories of communication are pertinent.

3 Russia's Justification of the War in Ukraine: A General Overview

In this contribution, we focus on the arguments used by Russia to invade Ukraine that appeal to a misappropriation of human rights. Nevertheless, in order to get a better understanding of this argumentation, it is important to look at the entire complex of arguments that Russia has used as a justification for the war. To this end, we provide a discussion of the three most prominent addresses of Vladimir Putin that have been essential in Russia's justification of the war: his speech on 21 February 2022 just before the full on invasion of Ukraine,[12] the declaration of war that Putin gave on 24 February 2022 on the day of the invasion,[13] and his speech on 21 February 2023, one year after

10 HP Grice, 'Logic and Conversation' in C Peter and J Morgan (eds), *Syntax and Semantics*, vol 3 (Academic Press 1975) 41.

11 See for example Robert M Entman, 'Framing Bias: Media in the Distribution of Power' (2007) 57 Journal of Communication 163 <DOI: 10.1111/j.1460–2466.2006.00336.x>; George Lakoff, *Don't Think of an Elephant! Know Your Values and Frame the Debate* (2014 edn., Chelsea Green Publishing 2004).

12 Vladimir V Putin, 'Address by the President of the Russian Federation' (Kremlin, Moscow, 21 February 2022) <http://en.kremlin.ru/events/president/news/67828> accessed 28 April 2025 (Putin Speech of 21 February 2022).

13 Vladimir V Putin, 'Address by the President of the Russian Federation' (Kremlin, Moscow, 24 February 2022) <http://en.kremlin.ru/events/president/news/67843> accessed 28 April 2025 (Putin Speech of 24 February 2022).

the invasion.[14] We used the English version of the speeches given on the website of the Kremlin, and in some cases we also used the original Russian version.

3.1 Speech Just before the War (21 February 2022)

Just before Russia invaded Ukraine, Putin delivered a speech on 21 February 2022 in which he anticipated a possible war and laid down Russia's terms for stopping such a war. The speech could be seen as a warning for the West, and for his own population. He started the speech with an elaborate history lesson about the relation between Ukraine and Russia, saying that Ukraine was *de facto* an inherent part of Russia:

> Since time immemorial, the people living in the south-west of what has historically been Russian land have called themselves Russians and Orthodox Christians. This was the case before the 17th century, when a portion of this territory rejoined the Russian state, and after.[15]

Putin claimed that the modern Ukrainian territory has been created by subsequent Bolshevik governments, led by Lenin, Stalin, and Khrushchev. In reality, according to Putin, Ukraine, like the other union republics, did not have any power of itself, but on paper, it had. When the USSR collapsed in the mid-1980s, the union republics claimed their independence, which could not be prevented by the weakened communist party. Instead, this was even encouraged by the different competing factions within the party, who were by that time involved in a power struggle, and who all saw the compliance with nationalist sentiments as a means to expand their support base. In sum, Putin suggests that Ukraine, being a sovereign nation state independent from Russia, must be seen as a mistake of history.

For Putin, this became especially apparent in 2014. In the West, this moment in time in Ukraine is usually described as the period of the Maidan revolution – an uprising of the Ukrainian people against a corrupt pro-Russian president. But Putin sees this differently. In his speech, he framed this as follows. A pro-Western government was installed in 2014, which is associated with Neo-Nazism and seen as a Western project, as a sign that NATO was

---

14 Vladimir V Putin, 'Presidential Address to Federal Assembly' (Gostiny Dvor, Moscow, 21 February 2023) <http://en.kremlin.ru/events/president/news/70565> accessed 28 April 2025 (Putin Speech of 21 February 2023).

15 Putin Speech of 21 February 2022 (n 12).

taking over in Ukraine. According to Putin, this was part of a larger movement where NATO, against agreements, had expanded into the Russian sphere of influence. Putin warned the Western world that Russia might have to act against Ukraine since NATO had effectively taken over control of the Ukrainian army, was at its borders in Ukraine, and was likely preparing a pre-emptive strike against Russia. According to Russia, the hate for and fear of Russia might explain such a possible pre-emptive strike. Putin also repeated his earlier demands: First, to prevent further NATO expansion. Second, to have the Alliance (NATO) refrain from deploying assault weapon systems on the Russian borders. And finally, rolling back the bloc's (NATO) military capability and infrastructure in Europe to where they were in 1997, when the NATO-Russia Founding Act was signed. Putin further added:

> I would like to be clear and straightforward: in the current circumstances, when our proposals for an equal dialogue on fundamental issues have actually remained unanswered by the United States and NATO, when the level of threats to our country has increased significantly, Russia has every right to respond in order to ensure its security. That is exactly what we will do.[16]

The speech ended by saying that steps would immediately be taken to recognise the independence and sovereignty of the Donetsk People's Republic and the Luhansk People's Republic and that '[w]e want those who seized and continue to hold power in Kiev to immediately stop hostilities. Otherwise, the responsibility for the possible continuation of the bloodshed will lie entirely on the conscience of Ukraine's ruling regime'. As such, the speech contained an ultimatum consisting of two parts: (i) prevent further NATO expansion and diminish NATO presence, (ii) stop the bloodshed in the Donbas by the 'Kiev regime'.

3.2 Speech at the Start of the War (22 February 2022)

When Russia invaded Ukraine a few days later, Putin's speech, which was *de facto* a declaration of war, was more diffuse. It largely consisted of a lament about the Western world, NATO, and especially the US, that had been diminishing the role of Russia in the world, and whose invasions in Libya, Iraq, Syria, and Belgrade had brought disaster to the world. It repeated the threat of NATO towards Russia but presented as the main reason to invade Ukraine,

16 Putin Speech of 21 February 2022 (n 12).

the liberation of the people who have been subject to genocide from the 'Kiev regime'. The goal was to liberate and denazify Ukraine:

> In this context, in accordance with Article 51 (Chapter VII) of the UN Charter,[17] with permission of Russia's Federation Council, and in execution of the treaties of friendship and mutual assistance with the Donetsk People's Republic and the Lugansk People's Republic, ratified by the Federal Assembly on February 22, I made a decision to carry out a special military operation.
>
> The purpose of this operation is to protect people who, for eight years now, have been facing humiliation and genocide perpetrated by the Kiev regime. To this end, we will seek to demilitarise and denazify Ukraine, as well as bring to trial those who perpetrated numerous bloody crimes against civilians, including against citizens of the Russian Federation.[18]

In this fragment, Putin presents the invasion framed as a 'special military operation' in accordance with the treaty they signed with the Donetsk People's Republic and the Luhansk People's Republic. According to Putin, these are republics in the former territory of Ukraine that broke away from Ukraine. According to Russia, these republics represent the will of the people living there. In reality, these are regimes installed by Russia and governed from Moscow. To what extent they represent the will of the people living there is unknown since the referendums that were held before the regimes were installed were not transparent or recognised by the UN or Ukraine. Nevertheless, Putin creates the impression that the invasion was the necessary result of an international agreement. In addition, by referring to a text of the UN Charter, the invasion of Ukraine is also presented as being in accordance with international law because Russia acts out of self-defence, a term which Putin also uses himself in his speech of 24 February 2022:

> I reiterate: we are acting to defend ourselves from the threats created for us and from a worse peril than what is happening now. I am asking you, however hard this may be, to understand this and to work together with us so as to turn this tragic page as soon as possible and to move forward together, […].[19]

---

17 For the text of the relevant article, see *Charter of the United Nations* (adopted 26 June 1945, entered into force 24 October 1945) 1 UNTS XVI, art 51 <https://legal.un.org/repertory/art51.shtml> accessed 28 April 2025.

18 Putin Speech of 24 February 2022 (n 13).

19 Putin Speech of 24 February 2022 (n 13).

This shift from the military threat towards the issue of the human rights of the Russian-speaking population of the Donbas and Ukraine primarily had to do with the target audience of the message. The narrative of the NATO threat was also directed at the leaders of the Western world and meant to induce them to say no to a Ukrainian membership of NATO, whereas the story about the liberation of the Russians or Russian-speaking people in Ukraine and the denazification was primarily meant for the Russian home audience. Its goal was to provide them with a credible and emotionally appealing explanation for the Russian invasion. It was also accompanied by references to the Second World War, most notably the use of terms like genocide and Nazi.[20]

3.3 Speech One Year after the Start of the War (24 February 2023)

One year after the invasion, Putin gave another speech, in which he discussed the special military operation against Ukraine. The speech was clearly aimed at the home audience, even though it was also partly meant for the West. This speech also combined the narrative about the NATO threat, the NATO-expansion against agreements not to expand, and Ukraine as a Nazi-regime that kills Russians. According to Putin, it was not Russia that started the war, but the West. The Western world (governed by the 'Western elites') was presented as a cynical, unreliable, perverted world with disregard for international agreements and law, and which already in the 1930s had initiated the Ukraine-project, a project to turn Ukraine into a Nazi-state that could be used as a weapon against Russia. Russia, on the other hand, was presented as a peace-loving, reliable, multi-ethnic, and Christian nation, which would bring economic prosperity.

3.4 The Four Main Arguments

Based on these three speeches, it is possible to distinguish the following arguments provided by Russia to justify its invasion in Ukraine (until 2025 still framed as a 'special military operation'):
(1) Ukraine is not a sovereign nation state.
(2) Russia has to defend itself against Western aggression.
(3) The people in Donbass should be liberated from genocide.
(4) Russia did not start the war; the West did.

20 For a thorough analysis see ELJ Fortuin, 'Ukraine Commits Genocide on Russians: The Term "Genocide" in Russian Propaganda' (2022) 46 Russian Linguistics 313 <DOI: 10.1007/s11185-022-09258-5>.

If we look at other speeches and utterances by Putin or other Kremlin officials after the full scale invasion of 2022, we find that the same arguments are used, which shows that these four arguments are used in a consistent way. When the war started, the second and third arguments were explicitly given as arguments to start the war. In the next sections, we will focus on the third argument, since this pertains directly to the misappropriation of human rights. Note that we will also take into account quotes by other Russian politicians than Putin if relevant for the discussion.

4 The Liberation from Genocide Argument

In this section, we will provide an argumentative analysis of the argument that Russia has used to invade Ukraine, which has to do with human rights. These arguments can be found in one or more of the above discussed three speeches in the previous section. Following standard practice in argumentation theory, we present both a reconstruction of Russia's argumentation, the historical and political context in which the argument is used, and an evaluation of it. This evaluation concerns not only the soundness of the arguments, that is, whether they are applied appropriately, but also the validity and truthfulness of the underlying claims. In addition, the analysis addresses the presentational strategies employed in Russia's argumentation, including lexical choices and framing devices. Even though our analysis is primarily based on argumentation theory, it also takes into account legal perspectives where relevant. Before providing our argumentative analysis, we will first briefly give a historical background to understand the issue of the violation of human rights.

4.1 Historical Background

In February 2014, Russia invaded Ukraine by annexing Crimea. This was Russia's response to the ousting of the pro-Russian president Yanukovych and the installation of a new pro-Western government by the Ukrainian parliament. The protests on the Maidan Square were a response from a large group of Ukrainians who were shocked that Russia had pressured the pro-Russian president Yanukovych to suddenly not want to sign the free trade and association agreement with the EU. During the protests, protesters and a number of police officers were killed. On 22 February 2014, the Ukrainian parliament voted by a large majority (73% of the members of parliament) to remove Yanukovych from his office and to schedule an early presidential election for 25 May 2014, which resulted in the pro-Western government of Poroshenko. The reason given by parliament for his removal was that, because he fled the country, he was unable to carry out his duties, which was deemed to be against the constitution.[21] The removal of the president had characteristics of an actual popular revolution, which was supported by a majority of the population, even though it was not fully in accordance with the constitution.[22]

When Russia annexed Crimea, protests and armed uprisings erupted in Donetsk and Luhansk.[23] Pro-Russian separatists declared independence from Ukraine and installed self-declared People's Republics: the Donetsk People's Republic and the Luhansk People's Republic. Both are located in the Donbas region of eastern Ukraine, bordering Russia. These so-called republics were *de facto* controlled and installed by Russia without a democratic process. The governments were not internationally recognised except by Russia and very few other countries. Russia has provided military, political, and economic support to these republics since their formation. Although Russia initially denied direct military involvement, evidence has shown Russian troops, weapons, and leadership operating in the region.[24] Since Ukraine saw the territory of these republics as part of Ukraine, they started a military operation to reclaim these territories. The conflict between Ukraine and the Russia-backed separatists led to casualties on both sides, including civilians. There were two deals (Minsk I in 2014 and Minsk II in 2015) aimed at ending the war in eastern Ukraine between Ukrainian forces and Russian-backed separatists. These deals included things like ceasefires, withdrawal of heavy weapons, local elections in separatist regions, and greater autonomy for Donetsk and Luhansk. But the agreements were never fully implemented, and both sides accused each other of violations.

Since the Maidan revolution, Russia has framed the successive pro-Western Poroshenko and Zelensky governments (also referred to by Kremlin officials as the 'Kiev regime') as illegal and as Neo-Nazi. For Putin, the 'Kiev regime' is an illegal *junta* that was the result of a *coup d'état* or *putsch*.[25] The use of words

---

21 Yuriy Shveda and Joung Ho Park, 'Ukraine's Revolution of Dignity: The Dynamics of Euromaidan' (2016) 7 *Journal of Eurasian studies* 85, 88, 90 <DOI: 10.1016/j.euras.2015.10.007>.

22 For more information, see for example Daisy Sindelar, 'Was Yanukovych's Ouster Constitutional?' *Radio Free Europe/Radio Liberty* (23 February 2014) <www.rferl.org/a/was-yanukovychs-ouster-constitutional/25274346.html> accessed 28 April 2025.

23 For a timeline see Civic Monitoring, *Chronology of the Conflict* (2014) <https://civicmonitoring.org/747-2/> accessed 2 May 2025.

24 Ukraine and the Netherlands v Russia (dec) [GC] App nos 43800/14, 8019/16 and 28525/20 (ECtHR, 30 November 2022) <https://hudoc.echr.coe.int/eng#{%22itemid%22:[%22002-13989%22]}> accessed 2 June 2025.

25 The term *coup* (*d'état*) is used in the Putin Speech of 21 February 2022 (n 11), the Putin Speech of 24 February 2022 (n 12) and the Putin Speech of 21 February 2023 (n 13). Putin used the term *putsch* (*putč*) in an address of 18 March 2014 (Vladimir V Putin, 'Obrašče-

like *junta* clearly suggests the idea of illegal takeover of power in a country by a small group of military people. This framing is, obviously, not accurate. Even if the removal of Yanukovych was not in full accordance with the Ukrainian constitution,[26] it was not the result of a coup by a *junta*, but a decision of the Ukrainian Parliament. In Russia's rhetorical frame, the Ukrainian government is not just illegal, but also Neo-Nazi, a frame that functions to strengthen the argument that the government is illegal. For the presumed Neo-Nazi character of the 'Kiev regime', they referred to the presumed large presence of Neo-Nazis during the Maidan protests, for which no proof was given, and to the policies of the Poroshenko and Zelensky governments, most notably laws that were introduced in Ukraine. As a result of the Russian invasion, the newly installed Ukrainian government led by Poroshenko implemented a number of laws which banned the propagation of Nazi and Soviet symbols, and glorified and prevented criticism of historical political groups, which had fought for the independence of Ukraine, including groups with fascist and Nazi tendencies (UPA/OUN).[27] As a result, numerous cities and regions were renamed. These

---

nie Prezidenta Rossijskoj Federacii' (Kreml', Moskva, 18 March 2014) <http://kremlin.ru/events/president/news/20603> accessed 28 April 2025). The term *junta* is used in the Putin Speech of 24 February 2022 (n 13).

26 H Pleines, 'Assessing the legality of the power changes in Ukraine' Montesquieu Instituut (24 March 2014) < https://www.montesquieu-instituut.nl/id/vjicc5jt4ayk/nieuws/assessing_the_legality_of_the_power?colctx=vllzft76lfmu&start_002=644&utm> accessed 5 June 2025.

27 These are the following laws in English translation: Law of Ukraine of 4 February 2020 № 2539, 'On the Perpetuation of the Victory over Nazism in World War II of 1939–1945' https://uinp.gov.ua/dokumenty/normatyvno-pravovi-akty-rozrobleni-v-instytuti/zakony/the-law-on-the-perpetuation-of-the-victory-over-nazism-in-world-war-ii-of-1939-1945 accessed 26 May 2025; Law of Ukraine of 2 March 2020 № 2540, 'On Access to Archives of Repressive Agencies of Totalitarian Communist Regime of 1917–1991' https://uinp.gov.ua/dokumenty/normatyvno-pravovi-akty-rozrobleni-v-instytuti/zakony/the-law-on-access-to-archives-of-repressive-agencies-of-totalitarian-communist-regime-of-1917-1991 accessed 26 May 2025; Law of Ukraine of 2 March 2020 № 2558, 'On the Condemnation of the Communist and National Socialist (Nazi) Regimes, and Prohibition of Propaganda of their Symbols' https://uinp.gov.ua/dokumenty/normatyvno-pravovi-akty-rozrobleni-v-instytuti/zakony/the-law-on-the-condemnation-of-the-communist-and-national-socialist-nazi-regimes-and-prohibition-of-propaganda-of-their-symbols accessed 26 May 2025; Law of Ukraine of 2 March 2020 № 2538–1, 'On the Legal Status and Honoring the Memory of Fighters for Ukraine's Independence in the Twentieth Century' https://uinp.gov.ua/dokumenty/normatyvno-pravovi-akty-rozrobleni-v-instytuti/zakony/the-law-on-the-legal-status-and-honoring-the-memory-of-fighters-for-ukraines - independence-in-the-twentieth-century accessed 26 May 2025; Law of Ukraine of 9 April 2015 № 317-VIII, 'On the Condemnation of the Communist and National Socialist (Nazi) Regimes, and Prohibition of Propaganda of their Symbols' https://zakon.rada.gov.ua/laws/show/317-19?lang=uk#Text accessed 23 April 2022; Law of Ukraine of 1 July 2021

changes are part of a broader effort to reinforce Ukrainian national identity and to break away from the Soviet legacy. In Russia, the prohibition of the use of Soviet names was seen as a hostile and, therefore, 'Neo-Nazi' act, reminiscent of the Nazis that wanted to exterminate the Soviet-Union. This claim was further strengthened with reference to legislation that was introduced to honour Ukrainian independence fighters, regardless of whether they held controversial or extremist views in other areas. A prominent example is Stepan Bandera, who fought for Ukrainian independence during the 1920s to 1950s. However, he also espoused fascist views and was involved in acts of violence against Jews, Poles, and Soviets.[28] For Russia, this law clearly showed the Nazi-tendencies of the Poroshenko government. Finally, Ukraine also implemented laws which were seen by Russia as violating the human rights of Russians or Russian speakers. These were the language laws, which aim to strengthen the position of the state language, Ukrainian, at the expense of Russian and other minority languages such as Hungarian and Romanian.[29] The framing of the Ukrainian governments as Neo-Nazi is connected to Russia's claim that Ukraine is violating the human rights of the Russian-speaking people in Ukraine, which are systematically framed as Russians, notwithstanding research that shows that in Ukraine, many Russian-speaking people do in fact feel Ukrainian and not Russian.[30] The use of the term 'Neo-Nazi' and 'genocide' is part of a coherent and systematic rhetorical frame which draws an analogy between the Nazis and the Ukrainians. The genocide of the Jewish population by the Nazis is implicitly presented as similar to the acts of the 'Kiev regime'.[31] In the next section, we will address the genocide argument in detail.

Nº 1616-IX, 'On Indigenous Peoples of Ukraine' ('Zakon Ukraïny pro korinni narody Ukraïny') *Bulletin of the Verkhovna Rada of Ukraine* 2021, Nº 38, art 319 <https://zakon.rada.gov.ua/laws/show/1616-20?lang=en#Text> accessed 26 May 2025.

28 Andreas Umland, 'Irregular Militias and Radical Nationalism in Post-Euromaydan Ukraine: The Prehistory and Emergence of the "Azov" Battalion in 2014' (2019) 31 Terrorism and Political Violence 105, 115 <https://doi.org/10.1080/09546553.2018.1555974>.

29 Fortuin, 'Ukraine Commits Genocide on Russians' (n 20) 320–323, 338.

30 VJe Khmelko, 'Linhvo-Etnična Struktura Ukraïny: Rehional'ni Osoblyvosti Ta Tendenciï Zmin Za Roky Nezaležnosti' (2004) 32 Naukovi zapysky NaUKMA. Sociolohični nauky 3 <http://ekmair.ukma.edu.ua/bitstream/handle/123456789/8098/Khmelko_Linhvo-etnichna_struktura_Ukrainy.pdf?sequence=1&isAllowed=y> accessed 28 April 2025; Volodymyr Kulyk, 'Language Attitudes in Independent Ukraine: Differentiation and Evolution' (2017) 35 Harvard Ukrainian studies 265; Dominique Arel, 'Language, Status, and State Loyalty in Ukraine' (2017–2018) 35 Harvard Ukrainian studies 233.

31 Fortuin, 'Ukraine Commits Genocide on Russians' (n 20) 339.

4.2 The Genocide Argument

A major reason given by Russia to invade Ukraine was to stop 'humiliation and genocide perpetrated by the Kiev regime'.[32] Even though the term 'genocide' is used explicitly with respect to Donbas, it is sometimes also used without the Donbas reference, suggesting it applies to all the Russian-speaking areas of Ukraine or the whole of Ukraine. As we will explain below, this gives the audience the impression that what is true for Donbas is true for the whole of Ukraine. As such, Russia is deliberately playing with the ambiguity over whether something concerns only Donbas or all of Ukraine. This is connected to the fact that Russia needs an argument not just to 'liberate' Donbas, but all of Ukraine.[33]

A Pragma-Dialectical reconstruction of this liberation from genocide argument results in the following argumentation structure. Please note that, as explained in the note to the text section, we use Russian names (e.g. Russian Donbass instead of Ukrainian Donbas) when we cite or refer to Russian state discourse:[34]

---

32 Putin Speech of 24 February 2022 (n 13).

33 In his speeches, Putin uses different terms to characterise the violation of human rights in Ukraine, sometimes in combination with one another, for example in his speech of 21 February 2022, just before the invasion, he uses the term "horror and genocide" with respect to Donbas, and he talks about "discriminatory bills" (with respect to the language laws of Ukraine), but on 24 February 2022, in his declaration of war, he talks about "that atrocity, that genocide of the millions of people, humiliation and genocide perpetrated by the Kiev regime" when talking about Donbas. Other state officials, such as Lavrov, also used other terminology such as "oppression" for the whole of Ukraine (Mixail Čkanikov, 'Sergej Lavrov: Vse, Čto Zapad Xotel Sprovocirovat' u Nas, Načinaetsja u Nego' *Argumenty i Fakty* (8 October 2022) <https://aif.ru/politics/world/sergey_lavrov_vse_chto_zapad_hotel_sprovocirovat_u_nas_nachinaetsya_u_nego> accessed 2 June 2025). In all cases, it is clear that the terms used are about violations of human rights. For an overview of all the violations of human rights in Ukraine as perceived by Russia, see the 2023 rapport of the Russian state about the human rights situation in Ukraine: Ministry of Foreign Affairs of the Russian Federation, *Concept of the Humanitarian Policy of the Russian Federation Abroad* (31 July 2022) <https://mid.ru/en/foreign_policy/humanitarian_cooperation/1448658/> accessed 26 May 2025.

34 Most of the exact wording is taken over from the speech of 21 February 2022. The annotation used here is based on Frans H van Eemeren and A Francisca Snoeck Henkemans, *Argumentation. Analysis and Evaluation* (Routledge 2016). In this annotation method, the highest level concerns the standpoint (in this case: "The war against Ukraine is justified"), which gets a "1". Every sublevel (of supporting arguments) gets an extra ".1". When the arguments are related to each other, they also get the addition of a letter: a, b, c, etc., whereas each new independent argument on the same level gets a higher number: 2, 3, 4 etc. In the structure at hand, 1.1 indicates that we are dealing here with the first main argument, 1.1.1a–1.1.1f indicate the linked subarguments supporting the main argu-

1.1 It is Russia's Duty to Liberate the Russians in the People's Republics of Donbass from the Illegal Nazi-Government of Zelensky (and in Doing So, the Whole of Ukraine Must Be Liberated)

1.1.1a Almost 4 million people are facing horror and genocide
- Innocent civilians are being killed in the People's Republic of Donbass, and there is no end in sight
- They, like all Russian-speaking people in Ukraine, do not have the elementary right to live on their own land, to speak their own language, and to preserve their culture and traditions
- They, like all the inhabitants of Ukraine, have to live with laws which glorify their Nazi-past (and Neo-Nazis hate Russians and want to harm Russians)

1.1.1b The horror and genocide are an infringement of UN Security Council Resolution 2202 of 17 February 2015, which consolidated the Minsk Package of Measures of 12 February 2015

1.1.1c The liberation of Donbass/Ukraine is in accordance with Article 51 (Chapter VII) of the UN Charter

1.1.1d There is no other option to enforce those treaties than a military one
- The so-called civilised world, which our Western colleagues proclaimed themselves the only representatives of, prefers not to see the Kiev regime's crimes

1.1.1e The liberation is an execution of the Treaties of friendship and mutual assistance with the Donetsk People's Republic and the Lugansk People's Republic, ratified by the Federal Assembly in February 2022

1.1.1f Russia has a right to liberate the Russians in Ukraine and the Ukrainian people as a whole
- The Kiev regime is illegal and does not represent its people

4.3 Argument 1.1.1a

When talking about the claim made by Russia that they have to liberate the Russian-speaking people in Ukraine who are subject to genocide,[35] there are two important interrelated issues, which need to be cleared up: To which

ment. In view of the lengthy annotation of the lower levels of the structure, we chose to indicate them with square dots.

35 Like we mentioned in note 33, Putin often combines expressions ("horror and genocide" or "humiliation and genocide"), but since committing genocide is clearly a stronger and

geographical areas of Ukraine are these terms applied, and to which actions by Ukraine are they applied? As can be seen in our argumentation structure under 1.1.1a, the first reason given for the liberation argument is that the people in Donbas face horror and genocide (1.1.1a). This accusation of genocide refers to Ukraine's military actions to regain control over the eastern parts of the country. Putin frames Ukraine's military actions in that region as deliberate genocide on Russian-speaking people by the 'Neo-Nazi Kiev regime', without giving any proof for that. In Putin's speeches, there is, however, quite some ambiguity with respect to the claims about genocide. This can be illustrated with Putin's declaration of war in February 2022 (see 3.2 and repeated below):

> In this context, in accordance with Article 51 (Chapter VII) of the UN Charter, with permission of Russia's Federation Council, and in execution of the treaties of friendship and mutual assistance with the Donetsk People's Republic and the Lugansk People's Republic, ratified by the Federal Assembly on February 22, I made a decision to carry out a special military operation.
>
> The purpose of this operation is to protect people who, for eight years now, have been facing humiliation and genocide perpetrated by the Kiev regime. To this end, we will seek to demilitarise and denazify Ukraine, as well as bring to trial those who perpetrated numerous bloody crimes against civilians, including against citizens of the Russian Federation.[36]

In the first sentence of the second paragraph, Putin does not explicitly specify that the humiliation and genocide perpetrated by the 'Kiev regime' refer exclusively to the population of Donbas, although this can be inferred from the preceding context, in which he refers to the treaties of friendship and mutual assistance with the Donetsk and Lugansk People's Republics. However, instead of making this explicit – for instance, by stating 'to protect the people of the Donbas, who have been facing humiliation and genocide…' – he leaves it implicit. This creates the impression that his statement possibly applies to Ukraine as a whole, an interpretation that is reinforced by the subsequent sentence, which addresses the objectives of demilitarising and 'denazifying Ukraine', i.e., the *entire* country. But Putin can defend himself by saying that the whole of Ukraine needs to be invaded as a matter of self-defence, something which is backed up by his reference to Article 51 of the UN charter. By

more well-defined term, we will focus on that, leaving the vaguer terms out of our discussion.

36 Putin Speech of 24 February 2022 (n 13).

leaving such argumentative links implicit, Putin can suggest things, even though he is not literally saying them.

Something similar can be illustrated with respect to Putin's speech of 21 February 2022, where he talks about the killing and abuse of civilians in Donbas:

> Not a single day goes by without Donbass communities coming under shelling attacks. The recently formed large military force makes use of attack drones, heavy equipment, missiles, artillery and multiple rocket launchers. The killing of civilians, the blockade, the abuse of people, including children, women and the elderly, continues unabated. As we say, there is no end in sight to this. [...] [O]nly because these people did not agree with the West-supported coup in Ukraine in 2014 and opposed the transition towards the Neanderthal and aggressive nationalism and neo-Nazism which have been elevated in Ukraine to the rank of national policy.[37]

In the same speech, Putin also mentions the language laws of Ukraine and the law on minorities[38] and states that the goal of these laws is to root out the Russian language and culture in the whole of Ukraine, so not just the Donbas area. Note that Putin equates Russian-speaking with identifying as being Russian, even though Russian-speaking Ukrainians often identify with Ukraine and feel Ukrainian:[39]

> The policy to root out the Russian language and culture and promote assimilation carries on. The Verkhovna Rada has generated a steady flow of discriminatory bills, and the law on the so-called indigenous people has already come into force. People who identify as Russians and want to preserve their identity, language and culture are getting the signal that they are not wanted in Ukraine.
>
> Under the laws on education and the Ukrainian language as a state language, the Russian language has no place in schools or public spaces, even in ordinary shops. The law on the so-called vetting of officials and purging their ranks created a pathway for dealing with unwanted civil servants.[40]

Putin does not use the word 'genocide' with respect to the language laws, but talks about discrimination and rooting out the Russian language and culture.

---

37 Putin Speech of 21 February 2022 (n 12).

38 Law of Ukraine of 1 July 2021 № 1616-IX, 'On Indigenous Peoples of Ukraine' (n 27).

39 Kulyk (n 30).

40 Putin Speech of 21 February 2022 (n 12).

In his later speech on 30 September 2022, when Russia formalised the annexation of Donetsk, Luhansk (Donbas), and the Russian-speaking areas of Kherson and Zaporizhzhia (Russian-speaking areas outside of Donbas), Putin, however, appears to make more far-reaching claims. He claims that those who opposed the installation of the Poroshenko government were fighting for their right to speak their native language, to preserve their culture, traditions, and religion, and even for their very right to exist. This framing implies that speaking Russian in the whole of Ukraine entails a threat to one's life:

> We will always remember the heroes of the Russian Spring, those who refused to accept the neo-Nazi coup d'état in Ukraine in 2014, all those who died for the right to speak their native language, to preserve their culture, traditions and religion, and for the very right to live. We remember the soldiers of Donbass, the martyrs of the 'Odessa Khatyn', the victims of inhuman terrorist attacks carried out by the Kiev regime.[41]

Similarly, in his speech of 21 February 2023, one year after the full scale invasion, Putin suggests that one of the main reasons for the Russian invasion was 'to protect the people in our historical lands',[42] suggesting that Russia had to protect all the Russian-speaking people of Ukraine, not just those in Donbas. But when further illustrating this, he refers to Donbas, and argues that '[s]ince 2014, Donbass has been fighting for the right to live in their land and to speak their native tongue'.[43] Again, in this quote, it is argued that Russian speakers of Donbas, or perhaps of the whole of Ukraine, are not able to speak their own language.

Similar statements can be found with other Russian state officials. For instance, Minister of Foreign Affairs Sergey Lavrov, speaking at a session of the UN Human Rights Council (UNHRC) on 1 March 2022, talked about the language laws of Ukraine while defending the Russian invasion. He claimed that Russian-speaking people in Ukraine are killed only because they want to speak their native language: 'The Russian language is being driven out of schools and universities, from the public sphere, and even from everyday use. It is not uncommon that one can pay not only with their job or health,

41 Vladimir V Putin, 'Signing of treaties on accession of Donetsk and Lugansk people's republics and Zaporozhye and Kherson regions to Russia' (Kremlin, Moscow, 30 September 2022) <http://en.kremlin.ru/events/president/news/69465> accessed 26 September 2025.

42 Putin Speech of 21 February 2023 (n 14).

43 Putin Speech of 21 February 2023 (n 14).

but even with their life for the right to speak their native language.'[44] In describing this, Lavrov draws a parallel with the legislative practices of Nazi Germany, suggesting that the anti-Jewish legislation is similar to that of the language laws of Ukraine. The Nazi-context already elicits a connection with the genocide frame without using the word genocide itself. But this connection was also made in an explicit way: a member of the Council for the Development of Civil Society and Human Rights, Ukrainian-born journalist and Russian political figure Kirill Valerievich Vyshinsky, even argued when discussing this issue with Putin, that the Ukrainian language laws have led to genocide of the Russian-speaking people in Donbas, explicitly linking language policies to genocide:

> [F]rom my perspective, a certain logical chain has formed. It all starts with Russophobia, which then transforms and becomes formalized, including at the state level – in the Baltics, and as I've already mentioned, in Ukraine – into various forms of discrimination: linguistic, social, and so on. And one step further, Vladimir Vladimirovich, in my view, this leads to genocide. A vivid example of genocide against Russian-speaking people or representatives of the multiethnic Russian nation is the situation in Donbass, where people are subjected to physically unbearable conditions that make survival impossible, or they are simply killed.[45] (K. Vyshinsky addressing Putin at the Meeting of the Council for the Development of Civil Society and Human Rights, 9 December 2021, published on the Kremlin website).

This fragment was put on the website of the Kremlin, and Putin, during this address, did not refute this claim, as such implicitly agreeing with it. In fact, as discussed by Fortuin, claims about genocide and the Ukrainian language laws could be found more commonly in Russian propaganda.[46]

As has been argued elsewhere,[47] there is no proof whatsoever that Ukraine has been committing genocide in the Donbas region when they tried to regain control over their territories. This claim by Russia is obviously absurd. We will therefore focus on the issue of the language laws of Ukraine in relation to the

---

44 'Lavrov: za Pravo Govorit' na Russkom Jazyke na Ukraine Možno Poplatit'sja Žizn'ju' *TASS* (Moskva, 1 March 2022) <https://tass.ru/politika/13914295> accessed 28 April 2025. The text has been translated from Russian.

45 Vladimir Putin, 'Meeting of the Council for Civil Society and Human Rights' (Moscow, 9 December 2021) <http://kremlin.ru/events/president/news/67331> accessed 2 May 2025. The text has been translated from Russian.

46 Fortuin, 'Ukraine Commits Genocide on Russians' (n 20) f.i. 330, 334, 341.

47 Fortuin, 'Ukraine Commits Genocide on Russians' (n 20).

claims made by Russia. In order to assess whether the language laws of Ukraine are indeed discriminatory, aim to erase the Russian language and culture from Ukraine (claimed by Putin), and even involve killing (claimed by minister of foreign affairs Lavrov, and suggested by Putin) and can be seen as an instance of genocide or leading to genocide (claimed by a representative of the Council for the Development of Civil Society and Human Rights, and not refuted by Putin), we will now take a closer look at two laws which deal with language (2017 and 2019).

The Law on Education (2017)[48] designated Ukrainian as the language of all education. Instruction in other languages, such as Russian or Hungarian, is allowed only at the preschool (children of approximately 3–6 years old) and general secondary levels (children of approximately 6–15 years old),[49] and only alongside Ukrainian. The 2019 Law on Supporting the Functioning of the Ukrainian Language as the State Language regulates Ukrainian use across sectors, including media, education, healthcare, and the workplace, aiming to strengthen its societal role, often at the expense of Russian.[50] It mandates Ukrainian proficiency for citizens (article 16.1), allows employers to use it at work (article 20.1), and introduces phased measures such as requiring Ukrainian in publications, films, and cultural events. Ukrainian is also the default language in shops and restaurants unless clients request otherwise (article 30.1, 3). Furthermore, in 2021, a law concerning minorities was introduced in Ukraine, which did not improve the position of the Russian language.[51] Even though the law defines the legal status of indigenous peoples in Ukraine and creates legal guarantees for the full enjoyment of all human and fundamental freedoms of persons belonging to those peoples, it defines indigenous peoples in Ukraine as those peoples that do not have a state beyond Ukraine. This meant that Russians were not seen as indigenous to Ukraine.

---

48 Law of Ukraine of 5 September 2017 № 2145-VIII, 'On Education' [2022 revision based on № 1986-IX] *Bulletin of the Verkhovna Rada* 2017, № 38–39, art 380 <https://zakon.rada.gov.ua/laws/show/2145-19?lang=en#Text> accessed 26 May 2025; Law of Ukraine of 25 April 2019 № 2704-VIII, 'On Supporting the Functioning of the Ukrainian Language as the State Language' [2022 revision based on № 2229-IX] *Bulletin of the Verkhovna Rada of Ukraine* 2019, № 21, art 81 <https://zakon.rada.gov.ua/laws/show/2704-19?lang=en#Text> accessed 26 May 2025.

49 Futher details on the Ukrainian school system can be found on 'Education System in Ukraine' (*Ministry of Education and Science of Ukraine*) <https://emergency.mon.gov.ua/educationalsystem/> accessed 16 September 2025.

50 Law of Ukraine of 25 April 2019 № 2704-VIII, 'On Supporting the Functioning of the Ukrainian Language as the State Language' (n 48).

51 Law of Ukraine of 1 July 2021 № 1616-IX, 'On Indigenous Peoples of Ukraine' (n 27).

It is true that the language laws (2017, 2019) and the law which deals with indigenous peoples of Ukraine and minorities (2021) have been criticised by the Council of Europe's advisory body on constitutional matters, i.e., the European Commission for Democracy through Law, better known as the Venice Commission, in various Opinions. In its 2017 Opinion, the Venice Commission states that the less favourable treatment of Russian and other non-EU languages is difficult to justify and raises concerns of 'discrimination'.[52] It also has concerns about the constitutionality of the law.[53] The Venice Commission argues that the loss of education in Russian 'would amount to a disproportionate interference with the existing rights of persons belonging to national minorities',[54] and notes that '[i]n particular, the issue of discriminatory treatment of other minority languages – which are not official languages of the EU – would have to be addressed in this context'.[55] Furthermore, the Venice Commission criticised the 2019 Ukrainian law on the state language for failing to balance promoting the state language with protecting minority linguistic rights.[56] Similar criticisms can be found in the Venice Commission's opinion from 2023 on Ukraine's 2021 law on national minorities, where it is suggested that the Ukrainian law should be revised, ensuring the rightful protection of minorities.[57]

---

52 Venice Commission, *Opinion on the Provisions of the Law on Education of 5 September 2017 which Concern the Use of the State Language and Minority and Other Languages in Education*, Opinion № 902/2017 (11 December 2017) <www.venice.coe.int/webforms/documents/default.aspx?pdffile=CDL-AD(2017)030-e> accessed 26 May 2025, s 124.

53 Venice Commission, *Opinion on the Provisions of the Law on Education of 5 September 2017* (n 52) s 114, fn 38.

54 Venice Commission, *Opinion on the provisions of the law on education of 5 September 2017* (n 52) ss 120, 122, 124.

55 Venice Commission, *Opinion on the provisions of the law on education of 5 September 2017* (n 52) ss 125, 25.

56 Venice Commission, *Opinion on the Law on Supporting the Functioning of the Ukrainian Language as the State Language, adopted by the Venice Commission at its 121st Plenary Session*, Opinion № 960/2019 (6–7 December 2019) < https://www.venice.coe.int/webforms/documents/?pdf=CDL-AD(2019)032-e> accessed 26 May 2025, ss 31, 44. The Advisory Committee on the Framework Convention for the Protection of National Minorities (an advisory board of the Council of Europe) similarly called for stronger legal safeguards for minority languages. Advisory Committee on the Framework Convention for the Protection of National Minorities, Council of Europe, *Fourth Opinion on Ukraine – adopted on 10 March 2017* (Council of Europe, 5 March 2018) <https://rm.coe.int/fourth-opinion-on-ukraine-adopted-on-10-march-2017-published-on-5-marc/16807930cf> accessed 26 May 2025.

57 Venice Commission, *Opinion on the Law on National Minorities (Communities), Ukraine*, CDL-AD(2023)021-e (9–10 June 2023, published 12 June 2023) < https://www.venice.coe.int/webforms/documents/default.aspx?pdffile = CDL-AD(2023)021-e> accessed 4 July

The Venice Commission, in its 2017 Opinion, does not state that it is a human right for minorities to have education in their native language. But the Commission has concerns about discrimination against Russian speakers in Ukraine,[58] which constitutes a human rights violation. However, the discriminatory nature of the Ukrainian language laws is, as we will explain, not a simple or even a black-and-white matter. In this context, it should be noted that the Venice Commission's view of the law as discriminatory at least partly depends on how far it aligns with the country's own legal commitments. The Venice Commission, in its 2017 Opinion, points out that Ukraine has in fact ratified international treaties on the protection of human rights (e.g. European Convention on Human Rights), which prohibit discrimination on the grounds of language and contain general guarantees for the protection of minorities, even though it does not automatically oblige a country to provide education in minority languages.[59]

As an argument of defence, it has been pointed out, for example, by Ukrainian lawyers and scholars, that similar laws to the Ukrainian laws on language and minorities can be found in EU countries or countries neighbouring

---

2025; see specifically the conclusion (pp 22–23), and section 2, where the Commission repeats its earlier criticism regarding language and education.

58 Tabory (1980) also claims that the right to have education in minority (non-state) language, or the right to use the minority language in communication with the government, etc., is usually not treated as a human right in multilateral instruments post–Second World War. See for example Tabory, 'Language Rights as Human Rights' (1980) 10 *Isr YB Hum Rts* 167. More recently, the guide on Article 2 of Protocol No 1 by the European Court of Human Rights discusses relevant case law and shows that, while the issue remains controversial, the Court has often not judged the absence of secondary education in a minority language to constitute a violation of human rights. See: European Court of Human Rights, Guide on Article 2 of Protocol No 1 to the European Convention on Human Rights – Right to education (28 February 2025) <https://ks.echr.coe.int/documents/d/echr-ks/guide_art_2_protocol_1_eng> accessed 1 July 2025.

59 Venice Commission, *Opinion on the Provisions of the Law on Education of 5 September 2017* (n 52) ss 28, 29, 114, fn 38. When considering the European context and the human rights treaties which prohibit discrimination and have been ratified by Ukraine, of specific importance is Article 14 of the European Convention on Human Rights and the connection to other rights mentioned therein, as well as Article 2 of Protocol No 1 of this Convention, which concerns the right to education (see: Council of Europe, *Convention for the Protection of Human Rights and Fundamental Freedoms* (European Convention on Human Rights, as amended, 4 November 1950) ETS No 5) <https://www.echr.coe.int/documents/d/echr/convention_ENG> accessed 15 August 2025.) It is also important to note that Ukraine, as is mentioned in section 29 of the 2017 Opinion of the Venice Commission, has acceded to instruments of the Council of Europe that safeguard the rights of minorities and their languages.

Ukraine.[60] This is also true for Ukrainian-speaking minorities in neighbouring countries, which do not have the right to monolingual education in their native language and do not benefit from agreements aimed at encouraging bilingual education.[61] In Europe, some countries, such as Belgium and Switzerland, provide legal protection for the language rights of their linguistic communities. However, there is no uniform standard for the protection of language rights across Europe. To give an example, in Latvia the language laws are in fact quite similar to that of Ukraine with respect to Russian speakers (even if the Latvian law allows for more education in Russian),[62] and in France, French is the only official language named in the constitution[63] while minority languages have a similar status to that of Russian in Ukraine (note that France also ratified the European Convention on Human Rights, but unlike Ukraine it did not ratify the Framework Convention for the Protection of National Minorities). In many European countries, immigrant communities lack the right to receive education in their mother tongue. Although this situation is not directly comparable to that of Ukraine, several linguists have noted that the current linguistic landscape of Ukraine results from a long and sometimes recent history of russification and from the settlement of Russian-speaking populations in the country. This also includes the deportation of the entire Crimean Tatar population by Stalin in 1944, which changed the linguistic landscape in Crimea, leading to the present situation where the large majority speaks Russian. But one can also think about the deliberate starvation of Ukrainian peasants in 1932–1933 (the Holodomor), which diminished the population in areas where Ukrainian was traditionally spoken. As such, in Ukraine, Russian can be seen as both a traditional and an immigrant language, to some extent comparable to the Baltic states, which, unlike Ukraine, did not sign the European Charter for Regional and Minority Languages, exactly for this reason.

60 Ivan Toronchuk and Volodymyr Markovskyi, 'The Implementation of the Venice Commission Recommendations on the Provision of the Minorities Language Rights in the Ukrainian Legislation' (2018) 5 European Journal of Law and Public Administration 54, 61.

61 Ivan Toronchuk and Volodymyr Markovskyi, 'The Implementation of the Venice Commission Recommendations on the Provision of the Minorities Language Rights in the Ukrainian Legislation' (2018) 5 European Journal of Law and Public Administration 54, 61.

62 For Latvia, see the extensive description given in Venice Commission, *Latvia - Opinion on the Recent Amendments to the Legislation on Education in Minority Languages*, Opinion № 975/2020 (18 June 2020) <https://www.venice.coe.int/webforms/documents/default.aspx?pdffile=CDL-AD(2020)012-e> accessed 15 August 2025.

63 For the French language situation, see Simo K. Määttä, 'The European Charter for Regional or Minority Languages, French Language Laws, and National Identity' (2005) 4(2) Language Policy 167, 170 <DOI: 10.1007/s10993-005-3518-4>.

In its 2023 Opinion on Ukraine, the Venice Commission also addresses this topic of the apparent imposition of more stringent standards on Ukraine than on other European states. In this Opinion, the Venice Commission refers to an earlier Opinion on Latvia from 2020,[64] stating that the Ukrainian situation is different from the Latvian one, since the Constitution of Ukraine, and not that of Latvia, safeguards the 'free development, use and protection of Russian'.[65] Furthermore, the Commission argues that because of its membership of the EU, Latvia can, in some cases, give a prioritised status to EU-languages in education, and treat Russian, which is not a foreign EU-language, as a minority language with less status than a foreign EU-language. This means that, according to the commission, in this respect, the differential treatment of Russian in Ukraine is different from the differential treatment of Russian in an EU-country such as Latvia. For Ukraine, which also aspires to become a member of the EU, it may appear as a double standard that the rights of the Russian language seem to carry less weight in an EU member state than in its own country. Nor are the feelings of discrimination among Russian speakers in Latvia likely to be any less pronounced than in Ukraine, merely because they live within the EU.

In its 2017 Opinion, the Venice Commission also takes into account that the Ukrainian language laws were a disproportionate interference with the *existing* rights of persons belonging to national minorities, and notes that:[66]

> [i]t [Article 7 of the draft law] actually allows to radically change the previous language regime, at least in secondary education, towards a system focused on the mandatory use of the Ukrainian language as the language of education. This could result in a substantial diminution in the opportunities available to persons belonging to national minorities to be taught in their languages, which

---

64 Venice Commission, *Latvia* (n 62) ss 109–114.

65 Venice Commission, *Opinion on the Law on National Minorities (Communities), Ukraine* (n 57) s 41.

66 At the same time, the Commission is aware that in actual practice the law cannot be implemented immediately due to a lack of qualified teachers. Therefore the Commission recommends 'to amend the transitional provision and to determine [...] a more realistic transitional period.' Venice Commission, *Opinion on the Provisions of the Law on Education of 5 September 2017* (n 52) s 82. The Commission also recommends the Ukrainian government to conserve 'at least, some prominent Russian schools as part of the historic and cultural identity and heritage of the concerned communities'. Venice Commission, *Opinion on the Provisions of the Law on Education of 5 September 2017* (n 52) s 115.

> would amount to a disproportionate interference with the existing rights of persons belonging to national minorities.[67]

The Venice Commission also states that '[i]n the context of the Framework Convention monitoring mechanism, changes from one model to another have been accepted as (possibly) being justified by the legitimate goal of any state to support and (re)vitalise its state language(s) in the case of e.g. Estonia and Latvia'.[68] This suggests that if it is Ukraine's goal to (re)vitalise the state language (Ukrainian), more far-going measures to promote the state language in Ukrainian might be permitted. But from a Ukrainian perspective, the existing situation was the result of a long period of deliberate attempts by Russia to promote Russian at the expense of Ukrainian.

In 2022 Ukraine also responded to the criticisms about its law on minorities, and defended its language policy, stating that '[d]espite the fact that Ukrainians made up the majority of the population of the Ukrainian SSR (72.73% of the total population according to the 1989 population census), they assimilated in terms of language as a result of the Russification policy, which provided a dominant status for Russian'.[69] Furthermore, the existing language law of 2012, which was replaced by the 2019 law, was introduced by the pro-Russian Yanukovych government, and resulted in a situation where in Russian-speaking parts of the country, Ukrainian de facto disappeared as the language of education, or of the government, de facto comparable to the opposite situation of Ukraine today. Without using the term 'discrimination', the Venice Commission noted in their Opinion about this law from the previous pro-Russian government that 'by strongly protecting the Russian language, without taking additional measures to confirm the role of Ukrainian as the State language and to ensure protection of other regional or minority languages, the Draft might increase existing linguistic divisions in the country rather than decreasing them'.[70]

---

67 Venice Commission, *Opinion on the Provisions of the Law on Education of 5 September 2017* (n 52) s 120.

68 Venice Commission, *Opinion on the Provisions of the Law on Education of 5 September 2017* (n 52) s 82.

69 Advisory Committee on the Framework Convention for the Protection of National Minorities, Council of Europe, *Fifth Report submitted by Ukraine Pursuant to Article 25, paragraph 2 of the Framework Convention for the Protection of National Minorities* (Council of Europe, 10 January 2022) 18 <https://rm.coe.int/5th-sr-ukraine-en/1680a52485> accessed 26 May 2025.

70 Venice Commission, *Opinion on the Draft Law on Languages in Ukraine, adopted by the Venice Commission at its 86th Plenary Session*, Opinion № 605/2010 (30 March 2011) <https://www.venice.coe.int/webforms/documents/default.aspx?pdffile=CDL-AD(2011)008-e> accessed 15 August 2025.

The Constitutional Court of Ukraine declared on 16 July 2019 that the Law on Education was non-discriminatory, and hence constitutional.[71] Nevertheless, the Venice Commission's findings in 2017 and 2019 say with regard to 'the differential treatment between the minorities speaking an official language of the EU and other national minorities,' that the Ukrainian arguments 'are not sufficient to outweigh the previous assessment of the Venice Commission and are not convincing from the perspective of human rights in general and the prohibition of discrimination in particular,' and recommended the repeal of the relevant provisions 'to the extent that it [the differential treatment] is not based on an objective and reasonable justification'.[72]

The preceding discussion shows that the topic of language laws is a complicated one, the evaluation of which strongly depends on the legal, political, and historical context, so that it, for instance, requires taking into account the legal framework of the country in question, as well as the treaties it has ratified and the Conventions and instruments it is a party to.

In sum, it is clear that the Ukrainian language laws negatively impact the Russian speakers in Ukraine. They raise issues of discrimination and diminish the role that the Russian language could play in Ukrainian society, something which is put forward by Putin. However, their primary goal is not to oppress the Russian-speaking minority or to eliminate the Russian language from Ukraine, as often suggested by Putin or other state officials, but to strengthen the unity of Ukraine via the sole official state language, which has been Ukrainian since 1989. The introduction of language legislation is also unlikely to lead to the disappearance of the Russian language in Ukraine, and the Russian language has a strong position in many parts of Ukraine. The Ukrainian language laws of 2017 and 2019 were introduced as a response to the 2012 language law of Ukraine introduced by the previous pro-Russian government, which promoted the use of Russian at the expense of Ukrainian. In addition, the laws of 2017, 2019, and 2021 also aim to protect the Ukrainian information

71 Constitutional Court of Ukraine, 'Summary to the Decision of the Grand Chamber of the Constitutional Court of Ukraine No. 10-r/2019 dated July 16, 2019 in the case upon the constitutional petition of 48 People's Deputies of Ukraine on the compliance of the Law of Ukraine "On Education" with the Constitution (constitutionality)' (16 July 2019) <https://view.officeapps.live.com/op/view.aspx?src=https%3A%2F%2Fweb.ccu.gov.ua%2Fsites%2Fdefault%2Ffiles%2Fdocs%2F10_r_2019_0.doc&wdOrigin=BROWSELINK > accessed 15 August 2025; Volodymyr Makarchuk and others, 'The adjudication of the language of education case in the Constitutional Court of Ukraine – a comparative analysis with ECtHR jurisprudence' (2020) 2 Law Review of Kyiv University of Law 94 <DOI: 10.36695/2219–5521.2.2020.16>.

72 Venice Commission, *Opinion on the Law on Supporting the Functioning of the Ukrainian Language* (n 56) s 44.

space.[73] That is, after the Russian invasion of 2014, the Ukrainian government wanted to prevent Russia from abusing the Russian-speaking minority in Ukraine for its political goals, for instance, through Russian propaganda aimed at Russian-speaking citizens. Therefore, the claim found in Russian propaganda that these language laws violate the human rights of Russian-speaking people or similar statements attribute false motives to the instalment of these laws and should be seen primarily as instruments of political agitation, even if there is indeed a concern about discrimination and the safeguarding of the rights of minorities and their languages.[74]

Moreover, Lavrov's claim that Russian-speaking people are killed only because they want to speak their native language is an unwarranted claim.[75] Indeed, people were killed, but this had nothing to do with genocide or with their native language, but with a country trying to regain control over its occupied territories. In the same vein, as is analysed in detail by Fortuin, restricting language policies cannot be equated with genocide.[76] Also, the claim that the language laws have caused genocide, as in our quote given above by Kirill Valerievich Vyshinsky, is fully unwarranted. This is clearly a causal fallacy (*post hoc ergo propter hoc*, literally 'after this, therefore because of this'), since there is no evidence whatsoever that the language laws of Ukraine led to the hostilities in the Donbas region, let alone genocide, and it is also not likely to assume that they did. In fact, the hostilities in Donbas were the result

73 The Ukrainian government's endeavour to protect its country's information space in a hybrid warfare is also described by Fortuin, 'Ukraine Commits Genocide on Russians' (n 20) 322–323. Original sources on the aim of the Ukrainian state to its information space include for instance, 'Bil'še Polovyny Pisen' na Radio Zvučat' Ukraïns'koju – Nacrada' *Ukrinform* (14 December 2018) <www.ukrinform.ua/rubric-society/2601314-bilse - polo vini-pisen-na-radio-zvucat-ukrainskou-nacrada.html> accessed 23 September 2025; National Security and Defense Council of Ukraine, 'Oleksiy Danilov: Russia Uses Information Terrorism against Ukraine, Which is Part of Hybrid Aggression' (3 February 2021) <https://www.rnbo.gov.ua/en/Diialnist/4804.html> accessed 23 September 2025; Ukaz Prezydenta Ukraïny 02.02.2021 № 43/2021, 'Pro Zastosuvannja Personal'nyx Special'nyh Ekonomičnyx ta Inšyx Obmežuval'nyx Zaxodiv (Sankcij)' (Prezydent Ukraïny Volodymyr Zelens'kyj, 2 February 2021) <https://www.president.gov.ua/documents/432021-36441?utm> accessed 23 September 2025.

The last source is the decree (№ 43/2021) of President Zelensky to sanction three Russian-speaking TV channels and the people related to them. Thereby he enacted the decision of the National Security and Defense Council of Ukraine, of which Oleksiy Danilov was the secretary at that time. The penultimate source also mentions this decision.

74 Fortuin, 'Ukraine Commits Genocide on Russians' (n 20) 322.

75 'Lavrov: za Pravo Govorit' na Russkom Jazyke na Ukraine' (n 44).

76 Fortuin, 'Ukraine Commits Genocide on Russians' (n 20) 340–341.

of the Russian invasion of 2014, and their support of the so-called people's republics of Donetsk and Luhansk, and the language laws of Ukraine can also be seen as strongly motivated by the Russian invasion. The argument as presented above can also be interpreted as a slippery slope fallacy, since the implementation of language laws is incorrectly presented as dangerous, since it will lead to a chain reaction resulting in the most serious crime against humanity – genocide.

Furthermore, even though Ukrainian laws glorify groups with questionable political views, the policies of the Ukrainian government themselves were not fascist or Nazi-inspired. In fact, the influence of right-wing political parties or Neo-Nazi political movements has significantly diminished in Ukraine, and is not different from other European countries, including Russia itself. There is also no proof that during the Maidan-protests, Neo-Nazis played an important role.[77] As such, the genocide or violation of human rights claim by Russia is partly based on misinformation about the Ukrainian language laws, and the actions of Ukraine to regain control over its lost territories, and partly an exaggeration and a hyperbole, fabricated to have a reason to invade Ukraine. It is a strawman fallacy since various standpoints are attributed to the government of Zelensky, for example, that they want to erase the Russian language from Ukraine, or even kill Russian-speakers, which is false.

4.4 Argument 1.1.1c

According to Putin, the liberation of Ukraine is in agreement with international law. That is, the 'Kiev regime' cannot be seen as a legal government, and since it does not represent the Russian-speaking people of Ukraine (specifically from Donbas, Zaporozhye, and Kherson regions), but is oppressing the Russian and Russian-speaking people in Ukraine, the Russian 'special military operation' of 2022 fully conforms to the 1970 UN Declaration on Principles of International Law. In the words of Lavrov:

> The question of the relationship between the right to self-determination and the principle of territorial integrity, after many years of debate, was resolved in the 1970 UN Declaration on Principles of International Law. It confirms the inviolability of the territorial integrity or political unity of states, provided that they have governments representing all the people living in a given territory. We know what severe oppression the Kiev regime subjected the Russian and Russian-speaking population to after the 2014 coup. It is obvious that the

77 See also Fortuin, 'Ukraine Commits Genocide on Russians' (n 20) 331.

> authorities in Kiev do not represent the residents of the Donbass, Zaporozhye and Kherson regions. The question of the conformity of referendums with the Constitution and the legislation of Ukraine does not affect their qualification under international law.[78]

Lavrov refers to principle 5 of the Resolution 2625 (XXV): 'Nothing in the foregoing paragraphs shall be construed as authorizing or encouraging any action which would dismember or impair, totally or in part, the territorial integrity or political unity of sovereign and independent States conducting themselves in compliance with the principle of equal rights and self-determination of peoples as described above and thus possessed of a government representing the whole people belonging to the territory without distinction as to race, creed or colour.'[79] In Lavrov's argumentation, the absence of a government, which represents all the people, i.e. the Russian-speaking people of the above-named territories, justifies Russia's support for the referendums and the annexation of the named territories. However, apart from this incorrect interpretation of the 1970 resolution,[80] Lavrov's claim that the democratically chosen and legitimate Zelensky government does not represent the whole people belonging to Ukraine is incorrect.[81] It is clear that Russia not only applies international law incorrectly, but it also clearly cherry-picks from it and uses it to deflect attention away from the Russian invasion. This can be illustrated with Lavrov's reference to the same 1970 Resolution 2625 (XXV) in 2015:

> Everyone must accept the fact that people have the right to independently choose their future without foreign interference in their internal affairs. In this connection, I suggest that we consider reaffirming and strengthening the rele-

---

78 Čkanikov (n 33) (see also the discussion in Olena Snigyr, 'Russian Strategic Narratives, 2022–2023' (2024) 68 Orbis 3, 17 <DOI: 10.1016/j.orbis.2023.11.002>).

79 United Nations General Assembly Sixth Committee (25th Session) 'Declaration on Principles of International Law concerning Friendly Relations and Cooperation among States in accordance with the Charter of the United Nations' (adopted 24 October 1970) UN Doc A/RES/2625(XXV) <https://digitallibrary.un.org/record/202170?v=pdf> accessed 2 June 2025.

80 Daniel Thürer and Thomas Burri, 'Secession', *Max Planck Encyclopedia of Public International Law* (2009) <https://opil.ouplaw.com/display/10.1093/law:epil/9780199231690/law-9780199231690-e1100?p=emailAm2EnwynJtupw&d=/10.1093/law:epil/9780199231690/law-9780199231690-e1100> accessed 2 June 2022.

81 See S Cavandoli and G Wilson, 'Distorting Fundamental Norms of International Law to Resurrect the Soviet Union: The International Law Context of Russia's Invasion of Ukraine' (2022) 69 Netherlands International Law Review 383; 392 <DOI: 10.1007/s40802-022-00219-9>.

> vant provisions of the 1970 Declaration on Principles of International Law concerning Friendly Relations and Co-operation among States in accordance with the UN Charter. The focus should be on the unacceptability of supporting the unconstitutional change of government. We must agree to use the UN Charter for joint risk management within increasingly complex international relations. In the early 1990s, the UN Secretariat prepared a handbook on the peaceful settlement of disputes between states. Maybe we need to update this handbook so that it incorporates the experience we have accumulated since its adoption.[82]

In this case, he refers to principle 1 that states that '[e]very State has the duty to refrain from organizing, instigating, assisting or participating in acts of civil strife or terrorist acts in another State or acquiescing in organized activities within its territory directed towards the commission of such acts, when the acts involve a threat or use of force'.[83] The Kremlin presents the Maidan revolution as something that was orchestrated by the West, and Lavrov wants the UN 1970 resolution to be reaffirmed and strengthened, such that it is even clearer that supporting 'unconstitutional change of government' would clearly fall under the resolution. As such, Russia has 'inverted' international law: its full-scale invasion is portrayed as consistent with international law, while the West's supportive stance towards the Maidan revolution is framed as a violation of international legal norms.

4.5 Arguments 1.1.1b, 1.1.1d, 1.1.1e, and 1.1.1f

According to argument 1.1.1b, the horror and genocide are an infringement of UN Security Council Resolution 2202 of 17 February 2015, which consolidated the Minsk Package of Measures of 12 February 2015. But as we already claimed above, Russia has never provided any evidence for genocide, and, in addition to that, the Minsk Agreements, which were a ceasefire and peace framework, failed immediately after their implementation. This was also due to the fact that Russia did not withdraw its military presence or influence, and the agreements were forced on Ukraine in a situation where Russian or separatist forces were advancing and Ukraine was losing ground.[84] The connected argument

82 Sergey Lavrov, 'Statement at the UN Security Council Open Debate on "Maintenance of International Peace and Security: Upholding the UN Charter"' (Ministry of Foreign Affairs of the Russian Federation, 9 February 2021) <https://www.mid.ru/en/foreign_policy/news/1583643/> accessed 30 April 2025.

83 UNGA Sixth Committee (n 79).

84 Kristian Åtland, 'War, Diplomacy, and More War: Why Did the Minsk Agreements Fail?' (2024) International Politics 1 <DOI: 10.1057/s41311–024-00637-x>.

1.1.1d given above states that Russia had no other option than to invade Ukraine, because of the horror and genocide (which is an infringement of the UN Security Council Resolution 2202 of 17 February 2015, and which is in accordance with Article 51 (Chapter VII) of the UN Charter). According to Russia, the West was looking away, such that Russia had to act by itself. Apart from the fact that Russia never showed evidence for genocide, it must be pointed out here, that even if crimes were committed by the Ukrainians, alternative courses of action were clearly available, and that the presupposition of crimes committed by Ukraine does not, in itself, justify an invasion under international law. Furthermore, the UN Security Council Resolution 2202 of 17 February 2015, which was about the full implementation of the Package of Measures for the implementation of the Minsk Agreements, had nothing to do with genocide. In this case, the reference to human rights violations and international agreements or international law must be seen as a smoke screen to disguise that Russia has no valid arguments to invade Ukraine.

The argument of the 'Kiev regime' being illegal (1.1.1f), is closely connected to the argument that the population of Ukraine did, in fact, *want* Ukraine to be either part of Russia or be in close union with Russia (1.1.1e). In his speech of 24 February 2022, Putin addresses the officers of the Ukrainian army to say that they should not want to fight for the Neo-Nazi Ukrainian government since this government does not serve the goal of the Ukrainian people.[85] According to Putin, the people of Crimea and Sevastopol have freely made a choice to reunite with Russia,[86] and the residents of the Donetsk and Luhansk People's Republics, and the Zaporozhye and Kherson regions, have determined their future at the referendums and made a clear choice, that is, to be with Russia, with their Motherland.[87] As such, according to Putin, becoming part of Russia is in fact the same as liberation from the 'Neo-Nazi Kiev regime'.

It is true that in a referendum, people in these regions voted to become part of Russia (in the case of Crimea and the self-declared People's Republics) or become independent from Russia and later become part of Russia. According to Russia, these elections were fully in accordance with international law. The validity of the legitimacy and fairness of the referendum in Crimea has, however, been disputed and is not recognised by the UN. And the same is true for the referendums that were held in the self-declared People's Republics of Luhansk and Donetsk. But any criticism of this is countered by the claim

85 Putin Speech of 24 February 2022 (n 13).
86 Putin Speech of 24 February 2022 (n 13).
87 Putin Speech of 21 February 2023 (n 14).

that the West habitually makes use of a double standard with respect to international law.[88] The double standard is also mentioned by Putin, for example, in his address in 2023, phrased in terms of hypocrisy.[89] Putin and other officials also frequently refer to Kosovo, whose independence in 2008 from Serbia is acknowledged by the West, whereas the West does not acknowledge Crimea's break-away from Ukraine. It is true that Russia raises a fair point with respect to Kosovo, but in doing so, it fails to mention that the Serbians committed human rights abuses against Kosovo Albanians, whereas no such abuses took place in Crimea.

The double standard argumentation or the hypocrisy argumentation is a legitimate argument if its goal is to come to a better understanding of international law and consistency in its application. In this case, however, the argument is an instance of a so-called *tu quoque* fallacy, i.e., a personal attack on the opponent by pointing out inconsistent behaviour. This *ad hominem* fallacy has the effect that the opponent is denounced as a serious discussion partner, and it conveniently diverts attention from Russia's bad actions to those of the US, NATO, or the West. By doing so, Russia does not have to deal with the potential criticisms that one can have with respect to the annexation of Crimea or the invasion of the whole of Ukraine. The argumentation does not hold, however, because the existence of other bad behaviour does not turn the behaviour at stake into acceptable behaviour.

4.6 Concluding Remarks about Russia's Appeals to 'Human Rights'

The liberation from genocide argument is an example of how Russia tries to build a narrative around the Second World War to play into the emotions of Russians and rally up the population to follow Putin. Again, it is a successful way to create an image of Ukraine, which wants to belong to the West, as the enemy, and Russia as the liberator. If we look more broadly at the discourse of human rights by the Russian government from the period 2013–2023, what is

88 See for example Ministry of Foreign Affairs of the Russian Federation, 'Foreign Minister Sergey Lavrov's remarks and answers to questions at the Masterclass working session held as part of the 2019 Paris Peace Forum, Paris, November 12, 2019' (12 November 2019) <https://www.mid.ru/tv/?id=1475618&lang=en> accessed 26 May 2025; Ministry of Foreign Affairs of the Russian Federation, 'Foreign Minister Sergey Lavrov's interview with Larry King's "Politicking" show on RT, Moscow, July 14, 2018' (14 July 2018) <https://www.mid.ru/en/foreign_policy/news/1574196/> accessed 26 May 2025.

89 Putin Speech of 21 February 2023 (n 14).

striking is that the term 'human rights' itself is clearly misappropriated in various ways.[90]

Firstly, Russia often presents itself as the protector of human rights outside of Russia, most notably with respect to Russian-speaking minorities. But as we have shown, in the case of Ukraine, Russia has abused the concept of human rights as a false argument to invade Ukraine. Russia has also pointed out that Russian-speaking minorities are oppressed in other countries, most notably the Baltic states. Even though Russia probably has genuine concerns about these minorities, the discussion raised by Russia about human rights is highly politicised and does not aim to resolve a dispute about the language rights of the Russian-speaking minorities. Russia sees the presence of Russian-speaking people as an indication that these countries are either part of the Russian sphere of influence or that they should have good political relations with Russia. As such, the presence of Russian-speaking people is conceived as a geopolitical factor by Russia.

Secondly, Russia sometimes accuses the West of violating human rights, for example, with respect to minorities or prisons in the US. This is usually done to provide a negative image of the West, and to deflect attention from accusations of the West that Russia is violating the human rights of its own population. Russian officials also frequently accuse the West of misappropriating human rights for political ends and using it as a geopolitical goal. To give an example, during his speech given at the UN Human Rights Council in 2018, Lavrov argues that '[t]here are continued attempts by some to adjust human rights to their own opportunistic interests. There remain dangerous trends to use human rights as a pretext to put pressure on certain 'unwelcome' or objectionable countries'.[91] In his speech, Lavrov defends Russia's support for the Assad regime in Syria and contends that Western states apply a double standard and abuse human rights. He argues that alleged human rights violations in Syria are instrumentalised to criticise Russia, while severe violations of the rights of the Russian-speaking population in Ukraine are overlooked or even

90 For the purpose of this chapter, we also looked more broadly into Russian political discourse to determine how the actual term 'human rights' is used. For this all posts from the website of the Kremlin and the Ministry of Foreign Affairs were analysed from 2014 until August 2024 where the term *human rights* or *prava čeloveka* was used.

91 'Lavrov Rasskazal o Popytkax Davlenija na Strany Temoj Prav Čeloveka' *RIA Novosti* (Moskva, 28 February 2018) <https://ria.ru/20180228/1515436773.html> accessed 26 May 2025. For Lavrov's complete speech for the Human Right Council, see Sergey Lavrov, 'Geneva / Lavrov Human Rights Council' (United Nations, Geneva, 28 February 2018) <https://media.un.org/avlibrary/en/asset/d210/d2101642> accessed 26 May 2025.

implicitly condoned by the West. This echoes other remarks by Russia that the West's, such as the EU's, assessment of human rights is selective.[92]

Again, Lavrov's reasoning is a clear instance of a *tu quoque* fallacy, since Russia deflects the attention from the concerns about the violation of human rights by pointing at other violations of human rights or questioning the sincerity of the goals of the accusers. Part of this strategy is not discussing the concerns about human rights by immediately attacking the person raising concerns (*ad hominem*). This can be illustrated with Russia's response to the annual US Country Reports on Human Rights Practices for 2018. On the one hand, Russia states that 'the report is noted for a patronising attitude and total disregard for the notions of sovereignty and non-interference in the internal affairs of states, which is a fundamental principle of international law that is sealed in the UN Charter'. As such, they argue that countries should not interfere with the internal affairs of other countries, even when violations of human rights are concerned. Besides this, Russia frames the accusations and concerns about human rights as ungrounded and based on anti-Russian sentiments, as such, ignoring the information that is being put forward, making itself immune to criticism:

> As for the section devoted to Russia, we regret to say that the authors have again failed, or more likely, refused to abandon anti-Russia stereotypes. They again used a traditional list of accusations, which hardly differs from the previous reports, in order to maintain a negative attitude towards Russia. The United States is using pseudo-documentary information and hackneyed anti-Russia banalities and clichés to accuse us of disregard for human rights, harassment of NGOs and human rights activists and 'deficient' democracy. Moreover, in addition to these ungrounded accusations, the authors also attempted to blame Russia for the human rights situation in Ukraine.[93]

The Russian rhetoric of the West's double standards establishes a distinct dichotomy between itself and the hypocritical West. The latter is portrayed as a violator of human rights, unreliable in adhering to international law, and guilty of applying double standards. Conversely, Russia presents itself as a

92 Ministry of Foreign Affairs of the Russian Federation, 'Comment by the Information and Press Department on the EU Annual Report on Human Rights and Democracy in the World in 2014' (24 June 2015) <https://mid.ru/en/foreign_policy/news/1510860/> accessed 26 May 2025.

93 Ministry of Foreign Affairs of the Russian Federation, 'Comment by the Information and Press Department on the US Department of State Human Rights Reports' (14 March 2019) <https://mid.ru/en/foreign_policy/news/1456212/> accessed 26 May 2025.

principled actor, committed to peace and compliance with international legal norms. Be that as it may, this rhetoric could not help Russia to regain its membership of the United Nations Human Rights Council in October 2023, after it had been expelled from this institution following its invasion in Ukraine.[94] In response, Russia has contended that such accusations constitute a politically motivated misuse of human rights discourse by Western actors, aimed at interfering in Russia's internal affairs.[95]

A third misappropriation of Russia's use of the term 'human rights' is when it refers to human rights organisations operating within Russia. They are systematically discredited by labelling them as 'foreign agents'. This classification not only delegitimises their work but also frames human rights as an inherently Western construct, alien to Russian society. By doing so, the Russian government effectively marginalises domestic human rights discourse and restricts the space for civil society activism. But at the same time, Russia presents itself as the protector of human rights in Russia. Putin stresses the excellent human rights situation in Russia,[96] and Russia has a Council for Civil Society and Human Rights.[97]

The above shows that Russia's strategic reinterpretation and misappropriation of human rights amounts to:

(i) on the one hand, the hyperbolic abuse of terms like 'genocide' with respect to the treatment of Russian-speaking minorities;
(ii) on the other hand, the misuse of the term 'human rights' for the situation in Russia, which is presented as an excellent human rights situation, and as something which the government finds very important, ignoring the reality – the gross violations of human rights in Russia;
(iii) the reference to alleged violations of human rights in Western countries is only to deflect attention away from Russia;
(iv) the attack on the West when they criticise Russia or Russia-backed countries with respect to the violations of human rights, stating that

94 James Landale, 'Russia Seeks to Rejoin UN's Human Rights Council' *BBC* (26 September 2023) <www.bbc.com/news/world-europe-66919358> accessed 28 April 2025.

95 Ministry of Foreign Affairs of the Russian Federation, 'Statement by the Deputy Head of the Delegation of the Russian Federation to the UN Human Rights Council at the Thematic Discussion "75th Anniversary of the Universal Declaration of Human Rights: Importance of Honoring International Obligations by States"' (23 June 2023) <https://mid.ru/en/foreign_policy/news/1890688/> accessed 26 May 2025.

96 'Putin Nazval Nezyblemymi Prava i Svobody Čeloveka v Rossii' *RBK* (29 November 2022) <www.rbc.ru/politics/29/11/2022/6385e3979a79471d015a2bc2> accessed 28 April 2025.

97 See for example Putin, *Meeting of the Council for Civil Society and Human Rights* (n 45).

the West politicises human rights, as such deflecting attention from the Western claims.

This all serves to shield the Russian state from accountability while simultaneously undermining the universality of human rights as a guiding principle in international law and diplomacy. The concept of human rights is frequently framed in a way that diverges from its universal application. This framing serves specific political purposes and undermines the broader human rights dialogue, both within Russia and internationally. Since 2012, Putin has introduced several laws that forbid 'foreign agents' (2012[98]), 'fake news' (2019[99]), 'disrespect to the authorities' (2019[100]), and spreading false information about the so-called 'special military operation' in Ukraine (2022,[101] 2023[102]). Many people have been put in prison because of these laws. Many others have fled the country. As is often the case in Russian propaganda, Russia has misappropriated the term 'human rights' in such a way that it has lost its original meaning.

5 Discussion

We have demonstrated that Russia has presented multiple justifications for its invasion of Ukraine, which are partly framed in terms of the relation to the perceived human rights situation within Ukraine, including the occupied territory of the Donbas region (Donetsk and Luhansk). If we look at the argumentation from a Pragma-Dialectical point of view, several violations of the dis-

98 Federal'nyj Zakon ot 20.07.2012 № 121-FZ, 'O Vnesenii Izmenenij v Otdel'nye Zakonodatel'nye Akty Rossijskoj Federacii v Časti Regulirovanija Dejatel'nosti Nekommerčeskix Organizacij, Vypolnjajuščix Funkcii Inostrannogo Agenta' <http://publication.pravo.gov.ru/Document/View/0001201207230003> accessed 2 May 2025.

99 Federal'nyj Zakon ot 18.03.2019 № 31-FZ, 'O Vnesenii Izmenenij v Stat'ju 15–3 Federal'nogo Zakona «Ob Informacii, Informacionnyx Texnologijax i o Zaščite Informacii»' <http://publication.pravo.gov.ru/Document/View/0001201903180031> accessed 2 May 2025.

100 Federal'nyj Zakon ot 18.03.2019 № 27-FZ, 'O Vnesenii Izmenenij v Kodeks Rossijskoj Federacii ob Administrativnyx Pravonarušenijax' <https://www.consultant.ru/document/cons_doc_LAW_320399/> accessed 2 May 2025.

101 Federal'nyj Zakon ot 26.03.2022 № 70-FZ, 'O Vnesenii Izmenenij v Kodeks Rossijskoj Federacii ob Administrativnyx Pravonarušenijax' <http://publication.pravo.gov.ru/Document/View/0001202306240012?index=1> accessed 2 May 2025.

102 Federal'nyj Zakon ot 04.08.2023 № 413-FZ, 'O Vnesenii Izmenenij v Ugolovnyj Kodeks Rossijskoj Federacii i Stat'i 31 i 151 Ugolovno-processual'nogo Kodeksa Rossijskoj Federacii' <http://publication.pravo.gov.ru/Document/View/0001202308040006> accessed 2 May 2025.

cussion rules can be discerned. A violation of the Pragma-Dialectical rules results in a fallacy, that is, in an incorrect discussion move.[103]

We start with Rule 1, which states that discussants may not prevent each other from advancing standpoints or from calling standpoints into question. Russia has been doing exactly that by discrediting the West as a serious discussion partner. Indeed, this is not literally preventing the West to express a standpoint or to call one of Russia's claims into question, but it has a similar result since it makes the West look untrustworthy and their standpoints remarks that need not be listened to. The attacks on Zelensky by portraying him as a Nazi or someone who is not democratically elected and having no support within Ukrainian society are clearly *ad hominem* fallacies, i.e., they attack the opponent on their characteristics instead of their argumentation.[104] In addition, Russia's various attacks on the West, i.e., the actions of which Russia is now accused, have previously been performed by the West itself, is a subtype of this fallacy: a *tu quoque* ('Look at yourself!'; in other disciplines also called a whataboutism).

A second type of violation concerns Rule 3, prohibiting attacks on a standpoint that is not the exact standpoint that the other party has put forward. Putin's distortion of the content of the language laws, framing them as a way to eliminate the Russian language or even the Russian speakers in Ukraine, is a clear example of a strawman fallacy.

Thirdly, Russia frequently introduces irrelevant arguments to justify its claims, which is a violation of Rule 4, which states, a.o., that standpoints may not be defended by argumentation that is not relevant to the standpoint. Instead of providing evidence for genocide, Russian officials point to the existence of far-right or Neo-Nazi groups in Ukraine or reference historical Ukrainian nationalist figures. In doing so, an association is suggested with Nazi-Germany, a nation that committed genocide. While these topics may initially appear to lend support to Russia's claims, closer scrutiny reveals that they have no direct relevance to the accusation of genocide. This deliberate misdirection serves to manipulate public perception and obscure the central issue.

In the fourth place, a very frequent type of fallacy in Russia's discourse violates Rule 6, according to which discussants may not falsely present something as an accepted starting point or falsely deny that something is an accepted starting point. Starting points refer, for instance, to shared knowledge, agreed-upon facts (e.g., geo-political and historical facts), and to mutually accepted

---

103 Frans H van Eemeren and Rob Grootendorst, 'Fallacies in Pragma-Dialectical Perspective' (1987) 1 Argumentation 283, 284, 297 <DOI: 10.1007/BF00136779>.

104 Below we consider them as violations of Rule 6 as well.

ethical and legal principles. In the ideal model, the discussants make a list of such starting points before entering the stage where arguments and criticisms are being exchanged, because, ultimately, starting points are the foundation of any argumentation. In reality, however, more often than not, starting points consist of explicit concessions or are implicitly agreed upon when they are given by the (institutional) context.

Russia's discourse is based on the presupposition that it shares with the West common ground, whereas in reality it does not. In Russia's justifications of the war against Ukraine, most of the argumentation is based on misinformation and misleading information about Ukraine: the illegality of Zelensky's presidency, the lack of support that Zelensky suffers from the Ukrainian population, the attribution of 'fascist' or 'Neo-Nazi' to the so-called 'Kiev regime', the promises that NATO would not expand, the pro-Russia mindedness of the Russian-speaking population of Ukraine, etc. Furthermore, the use of exaggerated terms, such as 'genocide' to describe Ukraine's language policies or the war in the Donbas region, distorts the concept of genocide as defined by the 1948 Genocide Convention,[105] or other definitions of genocide. While alleging genocide, Russia has failed to delineate how this accusation aligns with the legal definition of genocide.[106] The assertion that Ukraine violates human rights also lacks factual grounding and contradicts reports from international human rights organisations. Also with regard to other arguments do the Russian authorities fail to provide verifiable evidence to substantiate their claims – a characteristic feature of authoritarian regimes. Building on misinformation might persuade an ignorant audience, but due to this flaw in Russia's argumentation, its discourse can certainly not be considered as a serious attempt to convince a reasonable and critical audience.

In the fifth place, it has become clear that Russia has often made use of incorrectly applied argument schemes, which is a violation of Rule 8. An example is the false analogy with respect to the annexation of Crimea by Ukraine. Russia argues that since the West accepted that Kosovo broke away

105 *Convention on the Prevention and Punishment of the Crime of Genocide* (adopted 9 December 1948, entered into force 12 January 1951) 78 UNTS 277.

106 Note that Russia's refusal to respond to criticisms that the genocide claim is false can be considered as a violation of Rule 2, that commends discussants to defend a standpoint when they are requested to do so. In fact, not responding is a general property of Russian political discourse. Even if the facts are obvious, as, for example, in the case of the MH-17, which was shot down with help from Russia, Russia never acknowledged that previous claims they made about the MH-17 were wrong. See for example Egbert Fortuin, 'Het Ontleden van Russische Propaganda: De Drogreden' (*Leiden Rusland Blog*, 24 April 2015) <https://web.archive.org/web/20190428124255/https://www.leidenruslandblog.nl/articles/het-ontleden-van-russische-propaganda>.

from Serbia, it must also accept that Crimea became independent from Ukraine. This comparison is false since Russia refrains from arguing the similarities between these two cases and simply neglects the important differences between the two cases (see Section 4). Another example is the incorrectly applied causal argument scheme concerning the claim that the language laws automatically led to genocide. There is no reason at all to see a causal connection here, which makes this an instance of a so-called *post hoc ergo propter hoc* fallacy (also Section 4).

Lastly, the argumentation in Putin's speeches is presented in a very unclear way, which is a violation of Rule 10, i.e., where it forbids discussants to use insufficiently clear or confusingly ambiguous language. The argumentative discourse lacks clear argumentative indicators, and there are many remarks that seem to imply all sorts of things without stating them clearly.[107] Moreover, the speeches contain an abundance of irrelevant distractions, diverting attention from lacking evidence by overwhelming discussions with broad historical grievances and extraneous geopolitical concerns (which is actually a violation of the relevance rule, Rule 4, as well). It seems that Russia tries to persuade primarily by an overload of vaguely connected statements and claims, with the intention to make the audience lose sight of the arguments and prevent it from scrutinising their validity.

The inventory of the characteristics of Russia's argumentation to justify its war against Ukraine clearly shows its propagandistic nature. The argumentation only makes sense against the background of Russia's own narrative, i.e., its idiosyncratic account of the facts. This amounts to an all-encompassing alternative version of past and present reality – repeated in various speeches by Putin – to fit Russia's political goals. In this narrative, Ukraine as a nation state is essentially an anti-Russian Western project, controlled by NATO/the West, c.q. the US. It was founded in the nineteenth and twentieth centuries on what are historically Russian lands. Even though Russia was so benign as to accept the existence of Ukraine as a sovereign state, in 2014, there was an illegal *coup d'état* in which an illegal regime consisting of Neo-Nazis seized power. This 'Kiev regime' started to oppress the Russian population in Ukraine and committed acts of genocide, especially in Donbas. For that reason, Russia had to start a military operation in the background of the ongoing genocide of the Russians in Donbas in 2022, after its various attempts to achieve peace with Ukraine, which were neglected by the malign West.

107 For this reason, the analysis relies heavily on pragma-linguistic insights about language use, in particular the Relevance Maxim, to be discussed below (cf. Grice (n 10)).

The function of this narrative becomes particularly evident when examining Russia's claims concerning the human rights situation in Ukraine, including the occupied region of Donbas. Russia never seriously engaged in a debate about the language laws of Ukraine, nor did it express concerns about the Russian-speaking population in a serious way. Instead, these concerns were articulated using highly charged legal terminology, such as allegations of genocide by the illegal 'Neo-Nazi Kiev regime'. As such, the human rights talk of Russia can hardly be considered as a genuine attempt to seriously engage in a reasonable discussion with Ukraine or the West on this topic. Instead, its main goal is to persuade an ignorant audience by manipulating and misguiding with the intention to influence its opinion about Ukraine in a negative way and forcing support for Russia's standpoint that Ukraine should be invaded and punished. To this end, the Russian discourse makes use of subterfuge, distortion, and seemingly sophisticated half-truths to give verisimilitude to claims.[108] This clearly comes back in the misappropriation of human rights by Russia. Russia falsely accuses Ukraine of violating human rights with the aim of furthering its own political goals and to deflect attention from its real intentions and actions. Terms such as 'genocide' fit perfectly well in this strategy, especially since Russia stays far away from explaining how it interprets legal terms and regulations in this regard.[109]

As a final point, it is interesting to note that the so-called Gricean maxims for successful communication also demonstrate that propaganda is at stake.[110] By distorting truth (maxim of Quality), providing misleading levels of detail (maxim of Quantity), introducing irrelevant distractions (maxim of Relation), and using ambiguous language (maxim of Manner), Russia manipulates public perception to justify its actions. Recognising these violations is crucial for critically assessing political discourse and preventing the misuse of human rights frameworks for propagandistic purposes.[111]

108 For what is characteristic of the misappropriation of human rights in general, see Mégret (n 1) 255; De Búrca and Young (n 1) 205, 207, 213.

109 Russia thereby strategically uses the fact that human rights are often intentionally formulated in an amenable way, as human rights mean to include all nations and cultures and should therefore be open to different contestations and new ideas. De Búrca and Young (n 1) 211.

110 Grice (n 10).

111 For a Grician approach to hate speech, which shows similarities to Russia's discourse about Ukraine, see Assimakopoulos' Gricean approach in relation to hate speech in Stavros Assimakopoulos, 'Incitement to Discriminatory Hatred, Illocution and Perlocution' (2020) 11 Pragmatics and Society 177 <DOI: 10.1075/ps.18071.ass>.

6 Conclusion

This contribution has examined argumentative strategies employed by Russia to justify its full-scale invasion of Ukraine, particularly the invocation of human rights and international law. We focused on the liberation from genocide argument. By applying insights from communication and argumentation theory, a systematic analysis of the argumentation was conducted, showing that Russia's claims fail to meet the standards of sound communication and argumentation, violating fundamental principles of cooperative communication, argumentation, and international legal norms. Instead, the Russian discourse serves as a strategic propaganda device designed to manipulate domestic and international audiences.

This study has highlighted the deliberate distortions and misappropriation of human rights discourse. Russia's use of legal terminology, such as 'genocide', functions as a persuasive tool rather than a substantiated claim.[112] This and other uses of human rights terminology by Russian officials should not be interpreted as an effort to engage in legitimate legal discourse. Rather, such rhetoric serves to erode the meaning of legal and moral concepts by portraying Ukraine and its people as fundamentally immoral or responsible for grave crimes. This strategy not only distorts language (the meaning of terms like 'genocide') but also diminishes the importance of engaging in substantive and critical discussions about factual claims. Nevertheless, Russian authorities often present their assertions within a legal framework, thereby granting them an appearance of legitimacy while obscuring their actual ideological and expansionist objectives.

This propagandistic approach not only undermines the credibility of human rights discourse but also serves to legitimise aggressive foreign policy while suppressing dissent at home. Until now, the arguments used by Russia since 2022 have not changed very much. Even though some of these arguments are used primarily in Russia itself, some other arguments can also be heard in Europe, for example, in circles of extreme right or populist movements, or left-wing circles in Europe that are sympathetic towards Russia.

Understanding the mechanisms of rhetorical manipulation in Russian war propaganda is essential for countering disinformation and reinforcing the integrity of human rights and international law. Future research could extend this analysis to other authoritarian regimes that employ similar strategies,

112 A similar conclusion is reached in Roy Allison, 'Russia's Case for War against Ukraine: Legal Claims, Political Rhetoric, and Instrumentality in a Fracturing International Order' (2023) 71 Problems of Post-Communism 271 <DOI: 10.1080/10758216.2023.2254915>.

thereby contributing to a broader understanding of the role of propaganda in geopolitical conflicts. Recognising and deconstructing these narratives is a necessary step in safeguarding both democratic discourse and the fundamental principles of human rights.

Notes to the Text

Egbert Fortuin is the first author and Henrike Jansen, Levina de Wolf, and Wiktor Pawlowski are second authors.

In the running text we used the British Standards Institution transliteration of the Cyrillic alphabet. For the bibliography we used the academic transliteration. Many Ukrainian place names have both a Ukrainian (official) and a Russian variant. A well-known example is Ukrainian Київ (transliterated Kyiv) and Russian Киев (transliterated Kiev). Russian officials always use the Russian variant, to emphasise that they consider this the genuine name of the place. If we refer or cite Russian state officials we use the Russian names, but if we refer to these place names ourselves, we use the official Ukrainian ones.

Acknowledgements

We would like to express our gratitude to the reviewers, the editors of the volume, and in particular to Júlia Miklasová, for their valuable comments on our chapter, which have undoubtedly contributed to its improvement.

Appendix

The ten discussion rules in Pragma-Dialectics, taken from Van Eemeren and Garssen:[113]

1. *The freedom rule*: Discussants may not prevent each other from advancing standpoints or from calling standpoints into question.

---

113 Frans H. van Eemeren and Bart Garssen, 'Putting Pragma-Dialectics into Practice' in Jan Sobocan (ed), *Critical Thinking Education and Assessment: Can Higher Order Thinking be Tested?* (2nd edn, Windsor Studies in Argumentation 2022) <DOI: 10.22329/wsia.12.-2022>; Van Eemeren and Grootendorst, *A Systematic Theory of Argumentation* (n 4).

2. *The burden of proof rule*: Discussants who advance a standpoint may not refuse to defend this standpoint when requested to do so.
3. *The standpoint rule*: Attacks on standpoints may not bear on a standpoint that has not actually been put forward by the other party.
4. *The relevance rule*: Standpoints may not be defended by non-argumentation or argumentation that is not relevant to the standpoint.
5. *The unexpressed premise rule*: Discussants may not falsely attribute unexpressed premises to the other party or disown responsibility for their own implicit premises.
6. *The starting-point rule*: Discussants may not falsely present something as an accepted starting point or falsely deny that something is an accepted starting point.
7. *The validity rule*: Reasoning that in an argumentation is presented as formally conclusive may not be invalid in a logical sense.
8. *The argument scheme rule*: Standpoints may not be regarded as conclusively defended by argumentation that is not presented as based on formally conclusive reasoning if the defence does not take place by means of appropriate argument schemes that are applied correctly.
9. *The concluding rule*: Inconclusive defences of standpoints may not lead to maintaining these standpoints, and conclusive defences of standpoints may not lead to maintaining expressions of doubt concerning these standpoints.
10. *The usage rule*: Discussants may not use any formulations that are insufficiently clear or confusingly ambiguous, and they may not deliberately misinterpret the other party's formulations.

Bibliography

'Bil'še Polovyny Pisen' na Radio Zvučat' Ukraïns'koju – Nacrada' *Ukrinform* (14 December 2018) <www.ukrinform.ua/rubric-society/2601314-bilse-polovini-pisen-na-radio-zvucat-ukrainskou-nacrada.html>; accessed 23 September 2025.

Charter of the United Nations (adopted 26 June 1945, entered into force 24 October 1945) 1 UNTS XVI, art 51 <https://legal.un.org/repertory/art51.shtml> accessed 28 April 2025.

Convention on the Prevention and Punishment of the Crime of Genocide (adopted 9 December 1948, entered into force 12 January 1951) 78 UNTS 277.

'Education System in Ukraine' (*Ministry of Education and Science of Ukraine*) <https://emergency.mon.gov.ua/educationalsystem/> accessed 16 September 2025.

Federal'nyj Zakon ot 20.07.2012 № 121-FZ, 'O Vnesenii Izmenenij v Otdel'nye Zakonodatel'nye Akty Rossijskoj Federacii v Časti Regulirovanija Dejatel'nosti Nekommerčeskix Organizacij, Vypolnjajuščix Funkcii Inostrannogo Agenta' <http://publication.pravo.gov.ru/Document/View/0001201207230003> accessed 2 May 2025.

Federal'nyj Zakon ot 18.03.2019 № 27-FZ, 'O Vnesenii Izmenenij v Kodeks Rossijskoj Federacii ob Administrativnyx Pravonarušenijax' <https://www.consultant.ru/document/cons_doc_LAW_320399/> accessed 2 May 2025.

Federal'nyj Zakon ot 26.03.2022 № 70-FZ, 'O Vnesenii Izmenenij v Kodeks Rossijskoj Federacii ob Administrativnyx Pravonarušenijax' <http://publication.pravo.gov.ru/Document/View/0001202306240012?index=1> accessed 2 May 2025.

Federal'nyj Zakon ot 18.03.2019 № 31-FZ, 'O Vnesenii Izmenenij v Stat'ju 15–3 Federal'nogo Zakona «Ob Informacii, Informacionnyx Texnologijax i o Zaščite Informacii»' <http://publication.pravo.gov.ru/Document/View/0001201903180031> accessed 2 May 2025.

Federal'nyj Zakon ot 04.08.2023 № 413-FZ, 'O Vnesenii Izmenenij v Ugolovnyj Kodeks Rossijskoj Federacii i Stat'i 31 i 151 Ugolovno-processual'nogo Kodeksa Rossijskoj Federacii' <http://publication.pravo.gov.ru/Document/View/0001202308040006> accessed 2 May 2025.

'Lavrov Rasskazal o Popytkax Davlenija na Strany Temoj Prav Čeloveka' *RIA Novosti* (Moskva, 28 February 2018) <https://ria.ru/20180228/1515436773.html> accessed 26 May 2025.

'Lavrov: za Pravo Govorit' na Russkom Jazyke na Ukraine Možno Poplatit'sja Žizn'ju' *TASS* (Moskva, 1 March 2022) <https://tass.ru/politika/13914295> accessed 28 April 2025.

Law of Ukraine of 2 March 2020 № 2540, 'On Access to Archives of Repressive Agencies of Totalitarian Communist Regime of 1917–1991' <https://uinp.gov.ua/dokumenty/normatyvno-pravovi-akty-rozrobleni-v-instytuti/zakony/the-law-on-access-to-archives-of-repressive-agencies-of-totalitarian-communist-regime-of-1917-1991> accessed 26 May 2025.

Law of Ukraine of 9 April 2015 № 317-VIII, 'On the Condemnation of the Communist and National Socialist (Nazi) Regimes, and Prohibition of Propaganda of their Symbols' [2020 revision based on № 396-IX], *Bulletin of the Verkhovna Rada of Ukraine* 2015, № 26, art 219 <https://zakon.rada.gov.ua/laws/show/317-19?lang=en#Text> accessed 23 April 2022.

Law of Ukraine of 2 March 2020 № 2558, 'On the Condemnation of the Communist and National Socialist (Nazi) Regimes, and Prohibition of Propaganda of their Symbols' <https://uinp.gov.ua/dokumenty/normatyvno-pravovi-akty-rozrobleni-v-instytuti/zakony/the-law-on-the-condemnation-of-the-communist-and-national-socialist-nazi-regimes-and-prohibition-of-propaganda-of-their-symbols> accessed 26 May 2025.

Law of Ukraine of 5 September 2017 № 2145-VIII, 'On Education' [2022 revision based on № 1986-IX] *Bulletin of the Verkhovna Rada of Ukraine* 2017, № 38–39, art 380 <https://zakon.rada.gov.ua/laws/show/2145-19?lang=en#Text> accessed 26 May 2025.

Law of Ukraine of 1 July 2021 № 1616-IX, 'On Indigenous Peoples of Ukraine' ('Zakon Ukraïny pro korinni narody Ukraïny') *Bulletin of the Verkhovna Rada of Ukraine* 2021, № 38, art 319 <https://zakon.rada.gov.ua/laws/show/1616-20?lang=en#Text> accessed 26 May 2025.

Law of Ukraine of 2 March 2020 № 2538–1, 'On the Legal Status and Honoring the Memory of Fighters for Ukraine's Independence in the Twentieth Century' <https://uinp.gov.ua/dokumenty/normatyvno-pravovi-akty-rozrobleni-v-instytuti/zakony/the-law-on-the-legal-status-and-honoring-the-memory-of-fighters-for-ukraines-independence-in-the-twentieth-century> accessed 26 May 2025.

Law of Ukraine of 4 February 2020 № 2539, 'On the Perpetuation of the Victory over Nazism in World War II of 1939–1945' <https://uinp.gov.ua/dokumenty/normatyvno-pravovi-akty-rozrobleni-v-instytuti/zakony/the-law-on-the-perpetuation-of-the-victory-over-nazism-in-world-war-ii-of-1939-1945> accessed 26 May 2025.

Law of Ukraine of 25 April 2019 № 2704-VIII, 'On Supporting the Functioning of the Ukrainian Language as the State Language' [2022 revision based on № 2229-IX] *Bulletin of the Verkhovna Rada of Ukraine* 2019, № 21, art 81 <https://zakon.rada.gov.ua/laws/show/2704-19?lang=en#Text> accessed 26 May 2025.

'Putin Nazval Nezyblemymi Prava i Svobody Čeloveka v Rossii' *RBK* (29 November 2022) <www.rbc.ru/politics/29/11/2022/6385e3979a79471d015a2bc2> accessed 28 April 2025.

Ukraine and the Netherlands v Russia (dec) [GC] App nos 43800/14, 8019/16 and 28525/20 (ECtHR, 30 November 2022) <https://hudoc.echr.coe.int/eng#{%22itemid%22:[%22002-13989%22]}> accessed 2 June 2025.

Ukaz Prezydenta Ukraïny 02.02.2021 № 43/2021, 'Pro Zastosuvannja Personal'nyx Special'nyh Ekonomičnyx ta Inšyx Obmežuval'nyx Zaxodiv (Sankcij)' (Prezydent Ukraïny, Volodymyr Zelens'kyj, 2 February 2021) <https://www.president.gov.ua/documents/432021-36441?utm> accessed 23 September 2025.

Advisory Committee on the Framework Convention for the Protection of National Minorities, Council of Europe, *Fourth Opinion on Ukraine – adopted on 10 March 2017* (Council of Europe, 5 March 2018) <https://rm.coe.int/fourth-opinion-on-ukraine-adopted-on-10-march-2017-published-on-5-marc/16807930cf> accessed 26 May 2025.

Fifth Report submitted by Ukraine Pursuant to Article 25, paragraph 2 of the Framework Convention for the Protection of National Minorities (Council of Europe, 10 January 2022) <https://rm.coe.int/5th-sr-ukraine-en/1680a52485> accessed 26 May 2025

Allison R, 'Russia's Case for War against Ukraine: Legal Claims, Political Rhetoric, and Instrumentality in a Fracturing International Order' (2023) 71 Problems of Post-Communism 271 <DOI: 10.1080/10758216.2023.2254915>.

Arel D, 'Language, Status, and State Loyalty in Ukraine' (2017) 35 Harvard Ukrainian studies 233.

Assimakopoulos S, 'Incitement to Discriminatory Hatred, Illocution and Perlocution' (2020) 11 Pragmatics and Society 177 <DOI: 10.1075/ps.18071.ass>.

Åtland K, 'War, Diplomacy, and More War: Why Did the Minsk Agreements Fail?' (2024) International Politics 1 <DOI: 10.1057/s41311-024-00637-x>.

Beaver DI and Stanley J, *The Politics of Language* (Princeton University Press 2024).

Bob C, *Rights as Weapons: Instruments of Conflict, Tools of Power* (Princeton University Press 2019).

Cavandoli S and Wilson G, 'Distorting Fundamental Norms of International Law to Resurrect the Soviet Union: The International Law Context of Russia's Invasion of Ukraine' (2022) 69 Netherlands International Law Review 383 <DOI: 10.1007/s40802-022-00219-9>.

Civic Monitoring, *Chronology of the Conflict* (2014) <https://civicmonitoring.org/747-2/> accessed 2 May 2025.

Čkanikov M, 'Sergej Lavrov: Vse, Čto Zapad Xotel Sprovocirovat' u Nas, Načinaetsja u Nego' *Argumenty i Fakty* (8 October 2022) <https://aif.ru/politics/world/sergey_lavrov_vse_chto_zapad_hotel_sprovocirovat_u_nas_nachinaetsya_u_nego> accessed 2 June 2025.

Constitutional Court of Ukraine, 'Summary to the Decision of the Grand Chamber of the Constitutional Court of Ukraine No. 10,r/2019 dated July 16, 2019 in the case upon the constitutional petition of 48 People's Deputies of Ukraine on the compliance of the Law of Ukraine "On Education" with the Constitution (constitutionality)' (16 July 2019) <https://view.officeapps.live.com/op/view.aspx?src=https%3A%2F%2Fweb.ccu.gov.ua%2Fsites%2Fdefault%2Ffiles%2Fdocs%2F10_r_2019_0.doc&wdOrigin=BROWSELINK> accessed 15 August 2025.

Council of Europe, *Convention for the Protection of Human Rights and Fundamental Freedoms* (European Convention on Human Rights, as amended, 4 November 1950) ETS No 5 <https://www.echr.coe.int/documents/d/echr/convention_ENG> accessed 15 August 2025.

Cunningham SB, *The Idea of Propaganda: A Reconstruction* (Praeger 2002).

De Búrca G and Young KG, 'The (Mis)Appropriation of Human Rights by the New Global Right: An Introduction to the Symposium' (2023) 21 International Journal of Constitutional Law 205 <DOI: 10.1093/icon/moad019>.

Eemeren, FH van, *Strategic Maneuvering in Argumentative Discourse: Extending the Pragma-Dialectical Theory of Argumentation* (John Benjamins Publishing 2010).

Eemeren, FH van, *Argumentation Theory: A Pragma-Dialectical Perspective* (Springer 2018).

Eemeren, FH van and Garssen B, 'Putting Pragma-Dialectics into Practice' in Jan Sobocan (ed), *Critical Thinking Education and Assessment: Can Higher Order Thinking be Tested?* (2nd edn, Windsor Studies in Argumentation 2022) <DOI: 10.223 29/wsia.12.2022>.

Eemeren, FH van and Grootendorst R, 'Fallacies in Pragma-Dialectical Perspective' (1987) 1 Argumentation 283 <DOI: 10.1007/BF00136779>.

Eemeren, FH van and Grootendorst R, 'A Pragma-Dialectical Procedure for a Critical Discussion' (2003) 17 Argumentation 365 <DOI: 10.1023/A:1026334218681>.

Eemeren, FH van and Grootendorst R, *A Systematic Theory of Argumentation: The Pragma-Dialectical Approach* (Cambridge University Press 2004).

Eemeren, FH van and Snoeck Henkemans, AF, *Argumentation. Analysis and Evaluation* (Routledge 2016).

Entman RM, 'Framing Bias: Media in the Distribution of Power' (2007) 57 Journal of Communication 163 <DOI: 10.1111/j.1460-2466.2006.00336.x>.

European Court of Human Rights, *Guide on Article 2 of Protocol No 1 to the European Convention on Human Rights – Right to education* (28 February 2025) <https://ks.echr.coe.int/documents/d/echr-ks/guide_art_2_protocol_1_eng> accessed 1 July 2025.

Fortuin ELJ, 'Het Ontleden van Russische Propaganda: De Drogreden' (*Leiden Rusland Blog*, 24 April 2015) <https://web.archive.org/web/20190428124255/https://www.leidenruslandblog.nl/articles/het-ontleden-van-russische-propaganda>.

Fortuin ELJ, 'Ukraine Commits Genocide on Russians: The Term "Genocide" in Russian Propaganda' (2022) 46 Russian Linguistics 313 <DOI: 10.1007/s11185-022-09258-5>.

Green JA, Henderson C and Ruys T, 'Russia's Attack on Ukraine and the Jus Ad Bellum' (2022) 9 Journal on the Use of Force and International Law 4 <https://www.tandfonline.com/doi/full/10.1080/20531702.2022.2056803> accessed 26 May 2025.

Grice HP, 'Logic and Conversation' in C Peter and J Morgan (eds), *Syntax and Semantics*, vol 3 (Academic Press 1975).

Jowett GS and O'Donnell V, *Propaganda and Persuasion* (5th ed., Sage 2008).

Khmelko VJe, 'Linhvo-Etnična Struktura Ukraïny: Rehional'ni Osoblyvosti Ta Tendenciï Zmin Za Roky Nezaležnosti' (2004) 32 Naukovi zapysky NaUKMA. Sociolohični nauky <http://ekmair.ukma.edu.ua/bitstream/handle/123456789/8098/Khmelko_Linhvo-etnichna_struktura_Ukrainy.pdf?sequence=1&isAllowed=y> accessed 28 April 2025.

Kulyk V, 'Language Attitudes in Independent Ukraine: Differentiation and Evolution' (2017) 35 Harvard Ukrainian studies 265.

Lakoff G, *Don't Think of an Elephant! Know Your Values and Frame the Debate* (2014 edn., Chelsea Green Publishing 2004).

Landale J, 'Russia Seeks to Rejoin UN's Human Rights Council' *BBC* (26 September 2023) <www.bbc.com/news/world-europe-66919358> accessed 28 April 2025.

Lavrov S, 'Geneva / Lavrov Human Rights Council' (United Nations, Geneva, 28 February 2018) <https://media.un.org/avlibrary/en/asset/d210/d2101642> accessed 26 May 2025.

Lavrov S, 'Statement at the UN Security Council Open Debate on "Maintenance of International Peace and Security: Upholding the UN Charter"' (Ministry of Foreign Affairs of the Russian Federation, 9 February 2021) <https://www.mid.ru/en/foreign_policy/news/1583643/> accessed 30 April 2025.

Makarchuk V and others, 'The adjudication of the language of education case in the Constitutional Court of Ukraine – a comparative analysis with ECtHR jurisprudence' (2020) 2 Law Review of Kyiv University of Law 94 <DOI: 10.36695/2219-5521.2.2020.16>.

Määttä SK, 'The European Charter for Regional or Minority Languages, French Language Laws, and National Identity' (2005) 4 Language Policy 167 <DOI: 10.1007/s10993-005-3518-4>.

Mégret F, 'Human Rights Populism' (2022) 13 Humanity: An International Journal of Human Rights, Humanitarianism, and Development 240 <DOI: 10.1353/hum.2022.0010>.

Miklasová J, *Secession in International Law with a Special Reference to the Post-Soviet Space* (Brill Nijhoff 2023) <https://brill.com/display/title/68975?language=en> accessed 26 May 2025.

Ministry of Foreign Affairs of the Russian Federation, 'Comment by the Information and Press Department on the EU Annual Report on Human Rights and Democracy in the World in 2014' (24 June 2015) <https://mid.ru/en/foreign_policy/news/1510860/> accessed 26 May 2025.

Ministry of Foreign Affairs of the Russian Federation, 'Foreign Minister Sergey Lavrov's interview with Larry King's "Politicking" show on RT, Moscow, July 14, 2018' (14 July 2018) <https://www.mid.ru/en/foreign_policy/news/1574196/> accessed 26 May 2025.

Ministry of Foreign Affairs of the Russian Federation, 'Comment by the Information and Press Department on the US Department of State Human Rights Reports' (14 March 2019) <https://mid.ru/en/foreign_policy/news/1456212/> accessed 26 May 2025.

Ministry of Foreign Affairs of the Russian Federation, 'Foreign Minister Sergey Lavrov's remarks and answers to questions at the Masterclass working session held as part of the 2019 Paris Peace Forum, Paris, November 12, 2019' (12 November 2019) <https://www.mid.ru/tv/?id=1475618&lang=en> accessed 26 May 2025.

Ministry of Foreign Affairs of the Russian Federation, 'Concept of the Humanitarian Policy of the Russian Federation Abroad' (31 July 2022) <https://mid.ru/en/foreign_policy/humanitarian_cooperation/1448
658/> accessed 26 May 2025.

Ministry of Foreign Affairs of the Russian Federation, 'Statement by the Deputy Head of the Delegation of the Russian Federation to the UN Human Rights Council at the Thematic Discussion "75th Anniversary of the Universal Declaration of Human Rights: Importance of Honoring International Obligations by States"' (23 June 2023) <https://mid.ru/en/foreign_policy/news/1890688/> accessed 26 May 2025.

National Security and Defense Council of Ukraine, 'Oleksiy Danilov: Russia Uses Information Terrorism against Ukraine, Which is Part of Hybrid Aggression' (3 February 2021) <https://www.rnbo.gov.ua/en/Diialnist/4804.html> accessed 23 September 2025.

Pleines H, 'Assessing the legality of the power changes in Ukraine' *Montesquieu Instituut* (24 March 2014) <https://www.montesquieu-instituut.nl/id/vjicc5jt4ayk/nieuws/assessing_the_legality_of_the_power?colctx=vllzft76lfmu&start_002=644&utm> accessed 5 June 2025.

Prina F and Pentassuglia G, 'Ukraine's Law on National Minorities and 'Effective' Participation: Expanding or Diluting Standards?' (2023) 30 International Journal on Minority and Group Rights 880 <DOI: 10.1163/15718115-bja10138>.

Putin V, 'Obraščenie Prezidenta Rossijskoj Federacii' (Kreml', Moskva, 18 March 2014) <http://kremlin.ru/events/president/news/20603> accessed 28 April 2025.

Putin V, 'Meeting of the Council for Civil Society and Human Rights' (Moscow, 9 December 2021) <http://en.kremlin.ru/events/president/news/67331> accessed 2 May 2025.

Putin V, 'Address by the President of the Russian Federation' (Kremlin, Moscow, 21 February 2022) <http://en.kremlin.ru/events/president/news/67828> accessed 28 April 2025.

Putin V, 'Address by the President of the Russian Federation' (Kremlin, Moscow, 24 February 2022) <http://en.kremlin.ru/events/president/news/67843> accessed 28 April 2025.

Putin V, 'Signing of treaties on accession of Donetsk and Lugansk people's republics and Zaporozhye and Kherson regions to Russia' (Kremlin, Moscow, 30 September 2022) <http://en.kremlin.ru/events/president/news/69465> accessed 26 September 2025.

Putin V, 'Presidential Address to Federal Assembly' (Gostiny Dvor, Moscow, 21 February 2023) <http://en.kremlin.ru/events/president/news/70565> accessed 28 April 2025.

Shveda Y and Park JH, 'Ukraine's Revolution of Dignity: The Dynamics of Euromaidan' (2016) 7 Journal of Eurasian studies 85 <DOI:10.1016/j.euras.2015.10.007>.

Sindelar D, 'Was Yanukovych's Ouster Constitutional?' *Radio Free Europe/Radio Liberty* (23 February 2014) <www.rferl.org/a/was-yanukovychs-ouster-constitutional/25274346.html>; accessed 28 April 2025.

Smith BL, 'Propaganda', *Encyclopedia Britannica* (2016) <www.britannica.com/topic/propaganda> accessed 23 April 2022.

Snigyr O, 'Russian Strategic Narratives, 2022–2023' (2024) 68 Orbis 3 <DOI: 10.1016/j.orbis.2023.11.002>.

Sproule JM, 'Channels of Propaganda' (ERIC/EDINFO Press, Indiana University 1994) <https://eric.ed.gov/?id=ED372461> accessed 28 April 2025.

Stanley J, *How Propaganda Works* (Princeton University Press 2015).

Tabory M, 'Language Rights as Human Rights' (1980) 10 *Israel Yearbook on Human Rights* 167.

Thürer D and Burri T, 'Secession', *Max Planck Encyclopedia of Public International Law* (2009) <https://opil.ouplaw.com/display/10.1093/law:epil/9780199231690/law-9780199231690-e1100?p=emailAm2EnwynJtupw&d=/10.1093/law:epil/9780199231690/law-9780199231690-e1100> accessed 2 June 2022.

Toronchuk I and Markovskyi V, 'The Implementation of the Venice Commission Recommendations on the Provision of the Minorities Language Rights in the Ukrainian Legislation' (2018) 5 European Journal of Law and Public Administration 54 <https://lumenpublishing.com/journals/index.php/ejlpa/article/view/1139/pdf> accessed 15 August 2025.

Umland A, 'Irregular Militias and Radical Nationalism in Post-Euromaydan Ukraine: The Prehistory and Emergence of the "Azov" Battalion in 2014' (2019) 31 Terrorism and Political Violence 105 <https://doi.org/10.1080/09546553.2018.1555974>.

United Nations General Assembly Sixth Committee (25th Session) 'Declaration on Principles of International Law concerning Friendly Relations and Cooperation among States in accordance with the Charter of the United Nations' (adopted 24 October 1970) UN Doc A/RES/2625(XXV) <https://digitallibrary.un.org/record/202170?v=pdf> accessed 2 June 2025.

Venice Commission, *Opinion on the Law on National Minorities (Communities), Ukraine*, CDL-AD(2023)021-e (9–10 June 2023, published 12 June 2023) < https://www.venice.coe.int/webforms/documents/default.aspx?pdffile=CDL-AD(2023)021-e> accessed 4 July 2025.

Venice Commission, *Latvia – Opinion on the Recent Amendments to the Legislation on Education in Minority Languages*, Opinion № 975/2020 (18 June 2020) < https://www.venice.coe.int/webforms/documents/default.aspx?pdffile=CDL-AD(2020)012-e> accessed 15 August 2025.

Venice Commission, *Opinion on the Law on Supporting the Functioning of the Ukrainian Language as the State Language, adopted by the Venice Commission at its 121st Plen-*

ary Session, Opinion № 960/2019 (6–7 December 2019) <https://www.venice.coe.int/webforms/documents/?pdf=CDL-AD(2019)032-e> accessed 26 May 2025.

Venice Commission, *Opinion on the Provisions of the Law on Education of 5 September 2017 which Concern the Use of the State Language and Minority and Other Languages in Education*, Opinion № 902/2017 (11 December 2017) <www.venice.coe.int/webforms/documents/default.aspx?pdffile=CDL-AD(2017)030-e> accessed 26 May 2025.

Venice Commission, *Opinion on the Draft Law on Languages in Ukraine, adopted by the Venice Commission at its 86th Plenary Session*, Opinion № 605/2010 (30 March 2011) <https://www.venice.coe.int/webforms/documents/default.aspx?pdffile=CDL-AD(2011)008-e> accessed 15 August 2025.

PART 2

Fora and Actors of Human Rights Misappropriation

CHAPTER 6

Alternative and Competing Narratives in the International Human Rights System

Rosa Freedman

1 Introduction

Universality is at the heart of international human rights, with the central tenet being that all individuals have fundamental human rights by virtue of being born human. Yet, ever since the Universal Declaration of Human Rights was adopted in 1948, a sizeable number of states have tried to insist that human rights are not universal. Those states have attempted to undermine universality by using a range of discourses and tactics to challenge or undermine the international human rights project.

For some decades leading up to the 1990s, conflicts on human rights issues were often presented as conflicts between states' values. Some states went as far as invoking 'Asian values'[1] in opposition to the existence of a universal concept of human rights.[2] Other governments deploying cultural relativist discourses used cultural or religious values to justify limiting or undermining human rights.[3] Resolving such conflicts becomes politically sensitive, and compromise often appears unfeasible.[4] Although cultural sensitivities can affect the way a fact is perceived, it is more likely that 'disagreement over the facts merely reflects wishful thinking or wilful deception, a hypocritical avoidance of the fundamental rules of international conduct by lying',[5] such as

1 See, for example, Michael D. Barr, 'Lee Kuan Yew and the "Asian values" debate' (2000) 24 Asian Studies Review 309.

2 See, for example, World Conference on Human Rights, Report of the Regional Meeting for Asia of the World Conference on Human Rights, Bangkok, 29 March-2 April 1993 (A/CONF.157/ASRM/8, 1993).

3 Bilahari Kausikan, 'Asia's Different Standards' (1993) 92 Foreign Policy 24.

4 Volker Rittberger, Bernhard Zangl, Matthias Staisch, *International Organization: Polity, Politics and Policies* (Palgrave MacMillan 2006) 193–208.

5 Thomas M. Franck, 'Of Gnats and Camels: Is there a double standard at the United Nations?' (1984) 78 The American Journal of International Law, 811, 831–832.

where claims about "cultural sensitivities" are used as an attempt to justify oppression of LGBT individuals.[6]

In the 1993 Vienna Declaration and Program of Action, practitioners can first be seen as insisting that the door has been closed on these discussions, declaring in its first paragraph that 'The universal nature of these rights and freedoms is beyond question'.[7] Whilst it also, rather more ambiguously, said that 'the significance of national and regional particularities and various historical, cultural and religious backgrounds must be borne in mind',[8] this should not be seen as deviating from the general orientation of universality. Rather, it indicates that the method of securing compliance is a matter for the State's internal legal system, and that it is the duty of States to promote and protect human rights.

Although the universality battleground is comprehensively discussed in many academic and practitioner commentaries, there is less understanding of how states currently take forward cultural relativist approaches at intergovernmental bodies and through soft power. This chapter explores how states are trying to push back on human rights and undermine universality through the guise of misappropriating human rights discourses and the politicised tactics that they deploy.

The article begins by exploring and explaining politicisation of human rights, how it can be understood, and ways in which it manifests in intergovernmental bodies, with a specific focus on those tactics within the UN Human Rights Council. As such, two case studies are explored in Section 3 to understand the manifestation and impact of politicised tactics at the Council on the human rights project and the misappropriation of human rights. The article then turns to some of the other tactics deployed outside of intergovernmental bodies to undermine universal human rights. The concluding comments explore some of the motivations for states to follow these courses of conduct and some ways to counter these moves in order to protect and advance universal human rights. The chapter does not aim to provide a comprehensive study of all forms of attacks on international human rights law – to do so would require significantly more space and resources than possible within the constraints of one article – but rather to open discussions about the current tactics used to attack and undermine universal human rights.

---

6 Eric Heinze, 'Sexual Orientation and International Law: A Study in the Manufacture of Cross-Cultural "Sensitivity"' (2001) 22 Michigan Journal of International Law 283.

7 Vienna Declaration and Programme of Action, adopted by World Conference on Human Rights on 25 June 1993 (UN Doc A/CONF.157/23) para 1.

8 Ibid, para 5.

2 Politicisation

> Let me suggest that the word 'politicization' be retired from active service. Let me be frank, most of the people in this room work for governments or seek to effect the actions of governments: that is politics. For some people in this room to accuse others of being political is a bit like fish criticizing one another for being wet. (Sergio Viera de Mello[9])

The very nature of international organisations is political, and therefore some degree of politicisation will always exist, through discourse[10] and/or through tactics. Whether there is politicisation is often based on the eye of the beholder. Brown asserts that 'politicization seems to be something that states are quite willing to accuse each other of doing but that they never seem to admit to doing themselves'.[11] States with common political aims will not view those aims as being furthered as politicisation, while countries with opposing interests will often cry foul. The forms of politicisation have been well explored,[12] but less attention has been paid to the motives that generate policisation, which I categorise as progressive, pernicious, retractionist or regionalist:

- ***progressive politicisation*** – states use tactics within intergovernmental bodies to advance the development of human rights;
- ***pernicious politicisation*** – states use intergovernmental bodies to undermine the interpretation or implementation of particular fundamental rights and/or to justify the oppression of particular groups or individuals;
- ***retractionist politicisation*** – states seek to undermine the human rights project in its entirety.

The key difference between, for example, progressive politicisation and advancing human rights or indeed retractionist politicisation and cultural relativism is whether human rights discourse and political tactics are being

9 Commission's Are Sound, Problems Can Be Surmounted, High Commissioner Says as Main Human Rights Body Ends Session', OHCHR Press Release, 25 April 2003.

10 See, e.g. Gene Lyons, David Baldwin, Donald McNemar, 'The "Politicization" Issue in the UN Specialized Agencies' (1977) 32 Proceedings of the Academy of Political Science 89; Eric Heinze, 'Even-handedness and the Politics of Human Rights' (2008) 21 Harvard Human Rights Journal 7, 41.

11 Bartram S. Brown, The United States and the Politicization of the World Bank: Issues of international law and policy (first published 1992, Kegan Paul International 2024) p. 22.

12 See, for example, Rosa Freedman, 'Third generation' rights: is there room for hybrid constructs within International Human Rights Law?' (2014) 2 Cambridge Journal of International and Comparative Law 935; and Rosa Freedman 'Politicisation of human rights: Current battlegrounds and sites of contestation' (2024) 51 University of Western Australia Law Review 1.

used to advance those rights or misappropriated to undermine them. Central to the topology is that the focus is first on the tactics and then on the motivations. Politicisation itself is a neutral term, but the motives underpinning specific politicised discourse and actions enable us to understand how and why they have been deployed. This, in turn, enables better understanding of state and bloc actions and activities within the human rights arena.

Frequently the tactics deployed by states with different motives are similar to one another. The key element that separates the different types of politicisation is whether the strategies and tactics are used to advance human rights, undermine specific human rights, or derail the human rights project altogether. Crucially, states seeking to undermine or derail almost always do so by misappropriating progressive discourse and tactics, seeking to attack the human rights project from within rather than simply disengaging from the system. Dominguez-Redondo insists that politicisation provides a "blunt critique" of political processes. Her position has some merit when commentators do not explore the different ways in which politicisation manifests;[13] but she does not address the impact of pernicious or retractionist politicisation. It is only by exploring the different types of politicisation, often deployed at the same time, by different groups of states, that we can understand how politicisation impacts upon the human rights matrix.

3 Politicisation and Human Rights: Current Sites of Contestation

To understand how competing human rights narratives play out within the human rights matrix, particularly the use of pernicious and retractionist tactics, this section explores two sites of contestation at the UN Human Rights Council, the global political human rights body. These are battlegrounds involving many states and alliances. This enables understanding of the tactics deployed both to advance and to counter those agendas, and the ways in which the topology can be used to understand state motives. That, in turn, provides foundations for understanding and analysing the current narratives and tactics deployed in other arenas (discussed in Section 4).

---

13 Elvira Domínguez-Redondo, In Defence of Politicization of Human Rights: The UN Special Procedures (OUP 2020).

3.1 SOGI Rights and Rights of 'the Family'

A main battleground on the universality of human rights has long been the protection, or lack thereof, of fundamental rights for Sexual Orientation and Gender Identity (SOGI) minorities. The case study demonstrates the tensions between different states and blocs using similar tactics motivated by all three types of politicisation. From the early negotiations on the 1993 Vienna Declaration and Programme of Action to the present day, this issue has been a site of contestation of human rights in which progressive tactics and agendas have been countered by pernicious tactics, sometimes with the additional aim of retractionism by those states seeking to undermine universality of human rights. As such, advances have been slow, at best, and each step towards non-discrimination has met with attempts to block or undermine those moves.

Initial attempts to propose language recognising the SOGI minorities[14] were proposed by states seeking to protect that group for progressive motivations. Those attempts were immediately countered by proposals to delete the entire sentence about prohibited grounds of discrimination,[15] motivated by pernicious reasons from states that criminalized or oppressed SOGI minorities or acts, and therefore wanted to block any attempt to protect universally their human rights. The outcome was a simple statement condemning discrimination without listing any specifically prohibited grounds,[16] which played into the hands of those seeking to block SOGI protection. The final Declaration and Programme of Action devoted substantial attention to women's rights but made no mention of SOGI minorities.

It took until 2006 for SOGI to be placed into a UN human rights resolution (on extra-judicial, summary or arbitrary executions),[17] and until 2011 for a resolution specifically on the fundamental rights of SOGI minorities. Resolution

14 The sentence in question was the first sentence of Principle 8 of the Secretariat-proposed text: 'Respect for human rights and for fundamental freedoms for all human beings without distinction as to sex, language, or religions is a fundamental rule of human rights law…'. The second sentence of the proposed paragraph referred to the need to eliminate 'all forms of racism and racism, xenophobia and related intolerance'. See M.D. Kirby, 'International Legal Notes: Second World Conference on Human Rights, Vienna, Austria', *Australian Law Journal*, June 1993, pp 1–12.

15 M.D. Kirby, 'International Legal Notes: Second World Conference on Human Rights, Vienna, Austria', *Australian Law Journal*, June 1993, pp 1–12.

16 Douglas Sanders, 'Human rights and sexual orientation in international law' (2002) 25 International Journal of Public Administration 13.

17 UNCHR, 'Commission on Human Rights resolution 2000/31 Extrajudicial, summary or arbitrary executions' (20 April 2000) UN Doc E/CN.4/RES/2000/31.

17/19[18] commissioned a study and convened a panel session on SOGI rights. Until 2011 discussions on SOGI rights had been blocked by the OIC and many African countries.[19] Resolution 17/19 was an anomaly enabled by internal rifts within the Organisation of Islamic Cooperation (OIC) during the 'Arab Spring' uprisings resulting in those states being absent from the negotiating process and therefore neither blocking nor diluting the resolution.

A year later, when the panel took place,[20] the OIC was almost fully reunified. As the then UN Secretary-General Ban Ki-Moon was delivering a video address opening the Panel, almost every delegate from OIC member states that were in attendance stood up and filed out of the Council Chamber, seemingly to undermine the panel's legitimacy. South Africa, which had proposed the original resolution, and which has SOGI rights enshrined in its national Constitution, caved to pressure from regional allies and announced that it would not table a further resolution on SOGI. South Africa's *volte-face* was a sign of the growing momentum against SOGI rights. It took another five years for the Council to create a Special Procedures mandate on protecting SOGI persons from violence and discrimination.[21] The mandate's creation stirred great protest first at the Council and then at the UN General Assembly,[22] but to date it continues to be renewed periodically.

The tactics deployed throughout that time demonstrate the back-and-forth nature of bloc voting and peer-pressure in advancing both progressive and pernicious motivations on SOGI rights. At the same time, other attempts were made not only to block the protection of SOGI rights but also to advance agendas that could be used to criminalise or oppress SOGI minorities, thus undermining the universality of human rights. More than 70 countries still criminalise LGBTI people and their actions and still have state-sponsored

18 UNHRC, '17/19 Human rights, sexual orientation and gender identity' (14 July 2011) UN Doc A/HRC/RES/17/19.

19 Rosa Freedman, 'The United Nations Human Rights Council's Backwards Step on LGBT Rights', *IntLawGrrls*, 7 June 2013.

20 Stephan Gray, '"Milestone" LGBT Discussion at UN Human Rights Council Welcomed Despite Walkout' *Pink News* (8 March 2012) <www.thepinknews.com/2012/03/08/milestone-lgbt-discussion-at-un-human-rights-council-welcomed-despite-walkout/> accessed 30 September 2025.

21 UNHRC, 'Resolution adopted by the Human Rights Council on 30 June 2016 – 32/2: Protection against violence and discrimination based on sexual orientation and gender identity' (15 July 2016) UN Doc A/HRC/RES/32/2.

22 Rosa Freedman, 'Mandate Renewal of Independent Expert on Sexual Orientation and Gender Identity At Risk' (*IPI Global Observatory*, 10 July 2019) <https://theglobalobservatory.org/2019/07/mandate-renewal-independent-expert-sogi-at-risk/> accessed 30 September 2025.

measures that violate their fundamental rights.[23] Many of those same states were at the fore of these pernicious and retractionist attempts. One tactic they deployed was seeking to advance 'traditional values' or rights of 'the family' as a way of countering moves to protect SOGI minorities.

In September 2009, the Russian Federation, Belarus, Bolivia, China, Singapore and Sri Lanka, amongst others, introduced a draft resolution at the HRC entitled 'Promoting Human Rights and Fundamental Freedoms through a Better Understanding of Traditional Values of Humankind'.[24] Some supporters of the resolution emphasised 'the importance, among others, of traditional *family* values, which serve as a good and solid foundation in the strengthening of human rights principles and norms'.[25] Other states raised concerns that this approach could undermine women's rights and the rights of other minorities, or indeed 'legitimise human rights abuses'.[26] The resolution was adopted by a vote of 26 to 15, with 6 abstentions.[27]

In 2011 and 2012 Russia tabled similar resolutions with the OIC, the Group of Arab States and the African Group as co-sponsors.[28] The 'Traditional Values' agenda was advanced both to counter protections of SOGI minorities and also, more broadly, to challenge universality of human rights. China, for example, insisted that 'the education of traditional values' was consistent with 'the right

23 See, for example, Human Dignity Trust, *Map of Countries that Criminalise LGBT People* <www.humandignitytrust.org/lgbt-the-law/map-of-criminalisation/?type_filter_submitted=> n.d.

24 UNHRC, '12/... Promoting human rights and fundamental freedoms through a better understanding of traditional values of humankind' (A/HRC/12/L.13/Rev.1, 30 September 2009).

25 Emphasis added. Permanent Mission of the Republic of Indonesia, 'Statement by H.E. Mr. Dian Triansyah Djani of Indonesia. Explanation of Vote on "Human Rights and Traditional Values"', Human Rights Council 12th Session, 2 October 2009.

26 On the resolution 'Strengthening Respect for Human Rights'. D. Griffiths, 'Explanation of Vote by the United States on Traditional Values', Human Rights Council 12th Session, 1 October 2009.

27 UNHRC, 'Promoting human rights and fundamental freedoms through a better understanding of traditional values of humankind: resolution / adopted by the Human Rights Council' (12 October 2009) UN Doc A/HRC/Res/12/21.

28 See adopted by a vote of 24 to 14, with 7 abstentions, UNHRC, '16/3 Promoting human rights and fundamental freedoms through a better understanding of traditional values of humankind', (8 April 2011) UN Doc A/HRC/RES/16/3; adopted by a vote of 25 to 15, with 7 abstentions, UNHRC, '21/3 Promoting human rights and fundamental freedoms through a better understanding of traditional values of humankind: best practices' (9 October 2012) UN Doc A/HRC/RES/21/3.

of each country to freely choose their mode for promoting human rights according to their natural historical, cultural or other backgrounds'.[29]

The HRC Advisory Committee 2012 study on traditional values underscored the primacy of universality of human rights where there are any conflicts with 'traditional values'.[30] An Office of the High Commissioner for Human Rights (OHCHR) report on the same topic noted that 'traditional values could be invoked [...] to undermine the rights of the most marginalized and disadvantaged groups'.[31] After that time, the Russian Federation and its allies moved away from the traditional values agenda and took up a related strategy in an attempt to counter increasing Council focus and action on SOGI rights.

In March 2013, Tunisia, Egypt, Russia, Bangladesh, Qatar, Uganda, Morocco, Mauritania and Zimbabwe proposed a draft resolution on 'protection of the family'.[32] Egypt introduced the resolution, stating that it was needed to counterbalance 'the excessive focus at the international level on individual rights at the expense of family and collective rights', but then – noting the lack of support garnered – immediately withdrew it for consideration at a later session.

The following year 64 states co-sponsored a draft resolution[33] setting out the need for the family to be protected by the state.[34] A group of 32 states led by Ireland, Chile, Uruguay and France proposing an amendment to change the focus to 'the protection of the family and all its members [...] bearing in mind that, in different cultural, political and social systems, various forms of the family exist'.[35] In response, Pakistan, Saudi Arabia and the United Arab Emir-

---

29 Remarks of China on draft resolution A/HRC/21/L.2 transcribed from UN webcast and translated in English at Human Rights Council, 21st regular session, 36th meeting, 26 September 2012. See UNHRC, '21st regular session of the Human Rights Council (10–28 September, 5 November 2012)'.

30 UNHRC, 'Study of the Human Rights Council Advisory Committee on promoting human rights and fundamental freedoms through a better understanding of traditional values of humankind' (6 December 2012) UN Doc A/HRC/22/71.

31 UNHRC, 'Summary of information from States Members of the United Nations and other relevant stakeholders on best practices in the application of traditional values while promoting and protecting human rights and upholding human dignity' (17 June 2013) UN Doc A/HRC/24/22.

32 Draft resolution introduction by the representatives of Egypt, HRC, 'Protection of the family: draft resolution / Bangladesh, Egypt, Jordan, Libya, Mauritania, Morocco, Qatar, Russian Federation, Saudi Arabia, Tunisia, United Arab Emirates, Uganda, Zimbabwe' (19 March 2013) UN Doc A/HRC/22/L.25.

33 UNHRC, 'Protection of the Family' (25 June 2014) UN Doc A/HRC/26.L.20/Rev.1.

34 Ibid.

35 Amendment to draft resolution A/HRC/26/L.20/Rev.1, UN Doc A/HRC/26/L.37. See, UNHRC, 'Protection of the Family' (25 June 2014) UN Doc A/HRC/26.L.20/Rev.1; and UNHRC, 'Argentina, Austria, Chile, Colombia, Croatia, Czech Republic, Denmark, Es-

ates proposed their own counter-amendment, which would have inserted new language clarifying that only men and women can marry.[36] A no-action motion blocked both proposals. The resolution was adopted by a vote of 26 in favour, 14 against and 6 abstaining. Notably, states' positions on the 'protection of the family resolution' were nearly identical to those on the 'traditional values'.[37]

The 'core group' of states supporting the 'protection of the family' initiative continued their efforts, for instance with a similar resolution in 2015.[38] However, as anti-SOGI messaging from those sponsoring 'protection of the family' resolutions became more vocal, more states and from across different regions opposed the agenda. The OHCHR 2016 report on the topic[39] made clear that such anti-SOGI messaging and intent was not compatible with universal human rights and that the *family* was not a rights holder but rather the *individuals* within it hold human rights.[40] Since that time, no further attempts have been made to advance this agenda by those states that still seek to undermine the fundamental rights of SOGI minorities at home and globally. However, they are at the fore of attempts to undermine the ongoing work of the Special Procedures mandate holder, and the mandate itself, as previously discussed.

---

tonia, Finland, France, Germany, Greece, Guatemala, Hungary, Ireland, Italy, Lithuania, Malta, Netherlands, New Zealand, Norway, Poland, Portugal, Romania, Slovakia, Slovenia, Spain, Sweden, Switzerland, United Kingdom of Great Britain and Northern Ireland, United States of America, Uruguay: amendment to draft resolution A/HRC/26/L.20/Rev.1' (24 June 2014) UN Doc A/HRC/26/L.37.

36 UNHRC, 'Pakistan, Saudi Arabia, United Arab Emirates: amendment to draft resolution A/HRC/26/L.20/Rev.1. 26/... Protection of the family' (25 June 2014) UN Doc A/HRC/26/L.38.

37 UNHRC, 'Resolution adopted by the Human Rights Council: 26/11 Protection of the family' (16 July 2014) UN Doc A/HRC/RES/26/11.

38 Draft Resolution L.25 proposed by Bangladesh, Belarus, China, Côte d'Ivoire, Egypt, El Salvador, Mauritania, Morocco, Qatar, Russian Federation, Saudi Arabia and Tunisia. HRC, 'Protection of the family: contribution of the family to the realization of the right to an adequate standard of living for its members, particularly through its role in poverty eradication and achieving sustainable development' (1 July 2015) UN Doc HRC/29/L.25.

39 UNHRC, 'Protection of the family: contribution of the family to the realization of the right to an adequate standard of living for its members, particularly through its role in poverty eradication and achieving sustainable development', (29 January 2016) UN Doc A/HRC/31/3.

40 See, in particular, UN Doc A/HRC/31/3, *Ibid*, Part III.

3.2 Pushback on Fundamental Rights: 'Defamation of Religions'

A main pernicious tactic seen at the HRC is the attempt to advance (non-human) entities as rights-holders in order to limit existing human rights. This tactic can be used to limit the rights of specific minorities (as has been seen regarding SOGI) and/or to limit specific fundamental rights. It is that latter objective that underpins the 'defamation of religions' agenda. States trying to position religions as rights-holders attempted to protect them from defamation as a way of undermining or limiting both the right to freedom of expression and the right to freedom of religion or belief. This is clearly pernicious politicisation; it is also retractionist insofar as it aims to weaken the system's very purpose of protecting *humans* as rights-holders.

Despite the Vienna Declaration making clear that human rights are universal, disputes over the implications of universality continued to escalate. In 1999 the OIC moved from merely opposing initiatives to spearheading a conservative campaign aimed protecting Islam from defamation.[41] Initially concerns were raised about the exclusive focus on Islam. In response to those concerns and a proposal to call it 'Stereotyping of Religions', Pakistan revised the resolution's title to 'Defamation of Religions', and it was adopted without a vote, although the EU stated that it did not attach any legal meaning to the word 'defamation'.[42]

The following year, Pakistan again tabled the 'Defamation of Religions' resolution on behalf of the OIC. Proposals were made to add language on the right to change one's religion and the right to profess no religion.[43] European countries voiced concerns about the suggestion that religions are protected by human rights law, and the implication that negative statements about religions are equivalent to racist hate speech and hence merit the same type of state response. Pakistan modified the text to remove references to 'xenophobia', and the resolution was adopted by consensus, with the EU insisting that the issue not be raised again.

---

41 UN Doc E/CN.4/1999/SR.61, referring to the draft resolution in UN Doc E/CN.4/1999/L.40. See, UNCHR, 'Summary record of the 61st meeting' (19 October 1999) UN Doc E/CN.4/1999/SR.61 and; UNCHR, 'Defamation of Islam' (20 April 1999) UN Doc E/CN.4/1999/L.40.

42 Resolution 1999/82, on 'Defamation of religions' UNCHR 'Report on the 55th Session 22 March-30 April 1999' UN Doc E/CN.4/1999/167.

43 Amendments proposed by Australia, Austria, Belgium, Cyprus, Czech Republic, Denmark, Finland, France, Germany, Ireland, Italy, Luxembourg, Netherlands, Poland, Portugal, Romania, Spain, Sweden and the United Kingdom. UNCHR, 'Amendments to draft resolution E/CN.4/2000/L.6' UN Doc E/CN.4/2000/L.18, 2000.

Nevertheless, in 2001 Pakistan again tabled a defamation of religions resolution on behalf of the OIC. Western European and Others Group (WEOG) members called for a vote on the resolution.[44] They emphasized that religions cannot be rights-holders, and that only individuals – including adherents to a religion – are protected under human rights law.[45] The resolution was adopted by a vote of 28 in favour to 15 against, with 9 abstentions.[46] This pattern was repeated on several subsequent occasions. In 2002,[47] 2003,[48] 2004[49] and 2005.[50]

In the autumn of 2005, following the publication of cartoons depicting the Prophet Mohammed in the Danish newspaper *Jyllands-Posten*, the OIC tabled a 'Defamation of religions' resolution at the UN General Assembly. The resolution was adopted by 88 in favour, 52 against and 23 abstentions. However, the 'whole-UN' litmus test showed important regional and political dynamics. The vote showed that 16 African states who were not members of the OIC abstained on the resolution. Within the Asia-Pacific region, small island states opposed the resolution, with other Asia-Pacific states abstaining. Albania, which was the sole Eastern European Member State within the OIC, voted against the resolution.

After this time, Western and Eastern European states started to build an alliance to oppose the defamation of religions resolutions. The OIC, meanwhile, started to call for limitations to the right to freedom of expression to ensure 'respect for religions and beliefs'.[51] This alienated many states, as it shifted the focus away from human rights and towards protecting institutions,

---

44 Resolution 2001/4 adopted by vote of 28 to 15, with 9 abstentions, UNCHR 'Combating defamation of religions as a means to promote human rights, social harmony and religious and cultural diversity' (18 April 2001) UN Doc E/CN.4/RES/2001/4.

45 ECOSOC, 'Compte rendu analytique de la 61e séance' (4 December 2001) UN Doc E/CN.4/2001/Sr.61.

46 Resolution 2001/4, UNCHR 'Combating defamation of religions as a means to promote human rights, social harmony, and religious and cultural diversity' (18 April 2001) UN Doc E/CN.4/RES/2001/4.

47 Resolution 2002/9, adopted by 30 votes to 15, with 8 abstentions UNCHR, 'Combating defamation of religion' (15 April 2002) UN Doc E/CN.4/RES/2002/9.

48 Resolution 2003/4, adopted by 32 votes to 14, with 7 abstentions UNCHR, 'Combating defamation of religions'(14 April 2003) UN Doc E/CN.4/RES/2003/4.

49 Resolution 2004/6, adopted by 29 votes to 16, with 7 abstentions UNCHR, 'Combating defamation of religions' (13 April 2004) UN Doc E/CN.4/RES/2004/6.

50 Resolution 2005/3, adopted by a recorded vote of 31 to 16, with 5 abstentions UNCHR 'Combating defamation of religions' (12 April 2005) UN Doc E/CN.4/RES/2005/3.

51 See, e.g., Resolution 61/164 adopted by the UNGA on 19 December 2006, UNGA, '61/164. Combating defamation of religions' (21 February 2007) UN Doc A/RES/61/164, op 9.

symbols and ideas, as well as providing legitimacy for violating the rights of religious minorities.[52]

By 2010, there was far less support for the agenda despite the OIC changing the language to the 'incitement to religious hatred', which sounds more compatible with human rights. However, the OIC realised that the resolution would be defeated in 2011, so agreed to a compromise resolution: 'Combating intolerance, negative stereotyping and stigmatisation of, and discrimination, incitement to violence and violence against, persons based on religion or belief'.[53] That resolution substantially built upon work ongoing at OHCHR,[54] which was formalised in the Rabat Action Plan in 2012.[55] It recognises that persons, not religions, benefit from protections under human rights law and that denigration of persons based on their religions does not necessarily constitute an incitement to religious hatred. The resolution was adopted by consensus.

Over the last decade, the OIC's 'defamation' agenda has continued to be used to block efforts by 'Western' states to introduce progressive content into resolutions on the right to Freedom of Religion or Belief. More recently there has been concern that the agenda may be brought back, particularly given the 2020 update of the Article 21 of the OIC's Cairo Declaration on Human Rights to foreground defamation of religions over freedom of expression.[56] That move has been criticised as undermining fundamental human rights.[57] In 2021 a

52 UNGA, 'Summary record of the 46th meeting: 3rd Committee, held at Headquarters, New York, on Monday, 24 November 2008, General Assembly, 63rd session' (24 November 2008) UN Doc A/C.3/63/SR.46.

53 Resolution 16/18 adopted on 24 March 2011. UNHRC, '16/18 Combating intolerance, negative stereotyping and stigmatization of, and discrimination, incitement to violence and violence against, persons based on religion or belief' (12 April 2011) UN Doc A/HRC/RES/16/18.

54 See, e.g., OHCHR, 'Expert seminar on the links between articles 19 and 20 of the International Covenant on Civil and Political Rights (ICCPR): Freedom of expression and advocacy of religious hatred that constitutes incitement to discrimination, hostility or violence', October 2008; OHCHR, '2011 Expert workshops on the prohibition of incitement to national, racial or religious hatred'.

55 UNGA, 'Report of the United Nations High Commissioner for Human Rights on the expert workshops on the prohibition of incitement to national, racial or religious hatred' (11 January 2013) UN Doc A/HRC/22/17/Add.4.

56 OIC, 'The Cairo Declaration of the Organization of Islamic Cooperation on Human Rights' (24 December 2020).

57 UNHRC, 'Countering Islamophobia/anti-Muslim hatred to eliminate discrimination and intolerance based on religion or belief' (13 April 2021) UN Doc A/HRC/46/30; David Kaye, 'Promotion and protection of the right to freedom of opinion and expression: note / by the Secretary-General' (28 July 2020) UN Doc A/75/261.

group of UN independent experts[58] issued a statement condemning attempts to revive the agenda.[59] The concern is that some states are returning to the agenda to undermine existing human rights, appeal to domestic audiences and/or justify discriminatory laws such as on blasphemy.

The June 2023 HRC session saw the most concerning challenge to the (increasingly fragile) consensus on this issue area. On 12 July 2023 the Human Rights Council adopted Resolution 53/1 on 'Countering religious hatred constituting incitement to discrimination, hostility or violence' as a direct response to the burning of the Quran in Sweden weeks earlier. The resolution was adopted by a vote of 28 to 7 with 12 abstentions. The resolution prioritises religions over individuals and effectively insists that States criminalise "the deliberate and public burning of the Holy Qur'an or any other holy book". The argument is that such acts are incitement to discrimination, hostility or violence, which violates ICCPR Article 20(2). But that obligation relates to protecting individuals from such acts, not to protecting religions or other entities.

Burning the Quran is an offensive act targeting a religious symbol, but offensive acts alone do not meet the Article 20(2) International Covenant on Civil and Political Rights (ICCPR) threshold of "advocacy of religious hatred that constitutes incitement to discrimination, hostility or violence". They are not prohibited by international human rights law. Conversely, calls for States to criminalise those acts are calls for States to violate human rights obligations. Resolution 53/1 goes beyond the Rabat Plan of Action, which makes clear that limitations under Article 20(2) ICCPR must also meet the three-part test under Article 19(3) of the ICCPR. That test requires that any limitations on freedom of expression are legally precise, pursue a legitimate aim and are necessary and proportionate to that aim. Instead, this new resolution undermines those safeguards.

It is important to understand the politics involved in this vote. Council members from the OIC could be expected to vote in favour. They were joined by Argentina, Bolivia, Cameroon, China, Cuba, India, South Africa, Ukraine and Vietnam. Countries voting against were: Belgium, Costa Rica, Czechia,

---

58 The experts Mr Ahmed Shaheed (Special Rapporteur on freedom of religion or belief), Ms Irene Khan (Special Rapporteur on the promotion and protection of freedom of opinion and expression), Mr Fernand de Varennes (Special Rapporteur on minority issues), Mr Clément Nyaletsossi Voule (Special Rapporteur on the right to peaceful assembly and of association) and Ms Fionnuala Ní Aoláin (Special Rapporteur on the promotion and protection of human rights while countering terrorism).

59 OHCHR, 'Historic consensus on freedoms of religion and expression at risk, say UN experts', Press Release, 23 March 2021.

Finland, France, Germany, Lithuania, Luxembourg, Montenegro, Romania, the United Kingdom and the United States. And Benin, Chile, Georgia, Honduras, Mexico, Nepal and Paraguay abstained. It would be crude at this stage to ascribe motives to states for voting for the resolution. Some may be motivated by pernicious or retractionist politicisation, others by political, regional or ideological alliances, and a further group may be motivated by viewing the resolution as benign rather than recognising the challenges it poses to universality and to fundamental human rights.

4 Tactics and Vehicles for Advancing Competing Human Rights Narratives

States that seek to push back on human rights use tactics to advance their agendas through the UN human rights bodies and other multilateral fora, together with bilateral agreements and arrangements. Most of those states do not explicitly reject human rights; rather, they appear to engage with the bodies and mechanisms, yet do so to dilute and undermine fundamental rights. This section explores the tactics and initiatives that they deploy.

State actors inimical to fundamental rights oppose them by advancing agendas that undermine existing protections. This often is manifested through advancing development over human rights, which includes attempts to make some states rights holder *vis-à-vis* other states through TGR on the right to development, international solidarity, or on an equitable and democratic order.[60] That tactic is also deployed to make non-humans rights-holders (e.g. religions or the family) in order to undermine fundamental rights, such as freedom of expression, or the rights of minority groups, such as SOGI individuals. In these ways, states advance retractionist or pernicious agendas to undermine human rights.

States also deploy a discourse emphasising socio-economic rights and development, seeking to prioritise them over other rights despite the Vienna consensus that all rights are indivisible, interdependent and interrelated. However, they select which ESCRs to prioritise, and avoid altogether the central principles of non-discrimination, minority rights and accountability. That tactic, then, appears to be an effort to avoid human rights and to block scrutiny of domestic abuses rather than an ideological position on the substance of rights.

---

60 See, for example, Rosa Freedman, 'Third generation' rights: is there room for hybrid constructs within International Human Rights Law?' (2014) 2 Cambridge Journal of International and Comparative Law 935.

States advance those agendas by forming coalitions specifically to attack human rights, spearheaded by states that prioritise those narratives, and bolstered by countries who join for other reasons. Those groups then advance those agendas through joint statements, sponsoring resolutions, proposing new mandates and mechanisms as well as bloc voting. They often use language that mirrors human rights phrases yet undermine rights protection. Those tactics are deployed to advance what seem to be benign issues but are attempts to erode or destroy existing human rights. States using the language of state sovereignty and/or cultural relativism often do so as a justification, excuse or reason for eroding, undermining or avoiding human rights obligations. This usually involves discourse and language of post-colonialism or anti-'Western' rhetoric, or references to religion and culture.

While much is already known about soft power in international human rights bodies,[61] there are other initiatives that need more research and discussion. There are, for example, three main initiatives spearheaded by China, although other countries have joined. The first is rights-free development. The changing narratives from human rights to development are part of the shift from obligations on states and towards protecting state sovereignty. This has been advanced within human rights bodies and mechanisms, being complemented by development activities and initiatives, often financed by China, that explicitly do not require rights compliance or implementation. This is in direct contrast with development and aid from Global North countries and from multilateral institutions that centre and adopt human rights standards and safeguards.

China's development banks and its BRI initiatives offer 'no strings' loans. BRI is a USD trillion infrastructure and investment programme that often finances projects in countries without access to alternative investors. This has secured China considerable goodwill among developing countries. BRI initiatives have the effect of bolstering authoritarianism because they ignore human rights and environmental standards,[62] leading to considerable human rights violations in some projects financed and constructed by Chinese state-

61 Joseph S. Nye, *Soft Power: The Means to Success in World Politics* (Public Affairs 2004); Joseph S. Nye, 'Soft power: the evolution of a concept' (2021) 14 Journal of Political Power 196; Christopher Walker, 'The Authoritarian Threat: The Hijacking of "Soft Power"' (2016) 27 (1) Journal of democracy 49.

62 Hugh Williamson, 'China: One belt, one road, lots of obligations' *Human Rights Watch* (12 May 2017) <www.hrw.org/news/2017/05/12/china-one-belt-one-road-lots-obligations> accessed 30 September 2025.

owned banks and companies.[63] In 2021 China took another step in its plan for global development by creating and promoting the Global Development Initiative.[64] This has been critiqued as not being "as innocent as it seems",[65] and has been noted by some observers as being another attempt "to break Western hegemony over global human-rights governance."[66]

In these ways, China has financial and political leverage for support – including votes – for its agendas in international organisations and multilateral institutions. Recipient states are silent or even supportive of China's domestic human rights record, also supporting China's pernicious and retractionist agendas on human rights. One clear example is Pakistan, a major BRI recipient that remains silent about China's violations of Muslims in Xinjiang. China uses BRI to create coercive economic and political alliances, whilst at the same time advancing Chinese hegemony.

Another agenda led by China is called win-win/mutually beneficial cooperation. This was started by China in 2015.[67] China began to advance it visibly in human rights bodies in 2018. In 2020 the HRC adopted a resolution, proposed by China, on 'mutually beneficial cooperation'[68] that heralded the culmination of China's efforts at the Council to advance state sovereignty and undermine accountability for human rights violations. The 2018 resolution proposed a 'win-win' for states by replacing the idea of holding them accountable for

63 See, for example, Yasmin Dagne et al., 'We're Leaving Everything Behind": The Impact of Guinea's Souapiti Dam on Displaced Communities' *Human Rights Watch* (16 April 2020) <https://www.hrw.org/report/2020/04/16/were-leaving-everything-behind/impact-guineas-souapiti-dam-displaced-communities> accessed 30 September 2025; Neelam Deo, Amit Bhandari, 'The intensifying backlash against BRI' *Gateway House* (31 May 2018) <www.gatewayhouse.in/bri-debt-backlash/> accessed 30 September 2025.

64 Mercedes Page 'Unpacking China's Global Development Initiative' *The Interpreter* (1 August 2022) <www.lowyinstitute.org/the-interpreter/unpacking-china-s-global-development-initiative> accessed 30 September 2025.

65 'China's Global Development Initiative is not as innocent as it sounds' *The Economist* (9 June 2022) <www.economist.com/china/2022/06/09/chinas-global-development-initiative-is-not-as-innocent-as-it-sounds> accessed 30 September 2025.

66 Joseph Lemoine, Yomna Gaafar, 'There's more to China's new Global Development Initiative than meets the eye' Atlantic Council (18 August 2022) <https://www.atlanticcouncil.org/blogs/new-atlanticist/theres-more-to-chinas-new-global-development-initiative-than-meets-the-eye/> accessed 30 September 2025.

67 Ministry of Foreign Affairs of the People's Republic of China, 'Statement. by H.E. Xi Jinping: Working Together to Forge a New Partnership of Win-win Cooperation and Create a Community of Shared Future for Mankind', General Debate of the 70th Session of the UNGA, 28 September 2015.

68 UNHRC, 'Promoting mutually beneficial cooperation in the field of human rights: resolution / adopted by the Human Rights Council on 22 June 2020' (2 July 2020) UN Doc A/HRC/RES/43/21.

violations and instead implementing a commitment to dialogue about human rights. Crucially, China also sought to remove civil society from Council proceedings and activities. The 2020 resolution went further. It repositions international human rights law as a matter of inter-state relations while ignoring states' legal responsibilities to protect human rights. The resolution treats human rights as subject to negotiation and compromise. China claims that the initiative is intended to address human rights being used to interfere in other countries' internal affairs, 'poisoning the global atmosphere of human rights governance'.[69]

China's initiatives aimed at undermining human rights also include the South-South Forum on Human Rights. It was created in 2017 and builds on the development and economic initiative of South-South Cooperation. However, instead of seeking to advance development, the South-South Forum seeks to undermine human rights. At the first of its bi-annual meetings, the Forum passed a Beijing Declaration on human rights, reflecting China's vision for human rights governance. China's foreign minister advocated diversity and localisation, claiming China had 'blazed an oriental pathway toward modernization'.[70] The 2021 meeting platformed a range of speakers that set out and championed the same positions that China has taken on human rights.[71]

China views human rights as separate from state obligations to protect individuals from abuse. This position was set out by Tom Zwart, a professor at Utrecht University who came under criticism for taking money from China to conduct human rights research and whose research was questioned in terms of its independence.[72] Zwart argued at the forum that human rights have been a 'liberal social engineering project'.[73] China also rejects universality of rights, instead insisting that they are government policies and that every country should be able to define and implement human rights in their own way. Speakers at the Forum reflected that position. They foregrounded economic development and welfare policies, insisted that collective rights are

69 OHCHR, 'China's Reply to the Questionnaire of the Human Rights Council Advisory Committee on the Role of Technical Assistance and Capacity Building in Fostering Mutually Beneficial Cooperation', August 2019.

70 H.E. Wang Yi, 'Advance the Global Human Rights Cause and Build a Community with a Shared Future for Mankind', Speech at the opening ceremony of the first South–South human rights forum, Beijing, 7 December 2017.

71 For more on the specific talks given and the speakers' biographies, see Lu Guangjin, Zhang Wei (eds.), *The South-South Dialogue on Human Rights* (Brill Nijhoff 2021).

72 HOP, Riest Agterberg 'UU professor under fire after decision from Vrije Universiteit about China' *DUB* (26 January 2022) <https://dub.uu.nl/en/news/uu-professor-under-fire-after-decision-vrije-universiteit-about-china> accessed 30 September 2025.

73 EU Political Report, 'Counter China's Devious Human Rights Propaganda', January 2022.

more important than individual ones, and argued that CPRs can be restricted for the collective interest.

There are broader initiatives that are used to achieve similar objectives. For example, some regional institutions are used to undermine universal rights by instead promoting state sovereignty, security, development and diversity as more important than human rights. China and Russia have created and led such organisations. Unlike their liberal counterparts that advance cooperation amongst members, these institutions protect authoritarian regimes from domestic or external threats. There has been a significant rise in the number of these organisations since the end of the Cold War. In form, they appear like 'Western' organisations, but in substance they advance autocratic norms and objectives. They seemingly seek to challenge liberal institutions and frameworks by working in the same areas and on the same issues but using illiberal tactics and advancing illiberal agendas. The Collective Security Treaty Organization (2002) was founded to mimic and counter the North Atlantic Treaty Organization; the Eurasian Economic Union (2014) did the same regarding the EU; and the SCO (2001) has the mandate to counter 'Western' hegemony.[74] These organisations are used as a cover for undermining human rights and for justifying violations. The SCO claims to be combatting the 'three evils of terrorism, separatism and religious extremism'[75] and while doing so actively encourages human rights violations under the cover of its Anti-Terrorism Treaty. The Collective Security Treaty Organization has been used as an excuse for Russia to send troops to crack down on dissent in former Soviet Republics, including Kazakhstan in 2022.

A similar tactic used is the rise of sham non-governmental organisations (NGOs), illiberal transnational networks and government-sponsored supposed-civil society actors, all of which are shills for states. Those organisations advance state objectives and also provide the illusion of a thriving civil society whilst in reality preventing legitimate associations from doing their work. Some of those states crackdown on civil society actors domestically, through legislation that restricts and monitors their activities at best or even labels them terrorists or criminals. Moreover, they have prevented their activities within international human rights bodies, sometimes by blocking the accredit-

---

74 See, for example, Alexander Cooley, Daniel H. Nexon, 'The Illiberal Tide: Why the International Order Is Tilting towards Autocracy' *Foreign Affairs* (26 March 2021) <www.foreignaffairs.com/united-states/illiberal-tide> accessed 30. September 2025.

75 Stephen Aris, 'The Shanghai Cooperation Organisation: "Tackling the Three Evils": A Regional Response to Non-Traditional Security Challenges or an Anti-Western Bloc?' (2009) 61 *Europe-Asia Studies* 457.

ation needed for UN participation[76] or even preventing human rights defenders from physically accessing those bodies.[77] China and Russia have led attempts to silence legitimate NGOs at UN human rights bodies,[78] and have used sham organisations to flood speakers lists at those bodies.[79]

Other tactics employed to advance competing narratives include the use of state-sponsored media and social media. States also use 'sharp power', an approach to international affairs that employs censorship or manipulative and subversive policies as a projection of state power, targeting think tanks, media, academia and other spheres in democratic countries.[80] In particular, there has been an increased interest in influencing research institutions, including universities, policy institutes and think tanks in 'Western' countries. Within academia there is increasingly reliance on student fees – particularly international student fees – to fund those institutions. States, such as China and Saudi Arabia, have increasingly provided scholarships for students. Those students receive legitimacy for their research and later work, which is particularly important as many of them may go on to work in their home country's public or private sectors. It also allows states to direct the type and nature of research being undertaken within those universities, as many of the students writing dissertations will focus on their home state. States may also provide capital funding for research centres or institutes, which influences the independence of their research and work. There has also been increased surveil-

---

76 See, e.g., Rana Siu Inboden, 'China at the UN: Choking Civil Society' (2021) 32 (3) *Journal of Democracy* 124 <www.journalofdemocracy.org/articles/china-at-the-un-choking-civil-society/> accessed 30 September 2025; and e.g. Rosa Freedman, Samuel Gordon, 'Civil Society and the UN Human Rights System' in Bertrand Ramcharan et. Al (eds), *The Protection Roles of Human Rights NGOs* (Brill 2022).

77 Rosa Freedman, Ruth Houghton, 'Two Steps Forward, One Step Back: Politicisation of the Human Rights Council' (2017) 17 *Human Rights Law Review* 753 <https://academic.oup.com/hrlr/article/17/4/753/4430990> accessed 30 September 2025.

78 Rana Siu Inboden, 'China at the UN: Choking Civil Society' (2021) 32 (3) *Journal of Democracy* 124 <www.journalofdemocracy.org/articles/china-at-the-un-choking-civil-society/> accessed 30 September 2025; Human Rights Watch, *The Costs of International Advocacy: China's Interference in United Nations Human Rights Mechanisms* (2017) <www.hrw.org/sites/default/files/report_pdf/chinaun0917_web.pdf> accessed 30 September 2025.

79 Ron Synovitz, 'Attack of the GONGOs: Government Organized NGOs Attack Warsaw Meeting' *Radio Free Europe/Radio Liberty* (30 September 2019) <www.rferl.org/a/attack-of-the-gongos-government-rganized-ngos-flood-warsaw-meeting/30191944.html> accessed 30 September 2025.

80 Christopher Walker, 'What Is 'Sharp Power'?' (2018) 29 (3) *Journal of Democracy* 9 <www.journalofdemocracy.org/articles/what-is-sharp-power/> accessed 30 September 2025.

lance of students and academics at home and abroad, particularly from China but also from other repressive regimes.[81]

5 Concluding Observations

It is one thing to understand and explore the tactics deployed but quite another to ascribe political or politicised motivations to those states. Of course, each state will have different motivations, even where some similarities exist, but it is important to note some clear themes and objectives. Some states engage in these tactics to block scrutiny of some or all of their human rights record. For some, this means advancing and engaging with specific types of rights or mechanisms in order to shield themselves from criticism for not engaging with other rights. For example, sponsoring and engaging with mandates and mechanisms on specific rights and using that to deflect attention away from their grave abuses of other rights.

Others deploy these discourses and actions as a method for avoiding scrutiny of human rights abuses altogether. This involves prioritising state sovereignty over human rights and thus using sovereignty as a method of avoiding

81 For more information, see, for example, Saipira Furstenberg, Tena Prelec, John Heathershaw, 'The Internationalization of Universities and the Repression of Academic Freedom' (*Freedom House*, Special Report 2020) <https://freedomhouse.org/report/special-report/2020/internationalization-universities-and-repression-academic-freedom> accessed 30 September 2025; International Center for Not-for-Profit Law, 'Academic Freedom and the Freedom of Opinion and Expression', 30 April 2020 <www.ohchr.org/sites/default/files/Documents/Issues/Opinion/Submissions/NGOs/ICNL1.pdf> accessed 30 September 2025; 'China: Government threats to academic freedom abroad' *Human Rights Watch* (21 March 2019) <www.hrw.org/news/2019/03/21/china-government-threats-academic-freedom-abroad> accessed 30 September 2025; Tim Swanston, 'Drew Pavlou, critic of University of Queensland's links to Chinese Government bodies, suspended for two years'. *ABC News (Australia)* (29 May 2020) <https://www.abc.net.au/news/2020-05-29/drew-pavlou-suspended-university-queensland/12302350> accessed 30 September 2025; Will Knight, 'MIT cuts ties with a Chinese AI firm amid human rights concerns' *Wired* (21 April 2020) <https://www.wired.com/story/mit-cuts-ties-chinese-ai-firm-human-rights/> accessed 30 September 2025; 'The Chinese Government Cannot Be Allowed to Undermine Academic Freedom' *Human Rights Watch* (8 November 2019) <https://www.hrw.org/news/2019/11/08/chinese-government-cannot-be-allowed-undermine-academic-freedom> accessed 30 September 2025; Human Rights Watch, 'Resisting Chinese Government Efforts to Undermine Academic Freedom Abroad: A Code of Conduct for Colleges, Universities, and Academic Institutions Worldwide' 19 March 2021 <https://www.hrw.org/sites/default/files/supporting_resources/190321_china_academic_freedom_coc_0.pdf> accessed 30 September 2025.

legal obligations. This is particularly the case for those states that advance rights-free development (rather than development as a human right) as an alternative to human rights. Another motivation is to avoid specific human rights obligations, particularly toward minorities. Cultural relativist arguments are used in an attempt to justify or excuse human rights violations. Then there is the group of states seeking greater representation of their own human rights ideologies, particularly on TGR. Many of those states view TGR as a method to redress or remedy colonial harms. Those rights often are then taken up and used by other regimes as a cover or excuse for their domestic human rights failures.

A main question that needs to be addressed is 'Why?' For what purpose do state actors inimical to fundamental rights oppose them by advancing agendas that undermine existing protections? It seems counterintuitive to advance retractionist or pernicious agendas to undermine rights rather than simply walking away from the system itself. Why advance those agendas by forming coalitions specifically to attack human rights, spearheaded by states that prioritise those narratives, and bolstered by countries who join for other reasons? Why then advance those agendas through joint statements, sponsoring resolutions, proposing new mandates and mechanisms as well as bloc voting? Why use language that mirrors human rights phrases yet undermine rights protection?

And there are other tactics being deployed elsewhere in the system. In particular, the rising number of 'independent experts' from China that are standing for election to UN human rights treaty bodies and special procedures mandates, which is concerning given that those parts of the system create a wealth of human rights jurisprudence.

Of course, some states may be seeking to appeal to domestic or regional audiences, particularly on issues relating to (neo)colonialism, history, culture and/or religion. However, other governments do so despite domestic populations opposing those positions. Within autocratic regimes, for example, domestic populations have limited opportunity to challenge the government's positions on human rights, and even more so when civil society is repressed or is simply a shill for the state. Furthermore, the realities of international relations and geopolitics means that these tactics are also advanced or supported by states that have political or economic alliances or ties with more powerful proponents of these discourses and actions. That support may be an overt or tacit condition of 'weaker' states having relationships with more 'powerful' countries.

There is also the motivation of seeking to undermine human rights movements' ability to topple illiberal regimes. Human rights are a tool to lobby for effective political change, and their power in this regard may be a key motivating factor for countries to seek to undermine the human rights project rather than simply turn their backs on it. To do so, as we have seen, those state misappropriate human rights language, discourse and institutions to subvert and undermine the very project that gives hope to the people living within their regimes.

The realities of the world within which human rights operate mean that it is crucial to understand the tactics deployed to undermine human rights in order to counter them and therefore to develop, promote and protect those rights. In general terms, human rights narratives are advanced through a pendulum movement. In other words, as progressive agendas move forward, competing retractionist or pernicious narratives are promoted to counter such progress. There are no 'magic bullets' available to counter these tactics, but there needs to be understanding of them in order to promote progressive objectives on human rights. A mixture of pragmatism and principle is required to progressively promote human rights and counter attempts to undermine the human rights project.

Bibliography

Articles

Aris, Stephen, 'The Shanghai Cooperation Organisation: "Tackling the Three Evils": A Regional Response to Non-Traditional Security Challenges or an Anti-Western Bloc?' (2009) 61 *Europe-Asia Studies* 457.

Barr, Michael D., 'Lee Kuan Yew and the "Asian values" debate' (2000) 24 Asian Studies Review 309.

Domínguez-Redondo, Elvira, In Defence of Politicization of Human Rights: The UN Special Procedures (OUP 2020).

Franck, Thomas M., 'Of Gnats and Camels: Is there a double standard at the United Nations?' (1984) 78 The American Journal of International Law, 811, 831-832.

Freedman, Rosa, 'Third generation' rights: is there room for hybrid constructs within International Human Rights Law?' (2014) 2 Cambridge Journal of International and Comparative Law 935;

Freedman, Rosa, 'Politicisation of human rights: Current battlegrounds and sites of contestation' (2024) 51 University of Western Australia Law Review 1.

Freedman, Rosa and Ruth Houghton, 'Two Steps Forward, One Step Back: Politicisation of the Human Rights Council' (2017) 17 *Human Rights Law Review* 753 <https://academic.oup.com/hrlr/article/17/4/753/4430990> accessed 30 September 2025.

Heinze, Eric, 'Sexual Orientation and International Law: A Study in the Manufacture of Cross-Cultural "Sensitivity"' (2001) 22 Michigan Journal of International Law 283.

Inboden, Rana Siu, 'China at the UN: Choking Civil Society' (2021) 32 (3) *Journal of Democracy* 124 <www.journalofdemocracy.org/articles/china-at-the-un-choking-civil-society/> accessed 30 September 2025

Kausikan, Bilahari, 'Asia's Different Standards' (1993) 92 Foreign Policy 24.

Kirby, M.D., 'International Legal Notes: Second World Conference on Human Rights, Vienna, Austria', *Australian Law Journal*, June 1993, pp 1-12.

Lyons, Gene, David Baldwin, Donald McNemar, 'The "Politicization" Issue in the UN Specialized Agencies' (1977) 32 Proceedings of the Academy of Political Science 89; Eric Heinze, 'Even-handedness and the Politics of Human Rights' (2008) 21 Harvard Human Rights Journal 7, 41.

Nye, Joseph S., *Soft Power: The Means to Success in World Politics* (Public Affairs 2004)

Nye, Joseph S., 'Soft power: the evolution of a concept' (2021) 14 Journal of Political Power 196

Sanders, Douglas, 'Human rights and sexual orientation in international law' (2002) 25 International Journal of Public Administration 13.

Walker, Christopher, 'The Authoritarian Threat: The Hijacking of "Soft Power"' (2016) 27 (1) Journal of democracy 49.

Christopher Walker, 'What Is 'Sharp Power'?' (2018) 29 (3) *Journal of Democracy* 9 <www.journalofdemocracy.org/articles/what-is-sharp-power/> accessed 30 September 2025.

Books and Book Chapters

Brown, Bartram S., The United States and the Politicization of the World Bank: Issues of international law and policy (first published 1992, Kegan Paul International 2024).

Freedman, Rosa and Samuel Gordon, 'Civil Society and the UN Human Rights System' in Bertrand Ramcharan et. Al (eds), *The Protection Roles of Human Rights NGOs* (Brill 2022).

Guangjin, Lu and Zhang Wei (eds.), *The South-South Dialogue on Human Rights* (Brill Nijhoff 2021).

Rittberger, Volker, Bernhard Zangl, Matthias Staisch, *International Organization: Polity, Politics and Policies* (Palgrave MacMillan 2006)

UN Documents

ECOSOC, 'Compte rendu analytique de la 61e séance' (4 December 2001) UN Doc E/CN.4/2001/Sr.61.

OIC, 'The Cairo Declaration of the Organization of Islamic Cooperation on Human Rights' (24 December 2020).

Vienna Declaration and Programme of Action, adopted by World Conference on Human Rights on 25 June 1993 (UN doc A/CONF.157/23).

World Conference on Human Rights, Report of the Regional Meeting for Asia of the World Conference on Human Rights, Bangkok, 29 March-2 April 1993 (A/CONF.157/ASRM/8, 1993).

UNCHR, 'Commission on Human Rights resolution 2000/31 Extrajudicial, summary or arbitrary executions' (20 April 2000) UN Doc E/CN.4/RES/2000/31.

UNCHR 'Report on the 55th Session 22 March-30 April 1999' UN Doc E/CN.4/1999/167.

UNCHR 'Combating defamation of religions as a means to promote human rights, social harmony and religious and cultural diversity' (18 April 2001) UN Doc E/CN.4/RES/2001/4.

UNCHR, 'Combating defamation of religion' (15 April 2002) UN Doc E/CN.4/RES/2002/9.

UNCHR, 'Combating defamation of religions'(14 April 2003) UN Doc E/CN.4/RES/2003/4.

UNCHR, 'Combating defamation of religions' (13 April 2004) UN Doc E/CN.4/RES/2004/6.

UNCHR 'Combating defamation of religions' (12 April 2005) UN Doc E/CN.4/RES/2005/3.

UNGA, '61/164. Combating defamation of religions' (21 February 2007) UN Doc A/RES/61/164.

UNGA, 'Summary record of the 46th meeting: 3rd Committee, held at Headquarters, New York, on Monday, 24 November 2008, General Assembly, 63rd session' (24 November 2008) UN Doc A/C.3/63/SR.46.

UNGA, 'Report of the United Nations High Commissioner for Human Rights on the expert workshops on the prohibition of incitement to national, racial or religious hatred' (11 January 2013) UN Doc A/HRC/22/17/Add.4.

UNHRC, '17/19 Human rights, sexual orientation and gender identity' (14 July 2011) Un Doc A/HRC/RES/17/19.

UNHRC, 'Resolution adopted by the Human Rights Council on 30 June 2016 – 32/2: Protection against violence and discrimination based on sexual orientation and gender identity' (15 July 2016) Un Doc A/HRC/RES/32/2.

UNHRC, '12/ … Promoting human rights and fundamental freedoms through a better understanding of traditional values of humankind' (A/HRC/12/L.13/Rev.1, 30 September 2009).

UNHRC, 'Promoting human rights and fundamental freedoms through a better understanding of traditional values of humankind: resolution / adopted by the Human Rights Council' (12 October 2009) UN Doc A/HRC/Res/12/21.

UNHRC, '16/3 Promoting human rights and fundamental freedoms through a better understanding of traditional values of humankind', (8 April 2011) UN Doc A/HRC/RES/16/3

UNHRC, '21/3 Promoting human rights and fundamental freedoms through a better understanding of traditional values of humankind: best practices' (9 October 2012) Un Doc A/HRC/RES/21/3.

UNHRC, 'Study of the Human Rights Council Advisory Committee on promoting human rights and fundamental freedoms through a better understanding of traditional values of humankind' (6 December 2012) UN Doc A/HRC/22/71.

UNHRC, 'Summary of information from States Members of the United Nations and other relevant stakeholders on best practices in the application of traditional values while promoting and protecting human rights and upholding human dignity' (17 June 2013) UN Doc A/HRC/24/22.

UNHRC, 'Resolution adopted by the Human Rights Council: 26/11 Protection of the family'(16 July 2014) UN Doc A/HRC/RES/26/11.

UNHRC, 'Protection of the family: contribution of the family to the realization of the right to an adequate standard of living for its members, particularly through its role in poverty eradication and achieving sustainable development', (29 January 2016) UN Doc A/HRC/31/3.

UNHRC, '16/18 Combating intolerance, negative stereotyping and stigmatization of, and discrimination, incitement to violence and violence against, persons based on religion or belief' (12 April 2011) UN Doc A/HRC/RES/16/18.

UNHRC, 'Countering Islamophobia/anti-Muslim hatred to eliminate discrimination and intolerance based on religion or belief' (13 April 2021) UN Doc A/HRC/46/30; David Kaye, 'Promotion and protection of the right to freedom of opinion and expression: note / by the Secretary-General' (28 July 2020) UN Doc A/75/261.

UNHRC, 'Promoting mutually beneficial cooperation in the field of human rights: resolution / adopted by the Human Rights Council on 22 June 2020' (2 July 2020) UN Doc A/HRC/RES/43/21.

Reports

Furstenberg, Saipira, Tena Prelec, John Heathershaw, 'The Internationalization of Universities and the Repression of Academic Freedom' (*Freedom House*, Special Report 2020) <https://freedomhouse.org/report/special-report/2020/internationalization-universities-and-repression-academic-freedom> accessed 30 September 2025

Human Rights Watch, 'China: Government threats to academic freedom abroad' *Human Rights Watch* (21 March 2019) <www.hrw.org/news/2019/03/21/china-government-threats-academic-freedom-abroad> accessed 30 September 2025

Human Rights Watch, 'The Chinese Government Cannot Be Allowed to Undermine Academic Freedom' *Human Rights Watch* (8 November 2019) <https://www.hrw.org/news/2019/11/08/chinese-government-cannot-be-allowed-undermine-academic-freedom> accessed 30 September 2025

Human Rights Watch, 'Resisting Chinese Government Efforts to Undermine Academic Freedom Abroad: A Code of Conduct for Colleges, Universities, and Academic Institutions Worldwide' 19 March 2021 <https://www.hrw.org/sites/default/files/supporting_resources/190321_china_academic_freedom_coc_0.pdf> accessed 30 September 2025.

International Center for Not-for-Profit Law, 'Academic Freedom and the Freedom of Opinion and Expression', 30 April 2020 <www.ohchr.org/sites/default/files/Documents/Issues/Opinion/Submissions/NGOs/ICNL1.pdf> accessed 30 September 2025

Media

Cooley, Alexander, Daniel H. Nexon, 'The Illiberal Tide: Why the International Order Is Tilting towards Autocracy' *Foreign Affairs* (26 March 2021) <www.foreignaffairs.com/united-states/illiberal-tide> accessed 30. September 2025.

Dagne, Yasmin, et al., 'We're Leaving Everything Behind": The Impact of Guinea's Souapiti Dam on Displaced Communities' *Human Rights Watch* (16 April 2020) <https://www.hrw.org/report/2020/04/16/were-leaving-everything-behind/impact-guineas-souapiti-dam-displaced-communities> accessed 30 September 2025

Deo, Neelam, Amit Bhandari, 'The intensifying backlash against BRI' *Gateway House* (31 May 2018) <www.gatewayhouse.in/bri-debt-backlash/> accessed 30 September 2025.

Freedman, Rosa, 'The United Nations Human Rights Council's Backwards Step on LGBT Rights', *IntLawGrrls*, 7 June 2013.

Freedman, Rosa, 'Mandate Renewal of Independent Expert on Sexual Orientation and Gender Identity At Risk' (*IPI Global Observatory*, 10 July 2019) <https://theglobalobservatory.org/2019/07/mandate-renewal-independent-expert-sogi-at-risk/> accessed 30 September 2025.

Gray, Stephan, '"Milestone" LGBT Discussion at UN Human Rights Council Welcomed Despite Walkout' *Pink News* (8 March 2012) <www.thepinknews.com/2012/03/08/milestone-lgbt-discussion-at-un-human-rights-council-welcomed-despite-walkout/> accessed 30 September 2025.

HOP, Riest Agterberg 'UU professor under fire after decision from Vrije Universiteit about China' *DUB* (26 January 2022) <https://dub.uu.nl/en/news/uu-professor-under-fire-after-decision-vrije-universiteit-about-china> accessed 30 September

2025.Human Dignity Trust, *Map of Countries that Criminalise LGBT People* <www.humandignitytrust.org/lgbt-the-law/map-ofcriminalisationtype_filter_submitted= n.d.

Knight, Will, 'MIT cuts ties with a Chinese AI firm amid human rights concerns' *Wired* (21 April 2020) <https://www.wired.com/story/mit-cuts-ties-chinese-ai-firm-human-rights/> accessed 30 September 2025

Lemoine, Joseph, Yomna Gaafar, 'There's more to China's new Global Development Initiative than meets the eye' Atlantic Council (18 August 2022) <https://www.atlanticcouncil.org/blogs/new-atlanticist/theres-more-to-chinas-new-global-devel opment-initiative-than-meets-the-eye/> accessed 30 September 2025.

OHCHR, Commission's Are Sound, Problems Can be Surmounted, High Commissioner Says as Main Human Rights Body Ends Session', OHCHR Press Release, 25 April 2003.

OHCHR, 'Historic consensus on freedoms of religion and expression at risk, say UN experts', Press Release, 23 March 2021.

Page, Mercedes, 'Unpacking China's Global Development Initiative' *The Interpreter* (1 August 2022) <www.lowyinstitute.org/the-interpreter/unpacking-china-s-global-development-initiative> accessed 30 September 2025.

Swanston, Tim, 'Drew Pavlou, critic of University of Queensland's links to Chinese Government bodies, suspended for two years'*ABC News* (*Australia*) (29 May 2020) <https://www.abc.net.au/news/2020-05-29/drew-pavlou-suspended-university-queensland/12302350> accessed 30 September 2025

Synovitz, Ron, 'Attack of the GONGOs: Government Organized NGOs Attack Warsaw Meeting' *Radio Free Europe/Radio Liberty* (30 September 2019) <www.rferl.org/a/attack-of-the-gongos-government-rganized-ngos-flood-warsaw-meeting/30191944.html> accessed 30 September 2025.

The Economist, 'China's Global Development Initiative is not as innocent as it sounds' *The Economist* (9 June 2022) <www.economist.com/china/2022/06/09/chinas-global-development-initiative-is-not-as-innocent-as-it-sounds> accessed 30 September 2025.

Williamson, Hugh, 'China: One belt, one road, lots of obligations' *Human Rights Watch* (12 May 2017) <www.hrw.org/news/2017/05/12/china-one-belt-one-road-lots-obligations> accessed 30 September 2025.

CHAPTER 7

Misappropriating the Legacy of Nuremberg: The Putin Regime's Campaign to Redefine Human Rights and Defend the Perpetrators of Atrocity Crimes

Robert Horvath

Accountability for large-scale human rights abuses was one of the greatest achievements of the post–Cold War human rights order. Before the 1990s, the Nuremberg trials were the exception that proved the rule that sovereign states could commit atrocity crimes with impunity. The preamble of the Universal Declaration of Human Rights may have affirmed that 'disregard and contempt for human rights have resulted in barbarous acts which have outraged the conscience of mankind,' but the world community did little to prevent the recurrence of atrocity crimes. In 1979, Vietnam faced international condemnation when it put an end to the genocide in Cambodia. Olaf Palme, the Swedish prime minister, declared that 'one can never excuse an intervention in a neighbouring state.'[1] This indifference came to an end in the 1990s, when a paradigm shift, generated by a confluence of the human rights regime, genocide prevention, and international criminal justice, produced a profusion of new accountability institutions.[2] The creation of ad hoc international criminal tribunals for the former Yugoslavia (ICTY) and Rwanda (ICTR), and the signing of the Rome Statute on the International Criminal Court (ICC), appeared to mark the beginning of the end of the era of impunity. For the first time since Nuremberg, high state officials, including presidents and prime ministers, were being prosecuted for atrocity crimes against their own people.

This chapter is about the response of authoritarian great powers to this breakthrough. I argue that the Putin regime has played a leading role in challenging the norms and undermining the institutions of international criminal justice. Its strategy exemplified what Young and de Búrca have called the 'mis-

1 'Stockholm: M. Palme condamne l'intervention vietnamienne' *Le Monde* (Paris, 14–15 January 1979) 3.

2 Alexa Stiller, 'The Genesis of the Human Rights-Based International Criminal Justice System' in Jan Eckel and Daniel Stahl (eds), *Embattled visions. Human Rights Since 1992* (Wallstein-Verlag 2022).

appropriation of human rights': 'human rights language in the service of ends which are exclusionary, repressive, or anti-pluralist in character, highly retrogressive or reversing of previous commitments, and evasive of external monitoring or accountability.'[3] This chapter examines how the Putin regime misappropriated the norms, language, and procedures of international criminal justice, a field closely related to international human rights law and often concerned with the most egregious violations of human rights.

Despite its political repercussions, this theatre of Russia's conflict with the post–Cold War international human rights order has received surprisingly little academic attention. By comparison with the burgeoning field of scholarship on Russia's promotion of traditional values and the 'moralist international,'[4] the struggles over accountability for atrocity crimes have been largely neglected. The exception is the substantial body of research on Russia's difficulties with the European Court of Human Rights (ECtHR), which became a major instrument for Russian civil society activists to hold the Russian state accountable for the abuses committed by its security forces in Chechnya and elsewhere.[5] Despite the crucial role of local activists, the major study of the 'Strasbourg Effect' attributes Russia's estrangement from the ECtHR to Russia's 'anti-liberal history and ideology' and its 'opposition to ideas that are seen as civilization-wise alien.'[6]

Contrary to this cultural relativist interpretation, which mirrors the civilisational rhetoric of pro-Kremlin nationalist propagandists, this chapter highlights the political factors that shaped Russia's confrontation with international criminal justice. On the one hand, the inception of the Putin regime during a brutal war in Chechnya made its leaders acutely aware of the dangers of accountability. This sensitivity was aggravated by international condemnation of Russian aggression in Georgia, Ukraine, and Syria. On the other hand,

---

3 Gráinne de Búrca and Katharine G. Young, 'The (mis)appropriation of human rights by the new global right: An introduction to the Symposium,' (2003) 21 I·CON 205.

4 Cai Wilkinson, 'Putting "Traditional Values" Into Practice: The Rise and Contestation of Anti-Homopropaganda Laws in Russia.' (2014) 13 *Journal of Human Rights.* 363; Kristina Stoeckl, 'Double bind at the UN: Western actors, Russia, and the traditionalist agenda,' (2018) 7 *Global Constitutionalism*, 383; Kristina Stoeckl and Dmitry Uzlaner, *The Moralist International: Russia in the Global Culture Wars* (Fordham UP 2022).

5 See for instance, Lisa Mcintrosh Sundstrom, 'Russian NGOs and the European Court of Human Rights: A Spectrum of Approaches to Litigation' (2014) 36 *Human Rights Quarterly*, 844; Philip Leach, 'Egregious human rights violations in Chechnya: appraising the pursuit of justice,' in Lauri Malksoo and Wolfgang Benedek (eds) *Russia and the European Court of Human Rights: the Strasbourg effect* (Cambridge UP 2018).

6 Lauri Malksoo, 'Introduction' in Lauri Malksoo and Wolfgang Benedek (eds) *Russia and the European Court of Human Rights: the Strasbourg effect* (Cambridge UP 2018) 24–25.

Russia's autocratisation empowered two groups that played important roles in the politics of the Putin regime. The first were anti-Western nationalists who spearheaded Russia's challenge to the ICTY and other tribunals, and who acted as apologists for Russian aggression. The second were 'political technologists,' consultants who developed the techniques of manipulation that were used by the regime and its proxies to fortify authoritarianism. Political technologists were much more than spin doctors. Instead of shaping perceptions of events, they transformed the political landscape by creating a plethora of pro-regime and anti-regime parties and movements.[7] In the sphere of human rights, they created 'human rights NGOs' and 'human rights activists' that served both to confuse public perceptions and to harness human rights to the goals of the regime.[8]

This chapter examines three distinct phases of the Putin regime's misappropriation of international criminal justice. During the first phase (2004–2007), Russian diplomats and politicians countered international criticism of atrocities in Chechnya by taking up the banner of anti-racism and stigmatising Latvia and Estonia, both new EU-member states, as apologists of Nazism. During the second phase (2008–2013), the Russian government used the language of genocide prevention and R2P to justify aggression against Georgia. During the third phase (2014–2022), Russia mounted an assault on the system of international criminal justice. While staking an exclusive claim to the legacy of the Nuremberg Tribunal, it actively resisted any form of accountability and promoted the denial of atrocities in Bosnia and Ukraine.

1 Evading Accountability

Before the consolidation of Putin's dictatorship, post-Soviet Russia was a cautious supporter of international human rights. In February 1993, Russia voted at the UN in favour of the creation of the International Criminal Tribunal for the Former Yugoslavia (ICTY). A few months later, it sided with Western democracies against the proponents of 'Asian Values' at the UN's landmark Vienna

7 On political technologists, see Andrew Wilson, *Political technology: The globalisation of political manipulation* (Cambridge University Press, 2023).

8 An exemplary political technologist in the human rights arena is Maksim Grigor'ev, who headed two notorious GONGOs: a 'Foundation for the Study of the Problems of Democracy' and the 'International Public Tribunal on the Crimes of Ukrainian Neo-Nazis.' See 'O fonde,' https://democracyfund.ru/about.php.

Conference on Human Rights.[9] Despite international condemnation of the first war in Chechnya (1994–96), Russia signed the European Convention on Human Rights in 1998. Later that year, Russia took part in the drafting of the Rome Statute on the International Criminal Court. Its last major concession to the principle of accountability was its signature of the Rome Statute in September 2000, less than six months after Putin's inauguration as president.[10]

By then, it was clear that the Putin regime had serious reservations about international criminal justice. Putin's ascent to power was boosted by Russia's second war against Chechnya, which was marked by gross violations of international humanitarian law. Indiscriminate bombardment of population centres, massacres during punitive operations, and torture in filtration camps, were all documented by human rights activists. The discovery of mass graves containing the bodies of victims abducted from different regions of Chechnya was clear evidence that the Russian security forces were waging a systemic campaign of disappearances.[11] In May 2001, the Committee on Conscience of the United States Holocaust Memorial Museum placed Chechnya at the top of its Genocide Alert list, which had been created to sound warnings of potential genocides.[12]

This carnage provoked a clamour for accountability that was magnified by the recent indictment of Slobodan Milošević for crimes against humanity in Kosovo. As early as April 2000, one month after Putin's election to the presidency, the International Federation for Human Rights (FIDH) released a report documenting Russian atrocities and calling for the creation of an international criminal tribunal on Chechnya.[13] This demand was echoed by the International Commission of Jurists, which argued that the proposed court 'should investigate and punish those responsible – including at the highest level of the Russian State – for war crimes and crimes against humanity committed in the course of the conflict in Chechnya.'[14]

---

9 Kozyrev, A. Speech to World Conference on Human Rights: 4th plenary meeting, Tuesday, 15 June 1993, https://searchlibrary.ohchr.org/record/29884?ln=en&v=pdf accessed 30 May 2025.

10 'Irak ostaetskya v tsentre diskussii,' *Nezavisimaya Gazeta* (Moscow, 15 September 2000) https://www.ng.ru/world/2000-09-15/6_irak.html accessed 30 May 2025.

11 Matt Bivens, 'Kovalyov takes grim message to US,' *Moscow Times* (Moscow, 17 February 2003).

12 Emma Gilligan, *Terror in Chechnya: Russia and the Tragedy of Civilians in War* (Princeton University Press 2009): 1.

13 'Rights group seeks Chechnya war crimes tribunal,' Reuters News (3 April 2000).

14 International Commission of Jurists 'Jurists back call for an International Criminal Court on Chechnya,' (I4 April 2000) https://www.icj.org/jurists-back-call-for-an-international-criminal-court-on-chechnya/ accessed 23 April 2025.

Russia's vulnerability to human rights scrutiny was aggravated by a series of diplomatic setbacks. On 6 April 2000, the Parliamentary Assembly of the Council of Europe (PACE) voted to suspend the voting rights of the Russian delegation because of the flouting of the right to life in Chechnya.[15] Later that month, the UN's Human Rights Commission passed an EU-sponsored resolution expressing concern about 'disproportionate and indiscriminate use of Russian military force, including attacks against civilians' and about 'gross, widespread and flagrant violations of human rights… notably in the alleged "camps of filtration".' To end these atrocities, it urged the Russian government to create an independent commission of inquiry 'to establish the truth and identify those responsible, with a view to bringing them to justice and preventing impunity.'[16]

What accountability meant in practice was highlighted by the struggle to extradite Slobodan Milošević to The Hague after his ouster in a popular uprising in October 2000. For a regime facing a storm of criticism about atrocities in Chechnya, the prospect of an allied head of state in the dock at the ICTY for similar crimes was an ominous precedent. Russia's response was to question the court's objectivity and usefulness. In a Security Council debate in early 2001, Russia's UN ambassador Sergei Lavrov complained about the 'anti-Serb bias in the tribunal's work' and demanded a time frame for its closure.[17] A few weeks later, Foreign Minister Igor Ivanov criticised the ICTY as an obstacle to a durable peace. In an interview, he argued that 'the tribunal was formed at a time when Bosnia and the Balkans were in a state of war, when there were no democratic institutions or institutions of justice.' This phase was 'passing into history' because of the democratic transitions in the region. By abolishing the ICTY, 'we would promote the stabilization of the situation in Yugoslavia and in the Balkans as a whole.'[18] This hope was confounded by the arrest of Milošević in April 2001 and his transfer to The Hague. While Russia was careful to avoid criticising its Serbian ally, it blocked a UN Security Council resolution welcoming the extradition.[19]

15 Yurii Kovalenko, '"Sadovye gnomy" zashchitili prava cheloveka,' *Novye Izvestiya* (Moscow 8 April 2000).

16 UN Commission on Human Rights resolution 2000/58 'Situation in the Republic of Chechnya of the Russian Federation,' 25 April 2000, E/CN.4/RES/2000/58, https://www.refworld.org/docid/3b00f2ba44.html accessed 23 April 2025.

17 'Moscow wants war crimes court in the Hague shut,' Reuters News 13 February 2001.

18 'Russia favors end to tribunal for former Yugoslavia,' Associated Press (23 February 2001).

19 'Russia blocks Security Council approval of Milosevic arrest,' Agence France-Presse (29 June 2001).

During these clashes over Chechnya and the ICTY, Russia's position was essentially defensive. In international forums, its diplomats posed as defenders of impartial justice, peace, and democratisation. Their position was strengthened by the West's rapprochement with the Putin regime in the aftermath of the 11 September 2001 terrorist attacks on the United States. Both US and EU leaders hailed Putin's 'strategic choice' to collaborate in the War on Terror, and extolled the shared values that united Russia and the Western democracies.

The last serious attempt to hold Russia accountable for atrocities in Chechnya was provoked by the referendum held to legitimise Russia's puppet regime in April 2003. Rudolf Bindig, PACE's human rights rapporteur for Chechnya, tabled a resolution calling for the Council of Europe to propose 'the setting up of an ad hoc tribunal to try war crimes and crimes against humanity in the Chechen republic, modelled on the International Criminal Tribunal for the former Yugoslavia.'[20] Although the resolution was passed 97-27, it was ignored by CoE's Council of Ministers. Nevertheless, it was denounced by the Russian Foreign Ministry, whose spokesman called it 'openly anti-Russian' and insisted that 'no-one can deprive Russia of its right to enforce its own legal system on its own territory.'[21] Certainly European leaders lacked the political will to create a new tribunal. At the EU–Russia summit later that year, Silvio Berlusconi, the holder of the EU's rotating presidency, announced that he was acting as 'Putin's lawyer' and defended Russia's subjugation of Chechnya as a legitimate response to terrorism.[22]

2 Misappropriating Anti-racism

A new phase in Russia's confrontation with the new international criminal justice was inaugurated by the consolidation of the Putin regime after heavily manipulated parliamentary and presidential elections in 2003–2004.[23] Abandoning their defensive approach, Russian diplomats now went on the offensive by formulating their own critique of the human rights records of Western democracies. The focus of their criticism was the 'rehabilitation of nazism' in two new EU member states, Latvia and Estonia. In the process, Russia posi-

20 Malcolm Hawkes, 'A Tribunal for Chechnya?' *Moscow Times* (Moscow, 31 March 2003) 10.
21 Ibid.
22 'Italy's Berlusconi defends Russia's Putin at Summit,' Associated Press (7 November 2003).
23 On the elections, see Michael McFaul and Nikita Petrov, 'Russian Democracy in Eclipse: What the Elections Tell Us,' (2004) 15 *Journal of Democracy*, 20.

tioned itself as a standard-bearer of anti-racism and the principles of the UN's 2001 Durban Declaration. By aligning itself with a series of resolutions dating back to the mid-1990s, Russia was able to forge a diverse coalition of developing states and authoritarian regimes.

The new strategy was unveiled at the March 2004 session of the UN Human Rights Commission. Russian diplomats proposed a resolution on the 'Inadmissibility of certain practices that contribute to fuelling contemporary forms of racism, racial discrimination, xenophobia and related intolerance.' Their draft paid lip service to article 84 of the Durban Declaration, which had 'condemned the persistence and resurgence of neo-Nazism, neo-Fascism and violent nationalist prejudice.' Although the Russian resolution made no reference to specific countries, it was clearly directed against Latvia, where small rallies and memorialisation of the SS by a group of aged Nazi collaborators had attracted disproportionate attention in the Russian media. Little room for doubt was left by the resolution's second article, which expressed concern over 'the glorification of former members of the Waffen SS organization, in particular, erecting monuments and memorials as well as holding public demonstrations of former SS members.' The resolution passed 36-13, with four abstentions. On the same day, a European Union resolution on Chechnya, which called on the Russian authorities to take urgent measures to prevent violations of human rights, 'including the full and prompt prosecution of all perpetrators,' was overwhelmingly defeated, 23-12, with 18 abstentions.[24]

This reversal set the pattern for a succession of clashes at the UN, where Russia was trying to consolidate its position as the advocate of a new anti-racism norm. Introducing a similar resolution at the following year's session of the UN Human Rights Commission, Russia's deputy foreign minister Yurii Fedotov lambasted the latest march of SS veterans in Riga as 'a challenge to the basic norms of humanity, to the UN Human Rights Commission.'[25] In December 2005, and in each of the following three years, Russian diplomats achieved the adoption of similarly worded resolutions by the UN General Assembly.[26]

Russia's anti-fascist diplomacy was reinforced by the country's domestic transformation. During 2005–2008, Putin unleashed a 'preventive counter-revolution,' a set of measures that were designed to insulate the country

24 *United Nations Commission on Human Rights. Report on the Sixtieth Session (15 March - 23 April 2004)*, E/CN.4/2004/127.

25 'International community should not close its eyes to neo-nazi orgy in Riga,' RIA Novosti (17 March 2005).

26 UN (2009), 'Resolution adopted by the General Assembly,' A/RES/63/162.

from the 'coloured revolutions' sweeping across the post-Soviet space. Central to this counter-revolution was the mobilisation of loyalist supporters, who claimed that Russia's sovereignty was threatened by Western attempts to sow chaos by enlisting fascists as agents of revolution. This linkage of anti-fascism to counter-revolutionary politics became central to the public rhetoric of the Putin regime. The Kremlin's most important loyalist organisation was the 'anti-fascist democratic youth movement' Nashi (Ours), which staged a massive demonstration about the 'passing of the baton' to a new generation of anti-fascist youth. Nashi's best-known pamphlet, titled 'Ordinary Fascism,' divided Russia's democratic opposition into 'fascists' and 'fascist sympathisers.'[27] No less inflammatory was a series of articles on the Kremlin-aligned website, Regnum, about the 'Front against Russia.' One of them claimed that the EU had been fatally transformed into a Russophobic, 'fascist' force by the admission of new member states from Eastern Europe, above all the Baltic states.[28] Later that year, the articles were published as a single volume by Gleb Pavlovskii, a key Kremlin advisor and theorist of the 'preventive counter-revolution,' who provided a preface.[29] Soon afterwards Regnum's editor, Modest Kolerov, was appointed to head a Kremlin department that was tasked with combatting 'coloured revolution' in the former Soviet space.[30]

This ideological reorientation found expression at the highest levels of the Russian state. Writing in *Le Figaro* on the 60th anniversary of VE-Day, President Putin condemned the memorialisation of Nazism in the Baltic states, and reminded his readers that 'the decisions of the international community, including those of the Nuremberg tribunal, unambiguously condemn any form of cooperation with Nazism, regardless of place or time.'[31]

This posturing constituted misappropriation in two ways. On the one hand, it was used to justify curbs on fundamental human rights. During the course of the 'preventive counter-revolution,' the regime imposed controls on NGOs, suppressed opposition political parties, barred critics from access to television, and restricted public demonstrations. Civil and political rights enshrined in the constitution were nullified in practice. On the other hand, the campaign

27 Horvath, R. *Putin's 'Preventive Counter-Revolution': Post-Soviet Authoritarianism and the Spectre of Velvet Revolution* (Routledge 2013) 106.

28 Dmitrii Kondrashov, 'Front protiv Rossii: napravleniya agressii' (28 March 2005) http://www.regnum.ru/news/428347.html accessed 23 April 2025.

29 *Rossiya i "Sanitarnyi kordon,'* (Evropa 2005).

30 Oleg Kashin, Oleg (2005) 'Vladimir Putin naznachil barkhatnogo kontrrevolyutsionera,' *Kommersant"* (Moscow, 23 March 2005) https://www.kommersant.ru/doc/556859 accessed 23 April 2025.

31 Vladimir Poutine, 'Les leçons de la victoire sure le nazisme,' Le Figaro (Paris: 7 May 2005).

coincided with an intensifying struggle against accountability. While the Putin regime was posing as the custodian of the legacy of the Nuremberg Tribunal and lambasting Latvia for seeking 'a re-evaluation' of its verdict, it orchestrated a sustained and vitriolic campaign to discredit the ICTY.[32] Unlike the earlier legalistic and democratic language of its earlier criticisms, it now denounced the court as a threat to human rights.

This shift was exemplified by Russia's reaction to Milošević's sudden death in his cell at The Hague on 11 March 2006. Foreign Minister Sergei Lavrov immediately cast doubt on the official explanation of Milošević's death and declared that 'we ... have the right not to believe and not to trust those who are conducting the tests' for the autopsy. To underline the unreliability of the tribunal, he announced that Russia had requested the participation of a group of its doctors in the autopsy.[33] In the process, he helped to kindle conspiracy theories that Milošević was a victim of foul play. Lavrov's insinuations were amplified by the State Duma, which issued a statement calling for the abolition of the tribunal. According to the statement, the ICTY's decisions revealed double standards and 'an extreme degree of politicisation and bias.' Those responsible for Milosevic's death – 'an absolutely unacceptable' violation of human rights – should be held accountable in court.[34] This 'tragic chain of events,' concluded the document, was 'in obvious dissonance with calls in Europe for the unconditional observance of human rights and the rejection of double standards.'[35]

The Putin regime's attack on the ICTY as a human rights violator was refined in a second campaign at the end of the year. The focus was Vojislav Šešelj, a Serbian radical nationalist politician on trial for crimes against humanity and war crimes. On 10 November 2006, Šešelj had announced a hunger strike in protest over procedural issues, including the translation of court documents into Serbian. A week later, the Russian State Duma voted to ask the Russian Foreign Ministry to investigate the case. Konstantin Kosachev, chairman of the Duma's Foreign Affairs Committee, also proposed that the Duma's Committee for the Study of Human Rights Practices in Foreign Coun-

---

32 'Shestvie v Rige byvshikh esesovtsev,' Interfax (16 March 2005).

33 'Russia questions Milosevic autopsy results: Lavrov,' Agence France-Presse, 13 March 2006.

34 E. Spetsko, 'Duma vystupit za uprazdnenie Gaagskogo tribunala,' *Vedomosti* (Moscow, 14 March 2006), https://www.vedomosti.ru/library/articles/2006/03/14/duma-vystupit-za-uprazdnenie-gaagskogo-tribunala accessed 23 April 2025.

35 'Mezhdunarodnomu tribunalu po byvshei Yugoslavii tak i ne udalos' realizovat' ideyu svoegu sozdaniya,' *Regnum* (14 March 2006), https://regnum.ru/news/605611 accessed 23 April 2025.

tries (CSHRP) hold hearings on the treatment of Šešelj.[36] This committee, chaired by the nationalist ideologue Nataliya Narochnitskaya, was one of the crucibles of the Putin regime's assault on international human rights norms.[37] At its roundtable on the ICTY on 14 December, CSHRP made no pretence of objectivity. A statement announcing the event warned that if the ICTY failed to meet Šešelj's demands, it 'would be latest testimony to the total bankruptcy of The Hague tribunal, whose activity has long been a farce.'[38] In her opening address, Narochnitskaya denounced the ICTY as an instrument of Western power, which had been created 'not only to justify NATO's aggression against Yugoslavia, but also to punish someone, and to show what might happen to several other political leaders in different corners of the world.'[39] Her invective was echoed by a series of Duma deputies and academic jurists. The most inflammatory was Aleksandr Mezyaev, a professor of international law, who claimed to have 'experienced a state of shock' while observing the tribunal. According to him, Milošević was a peacemaker and a martyr, who had been murdered to cover up the truth about Western aggression: 'They killed him because proof was submitted during the defence part of the trial that the crimes he was accused of, especially in Kosovo, were actually committed by NATO countries.'[40]

The attack on the ICTY was amplified by several Kremlin-aligned structures. One was a new 'Committee in Memory of Slobodan Milošević,' founded by a group of prominent anti-Western nationalists, who denounced the ICTY an instrument for 'the annihilation of all active political figures who resisted the West's destruction of Yugoslavia.'[41] Another was the Institute for Democracy and Cooperation, a soft power initiative, with branches in New York and Paris, which had been announced by Putin in 2007.[42] Narochnitskaya headed

---

36 'Deputaty predlagayut provesti parlamentskie slushaniya po situatsii v Mezhdunarodnom tribunal po byvshei Yugoslavii,' RIA Novosti (17 November 2006).

37 Robert Horvath, 'The Reinvention of 'Traditional Values': Nataliya Narochnitskaya and Russia's Assault on Universal Human Rights,' (2016) 68 *Europe-Asia Studies*, 878.

38 Nataliya Narochnitskaya, 'Zayavlenie presedatelya komissii gosudarstvennoi Dumy,' (1 December 2006) https://web.archive.org/web/20071020033734/http://www.narochnitskaia.ru/cgi-bin/main.cgi?item=1r1371r061201190109 accessed 23 April 2025.

39 Aleksei Timofeev, 'Sudilishche nad serbskimi vozhdyami. V Gosudarstvennoi Dume sostoyalis' slushaniya o deyatel'nosti MTBYu,' Stoletie (25 December 2006) https://www.stoletie.ru/slavyanskoe_pole/sudilische_nad_serbskimi_vozhdyami.htm accessed 23 April 2025.

40 Ibid.

41 'Zapretit deyatel'nost' Gaagskogo sudilishcha,' *Russkii vestnik* (8 December 2006).

42 Ekaterina Grigor'eva, 'Rossiya profinansiuret evropeiskuyu demokratiyu,' *Izvestiya* (Moscow. 29 October 2007), p. 2.

the Paris branch, which became a venue for regular seminars and round-tables where Eurosceptics and conservatives mingled with Russian propagandists. Much of this activity was coordinated by IDC's 'Director of Studies,' John Laughland, a British activist and scholar. Laughland was best known for his involvement with the British Helsinki Human Rights Group, an election-monitoring organisation that became notorious for defending rigged elections in Eastern Europe.[43] He was also the English-speaking world's most outspoken critic of the ICTY. In 2007, he published a scathing indictment of the tribunal titled *Travesty: The trial of Slobodan Milošević and the corruption of international justice*.[44] A year later, under the aegis of IDC, he and Narochnitskaya co-edited a volume about the dangers posed by 'orange networks' of Western democracy promoters and NGOs.[45]

IDC's first target was Carla del Ponte, the former ICTY prosecutor. In her recently published memoirs, Del Ponte had claimed that the ICTY had failed to act on allegations that Kosovar insurgents had abducted ethnic Serbs and taken them to prisons in Albania to be killed by organ traffickers. In one of her first media appearances after her appointment, Narochnitskaya was interviewed on a television report about the allegations. The tone of the broadcast was set by the presenter, who likened the organ harvesting to 'tortures in the Third Reich's concentration camps.' He was backed up by Narochnitskaya, who offered unsubstantiated atrocity claims about a Serbian child 'roasted with apples, like a Christmas goose.' When the presenter asserted that Del Ponte 'knew everything but still was always against the Serbs,' Narochnitskaya agreed. Del Ponte, she declared, was 'the devil incarnate, absolutely enraged with hatred towards the Serbs and acting on certain orders, of course.'[46]

Russia's attack on the ICTY intensified during the annual UN Security Council hearings about its performance. After a report by the tribunal's new prosecutor, Russia's UN ambassador Vitalii Churkin rose to condemn the ICTY's 'inability to fulfill resolutions of the Security Council.'[47] Complaining that 'the Tribunal just ignores the mass extraction of human organs under

43 David Aaronovitch, 'PR man to Europe's nastiest regimes,' *The Guardian* (London, 30 November 2004) https://www.theguardian.com/media/2004/nov/30/pressandpublishing.marketingandpr accessed 23 April 2025.

44 John Laughland, *Travesty: The trial of Slobodan Milošević and the corruption of international justice* (Pluto 2007).

45 Natal'ya Narochnitskaya and John Laughland (eds) *Oranzhevye seti: ot Belgrada do Bishkeka* (Moscow: Aleteiya 2008).

46 'Russian pundits add to Del Ponte allegations of anti-Serb atrocities,' *BBC Monitoring Former Soviet Union* (9 April 2008).

47 'Rossiya zachitala obvinenie Gaagskomu tribunalu,' *Kommersant"* (Moscow, 6 June 2008).

various pretexts,' he demanded action in response to del Ponte's 'shocking revelations.'[48]

The hardening of Russia's position on the ICTY was exemplified by its reaction to the arrest in July 2008 of Radovan Karadžić, the fugitive ex-president of Republika Srpska. To a far greater degree than Slobodan Milošević, Karadžić was directly implicated in atrocity crimes in the former Yugoslavia. Despite his notoriety, the Russian Foreign Ministry used the occasion to impugn the 'biased approach' of the ICTY.[49] At the same time, Russian officials attacked the unfairness of the impending trial. Dmitrii Rogozin, now Russia's ambassador to NATO, claimed that Karadžić should sit in the dock alongside 'those who made the decision to bombard innocent civilians, hundreds of whom perished during the "democratisation" of the Balkans by the West.'[50] Konstantin Zatulin, the deputy chairman of the Duma Committee for CIS Affairs, accused the West of trying to make a scapegoat out of Karadžić. The Hague tribunal, he added, 'long ago forfeited a moral right to existence, and the last nail [in its coffin] was hammered by Del Ponte in her memoirs.'[51] In a similar vein, Sergei Markov lambasted the ICTY as an 'American court: 'the Americans were initiators of a punitive, aggressive operation against Serbs, and now they put Serbs on trial.' No less emphatic was Nikolai Churkin, a prominent senator in the Federation Council, who declared that 'The Hague Tribunal has no right to exist.'[52]

3 Misappropriating Genocide Prevention

The Kremlin's misappropriation of human rights underwent an important shift during the Russia-Georgia war in August 2008. For the first time, the Putin regime used the language of genocide prevention to justify military aggression against another state. According to regime officials and propagan-

48 'Moscow again calls for probe into abductions of Serbians in Kosovo,' *Interfax* (5 June 2008).

49 Yuliya Petrovskaya, 'Iskali Mladicha, vzyali Karadzhicha,' *Nezavisimaya Gazeta* (Moscow, 23 July 2008).

50 'Rogozin: v sluchae suda nad Karadzhichem nado sudit' i initsiatorom agressii protiv byvshei Yugoslavii,' Regnum (Moscow, 22 July 2008).

51 'Radovan Karadzic mozhet razdelit' sud'bu Milosevicha,' *Izvestiya*,(Moscow, 22 July 2008), https://iz.ru/news/430705 accessed 23 April 2025.

52 'Rossiya pomozhet vernut' mezhdunarodnomu pravosudiyu ob"ektivnost',' Regions.ru/Novosti Federatsii (23 July 2008).

dists, the Georgian assault on the separatist territory of South Ossetia on 7 August constituted genocide. This accusation was first raised by the neo-fascist philosopher Aleksandr Dugin, who claimed in a radio interview that Georgia had 'implemented genocide on an ethnic basis.'[53] Within 24 hours, his terminology was adopted by Premier Putin, who declared at a meeting with displaced persons that 'this is genocide.'[54]

During the weeks that followed, Russian officials created the impression that they were laying the groundwork for a major war crimes trial. On 14 August, Investigative Committee head Aleksandr Bastrykin announced the first genocide prosecution under Article 357 of Russia's Criminal Code.[55] The case was fortified by repeated reports that Georgian forces had massacred 2,000 civilians.[56] In fact, the actual toll was much lower. In 2009, Russian officials conceded that there were 162 documented South Ossetian civilian casualties, significantly lower than the number of Georgian civilians killed during Russia's counter-offensive.[57] Undeterred by the lack of evidence, the Investigative Committee produced a steady stream of announcements about the progress of its genocide case. In an interview with the government newspaper, Bastrykin announced a major expansion of the team that was collecting evidence about crimes that could 'only be compared with the atrocities of the fascists during the years of the [Second World] war.' When asked whether the genocide accusation had been confirmed, he replied: 'Completely.'[58] Two days later, Bastrykin announced to the media that 'everything we have assembled here will be heard by international judicial bodies.'[59]

The genocide allegation provided the principal justification for Russia's recognition of the separatist regions of South Ossetia and Abkhazia as independent states on 26 August. In a televised address, President Medvedev presented the decision as a reaction to the fact that the Georgian government had 'made

53 Aleksandr Dugin, interview with Matvei Ganapol'skii, *Ekho Moskvy* (Moscow, 8 August 2008) http://www.echo.msk.ru/programs/personalno/532383-echo/ accessed 15 August 2008.

54 'Comparison of Ossetian, Jewish people's genocide correct,' Interfax (30 August 2008).

55 Aleksandra Samarina and Viktoriya Kruchinina, 'Genotsid "po faktu",' *Nezavisimaya Gazeta* (Moscow, 15 August 2008).

56 'Dannye o zhertvakh vooruzhennogo konflikta na Kavkaze,' *Reuters* (10 August 2008).

57 Roy Allison, 'The Russian case for military intervention in Georgia: international law, norms and political calculation' (2009) 18 *European Security*, 183.

58 'Voina na unichtozhenie - ot pervogo litsa,' Rossiiskaya Gazeta (Moscow 26 August 2008).

59 'SKP RF kvalifitsiruet deistviyz gruzinskoi armii v Yuzhnoi Osetii kaka genotsid,' RIA Novosti (28 August 2008).

its choice: Saakashvili chose genocide to achieve his political goals.'[60] On the same day, Medvedev used an interview with the BBC to frame Russia's invasion as a humanitarian intervention. Russian peacekeepers had long upheld Georgia's sovereignty, he said, but 'after the genocide started by Saakashvili's regime, the situation changed, and our most important thing was to prevent a humanitarian catastrophe, to save the lives of people we were responsible for.'[61] He repeated the point on the state's propaganda platform, Russia Today: 'it is obvious that our decision is aimed at preventing the genocide, the elimination of a people, and helping them to get on their feet.'[62]

The genocide accusation also served as an instrument of propaganda against the Georgian government. On 3 September, President Medvedev announced that Georgia's president Saakashvili 'does not exist for us, he is a political corpse.'[63] This anathema was reinforced by a steady stream of media statements about the progress of the Investigative Committee's genocide inquiry. In an interview with *Zuricher Zeitung*, Bastrykin dismissed claims that the case was weakened by the debunking of early claims about 2,000 victims. 'According to Russian legislation,' he explained, 'the crime of genocide depends not on the number of victims, but on whether the actions are aimed at the destruction of an ethnic group.... and we found enough evidence of this.'[64] Ten days later, his deputy Aleksandr Sorochkin told a mass circulation newspaper that it was 'entirely possible' that the case about Georgian atrocity crimes would be heard by the ICC or the European Court of Human Rights.[65]

The culmination of this performative prosecutorial activism was the release of a Russian 'White Book' about Georgian war crimes. The newspaper *Komsomol'skaya Pravda* commented that 'the Investigative Committee is preparing a

---

60 'Dmitrii Medvedev vystupil s zayavleniem v svyazi s priznaniem nezavisimosti Yuzhnoi Osetii i Abkhazii,' (26 August 2008) http://kremlin.ru/events/president/news/1223 accessed 23 April 2025.

61 'Interv'yu telekompanii Bi-Bi-Si,' (26 August 2008), http://kremlin.ru/events/president/transcripts/1228 accessed 23 April 2025.

62 'Interv'yu telekompanii "Rasha tudei",' (26 August 2008) http://kremlin.ru/events/president/transcripts/1226 accessed 23 April 2025.

63 'Radovan Karadzic mozhet razdelit' sud'bu Miloshevicha,' *Izvestiya* (Moscow, 22 July 2008) https://iz.ru/news/430705 accessed 23 April 2025.

64 'Bastrykin: Glavnoe v rassledovanii po Yuzhnoi Osetii' ITAR-TASS (5 September 2008).

65 'Rukovoditel' voennogo sledstvennogo upravleniya Sledstvennogo komiteta pri prokurature Rossii Aleksandr Sorochkin: 'Rossiiskikh grazhdan nikomu ne pozvoleno ubivat' beznakazanno,' *Izvestiya* (Moscow, 17 September 2008) https://iz.ru/news/340600 accessed 23 April 2025.

Nuremberg Trial for Saakashvili.'[66] The point was reiterated by President Medvedev at a meeting with Bastrykin. Everything needed to be done, insisted Medvedev, to bring the White Book to the attention of 'interested persons in every country of the world [and] international organisations that are engaged in criminal prosecutions, courts if necessary.'[67]

In fact, the case was put on the backburner while the Kremlin responded to the new Obama administration's 'reset' of US–Russia relations. The only sign of activity was an interview granted by Bastrykin on the first anniversary of the war, when he boasted about the compilation of 355 volumes of case materials, and held out the prospect of an international criminal prosecution as 'the most promising path.'[68] No steps were taken on that path until 2011, when the Georgian parliament voted to recognise the 1860s Circassian genocide in imperial Russia. Russia retaliated by finally sending its materials about South Ossetia to the ICC. The aim, according to a Foreign Ministry spokesperson, was to resolve 'the issue of prosecuting officials of Georgia who committed crimes against RF citizens' by presenting evidence showing that Georgia's aim was 'to destroy the Ossetian population residing in the territory of the republic.'[69] This renewed push for accountability was short-lived. The Kremlin's lost interest in the subject because of developments both at home and in Georgia. In 2012, the Putin regime was shaken by pro-democracy protests. Later that year, the victory of a Russia-aligned party, 'Georgian Dream' in Georgian parliamentary elections, signalled the beginning of the end of Saakashvili's rule.

Russia's intervention in Georgia was an exemplary case of the misappropriation of human rights discourse and the norms of international criminal law. As Roy Allison observed in his analysis of the Russian case for intervention, 'there was no good evidence of mass atrocity crimes in the region or an imminent or actual threat of them.'[70] Authoritative human rights experts from both Human Rights Watch and Memorial debunked Russia's claims about atroci-

---

66 Dmitrii Steshin, 'Na storone Gruzii voevali diversanty iz Ukrainy, Chekhy, Turtsii I SShA,' *Komsomol'skaya Pravda* (Moscow, 24 December 2008) https://www.kp.ru/daily/24220/421763/ Accessed 23 April 2025.

67 'Dmitrii Medvedev vystupil s zayavleniem v svyazi s priznaniem nezavisimosti Yuzhnoi Osetii i Abkhazii,' (26 August 2008) http://kremlin.ru/events/president/news/1223 accessed 23 April 2025.

68 'Saakashvili zovyut v sud,' *Rossiiskaya Gazeta*, 6 August 2009.

69 'Georgia not cooperating with RF on S Ossetia for contrived reasons' ITAR-TASS (Moscow, 8 August 2011).

70 Roy Allison, 'The Russian case for military intervention in Georgia: international law, norms and political calculation' (2009) 18 *European Security*, 185.

ties and genocide.[71] In spite of their findings, the Russian leadership and investigative organs went through the motions of preparing an elaborate genocide case against the Georgian leadership. This charade had negligible legal consequences but considerable value as propaganda. It would also provide a template for Russian disinformation during its coming conflict with Ukraine.

4 The Rupture

Russia's annexation of Crimea and its armed intervention in the Donbass marked the culmination of its confrontation with international justice. Building on the strategy used against Georgia, Russia misappropriated first the language of human rights and then that of genocide prevention to justify military intervention and territorial aggrandisement. At the same time, it effectively declared war on the institutions of post–Cold War international criminal justice. On the one hand, it disengaged itself from existing international criminal tribunals, and tried to discredit the historic ICTY judgment classifying the Srebrenica massacre as an act of genocide. On the other, it staked an exclusive claim to the legacy of the Nuremberg Tribunal, which became the focus of a profusion of government programmes, conferences and commemorations. These activities were used to legitimise Russia's performative investigations of atrocity crimes allegedly committed by Ukraine's new government. They also served to weaken the impact of international efforts to investigate atrocities committed by Russian armed forces and their proxies.

The origins of this shift can be traced to the intensification of the Kremlin's anti-Western propaganda in the aftermath of massive pro-democracy protests in 2011–12. While the regime smeared pro-democracy activists as Western pawns and imposed new 'foreign agents' laws on civil society, Russian diplomats escalated their attacks on the ICTY. In late 2012, after the exoneration of two Croatian generals and a former leader of the Kosovo Liberation Army (KLA), Russia's Foreign Ministry released a statement accusing the ICTY of 'selective justice' that 'left unpunished individuals who are accused of committing crimes against humanity and war crimes.'[72] The accusation was ec-

71 'Tat'yana Lokshina: "O genotside v kavkazkom konflikte govorit' net osnovanii,' Deutsche Welle (25 August 2008); Anastasia Kirilenko, 'Pravozashchitniki ne nashli v Yuzhnoi Osetii sozhzhennoi vo vremya voiny tserkvi,' Kavkazskii uzel (10 October 2008) https://www.kavkaz-uzel.eu/articles/142728 accessed 23 April 2025.

72 'Moskva tverdo namerena dobivat'sya zaversheniya raboty Mezhdunarodnogo tribunala po byvshei Yugoslavii v sroki, ustanovlennye SB OON – MID RF,' ITAR-TASS (Moscow, 30 November 2012).

hoed by Konstantin Dolgov, the Foreign Ministry's Commissioner for Human Rights, Democracy and the Rule of Law, who claimed that the tribunal had freed 'people accused of thousands of crimes.'[73] A week later, Russia's ambassador told the UN Security Council that the ICTY's decisions 'are discrediting the idea of international criminal justice.'[74]

The war of words escalated in the aftermath of Ukraine's 'Revolution of Dignity,' which was misrepresented by the Putin regime as a coup perpetrated by Western-backed neo-Nazis. The need to defend human rights, especially those of Russian speakers, became a central justification for Russia's invasion of Crimea and its covert instigation of a 'separatist' insurgency in the Donbas. Addressing the Federation Council on 1 March 2014 before it authorised the use of Russian armed forces on Ukrainian territory, the chamber's Speaker Valentina Matvienko declared that the new Ukrainian government's rhetoric and decisions 'persuaded us that it was impossible to defend human rights in these conditions.'[75] Within weeks, a group of Duma deputies had drafted an elaborate critique of the human rights situation in Ukraine. Their statement denounced 'the unacceptable violation' of 'basic democratic rights and freedoms, which are enshrined in the Universal Declaration of Human Rights, the International Covenant on Civil and Political Rights, [and] the European Convention on the Defence of Human Rights and Basic Freedoms.' It accused the 'self-proclaimed regime' of 'consciously and everywhere' trampling fundamental freedoms, and listed five arrested 'participants in protest actions.' The list was headed by Pavel Gubarev, a neo-Nazi militant who had been acclaimed by a crowd as 'People's Governor' of Donetsk.[76]

The case against Ukraine was amplified by the Public Chamber, the Kremlin's platform for the management of loyal civil society organisations. In early March, the Duma speaker, Sergei Naryshkin, announced that he was creating a group of 'independent experts' from the Public Chamber to monitor the

---

73 'Deitstviya MTBYU ne vedut k torzhestvu verkhovenstva prava - upolnomochennyi MID RF,' RIA Novosti (Moscow 30 November 2012).

74 'Moskva tverdo namerena dobivat'sya zaversheniya raboty Mezhdunarodnogo tribunala po byvshei Yugoslavii v sroki, ustanovlennye SB OON – MID RF,' ITAR-TASS (Moscow, 30 November 2012).

75 Natal'ya Bashlykova, 'Sovet Federatsii razvyazal preszidentu ruki,' *Izvestiya* (Moscow, 3 March 2014).

76 'O politicheskikh repressiyakh na Ukraine,' *Parlamentskaya Gazeta,* 11 April 2014, https://www.pnp.ru/archive/2014/04/10/o-politicheskikh-repressiyakh-na-ukraine.html accessed 23 April 2025.

human rights situation in Ukraine.[77] The 'experts' included Vyacheslav Grib, deputy chair of the Public Chamber, who announced in mid-March that 'we have recorded tens of cases of gross violations of human rights in southeast Ukraine.' According to him, material collected from the testimony of refugees who had fled to Crimea was being prepared for submission to the UN and the European Court of Human Rights.[78]

On the international stage, Russian diplomats repeatedly invoked human rights abuses as the reason for intervention. Addressing the UN Human Rights Council on 3 March, Lavrov denounced the new Ukrainian government's measures on minority rights and lustration as an attack on human rights and freedoms.[79] When a similar line was advanced by Russia's UN Ambassador as a justification for intervention, US Ambassador Samantha Power remarked sarcastically that 'one might think that Moscow has just become the rapid response arm of the High Commissioner for Human Rights.'[80] Several weeks later, Russia's delegate to the Human Rights Council, Aleksandr Borodavkin, claimed that Ukraine was being terrorised by radical nationalists who 'have committed murders, tortures, arbitrary detentions and extrajudicial killings.' He also alleged that the new government in Kyiv was 'violating the right of freedom of mass media' by targeting journalists, bloggers and independent television stations.[81] Forty Western democracies responded with a statement that condemned Russia's use of an 'unsubstantiated narrative of human rights violations' to justify military intervention in Ukraine.[82]

Russia's narrative shifted to genocide accusations after the outbreak of fighting in southeast Ukraine, which was precipitated by the Russian paramili-

77 'Gosduma RF obratit'sya v Venetsianskuyu komissiyu po voprosu legitimnosti reshenii Rady,' *RBK-Ukraina* (1 March 2014) https://www.rbc.ua/rus/news/gosduma-rf-obratitsya-v-venetsianskuyu-komissiyu-po-voprosu-01032014143000 accessed 23 April 2025.

78 Elena Teslova, 'Narushenie prav cheloveka neobkhodima rassledovat'' *Izvestiya* (Moscow, 17 March 2014).

79 'New Ukrainian power intends to attack human rights, freedoms' ITAR-TASS (Moscow, 3 March 2014).

80 Usborne, David (2014), 'Ukraine crisis: Putin is 'on the wrong side of history, says President Obama' *Independent Online*, 3 March https://www.independent.co.uk/news/world/europe/ukraine-crisis-putin-is-on-the-wrong-side-of-history-says-president-obama-9166831.html accessed 23 April 2025.

81 'Plans imposing illegitimate government on Crimea cannot be carried out – Russian permanent representative in Geneva,' ITAR-TASS (Moscow, 19 March 2014).

82 'Joint statement by 42 States at the Human Rights Council on the situation in Ukraine,' (26 March 2014) https://geneva.usmission.gov/2014/03/26/joint-statement-by-42-states-at-the-human-rights-council-on-the-situation-in-ukraine/ accessed 23 April 2025.

taries who seized the town of Slavyansk in April 2014. When 48 pro-Russian militants died in a fire in Odessa's House of Unions during clashes with pro-Ukraine football gangs, the Kremlin denounced the incident as a premeditated atrocity. According to Lavrov, it was 'pure fascism.'[83] His indignation was soon drowned out by international outrage over Russia's involvement in the downing of the Malaysian airliner MH17 on 17 July. Russia's response was to launch a campaign about atrocities during Ukraine's 'anti-terrorist operation' in the Donbas. On 1 September, the Moscow branch of the Russian Red Cross announced the creation of a commission to gather evidence of Ukrainian war crimes for submission to the ICC and to Russia's own Investigative Committee.[84] A few weeks later, the Russian government newspaper published an article headlined 'Genocide' about mass graves discovered by Kremlin-backed paramilitary forces in Donbas.[85] The accusation was promptly taken up by the Investigative Committee, which announced on 30 September that it had opened a genocide case against the Ukrainian government, armed forces, and members of the far-right movement Right Sector.[86] In January 2015, it launched a second genocide prosecution over the Ukrainian army's bombardment of urban areas.[87] Later that year, a third case identified 30 Ukrainian government officials as perpetrators of genocide.[88]

Like Russia's earlier investigations of Georgia, these genocide prosecutions were a propaganda tool. But they also signalled a more unilateral stance towards international justice. In October 2014, Putin himself staked a special claim to the legacy of Nuremberg. In an interview with a Serbian newspaper, he lamented that 'unfortunately the "vaccine" against the Nazi virus, which had been developed at the Nuremberg Tribunal, is losing its effectiveness in some European states.' The evidence was 'open manifestations of neo-Nazism' in the Baltic states and Ukraine.[89] A few days later, Putin elaborated the case

---

83 'Rossiya ne pozvolit "zamesti pod kover" tragediyu v Odesse – Lavrov", ITAR-TASS (Moscow, 7 May 2014).

84 'RKK sobirate informatsiyu o voennykh prestupleniyakh na Ukraine dlya predostavleniya v Mezhdunarodnyi ugolovnyi sud, Sovbez OON I SK RF' ITAR-TASS (Moscow, 1 September 2014).

85 'Genotsid,' *Rossiiskaya Gazeta* (Moscow, 24 September 2024).

86 Petr Kozlov, 'Rossiiskie sledovateli vozbuzhdayut novye ugolovnye dela protiv ukrainskikh voennykh,' *Vedomosti* (Moscow, 2 October 2014).

87 'SKR vozbudil delo o genotside iz-za poslednikh obstrelov zhilykh raionov Donbassa,' Interfax (Moscow, 13 January 2015).

88 'Za genotsid i narusheniya prav grazhdan na yugo-vostoka Ukrainy SK RF privlek 30 dolzhnostnykh lits,' Interfax (Moscow, 3 September 2015).

89 'Interv'yu gazete "Politika",' (15 October 2014), http://kremlin.ru/events/president/news/46806 accessed 23 April 2025.

against Ukraine in an address to his Presidential Council for Human Rights and the Development of Civil Society. After paying lip service to the idea that 'all human rights and freedoms are of supreme value,' Putin claimed that Ukraine was the site of 'a large-scale crisis in terms of international law, the basic norms of the Universal Declaration of Human Rights and the Convention on Prevention and Punishment of the Crime of Genocide.' He proceeded to itemise Ukraine's alleged violation of these foundational documents, article by article.[90]

While the Putin regime posed as the custodian of the Nuremberg legacy, it began to disengage itself from the post–Cold War human rights and international criminal justice regime. One of the standard bearers of this rupture was Bastrykin. In his annual address to the Investigative Committee's collegium in February 2015, he called for the creation of a new 'objective' international criminal tribunal for Ukraine and for the removal of Article 15/4 of the Russian constitution, which affirmed the priority of Russia's international obligations over domestic legislation.[91] Although the tribunal never materialised, the Investigative Committee announced a series of new genocide prosecutions in 2015 and 2016. Article 15/4 was ultimately deleted by the 2020 constitutional referendum.

One of the first targets of the new unilateralism was the European Court of Human Rights (ECtHR). The court's conflictual relationship with Russia had been aggravated by rulings on the Yukos case and Russian atrocity crimes in Chechnya. At a meeting with Duma deputies in August 2014, Putin lambasted the court, which 'does not defend any rights but simply fulfils some kind of political function.'[92] Practical steps followed in July 2015. In response to an inquiry from Duma deputies, Russia's constitutional court held that it could overturn decisions of the ECtHR that conflicted with the Russian constitution. This decision was reinforced by legislation that confirmed the prerogative of the Constitutional Court to rule on the constitutionality of ECtHR judgments.[93]

---

90 'Meeting of the Presidential Council for Civil Society and Human Rights,' 14 October 2014, http://en.kremlin.ru/events/councils/by-council/18/46786 accessed 23 April 2025.

91 Maksim Solopov, 'Aleksandr Bastrykin predlozhil izmenit' Konstitutsiyu,' *RBK* (Moscow, 27 February 2015).

92 'Vstrecha s chlenami fraktsii politicheskikh partii v Gosudarstvennoi Dume,' 14 August 2014 http://special.kremlin.ru/catalog/regions/CR/events/46451 accessed 23 April 2025.

93 Anton Burkov, 'The use of European human rights law in Russian courts' in Lauri Malksoo and Wolfgang Benedek (eds) *Russia and the European Court of Human Rights: the Strasbourg effect* (Cambridge UP, 2018) 590–92.

A second rupture was with the ICC. Although Russia had signed the Rome statute, it had never ratified it. Even this symbolic connection was called into question in January 2016, when the ICC launched an investigation of ethnic cleansing of Georgian villages during the 2008 war.[94] In response, Maria Zakharova, the Russian Foreign Ministry spokesperson, signalled that Russia would reconsider its attitude towards an institution that had disappointed hopes that it would contribute to the rule of law and international stability.[95] The last straw was a statement by the ICC prosecutor that the invasion of Crimea constituted an 'armed conflict' between Russia and Ukraine. One day later, Putin signed a directive on Russia's withdrawal from the Rome Statute.[96]

A third object of Kremlin displeasure was the ICTY's rulings on genocide in the former Yugoslavia. In July 2015, Russia cast the sole veto against a UN Security Council resolution marking the 20th anniversary of the Srebrenica massacre. The resolution invoked the ICTY judgment on genocide at Srebrenica and affirmed that 'acceptance of the tragic events at Srebrenica as genocide is a prerequisite for reconciliation.'[97] Despite the fact that the resolution did not name the perpetrators, Russia's UN ambassador Churkin denounced it as 'unconstructive, confrontationalist and politically motivated.' Its sponsors, he claimed, had exploited the anniversary to promote 'intrusive human rights approaches' that threatened state sovereignty.[98] Churkin's veto was reinforced by an extensive campaign on Kremlin propaganda platforms to deny that Srebrenica was genocide.[99]

This denialism became more vociferous during the trial of Ratko Mladić, the Bosnian Serb general who had supervised the massacre. When the ICTY

---

94 Jo Biddle, 'ICC prosecutors to probe 2008 alleged war crimes in Georgia' Agence France-Presse (Paris, 27 January 2016).

95 Shaun Walker, 'Russia withdraws signature from international criminal court statute' The Guardian (London, 17 November 2016) <https://www.theguardian.com/world/2016/nov/16/russia-withdraws-signature-from-international-criminal-court-statute> accessed 23 April 2025.

96 'Rasporyazhenie prezidenta rossiiskoi federatsii,' 16 November 2016 <http://publication.pravo.gov.ru/Document/View/0001201611160018> accessed 23 April 2025.

97 UN Security Council draft resolution, 8 July 2015, S/2015/508 https://www.securitycouncilreport.org/un-documents/document/s2015508.php accessed 23 April 2025.

98 'Rossiya primenila veto pri golosovanii rezolyutsii Soveta Bezopasnosti OON po Bosnii i Gertsegovine,' 8 July 2015 <https://news.un.org/ru/story/2015/07/1266801> accessed 23 April 2025.

99 'Srebrenica massacre a crime, not genocide - Russian lawmaker' Sputnik News (Moscow, 14 July 2015) <https://sputnikglobe.com/20150714/1024621420.html>; 'UNSC Genocide vote designed to justify NATO bombing of Yugoslavia,' Sputnik News (Moscow, 12 July 2015) <https://sputnikglobe.com/20150712/1024525133.html>.

sentenced Mladić to life imprisonment for genocide in November 2017, the Russian Foreign Ministry condemned the verdict as 'the continuation of a politicized and biased policy that has prevailed in the activities of the ICTY.'[100] As usual, the official position was amplified by propaganda. Numerous experts were enlisted by state news agencies to discredit the judgment as a travesty of justice. The core message of this commentary was summed up by a RIA Novosti article that concluded: 'The sentencing of Mladić is the final point in the war that the West launched against Yugoslavia. The general has been convicted, but it was Mladić and all Serbs who are victorious.'[101] When Mladić's appeal was dismissed in 2021, the Kremlin unleashed a new round of denunciation. Commenting on the verdict, Russia's deputy UN ambassador declared that 'the ICTY went down in history as a tool of revenge rather than a body of justice.'[102]

One month later, a campaign against the ICTY's Srebrenica judgment was launched by the release of the reports from two 'International Expert Commissions' that had been created by the government of Republika Srpska to evaluate the events in Sarajevo and Srebrenica between 1992 and 1995. To lend credibility to their findings, each was headed by an Israeli holocaust historian. Gideon Greif, the chair of the Srebrenica Commission, had recently been appointed a professor at Belgrade University.[103] His report challenged the ICTY's Srebrenica judgment by drastically reducing the number of victims and by rejecting the genocide charge.[104] An instant scandal, the report provoked the German government to rescind an award to Greif for his holocaust scholarship.[105] By contrast, the Putin regime actively promoted Greif's report. On 14 September, the Gorchakov Foundation, a think tank linked to the Russian Foreign Ministry, held a conference about the reports under the chairmanship of Professor Elena Ponomareva, a Balkan expert at the Moscow State Institute of International Relations (MGIMO). In an interview with the Russian government newspaper, Ponomareva hailed the reports as 'serious and

100 'Moscow Says Ex-Bosnian Serb Military Commander Mladic Conviction Politicized,' Sputnik News (Moscow, 23 November 2017).

101 '"Vse eto lozh'!" Kak v Gaage sudili serbskogo generala Ratko Mladicha,' RIA (Moscow, 22 November 2017) <https://ria.ru/20171122/1509360121.html> accessed 23 April 2025.

102 'Russia's UN mission slams life sentence for Bosnian Serb commander Mladic,' TASS (Moscow, 9 June) <https://tass.com/world/1300531>.

103 Ronen Shnidman, 'Israelis to teach Serbs how to say "shalom",' *Jerusalem Post* (Jerusalem, 22 June 2019).

104 Kirill Borshchev 'Izrael'skii istorik: "V Srebrenitse ne bylo genotsida - ya povtoryu eto sto tysyach raz,' *Balkanist*, 15 June 2021, <https://balkanist.ru/izrailskij-istorik-v-srebrenitse-ne-bylo-genotsida-ya-povtoryu-eto-sto-tysyach-raz/> accessed 23 April 2025.

105 'German cancels Israeli historian for genocide award,' Deutsche Welle, 1 January 2022.

interdisciplinary.' According to her, 'today we have evidence showing that neither in Sarajevo nor in Srebrenica did the Serbs commit a genocide.'[106]

The onslaught against the ICTY proceeded in tandem with a massive campaign to position the Putin regime as the guardian of the Nuremberg legacy. This push was heralded by a major propaganda event, an 'international scientific conference' on 'The Lessons of Nuremberg,' which was held in November 2020 to mark the 75th anniversary of the beginning of the trials. Funded by presidential grants and widely covered in the state media, the lavish two-day event was clearly intended to send a message about the Kremlin's status as a privileged interpreter and custodian of the memory of Nuremberg. The political significance of the conference was underlined by speeches from President Putin and leading government officials, including Lavrov, Bastrykin, and Prosecutor-General Igor Krasnov. In his address, Putin claimed to be guided by the lessons of the tribunal:

> The lessons of Nuremberg are relevant today. We constantly refer to the lessons of the Nuremberg tribunal… in order to resist convincingly the international distortion and falsification of the events of the Second World War … false attempts at the rehabilitation and even the glorification of nazi criminals and their henchmen.

The duty of the entire world community, he added, was 'to stand in guard' over the tribunal's decisions, which 'lay at the foundations of the values of the postwar world order and the norms of international law.' Because attempts to undermine the Nuremberg judgments were a threat to global security, 'Russia raises these issues in every negotiating arena.'[107]

The Putin regime's credentials as a sentinel of the Nuremberg judgments were reinforced by two state-organised campaigns about Soviet victimhood. The first was a federal programme titled 'Without a Statute of Limitations,' which provided funding for a national essay competition, research projects, and online exhibitions about Nazi crimes against Soviet citizens during the Second World War. The second was organised around a new concept, 'the

106 Aleksandr Borisov 'Professor Elena Ponomareva: V BiG k serbam byli primeneny praktiki genotsida,' *Rossiiskaya Gazeta* (Moscow, 12 September 2021) <https://rg.ru/2021/09/12/professor-elena-ponomareva-v-big-k-serbam-byli-primeneny-praktiki-genocida.html> accessed 23 April 2025.

107 'Obrashchenie k uchastnikam foruma "Uroki Nyurnberga",' 20 November 2020 <http://kremlin.ru/events/president/news/64447> accessed 23 April 2025.

genocide of the Soviet people,' which became the subject of an annual commemoration on 19 April 2021.[108]

The language of genocide prevention provided a central justification for Russia's full-scale invasion of Ukraine in 2022. In a series of statements, Putin and senior officials charged that Ukraine was committing a 'genocide of Donbas people.' On 22 February 2022, Putin told journalists that it had become intolerable 'to wait for the continuation of this persecution…. this genocide of nearly four million people.'[109] In his national address two days later, he spoke of the urgent need 'to stop this nightmare, the genocide of millions of people.' The 'Special Military Operation,' he vowed, would not only 'demilitarise and denazify Ukraine but also bring to justice those who committed numerous bloody crimes against civilians.'[110]

In fact the misappropriation of the Nuremberg legacy provided a shield for Russian perpetrators of atrocity crimes. Faced with international condemnation of the mass killings of Ukrainian civilians by Russian forces in Bucha, the Russian Foreign Ministry dismissed the furore as a Western-organised provocation 'similar to Srebrenica.'[111] One day later, Bastrykin announced an investigation of this 'Ukrainian provocation' and reiterated the need to collect evidence for war crimes trials of Ukrainian military leaders.[112] What followed was a new wave of performative criminal justice. While the Investigative Committee announced new genocide cases, Kremlin-aligned NGOs organised a plethora of public events about Ukrainian human rights abuses and the need for 'Nuremberg-2.'[113]

108 Anton Weiss-Wendt, '"Genocide of the Soviet People": Putin's Russia Waging Lawfare by Means of History, 2018–2023,' (2024) 17 *Genocide Studies and Prevention* 1.

109 'Vladimir Putin otvetil na voprosy zhurnalistov,' 22 February 2022 <http://kremlin.ru/events/president/news/67838> accessed 23 April 2025.

110 'Obrashchenie Prezidenta Rossiiskoi Federatsii,' 24 February 2022 <http://kremlin.ru/events/president/news/67843> accessed 23 April 2025.

111 'Zakharova nazvala sponsorov provokatsii, podobnykh toi, chto byla v Buche,' RIA (Moscow, 6 April 2022).

112 'Predsedatel' SK Rossii provel v Donetske soveshchanie' 7 April 2022, <https://sledcom.ru/press/events/item/1671392/> accessed 23 April 2025.

113 See for instance the June 2022 session of the Zinoviev Club on Nuremberg-2. 'Zinov'evskii klub: Pochemu Rossiya prava. Nyurnberg-2 protiv sponsora zla – kollektivnogo Zapada,' <http://zinoviev.info/wps/archives/7514> accessed 23 April 2025.

5 Conclusion

Under the rule of Vladimir Putin, Russia became a standard-bearer of the struggle against international criminal justice. No other state did more to undermine the new tribunals, to discredit their judgments, and to shield perpetrators of atrocity crimes from accountability. Central to the Kremlin's strategy was the misappropriation of human rights and the norms and processes of international criminal law. Over the course of two decades, Russian diplomats posed as defenders of anti-racism norms and accused the new institutions of complicity in human rights violations. At the same time, the Kremlin positioned itself as a defender of accountability, and as an enforcer of international criminal justice. During the war with Georgia in 2008 and Ukraine after 2014, Russian leaders mimicked the language of genocide prevention and R2P. This cynical rhetoric was reinforced by prosecutors who embarked on a succession of performative investigations of non-existent genocide in both countries.

These campaigns were an important part of the human rights recession of the twenty-first century. By undermining the legitimacy of the new tribunals, the Putin regime weakened their capacity to deter perpetrators of atrocity crimes. By denying genocide in Bosnia, it subverted post-conflict reconciliation and democratisation in the former Yugoslavia. By claiming that its aggression in Georgia and Ukraine was preventing genocide, it debased the language of international justice.

The culmination of this process was a rupture between Russia and the institutions of post–Cold War international criminal justice. As the Putin regime waged a war of attrition against the ICTY and severed its ties to the Strasbourg Court and the ICC, it staked an exclusive claim to the legacy of the Nuremberg trials. This new misappropriation was founded on propaganda about the 'rehabilitation of Nazism' in post-Soviet states and on the concept of the 'genocide of the Soviet people.' In fact, the Russian state's misappropriation of Nuremberg was part of a course of action that negated the basic principles of that foundational moment. In Kremlin propaganda, the 'lessons of Nuremberg,' accompanied by a panoply of new war crimes investigations and war crimes tribunals, served as justification for an aggressive war and a smokescreen for genocidal atrocities.

Bibliography

Aaronovitch, D. 'PR man to Europe's nastiest regimes,' *The Guardian* (London, 30 November 2004) <https://www.theguardian.com/media/2004/nov/30/pressandpublishing.marketingandpr> 23 April 2025.

Allison, R. 'The Russian case for military intervention in Georgia: international law, norms and political calculation' (2009) 18 *European Security,* 183.

Bashlykova, N. 'Sovet Federatsii razvyazal preszidentu ruki,' *Izvestiya* (Moscow, 3 March 2014).

'Bastrykin: Glavnoe v rassledovanii po Yuzhnoi Osetii' ITAR-TASS (5 September 2008).

Biddle, J. 'ICC prosecutors to probe 2008 alleged war crimes in Georgia' Agence France-Presse (Paris, 27 January 2016).

Borisov, A. 'Professor Elena Ponomareva: V BiG k serbam byli primeneny praktiki genotsida,' *Rossiiskaya Gazeta* (Moscow, 12 September 2021) <https://rg.ru/2021/09/12/professor-elena-ponomareva-v-big-k-serbam-byli-primeneny-praktiki-genocida.html> accessed 23 April 2025.

Borshchev, K. 'Izrael'skii istorik: "V Srebrenitse ne bylo genotsida – ya povtoryu eto sto tysyach raz,' *Balkanist,* 15 June 2021, <https://balkanist.ru/izrailskij-istorik-v-srebrenitse-ne-bylo-genotsida-ya-povtoryu-eto-sto-tysyach-raz/> accessed 23 April 2025.

Burkov, A. 'The Use of European Human Rights Law in Russian Courts' in Lauri Malksoo and Wolfgang Benedek (eds) *Russia and the European Court of Human Rights: The Strasbourg effect* (Cambridge UP, 2018).

'Comparison of Ossetian, Jewish people's genocide correct,' Interfax (30 August 2008).

'Dannye o zhertvakh vooruzhennogo konflikta na Kavkaze,' *Reuters* (10 August 2008).

de Búrca, G. and Young, K. 'The (mis)appropriation of human rights by the new global right: An introduction to the Symposium,' (2003) 21 *I·CON,* 205.

'Deitstviya MTBYU ne vedut k torzhestvu verkhovenstva prava – upolnomochennyi MID RF,' RIA Novosti (Moscow 30 November 2012).

'Deputaty predlagayut provesti parlamentskie slushaniya po situatsii v Mezhdunarodnom tribunal po byvshei Yugoslavii,' RIA Novosti (17 November 2006).

'Dmitrii Medvedev vystupil s zayavleniem v svyazi s priznaniem nezavisimosti Yuzhnoi Osetii i Abkhazii,' (26 August 2008) <http://kremlin.ru/events/president/news/1223> accessed 23 April 2025.

'Dmitrii Medvedev vystupil s zayavleniem v svyazi s priznaniem nezavisimosti Yuzhnoi Osetii i Abkhazii,' (26 August 2008) <http://kremlin.ru/events/president/news/1223> accessed 23 April 2025.

Dugin, A. interview with Matvei Ganapol'skii, *Ekho Moskvy* (Moscow, 8 August 2008) <http://www.echo.msk.ru/programs/personalno/532383-echo/> Accessed 15 August 2008.

'Genotsid,' *Rossiiskaya Gazeta* (Moscow, 24 September 2024).

'Georgia not cooperating with RF on S Ossetia for contrived reasons' ITAR-TASS (Moscow, 8 August 2011).

'German cancels Israeli historian for genocide award,' Deutsche Welle, 1 January 2022.

Gilligan, E. *Terror in Chechnya: Russia and the Tragedy of Civilians in War* (Princeton University Press 2009).

'Gosduma RF obratit'sya v Venetsianskuyu komissiyu po voprosu legitimnosti reshenii Rady,' *RBK-Ukraina* (1 March 2014) https://www.rbc.ua/rus/news/gosduma-rf-obratitsya-v-venetsianskuyu-komissiyu-po-voprosu-01032014143000 accessed 23 April 2025.

Grigor'eva, E. 'Rossiya profinansiuret evropeiskuyu demokratiyu,' *Izvestiya* (Moscow. 29 October 2007), 2.

Hawkes, M. 'A Tribunal for Chechnya?' *Moscow Times* (Moscow, 31 March 2003) 10.

Horvath, R. *Putin's 'Preventive Counter-Revolution': Post-Soviet Authoritarianism and the Spectre of Velvet Revolution* (Routledge 2013).

Horvath, R. 'The Reinvention of 'Traditional Values': Nataliya Narochnitskaya and Russia's Assault on Universal Human Rights,' (2016) 68 *Europe-Asia Studies*, 878.

International Commission of Jurists 'Jurists back call for an International Criminal Court on Chechnya,' (14 April 2000) <https://www.icj.org/jurists-back-call-for-an-international-criminal-court-on-chechnya/> accessed 23 April 2025.

'International community should not close its eyes to neo-nazi orgy in Riga,' RIA Novosti (17 March 2005).

'Interv'yu telekompanii "Rasha tudei",' (26 August 2008) <http://kremlin.ru/events/president/transcripts/1226> accessed 23 April 2025.

'Interv'yu gazete "Politika",' (15 October 2014), <http://kremlin.ru/events/president/news/46806> accessed 23 April 2025.

'Interv'yu telekompanii Bi-Bi-Si,' (26 August 2008) <http://kremlin.ru/events/president/transcripts/1228> accessed 23 April 2025.

'Irak ostaetskya v tsentre diskussii,' *Nezavisimaya Gazeta* (Moscow, 15 September 2000) https://www.ng.ru/world/2000-09-15/6_irak.html accessed 30 May 2025.

'Italy's Berlusconi defends Russia's Putin at Summit,' Associated Press (7 November 2003).

'Joint statement by 42 States at the Human Rights Council on the situation in Ukraine,' (26 March 2014) <https://geneva.usmission.gov/2014/03/26/joint-statement-by-42-states-at-the-human-rights-council-on-the-situation-in-ukraine/> accessed 23 April 2025.

Kashin, O. (2005) 'Vladimir Putin naznachil barkhatnogo kontrrevolyutsionera,' *Kommersant"* (Moscow, 23 March 2005) <https://www.kommersant.ru/doc/556859> accessed 23 April 2025.

Kirilenko, A. 'Pravozashchitniki ne nashli v Yuzhnoi Osetii sozhzhennoi vo vremya voiny tserkvi,' Kavkazskii uzel (10 October 2008) <https://www.kavkaz-uzel.eu/articles/142728> accessed 23 April 2025.

Kondrashov, D. 'Front protiv Rossii: napravleniya agressii' (28 March 2005) <http://www.regnum.ru/news/428347.html> accessed 23 April 2025.

Kovalenko, Yu. '"Sadovye gnomy" zashchitili prava cheloveka,' *Novye Izvestiya* (Moscow 8 April 2000).

Kozlov, P. 'Rossiiskie Sledovateli…' 'Rossiiskie Sledovateli Vozbuzhdayut Novye Ugolovnye Dela Protiv Ukrainskikh Voennykh,' *Vedomosti* (Moscow, 2 October 2014).

Kozyrev, A. Speech to World Conference on Human Rights: 4th plenary meeting, Tuesday, 15 June 1993, https://searchlibrary.ohchr.org/record/29884?ln=en&v=pdf accessed 30 May 2025.

Laughland, J. *Travesty: The trial of Slobodan Milošević and the corruption of international justice* (Pluto 2007).

Leach, P. 'Egregious Human Rights Violations in Chechnya: Appraising the Pursuit of Justice,' in Lauri Malksoo and Wolfgang Benedek (eds) *Russia and the European Court of Human Rights: the Strasbourg effect* (Cambridge UP 2018).

Malksoo, L. 'Introduction' in L. Malksoo and W. Benedek (eds) *Russia and the European Court of Human Rights: the Strasbourg effect* (Cambridge UP 2018).

McFaul, M. and Petrov, N. 'Russian Democracy in Eclipse: What the Elections Tell Us,' (2004) 15 *Journal of Democracy*, 20.

'Meeting of the Presidential Council for Civil Society and Human Rights,' 14 October 2014, <http://en.kremlin.ru/events/councils/by-council/18/46786> accessed 23 April 2025.

'Mezhdunarodnomu tribunalu po byvshei Yugoslavii tak i ne udalos' realizovat' ideyu svoegu sozdaniya,' *Regnum* (14 March 2006), <https://regnum.ru/news/605611> accessed 23 April 2025.

'Moscow again calls for probe into abductions of Serbians in Kosovo,' *Interfax* (5 June 2008).

'Moscow Says Ex-Bosnian Serb Military Commander Mladic Conviction Politicized,' Sputnik News (Moscow, 23 November 2017).

'Moscow wants war crimes court in the Hague shut,' Reuters News 13 February 2001.

'Moskva tverdo namerena dobivat'sya zaversheniya raboty Mezhdunarodnogo tribunala po byvshei Yugoslavii v sroki, ustanovlennye SB OON – MID RF,' ITAR-TASS (Moscow, 30 November 2012).

Narochnitskaya, N. and Laughland, J. (eds) *Oranzhevye seti: ot Belgrada do Bishkeka* (Moscow: Aleteiya 2008).

Narochnitskaya, N. 'Zayavlenie presedatelya komissii gosudarstvennoi Dumy,' (1 December 2006) <https://web.archive.org/web/20071020033734/http://www.narochnitskaia.ru/cgi-bin/main.cgi?item=1r1371r061201190109> accessed 23 April 2025.

'New Ukrainian power intends to attack human rights, freedoms' ITAR-TASS (Moscow, 3 March 2014).

'O politicheskikh repressiyakh na Ukraine,' *Parlamentskaya Gazeta*, 11 April 2014, <https://www.pnp.ru/archive/2014/04/10/o-politicheskikh-repressiyakh-na-ukraine.html> accessed 23 April 2025.

'Obrashchenie k uchastnikam foruma "Uroki Nyurnberga",' 20 November 2020 <http://kremlin.ru/events/president/news/64447> accessed 23 April 2025.

'Obrashchenie Prezidenta Rossiiskoi Federatsii,' 24 February 2022.

Petrovskaya, Yu. 'Iskali Mladicha, Vzyali Karadzhicha,' *Nezavisimaya Gazeta* (Moscow, 23 July 2008).

'Plans imposing illegitimate government on Crimea cannot be carried out – Russian permanent representative in Geneva,' ITAR-TASS (Moscow, 19 March 2014).

Poutine, V. 'Les leçons de la victoire sure le nazisme,' *Le Figaro* (Paris: 7 May 2005).

'Predsedatel' SK Rossii provel v Donetske soveshchanie' 7 April 2022, <https://sledcom.ru/press/events/item/1671392/> accessed 23 April 2025.

'Radovan Karadzic mozhet razdelit' sud'bu Miloshevicha,' *Izvestiya* (Moscow, 22 July 2008) <https://iz.ru/news/430705accessed23April2025> accessed 23 April 2025.

'Rasporyazhenie prezidenta rossiiskoi federatsii,' 16 November 2016 <http://publication.pravo.gov.ru/Document/View/0001201611160018> accessed 23 April 2025.

'Rights group seeks Chechnya war crimes tribunal,' Reuters News (3 April 2000).

'RKK sobirate informatsiyu o voennykh prestupleniyakh na Ukraine dlya predostavleniya v Mezhdunarodnyi ugolovnyi sud, Sovbez OON I SK RF' ITAR-TASS (Moscow, 1 September 2014).

'Rogozin: v sluchae suda nad Karadzhichem nado sudit' i initsiatorom agressii protiv byvshei Yugoslavii,' Regnum (Moscow, 22 July 2008).

Rossiya i "Sanitarnyi kordon,' (Evropa 2005).

'Rossiya ne pozvolit "zamesti pod kover" tragediyu v Odesse – Lavrov", ITAR-TASS (Moscow, 7 May 2014).

'Rossiya pomozhet vernut' mezhdunarodnomu pravosudiyu ob"ektivnost',' Regions.ru/Novosti Federatsii (23 July 2008).

'Rossiya primenila veto pri golosovanii rezolyutsii Soveta Bezopasnosti OON po Bosnii i Gertsegovine,' 8 July 2015 <https://news.un.org/ru/story/2015/07/1266801> accessed 23 April 2025.

'Rossiya zachitala obvinenie Gaagskomu tribunalu,' *Kommersant"* (Moscow, 6 June 2008).

'Rukovoditel' voennogo sledstvennogo upravleniya Sledstvennogo komiteta pri prokurature Rossii Aleksandr Sorochkin: 'Rossiiskikh grazhdan nikomu ne pozvoleno ubivat' beznakazanno,' *Izvestiya* (Moscow, 17 September 2008) <https://iz.ru/news/340600> accessed 23 April 2025.

'Russia blocks Security Council approval of Milosevic arrest,' Agence France-Presse (29 June 2001).
'Russia favors end to tribunal for former Yugoslavia,' Associated Press (23 February 2001).
'Russia questions Milosevic autopsy results: Lavrov,' Agence France-Presse (13 March 2006).
'Russian pundits add to Del Ponte allegations of anti-Serb atrocities,' *BBC Monitoring Former Soviet Union* (9 April 2008).
'Russia's UN mission slams life sentence for Bosnian Serb commander Mladic,' TASS (Moscow, 9 June) <https://tass.com/world/1300531> accessed 23 April 2025.
'Saakashvili zovyut v sud,' *Rossiiskaya Gazeta*, 6 August 2009.
Samarina, A. and V. Kruchinina, 'Genotsid "po faktu",' *Nezavisimaya Gazeta* (Moscow, 15 August 2008).
'Shestvie v Rige byvshikh esesovtsev,' Interfax (Moscow, 16 March 2005).
Shnidman, R. 'Israelis to Teach Serbs How to Say "Shalom",' *Jerusalem Post* (Jerusalem, 22 June 2019).
'SKP RF kvalifitsiruet deistviyz gruzinskoi armii v Yuzhnoi Osetii kak genotsid,' RIA Novosti (28 August 2008).
'SKR vozbudil delo o genotside iz-za poslednikh obstrelov zhilykh raionov Donbassa,' Interfax (Moscow, 13 January 2015).
Solopov, M. 'Aleksandr Bastrykin predlozhil izmenit' Konstitutsiyu,' *RBK* (Moscow, 27 February 2015).
Spetsko, E. 'Duma vystupit za uprazdnenie Gaagskogo tribunala,' *Vedomosti* (Moscow, 14 March 2006), <https://www.vedomosti.ru/library/articles/2006/03/14/duma-vystupit-za-uprazdnenie-gaagskogo-tribunala> accessed 23 April 2025.
'Srebrenica massacre a crime, not genocide – Russian lawmaker' Sputnik News (Moscow, 14 July 2015) <https://sputnikglobe.com/20150714/1024621420.html> accessed 23 April 2025.
Steshin, D. 'Na storone Gruzii voevali diversanty iz Ukrainy, Chekhy, Turtsii i SShA,' *Komsomol'skaya Pravda* (Moscow, 24 December 2008).
Stiller, A. 'The Genesis of the Human Rights-Based International Criminal Justice System' in Jan Eckel and Daniel Stahl (eds), *Embattled visions. Human Rights Since 1992*. (Wallstein-Verlag 2022).
'Stockholm: M. Palme condamne l'intervention vietnamienne' *Le Monde* (Paris, 14–15 January 1979) 3.
Stoeckl, K. and Uzlaner, D. *The Moralist International: Russia in the Global Culture Wars* (Fordham UP 2022).
Stoeckl, K. 'Double bind at the UN: Western actors, Russia, and the traditionalist agenda,' (2018) 7 *Global Constitutionalism*, 383.

Sundstrom, L. 'Russian NGOs and the European Court of Human Rights: A Spectrum of Approaches to Litigation' (2014) 36 *Human Rights Quarterly*, 844.

'Tat'yana Lokshina: "O genotside v kavkazkom konflikte govorit' net osnovanii,' Deutsche Welle (25 August 2008).

Teslova, E. 'Narushenie prav cheloveka neobkhodima rassledovat" *Izvestiya* (Moscow, 17 March 2014).

Timofeev, A. 'Sudilishche nad serbskimi vozhdyami. V Gosudarstvennoi Dume sostoyalis' slushaniya o deyatel'nosti MTBYu,' Stoletie (25 December 2006) <https://www.stoletie.ru/slavyanskoe_pole/sudilische_nad_serbskimi_vozhdyami.htm> accessed 23 April 2025.

UN (2009), 'Resolution adopted by the General Assembly,' A/RES/63/162.

UN Commission on Human Rights resolution 2000/58 'Situation in the Republic of Chechnya of the Russian Federation,' 25 April 2000, E/CN.4/RES/2000/58 <https://www.refworld.org/docid/3b00f2ba44.html> accessed 23 April 2025.

'UNSC Genocide vote designed to justify NATO bombing of Yugoslavia,' Sputnik News (Moscow, 12 July 2015) <https://sputnikglobe.com/20150712/1024525133.html> accessed 23 April 2025.

UN Security Council draft resolution, 8 July 2015, S/2015/508 https://www.securitycouncilreport.org/un-documents/document/s2015508.php accessed 23 April 2025.

United Nations Commission on Human Rights. Report on the Sixtieth Session (*15 March – 23 April 2004*), E/CN.4/2004/127.

Usborne, D. (2014), 'Ukraine crisis: Putin is 'on the wrong side of history, says President Obama' *Independent Online*, 3 March <https://www.independent.co.uk/news/world/europe/ukraine-crisis-putin-is-on-the-wrong-side-of-history-says-president-obama-9166831.html> accessed 23 April 2025.

'Vladimir Putin otvetil na voprosy zhurnalistov,' 22 February 2022 <http://kremlin.ru/events/president/news/67838> accessed 23 April 2025.

'Voina na unichtozhenie – ot pervogo litsa,' *Rossiiskaya Gazeta* (Moscow 26 August 2008).

'"Vse eto lozh'!" Kak v Gaage sudili serbskogo generala Ratko Mladicha,' RIA (Moscow, 22 November 2017) <https://ria.ru/20171122/1509360121.html> accessed 23 April 2025.

'Vstrecha s chlenami fraktsii politicheskikh partii v Gosudarstvennoi Dume,' 14 August 2014 <http://special.kremlin.ru/catalog/regions/CR/events/46451> accessed 23 April 2025.

Walker, S. 'Russia withdraws signature from international criminal court statute' The Guardian (London, 17 November 2016) <https://www.theguardian.com/world/2016/nov/16/russia-withdraws-signature-from-international-criminal-court-statute> accessed 23 April 2025.

Weiss-Wendt, A. '"Genocide of the Soviet People": Putin's Russia Waging Lawfare by Means of History, 2018–2023,' (2024) 17 *Genocide Studies and Prevention*, 1.
Wilkinson, C. 'Putting "Traditional Values" Into Practice: The Rise and Contestation of Anti-Homopropaganda Laws in Russia.' (2014) 13 *Journal of Human Rights*, 363.
Wilson, A. *Political technology: The globalisation of political manipulation* (Cambridge University Press, 2023).
'Za genotsid i narusheniya prav grazhdan na yugo-vostoka Ukrainy SK RF privlek 30 dolzhnostnykh lits,' Interfax (Moscow, 3 September 2015).
'Zakharova nazvala sponsorov provokatsii, podobnykh toi, chto byla v Buche,' RIA (Moscow, 6 April 2022).
'Zapretit deyatel'nost' Gaagskogo sudilishcha,' *Russkii vestnik* (8 December 2006).
'Zinov'evskii klub: Pochemu Rossiya prava. Nyurnberg-2 protiv sponsora zla – kollektivnogo Zapada,' http://zinoviev.info/wps/archives/7514 accessed 23 April 2025.

CHAPTER 8

'The True Rights-Bearers': Victimhood and Citizenship in the Construals of the Legal Subject

Adriane Sanctis de Brito, Luciana Silva Reis, Ana Silva Rosa and Mariana Amaral

The Brazilian citizen is at the mercy of having his life, his physical integrity, his intangible heritage and women, especially their honour and sexual freedom, attacked without being able to defend themselves, due to mistaken public policies, especially the enactment of Law 10.826, of 2003 [Gun Control Statue], and criminal laws that, as enforced by the Judiciary, in fact determine impunity for criminals in the country, especially with the policies against incarceration that result in thousands of convicted criminals released from prison.' (AOR-EB, ADI 6119)

Local farmers are, without a doubt, among the biggest victims of the tortuous (lack of) public policy. They feel much more directly and immediately the impacts resulting from FUNAI's [National Foundation for the Indigenous People] change in orientation with the demarcations of indigenous lands. Many were stripped of their properties – and, consequently, of their own ability to subsist – without even the protection of due administrative legal process; many others go to bed, every night, surrounded by fear and anxiety that the next day will be the one in which they are dispossessed.' (Rural Union of Ilhéus, RE 1.017.365)

The driving force behind such gestures of consolidation is defensive: cornered by secular scientific and political elites for almost three hundred years, despite enjoying enormous popular acceptance and making up a living part of the moral consciousness of societies, religions have sought, since then, to avoid as much as they can the incessant attempt to banish them from social life under the epithets of ignorance, superstition, credulity, etc., which would be incompatible with individual autonomy, the greatest achievement of the Enlightenment era. (Marcelo Crivella, 2016, CCJ Opinion to PLC 160/2009)

> Today, the persecuted are not visible to our eyes, as they are being generated in the mother's womb, but the fact that they cannot be seen should not silence the conscience of those who have the power/duty to interfere, nor will it silence the voice of those who have always fought in favor of the true dignity and freedom of human beings. (National Conference of Bishops of Brazil – CNBB, ADPF 442)

1 Introduction

Victimhood is a recurring pattern in contemporary politics. Presenting oneself as part of a group victimised by antagonists is a powerful performance in the vindication of justice and legitimacy for one's actions. The individuals or ideas who are made into antagonists vary, often stemming from identity clashes. Since it denounces injustices entrenched in social structures and collective patterns of victimisation, victimhood politics can in fact contribute to advancements in the struggles for inclusion of marginalised groups in the 'social contract'. One could argue this was the case of the 1960s civil rights movements and part of the subsequent 'identity politics of diversity',[1] as well as an ingredient for the reconstruction of European democracies in the post-war period.[2] Yet victimhood performances are not limited to a particular historical context or political position.

With the rise of authoritarian, 'populist', or 'illiberal' leaders and movements, it is often observed that the same victimhood pattern is a fundamental part of the underlying values that drive their exclusionary demands, reactionary politics, and bigotry.[3] This should not come as a surprise. As socio-legal studies focused on criminal law have long shown, the 'victim' has consistently

1 Robert Horwitz, 'Politics as Victimhood, Victimhood as Politics' (2018) 30(3) *Journal of Policy History* 552.

2 Ruzha Smilova, 'The Ideational Core of Democratic Illiberalism' in András Sajó, Renáta Uitz and Stephen Holmes (eds), *Routledge Handbook of Illiberalism* (Routledge 2022).

3 Ruth Wodak, *The Politics of Fear: What Right-Wing Populist Discourses Mean* (SAGE Publications Ltd 2015) https://doi.org/10.4135/9781446270073; Horwitz (n 1) and Smilova (n 2). Besides the references, see also: Adriane Brito, Conrado Hubner, Fernando Sales, Mariana Amaral, Marina Barreto. *The Path to Autocracy: Current Strategies for Democratic Erosion* (Tinta da China 2023) (in Portuguese). The book analyses how penal populism – a political practice that disregards empirical evidence and expert opinion in the formulation of public security policies – has been mobilised by autocrats around the world. The construction of enemies and the restriction of citizenship rights for groups identified as such are among the tactics of penal populism. According to the authors, this political practice establishes a division between the society that must be protected and the outsiders that must be repressed.

been employed to legitimate repressive policies. The image of the victim combines the ideal rights-holder with someone who has been or may be victimised by a criminal, effectively excluding the latter from the protection of rights.[4] In that it becomes evident that the alignment with inclusion and diversity is not a necessary aspect of victimhood politics, but rather a contingency of social struggles and historical circumstances.

This chapter describes how the victimhood pattern has been a core feature of conservative and reactionary mobilisations in Brazil. The analysis presented here builds on broader results[5] about the use of legal language by such mobilisations. Our research dialogues with frameworks such as the '(mis)appropriation of human rights',[6] but we employ a descriptive-analytical approach that eschews classifying the uses of rights and other constitutional values as right or wrong, or coming in good or bad faith. This approach allows identifying detailed patterns of political and legal arguments that, although not exclusive to the right-wing spectrum,[7] point to potentially authoritarian uses of rights, as is the case with victimhood politics.

Our research analyses the use of legal language by Brazilian conservative and reactionary groups to advance their values and interests in three major areas of dispute: socio-environmental, moral-religious spheres, and public security. In Brazilian politics, these three coalitions are known in the Brazilian Congress by the acronym 'BBB', which stands for 'Beef, Bible, and Bullets'. Their general goals are promoting agribusiness interests, Christian values, and relaxed regulations on guns and the use of armed and militarised forces by the state.[8] Different arrangements of these three sectors have been present in

---

4 Jonathan Simon, *Governing Through Crime: How the War on Crime Transformed American Democracy and Created a Culture of Fear* (Oxford University Press 2019).

5 Adriane Brito, Luciana Reis, Ana Silva and Mariana Amaral, *The Law of the Beef, the Bullet, the Bible: Democratic Crisis in Disputes Over Rights* (Tinta-da-China Brasil 2024) (in Portuguese).

6 Gráinne De Búrca and Katharine G Young, 'The (Mis)Appropriation of Human Rights by the New Global Right: An Introduction to the Symposium' (2023) 21 *International Journal of Constitutional Law* 205.

7 See Section 4 for a discussion.

8 In addition to organising themselves in civil society associations, these forces also form caucuses in the National Congress. The statutes of these caucuses and the action plans of Agribusiness entities are some of the documents that summarize the interests of these actors, as well as submissions by pro-gun and pro-life associations in constitutional cases before the Federal Supreme Court. We explore these and other examples in the following section. For example, see *Statute of the Evangelical Parliamentary Front of the National Congress* (Frente Parlamentar Evangélica, 2023); *Work Plan 2018–2030 of the National Confederation of Agriculture* (Plano de Trabalho 2018–2030 da Confederação Nacional da Agricultura, 2018).

Brazilian politics for decades – if not longer –[9] but they have taken on new characteristics in recent years. First, the historical process of their formal representation in Congress today can be traced back to interest groups participating in the constituent assembly process that resulted in the 1988 Brazilian Constitution.[10] Second, the 'BBB' coalitions have gained political visibility and have effectively advanced their agenda during the Jair Bolsonaro government (2019–2022), whose candidacy was strongly supported by them.[11] All in all, elected representatives have been the centre of public debate and academic analysis. As a first step in grasping these articulations, our approach to the 'BBB' coalitions in Brazil departs from their caucus in congress, but also considers manifestations of a variety of civil society actors before the Legislative, Executive, and Judiciary branches. While not entirely homogeneous and not necessarily in agreement,[12] the actions of these groups are largely aligned with conservative or right-wing politics.[13]

We reviewed specialised literature on recent debates in each area and identified key cases where these groups mobilised through judicial cases and legislative proposals at the federal level. Our analysis spans the period from the enactment of the Brazilian Constitution in 1988 to 2023. Yet our study did not aim to be exhaustive. We applied two selection criteria to define our final set of cases. First, we prioritised issues that were central to political disputes during the Bolsonaro government, as identified in the specialised literature, and traced them back to their immediate antecedents when area-specific studies indicated strong interconnections. Second, we aimed to present sample cases

---

9 Brito, Reis, Silva, Amaral (n 5) 19–20.

10 Ibid 24–26, 66–69, 108–114.

11 Caio Pompeia, 'As cinco faces do agronegócio: mudanças climáticas e territórios indígenas' (2023) 66 *Revista de Antropologia* https://doi.org/10.11606/1678-9857.ra.2022.202839; Ronaldo Almeida, 'Bolsonaro presidente: conservadorismo, evangelismo e a crise brasileira' (2019) 38(1) *Novos Estudos Cebrap* 185; Paulo Gracino de Souza Junior and Carlos Henrique Pereira de Souza, Evangélicos e conservadorismo – afinidades eletivas: as novas configurações da democracia no Brasil (2020) 18(57) *Horizonte - Revista de Estudos de Teologia e Ciências da Religião;* Gabriel Feltran, 'A política como violência' (2021) 17(2) *Terceiro Milênio: Revista Crítica de Sociologia e Política.*

12 As Ronaldo de Almeida argues, actors often operate on different playing fields, but the outcomes of these actions – frequently misaligned and marked by divergences – are nonetheless significant for understanding what constitutes conservative waves. Ronaldo de Almeida, 'A onda quebrada – evangélicos e conservadorismo' (2017) 50 *Cadernos Pagu.*

13 Here, we use a broad interpretation of the terms 'right' and 'left' as relational categories that have historically been interchangeable and context-dependent. In this case, many of these actors can be classified as being on the right either because they identify as 'conservative' or because they hold non-progressive political positions on divisive political issues in Brazil.

that reflect the wide variety of issues addressed by each coalition and their aligned civil society manifestations.

Based on these criteria, we selected and conducted a qualitative analysis of 407 public documents[14] to map their legal arguments, especially those related to the vindication of rights (such as the right to development, the right to life, and the right to self-defence) and features presented as their 'true' subjectivities. We share André Céllard's perception that 'most methodologists agree that it is through repeated reading that one is finally able to perceive the similarities, relationships, and differences that can lead to an acceptable and reliable reconstruction'.[15] This is the way[16] a researcher may establish connections 'between [...their] problem and the various observations extracted from their documentation', and thus 'produce a coherent interpretation, and carry out a reconstruction of any aspect of a given society, at a particular moment in time'.[17]

At the Federal Supreme Court (STF), we accessed complete case files and selected manifestations from *amici curiae*, the Federal Public Prosecutor's Office, and the Office of the Attorney General. In the National Congress, we examined the full text of legislative proposals, the corresponding legal opinions, and – particularly in the Chamber of Deputies – the relevant excerpts of legislative debates on the subject. All materials were collected from the official websites of the respective institutions. In the case of the Chamber of Deputies

---

14 The set of public documents includes issues debated in the National Congress or cases brought before the Brazilian Federal Supreme Court (STF). The materials include justifications for bills, reports by thematic commissions, amici curiae in constitutional cases in the STF, and programmatic documents formulated by entities representing agriculture, sent to the Executive for the presidential elections.

15 André Cellard, 'A análise documental' in Jean Poupart (ed), *A pesquisa qualitativa: enfoques epistemológicos e metodológicos* (Vozes 2008) 304.

16 The documental systematisation that is partly explored in this chapter was also inspired by the grounded theory method, departing from close observation of a selected object to ultimately develop a substantive reading about a phenomenon. As Anne Laperrière explains, the grounded theory method is based on coding the data in three stages: first, coding 'all incidents, all units of meaning'; then, these initial codes are organised into a broader, more abstract identifier; finally, the third stage consists of elaborating a single category that 'should allow the inclusion of all data related to the researched phenomenon, or at least as much of it as possible'. Although we do not consider this chapter a comprehensive theoretical analysis, the initial stages of the grounded theory tecnique proved to be a fruitful exercise in the in-depth systematisation of the elements within the documents that informed this analysis. Anne Laperrière, 'A teorização enraizada (grounded theory): procedimento analítico e comparação com outras abordagens similares' in Jean Poupart (ed), *A pesquisa qualitativa: enfoques epistemológicos e metodológicos* (Vozes 2008) 361–364.

17 Céllard (n 15) 304.

and the Senate, we also utilised the 'Contact Us' service to locate proposals on specific topics. We also included materials prepared by agribusiness associations and rural unions addressed to the Federal Executive Branch.

Our conclusions suggest that analyses such as Robert Horwitz' are also applicable to the current dynamics in Brazil. As Horwitz states, 'even as conservative critics deplore the politics of victimhood, and reproach those whom they believe play the "victim card", they too engage in the exercise and claim the status of victim even as they disavow doing so – which only underscores how powerful and defining the dynamic of victimhood politics really is'.[18]

The mobilisation of victimhood transforms the legal meanings of the rights at stake and pushes for changes in democratic political culture. This includes redefining communal meanings of citizenship and the relationship between the state and citizens. We find that right-wing actors across different interest fields share one common self-perception: they present themselves as the 'true bearers' of rights, opposed to their alleged 'enemies' to be neutralised. In particular, by advancing points about who are the 'true rights-bearers', we observed that legal language mobilised by the 'BBB' coalitions create counterimages of 'lesser citizens', as discussed in Section 4. In the next section, we describe the 'BBB' coalitions, beyond their organisation as congressional caucuses, as broad societal actors in Brazilian politics. Section 3 describes and exemplifies the patterns of victimhood that appear in their legal and political discourses. Our findings highlight the need to engage in nuanced and critical reflections about how the dynamics of victimhood politics affects the deployment of human rights in securing demands for material redistribution and symbolic recognition.

2 Beef, Bible, and Bullets: Three Pillars of Brazilian Conservatism

The term 'bancada da bala' ('Bullet' caucus) first emerged in the Brazilian public debate at least twenty years ago. The expression emerged to refer to the group of parliamentarians opposing the bill that would later become the 'Disarmament Statute'. Around ten years later, the term gained popularity when the Brazilian press started using it to refer to congressmen coming from the security forces.[19] Since then, 'the bullet caucus' has entered the Brazilian political vocabulary, representing parliamentary groups that advocate

18 Horwitz (n. 1) 558.
19 Brito, Reis, Silva, Amaral (n 5).

not only for armaments but also for various issues related to more violent models of public security.[20]

The ruralist caucus, also known as the 'boi' (Beef), is a coalition of groups associated with agricultural and cattle raising activities. It is one of the oldest, most united, and influential groups in the National Congress. Since the colonial period and throughout history, rural elites have held positions of power and decision-making in Brazil. Despite processes of industrialisation, economic modernisation, and democratisation, they continue to exert massive influence in Brazilian politics. The current Agricultural Parliamentary Front was established between 1987 and 1988 during the drafting of the Constitution. At that time, the conservative nature of the ruralist caucus was evident in its opposition to agrarian reform, the expansion of social and labour rights, and democratisation processes in general, particularly popular participation in the legislative process.[21] Over the next 30 years, the ruralist bench grew stronger and became institutionalised, maintaining a complex relationship with the State.[22]

Finally, the origin of the 'Bible' caucus also dates back to the National Constituent Assembly in the 1980s. Fearing that the new Constitution would restore old privileges to the Catholic Church and address controversial issues such as the legalisation of abortion and drugs, as well as minority rights for the LGBTQIA+ population, feminists, and communists, constituent deputies from various political parties and religious organisations united under the banner of the Evangelical Parliamentary Front.[23] The moniker 'Bible caucus' originated during parliamentary debates in the 2000s. Initially, it was used to refer to evangelical parliamentarians. However, over time, it came to include Catholic and Christian parliamentarians who shared the values advocated by the group. Despite the religious diversity within this caucus, its members are usually united by their conservative stance on social customs. Their objective is to safeguard and promote a narrow moral perspective and uphold a specific notion of family.[24]

---

20 Ibid 24–63.

21 Regina Bruno, 'Bancada ruralista, conservadorismo e representação de interesses no Brasil contemporâneo' in *Questões agrárias, agrícolas e rurais: conjunturas e políticas públicas* (E-Papers 2017).

22 Caio Pompeia, *Formação Política do Agronegócio* (Elefante 2021).

23 Reginaldo Prandi and Renan W S Santos, 'Quem tem medo da bancada evangélica? Posições sobre moralidade e política no eleitorado brasileiro, no Congresso Nacional e na Frente Parlamentar Evangélica' (2017) 29 *Tempo Social* 187–214.

24 Flávia Biroli, Maria D Machado and Juan Marco Vaggione, *Gênero, neoconservadorismo e democracia* (Boitempo 2020).

The strength of the 'BBB' agenda gained prominence during the years of Bolsonaro's government. Both the representatives of the three caucuses in the Legislative branch and the demands present in the Executive's agenda gained importance and political influence.[25] A perspective that takes into account all three branches of government, however, reveals an even broader movement – one in which civil society actors, whether directly connected to the Executive and Legislative or not, also transformed similar agendas into reinforcing interventions within the Judiciary.[26] That is why, for the purposes of this analysis, we will use the term 'BBB' to refer not only to the mobilisation of each of the Legislative caucus but more broadly as to encompass diverse mobilisations coming from both elected representatives of civil society in each of the areas, and analyse issues brought to all three branches – the Legislative, the Executive, and the Judiciary.

Against this background, the next section explores how different groups of actors mobilised the category of 'victim'. The analysis reveals a recurring argumentative pattern, as the invocation of victimhood cuts across different cases and is articulated as a means of legitimising the restriction or the expansion of fundamental rights for certain groups.

25 Those actors maintained their strength – especially in the Legislative branch – even after Jair Bolsonaro left office. In May 2025, the Senate approved a Bill that changes the rules for environmental licenses. Environmentalists have called it the 'devastation Bill'. Even though it is still pending approval in the Chamber of Deputies, the move has been seen as a major victory for the Beef coalitions. Giovana Girardi, 'PL do licenciamento: Senado desmantela segurança ambiental e social do país' *Agência Pública* (22 May 2025). <https://apublica.org/2025/05/pl-do-licenciamento-senado-desmantela-seguranca-ambiental-e-social-do-pais/> accessed 26 May 2025. In 2024, groups connected to the Bible caucus celebrated when a Bill restricting the three current possibilities of legal abortion (pregnancy resulting from rape, risk to the woman's life, and cases of diagnosed foetal anencephaly) bypassed the usual legislative timeline and was setto be voted by representatives with no previous discussions on subcommissions. After intense mobilisation from civil society, the vote on the Bill was suspended. Nevertheless, the move revealed the power groups linked with the 'Bible' caucus. Bárbara Blum, 'Entenda o que muda com o PL que restringe o aborto legal em casos de estupro' *Folha de São Paulo* (São Paulo, 13 June 2024).<https://www1.folha.uol.com.br/equilibrioesaude/2024/06/entenda-o-que-muda-com-o-pl-que-restringe-o-aborto-legal-em-casos-de-estupro.shtml> accessed 26 Mat 2025. Finally, Bullet groups recently won a case judged by the STF. The Court ruled that the municipalities' patrimonial watch could now also be enforced through police power, expanding the role of public security forces. André Rithcer 'STF confirma competência de guardas municipais para fazer policiamento' *Agência Brasil* (Brasília, 21 February 2025). <https://agenciabrasil.ebc.com.br/justica/noticia/2025-02/stf-confirma-competencia-de-guardas-municipais-para-fazer-policiamento> accessed 26 May 2025.

26 Brito, Reis, Silva, Amaral (n 5).

3 Constructions of the Legal Subject in the 'BBB': The Victimhood Pattern

The notion that the country is facing a public security crisis is prevalent in most of the cases analysed in the field of debates on criminal policy, led by actors from the 'bullet' sector. These debates portray a country gripped by high crime rates, with a call for increased access to firearms and ammunition, as a means to argue for reduced external control over the actions of public security forces. According to this narrative, the 'nation' is being held 'hostage to bandits' and 'dominated by fear', as stated by Congressman Cabo Sabino in 2015 during discussions about the Congress Bill n. 4471/2012. The argument suggests that 'criminals' are victimising the entire nation. In defence of the 'victims', lawmakers and organisations associated with the 'bullet' sector advocate for loosening guns and ammunition control, citing the right to self-defence and the preservation of life, while opposing measures aimed at strengthening democratic oversight of public security forces.

The killing of 111 people imprisoned at the Carandiru facility in 1992, a massacre committed by the military police, is described as a 'successful operation'.[27] The establishment of the National Truth Commission, to investigate the crimes committed by state agents during Brazil's military dictatorship, is portrayed as a way to reopen 'already healed wounds, causing new tears of pain in people who do not accept possible slander, persecution, and injustice'.[28] Efforts to impose safeguards on police operations in the favelas of Rio de Janeiro, where dozens of civilians have been killed, is considered 'unconstitutional'.[29]

Public security agents are often depicted as 'heroes' who are 'at a disadvantage' when compared to 'criminals'. The 'criminals' are portrayed as well-equipped, well-structured, powerful, heavily armed, and in control of territories and entire communities.[30] On the other hand, the precariousness of the police infrastructure is emphasised, including inadequate work equipment,

---

27 Congressman Sargento Fahur, 'Speech on Bill 2.821/2021' (Chamber of Deputies, 2022). Proposed by Federal Deputy Captain Augusto, the bill aimed to pardon the police officers involved in the Carandiru Massacre, a massacre that occurred in a São Paulo prison in 1992.

28 Congressman Arolde de Oliveira, 'Speech on Bill 7.376/2010' (Chamber of Deputies, 2011). The aim of this bill was to establish a National Truth Commission to investigate crimes committed during the period of military dictatorship in Brazil (1964–1985).

29 Pro-Society Public Attorneys, 'Submission in ADPF 635' [2021] ADPF 635 (STF). This constitutional action sought to have the high levels of violence and police lethality in the state of Rio de Janeiro recognised as unconstitutional.

30 Pro-Society Public Attorneys, 'Submission in ADPF 635' [2021] ADPF 635 (STF).

insufficient personal protection, and low salaries. These arguments highlight the number of police officers killed in the line of duty[31], without acknowledging the high numbers of Brazilian police fatalities.

This contrast is used to emphasise the importance of the police, whose officials are seen as the only ones capable of confronting such a dangerous 'enemy'. It justifies the need for increased state investment in police careers and infrastructure, arguing they are not equipped on the same level as 'criminals'. In this scenario, 'good' people, as crime victims, should have the right to obtain firearms for self-defence under regulated conditions and after undergoing psychological tests.[32] This was the reasoning present not only in parliamentary debates, but also in Bolsonaro's justification to expand the circulation of firearms during his term in office.[33]

For individuals belonging to gun associations and legally owning firearms, exercising their rights to life, self-defence, and freedom is of tantamount importance. Commenting the case brought to the Supreme Court to reverse Jair Bolsonaro's regulations on firearms and ammunition in 2022, the Brazilian Army Reserve Officers Association (AOR-EB) argued, 'the Brazilian citizen is at the mercy of having his life, his physical integrity, his intangible heritage and women, especially their honour and sexual freedom, attacked without being able to defend themselves'.[34] The self-proclaimed Law-abiding citizens, willing to undergo 'psychological tests' and adhere to regulations in order to obtain weapons and ammunition for sports or personal protection, stand in stark contrast to 'criminals', 'outlaws', and 'drug dealers'.[35]

'Respectful citizens', in addition to being identified as victims of 'crime', are described as 'good people, coming from the most diverse segments of our

31 Congressman Cabo Sabino, 'Speech on Bill 4471/2012' (Chamber of Deputies, 2015). The aim of Bill 4471/2012 was to establish rules for investigating deaths and bodily injuries caused by state agents, such as police officers, and to reinforce the duty to investigate whenever the use of police force resulted in death or bodily harm.

32 Pro-Guns Association (PROARMAS), 'Submission in ADPF 668o' [2021] ADPF 668o (STF). This action challenged the constitutionality of decrees issued during the Bolsonaro administration that relaxed restrictions on the possession and carrying of guns in the country.

33 Brito, Reis, Silva, Amaral (n 5).

34 Brazilian Army Reserve Officers Association (AOR-EB), 'Submission in ADI 6119' [2022] ADI 6119 (STF). This action challenged the constitutionality of decrees issued during the Bolsonaro administration that relaxed restrictions on the possession and carrying of guns in the country.

35 Brazilian Practical Shooting Confederation (Confederação Brasileira de Tiro Prático - CBTP), 'Submission in ADI 6675' [2019] ADI 6675 (STF). The action challenged the constitutionality of decrees issued during the Bolsonaro administration that relaxed restrictions on the possession and carrying of guns in the country.

society; they are businessmen, doctors, traders, engineers, lawyers, farmers, members of the Armed Forces, the Judiciary, the Public Ministry, public servants, etc'.[36] This figure is also directly associated with the idea of the family, as a nucleus of good citizens who deserve protection of their rights, such as those to participate in gun sports, for example, in which 'wives and children also take part'.[37]

Just like the 'good citizens' and the 'heroic' police officers, the 'Beef' actors also depict themselves as members – and defenders – of a group of victimised individuals. Legal regulations imposing environmental fines, land regularisation policies, labour laws, and demarcation of indigenous lands are accused of harming honest rural workers, committed to the country's economic development. In addition to suffering the losses of political choices guided by what they deem to be ideological parameters, not aligned with the country's development, rural producers proclaim to be demonised by the media and by international environmental protection NGOs.[38] They argue those institutions would always wrongly characterise them as 'invaders and evildoers, always ready to plunder and abuse the countryside through violence'.[39]

The documents, for their part, portray agribusiness as the 'sustainer' of the Brazilian economy. They present the Brazilian farmer as a peaceful figure, a worker who invests their time, dreams, and work in the land. In this scenario, farmers are portrayed as 'those (...) whose hands are cracked, their faces are tanned, their feet are cracked from being immersed in mud, in clay; those who deliver our rice, our beans, our meat to the hands of our Brazilian brothers'.[40] These hard-working farmers are allegedly the ones negatively affected by, among other things, excessively restrictive environmental legislation. They

---

36 Shooting Federation of the State of Mato Grosso do Sul (Federação de Tiro do Estado do Mato Grosso do Sul – TiroMS), 'Submission in ADI 6675' [2021] ADI 6675 (STF).

37 Shooting Federation of the State of Mato Grosso do Sul (Federação de Tiro do Estado do Mato Grosso do Sul – TiroMS), 'Submission in ADI 6675' [2021] ADI 6675 (STF).

38 Congressman Paulo Piau, 'Speech on Bill 1.876/1999' (Chamber of Deputies, 2011); CongressmanAldo Rebelo, 'Speech on Bill 1.876/1999' (Chamber of Deputies, 2010). The bill addressed proposals for the new Brazilian Forest Code; Itamaraju Rural Union (Sindicato Rural de Itamaraju), 'Submission in RE 1.017.365' [2021] (STF). The Extraordinary Appeal nº. 1.017.365 addresses the constitutionality of the thesis establishing that Indigenous peoples in Brazil only have the right to claim the demarcation of lands they already occupied or disputed as of 1988, the year the current Brazilian Constitution was promulgated.

39 Brazilian Confederation of Agriculture and Livestock (Confederação da Agricultura e Pecuária no Brasil – CNA), 'Submission in R.E. 1.017.365' [2020] (STF).

40 Congressman Nelson Marchezan Junior, 'Speech onBill 1.876/1999' (Chamber of Deputies 2011).

would be the 'biggest victims' of the constitutionally guaranteed process of land demarcation for indigenous communities, what they call a 'tortuous public policy' that only generates 'fear and anxiety'.[41]

Descriptions of 'country life' often adopt nationalist tones, emphasising rural producers and rural culture as integral parts of the 'treasures of Brazilian social formation'. Furthermore, producers and landowners are portrayed not only as diligent workers and dreamers, but also as peaceful individuals who genuinely care for their land. They are supposedly 'always demonised, considered, in principle, as invaders and evildoers'. However, 'nothing could be more absurd, exaggerated and mistaken', since these farmers are committed to a 'legal, political and social effort to obtain peace and tranquillity in the countryside'.[42]

If actors from the 'bullet' field position themselves as defenders of 'good citizens' who are victims of 'criminality', and actors from the 'beef' field position themselves as defenders of farmers who are victimised by environmental fines and undue demarcations of indigenous lands, 'Bible' actors claim to defend a Christian majority persecuted by political and scientific elites.

They use, in some cases, rhetoric that compares the disputes faced in the present to the persecutions suffered by Christians in the past. In 2016, for instance, Congressman Marcelo Crivella, while commenting on the draft of what was then called the General Law of Religions, argued that Christians have been 'cornered by secular scientific and political elites for almost three hundred years'.[43] In other documents, they argue that churches are persecuted for supporting their faith and opposing social behaviours adopted by certain groups.[44] The idea of 'christophobia' is employed to refer to their consistent victimisation, while those supposedly against the right to life are considered to be part of a culture of death that the 'Bible' coalitions are fighting against.[45] They assert that they protect the family, women, children, adoles-

41 Ilhéus Rural Union (Sindicato Rural de Ilhéus), 'Submission in R.E. 1.017.365' [2021] (STF).

42 Brazilian Confederation of Agriculture and Livestock (Confederação da Agricultura e Pecuária no Brasil – CNA), 'Submission in R.E. 1.017.365' [2020] (STF).

43 Congressman Marcelo Crivella, 'Speech on Bill 160/2009' (Chamber of Deputies, 2016). The bill addressed proposals concerning the general law on religions.

44 National Council of Indigenous Evangelical Pastors and Leaders (Conselho Nacional de Pastores e Líderes Evangélicos Indígenas – CONPLEI), 'Submission in ADPF 811' [2021] ADPF 811 (STF). The constitutional action challenged the constitutionality of the prohibition of worship services, masses, and other collective religious activities during the Covid-19 pandemic.

45 Brito, Reis, Silva, Amaral (n 5).

cents, and unborn children – all of whom they consider to be naturally 'vulnerable', 'weak', and 'at risk' groups.[46]

In the debates about decriminalisation of abortion, the 'Bible' argues that the 'fragility' and the foetus's inability to defend itself necessitate a more assertive protective stance by the State. They suggest that the State should adopt a paradigm similar to that of a family relationship, where 'parents protect the lives of their children after birth (…); as a natural imperative, the State should therefore protect the right to life of the most vulnerable'.[47]

Some documents present an argument highlighting 'the role of law in safeguarding the most vulnerable individuals from those who possess strength or other advantages that could cause them irreparable harm'. It suggests that institutions have a 'responsibility to establish legal mechanisms' to protect unborn children. By doing so, the law would prevent the dominance of the 'law of the strongest' and the perpetration of violence against these groups.[48]

Abortion is also considered 'one of the most serious offenses against women',[49] and defending it would show disregard for the 'psychospiritual health of the woman'.[50] Building on those arguments, these groups characterize their position on abortion as a way to likewise protect women, portrayed as victims when it serves their purpose. When arguing for the prohibition of gender neutral bathrooms, some documents argue that those would 'facilitate the actions of sex offenders'. In this scenario, women and children would be the ones protected by the Bill, since they are identified as 'the main victims of sexual crimes in the country'.[51]

In many cases involving the rights of LGBTQIA+ people, particularly those related to gender, children and adolescents are often considered a 'vulnerable' group in need of protection. Some legislative proposals aim to restrict access to medical treatments available to the transgender population for children

---

46 Family and Succession Law Association (Associação de Direito de Família e das Sucessões) 'Submission in ADPF 442' [2017] ADPF 442 (STF). The action discusses the possibility of legal abortion up to the third month of pregnancy.

47 Life and Family Caucus (Frente Parlamentar da Família e Apoio à Vida) 'Submission in ADPF 442'[2018] ADPF 442 (STF).

48 Bill 478/2007 (Brazil). The bill, which remains pending in the legislature, aims to establish the Statute of the Unborn based on a limited legal definition of family and by restricting the conditions for legal abortion process.

49 Congresswoman Fatima Pelaes, 'Speech on Bill 478/2007' (Chamber of Deputies, 2014).

50 National Laity Council (Conselho Nacional do Laicato) 'Submission in ADPF 442' [2018] ADPF 442 (STF).

51 Bill 4.036/2021 (Brazil). The bill, which remains pending in the legislature, aims to prohibit the construction or creation of gender neutral bathrooms in public and private locations throughout the country.

and adolescents, arguing that they are in an 'obvious stage of formation'[52] or 'crossing the personality construction phase'.[53] This group is supposedly easily 'influenced' and could be 'vulnerable to societal trends', particularly in relation to their understanding of themselves as transgender individuals.[54] Therefore, it is argued that the State should be attentive to the 'unique needs and circumstances' of this group and prevent the implementation of 'treatments that may have unpredictable and lasting effects on their lives'.[55]

While in the 'bullet' field the figures of the 'good citizen' and the police officer are opposed to the criminal, and in the 'beef' field the opposition is between rural producers and indigenous people, NGOs, and environmentalists, here, the opposition is operationalised around the true defenders of groups deserving protection from the State versus those who seek to victimise those groups. The former proclaim to fight for the realisation of fundamental rights and the preservation of indispensable social structures, such as the family. They perceive themselves as standing against groups and individuals who persecute Christians, propagate the culture of death, disrespect fundamental rights, and attack the family as an institution.

On the other side, the group being opposed includes pro-abortion activists, the LGBTQIA+ community, human rights organisations, feminists, individuals and institutions advocating for drug regulation and less repressive public security models. They are often portrayed as ideological and accused of not being committed to the truth or the social well-being. Instead, they are believed to prioritise vested and financial interests, which are seen as threats to children, the family, and the social and political order.

4 Victimhood and Citizenship

The 'Brazilian citizen' becomes a victim of gun control regulations when '[... left] at the mercy of having his life, his physical integrity, his intangible heritage and women, especially their honour and sexual freedom, attacked with-

---

52 Bill 441/2023 (Brazil). The bill, which was formally withdrawn from the legislative process, aimed to criminalise gender reassignment procedures.

53 Bill 994/2023 (Brazil). The bill, which remains pending in the legislature, aims to prohibit transgenital surgery and gender reassignment treatment for individuals under the age of 21.

54 Bill 269/2023 (Brazil). The bill, which remains pending in the legislature, aims to prohibit puberty blockers for transgender minors, and hormonal therapy and gender reassignment surgery for those under 18 and 21 years old, respectively.

55 Bill 441/2023 (Brazil).

out being able to defend themselves'. Also in the context of law enforcement, the narrative literally pits 'good citizens' and police as 'heroes' against 'criminals'. That distinction is used to justify changes in the Disarmament Statute, for example, and to bolster efforts to enhance police forces.

In the field of 'beef', there is also a distinction. Farmers are seen as key players in Brazilian economic and social development, unjustly victimised by the imposition of environmental fines, land regularisation, labour laws, and the demarcation of indigenous lands. These perceived injustices, according to 'beef' groups, occur within a conflict-ridden, insecure, and violent environment, exacerbating the disorder. Therefore, regulations that favour ruralists in each of these areas are presented as an attempt to 'pacify' and 'harmonise' the situation. Similarly to bullet groups, 'beef' actors construct an image of a citizen whose rights have been violated. However, in the former case, the threats materialise more tangibly in the form of 'criminals', while in the latter case, indigenous peoples and environmental protection serve as a hidden focal point.

The construction of self-images and counter-images also plays a significant role in the study of the 'Bible' coalitions. Their rhetoric compares present disputes to past persecutions suffered by Christians, portraying them as a virtuous majority unfairly treated by the groups it opposes. This self-image claims to express the popular will and to be committed to protecting families and children, aligning with the real desires and dynamics of Brazilian society. These positive images are constructed to justify the expansion of church rights and the freedom for religious ministers to express their values.

The research reveals that these conservative and reactionary groups in Brazil articulate their demands before the Judiciary and Legislative powers by presenting themselves as victims or protectors of those they perceive as victimised. This strategy helps them construct an identity that justifies their actions and legitimises the implementation, and sometimes even the unrestricted expansion, of the rights they advocate. By positioning themselves as victims, these groups secure their own rights while limiting or suppressing the rights of those they perceive as victimisers.

In this way, a limited form of citizenship is established through victimisation. Not only literal narratives about victimised 'good citizens' push for certain meanings in the political debate, but so do arguments about who qualifies as legitimate rights-bearers. Both can be read as matters of citizenship, we argue.

Social science and legal studies about citizenship provide valuable lenses for thinking about current uses of legal language amid rising conservatism and declining democracies. They show that citizenship is largely contextual and political: 'the form and substance of citizenship are outcomes of competing interests, strategies and capacities within diverse political spaces'.[56] In this sense, different dimensions of citizenship that can be found in varying academic approaches prove to have mutual influence in actuality. The vocabulary of citizenship describes, for example, the membership to a certain political community, designating insiders and outsiders, where law (or its interpretations) transforms membership into a legal status usually associated with sets of civil, political, and social rights.[57]

In his classic Insurgent Citizenship, James Holston[58] identified the paradoxical nature of Brazilian citizenship, which has internalised the language of rights but often employs it in an instrumental and unequal manner – not necessarily to achieve universal social integration or equal political representation. The author shows how three very different foundations of rights are simultaneously present in the discourse of those engaging in practices of 'insurgent citizenship':[59] rights as privilege, contributor rights, and text-based rights. Only the latter appeal to anonymous universal citizenship, drawing on legal codes and especially the constitutional text as a basis for rights vindication. The other two perpetuate disjunctive notions of citizenship: the contributor conception portray rights-bearers as tax-payers, workers and mass consumers, and the privilege conception embraces the idea of citizenship as a 'distribution of inequality and injustice'[60] – it accepts that compensatory legal privileges (understood as rights), not structural changes, are the adequate path for addressing inequalities, and puts upon the citizen the burden of being a rights-bearer: 'because these rights can only be acquired by the right citizens, people who need to use them "have to chase after their rights"'.[61]

---

56 Kristian Stokke, 'Politics of Citizenship: Towards an Analytical Framework' (2017) 71 *Norsk Geografisk Tidsskrift – Norwegian Journal of Geography* 193, 193–207 https://doi.org/10.1080/00291951.2017.1369454.

57 Stokke (n 45) 204. Strokke argues that four dimensions (identifiable in the social sciences literature as 'citizenship as membership', 'citizenship as legal status', 'citizenship as rights' and 'citizenship as participation') are mutually constitutive pieces of '[how] the form and substance of citizenship reflect contextual power relations and political contentions.'

58 James Holston, *Insurgent Citizenship* (Princeton University Press 2008).

59 Ibid. Holston traces movements of contestation and reinvention of citizenship from the urban peripheries, especially among residents of favelas and illegal (self-built) subdivisions, who, although excluded, claim rights based on their urban experience and the promises of modernity.

60 Holston (n 47) 255.

61 Ibid 256.

Holston's analysis provides important insight into thinking about contemporary uses of rights language by conservative and reactionary groups. It prevents us from pinning disjunctive citizenship as solely a right-wing strategy, as it is a rather usual feature of actual democracies, in which 'the timing and substance of citizenship's development vary in different historical and national contexts [and] this development is never cumulative, linear, or evenly distributed. Rather, citizenship always simultaneously expands and erodes in uneven ways.'[62]

Building on that insight, we argue that the victimhood pattern is an important feature of the disjunctive conception of citizenship coming from right-wing legal mobilisations. Many of the arguments analysed suggest, with varying degrees of literalness, that victimised groups should receive support from the State and enjoy complete freedom, while others are subjected to control and neutralisation. The concept of citizenship based on victimhood alters the relationship between individuals and the State, as well as the understanding of democracy itself. In this constructed democracy of armed power, economic interests, religion, and violence, the State no longer guarantees universal rights but becomes a tool to directly fulfil the rights of a specific group: the victims. This group includes law-abiding citizens, police officers, farmers, landowners, and Christians. Consequently, democracy is construed as a system working primarily for these 'victimised' individuals.

This citizenship disjunction operated by the victimhood politics is part of a larger phenomenon diagnosed by the '(mis)appropriation' approach, where the effects of arguments and interpretations about human rights have broken away from the universalist traits of human rights – 'the basic commitments to recognition and protection for the equal human dignity, human freedom, and human welfare of all persons'.[63] We agree with the diagnosis that the use of human rights language for antipluralistic and undemocratic goals must be better examined and understood to find effective ways of response and resistance. Yet we see both this diagnosed phenomenon and its potential responses as recurrent patterns of the reality of rights interpretation. Legal language mobilisation – and its various 'appropriations' – often do drift away from universalist commitments. This has happened throughout the history of human rights practice and cannot be pinned down as deriving solely from right-wing politics. And a central trait of human rights language is offering tools of argu-

62 Ibid 15. This is not to say that this common feature of democracies cannot, in practice, contribute to democratic decline. Rather, certain uses of rights language – particularly when they promote discriminatory or anti-pluralistic visions of communal life – may in fact transform democratic political culture. See Brito, Reis, Silva, Amaral (n 5) 176–180.

63 De Búrca, Young n 6 209.

mentative and political counterengagement.[64] For that end, the victimhood narrative analysed in this chapter deserves special attention, given this has served the right-wing mobilisation of the very conception of citizenship.

5 Conclusion

By shedding light on the actions of conservatives and reactionaries in formal spaces of power, this research aimed to reveal how such groups mobilise political and legal institutions. Our analysis builds on the perception that the main analytical challenge of our current political context is to pick up the specific patterns of argumentation and coalition forming that drives conservative and reactionary groups in weaponizing this fluidity of human rights practice. Conservative and reactionary actors do so by using human rights characteristic vocabulary and imbuing their own meanings into it. In this process, they formulate unique interpretations of fundamental rights and the individuals they are intended to protect. Their use of the language of rights presents a strategy of disjunctive citizenship that drives rights politics further away from its humanist and pluralist dimensions. These actors, referring to themselves as the true subjects of law, position themselves against their perceived 'enemies,' who they believe must be neutralised.

At the heart of these transformations, the concept of victim plays a central role, linking the fields of law enforcement, religion, and politics in the 'conservative wave' witnessed in Brazil. 'True rights-bearers' are constructed in contrast to individuals or groups whose actions are deemed dangerous and whose claims are delegitimised. A relative image of citizenship emerges, dividing 'good' and 'lesser' citizens. By doing so, they not only transform the legal implications of fundamental rights but also impact the democratic political culture itself.

Bibliography

Almeida R, 'A onda quebrada – evangélicos e conservadorismo' (2017) *Cadernos Pagu*, 50.

Almeida R, 'Bolsonaro presidente: conservadorismo, evangelismo e a crise brasileira' (2019) 38(1) *Novos Estudos Cebrap*, 185.

---

64 See Brito, Reis, Silva, Amaral (n 5) 175 et seq.

Biroli F, Machado MD and Vaggione JM, *Gênero, neoconservadorismo e democracia* (Boitempo 2020).

Blum B, 'Entenda o que muda com o pl que restringe o aborto legal em casos de estupro' *Folha de São Paulo* (São Paulo, 13 June 2024) <https://www1.folha.uol.com.br/equilibrioesaude/2024/06/entenda-o-que-muda-com-o-pl-que-restringe-o-aborto-legal-em-casos-de-estupro.shtml> accessed 26 Mat 2025.

Brito A, Hubner C, Sales F, Amaral M and Barreto M, The Path to Autocracy: Current Strategies for Democratic Erosion (Tinta da China 2023) (in Portuguese).

Brito A, Reis L, Silva M and Amaral M, *The Law of the Beef, the Bullet, the Bible: Democratic Crisis in Disputes Over Rights* (Tinta da China 2024) (in Portuguese).

Bruno R, 'Bancada ruralista, conservadorismo e representação de interesses no Brasil contemporâneo' in *Questões agrárias, agrícolas e rurais: conjunturas e políticas públicas* (E-Papers 2017).

Céllard A, 'A análise documental' in Jean Poupart (ed), *A pesquisa qualitativa: enfoques pistemológicos e metodológicos* (Vozes 2008).

Feltran G, 'A política como violência' (2021) 17(2) *Terceiro Milênio: Revista Crítica de Sociologia e Política.*

Girardi G, 'PL do licenciamento: Senado desmantela segurança ambiental e social do país' *Agência Pública* (22 May 2025) <https://apublica.org/2025/05/pl-do-licenciamento-senado-desmantela-seguranca-ambiental-e-social-do-pais/> accessed 26 May 2025.

Horwitz R, 'Politics as Victimhood, Victimhood as Politics' (2018) 30(3) *Journal of Policy History* 552.

Holston J, *Insurgent Citizenship* (Princeton University Press 2008).

Laperrière A, 'A teorização enraizada (grounded theory): procedimento analítico e comparação com outras abordagens similares' in Jean Poupart (ed), *A pesquisa qualitativa: enfoques epistemológicos e metodológicos* (Vozes 2008).

Pompeia C, *Formação Política do Agronegócio* (Elefante 2021).

Pompeia C, 'As cinco faces do agronegócio: mudanças climáticas e territórios indígenas' (2023) 66 *Revista de Antropologia* https://doi.org/10.11606/1678-9857.ra.2022.202839.

Prandi R and Santos RWS, 'Quem tem medo da bancada evangélica? Posições sobre moralidade e política no eleitorado brasileiro, no Congresso Nacional e na Frente Parlamentar Evangélica' (2017) 29 *Tempo Social* 187–214.

André Rithcer 'STF confirma competência de guardas municipais para fazer policiamento' *Agência Brasil* (Brasília, 21 February 2025) <https://agenciabrasil.ebc.com.br/justica/noticia/2025-02/stf-confirma-competencia-de-guardas-municipais-para-fazer-policiamento> accessed 26 May 2025.

Smilova R, 'The Ideational Core of Democratic Illiberalism' in András Sajó, Renáta Uitz and Stephen Holmes (eds), *Routledge Handbook of Illiberalism* (Routledge 2022).

Simon J, *Governing Through Crime: How the War on Crime Transformed American Democracy and Created a Culture of Fear* (Oxford University Press 2019).

Souza Junior PG and Souza CHP, 'Evangélicos e conservadorismo – afinidades eletivas: as novas configurações da democracia no Brasil' (2020) 18(57) *Horizonte – Revista de Estudos de Teologia e Ciências da Religião* 1188.

Stokke K, 'Politics of Citizenship: Towards an Analytical Framework' (2017) 71 *Norsk Geografisk Tidsskrift – Norwegian Journal of Geography* 193 https://doi.org/10.1080/00291951.2017.1369454.

Wodak R, *The Politics of Fear: What Right-Wing Populist Discourses Mean* (SAGE Publications Ltd 2015) https://doi.org/10.4135/9781446270073.

PART 3

Critique of Human Rights Misappropriation

CHAPTER 9

Misappropriation of Human Rights as an Empty Frame

Işıl Aral

1 Introduction

In recent years, a growing number of scholarly writings have argued that human rights standards in various authoritarian regimes are experiencing a backlash. Most of these writings claim that these states either totally reject human rights as Western and neo-colonial or use them for their own interests by subverting their meaning. This phenomenon is commonly labelled as 'distortion' or 'abuse' and characterized as 'misappropriation'. For instance, Graínne De Búrca and Katharine Young organized a symposium in the International Journal of Constitutional Law in 2023 to discuss how populist, right-wing, and exclusionary policies in authoritarian regimes are undoing the long-fought gains of human rights law.[1] Many other scholars have likewise examined the impact that populism had on international human rights law.[2] This chapter conceptualizes these scholarly writings as misappropriation of human rights discourses and aims at bringing to light how they frame misappropriation as a problem by conducting a discourse analysis.[3] It investigates the narrative on the misappropriation of human rights by examining how the

1 Graínne De Búrca and Katharine G Young, 'The (Mis)Appropriation of Human Rights by the New Global Right: An Introduction to the Symposium', *International Journal of Constitutional Law,* 21/1 (2023), 205–223.

2 See Section 2. See also Tom Ginsburg, *Authoritarian International Law,* 114 American Journal of International Law 221 (2020), Samuel Moyn, *Not Enough: Human Rights in an Unequal World* (Harvard University Press 2018).

3 Discourse here is used to define engagement with a subject whether in speech or writing that creates a particular understanding to the exclusion of alternative ways of interpreting the same phenomena in order to claim authority over that subject. This definition draws from Andrea Bianchi's approach who defines discourse as 'what keeps certain practices and procedures in circulation while others are excluded' in Andrea Bianchi, 'Epistemic Communities' in Jean d'Aspremont and Sahib Singh (eds), *Concepts for International Law: Contributions to Disciplinary Thought* (Edward Elgar 2019) 258. For an extended discussion on discourse, see Michel Foucault, 'Order of Discourse' in Robert Young (ed), *Untying the Text: A Post-Structuralist Reader* (Routledge 1981) 48–78.

impact of populism on human rights law is projected as a problematic relationship, how this problem is situated in time and space.

What is mundane is not worth telling. When one wants to tell a story, whether it is in international law or in any other field, the story has to deal with change, crisis, problem, trouble, disaster, challenge, deadlock etc. International legal scholarship is abundant with writings on crisis. It can even be said that international law is a field of crisis.[4] International lawyers thrive in finding crises that they then try to solve. What happens around us can be turned into crises and then the legal vocabulary can be deployed to address these problems and provide solutions.[5] These crises, however, do not exist on their own and have to be created through a narrativization process. What happens in the world needs to be put in an order through a narrativization that will tell a story with a beginning, a middle and an end. In this narrative, the narrator must justify why the story needs to be told and why it deserves the audience's attention. This justification is typically established by presenting a crisis, which the international lawyer then addresses through the narrativization of facts and sources.

The legal scholarship on international human rights law has hosted several claims about a human rights crisis. The problems that scholars have raised about human rights are too many to count in an exhaustive manner.[6] The crisis on which this chapter focuses is constructed around the alleged misappropriation of human rights witnessed in recent years. Scholarship examining this misappropriation began to flourish in the 2010s, with much of the literature concentrating on the engagement of rising populist leaders with human rights. It is evident that many international lawyers have expressed concern about the impact of these leaders on the protection of human rights. The discourse on the effects of populism on human rights law is portrayed as a serious challenge that demands assessment by international lawyers. A common thread running through these accounts is the argument that populist politicians, through their divisive rhetoric, are undermining the protection of human rights and dismantling several decades of progress. As will be detailed in the following sections, over the past decade, international lawyers

---

4 Hilary Charlesworth, 'International Law: A Discipline of Crisis', *The Modern Law Review*, 65/3 (2002), 377–392, Makane Moïse Mbengue and Jean d'Aspremont (eds.), *Crisis Narratives in International Law* (Brill, 2021).

5 See generally, Martti Koskenniemi, 'The Politics of International Law–20 Years Later', *European Journal of International Law*, 20/1 (2009) 7–19.

6 Stephen Hopgood, *The Endtimes of Human Rights* (Cornell University Press 2013) 1, Gráinne De Búrca, *Reframing Human Rights in a Turbulent Era* (Oxford University Press 2021) 1, Eric Posner, *The Twilight of Human Rights Law* (Oxford University Press 2014).

have increasingly framed the relationship between populism and international human rights law as a crisis, offering their own narrativization of this relationship. According to these discourses, international human rights law is facing a crisis that must be acknowledged, critically examined, and addressed.

This chapter elucidates the narrativization techniques that international lawyers used to construct misappropriation of human rights discourses. Since international law discourses are constructed based on some narrativization strategies, it is possible to deconstruct these narratives into their components and understand the elements that allowed the framing of an alleged misappropriation of human rights as a crisis. In particular, it takes a critical look at three of these narrativization techniques, namely the construction of the formal, temporal, and spatial elements of the narrative to understand how they have been instrumental in the creation of these misappropriation discourses. The formal element explains how international lawyers drew the legal contours of these discourses and anchored the subject into a legal framework. The temporal element examines how scholars used the periodization of history to situate their discourses in time. The spatial element explores within which space this narrative has an impact.

This chapter claims that the argument about a possible misappropriation of human rights is an empty frame that does not have a meaning on its own. It is the scholarly writings that give it a meaning by explaining what they mean by the misappropriation of human rights. The scholarly writings on the misappropriation of human rights can be conceptualized as forming a narrative that tries to convey a similar argument. The narrative on misappropriation is one of many possible narratives that can be constructed in order to address the possible shortcomings of the contemporary human rights framework. The simplest definition that we can give to narrative is 'the representation of an event or a series of events'.[7] Narratives tell a story of change,[8] a story which has a beginning, a middle and an end.[9] Hayden White defined narrative as 'a metacode, a human universal on the basis of which transcultural messages

7 Porter Abbott, *The Cambridge Introduction to Narrative* (Cambridge University Press 2002) 12.
8 Ibid, 12.
9 Hayden White, 'The Structure of Historical Narrative' in Hayden White, *The Fiction of Narrative: Essays on History, Literature, and Theory, 1957–2007* (Robert Doran ed, Johns Hopkins University Press 2010) 112.

about the nature of a shared reality can be transmitted'.[10] Narrative allows us to translate what we see around us into words and becomes a repository of our interpretation of facts. It transforms the human experience into stories and produces an account of reality.[11] It names facts, events, values, identities, and allows us to make sense of our surroundings. It can be argued that there is no factual reality that exists independently from the narrative.[12]

The chapter conceptualizes the scholarly writings that discuss a possible misappropriation of human rights due to populist policies as a narrative and aims at bringing to light how it frames misappropriation as a problem. The chapter conducts a discourse analysis of scholarly writings arguing for a possible misappropriation of human rights and explains how international lawyers present their argument (2). It identifies three narrativization elements that are essential in building the narrative on the misappropriation of human rights. It examines the formal element that determines why the narrative pertains to international law (3). Then, it turns to the temporal element of the narrative to understand how a certain historical flow is created by this narrative and how it is situated in time (4). It further examines how the narrative is situated in space (5). By bringing these narrativization elements to light, the chapter demonstrates how international lawyers create new necessary causalities between historical events, legal sources, doctrines, judgments, and international practice to create meaning in a text and advance an argument.[13] The chapter finishes with some concluding remarks (6).

---

10 Hayden White, 'The Value of Narrativity in the Representation of Reality' (1980) 7 Critical Inquiry 5, 6. Hayden White differentiated between narrative and discourse, the former referring to an objective representation of facts where the narrator is almost absent, the latter a subjective account where the narrator's presence is easily identifiable. He added a third category that he called 'narrativizing discourse' which is identified with the absence of a narrator and 'the events seem to tell themselves'. See ibid, 7.

11 Roland Barthes, 'Le Discours de l'Histoire' (1967) 6 Social Science Information 63, 74.

12 As famously stated by Jacques Derrida, 'There is nothing outside of the text [there is no outside-text; il n'y a pas de hors-texte]' in Jacques Derrida, *Of Grammatology* (Johns Hopkins University Press 2016) 646. Similarly, White argued that there is no historical reality outside the discursive form, see Hayden White, *Metahistory: The Historical Imagination in Nineteenth-Century Europe* (Johns Hopkins University Press 1975) 5–27. On the narrative structure of history, see also Paul Ricoeur, *Time and Narrative* (University of Chicago Press 1988).

13 Paul Gewirtz 'Narrative and Rhetoric in the Law' in Peter Brooks and Paul Gewirtz (eds), *Law's Stories: Narrative and Rhetoric in the Law* (Yale University Press 1996) 4. See also Andrea Bianchi, 'Reflexive Butterfly Catching: Insights from a Situated Catcher' in Joost Pauwelyn, Ramses Wessel and Jan Wouters (eds), *Informal International Lawmaking* (Oxford University Press 2012).

2 The Misappropriation of Human Rights Discourses

The scholarly writings on the misappropriation of human rights argue that the approach of certain states to human rights constitutes a problem. These discourses criticize the ways in which primarily authoritarian states interpret and implement human rights. According to these scholarly writings, these states subvert human rights by abusing and distorting them, ultimately undermining the protection and advancement of human rights. According to Alston, 'the challenges the human rights movement now faces are fundamentally different from much of what has gone before'.[14] In that sense, for some international lawyers, populism poses a challenge to human rights that is unprecedented. While the human rights movement has faced various difficulties over time, countering the attacks of populism and other exclusionary policies is seen as requiring a new strategy. In other words, this is presented as a crisis unlike any before. However, this contention mirrors a familiar pattern in scholarly debates in international law: every new problem is framed as unique. When a scholar seeks to intervene in the literature, she must necessarily present something new which should constitute an original contribution. The crisis must be constructed as distinct from past episodes. In this regard, the claim that populism represents an entirely new challenge is part and parcel of the narrative practices of international law. This is not to deny that many scholars have acknowledged the persistent presence of human rights abuses throughout history. However, the contemporary discourse constructs the current challenge as distinct, thereby reinforcing the perception that this crisis demands a novel approach. This section outlines the contributions of international scholars to the ongoing debate concerning the alleged misappropriation of human rights.

In 2023, de Búrca and Young organized a symposium in the International Journal of Constitutional Law under the theme 'The (Mis)appropriation of Human Rights in the New Global Right'.[15] De Búrca and Young argued that we are witnessing an era in which the long-fought gains of human rights are being undone by the rise of right-wing politics. They coined the term 'misappropriation' to describe the use of the language of human rights for 'exclusionary, repressive, or antipluralist' ends.[16] Although they acknowledged the difficulty of determining the precise scope of human rights, their correct inter-

14 Philip Alston, 'The Populist Challenge to Human Rights', *Journal of Human Rights Practice*, 9/1 (2017) 2.

15 De Búrca and Young (n 1) 205–223.

16 Ibid, 213.

pretation, or the appropriate strategies for their implementation, they nevertheless contended that it was still possible to observe how authoritarian regimes were undoing the progress achieved in recent decades. They identified a new group of actors, which they called 'the New Global Right' encompassing illiberal, populist, conservative, and religious political actors. According to their analysis, the New Global Right did not reject the discourse of human rights outright; rather, it produced its own version of human rights, effectively reversing many of the gains made over previous decades. De Búrca and Young identified the 1993 Vienna World Conference on Human Rights as a pivotal moment that fostered broad consensus on human rights. Despite the significance they attributed to the Vienna Conference, they emphasized that, '[t]his Symposium avoids the twin pitfalls of presenting human rights either as a fixed body of positive law underpinned by clear consensus or as an unmoored set of open-ended signifiers capable of being filled with any content'.[17] This position allowed them to adopt an ambivalent stance regarding the scope of human rights: on the one hand, they refrained from offering a definitive list of rights; on the other, they advanced guiding concepts, such as human dignity, human freedom, and the welfare of all persons, that should inform our understanding of human rights.

After identifying the 1993 World Conference on Human Rights as a moment of global consensus, De Búrca and Young argued that this consensus has been ruptured by the policies of the New Global Right. Despite acknowledging the difficulty of defining the rigid contours, scope, or correct interpretation of human rights, they contended that authoritarian regimes in recent years have adopted approaches that fundamentally disregard the core values of human rights. These regimes that are characterized as authoritarian, populist, or conservative tend to prioritize certain rights over others, exclude particular groups from protection, or actively seek to reverse long-standing human rights commitments. The articles included in the Symposium examined the United States, Russia, Turkey, Brazil, India, Uganda, Nigeria, and Ghana. They traced how political actors in these states adopted strategies that, in the authors' view, undermined the 'genuine' protection of human rights. While some policies reflected continuity with earlier conservative approaches, others marked new strategies that contributed to reshaping or dismantling existing protections. De Búrca and Young proposed a set of guiding questions for contributors, aimed at identifying whether the policies in question promoted exclusionary, repressive, or anti-pluralist agendas; whether they sought to reverse the gains made in human rights since the adoption of the Universal Declar-

17 Ibid, 209.

ation of Human Rights; whether they established hierarchies among rights; and whether public policies obstructed the protection of certain rights. In their analysis, the authors pointed not only to state actors and populist politicians but also to religious groups that exert significant influence over public institutions. One key strategy employed by these actors, they argued, involved marginalizing rights that were incorporated into the human rights framework at a later stage. While the foundational rights of the UDHR were often embraced, more recently recognized rights were selectively dismissed, misappropriated, or outright rejected. Drawing on Śledzińska-Simon's work on populism, they referred to this as a 'buffet' approach to human rights – where populist leaders pick and choose rights based on their political agendas.[18]

In one of the earliest contributions to the literature on human rights backlash, Susan Marks focused on the United Kingdom, examining how conservative policies framed human rights as having gone 'too far', expanding into too many rights and exerting excessive institutional control.[19] She explored how media outlets, judges, and politicians criticized the European Court of Human Rights for allegedly intervening in the UK's internal affairs and dictating domestic law from Strasbourg. Marks observed that 'human rights are blamed for producing the very condition they purport to remedy, that is to say, subjection, insecurity, unfreedom'.[20] She noted that critics of the human rights movement, while expressing concern over its expansion, did not dismiss human rights altogether as a redundant or unproductive concept. Instead, they appropriated human rights language to present themselves as the true defenders of fundamental freedoms. Marks identified conservatives as the primary proponents of this narrative and argued that a key element of their criticism was the self-representation as the voice of the 'righteous man'.[21]

In his article Human Rights Populism, Frédéric Mégret critically examined recent populist trends that seek to push back against human rights.[22] He defined human rights populism as 'the use of human rights discourse by those whose politics are grounded in an appeal to ordinary "people" against an elite, even as their politics have traditionally been understood as anti-

18 Anna Śledzińska-Simon, 'Populists, Gender, and National Identity', International Journal of Constitutional Law, 18/2 (2020) 447–454.

19 Susan Marks, 'Backlash: The Undeclared War against Human Rights', European Human Rights Law Review, 4 (2014) 319–327.

20 Ibid, 323.

21 Ibid, 325.

22 Frédéric Mégret, 'Human Rights Populism', Humanity: An International Journal of Human Rights, Humanitarianism, and Development, 13/2 (2022) 240–259.

human rights'.[23] Unlike other forms of populism, whether national, economic, religious, or racial, Mégret argued that human rights populism does not wholly reject human rights discourse. Rather, it strategically appropriates the language of human rights to advance particular interests. The ambition of human rights populism, he claimed, is 'to construct a vision of "a people" defending *its* human rights'.[24] Mégret's case studies stood out from other scholarship due to his focus on Western states. He argued that the strong historical attachment to human rights in Western democracies has allowed populist actors to draw on this tradition to legitimize their agendas. His analysis centred on Western countries such as France, the United Kingdom, the United States, Canada, and Israel. By focusing on specific rights, Mégret demonstrated how progress made in certain areas has been instrumentalized to restrict the scope of other rights.

Philip Alston placed populist policies that challenge the progress of the human rights movement at the centre of his critique.[25] He stated that the 'populist agenda that has made such dramatic inroads recently is often avowedly nationalistic, xenophobic, misogynistic, and explicitly antagonistic to all or much of the human rights agenda'.[26] Deeply alarmed by populism's reaction to human rights, Alston warned that the challenges 'will undoubtedly be more severe and sustained than anything we have witnessed since the depths of the Cold War'.[27] According to Alston, the security concerns that emerged after 9/11 inflicted significant harm on certain fundamental freedoms, such as freedom of movement, privacy, and non-discrimination, which were often treated as necessary trade-offs. He further noted that civil society organizations are increasingly being displaced by state-sponsored NGOs that cannot function as impartial monitoring mechanisms of human rights. Regulations restricting or banning certain NGOs and limiting their funding, he argued, cause further damage to the vital role of civil society in protecting fundamental freedoms. Alston also highlighted how the human rights movement's focus on society's most marginalized groups has, in some cases, created resentment among broader segments of the population who feel unseen.

In his monograph *Human Rights and Populism*, Jolyon Ford questioned whether populism truly poses a significant challenge to human rights.[28] In addressing the relationship between populism and the recent human rights

23 Ibid, 241.
24 Ibid, 253.
25 Alston (n 14).
26 Ibid, 1–2.
27 Ibid, 3.
28 Jolyon Ford, *Human Rights and Populism* (Taylor & Francis 2023).

backlash, he adopted a cautious tone. Ford acknowledged that populism is not the sole cause of the backlash observed in recent years. He argued that there are multiple ways to frame the challenges the human rights movement has faced over time. While he recognized that the rise of populist leaders beginning in the 2010s has indeed created serious concerns regarding the protection of human rights, he resisted the temptation to treat populism as the singular explanation for the backlash. Instead, he examined how, among many other factors, populism has shaped the human rights movement in particular ways. According to Ford, the human rights project cannot be understood as a field of continuous evolution and progress; rather, its challenges stem from a range of complex causes. Instead of solely asking how populism has affected human rights, Ford provocatively asked, 'how did we, the human rights movement, do this to ourselves?'[29] He focused on the ways populism has targeted human rights law to probe deeper into the internal shortcomings of the human rights project, particularly its perceived failure to address the concerns of ordinary people, as highlighted by populist leaders.

The theme of the 2018 volume of the *Netherlands Yearbook of International Law* was 'Populism and International Law'. The chapters in the volume addressed various manifestations of populism in international law, including Trump's engagement with populism,[30] populism in Latin America[31] and Kenya,[32] populism's encounter with the World Bank[33] and the role of inter-

---

29 Ibid, 5.

30 Lukasz Gruszczynski and Jessica Lawrence, 'Trump, International Trade and Populism' in Janne E Nijman and Wouter G Werner, 'Populism and International Law: What Backlash and Which Rubicon?', *Netherlands Yearbook of International Law,* 49 (2018) 19, Aaron Fichtelber, 'Populist Paranoia and International Law' in Janne E Nijman and Wouter G Werner, 'Populism and International Law: What Backlash and Which Rubicon?', *Netherlands Yearbook of International Law,* 49 (2018) 45.

31 Alejandro Rodiles, 'Is There a "Populist" International Law (in Latin America)?' in Janne E Nijman and Wouter G Werner, 'Populism and International Law: What Backlash and Which Rubicon?', *Netherlands Yearbook of International Law,* 49 (2018) 69, Rene Urueña, 'Reclaiming the Keys to the Kingdom (of the World): Evangelicals and Human Rights in Latin America' in Janne E Nijman and Wouter G Werner, 'Populism and International Law: What Backlash and Which Rubicon?', *Netherlands Yearbook of International Law,* 49 (2018) 175.

32 Edwin Bikundo, 'People, Politics and Populism in International Criminal Law: The Mungiki as Kenyan Ethos and Kenyan Demos' in Janne E Nijman and Wouter G Werner, 'Populism and International Law: What Backlash and Which Rubicon?', *Netherlands Yearbook of International Law,* 49 (2018) 123.

33 Lys Kulamadayil, 'Addressing Economic Populism Through Law – A Case Study of the World Development Report 2017' in Janne E Nijman and Wouter G Werner, 'Populism and International Law: What Backlash and Which Rubicon?', *Netherlands Yearbook of International Law,* 49 (2018) 209.

national lawyers in perpetuating neoliberalism and populist backlash.[34] The chapter by Veronika Bilková focused on the relationship between populism and human rights.[35] She took the view that populism posed a threat to the effective protection of human rights. According to Bilková, one of the main characteristics of populists is their belief that the people form a homogenous group where differences regarding their ideological, social, or political beliefs can be disregarded as insignificant.[36] Populists believe in the existence of a people that unit around their shared values. Another main characteristic is their hostility against the elite who are not pursuing the interests of the real people. Plus, this elite aims to destroy the traditions and values that form the very core identity of this people. Populists posit themselves as the saviour of the real people who will defend these traditions and values in such a way that no other political movement can do so. In that sense, they are anti-democratic since they are the only ones that can represent the people.

Andrew Fagan addressed the challenges posed by what he called the 'demagogues' rather than populists in the way they juxtaposed human rights as a project against the 'ordinary people'.[37] He indicated that unless the human rights community responded to the challenges posed to human rights in liberal states, it risked 'an unedifying descent into a socially exclusive, politically unpopular credo for a diminishing number of supporters, with ever diminishing influence beyond their own social enclaves'.[38] In order to understand the impact of what he called the 'demagogic authoritarianism', Fagan examined the relationship between human rights and capitalism. He explored how the rights-based order goes hand in hand with neoliberal policies both supported by states with a liberal democracy and global financial institutions including the International Monetary Fund and World Bank. In his review of Gerald Neuman's edited volume *Human Rights in a Time of Populism*, he continued his focus on the connection between human rights and capitalism, a point he

34 Christine Schwöbel-Patel, 'Populism, International Law and the End of Keep Calm and Carry on Lawyering' in Janne E Nijman and Wouter G Werner, 'Populism and International Law: What Backlash and Which Rubicon?', *Netherlands Yearbook of International Law,* 49 (2018) 97.

35 Veronika Bilková, 'Populism and Human Rights' in Janne E Nijman and Wouter G Werner, 'Populism and International Law: What Backlash and Which Rubicon?', *Netherlands Yearbook of International Law,* 49 (2018) 143.

36 Ibid, 149.

37 Andrew Fagan, 'The Gentrification of Human Rights', *Human Rights Quarterly,* 41/2 (2019), 283–308.

38 Ibid, 285.

argued is missing in Neuman's approach to populism.[39] He claimed that a key reason for people's diminishing trust in liberal democracy and the rising power of populist leaders is the close connection of the rights-based order with neoliberal policies that created serious problems ranging from hunger to systemic inequality.[40]

Neuman's edited volume *Human Rights in a Time of Populism: Challenges and Responses* stemmed from a multidisciplinary conference that was organized at Harvard Law School in 2018. Neuman's chapter discussed what populism meant and provided a general account on its impact regarding the protection of human rights. In Neuman's view, 'populists have an exclusionary notion of the "real people" that they contrast with morally reprehensible elites; and populists claim to speak for the will of the "real people", which should not be constrained'.[41] Based on this definition, Neuman claimed that a major threat posed by populism is the exclusion of a certain group of people that are not considered 'real people'.[42] In particular, those who are seen as the 'powerful elite' or those that received favourable attention according to populists might be excluded from the protection of fundamental rights.[43] An important challenge to human rights posed by populists is their claim to represent the popular will in a way that denies the legitimacy of any form of opposition. This creates an anti-pluralist environment that rejects dissent and fosters authoritarian rule. The distinction drawn between the 'real people' and the 'powerful elite' or other favoured groups is reflected in their approach to human rights, where certain rights may receive greater protection than others. One significant impact of populism on human rights, as discussed by Neuman in his chapter, concerns the approach of populist leaders toward international human rights protection mechanisms. While Neuman's chapter outlined the concept of populism and sketched the general contours of its effects on human rights globally, the remaining chapters of the edited volume focused on individual states, offering detailed examinations of the challenges populism poses to human rights. The volume closely analysed the cases of the United States, the United Kingdom, Poland, Venezuela, Colombia, Turkey, and Myanmar. A common thread running through all the chapters is the argu-

---

39 Andrew Fagan, 'Human Rights in a Time of Populism: Challenges and Responses Ed. By Gerald L. Neuman', *Human Rights Quarterly*, 43/2 (2021), 416–421.

40 Ibid, 420–421.

41 Gerald Neuman, 'Populist Threats to the International Human Rights System', in Gerald Neuman (ed), *Human Rights in a Time of Populism: Challenges and Responses* (Cambridge University Press 2020) 2.

42 Ibid, 6.

43 Ibid.

ment that populism has had a detrimental impact on the protection of human rights.

An important intervention in the debate on populism and human rights was made by Kenneth Roth, then Executive Director of Human Rights Watch. In the 2018 World Report, Roth argued that populists tend to blame disadvantaged groups rather than offering genuine solutions to human rights problems.[44] He stated that the attacks of populists have targeted the values that lied at the heart of human rights including inclusivity, tolerance, and respect.[45] He further claimed that populists presented human rights as protecting only the terrorists and asylum seekers in a way that disregarded the majority in the society that also needed the same protection.[46] He provided examples from the Trump administration in the US, Marine Le Pen in France, and Geert Wilders in the Netherlands. He added that 'claims of unfettered majoritarianism, and the attacks on the checks and balances that constrain governmental power, are perhaps the greatest danger today to the future of democracy in the West. They threaten to reverse the accomplishments of the modern human rights movement'.[47]

Jure Vidmar's edited volume *European Populism and Human Rights* brings together 13 chapters assessing the impact of populism on the European public order.[48] Geographically limited to Council of Europe member states, the book examined how populist politics have affected democratic governance in Europe. The book is premised on the idea that right-wing populism is inherently detrimental to democratic institutions and the protection of human rights.[49] Unlike other edited volumes on the subject, *European Populism and Human Rights* did not focus on particular states but instead traced the broader relationship between populism, human rights, and democratic rule. In his introductory chapter, Vidmar defined procedural and substantive democracy and explained how democratic governance is embedded within human rights law, particularly in the jurisprudence of international human rights monitoring bodies. Building on this framework, the subsequent chapters explored how populism has emerged as a key driver of democratic regression in recent years.

44 Human Rights Watch, World Report 2018, available at: https://www.hrw.org/world-report/2018, 2.
45 Ibid.
46 Kenneth Roth, 'The Dangerous Rise of Populism: Global Attacks on Human Rights Values', *Journal of International Affairs*, Special 70th Anniversary Issue (2017) 79–80.
47 Ibid, 81.
48 Jure Vidmar (ed), *European Populism and Human Rights* (Brill Nijhoff 2020).
49 Ibid.

3 The Formal Element: Misappropriation as a Narrative of Obscurity

In the construction of international law narratives, the formal element identifies why the narrative falls within the domain of international law. It is the narrativization element that evidences how the narrative speaks the language of international law. The narratives that international lawyers create aim to persuade the audience that the argument put forward makes a convincing claim. International lawyers have to adopt a legal language and need to engrave their narrative into a legal framework. They need to demonstrate why the stories they tell are different from any other non-law stories. In that regard, the narrator needs to create the necessary links between facts and tie the narrative into an international law framework. Since facts do not in themselves incorporate a legal significance, it is the narrator's role to create the link between the facts and legal sources broadly construed to make them part of international law. It is argued here that the narrativization technique that allows the legal scholar to anchor the narrative into an international law framework and differentiate it from any other non-international law narrative is the construction of the formal element.

In the case of the misappropriation of human rights discourses, the main argument concerns the alleged backlash against international human rights law triggered by the rise of populist and exclusionary politics. It is contended that the protection of human rights is in decline across several states due to the growing influence of populist, nationalist, or authoritarian movements. Despite their emphasis on a human rights backlash, these writings rarely specify which particular rights are being affected. It is argued here that the obscurity in defining what constitutes 'human rights' forms the formal element of the narrative on the misappropriation of human. This ambiguity surrounding the scope of human rights is not incidental. It serves as the very mechanism by which scholars construct the narrative of misappropriation, precisely by avoiding any clear definition of what misappropriation entails. The obscurity of human rights allows the invocation of legal language and the framing of the issue as one of international legal concern. The strategic use of vague references to 'human rights' allows scholars to situate their arguments within the domain of international law, even in the absence of a clearly defined normative framework. The obscurity itself becomes a technique of legal narrativization: it enables the narrative to sound in the register of international law while avoiding the need to specify what this law requires. In that sense, the obscurity of the scope of human rights allows scholars to deploy the vocabulary and authority of human rights without necessarily explaining how misappropriation is opposed to a good interpretation. The idea of a backlash presupposes a clear understanding of what a 'proper' application or enforcement of human rights would entail. Yet, rather than articulating which rights are under threat or detailing the mechanisms through which their protection is being curtailed, these writings often rely on political rhetoric and focus their criticism on how political figures interpret and invoke human rights. In doing so, they engage less with institutional interpretations of human rights law and more with the ways politicians interact with and narrate what they call the 'human rights movement'.

Human rights are multifaceted, and there are numerous ways of defining and understanding them. Despite the difficulty, or even the impossibility, of offering a definitive account of what human rights are, any discussion about the detrimental impact of populism on human rights necessarily presupposes some conception of their scope. If there is talk of misappropriation, misuse, abuse, or backsliding, these terms acquire meaning only in relation to an assumed proper appropriation, use, or interpretation of human rights. Terms that signal a backlash against human rights do not have intrinsic meaning; they are intelligible only when contrasted with a particular understanding of what constitutes correct or genuine interpretation of human rights. The claim that human rights are being misappropriated implicitly relies on the existence of an authentic, accurate interpretation of human rights and on the possibility of identifying what human rights are and how they ought to be implemented. Misappropriation,[50] misuse,[51] subterfuge,[52] and mimicry[53] are all different expressions used in this narrative that claims human rights are being abused at the hand of authoritarian politicians. What these expressions conceal, however, is an underlying essentialist understanding of human rights. This underlying assumption cannot simply be set aside by acknowledging the multiplicity of ways in which human rights can be substantiated. Misappropriation, by its very nature, can only be understood in contrast to proper interpretation. Yet, within this narrative, there is little engagement with what constitutes correct interpretation; instead, the focus remains almost exclusively on identifying instances of misappropriation. This approach essentializes a particular conception of human rights without ever explicitly defining or clarifying what

50 *De Búrca and Young (n 1)*

51 Tímea Drinóczi and Agnieszka Bień-Kacała, *Illiberal Constitutionalism in Poland and Hungary: The Deterioration of Democracy, Misuse of Human Rights and Abuse of the Rule of Law* (Routledge 2021).

52 Farrah Ahmed, 'Constitutional Parasitism, Camouflage, and Pretense: Shaping Citizenship through Subterfuge', *International Journal of Constitutional Law*, 21/1 (2023) 285–307.

53 Mégret (n 22) 241.

that essence entails. Most scholars gesture vaguely towards values such as human dignity or equality as the core of human rights, but these broad terms do little to illuminate the specific content or contours of the presumed essence.

De Búrca and Young attempted to navigate this tension by acknowledging the persistent debate over which fundamental interests qualify as human rights, the scope these rights should have, and the appropriate means of their protection.[54] They acknowledged that defining what human rights are, or determining how they should be interpreted in specific contexts, is a complex and contested task. Nevertheless, they maintained that it remains possible to identify a phenomenon they termed 'misappropriation'. They defined the misappropriation of human rights as 'the deployment by a particular set of actors of a range of strategies and arguments … advanced in the language of protecting "human rights", but generally seeking to reverse or undo previous human rights developments and commitments'.[55]

According to de Búrca and Young, the consensus established by the 1993 World Conference on Human Rights in Vienna is being undermined by the populist and exclusionary right-wing policies of recent years.[56] However, it remains unclear what exactly this consensus entailed and why the scholars use the Vienna Conference as a contrasting point to the contemporary approach of certain states toward human rights. The scholars themselves acknowledged that 'given the open-ended character of so many rights provisions, it is not obvious that any particular interpretative move – whether conservative or progressive – can readily be characterized as transgressing the plausible boundaries of the field'.[57] If the scope of human rights is not easily determined and if there is a constant tension between different interpretative moves, it becomes difficult to pinpoint exactly which core values these populist policies violate. The contradiction in de Búrca and Young's argument largely stems from their recognition of the difficulty in defining human rights, despite their claim that populist states are misappropriating them. If the scope of human rights is continually debated and their proper application is subject to interpretation, then determining their misappropriation becomes equally impractical. They argued that their understanding of human rights is a system which is 'as a complex and dynamic one involving ongoing interaction between domestic and local cultures, institutions, prac-

54 De Búrca and Young (n 1) 206.
55 Ibid, 206–207.
56 Ibid, 207.
57 Ibid, 208.

tices, and values on the one hand, and the global framework of norms and values on the other, in shaping the corpus of human rights'[58] and that 'it may be difficult to assert that any particular or singular interpretation of a given right is wrong or illegitimate'.[59] By emphasizing the dynamic nature of the human rights system, the scholars avoid providing a clear definition of what proper interpretation looks like. If human rights do not have a fixed content and are instead a dynamic set of norms open to various interpretations, then the determination of what constitutes a 'good' or 'bad' appropriation depends on the perspective of the scholar. This fluid and unstable nature of human rights grants the scholar considerable flexibility in determining what should be accepted as an incorrect interpretation. In other words, a misappropriation of human rights is whatever the narrator defines as a distorted interpretation of these rights. The analysis thus becomes self-referential, as it is impossible to demonstrate what constitutes a 'good' interpretation while simultaneously arguing that human rights are being misappropriated. Unless the concept of misappropriation is clearly defined by explaining what constitutes a proper interpretation, any evaluation based on the misappropriation of human rights risks being self-referential.

The claim of misappropriation is grounded in the alleged existence of strategies designed to reverse previous human rights developments. The research questions posed by de Búrca and Young to investigate these strategies focus on issues such as the exclusion of certain rights from enforcement policies, particular interpretations of human rights that deviate from foundational human rights sources, the hierarchy of rights, censorship of civil society, bad faith practices, and a move away from international monitoring.[60] These questions serve to illustrate what misappropriation might look like, but they do not establish a clear parameter for distinguishing between a 'good' appropriation or interpretation and a misappropriation of human rights. As a result, these research questions fail to set a framework that could differentiate between these two concepts, thus reinforcing the self-referentiality of the argument.

An analysis of how international law scholars address the misappropriation, abuse, or distortion of human rights reveals a marked reluctance to engage with the substantive question of what human rights are. Rather than articulating a clear account of what constitutes a good or faithful interpretation of human rights, scholars frequently rely on the flexible and open-ended character of human rights norms, focusing instead on identifying and cri-

58 Ibid, 209.
59 Ibid, 210.
60 Ibid, 213.

tiquing what they regard as 'bad' interpretations or misappropriations. The formal element that anchors this narrative into international law appears to be the very obscurity of human rights. The invocation of international legal frameworks is justified not by the precision or clarity of human rights norms, but rather by their inherent ambiguity. Scholars leverage this definitional uncertainty to argue that human rights are being abused or misappropriated, often assuming, without substantial elaboration, that there exists a shared, intuitive understanding of what human rights are, what they mean, and how they ought to be interpreted in good faith.

Little effort is made to substantively define the 'correct', 'genuine', or 'appropriate' interpretation of human rights. Instead, there is an implicit expectation that, as international lawyers, we are presumed to recognize the proper application of human rights norms without the need for explicit articulation. In this respect, human rights are treated as if they possess an autonomous and self-evident existence, detached from the processes of narrative construction and contestation. They are presumed to be unquestionable promoters of human progress rather than contingent, historically and politically situated constructs requiring substantive elaboration. Indeed, this obscurity of human rights is, in itself, a strategically useful characteristic, as it offers a wide scope of manoeuvre to any scholar seeking to narrate instances of misappropriation without having to define what constitutes a proper or genuine interpretation. Consequently, the narrative on the misappropriation of human rights becomes self-referential: it critiques distortions of human rights without clearly delineating the substantive boundaries of its own subject matter. In failing to define the contours of 'genuine' human rights, the narrative ultimately relies on an assumed, but unarticulated, consensus, thereby undermining its own analytical coherence.

4 The Temporal Element: Misappropriation as a Narrative of Regress

In constructing narratives, the narrator must select relevant facts and establish connections between them to form a coherent story. The organization of these facts depends on the narrator's judgment, making the ordering of events an inherently arbitrary exercise.[61] This does not mean that there is no logic in

61 Reinhart Koselleck stated that 'all chronologies are products of certain cultures and are, in this respect, relative' in Reinhart Koselleck, *The Practice of Conceptual History: Timing History, Spacing Concepts* (Stanford University Press 2002) 106.

the ordering of things but rather this arbitrariness draws attention to the multiplicity of ways in which things can be ordered. The periodization of history is not a purely mechanical exercise; rather, it actively contributes to the normative framework of the narrative being constructed. The temporal element of a narrative situates it within a specific timeframe and determines the chronological boundaries through which an argument is advanced. It is the narrator who selects the temporal framework of the analysis, including the key events that will mark the beginning and end of the period under examination. Historical facts, events, treaties, principles, theories, the practices of international law actors, doctrines, academic writings, decisions, and judgments all serve as raw materials available to the narrator. These elements must be organized through a process of narrativization to generate meaning and construct a coherent narrative. The manner in which the narrator establishes causal links between these facts, and the intended effect of this causal sequencing, ultimately determines the rhythm and structure of the narrative. It is this temporal element that will determine whether the story is a story of progress or regress or whether it adopts a non-linear timeline.

It is possible to investigate how scholars who argue that human rights are being misappropriated periodize relevant materials and situate their narrative in history. The narrative on the misappropriation of human rights portrays recent developments as a problem requiring urgent attention. De Búrca and Young argued that the misappropriation of human rights could be defined as the undoing of previous commitments.[62] They stated that human rights have been in decline since the 1993 World Conference on Human Rights in Vienna, which is depicted as a pivotal moment that established a consensus on the scope of human rights.[63] According to the scholars, since then due to the populist and right-wing policies human rights have been in constant decline. This portrayal of recent developments as a form of regress enables the authors to advance a vision of what the ideal future of human rights should entail. If the present trajectory represents a deviation or decline, it logically follows that corrective measures must be taken to restore the 'genuine' implementation of human rights. The narrative of regress thus allows the scholars not merely to diagnose a crisis but also to prescribe a normative path for the future development of human rights law. In that sense, the narrative on misappropriation serves a dual function: it identifies perceived distortions in the current practice of human rights while simultaneously delineating a preferred normative direction for the field. By framing the recent history of human rights as a story

62 De Búrca and Young (n 1) 207.
63 Ibid.

of decline, scholars create the discursive space necessary to advocate for a particular vision of the future of international human rights law.

Marks based her analysis on the idea that there is a backlash against human rights in conservative circles in the UK. She traced the genealogy of the word 'backlash' and stated that '[i]n mechanics a backlash is a jarring reaction or "striking back" within a mechanism. Likewise, in social and political life a backlash came to signify a striking back in the form of a strongly negative reaction against something which is deemed to have gained popularity, prominence, influence or power'.[64] She then turned to the implications of framing recent developments as a backlash against human rights and examined how some critics have launched a direct attack on human rights, accusing it of curtailing freedoms and betraying its foundational promises.[65] In a similar line, Alston argued that 'an increasingly diverse array of governments have all expressed a desire to push back against key pillars of the international human rights regime'.[66] After examining the challenges faced by the human rights movement because of the rise of populism, Alston then continued to offer some actions that can be adopted to counter these challenges. In parallel, Bilková stated that populists 'undermine the normative consensus which has emerged in the international scene over the past decades and sap the public trust in human rights'.[67] She argued that populist leaders are doing a significant disservice to the protection of human rights by advancing a selective understanding of human rights.

It can be stated that the narrative on the misappropriation of human rights is a narrative of regress. It evaluates the developments witnessed from the early 1990s until now as a decline. The periodization employed in the narrative on the misappropriation of human rights portrays the history of human rights as one of the major achievements of the twentieth century. It is undeniable that the post–Second World War era witnessed the adoption of numerous human rights treaties and the establishment of various human rights institutions. In that sense, the history of human rights can readily be told as a story of progress.[68] However, it is equally possible to emphasize the persistent challenges associated with the enforcement of human rights throughout this

64 Marks (n 19) 322.
65 Ibid, 323.
66 Alston (n 14) 3.
67 Bilková (n 35) 144.
68 On the idea of progress, see Thomas Skouteris, *The Notion of Progress in International Law Discourse* (TMC Asser Press 2010), Oliver Diggelmann, 'The Periodization of the History of International Law' in Bardo Fassbender and Anne Peters (eds), *The Oxford Handbook of the History of International Law* (OUP 2012) 999, Júlia Miklasová and others,

period. In other words, rather than a singular narrative of steady advancement, the history of human rights can also be read as a more heterogeneous account, encompassing both progress and setbacks. The misappropriation narrative constructs an image wherein the human rights system was in a far better state prior to the rise of populist governments. It casts recent years as a period of backlash, suggesting that the hard-won gains of the previous century are being eroded. This claim, however, is not self-evident. It remains unclear why the human rights system is assumed to have been in a superior condition before the advent of populist regimes. Given that the narrative of misappropriation does not clearly define what constitutes good or genuine appropriation, it becomes difficult to identify the parameters by which the current period is deemed worse than previous decades. The narrative of misappropriation presents the history of human rights as a linear and progressive trajectory that is now being disrupted by a period of regress. This account relies on a periodization that frames recent developments as an anomaly within an otherwise progressive trajectory. However, it is far from self-evident that the current backlash against human rights, driven by populist policies, stands in stark opposition to the broader and more complex historical development of human rights.

5 The Spatial Element: Misappropriation as a Narrative of Non-Western States

Every international law narrative will have an impact over a spatial dimension. International law discourses necessarily include a spatial dimension and define a certain space where the law will have an impact. When one constructs an international law narrative, it will not only discuss the legal content of that subject matter, the international actors involved or how it is situated in time, but it will inevitably comprise a spatial dimension to indicate where the law will take effect. The narrator will have to construct the space where the normativity produced by the narrative will compel international law actors to act in a certain way. In that sense, space is a narrative construct and will be imagined and created since it does not exist unless one wants to have an effect upon others through the narrative.[69] Nonetheless, the creation of the narra-

---

'Editorial: Progress and International Law: A Cursed Relationship' in 84 (2024) ZaöRV 785.

69 Robert David Sack, *Human Territoriality: Its Theory and History* (CUP 1986) 30.

tive space is not a neutral exercise.[70] This is why Henri Lefebvre opined that we should not only 'see' the space but also conceptualize what it represents.[71] Space does not only consist of a material existence but should rather be construed as an abstract concept that does not exist prior to the narrative. It does not only refer to a natural territory or a geography where the law discussed will be applied but it carries with it social, political, and legal references as well.

Reflecting on the spatial element of a narrative is important mainly for three reasons. First, the space that has been created by the narrator defines the territory that will be controlled by the narrative.[72] It will impose boundaries within which the narrative will have an impact, exercise power, and modify relations between actors. It will dictate how they should behave in a certain context by advancing a normative framework to be followed. Second, another way of exercising power through the spatial dimension becomes evident when one thinks about the way space has been used in a narrative in order to include and exclude certain actors.[73] Said differently, space determines the beneficiaries, members, and also outsiders of the narrative by drawing boundaries. Third, the spatial element of the narrative might be used to shift the reader's focus from the narrator to the space that is being discussed.[74] Highlighting how the space is regulated in a particular context can displace the emphasis from the narrator to the territory and remove the former's agency in the creation of the latter. In that regard, it can serve to tell an impersonal story which seems to depict the world from an external point of view.

There are various ways of reading the misappropriation of human rights discourses in order to unpack the space that it creates. One way of conceptualizing the space in these discourses is to analyse the states that these writings put under their radar. At a first glance, it is easy to spot that the attention in these writings is mostly concentrated on a dozen of states. Most of the time, the argument that authoritarian regimes are misinterpreting human rights and using them for their own interests is directed against non-Western states

70 Michel Foucault is a prominent name whose works on the production and exercise of power were closely linked to spatiality. He argued that 'the anxiety of our era has to do fundamentally with space, no doubt a great deal more than with time' in Michel Foucault (Jay Miskowiec tr), 'Of Other Spaces' (1986) 16 Diacritics 22, 23. See also Jeremy Crampton and Stuart Elden (eds), *Space, Knowledge and Power: Foucault and Geography* (Ashgate 2007).

71 Henri Lefebvre, *The Production of Space* (Blackwell 1991) 93–94.

72 Robert David Sack, *Human Territoriality: Its Theory and History* (Cambridge University Press 1986) 32.

73 Ibid, 32.

74 Ibid, 33.

such as Brazil,[75] India,[76] Russia,[77] Turkey,[78] and Eastern European states such as Poland and Hungary.[79] It can be stated that the misappropriation of human rights populism discourses are very much concerned with non-Western states where populist leaders allegedly misinterpret human rights in order to advance their political interests.[80] The focus is on how the leaders of these non-Western states do not grasp the importance of human rights and merely use it as an instrument in their discourse. It is argued that they misuse, abuse or misinterpret human rights in a way that benefits their populist policies. In other words, Western states seem to be immune to the misuse of human rights as they constitute only a marginal portion of the overall case studies.

The scholarship is abundant in discussing the European origins of the contemporary human rights law.[81] Scholars have discussed at length how our current human rights system has been very much inspired by the developments witnessed in European states. The emergence of the contemporary human rights law in the aftermath of the Second World War is often presented as a result of domestic developments in Western states. In that sense, it is striking that these Western states who have provided the essence of the current human rights system have managed to spare themselves from the criticism of scholars who have analysed the impact of populism on human rights. The selection of case studies demonstrates without much difficulty that the universalization of a Western understanding of human rights has not been very successful in every state. Russia, Turkey, Brazil, and India seem to represent the key states where politicians misuse the human rights movement. These discourses seem to argue that populist leaders are not capable or willing to understand the true meaning and significance of human rights. In that

75 Marta R De Assis Machado, 'Antiabortion Legal Mobilization in Brazil: Human Rights as a Field of Contention', International Journal of Constitutional Law, 21/1 (2023), 308–338.

76 Ahmed (n 52).

77 Kristina Stoeckl, 'Traditional Values, Family, Homeschooling: The Role of Russia and the Russian Orthodox Church in Transnational Moral Conservative Networks and Their Efforts at Reshaping Human Rights', International Journal of Constitutional Law, 21/1 (2023) 224–242.

78 Başak Çalı and Esra Demir-Gürsel, 'Continuity and Change in Human Rights Appropriation: The Case of Turkey', International Journal of Constitutional Law, 21/1 (2023) 266–284.

79 Zoltán Szente, 'The Myth of Populist Constitutionalism in Hungary and Poland: Populist or Authoritarian Constitutionalism?', International Journal of Constitutional Law, 21/1 (2023) 127–155.

80 Some exceptions include Marks (n 19), Mégret (n 22), Roth (n 46).

81 Makau Mutua, 'Savages, Victims, and Saviors: The Metaphor of Human Rights', Harvard International Law Journal, 42 (2001), 201, Upendra Baxi, 'Voices of Suffering and the Future of Human Rights', Transnational Law & Contemporary Problems, 8 (1998) 125.

sense, these populist leaders fail in capturing the essence of human rights. It is striking that whenever the US is taken as a case study, it is usually referred to as the 'Trump administration'. It seems that the US is only going through a phase which should not be equated to the state itself. Whereas, in all other cases, scholars do not shy away from referring to the states where populism seems to represent a general policy that can be equated to the state itself.

In the special issue where they analysed the misappropriation of human rights, the cases that De Búrca and Young chose included Russia, Turkey, Brazil, India, Uganda, Nigeria, Ghana, Zambia, Kenya, and the Trump administration. It is clear from these cases that Western European states are in a good state in the way they use or practise human rights. It seems it is only non-Western states, with the exception of the Trump administration from the West, that have a problem with the interpretation of human rights. De Búrca and Young argued that '[e]ven the mature and embedded European human rights institutions risk playing into the hands of human rights misappropriation, and providing cover for bad faith or highly illiberal uses'.[82] They very briefly evaluated the response of the European Court of Human Rights in applications against Turkey and stated that the doctrines developed by the Court were being misinterpreted by the Turkish government in a way that renders the Court complicit in the misappropriation of human rights.[83] De Búrca and Young's approach to the European human rights institutions emphasized their historically old pedigree and well-established character. These European institutions were not, however, the centre of attention in their analysis since none of these institutions or states are part of the several case studies that the contributors examined. The criticism against the European Court of Human Rights fell short of analysing the possible misappropriations of human rights by the Court itself, its conservative approach in some cases or its failure to tackle the human rights backlash. The Court is rather portrayed as the victim of its own success whose doctrines developed with very good intentions have been turned against it.

The way the question of misappropriation has been shaped as based on authoritarian and populist governments constitutes a perspective that does not allow to investigate the shortcomings of the human rights system in Western states. The Western examples mainly focus on short-term governments, such as the Trump administration, and do not form the main focus of the

82 De Búrca and Young (n 1) 220.

83 Ibid, 220.

misappropriation narrative.[84] This makes one question the neo-colonial undertones of this narrative which structures its main problematic in such a way that its mostly non-Western states that are put under a radar for their failings for the protection of human rights. In other words, the misappropriation narrative can be conducive to an examination that helps to turn a blind eye to the non-implementation of human rights in the Western world.

6 Concluding Remarks

This chapter has examined the construction of the misappropriation of human rights narrative in legal scholarship. It has focused on how misappropriation is framed as a legal problem, and how it uses time and space. In doing so, it has identified the narrativization elements that have been central in the construction of this narrative. This discourse analysis is not intended to suggest that the issue should be abandoned and that states should not be criticized for their interpretation of the human rights framework. Rather, the chapter has sought to interrogate the narrative that human rights are being systematically misappropriated by populist, right-wing, and exclusionary political actors, and to explore how such a narrative is constructed and mobilized within legal discourse. This can help to better diagnose how the use of international law serves particular purposes. The aim of the discourse analysis conducted in this chapter is not to invalidate, discredit, or disprove the narrative of misappropriation. Rather, it seeks to expose the narrativization elements employed by scholars in constructing this narrative and to examine how the order imposed by the narrators might be questioned. In this sense, the chapter does not assert that there is a correct or incorrect way of constructing an international law narrative, nor does it propose a better or more accurate interpretation of a possible human rights crisis.

When human rights law is conceptualized as a discourse of making arguments at the disposal of international law actors, this allows to take a broader perspective on several grounds. First, such an approach explains how problems, challenges, or crises are created in international legal scholarship. It demonstrates the various purposes that invoking the language of human rights may serve in a particular discourse. Second, it allows a genealogical mode of inquiry rather than one based on linear periodization that reinforces a dichotomy between progress and regress. Third, it enables to unpack how

84 Jayne Huckerby and Sarah Knuckey, 'Appropriation and the Rewriting of Rights', International Journal of Constitutional Law, 21/1 (2023) 243–265, Alston (n 14).

the space where the discourse will have an impact is created. Conceptualizing scholarly writings on misappropriation as a narrative allow to demonstrate that it is equally possible to frame problems in human rights law from a different angle. In that sense, it helps to analyse how legal discourses are created and operationalized for different purposes. The human rights system was in crisis, is in crisis, and will always be in crisis. It will always be instrumentalized, misappropriated, and abused. Rather than evaluating the good and bad uses of human rights, the chapter sought to analyse how the discourse is employed in practice, and what this reveals about the broader dynamics of worldmaking in international law.

Bibliography

Abbott, Porter (2002), *The Cambridge Introduction to Narrative* (Cambridge University Press).

Ahmed, Farrah (2023) 'Constitutional Parasitism, Camouflage, and Pretense: Shaping Citizenship through Subterfuge' *International Journal of Constitutional Law*, 21 (1), 285–307.

Alston, Philip (2017), 'The Populist Challenge to Human Rights', *Journal of Human Rights Practice*, 9 (1), 1–15.

Barthes, Roland (1967) 'Le Discours de l'Histoire' 6 Social Science Information 63.

Baxi, Upendra (1998), 'Voices of Suffering and the Future of Human Rights', *Transnational Law & Contemporary Problems*, 8, 125.

Bianchi, Andrea (2019) 'Epistemic Communities' in Jean d'Aspremont and Sahib Singh (eds), *Concepts for International Law: Contributions to Disciplinary Thought* (Edward Elgar).

Bianchi, Andrea (2012) 'Reflexive Butterfly Catching: Insights from a Situated Catcher' in Joost Pauwelyn, Ramses Wessel and Jan Wouters (eds), *Informal International Lawmaking* (OUP).

Charlesworth, Hilary (2002) 'International Law: A Discipline of Crisis', *The Modern Law Review*, 65/3, 377–392.

Crampton, Jeremy and Stuart Elden (eds) (2007), *Space, Knowledge and Power: Foucault and Geography* (Ashgate).

Çalı, Başak and Esra Demir-Gürsel (2023) 'Continuity and Change in Human Rights Appropriation: The Case of Turkey', *International Journal of Constitutional Law*, 21 (1), 266–284.

De Búrca, Graínne and Young, Katharine G (2023), 'The (Mis) Appropriation of Human Rights by the New Global Right: An Introduction to the Symposium', *International Journal of Constitutional Law*, 21 (1), 205–223.

De Búrca, Gráinne (2021), *Reframing Human Rights in a Turbulent Era* (Oxford University Press).

Derrida, Jacques (2016) *Of Grammatology* (Johns Hopkins University Press).

Diggelmann, Oliver (2012) 'The Periodization of the History of International Law' in Bardo Fassbender and Anne Peters (eds), *The Oxford Handbook of the History of International Law* (Oxford University Press), 999.

Drinóczi, Tímea and Agnieszka Bień-Kacała (2021) *Illiberal Constitutionalism in Poland and Hungary: The Deterioration of Democracy, Misuse of Human Rights and Abuse of the Rule of Law* (Routledge).

Fagan, Andrew (2019), 'The Gentrification of Human Rights', *Human Rights Quarterly*, 41 (2), 283–308.

Fagan, Andrew (2021), 'Human Rights in a Time of Populism: Challenges and Responses ed. by Gerald L. Neuman', *Human Rights Quarterly*, 43 (2), 416–421.

Ford, Jolyon (2023), *Human Rights and Populism* (Taylor & Francis).

Foucault, Michel (1981) 'Order of Discourse' in Robert Young (ed), *Untying the Text: A Post-Structuralist Reader* (Routledge).

Foucault, Michel (Jay Miskowiec tr) (1986) 'Of Other Spaces' 16 Diacritics 22.

Gewirtz, Paul (1996) 'Narrative and Rhetoric in the Law' in Peter Brooks and Paul Gewirtz (eds), *Law's Stories: Narrative and Rhetoric in the Law* (Yale University Press).

Ginsburg, Tom (2020) *Authoritarian International Law*, 114 American Journal of International Law, 221.

Koselleck, Reinhart (2002), *The Practice of Conceptual History: Timing History, Spacing Concepts* (Stanford University Press).

Hopgood, Stephen (2013), *The Endtimes of Human Rights* (Cornell University Press).

Huckerby, Jayne and Sarah Knuckey (2023) 'Appropriation and the Rewriting of Rights', *International Journal of Constitutional Law*, 21/1, 243–265.

Koskenniemi, Martti (2009), 'The Politics of International Law–20 Years Later', *European Journal of International Law*, 20 (1), 7–19.

Lefebvre, Henri (1991) *The Production of Space* (Blackwell).

Machado, Marta R De Assis (2023) 'Antiabortion Legal Mobilization in Brazil: Human Rights as a Field of Contention', *International Journal of Constitutional Law*, 21/1, 308–338.

Marks, Susan (2014), 'Backlash: The Undeclared War Against Human Rights', *European Human Rights Law Review*, 4, 319–327.

Mégret, Frédéric (2022), 'Human Rights Populism', *Humanity: An International Journal of Human Rights, Humanitarianism, and Development*, 13 (2), 240–259.

Miklasová, Júlia and others (2024) 'Editorial: Progress and International Law: A Cursed Relationship' in 84 ZaöRV, 785.

Moyn, Samuel (2018), *Not Enough: Human Rights in an Unequal World* (Harvard University Press).

Mutua, Makau (2001), 'Savages, Victims, and Saviors: The Metaphor of Human Rights', *Harvard International Law Journal*, 42, 201.

Neuman, Gerald (ed.) (2020), *Human Rights in a Time of Populism: Challenges and Responses* (Cambridge University Press).

Nijman, Janne E and Werner, Wouter G (2018), 'Populism and International Law: What Backlash and Which Rubicon?', *Netherlands Yearbook of International Law*, 49, 3–17.

Posner, Eric (2014), *The Twilight of Human Rights Law* (Oxford University Press).

Ricoeur, Paul (1988), *Time and Narrative* (University of Chicago Press).

Roth, Kenneth (2017), 'The Dangerous Rise of Populism: Global Attacks on Human Rights Values', *Journal of International Affairs* (Special 70th Anniversary Issue), 79–84.

Sack, Robert David (1986), *Human Territoriality: Its Theory and History* (CUP).

Skouteris, Thomas (2010) *The Notion of Progress in International Law Discourse* (TMC Asser Press).

Stoeckl, Kristina (2023), 'Traditional Values, Family, Homeschooling: The Role of Russia and the Russian Orthodox Church in Transnational Moral Conservative Networks and Their Efforts at Reshaping Human Rights', *International Journal of Constitutional Law*, 21 (1), 224–242.

Śledzińska-Simon, Anna (2020), 'Populists, Gender, and National Identity', *International Journal of Constitutional Law*, 18 (2), 447–454.

Szente, Zoltán (2023), 'The Myth of Populist Constitutionalism in Hungary and Poland: Populist or Authoritarian Constitutionalism?', *International Journal of Constitutional Law*, 21 (1), 127–155.

Vidmar, Jure (ed.) (2020), *European Populism and Human Rights* (Brill Nijhoff).

White, Hayden (2010), 'The Structure of Historical Narrative' in Hayden White, *The Fiction of Narrative: Essays on History, Literature, and Theory, 1957–2007* (Robert Doran ed, Johns Hopkins University Press).

White, Hayden (1980), 'The Value of Narrativity in the Representation of Reality' 7 Critical Inquiry, 5.

White, Hayden (1975), *Metahistory: The Historical Imagination in Nineteenth-Century Europe* (Johns Hopkins University Press).

CHAPTER 10

Misappropriation: Who Fills the Space? An Examination of Misappropriation in Euthanasia Cases

Eve Lister

1 Introduction

The misappropriation paradigm is designed to enable identifiers to spotlight misuses of human rights by fellow state or civil society actors (misappropriators) – thus protecting human rights from distortion (or, misappropriations). There is no single definition of misappropriation, although indicators have been proposed as a means to identify it. These are primarily: behaviour which (a) represents a departure from an "existing body ... of human rights law",[1] (b) has a "repressive ... exclusionary aim or effect",[2] (c) operates as dignity-reducing, rather than dignity-enhancing,[3] and (d) shows evidence of "intentional distortion or deliberate polarisation".[4] I would argue that the indicators are quasi-legal: dignity and repression are concepts with definitions in law and fact,[5] "aim ... (and) intent" lends a mens rea component familiar to lawyers; "effect" is reminiscent of causation.

Questions arise regarding the interplay between these broad indicators and how they function collectively, who has authorial control over them, the

1 Gráinne De Búrca and Katherine Young, 'The (Mis)Appropriation of Human Rights by the New Global Right: An Introduction to the Symposium (New York School of Law, Working Paper No 23-32, 2023) 8.

2 Başak Çalı and Esra Demir-Gürsel, 'Continuity and Change in Human Rights Appropriation: The Case of Turkey' (Hertie School, Universität zu Berlin 2023) Forthcoming in *ICON* (2023) as part of the symposium on "The (Mis)appropriation of Human Rights by the New Global Right" edited by Gráinne de Búrca and Katharine Young, 1.

3 De Burca and Young (n 1) 8.

4 Farah Ahmed, 'Constitutional Parasitism, Camouflage, and Pretense: Shaping Citizenship through Subterfuge' (2023) 21 *International Journal of Constitutional Law* 285, 287.

5 Da Rosa and William Torres Laureano, 'The Dialectic of Emancipation and Repression in International Human Rights Law' (Master's Thesis, University of Sussex 2016) <https://sussex.figshare.com/articles/thesis/The_dialectic_of_emancipation_and_repression_in_international_human_rights_law/23435210/1> accessed 15 April 2025.

behaviour that constitutes them, and the threshold at which they can be considered met.

Arguably, questions concerning the practical functionality of the misappropriation paradigm should be addressed within the indicators themselves. This would ensure that there are sufficient distinctions between a misappropriation in the quasi-legal sense as proposed by De Búrca and Young; and what I may term a misapplication (a poor, but not intentionally manipulative, use of rights), as well as a pure human rights breach.

The architects of misappropriation may argue that the paradigm is quasi-legal, and not doctrinal, therefore responses to these queries are inherently open-ended, perhaps as, given their quasi-legal character, assigning a fixed character to the indicators would be undesirable. However, scholars have demarked these indicators as "red flags which strengthen the probability"[6] of misappropriation and doing so clearly justifies further socio-legal scrutiny, as they do, by their purposive design, constitute the foundation of a misappropriation finding.

In unravelling the misappropriation indicators, I will expose their lack of settled normative content, arguing that the misappropriation paradigm is unduly broad in its current form.

The tension between the theoretical indicators and their practical realisation is an interesting one to unpick in the context of euthanasia cases, which are socially contentious and directly impact vulnerable communities.

Through analysis of euthanasia, and potential misappropriations of the right to life and human rights therein, I will draw attention to the visible symmetries between acceptable uses (in which there were no human rights violation) and perceived abuses (which I will examine as potential misappropriations using the indicator posited by the designers of the misappropriation concept), to argue that the indicators are not fit for purpose within the misappropriation framework.

I have chosen cases concerning euthanasia in which abuses of the right to life were found, and not found, to demonstrate that the indicators used for misappropriation can be perceived as arising depending upon the identifier, and they arise throughout in various cases without meaningful consistency, making the indicators an unsteady foundation upon which to find misappropriations.

It is important to note that the architects of the misappropriation framework present misappropriations as distinct from breaches of human rights. However, cases which recognise euthanasia as being in breach of human

6 De Burca and Young (n 1) 8.

rights law provide useful analogies, as, invariably, the misappropriation indicators remain at play therein, and the argumentative basis for illegality is often framed in similar substantive terms: in the sense that they breach fundamental first principles, such as dignity, as included within the indicators.

However, as I will demonstrate, findings of the misappropriation or non-misappropriation of rights do not turn on the presence or absence of these indicators. Rather, these indicators behave as open-textured norms; so, the actors involved in misappropriation claims can selectively sculpt and inject them with meaning. The cases have been chosen to reflect the plurality of the indicator(s), and misappropriation findings as a whole.

I have chosen euthanasia and the right to life as the object of the chapter because it offers an interesting prism through which to view misappropriation. Mugabi has characterised the right to life as being of paramount importance, as: "(a) global spectrum of human rights regimes has held (the right to life) … with greatest regard … the most important of all rights".[7] The primacy of this right makes it crucial for quasi-legal sanctions to interact with. Furthermore, the analysis in this chapter may subvert and mirror studies on the oft-recognised misappropriation of reproductive rights; the right to and sanctity of life, hierarchies of rights and principles, and infringement of autonomy are at play in euthanasia examples. As a central site of conflict, and subject to arguably widescale misappropriations as to its start and end,[8] the interactions between the right to life and the misappropriation paradigm are significant and should be studied from points of origin and end. This chapter examines the latter, though welcomes further analysis of the former.

I have fenced the scope of discussion to the lens of euthanasia only in this chapter for a few reasons. Firstly, euthanasia offers the kind of complex, emotive context in which human rights rhetoric can, and does, have a very significant role to play in readdressing power imbalances between claimants (Persons with Disabilities, PWDs) and lawmakers (who are often said to be paternalistic and exclusionary towards the former).

I choose it as a prism as an alternative to abortion (which exists in tension with the perceived start of the right to life): both for the constraints of time and based on polarity: euthanasia remains subject to greater criminality than

---

7 Ivan Mugabi, 'Right to Life Cases in the Jurisprudence of the European Court of Human Rights: A Critical Analysis' (2023) 1 *Kabale University* 1 [1].

8 Elizabeth Chloe Romanis, 'Is "Viability" Viable? Abortion, Conceptual Confusion and the Law in England and Wales and the United States' (2020) 7 *Journal of Law and the Biosciences lsaa059*, [59].

abortion;[9] and, euthanasia is more immediately urgent and fast-moving politically (certainly in the UK, where I live and work), and I would personally characterise it as more socio-legally fraught.[10]

The topic also offers an interesting foreground with which to examine the politics of misappropriation: it encompasses quite distinct socio-legal dimensions, worthy of its own analytical space. Whilst abortion discussions centre on balancing perceived interests (generally separated into the interests of the pregnant woman, and the foetus, the balance of which varies depending upon the point of gestation); euthanasia's ethical issues mirror the misappropriation indicators in many ways. For instance, dignity, repression, and exclusion are all concepts that PWDs verbalise in campaigns both for and against euthanasia, with wide interpretive bandwidth which is firmly rooted in rights rhetoric.

It is important to acknowledge that those affected by euthanasia decisions are often PWDs, and interpretations of the right to life in euthanasia cases ultimately concern the end of their lives. I do not live with physical disabilities, and therefore am not able to understand the nuances of living with disabilities, and the ways that viewpoints on assisted dying, and disability rights, shape the lived experiences of those who do. I am also conscious that PWDs' lives are often culturally shaped by the disabilities they live with, and the ableist world in which they live, which unfortunately is reflected within legal scholarship. PWDs' active participation and, therefore, their perspective, is often excluded from legal spaces and is either ignored entirely or treated with a distant paternalism. Though I have not been able to conduct empirical research with PWDs to learn from this lived testimony, the socio-legal approach I adopt in this chapter is useful because it illuminates shortcomings in indicators a-d and calls into question the potential scope for the misappropriation framework to reinforce biases, exclusion, and potential harm for PWDs. I have drawn upon existing data and accounts from PWDs in good faith, in the belief that their readings of dignity, repression, and autonomy are diverse, nuanced, and important within legal interpretivism. I do not present this work as the only, or the most significant, finding on the matter. Disability campaigners have long

---

9 Maria Silvestre, Iratxe Aristegui and Usue Beloki, 'Abortion and Euthanasia: Explanatory Factors of an Association in Thanatos. Analysis of the European Values Study' (2022) 4 *Frontiers in Political Science* <https://www.frontiersin.org/journals/political-science/articles/10.3389/fpos.2022.966711/full> accessed 17 June 2025.

10 Gordon Brown, 'MPs Have Personal Beliefs, but Also Solemn Duties: That's Why They Must Reject the Assisted Dying Bill This Week' (*The Guardian*, 16 June 2025) <https://www.theguardian.com/commentisfree/2025/jun/16/mps-assisted-dying-bill-law-palliative-care> accessed 14 June 2025.

vocalised their anger at exclusion from legislative decision-making,[11] and legal frameworks more broadly, despite the pivotal impact legislation around euthanasia has on them. This chapter explores the ways in which the misappropriation indicators could play into, and replicate, this pattern. Specifically, I will reveal how the complexity inherent to euthanasia cases exceeds the scope of misappropriation indicators a-d.

I argue that each designated misappropriation criteria lack a stable normative foundation by exploring widely varied depictions of it by scholars, PWDs, and judges through this chapter. I will adopt a chronological approach to mirror the misappropriation criteria.

As a basis, Section 2 will examine the purpose and utility of the misappropriation paradigm. In Section 3, I will frame the concept of euthanasia and end-of-life treatment for our purposes.

Next, in Section 4, the main section of this chapter, I will critique the first misappropriation requirement for a departure from a settled body of law in this context, presenting the wide jurisprudential variation surrounding the legality of euthanasia globally to call into question the presence of a settled body of law. In this section, I will also analyse potential responses to this argument, by critiquing the potential polarity in the meaning of settled, and examining the settled variation position. The settled variation position states that euthanasia cases are unsettled to the extent that there is consistently very wide jurisprudential variation, and the consistency of this variation renders it a settled body of law.

I will rebut this viewpoint, starting by critiquing settled in this framing as devoid of its natural meaning, and pointing out that it falls short of synonymous concepts of harmony, coherence, and unification. I will also argue that the concept of settled body of law when given its natural meaning would reasonably anticipate cohesive findings; and that the architects of the misappropriation concept therefore ought to re-examine the ontological assumptions underscoring settled law as the paradigm continues to develop and may clarify whether the requirement for settled is substantive or procedural.

I argue that interpreting wide jurisprudential variation, oscillating from complete lawfulness to complete lawlessness, as settled, thus constituting a body of law by its unsettlement frustrates the purpose of the misappropriation paradigm: which, in essence, was constructed to flag distortions, manipulations, or bad-faith readings of human rights.

---

11 A O'Grady and others, 'Disability, Social Exclusion, and the Consequential Experience of Justiciable Problems' (2004) 19(3) *Disability & Society* 235–252 <https://www.tandfonline.com/doi/full/10.1080/0968759042000204158> accessed 16 April 2025.

This section identifies that this area of law is not settled, but I will also challenge the assumption that euthanasia must therefore be excluded from the misappropriation paradigm on this basis. I would rather recommend that the indicators for misappropriation be refined: who and how they are defined in the course of the quasi-legal mechanism should be more consciously examined.

In this context, a lack of settled law to stray from could lead to a complete exclusion of euthanasia matters from the misappropriation framework, and some may perceive this as the best way forward, as these socially contentious issues can be politically and legally volatile.

However, the exclusion of euthanasia from the misappropriation paradigm creates tension between the purposive dimension of misappropriation and the precedent style of this indicator. It is important to note that distortions of rights rhetoric can and do still occur in socially contentious, therefore unsettled, socio-legal environments. Arguably, such manipulation, which is at the core of misappropriation, is perhaps more likely to occur due to the great sensitivity of the context.

Therefore, excluding these cases from the misappropriation paradigm risks leaving crucial human rights (in this case, the right to life) without the useful functionality of a quasi-legal mechanism to oversee its appropriate use and flag misuses. This also curtails misappropriation and may build a perception of it as only half-useful: and rather than as broad quasi-legal collective mechanism for rights enforcement, it may be seen as substantively without teeth.

I also argue that interpreting euthanasia law as settled sets up an opportunity to circumvent meaningful engagement with other misappropriation indicators: and prevents discussions and debates on what is dignity-enhancing, who decides this, and how a perceived threshold can be quantified. This could stimulate active participatory debate among PWDs in a euthanasia context: to circumnavigate this to avoid complex discussions based on a narrow interpretation of settled and departure is a missed opportunity. In this sense, it is precisely the variation within euthanasia cases that means they ought to be at least able to be ensnared by the misappropriation framework. I argue that variation in case matters is inherent in socially contentious subjects, as in euthanasia; and that this should not preclude them from the misappropriation framework.

I argue that it is not only much more interesting but also much more legally imaginative, to engage directly with the unsettled nature of jurisprudence surrounding euthanasia, as an inherent part of its socially contentious subject matter and engage PWDs as active participants in helping to scope findings of misappropriation in matters of euthanasia.

Having established the inconsistent body of law herein, I will examine uncertainty around further indicators of misappropriation in Section 5: using deductive analysis to unravel the requirement that decisions be "exclusionary or repressive in aim or effect".[12] I will argue that the question of how exclusionary or repressive a use is (in aim or effect) turns upon varied legal and ontological arguments which are inherently divided for socially contentious topics such as euthanasia, and thus raise complex policy and ontological questions. This section will include a critique of how some additional indicators, including dignity, are flagged by misappropriation creators within the euthanasia space, and who can flag and define them. In this section, I will reveal that some PWDs position these concepts in a way entirely distinct from their orthodox legal interpretation: and will call upon misappropriation authors to consider this diversity of viewpoints in their indicators. I posit that these indicators fall short due to the substantial variation across legal, philosophical, and socio-political interpretations of them; I will illustrate this variation by analysing jurisprudence, scholarship, and testimony from PWDs.

I will argue that euthanasia is innately polarising by the social contention which surrounds it. However, I will posit that this is typical for complex human rights issues, and the indicator fails to consider the broader context of power between the identifier finding the misappropriation, and the identified misappropriator. This indicator ultimately leaves questions behind. For instance, in the context of inherently polarising issues such as euthanasia, who is impacted by the polarity which constitutes misappropriation, and, in the context of sensitive PWD issues, who decides what is sufficiently polarising?

In the conclusion, I argue that, in the context of a socially contentious topic such as euthanasia, misappropriation indicators A-D are vulnerable to being injected with dominant cultural values. This may lead to distortions of these concepts as they pertain to the experiences and interests of PWDs, whose participation in the shaping of these norms is often marginalised and ignored, but who will be most directly impacted by euthanasia findings.

As a whole, this chapter aims to raise questions as to the wide scope of the indicators and their potentially negative impact on the rights of PWDs in the context of euthanasia.

---

12 De Burca and Young (n 1) [5].

2 Misappropriation: An Outline

I will now construct the misappropriation paradigm by analysing what it purports to do, and how, to foreground a subsequent analysis of its conceptual shortcomings. Recently, scholars and practitioners have made a concerted effort to catalogue perceived "misuses of human rights language",[13] as distinct from pure human rights breaches. The paradigm aims to taxonomise "attempts to make concerted, often illiberal legal change in the field of human rights";[14] and Indicators A-D cumulate to signpost to a misappropriation of rights. Scholars have explored misappropriations in India, Russia, Turkey, Brazil, the US, Nigeria, Uganda, and Ghana,[15] indicating that manipulations of human rights, as distinct from breaches of human rights, are endemic and widespread. Research differentiates misappropriations from rights breaches on the basis that they involve an actor "knowingly disguising, masking, (and) misdirecting attention from the true nature of its actions",[16] to "consciously promote a distinctive and distorted conception of human rights".[17] Importantly, none of the indicators require an individual human rights violation to have occurred for a misappropriation to be flagged: there is also no prescribed form, shape, or arena in which an act must occur to be categorised as such. The broad scope of the indicators, in this sense, provides the misappropriation concept with a wide scope and flexibility, which, arguably, represents the expansion of our understanding of the threats facing human rights. Human rights rhetoric is becoming increasingly right-wing.[18] Yet, until now, human rights scholarship has tended to leave the linguistic framing of rights somewhat unexamined, perhaps because of an assumption that research on the matter would be in the domain of political scientists. However, illuminating a contortion or manipulation of rights, rather than the outright abuse of them, enables practitioners to better understand the arterial network which nurtures subsequent, systemic human rights crises. By successfully cataloguing the manipulation of human rights concepts, which is designed to erode human rights values, lawyers will arguably be better placed to pre-empt and prevent

---

13 De Burca and Young (n 1) 1.

14 Ibid.

15 Ibid.

16 Ahmed (n 4) 285.

17 De Burca and Young (n 1) 4.

18 Leah Wilson, 'The Rise of "Right-Wing" Human Rights Rhetoric: A Palestinian & Israeli Case Study'. (The Social Practice of Human Rights, University of Dayton) 2023 73 <https://ecommons.udayton.edu/human_rights/2019/events/73/> accessed 19 October 2024.

the denigration of rights values. By focusing on rights-framing, the misappropriation paradigm contextualises human rights abuses as the outcome of a broader systematic campaign of rights contortion and acknowledges the reality that threats to rights begin long before an individual, actionable breach takes place. Scholarship has long critiqued the specific focus on singular breaches, arguing this has built a model that fails to achieve collective equality and dignity:[19] principles which are at the core of human rights.

The misappropriation paradigm seems to respond to this line of thought. Calı and Demir-Gürsel characterise misappropriations as specifically designed to harm vulnerable groups.[20] They involve powerful actors (misappropriators) distinguishing between supposed authentic and inauthentic[21] rights holders to exclude these inauthentic groups from rights protection, and to justify their ongoing marginalisation.[22] These authentic right holders are often white, heterosexual, and middle-aged, with conservative political views;[23] whilst inauthentic right holders are those who belong to an underrepresented group; non-white, LGBTQ, women, and/or political activists who have, or are presumed to have, progressive politics due to their sexuality or gender identity.24 Sanders argues that misappropriator(s) are typically "well-organised Conservative coalitions within lobbying, activist training, strategic litigation, and public awareness campaigns",[25] which use progressive framing to systematically "spoil rights norms".[26]

In 2021, the Report on the Commission on Inalienable Rights (under the Trump administration) called for a roll-back of rights on the basis that human rights in their current form were the result of "manipula(tion) [...] (and constituted) ominous new threats".[27] They argued that truly fundamental rights

19 Samuel Moyn, 'A Powerless Companion: Human Rights in the Age of Neoliberalism' (2015) 77 Law and Contemporary Problems 147.

20 Çalı and Demir-Gürsel (n 2).

21 Ahmed (n 4) [287].

22 Çalı and Demir-Gürsel (n 2) 2.

23 Ibid.

24 Amnesty International, 'India/ Egypt: Ongoing Human Rights Crisis in Both Countries Must Be Addressed' (Amnesty International, 26 January 2023) <https://www.amnesty.org/en/latest/news/2023/01/india-egypt-ongoing-human-rights-crisis-in-both-countries-must-be-addressed/> accessed 12 September 2023.

25 Rebecca Sanders, 'Norm Spoiling: Undermining the International Women's Rights Agenda' (2018) 94 International Affairs Journal 271, 273.

26 Ibid., 271.

27 Michael R Pompeo, '*Report of the Commission on Unalienable Rights*' (Office of Policy Planning, US Department of State 2021) Commission Report 4 https://2017-2021.state.

had been exaggerated beyond their purpose and natural meaning,[28] as set out in the "distinctive US Constitution",[29] and caused by "international institutions' expansion (and) the overuse (of) rights language".[30]

The report neatly encapsulates the hierarchy of rights and rights-holders inherent to misappropriation. It adopts a singular materialist approach, selectively confining the natural meaning of rights to those iterated in the US Constitution. This originalist reading effectively marries rights framing to "Conservative aims (and ends)".[31]

Doing so was a highly politicised choice made based on right-wing values: it reflects an intent to constrain the evolution of rights concepts to centuries-old iterations. This conservativism is a through line within the report; the freedoms of speech and religion of conservative actors are characterised as fundamental and inalienable,[32] whilst rights to equal treatment and non-discrimination of LGBTQIA people[33] amounted to undue over-expansion. Thus, the former were presented as worthy of protection; the latter rights were identified as threats to human rights because they represented an over-extension of "real" human rights principles, and thus needed to be stripped back.

Importantly, misappropriation is a dualistic process: there is an outward commitment to human rights, which helps misappropriators avoid geopolitical condemnation and confrontation.[34] This perceived rights enthusiasm helps construct a façade of value compliance, which, combined with regressive rights interpretation, distorts the normative character of rights principles over time.

As misappropriations of rights tend to target marginalised people as inauthentic rights-holders, the paradigm seeks to spotlight an imbalance of

---

gov/wp-content/uploads/2020/08/Report-of-the-Commission-on-Unalienable-Rights.pdf accessed 14 September 2023.

28 Ibid.

29 Ibid., 8.

30 Ibid., 6.

31 Jayne Huckerby and Sarah Knuckey, 'Appropriating Rights: Who Rewrites Rights and How? Instead of Blunt Rejection, the Global New Right Is Pursuing a Project of So-Called Rights Renewal' (Open Global Rights, 14 June 2023) <https://www.openglobalrights.org/appropriating-rights-who-rewrites-how/> accessed 5 October 2023.

32 Michael R Pompeo (n 27) 14.

33 Ari Shaw and others, 'Comment on the "Commission on Unalienable Rights"' (Williams Institute, UCLA School of Law, April 2020) 1 <https://williamsinstitute.law.ucla.edu/wp-content/uploads/Comment-CUR-Apr-2020.pdf> accessed 20 September 2023.

34 Aya Fujimura-Fanselow, Jayne Huckerby and Sarah Knuckey, 'An Exercise in Doublespeak: Pompeo's Flawed "Unalienable Rights" Commission' (Just Security, 29 July 2020) <https://www.justsecurity.org/71705/an-exercise-in-doublespeak-pompeos-flawed-unalienable-rights-commission/> accessed 10 October 2023.

power between the dominant misappropriator and the dominated rights-holder. It reminds us that rights can be fragmented swiftly and extensively, sometimes leading to complete reversal of the institutional protection the rights initially sought to ensure. The campaign to legalise abortion in the US was systematic and prolonged;[35] and yet reproductive rights went from being characterised by legal scholars as "relatively secure"[36] to being repealed[37] within just over a decade. Pro-life campaigners focused on the unborn child as the authentic rights-holder of the first right-to-life, a powerful semantic framework that has left women's reproductive rights in tatters.

Using rights framing to justify threats to human rights values can also make abuse of rights more challenging to detect; obscuring the intention or true values of an actor in the rights process, and, insofar as it works to successfully justify rights distortion, may become more widespread, leading to collective distortions of human rights norms, denigrating rights consciousness. This distortion of the meaning of rights serves to normalise rights abuses where they do occur[38] on a broader scale,[39] and helps lead to disenfranchisement with the rights framework which we see within scholarship[40] more broadly.[41]

I have foregrounded this chapter with this analysis of the rights landscape to recognise the good intentions of the misappropriation paradigm. I understand that a framework to catalogue, and thus attempt to safeguard, human rights concepts from manipulation in the face of complex, underhanded threats is necessary. Global concerns about the sluggishness and

---

35 Claire M Adkins, *The Impact of Roe v. Wade (1973) on the American Abortion Rights Movement* (Senior Honours Project, James Madison University) [2017] 6.

36 Carol Sanger, 'Decisional Dignity: Teenage Abortion, Bypass Hearings, and the Misuse of Law' (2009) 18 Colum. J Gender & L 409, 410.

37 Nicolas Avril, 'As Abortion Rights Come under Attack Globally, How Do We Provide Women with Access to Vital Information about Their Reproductive Choices?' *Action for Global Health* (13 December 2022) <https://actionforglobalhealth.org.uk/as-abortion-rights-come-under-attack-globally-how-do-we-provide-women-with-access-to-vital-information-about-their-reproductive-choices/#:~:text=Women%20and%20girls'%20reproductive%20rights,or%20moderately%20restrictive%20abortion%20laws*> accessed 7 October 2023.

38 Lisa Schlein, 'UN: Human Rights Defenders Under Attack in Guatemala' *VOA News* (26 May 2019) <https://www.voanews.com/a/human-rights-defenders-under-attack-in-guatemala/4932963.html> accessed 12 October 2023.

39 Olivia Beavers, 'National Security Experts Warn of Rise in Authoritarianism' *The Hill* (26 February 2019) <https://thehill.com/policy/national-security/431646-national-security-experts-warn-of-rise-in-authoritarianism-efforts/> accessed 9 October 2023.

40 Such as in Moyn (n 19).

41 P O'Connell, 'On Reconciling Irreconcilables: Neo-Liberal Globalisation and Human Rights' (2007) 7 Human Rights Law Review, 483.

inaccessibility of human rights courts also enhance the perceived utility of a quasi-legal paradigm. The concept of misappropriations is useful: this can be seen in the democratic, collective critique of pathological misuses of rights in the Commission on Unalienable Rights Report,[42] in which a wide range of legal scholars and practitioners publicly challenged President Trump's iteration of human rights as a "reworking of the human rights canon".[43] Significantly here is the term "reworking": it is emblematic of the manipulation component central to misappropriation and distinguishes it from a breach of human rights. Scholarly engagement with this deliberate manipulation of rights in the report arguably led to the subsequent (and unequivocal) disavowal of the reporting Commission by the Biden administration.[44]

However, given the emotionally charged scenarios in which misappropriations are identified, and the politically punitive consequences of them, the indicators used to do so must have a firm normative foundation. If the open-textured, plural nature of the current indicators is not acknowledged and channelled, there is a risk of gap-filling by identifiers which may further entrench majoritarian cultural discourse as to the correct or right use of human rights: the classical concern of the tyranny of the majority which rights purport to safeguard against.[45] Actors which tend to adopt a critical view of human rights institutionalisation, perhaps existing at the fringes of the orthodox human rights narrative at-scale, may be more vulnerable to being excluded from the norm-construction of misappropriation.

To foreground my argument that misappropriation indicators lack settled normative content, I will now unpick the relevant law surrounding the right to life and euthanasia.

---

42 Kenneth Roth, 'Pompeo's Commission on Unalienable Rights Will Endanger Everyone's Human Rights' *Human Rights Watch* (27 August 2020) <https://www.hrw.org/news/2020/08/27/pompeos-commission-unalienable-rights-will-endanger-everyones-human-rights> accessed 25 September 2023.

43 Jayne Huckerby and Sarah Knuckey, 'Appropriation and the Rewriting of Human Rights' (2023) 21 Int J Const L 243, 244.

44 The White House, 'Remarks by President Biden and First Lady Jill Biden at the 2023 Human Rights Campaign National Dinner' (15 October 2023) <https://www.whitehouse.gov/briefing-room/speeches-remarks/2023/10/15/remarks-by-president-biden-and-first-lady-jill-biden-at-the-2023-human-rights-campaign-national-dinner/> accessed 7 November 2023.

45 Nick Henneberry, 'Democracy Requires the Limitation of the Rule of the Majority' (2007) 13 UCL Jurisprud L 255.

3 The Right to Life and Euthanasia

It is clear that the right to life is of paramount importance.[46] It is enshrined in Article 6 of the International Covenant on Civil and Political Rights, which states that "every human being has the inherent right to life [and] no one shall be arbitrarily deprived of his life".[47] As a "basic value of democratic societies",[48] there are no derogations to the right.[49] It is widely depicted as highest in a rights hierarchy, being "fundamental and supreme".[50] However, despite being characterised as "the first right",[51] in practice, the right to life is arguably unpredictable in scope,[52] especially temporally; the point at which a right to life ends is significant for the legality of euthanasia, and this question remains subject to debate.

To preface, in using the term euthanasia, I am adopting Manzione's definition of the concept as "broadly encompass(ing) all methods of ending one's life sooner than nature would ... whether by the patient himself, or a friend, spouse, child, or health care practitioner ... the individual requesting death is a person undergoing medical treatment for a life-ending disease and not a person considering death (suicide) due to mental illness".[53] I may also use the terms passive, active, voluntary, and involuntary euthanasia which were influenced by Manzione's modifying terms analysis. Voluntary euthanasia[54] involves an act that ends life being performed by another to end the life of Actor B, with Actor B's immediate consent (often at their request). Conversely, involuntary euthanasia involves an act that ends life being performed without the consent of Actor B (where they are incapacitated, so consent cannot be retrieved).

---

46 *McCann v UK* [1995] 18984/9, 37 (European Court of Human Rights).

47 Art 6, International Covenant on Civil and Political Rights, GA Res 2200A https://www.ohchr.org/en/instruments-mechanisms/instruments/international-covenant-civil-and-political-rights accessed 23 October 2025.

48 Ibid., para 147.

49 Douwe Korff, 'The Right to Life: A Guide to the Implementation of Article 2 of the European Convention on Human Rights' (Council of Europe, Human Rights Handbook No. 8, 2006) <https://ssrn.com/abstract=1288555> accessed 21 August 2023.

50 Claire de La Hougue and Gregor Puppinck, 'Assisted Suicide under the ECHR' (2014) 18 IJHR 735, 745.

51 Ibid.

52 Chiara Cosentino, 'Safe and Legal Abortion: An Emerging Human Right? The Long-Lasting Dispute with State Sovereignty in ECHR Jurisprudence' (2015) 15 HRLR 569, 572.

53 Lara L Manzione, 'Is There a Right to Die?: A Comparative Study of Three Societies (Australia, Netherlands, United States)' (2002) 30 Golden Gate University School of Law 443, 443.

54 Ibid., 445.

Passive euthanasia[55] or a withdrawal of treatment refers to withholding or omitting treatment or action to intentionally let Actor B die, and active euthanasia[56] refers to the deliberate act of a physician to end Actor B's life (such as by administering drugs). The distinction between passive and active euthanasia is contentious across scholarship and law: to the extent that eminent scholarship has presented its legality as continuing to hang in the balance.[57] Indeed, the broad-strokes distinctions made between subcategories of euthanasia also remain contentious, and their descriptions vary from source to source: one scholar categorises the sub-types as a series of "euphemism(s)".[58] This certainly creates an unsettled backdrop, which perhaps sets up theoretical tension with the requirement for a settled body of law from which to depart. In light of this contention, I will use euthanasia as an umbrella term to refer to ending another's life throughout this chapter.

There is evident tension between euthanasia and the human right to life. Wake and Gondarra have argued that the right to life was founded on the principle of the "sanctity of life ...[59] as a consequence, human life cannot be deliberately taken".[60]

According to fundamental first principles as iterated by Locke,[61] the right to life is inalienable.[62] This specific, loaded wording harks back to Thomas Jefferson's framing of the rights of man,[63] and reinforces a view that the right to life is "unable to be given ... or taken away",[64] despite what some scholars view as attempts to do so through euthanasia.[65]

The inalienability of the right to life is contentious, particularly in the sense of how it functions in light of conflicts with other rights and legal practices:[66]

---

55 Ibid.

56 Ibid., 446.

57 Hazel Biggs, 'Euthanasia and Death with Dignity: Still Poised on the Fulcrum of Homicide' (1996) 1 Criminal Law Review 878, 879.

58 Heather Lardy, 'Euthanasia and Euphemism' (1997) 1 Edinburgh Law Review 227.

59 Wake and Gondarra vs Northern Territory of Australia and Asche (Administrator of the Northern Territory) [1996] NTSCFC 56, 42 [7(a)] (Angel J).

60 Ibid.

61 Gary D Glenn, 'Inalienable Rights and Locke's Argument for Limited Government: Political Implications of a Right to Suicide' (1984) 46 Journal of Politics 80, 80.

62 Joel Feinberg, 'Voluntary Euthanasia and the Inalienable Right to Life' (1978) 7(2) Philosophy and Public Affairs 93.

63 Ibid.

64 Ibid., 93.

65 Ibid.

66 John O'Manique, 'Universal and Inalienable Rights: A Search for Foundations' (1990) 12 HRQ 465.

such as how the persisting (if decreasing) state practice of capital punishment can be reconciled with it.

However, I would argue that the fundamentality of the right to life is baked into the structure of the right itself: it is the only right without any derogations in international human rights treaties; and as such, the state cannot "override, impair or detract from" it.[67] Its hierarchical primacy is clear in the right to life's placement in conventions more broadly, which has led to a perception of it as the "first"[68] right from which all subsequent human rights flow.

On the basis that the right to life is inalienable, it could be said that the unlawfulness of euthanasia naturally follows.[69] Scholars and campaigners against euthanasia have often stated that it is both immoral and unlawful primarily by virtue of its direct and inherent incompatibility with the right to life.[70] From this perspective, by directly causing life to end, euthanasia frustrates the very essence of the right to life.

Yet, PWDs who campaign for the legalisation of euthanasia often do so using a rights framework; they interpret the right to life as the right to a dignified life,[71] therefore accompanied by a right to non-interference where an individual wishes to end an undignified life.[72] Campaigners also invoke principles of self-determination and consent;[73] the right of consenting adults to make autonomous choices,[74] and have argued that the inaccessibility of euthanasia violates the fundamental right to respect for private and family life.[75] The success of these legal arguments aside, they reveal tensions within the concept of the right to life, and between it and other human rights principles: tensions and polarity which create scope for misinterpretations, or misappropriations, of rights.

67 Ibid., 43.

68 Gregor Puppinck and Claire de La Hougue, 'The Right to Assisted Suicide in the Case Law of the European Court of Human Rights' [2014] 18(7–8) The International Journal of Human Rights 735, 745.

69 Subhash Chandra Singh, 'Euthanasia and Assisted Suicide: Revisiting the Sanctity of Life Principle' (2012) 54 Journal of the Indian Law Institute 196.

70 Lord Goff, 'Last Rights: Euthanasia, the Sanctity of Life, and the Law in the Netherlands and the Northern Territory of Australia' (1998) 47 Int & Comp L Q 362.

71 *Sanles Sanles v Spain (Decision)* [2000] ECtHR (app no 22151/21).

72 Ibid., para 5.

73 *Daniel Karsai v Hungary* App no 32312/23 (ECtHR, 20 March 2024).

74 Wilson J, 'Is Respect for Autonomy Defensible?' (2007) J Med Ethics 33 353.

75 *Koch v Germany (n 87)* 2.

4 A "Settled" Body of Law

On this basis, I will now explore indicator a: the requirement for a departure from a settled body of law to constitute a misappropriation. Firstly, the concept of "a departure from a settled body of law"[76] can be read in several ways. Perhaps, this requires a settled body of law as a pre-requisite for a 'departure', thus ensnaring decisions that are atypical within their context as misappropriations. In this sense, where there is no 'settlement' in the law, there is a 'failure' to meet a threshold inherent to misappropriation, and there can be no 'departure' based on the palpable unsettlement of euthanasia in the socio-legal landscape. This may be seen as a kind of 'exclusionary' failure, and perhaps indicates that euthanasia cases would be excluded from the misappropriation paradigm based on the varied jurisprudence on the matter globally. Alternatively, perhaps we can view 'departure' as a twin of 'settled': where the legality of euthanasia is regularly 'departed' from across jurisdictions, it is consistent enough to be deemed 'settled'. In this framing, the 'body of law' is settled by its variation, and there is no scope for the misappropriation framework to be engaged.

In both of these prior instances, euthanasia would be deemed incompatible with the misappropriation framework, though for antithetical reasons.

The interpretive variation of 'settled' and 'departure' builds an interesting tension between misappropriation and euthanasia. I will examine the settled body of law question from two dimensions: firstly, examining whether it can be said that the body of euthanasia law is 'settled' (either as to the legality of euthanasia being consistent across jurisdictions, or as to the level of jurisprudential variation being consistent), and then examining whether an 'unsettled' body of law means that there can be no 'departure from' it, therefore failing a central misappropriation indicator and potentially excluding euthanasia cases from the misappropriation framework in its entirety. I will also critique the negative impacts of the latter.

Firstly, perhaps the requirement for a 'settled body of law' requires cohesion in law internationally: though, there are great variations in legal systems by-design, so this is unlikely. Alternatively, perhaps settlement can be met by having a body of cohesive law within a nation, so that a resident of a nation is able to foresee whether certain conduct would constitute a breach. I will argue that, as there are variations in the legality of euthanasia, the scope of the 'right to life' is unsettled from both perspectives, and the resulting body of law which it creates is too variable within and across states to be deemed settled.

76 De Burca and Young (n 1).

As to the first interpretation of settled: international cohesion around socially contentious topics is neither reasonable, likely, nor useful, particularly in a human rights framework. Legg has argued that in contentious case matters the margin of appreciation doctrine is utilised, because cultural, religious, and social values differ so broadly across states, the doctrine permits (and thus encourages) wide variation across State practice,[77] insofar as a finding fits the given State in which it is made. Normative variations across states in these instances imply that not only is a human rights court unlikely to intervene and alter national court findings, but the court must not do so as they are "legally required to exercise a degree of restraint in its review of Convention compliance".[78] This creates a culture of deference in which courts will offer a "subsidiarity in their human rights jurisprudence";[79] and it erodes a substantive, natural meaning of a settled body of law. Perhaps it can be argued that the settled character of the law lies in the collective expectation of procedural and substantive deference to national courts in interpreting the right to life. From this perspective, perhaps euthanasia cases are settled, in a sense.

However, it is reasonable to assume that the architects of the misappropriation paradigm did not intend for its indicators to be purely procedural in character, based on the expansive approach taken in their shaping of the paradigm to date. De Búrca and Young depict the framework as intending to "identify intersecting moves ... to reject equality ... distort ... rights ... across different sites, strategies, and actors".[80] Whilst the indicators are currently tentative and developing, it would be antithetical to the aim of spotlighting "the reversal... distortion ... or undo(ing) of previous human rights developments",[81] for the paradigm's applicability to close upon a sense of precedent from a set of developments. As the misappropriation concept develops, observations of it occurring over the long term do, too: and it becomes more self-binding for findings of misappropriation to hold on the basis that they depart from established human rights use. Arguably, misappropriations, and how they use and distort human rights, have developed over the years. One example is the US invasion of Iraq: De Búrca and Young's positions are that "the discourse of

---

77 Andrew Legg, *The Margin of Appreciation in International Human Rights Law: Deference and Proportionality* (Online Edition, Oxford Academic Press 2012) 7.

78 *SAS v France* (2014) ECHR 43835/11, para 154.

79 Andreas Follesdal and Nino Tsereteli, 'The Margin of Appreciation in Europe and Beyond' (2016) 20 The IJHR 1055, 1055.

80 De Burca and Young (n 1) 17.

81 De Burca and Young (n 1) 2.

human rights was instrumentalised for war mongering".[82] Insofar as this distortion of law has occurred in the past, perhaps future, similar uses of it will be seen as harmonious and cohesive, also falling shy of the requirement that they depart from a settled body of law.

However, even if we assume that deference to states through the margin of appreciation is settled, there is arguably still uncertainty within the degree of deference posited in euthanasia cases. Some cases, such as *Pretty v UK*,[83] arguably present the margin of appreciation as functioning as pure deference to national court findings and preferences in euthanasia cases. Therein, the ECHR emphasised that if a State *were* to recognise a right to die (whether in the form of active or passive euthanasia) doing so would not violate the right to life insofar as national courts justified this decision.[84] However, in other cases, the ECHR has stated that there must be a (national) "legal framework in place to regulate … decisions taken … with *sufficient precision*",[85] implying that there is a normative threshold against which the lawfulness of euthanasia may be measured, thus diluting the degree of deference applied. Therefore, states are required to "precisely regulate the decision-making process"[86] behind their findings on euthanasia (whether it is to legalise voluntary, involuntary, active, or passive euthanasia, or criminalising some or all of these subcategories).[87] Therefore, even in a legal context in which state deference is a settled matter, a degree of uncertainty remains in the degree of this deference, as case law implies it is qualified to an unclear extent. This arguably undermines the first potential interpretation of a settled body of law, as being met based on consistent variation. Arguably even where variation is anticipated, its degree remains unsettled.

Nations do adopt very different approaches to euthanasia and the right to life. In *Pretty v UK*,[88] the ECHR held that Article 2 does not encompass a right to die "whether at the hands of a third person in the form of assisted suicide, or with the assistance of a public authority",[89] in the form of passive euthanasia. This is an interesting framing. On the one hand, euthanasia is not per se a violation of the right to life, but nor is it encapsulated within the right itself,

---

82 Stephen Kinzer, 'Overthrow: America's century of regime change from Hawaii to Iraq' (2006) 45.

83 *Pretty v United Kingdom (Chamber, App no 2346/02)* (2002) 35 EHRR 1.

84 Ibid.

85 *Lambert v France* (Grand Chamber, App no 46043/14 [2015], ECHR 545, [143].

86 Ibid.

87 *Koch v Germany* (Chamber, App no 497/09) (2012) ECHR 1350.

88 *Pretty v United Kingdom* (n 83) [40].

89 *Pretty v United Kingdom* (n 83) [65].

thus legal euthanasia is not necessarily safeguarded. In this finding, euthanasia sits in a liminal space, neither inherently permitted nor inherently outlawed as a general principle.

Furthermore, in *Haas v Switzerland*,[90] state refusal to provide active euthanasia did not contravene the right to life; giving weight to the reasoning in *Pretty* that the right to life did not encompass a "diametrically opposing right to death".[91] It was also held that a refusal to allow euthanasia did not violate the applicants' dignity or autonomy.[92] However, neither finding was absolute; nor can the law therein be considered settled.

Whilst acknowledging the absence of a diametric right to die, judges in *Pretty* "refused to exclude the fact that ... preventing the applicant from ... exercising her choice to end an undignified life ... interfered with her right to privacy and family life"[93] – which implies that principles of autonomy and competing rights interests exist in tension with the right to life in euthanasia. Euthanasia cases arguably present a more complex factual and legal matrix than the requirement of settled law can reflect. From this perspective, uncertainties continue within each case. This is because tensions are inherent to euthanasia: competing interests, suffering, harm, and rights interplay.

There are other examples in which the law is unsettled within individual nations.

In 1995, active voluntary euthanasia was legalised under certain criteria in the Northern Territory of Australia,[94] but the act was repealed nine months after it came into effect.[95] This was a legislative reaction to the President of the Australian Medical Association seeking a Supreme Court judgement because legalising euthanasia violated the inalienable right to life and was consequentially invalid.[96] In this instance, even individual state entities are in tension.

The variation within euthanasia reflects deep contestation surrounding it, which can result in disparities that present as arbitrary and unpredictable. In South Africa, only voluntary passive euthanasia is practically permitted,[97] whilst in the Netherlands, legislation granted immunity to doctors practicing

90 *Haas v Switzerland* (Chambers, App no 31322/07) (2011) ECHR 242.
91 *Pretty v United Kingdom* (n 83).
92 *Haas v Switzerland* (n 90).
93 Ibid.
94 Antoon A Leenaars, 'Suicide, Assisted Suicide and Euthanasia: International Perspectives' (2001) 18 Irish Journal of Psychological Medicine 33, 35.
95 Ibid.
96 Wake and Gondarra vs Northern Territory of Australia and Asche (Administrator of the Northern Territory) (n 59) [5] (Martin CJ, Mildren J).
97 Todd Skinner, *Decriminalising Voluntary Active Euthanasia through the Recognition of Fundamental Human Tights: A Comparison of South Africa and Foreign Jurisdictions*

(initially passive) euthanasia almost 30 years ago,[98] which was later extended to active assisted suicide.[99] Disparities in euthanasia policy even persist on a domestic level. In the US: Oregon, California, Vermont, Washington, Montana, Columbia, and Colorado all legally recognise assisted suicide in legislation,[100] whilst several states criminalise the practice outright. Though federal systems accommodate variation in law, diametric trends that veer between custodial sentences for euthanasia[101] to deliberate, thoughtful frameworks for the systematic provision of life-ending treatment[102] in close cultural and temporal proximity are a stark example of the contestations at play.

Moreover, there are broader reasons that a finding of a body of settled law based on procedural deference to states is problematic in effect as well as in theory, as it may exclude meaningful application of the misappropriation concept to euthanasia cases entirely.

Whilst it is important to note that designers of misappropriation have not specified the primacy of any one criterion over another and that the indicators represent general proposals for misappropriation findings, the indicators do currently constitute our indicative framework through which we may identify a misappropriation.

Furthermore, the departure from a settled body of law calls upon a concept of precedent, and, if there is no settled body of law, euthanasia may fail at the first hurdle in a misappropriation framework.

In the context of a quasi-legal framework, likely to operate in fast, reactive, politically sensitive environments: events which have led to reduction of dignity, excluded people, and been repressive may be excluded from misappropriation purely on the basis that euthanasia law is inherently contentious.

When introducing this chapter, I laid out the utility of the misappropriation concept, on the basis that it constitutes an interesting quasi-legal framework that could have a meaningful impact on the collective policing of rights dis-

(University of Pretoria 2021) 9 <https://repository.up.ac.za/bitstream/handle/2263/84100/Skinner_Decriminalising_2021.pdf?sequence=3> accessed 21 October 2023.

98 GK Kimsma, 'Death by Request in The Netherlands: Facts, the Legal Context and Effects on Physicians, Patients and Families' (2010) *Medicine, Health, Care and Philosophy* 355, 356.

99 Ibid.

100 Roger Collier, 'Assisted Death Gaining Acceptance in US' (2017) 189 Canadian Medical Association Journal 118.

101 Anna Betts, 'US Woman Sentenced to a Year in Prison for Shooting Terminally Ill Husband' *The Guardian* (3 March 2025) <https://www.theguardian.com/us-news/2025/mar/03/florida-prison-sentence-killing-ill-husband> accessed 16 April 2025.

102 Jonathan S Cohen and others, 'Attitudes toward Assisted Suicide and Euthanasia among Physicians in Washington State' (1994) 331 *New England Journal of Medicine* 89.

tortion. It would be undesirable and arbitrary, for euthanasia, as a socially significant, sensitive human rights issue, to be excluded from a collective mechanism designed to safeguard against the distortion of human rights.

Indeed, the architects of this quasi-legal mechanism did not exclude the right to life from its remit, nor did they exclude any specific right as external to it. Instead, misappropriation authors have presented the framework expansively, emphasising that, in essence, it purports to flag up manipulations of rights. This purpose is contradicted by the potential for its indicator to potentially disqualify euthanasia cases from its remit, indicating a chasm between the essence of misappropriation, and its quasi-legal indicators.

Moreover, distortion and manipulation of rights rhetoric can and does still occur in characteristically contentious legal realms, including euthanasia, and could occur in the pursuit of granting or disallowing euthanasia.

If we consider the classically deserving rights holder in a misappropriation: they are often religious, politically conservative, heterosexual, and white; historically, PWDs have rarely been empowered as authors or owners of rights, rather as rights recipients in a paternalistic framing. It is not uncommon to see religious organisations campaign against euthanasia by using religious imagery and verbiage in campaigns to proclaim the "sanctity of … and right to… life"; framing euthanasia as "turn(ing) doctors into killers …" and nurses with "blood on their hands"; and presenting lawmakers advocating for euthanasia as "speaking for death":[103] it can be hard to see where the need for a socially settled consensus is relevant. The loaded language parallels many of the already recognised misappropriations echoed by the Trump administration, in which then Secretary of State Pompeo states: "Gross violations continue throughout the world … sometimes even in the name of human rights." This perhaps implies that, in analysing the lawfulness of euthanasia in any given case, related human rights principles, including dignity, autonomy, harm, and loss (which turn upon facts as well as law) would play significant roles in a finding of a breach or a misappropriation. There is a parallel to be drawn to the indicators: context clues of the impacts upon dignity, how repressive and polarising a finding is may offer interesting measurements of the contention of a decision, but, if a decision does represent a distortion of the kind the misappropriation architects sought to shine a light on, it is not conceptually justifiable that that scenario be excused from the paradigm due to the law in the area being very varied. I also point to these parallels in language to ask

103 Alexandra Teng, 'Don't Turn Doctors into Killers – Stand against Assisted Suicide' *Christian Concern* (1 May 2024) <https://christianconcern.com/news/dont-turn-doctors-into-killers-stand-against-assisted-suicide/> accessed 17 June 2025.

whether cohesion in policy is so significant in a broader context of distorting rhetoric, which has the potential to harm and exclude PWDs from a fundamental action we are all otherwise free to do (end our lives). Perhaps, if our instinct regarding the distinction between an anti-euthanasia example and Pompeo's misappropriation is that whether the campaign is made in good faith is determinative, then the requirement for a departure from a cohesive body of law seems less relevant than it has been posited to be.

In this section, I presented the diversity across legal findings on euthanasia (both vertically and horizontally, across and within nations). I have also critiqued the assumptions within indicator A (a departure of a body of settled law). I argued that, if we view euthanasia case law as inherently unsettled, thus excluding it from the misappropriation paradigm, we are unnecessarily confining the utility of misappropriation. I also argued that, alternatively, viewing euthanasia cases as settled in the fact that there is huge jurisprudential variation also excludes euthanasia from the misappropriation paradigm. I argued that this artificially excludes euthanasia, as an evolving, socially contentious topic, from receiving the same quasi-legal scrutiny, although distortion and manipulation of rights can still occur in these instances. I argued that this exclusionary impact is undesirable and contradicts the essence of misappropriation (to encapsulate distortion of rights). This section has unravelled the first indicator, arguing that the requirement for a departure from a settled body of law may be interpreted diversely, but, as it can have an artificially exclusionary impact on euthanasia cases (despite whether there is tangible distortion or rights manipulation at play), purely on the basis that this area of law is contentious.

On this basis, this indicator must be reformed. The remaining part of this chapter will examine subsequent indicators.

5 Dignity, Exclusion, and Polarisation

In this last part of the chapter, I will briefly unpick the broad scope, thus vacuous character, of associated indicators: mainly dignity, but also, briefly, exclusion and repression as well as polarisation.

This section intends to question the presumed substance of these concepts as they interrelate. It further supports the overall unsettled character of the law in this area, pointing to the tensions at play within misappropriation as a quasi-legal mechanism. According to its proponents, misappropriations are uses of human rights law which have an (b) exclusionary and repressive aim or effect, (c) are dignity-reducing rather than dignity-enhancing and are (d) intentionally polarising.

To position my analysis, I will start by acknowledging the interrelations between these criteria. They are descriptive and seem to speak to and feed into one another in this framework. In constructing the paradigm, Young and De Burca depicted subsequent criteria from a recognised pattern of uses of rights which were "anti-pluralist in character",[104] in which "the repress(ion) and exclusion of individuals ... (came alongside) consolidating authority and avoiding accountability",[105] inferring a correlation between several coalescing behaviours to amount to a misappropriation.

In so doing, I will lay out the disparities in the meaning of these indicator terms. For De Búrca and Young, the given meaning assigned to them is likely different than the bioethics and activist frameworks often presented by PWDs and campaigners for and against euthanasia. This aims to demonstrate the complexities and tensions between these indicators and euthanasia instances, and also to emphasise that these criteria are exceedingly imprecise and non-specific, which could lead to the imposing of one's values of dignity and repression by lawmakers.

For instance, some PWDs have framed inclusion through the right to self-determination – as a right to autonomously choose to end their lives through euthanasia.[106] In *Pretty*, the claimant was a woman with advanced motor neurone disease, who intended to end her life because her condition was "untreatable ... terminal ... (and) rapidly deteriorating".[107] She feared the distressing final stages of the disease and sought legal action on the basis that she would be able to "control how and when she dies".[108] In campaigning to actively control her death, Mrs Pretty arguably sought power over her medical treatment and the end of her life: she wanted to be included in being able to choose to end an undignified life, which, "with her physical incapacity, she could not do without help".[109] Mrs Pretty suffered greatly, experiencing a

104 De Burca and Young (n 1) 2.

105 Ibid.

106 *The Views of Disabled People within the Assisted Dying Debate* (My Death, My Decision, 13 May 2024) <https://www.mydeath-mydecision.org.uk/2024/05/13/the-views-of-disabled-people-within-the-assisted-dying-debate/> accessed 16 April 2025.

107 Susan Milns, 'Death, Dignity and Discrimination: The Case of Pretty v. United Kingdom' (2019) 20 *German Law Journal* 1, 1 <https://www-cambridge-org.libproxy.ucl.ac.uk/core/journals/german-law-journal/article/death-dignity-and-discrimination-the-case-of-pretty-v-united-kingdom/875F1A6C1779CC09C4860D0D402D2158> accessed 15 April 2025.

108 *Pretty v United Kingdom* (n 83) [8].

109 *Pretty v Director of Public Prosecutions* [2001] UKHL 61, [2001] 1 AC 800 (HL), [para 15].

"painful and public death"[110] as the final stages of motor neurone disease left her unable to breathe.

In attempting to realise a right to die, Mrs Pretty submitted that dying in this manner constituted "degrading treatment"[111] akin to torture, calling for dignity in death. The court explored dignity with reference to *Rodriguez*,[112] in which Sopinka J argued that a central part of "the persona and dignity of the human being (is) that ... he or she have the autonomy to decide what is best for his or her body".[113] The judges in *Pretty* further separately reinforced that "choices concerning one's own body"[114] exists at the core of dignity. Despite this, the court in Pretty did not accept the claim that denying her the right to die constituted a breach of the right to be free from torture and degradation, and Pretty was not able to access euthanasia. As illustrated, socio-legal concepts of autonomy, consent (and even freedom from torture), turn upon strong-held individual experiences of Mrs Pretty as a person with disabilities, which able-bodied people and lawmakers are far removed from.

Tension persists in our understanding of dignity. Millns has convincingly argued that "dignity and degradation are two sides of the same coin".[115] In arguing as such, she examines the "neat link" made between the two in the Kudla case: that "under [Article 3] the state must ensure that a person is detained in conditions which are compatible with respect for his human dignity...".[116] Laureano Da Rosa frames repression as "a movement opposite to emancipation ... working towards fewer rights and freedom, representing violence towards individuals or groups".[117] In a context in which she sought to avoid a frightening death and was unable to do so, Mrs Pretty's death may be considered representative of violence.

However, other PWDs frame a dignified life as necessitating a social structure in which "assistance to live, not assistance to die"[118] is provided, which arguably positions a decision to die as inherently repressive.[119] From this per-

110 Millns (n 86).
111 Ibid.
112 *Rodriguez v Attorney General of Canada* [1994] 2 Law Reports of Canada 136 (SCC).
113 Ibid., [192] (Sopinka J).
114 Ibid., [197] (Lamer C.J. and L'Heureux-Dubé, Cory and McLachlin JJ).
115 Millns, 'Death, Dignity and Discrimination' (n 107).
116 *Kudla v. Poland* [2000] ECHR 30210/96 (GC) [94].
117 Rosa and Laureano (n 5) 25.
118 Morgan Houlihan, 'Euthanasia: A Threat to Disabled Lives' *Contexts* (11 May 2022) <https://contexts.org/blog/euthanasia-a-threat-to-disabled-lives/> accessed 14 September 2023.
119 Graham Box and Kenneth Chambaere, 'Views of Disability Rights Organisations on Assisted Dying Legislation in England, Wales and Scotland' (2021) 47 J Med Ethics 64, 67.

spective, a choice to end one's life is repressive in that, as argued by Blaser, "life ending decisions take place in a social and economic context".[120] PWDs may rely heavily on care from family or other sources and may be unable to work to generate an income, and there is a concern among pro-life campaigners that the feeling of being a burden[121] may motivate decisions to end their lives based on socio-economic vulnerability and a perception of a lack of other available choices. PWDs have also critiqued the perception of mutual exclusivity between being able-bodied and leading a fulfilling life, which arguably "draws strength from ableist assumptions about the inherent quality of life, or worth of the life of a person with a disability".[122]

Disability Rights depicted the passing of an assisted dying bill as "a profound betrayal (to) disabled people … (as it could) reinforce societal biases that view disabled people's lives as less valuable".[123] This implies that inclusion through the lens of the legal right to seek assistance to end their life, as most people can do without legal assistance, excludes them from living meaningful lives, and thus has been presented as an indignity. This is to show that these broad, expansive concepts are just that, and in developing a framework for a quasi-legal mechanism to encourage compliance with human rights law, we must be intentional and sensitive in selecting the viewpoints we choose to define these concepts by.

Comparative jurisdictional studies of Belgium, Canada, Luxembourg, Colombia, the Netherlands, and five US states (all of which legally regulate euthanasia), lay claim to research that finds that "there is no evidence that vulnerable patients have … received euthanasia or assisted suicide at rates

---

120 Art Blaser, 'Euthanasia and Human Rights Law: Compatible or Contradictory?' (International Studies Association 41st Annual Convention, Loss Angeles, 14–18 March 2000) https://ciaotest.cc.columbia.edu/isa/bla01/#:~:text=This%20paper%20is%20a%20preliminary,global%20bodies%2C%20governmental%20and%20nongovernmental accessed 15 April 2025, 2.

121 Sonia Sodha, 'In the Rush towards a Law on Assisted Dying, the Vulnerable Have Become Expendable' *The Observer* (13 April 2025) <https://www.theguardian.com/commentisfree/2025/apr/13/in-the-rush-towards-a-law-on-assisted-dying-the-vulnerable-have-become-expendable> accessed 16 April 2025.

122 United Nations Human Rights Office of the High Commissioner, 'Disability Is Not a Reason to Sanction Medically Assisted Dying - UN Experts' (25 January 2021) <https://www.ohchr.org/en/press-releases/2021/01/disability-not-reason-sanction-medically-assisted-dying-un-experts> accessed 20 September 2023.

123 Disability Rights UK, 'DR UK's Statement on Passing of Assisted Dying Bill | Disability Rights UK' <https://www.disabilityrightsuk.org/news/dr-uks-statement-passing-assisted-dying-bill?srsltid=AfmBOor-fltigqflBA6vQFA6BXTdw8Trj2wYWCwQgWCAwPt9Dylto5Zi> accessed 16 April 2025.

higher than in the general population".[124] It may be easy to assume this could be done from the dominant viewpoint, as a matter of pragmatism: a UK-wide survey of PWDs found that 76% would want the option to seek assisted dying if they were facing the end of their lives,[125] possibly implying that a blanket ban on euthanasia would repress the voices of those most likely to be affected by these decisions. Yet, this leads straight back to the majoritarian problem as posited at the start. The misappropriation paradigm aims to flag distortions of rights language. In a context in which inclusion and autonomy for PWDs have been articulated as a right to end one's life, with the same vigour with which dignity has been presented as an outright ban on euthanasia, distortion is very hard to spot, and the concepts therein (including dignity, polarisation, repression) have yet to be meaningfully located for the misappropriation paradigm.

6 Conclusion

In this chapter, I have argued that the misappropriation indicators lack sufficient normative clarity through a case study on euthanasia and the right to life. I aimed to raise questions as to the rationality of the proposed indicators by presenting contestation in their conceptual foundations across bioethical, socio-legal, and doctrinal interpretations of the right to life.

In doing so, I have raised questions as to the functionality of the current indicators in not only the misappropriation space but in socially contentious rights arenas more broadly; to encourage the shaping of the misappropriation requirements over time. I demonstrated the plasticity of the indicators in euthanasia instances to illuminate their changeability, and I will end by briefly exploring the potential outcomes of such uncertain indicators.

The absence of discernible misappropriation indicators leaves a chasm in the concept.

In light of this, identifiers who draw attention to what they perceive as misappropriations of rights may be vulnerable to plugging this conceptual void with culturally dominant iterations of human rights. Where the indicators are so conceptually expansive, thinkers may find themselves cherry-picking a single interpretation of the right to life as settled and could viably

124 Ezekiel K Emanuel and others, 'Attitudes and Practices of Euthanasia and Physician-Assisted Suicide in the United States, Canada, and Europe' (2016) 316 JAMA 79, 79.

125 Dignity in Dying, 'Just 8% of disabled people surveyed believe disability rights groups should maintain their opposition to assisted dying' (11 December 2013) <https://www.dignityindying.org.uk/news/just-8-disabled-people-surveyed-believe-disability-rights-groups-maintain-opposition-assisted-dying/> accessed 20 September 2023.

argue that legalising assisted suicide and passive euthanasia, or allowing passive euthanasia only, or allowing neither passive euthanasia nor assisted suicide may individually and/or collectively align with or fundamentally contradict the right to life under the indicators offered. The potential for identifiers to be able to give meaning to these principled indicators in a wider context of ongoing political divisiveness is worrying.

Firstly, the breadth of the indicators has the potential to grant authorial scope to the author identifying a misappropriation, which creates tension with the fundamental purpose of rights being to protect against the tyranny of the majority. I would argue this is not purely a problem of a wide-scope creating a vulnerability to bad-faith abuse, instead, I would argue that even good-faith identifiers can shape the quasi-legal perception of rights compliance and rights abuse in their image. Arguably, this will empower a kind of rights distortion that the misappropriation paradigm was designed to safeguard against. In this sense, the misappropriation concept can splinter fundamental human rights values such as dignity, equality, respect, and autonomy by enabling their re-design in a majoritarian image. However, the iterated intention of the paradigm: to identify rights distortions and bad-faith actors; and to spot abuse in disguise, is an aspirational framework. As the misappropriation framework develops, I look forward to engaging with scholarship that further examines the proposed requirements and hope to see ongoing awareness of who can shape them as being pivotal in how they are to be defined. I do not intend to posit solutions, only to broaden the scope of discussion and reiterate the call for a re-examination of the chosen indicators.

Bibliography

Cases

Chamber judgment, Koch v Germany (Application No 19071/12).
Chamber judgment, Pretty v United Kingdom (Application No 29040/02).
Daniel Karsai v Hungary (Application No 32312/23, ECtHR, 20 March 2024).
Haas v Switzerland, App No 31322/07 (ECtHR, 2011).
Koch v Germany (2012) ECHR 497/09.
Kudla v Poland [Grand Chamber] App No 30210/96, ECHR (26 October 2000).
Lambert v France (2015) ECHR 46043/14.
McCann v UK (1995) ECHR 18984/91.
Pretty v UK (2002) ECHR 2346/02.
Rodriguez v Attorney General of Canada [1994] LRC (3) 136.

Rosa and Laureano (Da Rosa and Torres Laureano thesis referenced at n 5).
SAS v France (2014) ECHR 43835/11.
Sanles Sanles v Spain (dec) (2000) ECtHR 22151/21 & others.

Journal Articles

Adkins CM, 'The Impact of Roe v Wade (1973) on the American Abortion Rights Movement' (n 36).
Ahmed F, 'Constitutional Parasitism, Camouflage, and Pretense: Shaping Citizenship through Subterfuge' (2023) 21 International Journal of Constitutional Law 285.
Aristegui I, Beloki U and Silvestre M, 'Abortion and Euthanasia: Explanatory Factors of an Association in Thanatos: Analysis of the European Values Study' (2022) 4 Frontiers in Political Science.
Biggs H, 'Euthanasia and Death with Dignity: Still Poised on the Fulcrum of Homicide' (1996) 1 Criminal Law Review 878.
Blaser A, 'Euthanasia and Human Rights Law: Compatible or Contradictory?' 2.
Box G and Chambaere K, 'Views of Disability Rights Organisations on Assisted Dying Legislation in England, Wales and Scotland' (2021) 47 Journal of Medical Ethics 64.
Çalı B and Demir-Gürsel E, 'Continuity and Change in Human Rights Appropriation: The Case of Turkey' (Hertie School/Humboldt-Universität zu Berlin, forthcoming in ICON 2023).
Cohen JS et al, 'Attitudes toward Assisted Suicide and Euthanasia among Physicians in Washington State' (1994) 331 New England Journal of Medicine 89.
Collier R, 'Assisted Death Gaining Acceptance in US' (2017) 189 Canadian Medical Association Journal 118.
Cosentino C, 'Safe and Legal Abortion: An Emerging Human Right? The Long-Lasting Dispute with State Sovereignty in ECHR Jurisprudence' (2015) 15 Human Rights Law Review 569.
De Burca G and Young K, 'The (Mis)Appropriation of Human Rights by the New Global Right: An Introduction to the Symposium' (2023) Working Paper No 23-32, New York University School of Law.
de La Hougue C and Puppinck G, 'Assisted Suicide under the ECHR' (2014) 18 International Journal of Human Rights 735.
Emanuel ZK et al, 'Attitudes and Practices of Euthanasia and Physician-Assisted Suicide in the United States, Canada, and Europe' (2016) 316 Journal of the American Medical Association 79.
Feinberg J, 'Voluntary Euthanasia and the Inalienable Right to Life' (1978) 7 Philosophy and Public Affairs 93.
Follesdal A and Tsereteli N, 'The Margin of Appreciation in Europe and Beyond' (2016) 20 International Journal of Human Rights 1055.

Glenn GD, 'Inalienable Rights and Locke's Argument for Limited Government: Political Implications of a Right to Suicide' (1984) 46 Journal of Politics 80.
Henneberry N, 'Democracy Requires the Limitation of the Rule of the Majority' (2007) 13 UCL Jurisprudence Law Journal 255.
Huckerby J and Knuckey S, 'Appropriation and the Rewriting of Human Rights' (2023) 21 International Journal of Constitutional Law 243; and also 'Appropriating Rights: Who Rewrites Rights and How?' Open Global Rights (14 June 2023).
Kimsma GK, 'Death by Request in the Netherlands: Facts, the Legal Context and Effects on Physicians, Patients and Families' (2010) 13 Medicine, Health Care and Philosophy 355.
Korff D, The Right to Life: A Guide to the Implementation of Article 2 of the European Convention on Human Rights (Council of Europe, Human Rights Handbook No 8, 2006).
Lardy H, 'Euthanasia and Euphemism' (1997) 1 Edinburgh Law Review 227.
Leenaars AA, 'Suicide, Assisted Suicide and Euthanasia: International Perspectives' (2001) 18 Irish Journal of Psychological Medicine 33.
Goff L, 'Last Rights: Euthanasia, the Sanctity of Life, and the Law in the Netherlands and the Northern Territory of Australia' (1998) 47 International & Comparative Law Quarterly 362.
Manzione LL, 'Is There a Right to Die?: A Comparative Study of Three Societies (Australia, Netherlands, United States)' (2002) 30 Golden Gate University Law Review 443.
Mugabi I, 'Right to Life Cases in the Jurisprudence of the European Court of Human Rights: A Critical Analysis' (2023) 1 Kabale University Law Review 1.
Moyn S, 'A Powerless Companion: Human Rights in the Age of Neoliberalism' (2015) 77 Law and Contemporary Problems 147.
O'Connell P, 'On Reconciling Irreconcilables: Neo-Liberal Globalisation and Human Rights' (2007) 7 Human Rights Law Review 483.
O'Grady A et al, 'Disability, Social Exclusion, and the Consequential Experience of Justiciable Problems' [2004] Disability & Society.
O'Manique J, 'Universal and Inalienable Rights: A Search for Foundations' (1990) 12 Human Rights Quarterly 465.
Puppinck G and de La Hougue C, 'The Right to Assisted Suicide in the Case Law of the European Court of Human Rights' [2014] 18(7-8) International Journal of Human Rights 735.
Romanis EC, 'Is "Viability" Viable? Abortion, Conceptual Confusion and the Law in England and Wales and the United States' (2020) 7 Journal of Law and the Biosciences lsaa059.
Roth K, 'Pompeo's Commission on Unalienable Rights Will Endanger Everyone's Human Rights' (Human Rights Watch, 27 August 2020).

Sanger C, 'Decisional Dignity: Teenage Abortion, Bypass Hearings, and the Misuse of Law' (2009) 18 Columbia Journal of Gender and Law 409.
Sanders R, 'Norm Spoiling: Undermining the International Women's Rights Agenda' (2018) 94 International Affairs 271.
Singh SC, 'Euthanasia and Assisted Suicide: Revisiting the Sanctity of Life Principle' (2012) 54 Journal of the Indian Law Institute 196.
Skinner T, 'Decriminalising Voluntary Active Euthanasia through the Recognition of Fundamental Human Rights: A Comparison of South Africa and Foreign Jurisdictions' (2021) University of Pretoria LLD thesis.
Wilson J, 'Is Respect for Autonomy Defensible?' (2007) 33 Journal of Medical Ethics.
Wilson L, 'The Rise of "Right-Wing" Human Rights Rhetoric: A Palestinian & Israeli Case Study'.

Books

Legg A, The Margin of Appreciation in International Human Rights Law: Deference and Proportionality (Oxford University Press 2012).
Kinzer S, Overthrow: America's Century of Regime Change from Hawaii to Iraq (2006).
Perugini N & Gordon N, The Human Right to Dominate (2015).

Newspaper Articles

Betts A, 'US Woman Sentenced to a Year in Prison for Shooting Terminally Ill Husband' The Guardian (3 March 2025).
Brown G, 'MPs Have Personal Beliefs, but Also Solemn Duties: That's Why They Must Reject the Assisted Dying Bill This Week' The Guardian (16 June 2025).
Beavers O, 'National Security Experts Warn of Rise in Authoritarianism' The Hill (26 February 2019).
Sodha S, 'In the Rush towards a Law on Assisted Dying, the Vulnerable Have Become Expendable' The Observer (13 April 2025).

Blog Posts

Avril N, 'As Abortion Rights Come under Attack Globally, How Do We Provide Women with Access to Vital Information about Their Reproductive Choices?' Action for Global Health (13 December 2022).
Fujimura-Fanselow A, Huckerby J & Knuckey S, 'An Exercise in Doublespeak: Pompeo's Flawed "Unalienable Rights" Commission' Just Security (29 July 2020).
Houlihan M, 'Euthanasia: A Threat to Disabled Lives' Contexts (11 May 2022).

Teng A, 'Don't Turn Doctors into Killers – Stand against Assisted Suicide' Christian Concern (1 May 2024).
The White House, 'Remarks by President Biden and First Lady Jill Biden at the 2023 Human Rights Campaign National Dinner' (15 October 2023).
'Death, Dignity and Discrimination: The Case of Pretty v United Kingdom' German Law Journal.
Dignity in Dying: JUST 8% OF DISABLED PEOPLE SURVEYED BELIEVE DISABILITY RIGHTS GROUPS SHOULD MAINTAIN THEIR OPPOSITION TO ASSISTED DYING.'
'The Views of Disabled People within the Assisted Dying Debate' My Death, My Decision (13 May 2024).

Reports

Amnesty International, India/Egypt: Ongoing Human Rights Crisis in Both Countries Must Be Addressed (26 January 2023).
Disability Rights UK, 'Statement on Passing of Assisted Dying Bill'.
Pompeo MR, Report of the Commission on Unalienable Rights (Office of Policy Planning, US Department of State, 2021).
Schlein L, 'UN: Human Rights Defenders Under Attack in Guatemala' (VOA News, 26 May 2019).
Steyn L and others, Judgments – The Queen on the Application of Mrs Dianne Pretty v Director of Public Prosecutions and Secretary of State for the Home Department (UK Parliament).
UN OHCHR, 'Disability Is Not a Reason to Sanction Medically Assisted Dying – UN Experts' (25 January 2021).

Treaties

International Covenant on Civil and Political Rights, GA Res 2200A (XXI) 16 Dec 1966, Art 6

CHAPTER 11

A Change from Within: Beyond Human Rights

Dorjana Bojanovska Popovska

1 Introduction

In the post-1989 context, there seemed to be a liberal consensus. The post-Soviet space was predominantly composed of states transitioning towards democracy with international institutions providing support whilst developing standards to be complied with in the process. Constitutional democracy guarded by supranational institutions became the 'global normal'. Both national constitutions anchored in unifying principles such as constitutional patriotism and cosmopolitan solidarity[1] and supranational treaties anchored in shared traditions, values, and interests reiterated their commitment to human rights and the rule of law. As protections in human rights law were set as minimum standards their expansion seemed predetermined. The development of the evolutionary interpretation in international law[2] and the living instrument doctrine by domestic and international courts pointed in the same direction.[3] The birth and development of multilevel constitutionalism presupposed dilution of national sovereignty, as common values and objectives became an end in themselves.[4] Liberal internationalism was thus both a guiding light and an additional check on power, underpinning a consensual surrendering of national sovereignty.

---

1 Jürgen Habermas, *Between Facts and Norms: Contributions to a Discourse Theory of Law and Democracy* (MIT Press 1996).

2 Geraldo Vidigal, 'Evolutionary Interpretation and International Law' (2021) 24 Journal of International Economic Law 203.

3 See Vicki Jackson, 'Constitutions as "Living Trees"? Comparative Constitutional Law and Interpretive Metaphors' (2006) 75 Georgetown Law Faculty Publications and Other Works 921; George Letsas, 'The ECHR as a Living Instrument: Its Meaning and Legitimacy' in Andreas Føllesdal, Birgit Peters and Geir Ulfstein (eds), *Constituting Europe: The European Court of Human Rights in a National, European and Global Context* (Cambridge University Press 2013). Jayanta Boruah, 'Living Tree Doctrine: Role of Indian Judiciary against Constitutional Silence in India' (Social Science Research Network, 24 May 2019) <https://papers.ssrn.com/abstract=3787907> accessed 22 May 2025.

4 András Sajó and Renáta Uitz, 'Multi-Layered Constitutionalism, Globalization, and the Revival of the Nation State' in András Sajó and Renáta Uitz (eds), *The Constitution of Freedom: An Introduction to Legal Constitutionalism* (Oxford University Press 2017).

In the past decades, however, the reassertion of old and new il/anti-liberalisms both as an intellectual undertaking and political planform, pernicious polarization,[5] and the rise of ethno-nationalism[6] served as a pretext for the resurgence of national sovereignty and the closing of societies. One of the distinguishing features in this context is the tendency of dominant narratives and discourses to recalibrate established concepts and principles, reframing them through terms once considered dissonant. On an institutional level, this ambiguous merger has manifested in the decoupling of liberalism and democracy[7] by new forms of intelligent authoritarianisms that work on all levels – national and supranational. Contemporary illiberal challengers do not completely abandon the liberal paradigm and its institutional architecture but (ab)use it[8] by exploiting liberal constitutionalism's internal disagreements[9] and its authoritarian elements as relics from an unfinished project.[10] Such colouring within the lines and pushing their limits,[11] instead of completely breaking the rules of the game has thus, allowed them to transform the meaning of democracy and the role of human rights from within. Yet, these transformations occur without articulating a "clear alternative version of an all-encompassing or comprehensive ideology" or a coherent vision of society.[12] As all tools serve the purpose of concentrating power in the executive branch, they also work to unbind it from the constraints of "social diversity or political

5 Murat Somer and Jennifer McCoy, 'Toward a Theory of Pernicious Polarization and How It Harms Democracies: Comparative Evidence and Possible Remedies' (2019) 681 The ANNALS of the American Academy of Political and Social Science 234.

6 Robert Schertzer and Eric Taylor Woods, 'What Is Old Is New Again: The Deep Roots of Ethnic Nationalism in the Digital Age' (2024) 30 Nations and Nationalism 414.

7 Fareed Zakaria, 'The Rise of Illiberal Democracy' (1997) 76 Foreign Affairs 22.

8 Andras Sajó, *Ruling by Cheating* (Cambridge University Press 2021).; David Landau, 'Abusive Constitutionalism' (2013) 47 U.C. Davis Law Review 189; Kim Lane Scheppele, 'The Rule of Law and the Frankenstate: Why Governance Checklists Do Not Work' (2013) 26 Governance 559.

9 Gráinne de Búrca and Katharine G Young, 'The (Mis)Appropriation of Human Rights by the New Global Right: An Introduction to the Symposium' (2023) 21 International Journal of Constitutional Law 205.

10 Sajó, *Ruling by Cheating* (n 8). 23.

11 Tímea Drinóczi and Agnieszka Bień-Kacała, 'WEBINAR 8: HUNGARY & POLAND - The Year 2020: Lessons Learned from the Hungarian and Polish Management of the COVID-19 Crisis and Beyond' (*IACL*, 23 November 2020) <https://www.iacl-democracy-2020.org/blog/2016/3/23/blog-post-sample-9wntn-6ye75-hwawc-xx9lz-p6k2z-y8y6h-cplw4-4bcr5-t2hdf-pt4np-nzc2g-f64jl-c53x4-d693x-ycry5-xahmf> accessed 12 April 2025.

12 András Sajó, Renáta Uitz and Stephen Holmes, 'Preface', *Routledge Handbook of Illiberalism* (Routledge 2021).

pluralism (i.e. in the name of higher values such as Christianity, Hindutva, Islam, the common good, or peace and harmony)."[13]

The misappropriation of rights is appropriately situated as another strategy operating within these contemporary trajectories[14] – what started as counter movement against progressive inclusive human rights[15] has become a mechanism in a multilevel, multidirectional efforts to undermine constitutional democracy. Building on, rather than departing from, the core notion of misappropriation, the chapter shifts the focus from micro-strategies to a broader understanding of the forces and tools employed in this context. Focusing primarily on the European experience, the chapter identifies complementing strategies that are used by the same actors on national and supranational levels towards undoing democratic structures from within. The chapter situates the misappropriation of rights alongside other concepts and tools that work in the direction of power concentration and maximization. It also positions it as another driver of the reconceptualization of the public sphere that ultimately erodes the egalitarian foundations of constitutional democracy by promoting exclusionary definitions of citizenship. Thus, Part 1 will look at complementing strategies for unbounding power, and more particularly the reinterpretation of legal hierarchies and values. Part 2 will examine the misappropriation of rights as an element within a broader process of reconceptualizing the public sphere, with particular attention on the reconfiguration of actors that operate within it and on the role of religion in such reconceptualization.

2 Misappropriation of Rights and Beyond: Complementing Strategies for Unbounding Power

The collection of essays on human rights misappropriations show how they reshape and distort human rights "by emphasizing different sources, values, or particular rights, or by seeking to exclude certain groups or rights from protection," to "avoid, disrupt, or exclude external or independent mechanisms of accountability" often "through tropes of national sovereignty, anti-expertise, or anti-elitism."[16] These strategies often, but not always, go in parallel with

13 Ibid.

14 'Democracies in Decline' (*Freedom House*, 25 January 2024) <https://freedomhouse.org/issues/democracies-decline> accessed 22 April 2025.

15 Elizabeth S Corredor, 'Unpacking "Gender Ideology" and the Global Right's Antigender Countermovement' (2019) 44 SIGNS 613.

16 de Búrca and Young (n 9).

strategies of counter-norm pushing[17] and/or distorting scientific data as evidence[18] and fit into a larger trend of (ab)use of concepts and adopting strategies to restrain inter- and supranational organizations[19] and instruments with the goal of power maximization on the national level.[20] Instead of pursuing exit strategies or efforts to "undo" international organizations, they seek to reinterpret and transform their foundations and standards by limiting their competences and promoting a vision of democracy decoupled from constitutionalism. They thus work both in the direction of limiting the effects of international norms as well as transforming their function.

2.1 Repositioning Legal Hierarchies

One example of how misappropriation operates is the use of the Universal Declaration of Human Rights (UDHR) as an interpretive tool to advance a narrow, originalist reading of rights.[21] The over-reliance on the "UDHR as the most authoritative – and indeed last – word on human rights meaning"[22] however reflects broader implementation of "whatever works" strategies operationalized by illiberal challengers in numerous venues aimed at limiting external checks on power. One such strategy is the repositioning of legal hier-

17 Alexander Baturo, 'Russia's Global Anti-Nazism Campaign: Seeking Support in International Organizations - IGCC' (University of California Institute on Global Conflict and Cooperation, 14 April 2023) <https://ucigcc.org/publication/russias-global-anti-nazism-campaign-seeking-support-in-international-organizations/> accessed 2 June 2025.

18 Allison Carnegie, Richard Clark and Noah Zucker, 'Global Governance under Populism: The Challenge of Information Suppression - IGCC' (University of California Institute on Global Conflict and Cooperation, 14 February 2024) <https://ucigcc.org/publication/global-governance-under-populism-the-challenge-of-information-suppression/> accessed 2 June 2025.

19 See Christina Cottiero and others, 'Illiberal Regimes and International Organizations' [2024] The Review of International Organizations. Especially: Jana Lipps and Marc S Jacob, 'Undermining Liberal International Organizations from within: Evidence from the Parliamentary Assembly of the Council of Europe' [2024] The Review of International Organizations.

20 Kim Lane Scheppele, 'Asymmetric Rupture: Stabilizing Democratic Transitions 2.0 with Transnational Law' in Michal Bobek and others (eds), *Transition 2.0: Re-establishing Constitutional Democracy in EU Member States* (Nomos Verlagsgesellschaft mbH und Co KG 2023).

21 Jayne Huckerby and Sarah Knuckey, 'Appropriation and the Rewriting of Rights' (2023) 21 International Journal of Constitutional Law 243; Kristina Stoeckl, 'Traditional Values, Family, Homeschooling: The Role of Russia and the Russian Orthodox Church in Transnational Moral Conservative Networks and Their Efforts at Reshaping Human Rights' (2023) 21 International Journal of Constitutional Law 224.

22 de Búrca and Young (n 9).

archies, either to limit the application of international and supranational binding norms or to achieve specific goals that alter the functioning of international institutions.

As the former seeks to circumvent accountability, sovereigntist claims – articulated through the notion of constitutional identity – have frequently served as instruments towards this end, manifesting in various forms within European regional institutions. Beyond the blatant non-implementation of judgments,[23] more extreme instances – such as the Russian example – involve the invocation of state sovereignty to justify constraints on the execution of European Court of Human Rights (ECtHR) judgments, initially through apex courts, and subsequently via constitutional amendments.[24] Within the EU context, the ambiguous language of Article 4 (2) TEU, which obliges the Union to respect the national identities of Member States, has allowed national apex courts to invoke constitutional identity to limit and, at times, negate the primacy of EU law.[25]

This practice has been employed in both troubled and so-called consolidated democracies,[26] including in jurisdictions where constitutional identity is not explicitly enshrined in the constitutional text.[27] Certainly, in a setting of operating multilevel constitutionalism not all constitutional conflicts are aimed towards transforming the normative salience of international institutions. In fact, the employment of constitutional identity can be constructive

23 George Stafford and Jakub Jaraczewski, 'Taking European Judgments Seriously' [2022] Verfassungsblog <https://verfassungsblog.de/taking-european-judgments-seriously/> ac cessed 20 April 2025.

24 Lauri Mälksoo, 'Russia's Constitutional Court Defies the European Court of Human Rights: Constitutional Court of the Russian Federation Judgment of 14 July 2015, No 21-П/2015' (2016) 12 European Constitutional Law Review 377.

25 Gábor Halmai and Julian Scholtes, 'Illiberal Constitutionalism and the Abuse of Constitutional Identity' in Ran Hirschl and Yaniv Roznai (eds), *Deciphering the Genome of Constitutionalism: The Foundations and Future of Constitutional Identity* (Cambridge University Press 2024).

26 For France see Decision no. 2006-540 DC of 27 July 2006 (French Constitutional Council) confirmed by Decision no. 2017-749 DC of 31 July 2017 (French Constitutional Council); For Italy see Italian Constitutional Court, Judgment No 183/1973 (Italy, 18 December 1973); For Germany see Bundesverfassungsgericht, Judgment 2 BvR 2134/92 and 2 BvR 2159/92 (Germany, 12 October 1993) and BVerfGE. Bundesverfassungsgericht, Judgment 2 BvE 2/08 (Lissabon) (Germany, 30 June 2009) BVerfGE.

27 Petersen Niels and Wasilczyk Patrick, 'The Primacy of EU Law and the Polish Constitutional Law Judgment' (Policy Department for Citizens' Rights and Constitutional Affairs 2022) PE 734.568.

when "[remaining] within the confines of constitutional pluralism's normative core;" meaning that it is expressed through the values in Article 2 TEU.[28]

However, recent examples of the abuse of constitutional identity by illiberal actors[29] have reviled the dangers the concept poses to European integration,[30] as well as its inherent potential to serve as a tool for consolidating power. Constitutional identity has been employed as a legal instrument to actively defy implementation of EU laws and policies (for example immigration and asylum policies[31]) as well as to dismantle guarantees for judicial independence.[32] More recently, it has also been directly operationalized to curb dissent and evade accountability. For example, in Hungary, the concept has been interpreted in existential terms, with the Constitution establishing the defence and protection of constitutional identity as a core obligation of all state organs.[33] In addition, a specialized body with vague competences – the National Sovereignty Protection Office – is tasked with safeguarding constitutional identity against external influence thus, framing the perceived threat as originating from the outside. Further legal changes mandate the Office to advise the government on establishing a register for foreign-funded entities influencing public life; such entities would thereafter be obliged to obtain tax authority approval to receive foreign funds. Echoing other so-called foreign agent laws, a well-known tool in the illiberal/authoritarian playbook,[34] this measure ultimately aims to suppress dissent and evade accountability and monitoring by both international

28 Ana Bobić, 'Constructive Versus Destructive Conflict: Taking Stock of the Recent Constitutional Jurisprudence in the EU' (2020) 22 Cambridge Yearbook of European Legal Studies 60. For an alternative framing of constitutional identity review by national courts vis-a-vis the EU see Luke Dimitrios Spieker, 'Framing and Managing Constitutional Identity Conflicts: How to Stabilize the Modus Vivendi between the Court of Justice and National Constitutional Courts' (2020) 57 Common Market Law Review 361.

29 Halmai and Scholtes (n 25).

30 R Daniel Kelemen and Laurent Pech, 'The Uses and Abuses of Constitutional Pluralism: Undermining the Rule of Law in the Name of Constitutional Identity in Hungary and Poland' (2019) 21 Cambridge Yearbook of European Legal Studies 59.

31 Hungarian Constitutional Court, Decision 22/2016 (XII.5.) AB.

32 Anna Śledzińska-Simon and Michał Ziółkowski, 'Constitutional Identity in Poland: Is the Emperor Putting On the Old Clothes of Sovereignty?' in Christian Calliess and Gerhard van der Schyff (eds), *Constitutional Identity in a Europe of Multilevel Constitutionalism* (Cambridge University Press 2019).

33 András Sajó, 'The Constitution of Illiberal Democracy as a Theory About Society' [2019] Polish Sociological Review 395.

34 Iskra Kirova, 'Foreign Agent Laws in the Authoritarian Playbook' (*Human Rights Watch*, 19 September 2024) <https://www.hrw.org/news/2024/09/19/foreign-agent-laws-authoritarian-playbook> accessed 20 April 2025.

bodies and civil society organizations, thereby weakening established mechanisms for holding state power in check.[35]

While these examples demonstrate how practices of reordering legal hierarchies undermine the primacy of international legal norms, the next example illustrates how dubious legal hierarchies are introduced within organizational frameworks to enhance decision-making power through mechanisms of unanimity – echoing a vision of the return of the balance of power to nation-states. In 2020, Polish Prime Minister Morawiecki made efforts to interpret the adopted European Council conclusions about the implementation of the novel EU conditionality mechanism, as a permanent act of the European law, close to primary law and above regulations.[36] He suggested that future regulations must be in line with conclusions which would require unanimity to be altered. Such interpretation places conclusions – non-binding, non-legal instruments – above regulations that have a legal binding force. As Uitz points out while his take "may be unorthodox, his public statement clearly echoes a keen interest in shaping EU law through novel means, with reference to the weight of unanimity between national governments."[37] This fits within a paradigm where exit strategies are abandoned and instead the transformation of the EU is adopted as a strategy; aiming to renegotiate the EU as a community of values and limit its legal authority by diluting it with further reinforcement of unanimity in decision-making. While this may be only a single example and not indicative of an established or emerging trend, it should serve as a cautionary tale and a possible point of reference for future developments.

2.2 Reinterpreting Values

Reinterpreting the UDHR fits into a larger strategy of reinterpreting principles and values as guidelines for future legal framing. Values are at the core of the founding documents of all national and international legal systems. However, whereas legal norms are understood "as a result of clearly delineated procedures and established methods of interpretation and application" values are

35 See further: Renáta Uitz, 'A Threat to the Core' [2025] Verfassungsblog <https://verfassungsblog.de/hungary-transparency-law-foreign-funding/> accessed 2 June 2025.

36 Alexandra Brzozowski and Monika Mojak, 'Rule-of-Law Split Looms over Poland's Ruling Coalition - Euractiv' (11 December 2020) <https://www.euractiv.com/section/politics/short_news/rule-of-law-split-looms-over-polands-ruling-coalition/> accessed 19 April 2025. in Renáta Uitz, 'The Rule of Law in the EU: Crisis, Differentiation, Conditionality' (2022) 7 European Papers 929.

37 Uitz, 'The Rule of Law in the EU: Crisis, Differentiation, Conditionality' (n 42).

mostly understood to be fuzzy with their content, application and the legal effect being largely debated.[38] While the application and normativity or values is usually determined by additional norms that give them legal effect, their content, rather meaning is often contested and thus, prone to (re)interpretation. The failed attempt to smuggle traditional values into the (re)interpretation of Article 29 of the UDHR is one example illustrative to this.[39]

The developments on the EU level show that reinterpretation of values works even in a union of "values and laws" where the values of democracy, human rights and the rule of law have a strong normative standing with subsequent mechanisms in place to uphold them (even though its effectiveness has been debated).[40] Yet, they have been continuously contested by illiberal challengers who face repercussions for their blatant disregard. Using the language of rights to justify the violation of the rights of certain groups protected under EU law is only one part of the story. In addition, illiberal challengers have employed the reinterpretation of values to undermine the Union's core integrity, primarily by redefining the meaning of democracy and the rule of law as foundational values.

One strategy has been to interpret democracy as decoupled from liberalism[41] as opposed to the Union's own understanding as a union of constitutional democracies united by common interests.[42] The proposed minimalist conception of democracy that only requires a performative act of elections – considered free and fair only by formalistic standards,[43] ultimately seeks to

38 Christoph Konrath, 'Values and Laws' in Regina Polak and Patrick Rohs (eds), *Values – Politics – Religion: The European Values Study: In-depth Analysis – Interdisciplinary Perspectives – Future Prospects* (Springer International Publishing 2023).

39 Stoeckl (n 21).

40 They are understood as common to all Member States, inherent part of integration. See further Kim Lane Scheppele, Dimitry Vladimirovich Kochenov and Barbara Grabowska-Moroz, 'EU Values Are Law, after All: Enforcing EU Values through Systemic Infringement Actions by the European Commission and the Member States of the European Union' (2021) 39 Yearbook of European Law 3.

41 Marc F Plattner, 'Illiberal Democracy and the Struggle on the Right' 30 Journal of Democracy 5.

42 Armin Von Bogdandy, 'Ways to Frame the European Rule of Law: Rechtsgemeinschaft, Trust, Revolution, and Kantian Peace' (2018) 14 European Constitutional Law Review 675.

43 Consider here that a practice is evolving where observers parallel to the OSCE ODIHR monitoring mission observers are invited to defend otherwise flawed elections. Such was the case of the last election cycle in Hungary when friendly politicians, some of which from the EU, journalists and civil society activists were invited to endorse and if need be defend the electoral process against critiques steaming primarily from the ODIHR. See Anton Shekhovtsov, 'Government-Friendly Election Observers at the 2022 Hungarian Parliamentary Elections' (EPDE 2022).

disregard violations of EU laws and standards for human rights protection most notably, freedom of expression and the media and assembly.

The same strategy has also been used in front of the ECtHR, a court already criticized for either not doing enough or doing too little too late in the face of raising illiberalism and autocratic legalism.[44] In a recent analysis Uitz has shown that the "contestation about the concept of democracy is at the heart of the ongoing recalibration of human rights" in front of the court.[45] The end goal: shifting the meaning of the concept of democracy from its understanding "as a form of self-government for a diverse, pluralistic society" to a "purely majoritarian (procedural) conception of democracy."[46] She warns that if this shift is successful the foundations of the European human rights acquis will follow.[47]

Another strategy has been to strip the already contested principle of the rule of law[48] of any meaning other than a weapon in the hands of elites and the EU. At times, this narrative is coupled with arguments about democracy, as illiberal challengers accuse the EU of using the rule of law to suppress dissent and to "switch off democratically constituted institutions of the nation-states."[49] In contrast to the established understanding of the rule of law as a mechanism to limit power and "enforce ... legal limits to political discretion,"[50] this reconceptualization serves to justify the unrestrained exercise of state power, free from external accountability. These efforts not only seek to restrict the reach of international norms and regulations but also aim to invert the meaning of legal principles and values, thereby altering their interpretation in ways that carry significant normative consequences.

---

44 Başak Çalı and Esra Demir-Gürsel, 'The Council of Europe's Responses to the Decay of the Rule of Law and Human Rights Protections: A Comparative Appraisal' (2021) 2 Human Rights Law Review 165.

45 Renáta Uitz, 'Recalibrating Human Rights in Europe: A Call to Awaken the Principle of Non-Retrogression' [forthcoming] ECTHR Law Review.

46 Renáta Uitz, 'Recalibrating Human Rights in Europe: A Call to Awaken the Principle of Non-Retrogression' [forthcoming] ECTHR Law Review.

47 Ibid.

48 Jeremy Waldron, 'Is the Rule of Law an Essentially Contested Concept (In Florida)?' (2002) 21 Law and Philosophy 137.

49 Co-Chairman Prof. Ryszard Legutko on the State of the Union Speech' (16 September 2020) ecrgroup.eu in Uitz, 'The Rule of Law in the EU: Crisis, Differentiation, Conditionality' (n 42).

50 José María Maravall, 'The Rule of Law as a Political Weapon' in Adam Przeworski and José María Maravall (eds), *Democracy and the Rule of Law* (Cambridge University Press 2003).

These efforts often calumniate in more comprehensive alternative visions and possible futures of the EU. The Joint Declaration on the Future of Europe, signed in 2021 by EU political parties from 16 countries, offered a glimpse into a possible future as envisioned by the right-wing block of the EU.[51] Another example is the publication on the future of the EU by Ordo Iuris Institute and the Mathias Corvinus Collegium, titled The Great Reset.[52] Both documents – one emerging from within the EU, the other from outside – identify the same root problems: a democratic deficit and ideological imposition. Their proposed solution lies in restoring member state sovereignty and returning to a European common heritage defined along religious lines (see below).

3 Misappropriation of Rights and Beyond: Reconceptualizing the Public Sphere

The enlightenment idea of the public/private divide is one of the foundations of nation state. It emerged as a product of a long history of doctrines of state supremacy and sovereignty in the sixteenth and seventeenth centuries developed in a context of church-state and religious competition post-Reformation. A product of liberal intellectual and institutional design, the public/private divide is a concept about the very nature and functioning of democracy and setting limits on state power. As a concept limiting state power, it not only foresees realms from which state authority should be excluded but also provides rules on the acceptable justifications of state action as well as public deliberation. In between, the concept of the public sphere as the foundation of participatory democracy, bridges the divide understood as a forum where rational arguments are brought into public debates by interested parties on issues concerning the polity.[53]

Contemporary trajectories have prompted a reconceptualization of the public sphere.[54] In addition to standard critiques of the private/public divide

51 'Joint Declaration on the Future of Europe: A Manifesto for the "Freedom of Nations"' (*Counting Stars*) <https://www.outono.net/elentir/2021/07/02/joint-declaration-on-the-future-of-europe-a-manifesto-for-the-freedom-of-nations/> accessed 22 April 2025.

52 Rodrigo Ballester and others, 'The Great Reset' (Foundation Institute for Legal Culture Ordo Iuris and Mathias Corvinus Collegium 2025).

53 Jürgen Habermas, *The Structural Transformation of the Public Sphere* (MIT Press 1991).

54 Mark Eisenegger and Mike S Schäfer, 'Editorial: Reconceptualizing Public Sphere(s) in the Digital Age? On the Role and Future of Public Sphere Theory' (2023) 33 Communication Theory 61.

from feminist[55] and postcolonial perspectives,[56] technological advancement blurring the lines between the public/private sector has been one of the main drivers for the reconceptualization of the public sphere in an age where activities digital platforms are the main vehicle of public participation as well as one of the greatest threats to democracies.[57] In parallel two other developments have prompted reconceptualization of the public sphere: (1) the deprivatization of religion and the recalibration of the place of religion in the public sphere; (2) the reconceptualization of the actors that operate within it. The concept of misappropriation of rights fits into and adds a perspective in this larger paradigm shift.

3.1 The Return of Religion in the Public Sphere

The casting of the constitutional nation-state as a neutral arbiter was a consequence of the process of institutional differentiation and the development of religious tolerance into equal citizenship. In a de-facto pluralistic state and a growingly pluralistic world (not that homogeneity was ever a reality) neutrality was a necessity in the road towards equal citizenship in its formal and substantive dimensions.[58] The need for state neutrality, the absence of religion and other comprehensive doctrines in the public sphere and in the exercise of state power,[59] rests on the equal accessibility of public decisions, respect of individual autonomy[60] as well as the divisive nature of religious reasons.[61]

---

55 Ulla Wischermann and Ilze Klavina Mueller, 'Feminist Theories on the Separation of the Private and the Public: Looking Back, Looking Forward' (2004) 20 Women in German Yearbook 184.

56 Simon Susen, 'Critical Notes on Habermas's Theory of the Public Sphere' (2011) 5 Sociological Analysis 37.

57 Ines Mergel, 'Study on the Impact of Digital Transformation on Democracy and Good Governance' (Council of Europe, CDDG 2021) CDDG(2021)4 Final.

58 Dorjana Bojanovska Popovska and Francesca Raimondo, 'Formal and Substantive Aspects of Citizenship and Its Connection to Religion. Definition, Practices and Comparative Perspectives' (2021) 29 Quaderni di diritto e politica ecclesiastica, Rivista trimestrale 509.

59 John Rawls, *A Theory of Justice* (Harvard University Press 2005).; John Rawls, *Political Liberalism* (Columbia University Press 1993). Ronald Dworkin, *A Matter of Principle* (Harvard University Press 1985).

60 Since the exercise of autonomy may lead to the acceptance of any of a variety of conceptions of the good, respect for each person's autonomy requires the state to be neutral between different views of the good life. Andrew D. Mason, "Autonomy, Liberalism and State Neutrality," *The Philosophical Quarterly (1950-)* 40, no. 161 (1990): 433.

61 Laborde, "Justificatory Secularism," 167.

The so-called post-secular paradigm and the de-privatization of religion in the modern world[62] brought upon the rethinking/revisiting of these notions. As the presence of religious arguments in the public sphere was seen as less problematic,[63] they could be used or simply translated into secular terms to become accessible and thus, become equal part of public debates.[64] Fifteen years ago, however, Urbinati signalled the dangers and potential side effects of such openness in contexts where a strong majority religion is present, as it can lead to "directly [recognizing] the cultural patrimony of the large majority of the population."[65] She warned that such tarnishing of pluralism is dangerous, as pluralism is key to an open and safe public sphere, without it "a constitutional democracy may generate decisions that are not more liberal or tolerant than those made in a non-constitutional democracy."[66]

Scholarship on the rise of strong religion has further examined these dangers, pinpointing its influence on general norms. Particularly on how religiously based preferences – whether translated or not – are being inserted into national constitutions, international treaties, and the jurisprudence of apex courts, ultimately undermining equality and specific rights.[67]

The examples in the collection of essays on the misappropriation of rights fit into this trend as their operationalization is not only about establishing a priority of specific rights over others but about smuggling religious precepts into the international human rights system, its standards and norms. Thus, they fit into a larger trend of abusing concepts and mechanisms that ultimately lead to the erosion of the egalitarian foundation of constitutional democracy through adopting exclusionary definitions of citizenship and limiting of rights.

They operate in a period marked by the rise of Christian-based alternatives to constitutionalism. On an intellectual level, conservative Catholic intellec-

62 José Casanova, *Public Religions in the Modern World* (University of Chicago Press 1994).

63 Jürgen Habermas, 'Religion in the Public Sphere' (2006) 14 European Journal of Philosophy - 1.

64 Ibid., John Rawls, 'The Idea of Public Reason Revisited' (1997) 64 The University of Chicago Law Review 765.

65 Urbinati, "Laïcité in Reverse: Mono-Religious Democracies' and the Issue of Religion in the Public Sphere," 18.

66 Ibid.

67 András Sajó, 'Preliminaries to a Concept of Constitutional Secularism' in Susanna Mancini and Michel Rosenfeld (eds), *Constitutional Secularism in an Age of Religious Revival* (Oxford University Press 2014); Gabriel Abraham Almond, R Scott Appleby and Emmanuel Sivan, *Strong Religion : The Rise of Fundamentalisms around the World* (University of Chicago Press 2003); Gila Stopler, 'The Challenge of Strong Religion in the Liberal State' (2014) 32 Boston University International Law Journal 411.

tuals have advocated for the revival of integralism[68] as an alternative to democracy,[69] focusing on the return of natural law and rights, as well as the new/old conception of common good constitutionalism as an interpretative tool.[70] Thus, intellectual pursuits extend beyond simply maintaining an originalist or back-to-basics constrained interpretation of treaties and constitutions,[71] offering alternatives that go beyond originalism and into their own living instrument doctrine.[72] They operate in a time of recalibrating majority-minority dynamics in the politics of victimhood, where Christianity, as a victim of modernity, is not only used as a narrative tool but also as rhetoric that influences the jurisprudence of apex courts[73] and government policies.[74]

One strategy is the instrumentalization of the concept of constitutional identity, beyond its use as a tool to circumvent checks on power, to redefine citizenship and belonging. When adopted, a homogeneous interpretation of the constitution and its binding traits along religious and ethnocultural lines[75] not only erodes the egalitarian foundations of constitutional democracy but also allows for the exclusion of legal protections for certain groups or the legitimization of discriminatory policies, often protected by international human rights law.[76] This constitutes an abuse rather than use of the concept

68 Gladden Pappin, 'Contemporary Christian Criticism of Liberalism' in András Sajó, Renáta Uitz and Stephen Holmes (eds), *Routledge Handbook of Illiberalism* (Routledge 2022).

69 Patrick J Deneen, *Why Liberalism Failed* (Yale University Press 2019).

70 Adrian Vermeule, *Common Good Constitutionalism* (Polity 2022).

71 Huckerby and Knuckey (n 21); Stoeckl (n 21).

72 Adrian Vermeule, 'Beyond Originalism' (*The Atlantic*, 31 March 2020) <https://www.theatlantic.com/ideas/archive/2020/03/common-good-constitutionalism/609037/> accessed 23 April 2025.

73 Hannah Bailey, 'A New Minority in the Courts: How the Rhetoric of Christian Victimhood and the Supreme Court Are Transforming the Free Exercise Clause' (2023) 73 Syracuse Law Review 199.

74 'Eradicating Anti-Christian Bias' (*The White House*, 6 February 2025) <https://www.whitehouse.gov/presidential-actions/2025/02/eradicating-anti-christian-bias/> accessed 23 April 2025; 'Hungarian Foreign Minister Warns About Christianity Being the Most Persecuted Religion' (6 July 2022) <https://hungarytoday.hu/hungarian-foreign-minister-warns-about-christianity-being-the-most-persecuted-religion/> accessed 23 April 2025.

75 Kriszta Kovács, 'The Rise of an Ethnocultural Constitutional Identity in the Jurisprudence of the East Central European Courts' (2017) 18 German Law Journal 1703.

76 See Julian Scholtes, 'Abusing Constitutional Identity' (2021) 22 German Law Journal 534.; Federico Fabbrini and András Sajó, 'The Dangers of Constitutional Identity' (2019) 25 European Law Journal 457.

of constitutional identity, traditional understood as an inclusive concept serving as a binding glue of a non-homogenous nation brought together under the umbrella of the common constitutional order.[77]

Another strategy is the instrumentalization of Christianity – whether as culture, heritage, or through emergent forms of Christian democracy. Invoked by both state and non-state actors, contested narratives about the Christian roots and traditions of nation-states and of Europe[78] have served as a pretext for efforts aimed at rejecting constitutionalism and resisting advances in human rights. More particularly, the defence of a "Christian Europe" has often become central to efforts aimed at curtailing the promotion of women's rights and the rights of sexual minorities.[79] Illiberal state actors have also used this narrative trope "to avowedly illiberal political projects with questionable democratic credentials."[80] Once in power, they often codify traditional conceptions of gender roles and the family into law, while seeking to circumvent international human rights obligations. Note that the aspirations to transform Europe along the lines of its pre-modern Christian roots materialize in contexts beyond the state – as a vision for a reformed Europe as well as the word.[81]

These narratives exist across the illiberal/liberal divide and play out in courts where the content and definition of citizenship is renegotiated. In Italy for example, defining the crucifix as part of the cultural identity of the nation, was enough to satisfy Italian legislators and courts that its mandatory presence in public schools does not infringe on religious freedom and equality.[82] The approach defined a common Catholic identity of the nation

77 Michel Rosenfeld, 'Deconstructing Constitutional Identity in Light of the Turn to Populism' in Ran Hirschl and Yaniv Roznai (eds), *Deciphering the Genome of Constitutionalism: The Foundations and Future of Constitutional Identity* (Cambridge University Press 2024).

78 Sante Lesti, *Il Mito Delle Radici Cristiane Dell'Europa* (Einaudi Storia 2024).

79 Neil Datta, 'Modern-Day Crusaders in Europe. Tradition, Family and Property: Analysis of a Transnational, Ultra-Conservative, Catholic-Inspired Influence Network' (EPF 2020).

80 Fabio Wolkenstein, 'Christian Europe Redux' (2023) 61 JCMS: Journal of Common Market Studies 636.

81 'Joint Declaration on the Future of Europe: A Manifesto for the "Freedom of Nations"' (n 57); Neil Datta, 'Restoring the Natural Order' (EPF 2018).

82 Consiglio di Stato, Decision No 556/2006 (Italy, 13 February 2006); Corte di Cassazione, Decision No 439/2000 (Italy, 2000). See further: Lautsi v Italy App no 30814/06 (GC, 18 March 2011)

ought to "[provide] cultural and ethical principles on which full citizenship is based."[83] Furthermore, specific Courts have had no problem secularizing the meaning of the crucifix, either by affording it a "secondary meaning"[84] or by representing it as a symbol of "universal value, independent of specific religious connotation"[85] – approaches that "only dilute the authentic testimony of religions."[86]

Finally, particularly within illiberal populist contexts, exclusionary policies are enacted under the guise of a new model of Christian Democracy. This model bears little resemblance to Christian Democracy developed in the nineteenth and twentieth centuries. The term "Christian" is employed in a vague, identitarian, and exclusionary manner – framed as appealing to the majority, but in reality catering only to the agenda of the state/political apparatus.[87] In this context, religion is more about who belongs where in the friend-enemy dichotomy and less about belief.[88] As such, it is less about genuine Christian principles and more about instrumentalizing religious symbols and narratives to feed appetites for complete state take-over.

As a finally note, the reconceptualization of the public sphere and space has also worked in a direction of limiting the presence of religion, and especially religious symbols.[89] What these processes have in common as that, like the practices explained above, they allow for state power to penetrate where it was once not allowed to do so and that they allow for the renegotiation of the boundaries of constitutional democracy.[90]

83 Ferrari and Pastorelli, *Religion in Public Spaces*, 140.

84 American Legion v American Humanist Association 588 US ___ (2019). See further: Eric Yordy and Elizabeth Brown, 'Secondary Meaning and Religion: An Analysis of Religious Symbols in the Courts' (2020) 28 William & Mary Bill of Rights Journal 1025.

85 Consiglio di Stato, Judgment No 63/1988 (Italy, 1988).

86 Annicchino and Gedicks, "Cross, Crucifix, Culture: An Approach to the Constitutional Meaning of Confessional Symbols, 139.

87 Jan-Werner Mueller, '"False Advertising": Christian Democracy or Illiberal Democracy?' (*Balkan Insight*, 3 February 2020) <https://balkaninsight.com/2020/02/03/false-advertising-christian-democracy-or-illiberal-democracy/> accessed 21 April 2025.

88 Nadia Marzouki, Duncan Mcdonnell and Olivier Roy, *Saving the People. How Populists Hijack Religion* (Hurst Publishers 2016).

89 *Belcacemi and Oussar v Belgium* [2017] European Court of Human Rights 37798/13; *SAS v France* [2014] European Court of Human Rights 43835/11.

90 Dorjana Bojanovska Popovska, *State, Religion and Constitutions: The Limits of Constitutional Secularism* (Routledge forthcoming).

3.2 Reconceptualizing the Actors in the Public Sphere

Forces beyond the state have long been norm entrepreneurs,[91] using existing legal avenues to advance their goals and slowly or more rapidly shift and shape our common reality.[92] Beyond participatory law-making and features rooted in direct democracy, organized civic participation and flourishes through the perseverance and engagement of civil society organizations (CSOs) and non-governmental organizations (NGOs) in the public sphere. In times when courts and judges are key actors, the role of CSOs and NGOs is even more emphasized as they formulate disputes[93] and as friends of the court can influence outcomes and legal reasoning. CSOs and NGOs representing the interests of fragments of society or society as a whole, have a very important role in the public sphere as well as in their function of holding governments accountable to their constituencies.

Recent events have prompted the rethinking of the actors in the public sphere, more specifically regarding the nature of CSOs and NGOs and their relationships with states. This reconceptualization is at the core of the misappropriation conundrum. First, the rise and successes of rival[94] right-wing,[95] conservative transnational advocacy networks have challenged the post-1989 dominant view that human rights NGOs are predominantly a monolith group. Primarily, they challenge the view that they are a predominantly progressive force aimed at promoting and widening the scope of human rights protection – a conundrum in the core of the misappropriation of rights.

Second, they challenge the predominant view about the way transnational networks organize. The forming of transitional alliances and networks among civil society actors are traditional understood as bottom-up processes, where organizations with similar interests and goals come together to achieve common strategic aims.[96] Today, many organizations registered and working in national contexts are by their traits distinguishable as antennae of the trans-

91 Margaret E Keck and Kathryn A Sikkink, *Activists beyond Borders* (Cornell University Press 1998).

92 Cass R Sunstein, 'Social Norms and Social Roles' (1996) 96 Columbia Law Review 903.

93 Duncan Kennedy, 'Three Globalizations of Law and Legal Thought' in David M Trubek and Alvaro Santos (eds), *The New Law and Economic Development: A Critical Appraisal* (Cambridge University Press 2006).

94 Laura Landolt, 'Rival Transnational Advocacy Networks and Middle East Politics at the UN Human Rights' in Anthony Tirado Chase (ed), *The Routledge Handbook on Human Rights and the Middle East and North Africa* (Routledge 2016).

95 Clifford Bob, 'The Global Right Wing and Theories of Transnational Advocacy' (2013) 48 The International Spectator.

96 Keck and Sikkink (n 97).

national, socially conservative network.[97] As such, the relationship between the network and the national organizations is top down, where the agenda setting and the modes and models of operations and strategies are communicated top down.

Third, the relationship and the work of these organizations is often kept under the cloak of secrecy,[98] as opposed to the very public promotion of activities that NGOs' use to raise awareness of their aims and work. Even though these transitional conservative networks are responsible for submitting policy initiatives at a national, the European Union and the Council of Europe levels[99] their overall goals and strategies remain unavailable to the public.

Fourth, growing literature has also seen a shift in the way certain networks engage with political parties and even more so with the state, in illiberal democracies but not exclusively. Thus, as Krizsán and Roggeband have suggested in processes of de-democratization there is a need to reconfigure state-movement relationships.[100] Governments have recently "[attempted] to reorganize civic space through a dual process of selective in- and exclusion of civil society organizations."[101] For the state, this collaboration offers legitimacy to practices otherwise questionable from a human rights perceptive. Engaging with the state in turn has allowed these networks to influence policies in line with their aims ultimately leading to erosion of rights.

A parallel process has been the emergence or rather creation of so-called government-organized NGOs (GONGOs) as "entities [that] mimic the appearance of civil society activism while operating under tight government control."[102] Sponsored by the state they are "used to influence the realm of civil society in ways that directly legitimize state power and maintain an appearance of democracy."[103] Beyond the state, they combine with other similarly oriented organizations or act in their own capacity to engage with international organizations where they are "instrumentalized to propagate authori-

97 Datta (n 85).

98 Datta (n 87).

99 Ibid.

100 Andrea Krizsán and Conny Roggeband, 'Reconfiguring State–Movement Relations in the Context of De-Democratization1' (2021) 28 Social Politics: International Studies in Gender, State & Society 604.

101 Conny Roggeband and Andrea Krizsán, 'The Selective Closure of Civic Space' (2021) 12 Global Policy 23.

102 Sebastien Peyrouse, *Unmasking GONGOS as Agents of Illiberalism: A Case Study of the OSCE* (IERES 2024).

103 Roggeband and Krizsán (n 107).

tarian narratives…[c]laiming to voice the collective views of their population."[104]

All these processes have contributed to a more centralized structure of CSOs and NGOs operating in the public sphere – controlled top down by either state or non-state actors. As such they have contributed directly to both erosion of international human rights protection and national constitutional safeguards of power.

4 Conclusion

This chapter has demonstrated that the misappropriation of rights is one strategy in a broader repertoire of strategies employed by illiberal actors to concentrate power and undermine constitutional safeguards and democratic institutions. Alongside practices such as the reinterpretation of values, the repositioning of legal hierarchies, and the instrumentalization of religion and controlling the public sphere, the misappropriation of rights contributes to a systemic transformation of national and supranational legal orders. These strategies do not seek to abandon international institutions or legal frameworks; instead, they aim to reinterpret foundational concepts and turn them on their head. The goal is not exit, but transformation – reshaping the function and authority of international institutions from within. This broader trend of reinterpreting values, norms, and legal hierarchies poses a threat to the foundations of constitutional democracies and the international and regional organizations. Recognizing the interplay among these mechanisms and deployed strategies is essential to understanding the erosion of constraints of power from within.

Bibliography

Alexandra Brzozowski and Mojak M, 'Rule-of-Law Split Looms over Poland's Ruling Coalition – Euractiv' (11 December 2020) <https://www.euractiv.com/section/politics/short_news/rule-of-law-split-looms-over-polands-ruling-coalition/> accessed 19 April 2025.

Almond GA, Appleby RS and Sivan E, *Strong Religion : The Rise of Fundamentalisms around the World* (University of Chicago Press 2003).

104 Peyrouse (n 108).

Annicchino P and Gedicks FM, 'Cross, Crucifix, Culture: An Approach to the Constitutional Meaning of Confessional Symbols' (2013) 88 EUI Working Paper RSCAS.

Bailey H, 'A New Minority in the Courts: How the Rhetoric of Christian Victimhood and the Supreme Court Are Transforming the Free Exercise Clause' (2023) 73 Syracuse Law Review 199.

Ballester R and others, 'The Great Reset' (Foundation Institute for Legal Culture Ordo Iuris and Mathias Corvinus Collegium 2025).

Baturo A, 'Russia's Global Anti-Nazism Campaign: Seeking Support in International Organizations – IGCC' (University of California Institute on Global Conflict and Cooperation, 14 April 2023) <https://ucigcc.org/publication/russias-global-anti-nazism-campaign-seeking-support-in-international-organizations/> accessed 2 June 2025.

Bob C, 'The Global Right Wing and Theories of Transnational Advocacy' (2013) 48 The International Spectator.

Bobić A, 'Constructive Versus Destructive Conflict: Taking Stock of the Recent Constitutional Jurisprudence in the EU' (2020) 22 Cambridge Yearbook of European Legal Studies 60.

Bojanovska Popovska D, *State, Religion and Constitutions: The Limits of Constitutional Secularism* (Routledge forthcoming).

Bojanovska Popovska D and Raimondo F, 'Formal and Substantive Aspects of Citizenship and Its Connection to Religion. Definition, Practices and Comparative Perspectives' (2021) 29 Quaderni di diritto e politica ecclesiastica, Rivista trimestrale 509.

Boruah J, 'Living Tree Doctrine: Role of Indian Judiciary against Constitutional Silence in India' (Social Science Research Network, 24 May 2019) <https://papers.ssrn.com/abstract=3787907> accessed 22 May 2025.

Çalı B and Demir-Gürsel E, 'The Council of Europe's Responses to the Decay of the Rule of Law and Human Rights Protections: A Comparative Appraisal' (2021) 2 Human Rights Law Review 165.

Carnegie A, Clark R and Zucker N, 'Global Governance under Populism: The Challenge of Information Suppression – IGCC' (University of California Institute on Global Conflict and Cooperation, 14 February 2024) <https://ucigcc.org/publication/global-governance-under-populism-the-challenge-of-information-suppression/> accessed 2 June 2025.

Casanova J, *Public Religions in the Modern World* (University of Chicago Press 1994).

Corredor ES, 'Unpacking "Gender Ideology" and the Global Right's Antigender Countermovement' (2019) 44 SIGNS 613.

Cottiero C and others, 'Illiberal Regimes and International Organizations' [2024] The Review of International Organizations.

Datta N, 'Restoring the Natural Order' (EPF 2018).

Datta N, 'Modern-Day Crusaders in Europe. Tradition, Family and Property: Analysis of a Transnational, Ultra-Conservative, Catholic-Inspired Influence Network' (EPF 2020).

de Búrca G and Young KG, 'The (Mis)Appropriation of Human Rights by the New Global Right: An Introduction to the Symposium' (2023) 21 International Journal of Constitutional Law 205.

'Democracies in Decline' (*Freedom House*, 25 January 2024) <https://freedomhouse.org/issues/democracies-decline> accessed 22 April 2025.

Deneen PJ, *Why Liberalism Failed* (Yale University Press 2019).

Dworkin R, *A Matter of Principle* (Harvard University Press 1985).

Eisenegger M and Schäfer MS, 'Editorial: Reconceptualizing Public Sphere(s) in the Digital Age? On the Role and Future of Public Sphere Theory' (2023) 33 Communication Theory 61.

'Eradicating Anti-Christian Bias' (*The White House*, 6 February 2025) <https://www.whitehouse.gov/presidential-actions/2025/02/eradicating-anti-christian-bias/> ac cessed 23 April 2025.

Fabbrini F and Sajó A, 'The Dangers of Constitutional Identity' (2019) 25 European Law Journal 457.

Ferrari S and Pastorelli S (eds), *Religion in Public Spaces: A European Perspective* (Routledge 2012).

Habermas J, *The Structural Transformation of the Public Sphere* (MIT Press 1991).

Habermas J, *Between Facts and Norms: Contributions to a Discourse Theory of Law and Democracy* (MIT Press 1996).

Habermas J, 'Religion in the Public Sphere' (2006) 14 European Journal of Philosophy – 1.

Halmai G and Scholtes J, 'Illiberal Constitutionalism and the Abuse of Constitutional Identity' in Ran Hirschl and Yaniv Roznai (eds), *Deciphering the Genome of Constitutionalism: The Foundations and Future of Constitutional Identity* (Cambridge University Press 2024).

Huckerby J and Knuckey S, 'Appropriation and the Rewriting of Rights' (2023) 21 International Journal of Constitutional Law 243.

'Hungarian Foreign Minister Warns About Christianity Being the Most Persecuted Religion' (6 July 2022) <https://hungarytoday.hu/hungarian-foreign-minister-warns-about-christianity-being-the-most-persecuted-religion/> accessed 23 April 2025.

Jackson V, 'Constitutions as "Living Trees"? Comparative Constitutional Law and Interpretive Metaphors' (2006) 75 Georgetown Law Faculty Publications and Other Works 921.

'Joint Declaration on the Future of Europe: A Manifesto for the "Freedom of Nations"' (*Counting Stars*) <https://www.outono.net/elentir/2021/07/02/joint-dec

laration-on-the-future-of-europe-a-manifesto-for-the-freedom-of-nations/> accessed 22 April 2025.

Keck ME and Sikkink KA, *Activists beyond Borders* (Cornell University Press 1998).

Kelemen RD and Pech L, 'The Uses and Abuses of Constitutional Pluralism: Undermining the Rule of Law in the Name of Constitutional Identity in Hungary and Poland' (2019) 21 Cambridge Yearbook of European Legal Studies 59.

Kennedy D, 'Three Globalizations of Law and Legal Thought' in David M Trubek and Alvaro Santos (eds), *The New Law and Economic Development: A Critical Appraisal* (Cambridge University Press 2006).

Kirova I, 'Foreign Agent Laws in the Authoritarian Playbook' (*Human Rights Watch*, 19 September 2024) <https://www.hrw.org/news/2024/09/19/foreign-agent-laws-authoritarian-playbook> accessed 20 April 2025.

Konrath C, 'Values and Laws' in Regina Polak and Patrick Rohs (eds), *Values – Politics – Religion: The European Values Study: In-depth Analysis – Interdisciplinary Perspectives – Future Prospects* (Springer International Publishing 2023).

Kovács K, 'The Rise of an Ethnocultural Constitutional Identity in the Jurisprudence of the East Central European Courts' (2017) 18 German Law Journal 1703.

Krizsán A and Roggeband C, 'Reconfiguring State–Movement Relations in the Context of De-Democratization1' (2021) 28 Social Politics: International Studies in Gender, State & Society 604.

Landau D, 'Abusive Constitutionalism' (2013) 47 U.C. Davis Law Review 189.

Landolt L, 'Rival Transnational Advocacy Networks and Middle East Politics at the Un Human Rights' in Anthony Tirado Chase (ed), *The Routledge Handbook on Human Rights and the Middle East and North Africa* (Routledge 2016).

Lesti S, *Il Mito Delle Radici Cristiane Dell'Europa* (Einaudi Storia 2024).

Letsas G, 'The ECHR as a Living Instrument: Its Meaning and Legitimacy' in Andreas Føllesdal, Birgit Peters and Geir Ulfstein (eds), *Constituting Europe: The European Court of Human Rights in a National, European and Global Context* (Cambridge University Press 2013).

Lipps J and Jacob MS, 'Undermining Liberal International Organizations from within: Evidence from the Parliamentary Assembly of the Council of Europe' [2024] The Review of International Organizations.

Mälksoo L, 'Russia's Constitutional Court Defies the European Court of Human Rights: Constitutional Court of the Russian Federation Judgment of 14 July 2015, No 21-П/2015' (2016) 12 European Constitutional Law Review 377.

Maravall JM, 'The Rule of Law as a Political Weapon' in Adam Przeworski and José María Maravall (eds), *Democracy and the Rule of Law* (Cambridge University Press 2003).

Marzouki N, Mcdonnell D and Roy O, *Saving the People. How Populists Hijack Religion* (Hurst Publishers 2016).

Mason AD, 'Autonomy, Liberalism andState Neutrality' (1990) 40 The Philosophical Quarterly (1950) 433.

McCoy J, Rahman T and Somer M, 'Polarization and the Global Crisis of Democracy: Common Patterns, Dynamics, and Pernicious Consequences for Democratic Polities' (2018) 62 American Behavioral Scientist 16.

Mergel I, 'Study on the Impact of Digital Transformation on Democracy and Good Governance' (Council of Europe, CDDG 2021) CDDG(2021)4 Final.

Mueller J-W, '"False Advertising": Christian Democracy or Illiberal Democracy?' (*Balkan Insight*, 3 February 2020) <https://balkaninsight.com/2020/02/03/false-advertising-christian-democracy-or-illiberal-democracy/> accessed 21 April 2025.

Niels P and Patrick W, 'The Primacy of EU Law and the Polish Constitutional Law Judgment' (Policy Department for Citizens' Rights and Constitutional Affairs 2022) PE 734.568.

Pappin G, 'Contemporary Christian Criticism of Liberalism' in András Sajó, Renáta Uitz and Stephen Holmes (eds), *Routledge Handbook of Illiberalism* (Routledge 2022).

Peyrouse S, *Unmasking GONGOS as Agents of Illiberalism: A Case Study of the OSCE* (IERES 2024).

Plattner MF, 'Illiberal Democracy and the Struggle on the Right' 30 Journal of Democracy 5.

Rawls J, *Political Liberalism* (Columbia University Press 1993).

Rawls J, 'The Idea of Public Reason Revisited' (1997) 64 The University of Chicago Law Review 765.

Rawls J, *A Theory of Justice* (Harvard University Press 2005).

Roggeband C and Krizsán A, 'The Selective Closure of Civic Space' (2021) 12 Global Policy 23.

Rosenfeld M, 'Deconstructing Constitutional Identity in Light of the Turn to Populism' in Ran Hirschl and Yaniv Roznai (eds), *Deciphering the Genome of Constitutionalism: The Foundations and Future of Constitutional Identity* (Cambridge University Press 2024).

Sajó A, 'Preliminaries to a Concept of Constitutional Secularism' in Susanna Mancini and Michel Rosenfeld (eds), *Constitutional Secularism in an Age of Religious Revival* (Oxford University Press 2014).

Sajó A, 'The Constitution of Illiberal Democracy as a Theory About Society' [2019] Polish Sociological Review 395.

Sajó A, *Ruling by Cheating* (Cambridge University Press 2021).

Sajó A and Uitz R, 'Multi-Layered Constitutionalism, Globalization, and the Revival of the Nation State' in András Sajó and Renáta Uitz (eds), *The Constitution of Freedom: An Introduction to Legal Constitutionalism* (Oxford University Press 2017).

Sajó A, Uitz R and Holmes S, 'Preface', *Routledge Handbook of Illiberalism* (Routledge 2021).

Scheppele KL, 'The Rule of Law and the Frankenstate: Why Governance Checklists Do Not Work' (2013) 26 Governance 559.

Scheppele KL, 'Asymmetric Rupture: Stabilizing Democratic Transitions 2.0 with Transnational Law' in Michal Bobek and others (eds), *Transition 2.0: Re-establishing Constitutional Democracy in EU Member States* (Nomos Verlagsgesellschaft mbH und Co KG 2023).

Scheppele KL, Kochenov DV and Grabowska-Moroz B, 'EU Values Are Law, after All: Enforcing EU Values through Systemic Infringement Actions by the European Commission and the Member States of the European Union' (2021) 39 Yearbook of European Law 3.

Schertzer R and Woods ET, 'What Is Old Is New Again: The Deep Roots of Ethnic Nationalism in the Digital Age' (2024) 30 Nations and Nationalism 414.

Scholtes J, 'Abusing Constitutional Identity' (2021) 22 German Law Journal 534.

Shekhovtsov A, 'Government-Friendly Election Observers at the 2022 Hungarian Parliamentary Elections' (EPDE 2022).

Śledzińska-Simon A and Ziółkowski M, 'Constitutional Identity in Poland: Is the Emperor Putting on the Old Clothes of Sovereignty?' in Christian Calliess and Gerhard van der Schyff (eds), *Constitutional Identity in a Europe of Multilevel Constitutionalism* (Cambridge University Press 2019).

Somer M and McCoy J, 'Toward a Theory of Pernicious Polarization and How It Harms Democracies: Comparative Evidence and Possible Remedies' (2019) 681 The ANNALS of the American Academy of Political and Social Science 234.

Spieker LD, 'Framing and Managing Constitutional Identity Conflicts: How to Stabilize the Modus Vivendi between the Court of Justice and National Constitutional Courts' (2020) 57 Common Market Law Review 361.

Stafford G and Jaraczewski J, 'Taking European Judgments Seriously' [2022] Verfassungsblog <https://verfassungsblog.de/taking-european-judgments-seriously/> accessed 20 April 2025.

Stoeckl K, 'Traditional Values, Family, Homeschooling: The Role of Russia and the Russian Orthodox Church in Transnational Moral Conservative Networks and Their Efforts at Reshaping Human Rights' (2023) 21 International Journal of Constitutional Law 224.

Stopler G, 'The Challenge of Strong Religion in the Liberal State' (2014) 32 Boston University International Law Journal 411.

Sunstein CR, 'Social Norms and Social Roles' (1996) 96 Columbia Law Review 903.

Susen S, 'Critical Notes on Habermas's Theory of the Public Sphere' (2011) 5 Sociological Analysis 37.

Tímea Drinóczi and Bień-Kacała A, 'WEBINAR 8: HUNGARY & POLAND – The Year 2020: Lessons Learned from the Hungarian and Polish Management of the COVID-19 Crisis and Beyond' (*IACL*, 23 November 2020) <https://www.iacl-democracy-2020.org/blog/2016/3/23/blog-post-sample-9wntn-6ye75-hwawc-xx9lz-p6k2z-y8y6h-cplw4-4bcr5-t2hdf-pt4np-nzc2g-f64jl-c53x4-d693x-ycry5-xahmf> accessed 12 April 2025.

Uitz R, 'The Rule of Law in the EU: Crisis, Differentiation, Conditionality' (2022) 7 European Papers 929.

Uitz R, 'A Threat to the Core' [2025] Verfassungsblog <https://verfassungsblog.de/hungary-transparency-law-foreign-funding/> accessed 2 June 2025.

Uitz R, 'Recalibrating Human Rights in Europe: A Call to Awaken the Principle of Non-Retrogression' [forthcoming] ECTHR Law Review.

Urbinati N, 'Laïcité in Reverse: Mono-Religious Democracies' and the Issue of Religion in the Public Sphere' (2010) 17 Constellations 4.

Vermeule A, 'Beyond Originalism' (*The Atlantic*, 31 March 2020) <https://www.theatlantic.com/ideas/archive/2020/03/common-good-constitutionalism/609037/> accessed 23 April 2025.

Vermeule A, *Common Good Constitutionalism* (Polity 2022).

Vidigal G, 'Evolutionary Interpretation and International Law' (2021) 24 Journal of International Economic Law 203.

Von Bogdandy A, 'Ways to Frame the European Rule of Law: Rechtsgemeinschaft, Trust, Revolution, and Kantian Peace' (2018) 14 European Constitutional Law Review 675.

Waldron J, 'Is the Rule of Law an Essentially Contested Concept (In Florida)?' (2002) 21 Law and Philosophy 137.

Wischermann U and Mueller IK, 'Feminist Theories on the Separation of the Private and the Public: Looking Back, Looking Forward' (2004) 20 Women in German Yearbook 184.

Wolkenstein F, 'Christian Europe Redux' (2023) 61 JCMS: Journal of Common Market Studies 636.

Yordy E and Brown E, 'Secondary Meaning and Religion: An Analysis of Religious Symbols in the Courts' (2020) 28 William & Mary Bill of Rights Journal 1025.

Zakaria F, 'The Rise of Illiberal Democracy' (1997) 76 Foreign Affairs 22.

CHAPTER 12

Conclusions

Cathérine Van de Graaf, Paula Rhein-Fischer and Júlia Miklasová

This volume has explored the evolving concept of human rights misappropriation, examining the mechanisms, agents, and contexts in which human rights language is claimed, distorted, or instrumentalised. In this closing chapter, we evaluate the edited volume's contribution to the conceptual clarity of misappropriation of human rights and explore the potential of the misappropriation framework as a conceptual tool for future human rights scholarship. When reading across the 11 chapters of this edited volume, it becomes apparent that, although the contributing authors each examine the misappropriation of human rights from distinct perspectives or within specific contexts, they nonetheless often articulate shared concerns. As editors, we use this concluding chapter as an opportunity to add our own reflections to these common themes we identified.

This edited volume set out to offer answers to a set of central questions surrounding the phenomenon of human rights misappropriation. At its core, the volume asked: What are the constitutive elements of misappropriation, and how does it differ from more "ordinary" forms of abuse or distortion of human rights language? Our contributors examined the motives that drive actors to misappropriate human rights: ranging from restricting the legal rights of political opponents, to projecting legitimacy through the language of law, and shielding perpetrators from accountability through mechanisms of impunity. The volume explored where and how misappropriation takes place, and who the driving forces behind it are. Misappropriation can manifest in diverse fora and forms: through lawfare and the strategic use of legal procedures at the international or domestic level, in speeches, press statements, and media interventions, in legislative proposals, and even in the opening of frivolous domestic proceedings. The agents involved are equally varied, ranging from governments and political actors, courts and judges, to civil society associations.

Finally, the volume reflected critically on the concept itself. To what extent does "misappropriation" risk being dismissed as a subjective label, shaped by value judgments and power asymmetries? Does it risk marginalising diversified or non-Western approaches to human rights? And does the concept add analytical value beyond existing notions such as "abuse" or "distortion", or

© 2026 THE AUTHOR(S) | HTTPS://DOI.ORG/10.1163/9789004763005-014

does it merely repackage familiar critiques? The volume navigates through the murky waters of related concepts such as vernacularisation, appropriation and illiberalism while attempting to lay bare the elements that are necessary to speak of "misappropriation" and some indicators which can help identify the relevant practices from a more inductive point of view.

As the concluding chapter, the discussion aims to synthesise the insights developed throughout the preceding contributions and to offer our own reflections. This chapter is structured as follows. Section 1 revisits the conceptual foundation by reflecting critically on the concept of human rights, distinguishing appropriation from misappropriation, and reflecting on the constitutive and contextual elements of misappropriation, thereby consolidating and refining the analytical framework underpinning the volume. Section 2 addresses the conceptual limits of the term, with particular attention to its spatial and temporal dimensions, while Section 3 concludes by considering the limits of this edited volume and identifying directions for further research and scholarly engagement.

1 Human Rights Misappropriation

In the special issue titled "The (Mis)appropriation of Human Rights by the New Global Right" in the *International Journal of Constitutional Law*, de Búrca and Young define the (mis)appropriation of human rights as the "deployment by a particular set of actors of a range of strategies and arguments [...] advanced in the language of protecting 'human rights,' but generally seeking to reverse or undo previous human rights developments and commitments".[1] They further propose a set of eight criteria helping to identify this phenomenon.[2] As outlined in the introduction, this volume engages with de Búrca and Young's propositions and the findings of the special issue's case studies by testing both the concept and the relevance of the proposed criteria. This section highlights key foundational issues concerning the concept, particularly, its definition, its relationship to other neighbouring ideas and its constitutive and contextual elements.

1 G de Búrca and KG Young, 'The (Mis) appropriation of Human Rights by the New Global Right: An Introduction to the Symposium' (2023) 21 International Journal of Constitutional Law 206–207.

2 Ibid., 213–214.

1.1 Defining Human Rights

A first central concern is that any attempt to define the misappropriation of human rights will necessarily face the difficulty that there is no clear or widely shared understanding of what 'human rights' refers to. Several authors emphasised in their contribution that without such a shared understanding or approach, any demarcating of the use of human rights as a misappropriation will lack the necessary common starting point. In the chapter 'Misappropriation as an Empty Frame", Aral signalled that indeed it remains obscure "what 'human rights' means for the narrative". She argued: "If there is talk of misappropriation, misuse, abuse, or backsliding, these terms acquire meaning only in relation to an assumed proper appropriation, use, or interpretation of human rights."[3] To come to an agreement that misappropriation has occurred will depend on how human rights are conceptualised by the onlooker.

The lack of a common understanding of human rights goes beyond disagreements about which human rights are protected and how far that protection extends. Rather this reflects fundamentally divergent ontological, epistemological, and normative assumptions about the nature, justification, and purpose of human rights.[4] Whether human rights are viewed as a powerful language or framing without any objective existence (discourse scholars), or rather as claims and aspirations that allow the *status quo* to be contested in favour of the oppressed (protest scholars) or instead as an entitlement that one has by virtue of being a human being (natural scholars) will inevitably have an impact on what is viewed as a misappropriation of those human rights.[5] De Búrca and Young recognise that indeed human rights have always been a site of contestation and disagreement. Throughout their seminal work "The (Mis)appropriation of Human Rights by the New Global Right: An Introduction to the Symposium", they refer to the misappropriation of human rights language, the human rights system and in some instances human rights law in particular.[6] Hoping to sidestep the hurdle of positioning themselves vis-à-vis a thick moral or political theory of rights, de Búrca and Young took the basis commitment to "recognition and protection for the equal human dignity, human freedom, and human welfare of all persons" as a starting point for the recognition of when misappropriation of human rights takes place. They went on to state that: "legal protection for human rights should be dignity-

3 See chapter by Aral.

4 This divergence is situated at a metatheoretical level rather than a merely practical or doctrinal one, M-B Dembour. 'What Are Human Rights? Four Schools of Thought' (2010) 32 Human Rights Quarterly 1.

5 Ibid., 4–8.

6 De Búrca and Young (n 1) 206, 207.

enhancing rather than dignity undermining, recognizing rather than denying the equality of humans, universalist in orientation rather than strictly sovereigntist, welfare-promoting rather than welfare reducing, and accepting rather than rejecting of mechanisms of accountability". Yet, in the chapter 'Misappropriation or Vernacularisation in the Global South? The 'Family Love Alliance' and the Modernist Islamic Appropriation of Human Rights in Indonesia', Nugraha argued that through a process of human rights "vernacularisation" – that is, their reinterpretation in different contexts –, we may also end up with a "resulting hybrid (that) may not necessarily align with how we conceive dignity, freedom, and welfare".[7] He notes critically that the concept of de Búrca and Young has not accounted for the inescapable reality that human rights take on different forms as they diffuse within particular societies.[8]

In the special issue by de Búrca and Young, ultraconservative or illiberal human rights (mis)appropriation should constitute "a departure from the existing international human rights law, and particularly from developments post-dating the Universal Declaration of Human Rights (UDHR)".[9] Yet, Lister, in the chapter 'Misappropriation: The Semantics of Power', argues that the paradigm is simply too unsettled and how exclusionary or repressive a use of human rights is "turns upon varied legal and ontological arguments which are inherently divided for socially contentious topics".[10] Thus, by the very act of labelling a claim as "misappropriated", one exercises authority over the discourse, potentially reproducing hierarchies of interpretation. Aral stressed in her chapter that the failing "to define the contours of 'genuine' human rights, the narrative ultimately relies on an assumed, but unarticulated, consensus" undermines the framework's analytical coherence.[11] She cautions that the term can become an empty vessel, applied indiscriminately whenever actors disagree with prevailing interpretations of human rights. Bojanovska Popovska adds a constructive note in the chapter 'A Change from Within: Beyond Human Rights', urging that attention to misappropriation should not preclude the possibility of reform from within. She emphasises that the human rights project's resilience depends not on rigid protection of existing

7 Later in this conclusion, we will come back to the comparison of the concept of vernacularisation to (mis)appropriation.
8 See chapter by Nugraha.
9 De Búrca and Young (n 1), 213.
10 See chapter by Lister.
11 See chapter by Aral.

interpretations but on adaptive, context-sensitive engagement with contested meanings.[12]

Ultimately, the debate is one about whether there is a core of human rights about which there is a universal consensus – a question that has been debated for decades.[13] It is difficult to think the concept of misappropriation without that universal core as it serves as the key reference point for this concept. In any case, it is important that scholars who believe in such a universal core and further engage with the concept state clearly how they approach human rights and what is the actual content of a right that they present as being misappropriated.[14]

1.2 Defining and Distinguishing (Mis)Appropriation

As outlined in the introduction, several contributors to this volume observe that the concept of misappropriation of human rights bears significant resemblance to related concepts, which in part overlap with the misappropriation concept. This section revisits these competing concepts in order to examine the distinctive conceptual contribution that misappropriation of human rights offers. Additionally, we reflect on the relationship and interplay among these ideas and concepts.

1.2.1 Appropriation

While the prefix 'mis' gives the concept of misappropriation a clear negative connotation, "appropriation" as such is more neutral. De Búrca and Young's consistent use of (mis)appropriation with 'mis' in brackets indicates that they also apply their criticism against the relevant human rights invocations by primarily right-wing actors to 'appropriations' of human rights. The brackets then suggest an awareness of the inherent proximity between appropriation and misappropriation. However, 'appropriation' can also be used to refer to 'proper appropriation' of human rights, "misappropriation" then serving as the exact opposite of 'appropriation'. Indeed 'misappropriation' calls for an ant-

12 See chapter by Bojanovska Popovska.

13 See only J Donnelly, 'Cultural Relativism and Universal Human Rights' (1984) 6 Human Rights Quarterly 400; 'The Relative Universality of Human Rights' (2007) 29(2) Human Rights Quarterly 281; T Franck, 'Are Human Rights Universal?' (2001) 80 Council on Foreign Relations 191; E Brems, *Human Rights: Universality and Diversity* (Martinus Nijhoff 2001).

14 Later in this conclusion, we come back to the need for concretising the meaning of human rights for the misappropriation framework to make a useful contribution.

onym, as Aral rightly stresses: 'Misappropriation, by its very nature, can only be understood in contrast to proper appropriation.' Without illuminating concretely what the specific content is or what the contours are of the presumed essence of a right, scholars' assessment will inevitably remain vague. This aspect ultimately amounts to the argument that the content of human rights cannot be universally defined.

This reasoning holds true for use, abuse and misuse as well.

1.2.2 Abuse

Abuse is a concept that is primarily used in relation to rights in international law. In this context, among other things, it refers to the use of a legal right for an end different from that for which it was conferred.[15] The concept of misappropriation of human rights links in with this as it also requires – as we argue here – that human rights are invoked for other purposes than those they are usually associated with.[16] In this respect it also offers many similarities with the notion of "abusive constitutionalism" coined, among others, by Landau[17] to denote "the use of mechanisms of constitutional change in order to make a state significantly less democratic than it was before".[18]

In our view, abuse is the more general term and misappropriation thus always a form of abuse or abusive constitutionalism. However, misappropriation, as conceptualised here, can be considered as more specific in two respects: first, it puts a stronger emphasis on the fact that what is being misappropriated is formally agreed with and is thus "appropriated". In this respect, misappropriation is a particularly cunning and at the same time particularly subtle form of abuse. Second, while abuse is not always conceptualised as requiring any bad faith element, this element should be seen as a constitutive element for misappropriation.[19]

15 A Kiss, 'Abuse of Rights' MPEPIL (online edn OUP 2006) par 1; see also the introduction of this volume.

16 See introduction of this volume, and Section 1.2.3.

17 D Landau, 'Abusive Constitutionalism' (2013) 47 U.C. Davis L. Rev. 189; D Landau and R Dixon, *Abusive Constitutional Borrowing. Legal Globalization and the Subversion of Liberal Democracy* (Oxford University Press 2021) 27; see also J Petrov, 'How to Detect Abusive Constitutional Practices' (2024) 2 European Constitutional Law Review 1; see also introduction of this volume.

18 Landau (n 17) 195.

19 See below 1.2.3 and introduction. See Kiss (n 15) paras 4–6.

1.2.3 Vernacularisation

Vernacularisation is one such concept that cannot easily be distinguished from malicious abuse of human rights. As mentioned by de Búrca and Young in their introduction, 'human rights are so often "remade in the vernacular"'.[20] Merry conceptualised vernacularisation as "the extraction of ideas and practices from the universal sphere of international organizations and their translation into ideas and practices that resonate with the values and ways of doing things in local contexts".[21]

Nugraha argued that in fact: "resulting vernacularised conceptions may not necessarily align with our own sensibilities".[22] He stated that, "on the very contrary, vernacular human rights, as conditioned by local knowledge and values, may strike international human rights lawyers as 'revers[ing] or undo [ing] previous human rights developments and commitments' at the global level, even though from a local perspective, it is neither a 'progress' nor 'regress'".[23] A myriad of actors can engage in vernacularisation. For example, Genoud refers to 'vernacularisation from above' as a process where corporate or rather financial actors directly appropriate human rights in order to better serve their interests.[24]

Although there may be cases of such "vernacularisation from above", vernacularisation usually occurs in decentralised, organic, and often accidental processes. This is what distinguishes this notion from misappropriation where the use of human rights language is rather controlled, deliberate, and more systematic.

1.2.4 Contested or Novel Interpretation of Human Rights

This volume also made us reflect on the continuous misappropriation of human rights during the adjudication process at regional human rights courts and other supervisory mechanisms. In the configuration of applicant versus state, state agents and the lawyers representing the state will regularly under-

---

20 De Búrca and Young (n 1) 209. They refer to: 3 S Engle Merry, 'Transnational Human Rights and Local Activism: Mapping the Middle' (2006) 108 Am Anthropologist 38.

21 S Engle Merry, 'The Global Travel of Women's Human Rights' (New York University 2017) https://as.nyu.edu/content/dam/nyu-as/asSilverDialogues/documents/S%20Merry%20Resonance%20Dilemma%20silver%20prof%20article1.pdf accessed 5 November 2025; S Engle Merry, *The Seductions of Quantification: Measuring Human Rights, Gender Violence, and Sex Trafficking* (The University of Chicago Press 2016) 110–111.

22 See chapter by Nugraha.

23 Ibid.

24 C Genoud, 'Vernacularisation from Above: Finance's Appropriation of Human Rights in Land Governance' (2020) 25 The International Journal of Human Rights 1356.

stand that the invoked violation of human rights they are defending themselves against constitutes, in fact, a misappropriation of human rights. It is certainly imaginable that misappropriation of human rights takes place even before courts. However, the concept should be distinguished from the mere contested interpretations of human rights.[25]

Identifying distinctive features between contested interpretation and misappropriation already touches much on the constitutive elements of misappropriation which will be dealt with in more detail below.[26] Indeed, the differences appear to be three-fold: First, the examples that this volume identified as misappropriation suggest that misappropriation possesses some systemic element as it is usually part of a general policy and does not simply occur in relation to a specific case or proceeding. Second, while contested interpretations may be far-fetched, strange or even absurd, the misappropriation concept is reserved for "more extreme" cases in that it relates to invocations of human rights that turn against the instrument of human rights as such. Third, we argue that the actor, to "misappropriate" must act in bad faith, precisely to make the distinction from regular contested interpretation clearer: where they invoke human rights because they genuinely believe that a certain right has a particular content, we remain in the realm of interpretation. Misappropriation presupposes that the actor invokes human rights precisely to undermine the instrument of human rights.[27]

Of course, the distinction remains difficult to make. This is particularly interesting when it comes to actors that are usually not suspected of "misappropriating" human rights: progressive actors who invoke human rights to strive for an extension of particular rights, like an expansion of rights protection beyond the individual, to include non-human entities such as forests and rivers.[28] These expansive interpretations can sometimes entail a radical limitation or even result in non-recognition of competing human rights. While from the perspective of these activists, and perhaps even many human rights scholars, they are precisely acting to achieve a better human rights protection, this depends on the perspective: the competing rights-holder whose rights are put aside may be of a different view. Again, this is the consequence of problem that it is difficult to establish what the universal core of human rights is. This is

---

25 Compare De Búrca and Young's distinction from "genuine, even if contested, invocation of human rights" in De Búrca and Young (n 1), 212.

26 See Section 1.2 and in particular Section 1.2.3.

27 Compare Section 1.2.3 for bad faith as a constitutive element of misappropriation; see introduction for.

28 Compare A Huneeus, 'When Illiberals Embrace Human Rights' (2019) 113 AJIL Unbound 380.

not to say that all actors stemming from the "protest school of thought" who use human rights to – in their view – further social or environmental justice[29] should be seen as misappropriating human rights whenever their claims are radical enough to attack some core human rights norms. Still, it is worth in our view to further explore the possibility that misappropriation should not be reserved for "non-progressive", conservative actors, but is neutral vis-à-vis the political current of the actor.[30]

1.2.5 Illiberalism

In their special issue, de Búrca and Young already explicitly linked human rights (mis)appropriation to illiberalism by phrasing it as illiberal (mis)appropriation, thereby suggesting it is part of the playbook of illiberal coalitions. In the chapter 'A Change from Within: Beyond Human Rights', Bojanovska Popovska reflects on how the misappropriation of rights can in fact be approached as "one strategy in a broader repertoire of strategies employed by illiberal actors to concentrate power and undermine constitutional safeguards and democratic institutions".[31] Understood in this way, illiberalism is the ideology and institutional setting that misappropriation is grounded in; misappropriation in turn is a tool to realise illiberal politics.

1.3 The Constitutive and Indicative Elements of Misappropriation of Human Rights

Taken together, the chapters reveal the complex interplay between agency, narrative, and structure in misappropriation. Agents range from states to non-state actors, employing strategies that are rhetorical, legal, and political.

1.3.1 Fora and Agents

Misappropriation of human rights can occur in all three branches of the state: the parliament – e.g., when a bill is justified by human rights although their meaning is completely reversed –, the executive – e.g., when the members of the government, in public speeches, create a hierarchy of human rights prioritising the freedom of religion or right to life over other rights –, or the judiciary – e.g., when judges, during court proceedings, position themselves as

29 See Dembour (n 4) 3 et seq.
30 Compare chapter by Freedman – progressive, pernicious and retractionist politicisation.
31 See chapter by Bojanovska Popovska.

neutral defenders of the law or democracy to mask strategic misuse. Moreover, human misappropriation can also take place at the international level, whether within human rights bodies, such as the UN Human Rights Council, where States use human rights language and political tactics to advance competing discourses; through multilateral fora; or even bilaterally, when human rights rhetoric is abused to justify aggression and to deflect attention from a State's own violations.

An integrated reading of the volume highlights the multiplicity of actors who wield human rights not merely for protection but for strategic ends. Horvath's work illustrates the active role of state power in defending perpetrators of atrocity and reshaping the interpretation of international law, showing that misappropriation is simultaneously a tactic of self-preservation and political legitimisation.

Yet, as Bojanovska Popovska remind us, transnationally organised civil society organizations (CSOs) and non-governmental organizations (NGOs) can play equally decisive roles, either by reinforcing dominant narratives or by challenging them in ways that inadvertently facilitate misappropriation. Sanctis de Brito and others underscore the role of the 'BBB' (Beef, Bible and Bullets) coalitions, encompassing not only the legislative caucuses, but also various civil society actors, in using legal language, particularly concerning the vindication of rights and their 'true-bearers,' to advance their interests and values within the Brazilian political and legal context.

While the special issue of de Búrca and Young and also most of our contributions focused in particular on right-wing and ultra-conservative actors, we argue that this focus is possibly too narrow. Although the human rights project historically roots in efforts to protect individuals against state arbitrariness,[32] regardless of its political origin, human rights activists and scholars today are often identified with the progressive left. Indeed, systematic violations of human rights are without any doubt a sign of right-wing illiberal regimes, making human rights a bulwark especially against threats from the political right. From this perspective, it is not surprising that "misappropriations" of human rights have so far primarily been searched for in practices of right-wing and ultra-conservative actors. However, it should not be overseen that also socialist illiberal regimes such as those in Venezuela under Hugo Chávez or Nicolas Maduro or Nicaragua under Daniel Ortega also tend(ed) to justify illiberal policies with human rights language, namely, the necessity to protect social and collective rights as well as the right to security or the "right to live in

32 E Bates, 'History' in D Moeckli, S Shah, S Sivakumaran (eds), *International Human Rights Law* (4th edn, OUP 2022).

peace" – the latter ones being used to justify repressions against the opposition.[33] China, to which Freedman devoted her attention, is another example that does not fit in the camp of ultra-conservative right-wing actors, although practices of misappropriation can be identified there.

This analysis suggests that human rights misappropriation can occur at any level of political organisation – domestic, international, and even transnational – and stem from any actor, regardless of whether it is a state or a non-state actor, and regardless of the political current. The latter holds as long as two requirements are fulfilled: first, the actor must hold (political) power for the relevant practice to have some effect and, second, the actor must interact with law, allowing it to be recognised as a voice within the legal discourse at all.

1.3.2 Strategies

Across the volume, a recurring concern is the range of tactics through which misappropriation occurs. These extend from semantic manipulation to institutional strategies and public diplomacy. Freedman, Horvath, and Wilkinson collectively give examples of the formal and institutional mechanisms of misappropriation: coalition-building in multilateral fora, agenda-setting in rights institutions, and leveraging global development initiatives as mechanisms for reframing human rights priorities. Such strategies underscore the sophistication of statecraft in the contemporary human rights system: misappropriation is rarely *ad hoc*; it is deliberate and often highly coordinated.

At the discursive level, contributions by Maslova and Lipatova, Celik, Nugraha, and Fortuin and others, reveal more subtle mechanisms. Ambiguity, selective citation, and misrepresentation of legal norms allow actors to craft narratives that appear authoritative while diverging from established principles. These techniques exploit gaps in enforcement, public knowledge, and normative consensus, showing that misappropriation is as much a communi-

---

33 See, e.g. Maduro N, transl by La Riva G, 'Nicolás Maduro's Speech on Venezuela's New Anti-blockade Law to Resist U.S. Imperialism' (Liberation School, 16 December 2020) <https://www.liberationschool.org/nicolas-maduros-anti-blockade-law-speech> accessed 9 June 2026; implicitly also Chávez H, 'Strike at the Helm' (Caracas, 20 October 2012) <https://mronline.org/2015/04/01/strike-at-the-helm/> accessed 5 November 2025: "We must implant social property with the spirit of socialism, all down the line, from agricultural work […] to the system of distribution and consumption of the local producers"; Murillo R, 'Speech' (26 June 2018) <http://www.psuv.org.ve/temas/noticias/rosario-murillo-nicaragua-pueblo-paz-derecha-violencia-seguridad-oposicion-agenda-planes-desestabilizacion/> accessed 5 November 2025.

cative practice as a legal or political one. Celik's chapter 'The Strategic Deployment of 'Hate Speech' in Turkey: Misappropriation of Human Rights?' exemplifies the interaction between rhetorical manipulation by political leaders and selective enforcement by state institutions. Ambiguities in law can create loopholes that allow norms to be applied inconsistently, enabling the exercise of power in ways that may undermine rights or accountability. Similarly, Fortuin and others' application of Gricean maxims demonstrates that violations of communicative norms – misleading detail, irrelevant argumentation, and strategic fallacies – are not peripheral but central to misappropriation. Freedman's analysis of diplomatic and practical legal strategies to undermine the universality of human rights within the international human rights system and Wilkinson's study of Russia's promotion of "traditional values" demonstrates that misappropriation is not a matter of denial; rather, it often involves the construction of alternative frameworks that compete with liberal human rights norms.

De Búrca and Young's focus excluded what they named 'the distinctive Chinese model' as it is not considered part of the populist and/or religious right-wing coalitions.[34] Testing the stated distinctiveness, this edited volume does engage with the Chinese focus on traditional values and the strategies in advancing state sovereignty by limiting legal responsibilities towards human rights protection. As Freedman argues, China's main strategies to subvert "Western hegemony over global human-rights governance" consist in, first, shifting the discourse from human rights to development, notably through its development banks and infrastructure and investment programmes, second, promoting an agenda of "mutually beneficial cooperation" in human rights bodies, seeking to advance dialogue rather than accountability, and third, establishing the South-South Forum on Human Rights, striving to undermine human rights.

The chapter '"The True Right Bearers" Victimhood and Citizenship in the Construals of the Legal Subject' by Sanctis de Brito and others expands this discussion by interrogating the notion of victimhood and the legal subject. Misappropriation, in their account, is exercised through selective claims about who constitutes a legitimate rights-bearer. By privileging particular identities or narratives of suffering, actors can reconfigure the normative landscape, reshaping obligations and redirecting moral authority. Their use of the language of rights reflects a strategy of disjunctive citizenship that distances rights politics from its humanist and pluralist dimensions, as they claim to be the true subjects of law and define themselves against perceived "enemies" to be neutralised.

---

34 De Búrca and Young (n 1) 207.

Besides a discursive process, misappropriation can involve the erosion of procedural safeguards as well as the misuse of judicial process including *ex officio* investigations. Celik signals that, in her example of Turkey, state and quasi-legal institutions, including TİHEK and RTÜK, exercise discretion not merely in response to complaints but through proactive interventions.

Together, these analyses confirm that misappropriation operates across multiple dimensions: legal, discursive, political, procedural, and social.

1.3.3 Synthesis: The Constitutive and Indicative Elements of Misappropriation

From these findings, it is possible to extrapolate the constitutive elements – that are *necessary* to speak of "misappropriation" – as well as some indicators which, while they are not necessary, help identifying the relevant practices from a more inductive point of view, especially in borderline cases.

Naturally, some of these elements will be subject to the same critique as that raised against the definitional elements put forward De Búrca and Young. This applies above all to the critique by those who doubt that there is any objective consensus about a "core" of human rights norms. The following elements should therefore primarily be understood as a refinement of the existing definition of misappropriation addressed to those who believe in some universal core. These elements are, however, not able to solve the seemingly eternal debate about whether there is such a core and what exact form it takes.

With this reservation, we argue misappropriation requires the following constitutive elements: misappropriation is (1) the affirmative use of human rights language (appropriation), (2) that distorts core norms of human rights about which there is wide agreement (and the content of which should be stated clearly by those who use the concept of misappropriation), (3) by actors with political power and engaged in legal discourse, (4) for purposes other than those normally associated with human rights argumentation, specifically to undermine the human rights project as such (bad faith).

The identified strategies of misappropriation can mainly serve as indicators, helping to identify especially the crucial element of bad faith – about which there is usually the greatest uncertainty, and which needs to be deduced from objective circumstances.[35] From this perspective, it can be a sign of an intent to undermine the human rights project that the actor uses (i) institutional

35 See introduction of this volume.

strategies such as coalition-building in multilateral fora, agenda-setting in rights institutions, and leveraging global development initiatives to change the agenda of human rights, or (ii) discursive strategies such as deliberate ambiguity, selective citation, and misrepresentation of legal norms, shifting the discourse from human rights to development, promoting an agenda of "mutually beneficial cooperation" in human rights bodies, or making selective claims about who constitutes a legitimate rights-bearer. The more systematic these strategies appear, the more likely it is that one can speak of "misappropriation".

The constitutive elements suggested here largely overlap with but further refine de Búrca and Young's two-pronged definition. According to this definition, misappropriation is the "deployment by a particular set of actors of a range of strategies and arguments [...] advanced in the language of protecting 'human rights,' but generally seeking to reverse or undo previous human rights developments and commitments".[36] However, the elements suggested here are more specific with regard to the positive connotation of human rights language, the object of misappropriation, the nature of the relevant actor and the necessity of an element of bad faith. Similarly, the indicators identified here, which are not exhaustive, are to be understood not in opposition but to complement and further specify the eight indicators as identified by de Búrca and Young.[37]

2 Conceptual Dimensions of the Misappropriation of Human Rights

2.1 Spatial Aspects: The Geography of Misappropriation

As the focus of their study, de Búrca and Young refer to the New Global Right as an "array of national and transnational coalitions of populist and conservative political and religious actors".[38] The special issue included case studies from Brazil, Ghana, India, Nigeria, Russia, Turkey, Uganda, and the United States (under the former Trump administration). They discuss the issue of organised religious groups who are locally often the majority and thus can wield significant political power. This edited volume includes examples, among others,

36 De Búrca and Young (n 1) 207; for more details, see introduction of this volume.
37 De Búrca and Young (n 1) 213; see also introduction of this volume.
38 De Búrca and Young (n 1) 207.

from Brazil, China, Indonesia, Russia, and Turkey. Yet, this volume also casts doubt as to whether the concept can easily be transposed beyond across the world or whether in fact, as Nugraha states, "it turns out to be only meaningful within the societal and political contexts where de Búrca and Young operate".[39] Nugraha argues that his case study of the advocacy by the Family Love Alliance can be seen a warning against "applying concepts rooted in a particular context onto distinct realities".[40]

Meanwhile Aral criticises exactly the refusal of the West to take a hard look at itself by focusing on non-Western states and thereby suggest the misappropriation concept is blind vis-à-vis human rights distortions of Western states.[41] A planned chapter on US misappropriation of human rights under the Trump administration could not be delivered, leaving an area that remains open for further scholarly exploration. Rather than viewing this as a shortcoming, we see it as an invitation for continued debate and new research beyond the pages of this volume. In the chapter of Bojanovska Popovska, we read that both so-called consolidated and backsliding democracies have relied on Article 4(2) TEU which obliges the European Union to respect the national identities of its Member States.[42] Yet, national identity – at least in some cases – appears to be a repackaging of sovereignty and is used to evade accountability and curb dissent.[43] This chapter demonstrates that Western actors are by no means exempt from scrutiny, even if such analysis remains underdeveloped.

2.2 Temporal Aspects

The chapters in this volume converge on the insight that misappropriation is not a novel development; rather, it is a recurrent feature of rights discourse. Aral stresses that 'the history of human rights can also be read as a more heterogeneous account, encompassing both progress and setbacks'. Freedman used the term 'pendulum movement' to capture this process, stating that, inevitably, the furthering of progressive agendas, will be followed by a promotion of competing retractionist narratives to counter such progress. Similarly, Sanctis de Brito and others consider that the phenomenon that "legal language mobilisation" drifts away from the universalist approach of rights is a "recur-

39 See chapter by Nugraha.
40 Ibid.
41 See chapter by Aral.
42 N Petersen and P Wasilczyk, 'The Primacy of EU Law and the Polish Constitutional Law Judgment' (Policy Department for Citizens' Rights and Constitutional Affairs 2022) PE 734.568.
43 See chapter by Bojanovska Popovska.

rent patterns of the reality of rights interpretation" has occurred "throughout the history of human rights practice".

From a temporal perspective, misappropriation should perhaps not be understood as an entirely new phenomenon but as a recurring feature of engagement with human rights (discourse). As Aral mentions, while the ups and downs of the human rights movement are recognised in the work of de Búrca and Young, populism is positioned as an unprecedented challenge to the movement which makes new strategies necessary. We are not sure that this is true. What is truly novel, perhaps, is the speed and scale at which misappropriation can occur in the digital age, amplifying the effects of narrative control and institutional influence.

Another temporal question is to what extent the understanding of what an "appropriate" use of human rights is and hence, as opposed to this, a misappropriation *changes in time*. Interestingly, de Búrca and Young identified the "departure from the existing international human rights law, and particularly from developments post-dating the Universal Declaration of Human Rights" as one of their eight indicators of misappropriation, making misappropriation itself a concept to identify and safeguard against (attempted) regressive changes of the content of human rights. Yet, even if the speed of change may be slower in their core than in their peripheries, it would be unrealistic to claim that human rights' content is immutable. Neither is therefore the content of misappropriation. The difficulties involved in determining whether a relevant change has occurred mirror those raised by critics of the very concept itself: who determines the content of human rights, and on what basis can we say it has evolved? Should the mere number of states or courts endorsing a position be decisive? And does it matter whether the change reflects a more or less protective understanding of rights, given that the threshold for a human rights regression may be considerably higher?

3 Looking Ahead: Research Opportunities and Constraints

In this section, we reflect on the limits of this edited volume and signal how the roads non taken can be opportunities for future research.

3.1 Misappropriation as a Methodological Framework

The misappropriation of human rights as a framework risks overextension, particularly when applied indiscriminately to any challenge or reinterpretation of human rights. It also carries epistemic hazards: by focusing attention on misappropriation, one may inadvertently reinforce hierarchies or marginalise alternative, locally grounded interpretations of rights. As Aral, Lister, and Bojanovska Popovska all emphasise, scholars must navigate these tensions carefully, combining conceptual rigor with an openness to the dynamic evolution of human rights.

The contributors collectively highlight the methodological challenges in studying misappropriation. Analyses across institutions and actors, such as those by Maslova and Lipatova and Celik underscore the difficulty of establishing baseline norms against which misappropriation can be measured. Nugraha and Fortuin and others demonstrate that context-specific investigations, attentive to both legal frameworks and cultural discourse, are essential for understanding the dynamics of misappropriation in practice. Moreover, scholars must remain reflexive about their own positionality, acknowledging that what is labelled misappropriation may be shaped as much by analytical frameworks as by the actions of the subjects themselves.

As what discussed above, Aral rightly stressed that without illuminating concretely what the specific content is, or the contours are of the presumed essence of a right, scholars' assessment will inevitably remain vague. Aral criticised that scholars who have published on misappropriation rarely specify which particular rights are being affected.[44] As such, a central finding can be that for the concept of human rights misappropriation to be useful, it is necessary to highlight at the micro level where exactly the distortion occurs. De Búrca and Young captured this under point 7 in their list of indicators as "the fact that the human rights invocation is a reversal of previous rhetorical or legal strategies of the actor". Demonstrating *conclusively* that a state – or even a group of states – has misappropriated human rights is often impossible due to evidentiary constraints. However, by focusing on a specific strand of case law, or the evolution of political statements by a particular State or non-State actor or institution, scholars can often identify and infer *convincing* patterns. It is important that the elements identified above remain constant across case studies. At the same time, it is essential to remain cautious and consider alternative explanations for practices that may appear as misappropriation.

Despite these limits, the volume affirms the continued relevance of the misappropriation concept as a lens for critical engagement. By drawing attention to the mechanisms, agents, and consequences of strategic claims over

44 However, compare this with contributions in this volume that examine the phenomenon in relation to the operation of specific rights, see especially chapters by Freedman and Sanctis de Brito et al.

human rights, it equips scholars and practitioners with a vocabulary and analytical framework to identify, interrogate, and respond to challenges to the normative order. To recognise that misappropriation of human rights occurs is a valuable insight to obtain about any given situation or actor. Nevertheless, methodologically, interdisciplinary and context-sensitive approaches acknowledging one's own positionality will be essential, combining legal, political, and discursive analyses to capture the complexity of misappropriation in practice.

3.2 Future Research and Call to Action?

Looking ahead, research should attend not only to state actors but also to transnational, commercial, and Big Tech actors, whose influence increasingly shapes rights discourse. We already referred briefly to the role of other actors besides states when discussing the competing concepts of misappropriation in Section 1 of this final chapter. When one thinks about exploitation of human rights language one would inevitably think of commercial actors trying to wash their operations in human rights language for monetary or other profit. In addition to state actors, corporate actors can equally be involved in the misappropriation of human rights, a phenomenon that merits rigorous examination.[45] This was demonstrated by the earlier cited example of financial actors who appropriate human rights to serve their own interests and thereby cement unequal power relations related to land grabbing illustrates. It is worth exploring further to what extent such practices differ from misappropriations by states in their motives, strategies and in the ways to deal with them.

As confirmed throughout the volume but put eloquently by Freedman in her contribution: "There are no 'magic bullets' available to counter these tactics, but there needs to be understanding of them in order to promote progressive objectives on human rights." While 'magic bullets' may not be available, depending on the type of actor, there could be potential avenues for meaningful action. In 'Human Rights Populism', Mégret argues that responses to the manipulation of human rights discourse must move beyond a purely defensive posture. As such, one avenue could be a reform which acknowledges the internal contestations within the human rights project, rather than denying them. As Mégret suggests, this involves a willingness to re-examine the political and normative foundations of human rights, fostering a more pluralistic

45 Such actors were briefly mentioned in de Búrca and Young's introduction, De Búrca and Young (n 1) 206.

and self-reflective framework capable of withstanding misappropriation. At the inter-State and diplomatic level, efforts could focus on reinforcing *opinio juris* and promoting the good-faith interpretation and application of human rights treaties. This entails active engagement by States in international and regional fora to counter bad-faith or instrumental uses of human rights language. Before courts and treaty bodies, awareness of the potential for manipulation of rights claims could inform contextual analysis. For instance, under provisions such as Article 18 of the European Convention on Human Rights, which concerns restrictions applied for ulterior purposes, judicial engagement with a broader context of misappropriation can help differentiate between the genuine invocation and the strategic instrumentalisation of rights.

3.3 Conclusion

This concluding chapter highlights an important paradox: misappropriation is at once a useful analytical frame and a concept whose vagueness can obscure as much as it clarifies. The challenge lies in balancing sensitivity to manipulation with recognition of legitimate contestation. By drawing on cross-national empirical cases, the chapters in this volume offer a pathway forward: misappropriation should be understood as a relational, context-dependent phenomenon, requiring careful attention to both actor intention and structural conditions.

Bibliography

Monographs

Brems E, *Human Rights: Universality and Diversity* (Martinus Nijhoff 2001).

Engle Merry S, *The Seductions of Quantification: Measuring Human Rights, Gender Violence, and Sex Trafficking* (The University of Chicago Press 2016).

Landau D and Dixon R, *Abusive Constitutional Borrowing. Legal Globalization and the Subversion of Liberal Democracy* (Oxford University Press 2021).

Journal Articles

De Búrca G and Young K, 'The (Mis)appropriation of Human Rights by the New Global Right: An Introduction to the Symposium' (2023) 21 International Journal of Constitutional Law 205.

Dembour M-B, 'What Are Human Rights? Four Schools of Thought' (2010) 32 Human Rights Quarterly 1
Donnelly J, 'Cultural Relativism and Universal Human Rights' (1984) 6 Human Rights Quarterly 400.
Donnelly J, 'The Relative Universality of Human Rights', (2007) 29(2) Human Rights Quarterly 281.
Genoud C, 'Vernacularisation from Above: Finance's Appropriation of Human Rights in Land Governance' (2020) 25 The International Journal of Human Rights 1356.
Huneeus A, 'When Illiberals Embrace Human Rights' (2019) 113 AJIL Unbound 380.
Engle Merry S, 'Transnational Human Rights and Local Activism: Mapping the Middle' (2006) 108 Am Anthropologist 38.
Franck T, 'Are Human Rights Universal?' (2001) 80 Council on Foreign Relations 191.
Landau D, 'Abusive Constitutionalism' (2013) 47 University of California, Davis 189.
Petrov J, 'How to Detect Abusive Constitutional Practices' (2024) 2 European Constitutional Law Review 1.

Studies

Petersen N and Wasilczyk P, 'The Primacy of EU Law and the Polish Constitutional Law Judgment' (Policy Department for Citizens' Rights and Constitutional Affairs 2022) PE 734.568.

Contributions in Edited Volumes

Bates E, 'History' in Moeckli M, Shah S, Sivakumaran S (eds), *International Human Rights Law* (4th edn, OUP 2022).
Kiss A, 'Abuse of Rights' MPEPIL (online edn, OUP 2006).

Online Publications

Engle Merry S, 'The Global Travel of Women's Human Rights' (New York University 2017) https://as.nyu.edu/content/dam/nyu-as/asSilverDialogues/documents/S%20Merry%20Resonance%20Dilemma%20silver%20prof%20article1.pdf accessed 5 November 2025.

Speeches

Chávez H, 'Strike at the Helm' (Caracas, 20 October 2012) <https://mronline.org/2015/04/01/strike-at-the-helm/> accessed 5 November 2025.

Maduro N, transl by La Riva G, 'Nicolás Maduro's Speech on Venezuela's New Anti-blockade Law to Resist U.S. Imperialism' (*Liberation School*, 16 December 2020) <https://www.liberationschool.org/nicolas-maduros-anti-blockade-law-speech> accessed 9 June 2026.

Murillo R, 'Speech' (26 June 2018) <http://www.psuv.org.ve/temas/noticias/rosario-murillo-nicaragua-pueblo-paz-derecha-violencia-seguridad-oposicion-agenda-planes-desestabilizacion/> accessed 5 November 2025.

Epilogue

(Mis)appropriation of Human Rights

Gráinne de Búrca and Katharine G. Young

The openness to appropriation and adaptation of human rights language is one of its appealing and practical features. This adaptability allows for the resilience and capacity of law and institutions to respond to injustice, to acknowledge hitherto unrecognized harms and to include new kinds of rights, particularly in relation to those who have previously been marginalized. We understand human rights as a dense and evolving praxis, rooted (in terms of positive law and normative inspiration) in a range of international texts including but not limited to the UDHR and the array of UN and regional human rights treaties and instruments which preceded and followed this, and advanced by the engagement of those whose rights are affected and by their supporters and advocates with a multiplicity of institutions and actors tasked with promoting and protecting those rights.[1] In that sense we understand human rights neither as a fixed body of law and practice, nor as an infinitely malleable one, constrained as it is by a fundamental set of commitments to the protection and advancement of human dignity, equality and freedom, and to a complex system of external as well as internal accountability. And when we introduced the concept of "human rights (mis)appropriation" in 2022, we sought to illuminate a disturbing phenomenon, which is not by any means the first or only instance of mis-appropriation of human rights language, and which is not a phenomenon only to be found on the far-right of the political spectrum, but which we see nonetheless as a distinctive set of connected and even coordinated developments in the current geopolitical era. We sought to highlight a series of rising trends in authoritarianism and constitutional reordering: the widespread and at times concerted conscription of human rights discourse by governments and other actors who deliberately deploy its vocabulary and sometimes its instruments, not to expand the scope for inclusion, but to evade accountability and to weaken or substantially revisit prior settled meanings, or to upend and re-orient formerly progressive or pro-

1 For a fuller account, see e.g. G de Burca, *Reframing Human Rights in a Turbulent Era* (OUP 2021).

tected legal rights towards illiberal and repressive rather than emancipatory or inclusive ends.[2]

Our conceptual framework – building on long-standing critiques of rights indeterminacy and contradiction[3] as well as on contemporary analyses of their weaponization and abuse[4] – emerged from the study of eight distinctive contexts, spanning different political and constitutional systems, western as well as eastern, global north as well as global south. From Russia's orchestrated manipulation of "traditional family values" to Brazil's populist inversions, from Uganda's, Nigeria's and Ghana's defense of "proper sexual rights" in African traditions, to backsliding developments for the protections of inclusion or democracy in India, Turkey, and the United States, we identified patterns that transcended traditional North–South divisions. We offered eight indicators to crystallize or at least to organize these preliminary findings, revealing in particular how elements of ultraconservative religious groupings, populist nationalism, and authoritarianism converged in the (often coordinated or deliberately aligned) practices of actors and strategies in what we termed "the new Global Right".[5]

The present volume extends and interrogates our inquiry in significant ways, and helpfully probes the limits and the usefulness of the category of (mis)appropriation, both from a critical and theoretical perspective but also more practically to see whether it fits with a range of developments in jurisdictions including Indonesia, China, and elsewhere. Russia's prominence in the pages of this collection reflects an extended pedigree of human rights invocation and misuse by that government over recent decades – long predating the country-peer indicator of human rights recalcitrance seen in its 2022 suspension from the UN Human Rights Council.[6] The contributors demonstrate how Russia's government-organized non-government organizations (GONGOs), its distortion of anti-racism and hate speech protections in international settings, and its evasion of accountability through ostensibly rights-

2 G de Búrca and K Young, 'The (Mis)appropriation of Human Rights by the New Global Right: An Introduction to the Symposium' (2023) 21 International Journal of Constitutional Law 205, 207.

3 D Kennedy, *A Critique of Adjudication: Fin de Siècle* (Harvard University Press 1997).

4 C Bob, *Rights as Weapons: Instruments of Conflict, Tools of Power* (Princeton University Press 2019); D Landau & R Dixon, *Abusive Constitutional Borrowing: Legal Globalization and the Subversion of Liberal Democracy* (OUP 2021); K L Scheppele, 'The Opportunism of Populists and the Defense of Constitutional Liberalism' (2019) 20 German L. J. 314.

5 As we summarized in https://www.openglobalrights.org/misappropriation-human-rights/, such indicators operate as red flags to warn of that possibility, even as no single one can definitely identify such a use. These indicators are set out in the introduction to this volume.

6 UN GA Res. ES-11/3 (April 7, 2022) (93 in favor, 24 against, 58 abstentions).

defending rhetoric have become templates for emulation by other authoritarian and populist right-wing movements and governments.[7] Again, such pretextual uses of human rights language and even law are certainly not new, as several of the contributions to this volume indicate. However, we argue that their appearance in this particular shape as part of the advancement of a transnational illiberal set of agendas, which share many features – and funders – at a time of growing populism (or demagogy), in a era of changing communication technologies, and in the context of widespread grievance politics, all call for close, cross-country analysis and further research.[8] As the editors to this volume note, drawing on recent human rights pronouncements by the second Trump Administration in the United States, human rights (mis)appropriation now occupies a "central stage" of contemporary domestic and transnational politics.[9]

The collection also moves beyond this context to examine other different legal usages and arguments around human rights, beyond the example of Russia and in other jurisdictions. For example, a group using strategic litigation in Indonesia to assert religious objections to sexual and gender rights[10] and the advocacy by persons with disabilities around euthanasia legalization in the United Kingdom and Europe[11] reveal trajectories of human rights contestation that problematizes any easy diagnosis of (mis)appropriation. Such developments underscore the importance of distinguishing between legitimate vernacularization[12] – the good-faith adaptation and translation of nominally "universal" principles to local contexts – and cynical misappropriation, – even while acknowledging the difficulty in some circumstances of doing so. These scholarly contributions also emphasize the inevitable closeness of the human

7 R Horvath, 'Misappropriating the Legacy of Nuremberg: the Putin Regime's Campaign to Redefine Human Rights and Defend the Perpetrators of Atrocity Crimes'. See also C Wilkinson, 'Beyond LGBT Rights: Russia's "Traditional Values" Statecraft'; D Bojanovska Popovska, 'A Change from Within: Beyond Human Rights'. For analogues in Turkey, see E Celik, 'The Strategic Deployment of 'Hate Speech' in Turkey: Misappropriation of Human Rights?'.

8 Our study tacks closest to thick description in the interdisciplinary methods available in comparative constitutional studies: R Hirschl, *Comparative Matters* (OUP 2014).

9 J Miklasová, P Rhein-Fischer and C Van de Graaf, 'Introduction'.

10 I Y Nugraha, 'Misappropriation or Vernacularisation in the Global South? The 'Family Love Alliance' and the Modernist Islamic Appropriation of Human Rights in Indonesia'.

11 E Lister, 'Misappropriation: Who Fills the Space? An Examination of Misappropriation in Euthanasia Cases'.

12 P Levitt and S E Merry, 'Vernacularization on the Ground: Local Uses of Global Women's Rights in Peru, China, India and the United States' (2009) 9 Global Networks 441; K Young and J Perelman, 'Rights as Footprints: A New Metaphor for Contemporary Human Rights Practice' (2010) 9 Nw. J. Hum. Rts. 27.

rights frame to highly fractious moral disagreement, around the value of life, for example (as with settling euthanasia and abortion questions in law), or the jealous guarding of "family values" or "religious consensus" against a perceived hostile and dominant "West". In this context, we maintain that our indicators are a useful starting point for detecting bad faith and illiberal uses of human rights, even as constitutional democratic approaches to reasonable disagreement and the balancing of competing rights and interests in context such as euthanasia and abortion remain themselves unsettled.[13] Various chapters in the book which acknowledge the pendulum movement of politics,[14] and bring thicker descriptions to the selective presentation of victimhood,[15] exemplify these insights. Further, as we see a growth in newer articulations and institutionalizations of expanded rights – such as the right to a clean and healthy environment, the right to health care, the right to housing[16] –, the capacity for contradiction and rights-conflict will certainly continue as it always has. This points to the need for us to both understand the inevitability and desirability of appropriation and adaptation of human rights, but also to be alert to and vigilant about their cynical misuse, illiberal invocation and (mis)appropriation.

Alongside the richly probing, critical and constructive inquiries established within these chapters, we find methodological diversity put to great use: the book contains an impressive blend of social scientific, critical and legal scholarship. One chapter, for example, draws on communication and argumentation theory, and traces how government "spin" has evolved, in Russia, into sophisticated techniques of technological manipulation.[17] This analysis proves particularly prescient as artificial intelligence threatens to untether rights discourse entirely from reality, accelerating the "semiotic crisis" of rights as "empty signifiers", foreshadowed in our examples.[18] Other authors engage with methodologies of critical legal studies and narrative and the law to

---

13 As made clear by a comparative analysis of the U.S. Supreme Court's decision in *Dobbs v. Jackson Women's Health Org.*, 597 U.S. 215 (2022); K G Young, 'Human Rights in the Constitutional Era of *Dobbs*' (2025) 56 Colum. Hum. Rts. L. Rev. 912 (2025).

14 R Freedman, 'Alternative and Competing Narratives in the International Human Rights System'.

15 A Sanctis de Brito et al, "'The True Right Bearers': Victimhood and Citizenship in the Construals of the Legal Subject'

16 M Langford & K G Young, 'Introduction: The Plural Worlds of Economic and Social Rights', in M Langford & K G Young (eds), *The Oxford Handbook of Economic and Social Rights* (forthcoming).

17 E Fortuin, H Jansen, L de Wolf and W Pawłowski, 'Russia's Arguments to Justify the War in Ukraine and Their Abuse of Human Rights Appeals'.

18 D Kennedy (n 3).

more fundamentally question and challenge the concept of misappropriation, based on critical approaches to positionality and to claims of crisis,[19] and to unearth the open-texture of our (descriptive, although irreducibly normative) indicators.[20] These critiques point to the possible misappropriation and manipulation of the (mis)appropriation framework itself.

Cathérine Van de Graaf, Júlia Miklasová, and Paula Rhein-Fischer have assembled a valuable, timely and critically important collection of human rights scholarship. By connecting seemingly disparate practices across jurisdictions, they reveal how human rights misappropriation has become a central challenge in contemporary international law and constitutional politics. Their contributors illuminate which rights prove most susceptible to manipulation – as we repeatedly see rights-claims concerning gender, religion, speech, family life, equality, dignity and life, reappearing in these pages, as were discussed in our original symposium. The contributors also trace connections to broader assaults on constitutional democracy and the rule of law, through the manipulation of human rights language to disentrench electoral integrity, judicial independence and democratic governance, and to manipulate cultural and material anxieties and grievance in order to increase and entrench political power.[21] The distortion of language and meaning and the inversion of guarantees and protections which human rights (mis)appropriation entails is also often used strategically to distract from other substantive issues such as growing inequality or corruption, and to target unpopular or vulnerable groups such as migrants or LGBTQ communities. These findings suggest that the diagnosis and identification of these trends is a first, vital step in human rights resilience, and that further analysis of the guardrails that lie elsewhere, such as in constitutional politics, political economy, and technological and environmental regulation, must urgently follow.

19 I Aral, 'Misappropriation of Human Rights as an Empty Frame'.

20 E Lister, 'Misappropriation: Who Fills the Space? An Examination of Misappropriation in Euthanasia Cases'.

21 Emblematic, in a wide literature, is the comparative collection by M Graber, M Tushnet and S Levinson (eds.), *Constitutional Democracy in Crisis?* (OUP 2018).

Index

© 2026 THE AUTHOR(S) | HTTPS://DOI.ORG/10.1163/9789004763005-016

www.ingramcontent.com/pod-product-compliance
Lightning Source LLC
LaVergne TN
LVHW020717290926
849104LV00003B/24
9789004737068